OTHE
THE S

MW01612978

1. *The A to Z of Buddhism* b~~y Charles S. Prebish, 2001. Out of Print. See No. 124.~~
2. *The A to Z of Catholicism* by William J. Collinge, 2001.
3. *The A to Z of Hinduism* by Bruce M. Sullivan, 2001.
4. *The A to Z of Islam* by Ludwig W. Adamec, 2002. *Out of Print. See No. 123.*
5. *The A to Z of Slavery and Abolition* by Martin A. Klein, 2002.
6. *Terrorism: Assassins to Zealots* by Sean Kendall Anderson and Stephen Sloan, 2003.
7. *The A to Z of the Korean War* by Paul M. Edwards, 2005.
8. *The A to Z of the Cold War* by Joseph Smith and Simon Davis, 2005.
9. *The A to Z of the Vietnam War* by Edwin E. Moise, 2005.
10. *The A to Z of Science Fiction Literature* by Brian Stableford, 2005.
11. *The A to Z of the Holocaust* by Jack R. Fischel, 2005.
12. *The A to Z of Washington, D.C.* by Robert Benedetto, Jane Donovan, and Kathleen DuVall, 2005.
13. *The A to Z of Taoism* by Julian F. Pas, 2006.
14. *The A to Z of the Renaissance* by Charles G. Nauert, 2006.
15. *The A to Z of Shinto* by Stuart D. B. Picken, 2006.
16. *The A to Z of Byzantium* by John H. Rosser, 2006.
17. *The A to Z of the Civil War* by Terry L. Jones, 2006.
18. *The A to Z of the Friends (Quakers)* by Margery Post Abbott, Mary Ellen Chijioke, Pink Dandelion, and John William Oliver Jr., 2006.
19. *The A to Z of Feminism* by Janet K. Boles and Diane Long Hoeveler, 2006.
20. *The A to Z of New Religious Movements* by George D. Chryssides, 2006.
21. *The A to Z of Multinational Peacekeeping* by Terry M. Mays, 2006.
22. *The A to Z of Lutheranism* by Günther Gassmann with Duane H. Larson and Mark W. Oldenburg, 2007.
23. *The A to Z of the French Revolution* by Paul R. Hanson, 2007.
24. *The A to Z of the Persian Gulf War 1990–1991* by Clayton R. Newell, 2007.
25. *The A to Z of Revolutionary America* by Terry M. Mays, 2007.
26. *The A to Z of the Olympic Movement* by Bill Mallon with Ian Buchanan, 2007.
27. *The A to Z of the Discovery and Exploration of Australia* by Alan Day, 2009.
28. *The A to Z of the United Nations* by Jacques Fomerand, 2009.
29. *The A to Z of the "Dirty Wars"* by David Kohut, Olga Vilella, and Beatrice Julian, 2009.
30. *The A to Z of the Vikings* by Katherine Holman, 2009.
31. *The A to Z from the Great War to the Great Depression* by Neil A. Wynn, 2009.
32. *The A to Z of the Crusades* by Corliss K. Slack, 2009.
33. *The A to Z of New Age Movements* by Michael York, 2009.
34. *The A to Z of Unitarian Universalism* by Mark W. Harris, 2009.
35. *The A to Z of the Kurds* by Michael M. Gunter, 2009.
36. *The A to Z of Utopianism* by James M. Morris and Andrea L. Kross, 2009.
37. *The A to Z of the Civil War and Reconstruction* by William L. Richter, 2009.

185. *The A to Z of Irish Cinema* by Roderick Flynn and Patrick Brereton, 2010.
186. *The A to Z of Modern Chinese Literature* by Li-hua Ying, 2010.
187. *The A to Z of Modern Japanese Literature and Theater* by J. Scott Miller, 2010.
188. *The A to Z of Old-Time Radio* by Robert C. Reinehr and Jon D. Swartz, 2010.
189. *The A to Z of Polish Cinema* by Marek Haltof, 2010.
190. *The A to Z of Postwar German Literature* by William Grange, 2010.
191. *The A to Z of Russian and Soviet Cinema* by Peter Rollberg, 2010.
192. *The A to Z of Russian Theater* by Laurence Senelick, 2010.
193. *The A to Z of Sacred Music* by Joseph P. Swain, 2010.
194. *The A to Z of Animation and Cartoons* by Nichola Dobson, 2010.
195. *The A to Z of Afghan Wars, Revolutions, and Insurgencies* by Ludwig W. Adamec, 2010.
196. *The A to Z of Ancient Egyptian Warfare* by Robert G. Morkot, 2010.
197. *The A to Z of the British and Irish Civil Wars 1637–1660* by Martyn Bennett, 2010.
198. *The A to Z of the Chinese Civil War* by Edwin Pak-wah Leung, 2010.
199. *The A to Z of Ancient Greek Warfare* by Iain Spence, 2010.
200. *The A to Z of the Anglo–Boer War* by Fransjohan Pretorius, 2010.
201. *The A to Z of the Crimean War* by Guy Arnold, 2010.
202. *The A to Z of the Zulu Wars* by John Laband, 2010.
203. *The A to Z of the Wars of the French Revolution* by Steven T. Ross, 2010.
204. *The A to Z of the Hong Kong SAR and the Macao SAR* by Ming K. Chan and Shiu-hing Lo, 2010.
205. *The A to Z of Australia* by James C. Docherty, 2010.
206. *The A to Z of Burma (Myanmar)* by Donald M. Seekins, 2010.
207. *The A to Z of the Gulf Arab States* by Malcolm C. Peck, 2010.
208. *The A to Z of India* by Surjit Mansingh, 2010.
209. *The A to Z of Iran* by John H. Lorentz, 2010.
210. *The A to Z of Israel* by Bernard Reich and David H. Goldberg, 2010.
211. *The A to Z of Laos* by Martin Stuart-Fox, 2010.
212. *The A to Z of Malaysia* by Ooi Keat Gin, 2010.
213. *The A to Z of Modern China (1800–1949)* by James Z. Gao, 2010.
214. *The A to Z of the Philippines* by Artemio R. Guillermo and May Kyi Win, 2010.
215. *The A to Z of Taiwan (Republic of China)* by John F. Copper, 2010.
216. *The A to Z of the People's Republic of China* by Lawrence R. Sullivan, 2010.
217. *The A to Z of Vietnam* by Bruce M. Lockhart and William J. Duiker, 2010.
218. *The A to Z of Bosnia and Herzegovina* by Ante Cuvalo, 2010.
219. *The A to Z of Modern Greece* by Dimitris Keridis, 2010.
220. *The A to Z of Austria* by Paula Sutter Fichtner, 2010.
221. *The A to Z of Belarus* by Vitali Silitski and Jan Zaprudnik, 2010.
222. *The A to Z of Belgium* by Robert Stallaerts, 2010.
223. *The A to Z of Bulgaria* by Raymond Detrez, 2010.

224. *The A to Z of Contemporary Germany* by Derek Lewis with Ulrike Zitzlsperger, 2010.
225. *The A to Z of the Contemporary United Kingdom* by Kenneth J. Panton and Keith A. Cowlard, 2010.
226. *The A to Z of Denmark* by Alastair H. Thomas, 2010.
227. *The A to Z of France* by Gino Raymond, 2010.
228. *The A to Z of Georgia* by Alexander Mikaberidze, 2010.
229. *The A to Z of Iceland* by Gudmundur Halfdanarson, 2010.
230. *The A to Z of Latvia* by Andrejs Plakans, 2010.
231. *The A to Z of Modern Italy* by Mark F. Gilbert and K. Robert Nilsson, 2010.
232. *The A to Z of Moldova* by Andrei Brezianu and Vlad Spânu, 2010.
233. *The A to Z of the Netherlands* by Joop W. Koopmans and Arend H. Huussen Jr., 2010.
234. *The A to Z of Norway* by Jan Sjåvik, 2010.
235. *The A to Z of the Republic of Macedonia* by Dimitar Bechev, 2010.
236. *The A to Z of Slovakia* by Stanislav J. Kirschbaum, 2010.
237. *The A to Z of Slovenia* by Leopoldina Plut-Pregelj and Carole Rogel, 2010.
238. *The A to Z of Spain* by Angel Smith, 2010.
239. *The A to Z of Sweden* by Irene Scobbie, 2010.
240. *The A to Z of Turkey* by Metin Heper and Nur Bilge Criss, 2010.
241. *The A to Z of Ukraine* by Zenon E. Kohut, Bohdan Y. Nebesio, and Myroslav Yurkevich, 2010.
242. *The A to Z of Mexico* by Marvin Alisky, 2010.
243. *The A to Z of U.S. Diplomacy from World War I through World War II* by Martin Folly and Niall Palmer, 2010.
244. *The A to Z of Spanish Cinema* by Alberto Mira, 2010.
245. *The A to Z of the Reformation and Counter-Reformation* by Michael Mullett, 2010.

The A to Z of Burma (Myanmar)

Donald M. Seekins

The A to Z Guide Series, No. 206

The Scarecrow Press, Inc.
Lanham • Toronto • Plymouth, UK
2010

Published by Scarecrow Press, Inc.
A wholly owned subsidiary of
The Rowman & Littlefield Publishing Group, Inc.
4501 Forbes Boulevard, Suite 200, Lanham, Maryland 20706
http://www.scarecrowpress.com

Estover Road, Plymouth PL6 7PY, United Kingdom

British Library Cataloguing in Publication Information Available

Library of Congress Cataloging-in-Publication Data

The hardback version of this book was cataloged by the Library of Congress
as follows:

Seekins, Donald M.
  Historical dictionary of Burma (Myanmar) / Donald M. Seekins.
     p. cm.—(Historical dictionaries of Asia, Oceania, and the Middle East ; no.
59)
  Includes bibliographical references.
  1. Burma–History–Dictionaries. I. Title. II. Series: Historical dictionaries of
Asia, Oceania, and the Middle East ; 59.
DS528.34.S44 2006
959.1003–dc22   2006001432

ISBN 978-0-8108-7635-4 (pbk. : alk. paper)

∞™ The paper used in this publication meets the minimum requirements of
American National Standard for Information Sciences—Permanence of Paper
for Printed Library Materials   ISO Z39.48-1992.
Printed in the United States

Contents

Editor's Foreword

When Burma first became independent, there were valid reasons to expect it to be a relative success in the region. It was well endowed with natural resources, reasonably compact, and had some talented leaders with broad public support. Yet while its neighbors are presently known for political progress and occasionally economic "miracles," Burma has slipped back and become a rare laggard and even sometimes a pariah. Politically, it is run by one of the world's few remaining military regimes, which stubbornly rejects any democratization that could undermine its control. Economically, the situation has continued to worsen, for the bulk of the population at least, while any wealth is monopolized by a small elite, and the greatest source of riches is drugs. This can hardly be compensated for by superficial reforms or name changes—from Burma to Myanmar—or promises of better times to come. Nor can it be justified by the past, although it is somewhat easier to understand today against the background of yesterday, a long history marked by many problems that are yet to be resolved.

Although it is simple enough to say in an offhanded way what has gone wrong, it is not that easy to explain it more cogently. That requires countless details, without which it is difficult to make sense of the situation. It is because of the details that *The A to Z of Burma (Myanmar)* must be welcomed. It provides an exceptional overview of the country, both today and yesterday, and also perhaps clues about tomorrow. The dictionary section has hundreds of entries on notable leaders throughout history, the more significant events that shaped that history, and the groups and institutions that currently prevail. Other entries look into the economy, society, culture, and religion as well as its many different ethnic groups. This admittedly complex situation is summed up in the introduction and also traced over the centuries in the chronology. The bibliography points to other sources of information (although not as many as one would hope for), making this volume particularly useful.

This volume was written by Donald M. Seekins. Dr. Seekins, who is currently a professor of political science at the College of International Studies of Meio University, has spent much of his career in Asia, especially Japan and parts of Southeast Asia. He has visited Burma frequently and has specialized in the country's political history. Over the years he has written many papers and articles on various aspects of the country, as well as a book on the most important feature, namely the military regime, the aptly titled *The Disorder in Order: The Army-State in Burma since 1962*. Despite his concentration on the current and recent past, it is obvious from this historical dictionary that Dr. Seekins is familiar with the earlier periods as well and with the many intricacies that make Burma, despite its rather lackluster performance, a country for which one can develop considerable affection and a hope of better things to come.

Jon Woronoff
Series Editor

Acknowledgments

While preparing the volume, I received invaluable assistance from many people inside Burma, who—given present conditions—I cannot acknowledge by name. Professor Sean Turnell, director of the Burma Economic Watch at Macquarie University in Australia, provided much-needed comments on contemporary economic trends, including the Myanmar government's mysterious system of multiple *kyat*-dollar exchange rates.

I also wish to thank my wife Reiko and son Ken for their patience during those long days and evenings when I've been seated in front of the computer, absorbed in hammering out the minutiae of historical and contemporary Burma.

Daw May Kyi Win, who was curator of the Donn V. Hart Southeast Asia Collection at Northern Illinois University, compiled the bibliography, which has been revised and updated. I wish to dedicate this volume to May Kyi Win, a most conscientious and dedicated scholar whose untimely passing in 2002 has been felt keenly by the Burma studies community.

Reader's Notes

Although for most languages the choice of formal transliteration is a relatively scholarly decision, perhaps also influenced by habit and preference, in the case of Burma—or Myanmar—it is much more complex. In 1989, the Adaptation of Expressions Law promulgated by the State Law and Order Restoration Council provided a new romanization for geographical and ethnic group names. However, many writers, myself included, have chosen to use the old romanization, which dates from the British colonial era. Whether to refer to the country as "Burma" or "Myanmar" or its major city as "Rangoon" or "Yangon," etc., has become a politically charged issue. Those who prefer the old names, including Burmese dissidents living abroad, often use them to express their belief that the post-1988 martial law government is illegitimate. My reason for using them is different: There is no international consensus on which set of names should be used. The governments of the United States and the United Kingdom continue to use the old terminology, while the United Nations and most Asian countries, including Japan, have switched to the new one. Perhaps in the future there will be agreement on this matter that will satisfy all parties involved. But it will most likely be a long time in coming, given the close symbolic connection between the controversy over names and the bitter and unresolved standoff between the prodemocracy movement and the martial law regime since 1988.

It should be pointed out that many of the old names have less linguistic integrity than the post-1989 ones; for example, the pronunciation in spoken Burmese of the name of a town located northeast of Rangoon is much closer to the post-1989 *Bago* than it is to the old version, *Pegu*. However, the military government's claim that the new official country name, *Myanmar*, is ethnically neutral and inclusive of all the country's ethnic groups (roughly equivalent to the use of *British* to refer to the peoples of the United Kingdom) is patently untrue: In the

Burmese language, both *Myanmar* and *Burma* (*Myanma, Bama*) refer to the politically and numerically dominant Burman (Bamar) ethnic group, who make up about two-thirds of the population. There is, in fact, no ethnically neutral name to refer to the country or its inhabitants. In this volume, the following procedure is used to manage the disparity in old and new names: in the dictionary entries, the first time a geographic or ethnic group name is used, the old version is followed by the new version in parentheses, for example Rangoon (Yangon), Irrawaddy (Ayeyarwady) River, Karens (Kayins). Thereafter in the text the old version is used exclusively for each dictionary entry. Some names are the same under both the old and new systems, for example, Mandalay, Sagaing, Chins, which is indicated by the lack of a parenthetic entry on first mention. There is also a table following this note in which the old and new names are listed, so that persons familiar with the old nomenclature can easily find the post-1989 renditions.

The entry *Shan (Tai)* is different in that while the initial term *Shan* is used in both the old and new versions of Burmese ethnic and place names, *Tai* is the term used by the Shans in their own language to refer to themselves. Also, some Chinese terms are given first in the Wade Giles or old romanization, followed by the *pinyin* romanization in parentheses, for example, *Chungking (Chongqing), Kuomintang (Guomindang).*

In the dictionary entries, cross-references to terms that are defined elsewhere in the dictionary are in boldface type.

Burmese personal names are often confusing for Westerners because there are no family names (with the exception of some ethnic minorities, such as the Kachins), making it difficult if not impossible, on the basis of name alone, to trace blood or marriage relationships between people. Usually, a name consists of one or more (usually two or three) syllables; the initial sound of the first syllable has traditionally been chosen in accordance with the day on which the person was born, though an individual may change his or her name for a variety of reasons, including upon the advice of astrologers. Upon marriage, women do not assume their husband's name in any form. In addition, both men and women are usually addressed by sex- and status-specific honorifics placed before the name: for men, *Maung* (literally, younger brother), *Ko* (elder brother), and *U* (uncle); for women, *Ma* (for a younger woman) and *Daw* (aunt, for an older or married woman): thus, U Nu, Daw Aung

San Suu Kyi, Ma Thida. Many ethnic minorities have their own titles. For example, a Mon woman will be addressed as *Mi* (the equivalent of *Daw* or *Ma*) before her name, a Mon man as *Nai* (the equivalent of *U*). In the entries, the honorific is not reflected in the alphabetical arrangement.

Certain persons, for example, *Bogyoke* Aung San, have special titles, in this case meaning literally "major general." The term *Thakin* ("master") is often used in front of the names of persons who were involved in the struggle for independence, for example, Thakin Mya, Thakin Kodaw Hmaing. Buddhist monks have their own terms of address, for example, *pongyi, sayadaw. Saya,* meaning "teacher" (for women, *sayama*), is often used to address not only teachers, professors, or physicians but also adult persons who because of their skill or experience are deemed worthy of this title.

A source of confusion for both speakers of Burmese and of Western languages is the large number of persons who (though unrelated) have the same or similar names. For example, there are three prominent "Tin Oos" (or two "Tin Oos" and one "Tin U") in modern Burmese history: to differentiate between them, they are given prefixes in a manner frequently resorted to by Burmese people: "MI Tin Oo" was the director of Military Intelligence until he was purged in 1983; "S-2 Tin Oo" was a member of the State Law and Order Restoration Council/State Peace and Development Council, with the office of Secretary-2; and "NLD Tin U" is a former defense minister who now occupies a leadership position within the National League for Democracy.

The terms "Burman" and "Burmese" are also confusing (both are part of the old nomenclature; the post-1989 equivalents are "Bamar" and "Myanmar"). During the colonial period, the British used these terms interchangeably. But in most postcolonial era writing, the former refers to the dominant ethnic group, while the latter refers to nationals of the country regardless of ethnicity. Thus, a Karen could be described as "Burmese," though in fact many members of this group, and other minority groups as well, insist on being identified specifically as members of their own community as distinct from the "Burmese." In other words, in certain contexts, "Burman" and "Burmese" remain synonymous.

Burma's currency is the *kyat* (approximately pronounced "chat"), which because of the country's economic weaknesses has steadily depreciated against the U.S. dollar on the free market. In 2005, the *kyat* (abbreviated K) was over 1,000 to the dollar on the free market. There is, however, an official exchange rate, which has remained steady at around K6.00 = US$1.00 for many years. Fortunately, foreign visitors to the country with hard currency can take advantage of the free market rate.

In November 2005, the State Peace and Development Council commenced the relocation of civil servants to Pyinmana, in the central part of the country, where the junta has been constructing a heavily fortified compound that will serve as their new military headquarters (the "War Office") and a new national capital, replacing Rangoon (Yangon). The capital's relocation caught both Burmese and foreign observers by surprise, and it seems to indicate a determination by the military elite to isolate themselves not only from foreign countries, but also from their own people, in the event that there is a repetition of the massive prodemocracy demonstrations of 1988.

Old and New Place Names

The following is a guide to geographical place names in Burma (Myanmar) and their alteration, as issued by the State Law and Order Restoration Council in the June 1989 Adaptation of Expressions Law:

Old	New
Burma	Myanmar
Union of Burma	Union of Myanmar
Akyab (Sittwe)	Sittway
Arakan State	Rakhine State
Arakan Yoma	Rakhine Yoma
Ava	Inwa
Bassein	Pathein
Bassein River	Pathein River
Chindwin River	Chindwinn River
Irrawaddy Delta	Ayeyarwady Delta
Irrawaddy Division	Ayeyarwady Division
Irrawaddy River	Ayeyarwady River
Karen State	Kayin State
Keng Tung (Kengtung)	Kyaingtong
Kyaukpyu	Kyaukphyu
Magwe	Magway
Magwe Division	Magway Division
Maymyo	Pyin U Lwin
Mergui	Myeik, Beik
Mergui Archipelago	Myeik (Beik) Archipelago
Moulmein	Mawlamyine
Pa-an	Hpa-an
Pagan	Bagan
Pegu	Bago

Pegu Division	Bago Division
Pegu River	Bago River
Pegu Yoma	Bago Yoma
Prome	Pyay
Rangoon	Yangon
Rangoon Division	Yangon Division
Rangoon River	Yangon River
Salween River	Thanlwin River
Sandoway	Thandwe
Sittang River	Sittoung River
Syriam	Thanlyin
Tavoy	Dawei
Tenasserim Division	Tanintharyi Division
Toungoo	Taungoo
Yenangyaung	Yaynangyoung

List of Abbreviations and Acronyms

ABFSU	All Burma Federation of Student Unions
ABSDF	All Burma Students' Democratic Front
ABSU	All Burma Students Union
ABYMU	All Burma Young Monks' Union
AFO	Anti-Fascist Organization
AFPFL	Anti-Fascist People's Freedom League
ALD	Arakan League for Democracy
ANC	Arakan National Congress
ARMA	All Ramanya Mon Association
ARNO	Arakan Rohingya National Organization
ASEAN	Association of Southeast Asian Nations
BDA	Burma Defence Army
BIA	Burma Independence Army
BIMSTEC	Bangladesh-India-Myanmar-Sri Lanka-Thailand Economic Cooperation
BNA	Burma National Army
BSPP	Burma Socialist Programme Party
CNF	Chin National Front
CPB	Communist Party of Burma
CRPP	Committee Representing the People's Parliament
DAB	Democratic Alliance of Burma
DDSI	Directorate of Defense Services Intelligence
DKBA	Democratic Karen Buddhist Army
DPNS	Democratic Party for a New Society
DSA	Defence Services Academy
DSC	Defence Services Compound
DSI	Defence Services Institute
FACE	Frontier Areas Committee of Enquiry

GCBA	General Council of Burmese Associations
GCSS	General Council of Sangha Sammeggi
INGO	International Nongovernmental Organization
IUAB	Internal Unity Advisory Board
K	*kyat*
KIA/KIO	Kachin Independence Army/Organization
KMT	Kuomintang (Guomindang)
KNA	Karen National Association
KNLA	Karen National Liberation Army
KNPP	Karenni National Progressive Party
KNU	Karen National Union
LID	Light Infantry Divisions
MI	Military Intelligence
MIS	Military Intelligence Service
MMCWA	Myanmar Maternal and Child Welfare Association
MNDAA/MNDAP	Myanmar National Democratic Alliance Army/Party
MPF	Myanmar Police Force
MTA	Mong Tai Army
NC	National Convention
NCGUB	National Coalition Government of the Union of Burma
NCUB	National Council of the Union of Burma
NDA	New Democratic Army
NDAA—ESS	National Democratic Alliance Army—Eastern Shan State
NDF	National Democratic Front
NGO	Nongovernmental Organization
NIB	National Intelligence Bureau
NLD	National League for Democracy
NLD—LA	National League for Democracy—Liberated Areas
NMSP	New Mon State Party
NSCN	National Socialist Council of Nagaland
NUF	National Unity Front
NUP	National Unity Party
OSS	Office of Strategic Studies

OTS	Officers Training School
PBF	Patriotic Burmese Forces
PBS	Press Scrutiny Board
PC	People's Council
PDP	Parliamentary Democracy Party
PRC	People's Republic of China
PVO	People's Volunteer Organization
RC	Revolutionary Council
RIT	Rangoon Institute of Technology
RMC	Regional Military Commands
RUSU	Rangoon University Students Union
SACs	Security and Administration Councils
SLORC	State Law and Order Restoration Council
SNLD	Shan Nationalities League for Democracy
SPB	Socialist Party of Burma
SPDC	State Peace and Development Council
SSA (South)	Shan State Army (South)
UFU	United Frontier Union
UNDP	United Nations Development Program
UNLD	United Nationalities League for Democracy
USDA	Union Solidarity and Development Association
UWSA	United Wa State Army
YCDC	Yangon City Development Committee
YMBA	Young Men's Buddhist Association

UPPER BURMA

2nd Edition.

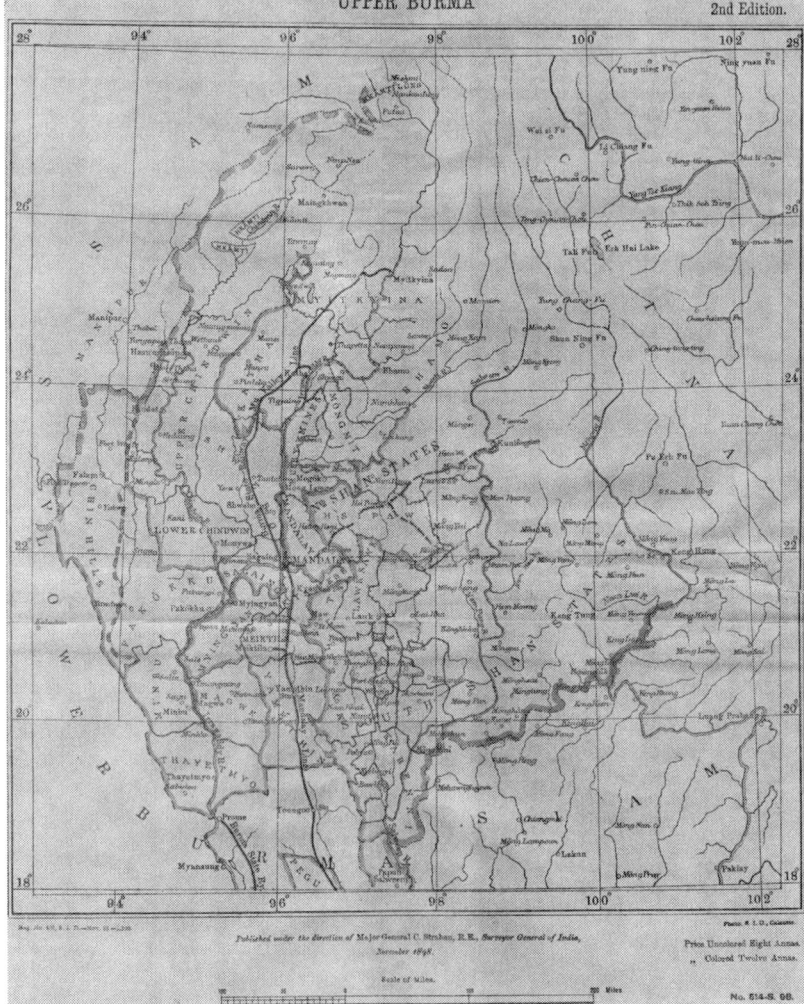

Published under the direction of Major General C. Strahan, R.E., Surveyor General of India,
December 1898.

Scale of Miles.

Price Uncoloured Eight Annas.
„ Coloured Twelve Annas.

No. 514-S. 98.

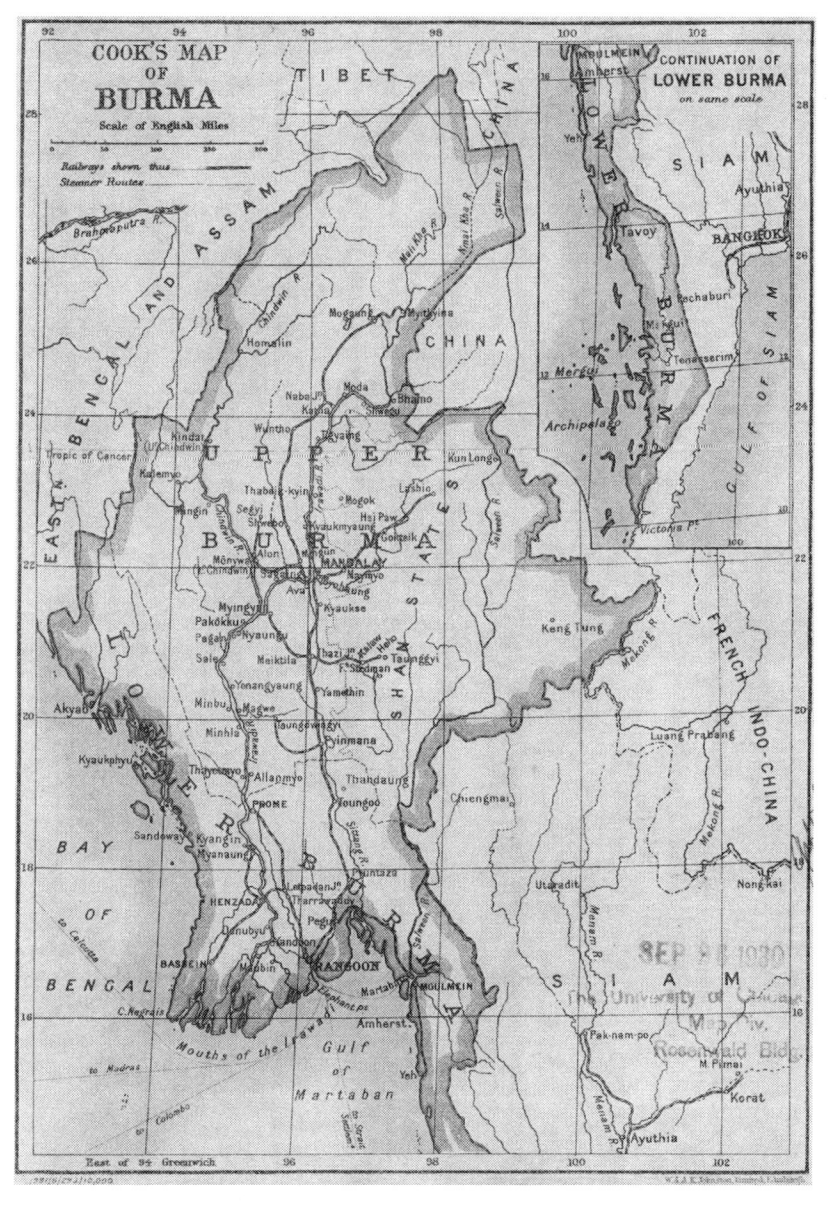

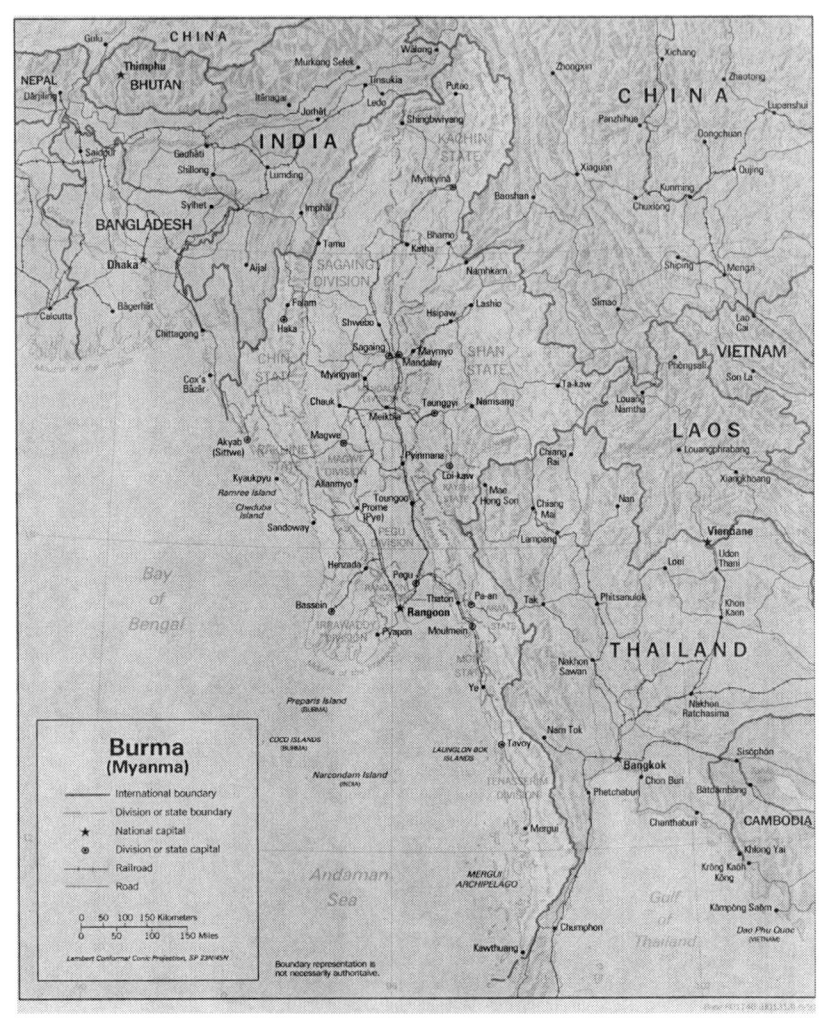

Burma
(Myanmar)

Chronology

Prehistory and Early History to 1000 CE

ca. 10,000 BCE–6,000 BCE Neolithic wall paintings appear in Padhalin Cave, Shan State.

563 BCE–483 BCE Gotama Buddha's lifetime, which according to Burmese legend witnessed construction of Shwe Dagon Pagoda, casting of Maha Muni Buddha image.

ca. third century BCE According to legend, Indian Emperor Asoka (r. 268–233 BCE) sends Buddhist missionaries to Thaton.

seventh century CE Chinese records describe Pyu state of Sri Ksetra (Thayekhittaya).

849 CE Founding of Pagan as a walled city by Burmans.

Dynastic Burma (1000–1824)

1044 King Anawrahta establishes Pagan Dynasty (1044–ca. 1325).

1287 King Wareru establishes state at Martaban in Lower Burma.

late 13th century Keng Tung founded by Shan (Tai) ruler.

1364 Establishment of Ava as capital in Upper Burma (Ava Period, 1364–1555).

1453–1472 Reign of Mon queen, Shinsawbu (Banya Thaw), at Hanthawaddy.

1486 Minkyinyo establishes Toungoo Dynasty (1486–1752).

1551–1581   Reign of Bayinnaung, preeminent Burman conqueror-king.

1600–1613   Portuguese Felipe de Brito controls Syriam.

1635   Toungoo Dynasty capital is moved from Pegu to Ava in Upper Burma by King Thalun.

1752   Alaungpaya establishes Konbaung Dynasty (1752–1885), capital at Shwebo.

1755   Alaungpaya establishes Rangoon (*Yangoun*), "End of Strife."

1757   Alaungpaya captures Pegu, extinguishes Mon independence.

1767   **March:** King Hsinbyushin captures and pillages Siamese capital of Ayuthaya.

1770   Kaungton peace treaty between Burma and China after war (1766–1769).

1784–1785   King Bodawpaya conquers Arakan, brings Maha Muni Buddha image back to Upper Burma.

British Colonial Period (1825–1941)

1824–1826   First Anglo-Burmese War; ends with Treaty of Yandabo.

1826   **February 24:** British annex Arakan and Tenasserim.

1852   **April–December:** Second Anglo-Burmese War; ends with annexation of Lower Burma (Pegu), including Rangoon, which becomes British colonial capital.

1871–1872   King Mindon (r. 1853–1878) holds Fifth Great Buddhist Council at Mandalay.

1881   Karen National Association (KNA) founded.

1885   **November 14–28:** Third Anglo-Burmese War.

1886   **January 1:** British proclaim annexation of all of Burma, as province of British India.

1885–ca. 1890   British Pacification of Burma.

1906 Young Men's Buddhist Association established in Rangoon.

1920 **March:** General Council of Burmese Associations (GCBA) established. **December:** First student strike in connection with Rangoon University Act.

1923 **January:** "Dyarchy" reforms implemented by British.

1930 **December 22:** Saya San Rebellion begins in Tharrawaddy District.

1931 **August:** Saya San captured by British, executed in November.

1936 **February 25:** Student strike at Rangoon University protests expulsion of Ko Nu, Ko Aung San.

1937 **April 1:** Government of Burma Act implemented; Burma separated from India.

1938–early 1939 Oilfield workers' strike; massive demonstrations in Rangoon; death of Bo Aung Gyaw, student activist mortally wounded in protest on December 20, 1938.

1940 **August:** Aung San leaves Burma for China to seek foreign assistance for independence struggle. **November:** Aung San arrives in Japan.

1941 **April–October:** Thirty Comrades receive military training from Japanese on Hainan Island. **December 8:** Pacific War begins. **December 28:** Burma Independence Army (BIA) established in Bangkok.

JAPANESE OCCUPATION (1942–1945) AND STEPS TOWARD INDEPENDENCE (1947)

1943 **August 1:** Japanese proclaim Burma an "independent" nation within the Greater East Asia Co-Prosperity Sphere; Dr. Ba Maw serves as *Nain-ngandaw Adipadi* or head of state.

1944 **March–June:** Imphal Offensive by Japanese into northeastern India. **August:** Anti-Fascist Organization founded, led by Aung San, communists.

1945   March 27: Aung San leads rising of Burma National Army against Japanese; anniversary known as Resistance Day/Armed Forces Day. **May:** Rangoon, evacuated by Japanese, recaptured by Allies.

1947   January 27: Aung San-Attlee Agreement signed. **February 12:** Panglong Agreement concluded by Aung San and Frontier Area Leaders (anniversary is Union Day). **July 19:** Aung San and members of his Interim Government cabinet assassinated. **October 17:** Nu-Attlee Agreement signed.

PARLIAMENTARY PERIOD (1948–1962)

1948   January 4: Burma becomes independent from British rule; U Nu is prime minister. **March 28:** Communist Party of Burma, mainstream faction under Than Tun, begins armed struggle.

1949   January: Karen National Union rebels against U Nu government; Burma afflicted by civil war, insurgency, with large areas under control of communists, Karens, and others.

1950   January–March: Kuomintang troops enter Shan State to establish anticommunist base.

1951   June: Burma's first general election begins; polling not complete until following year; Anti-Fascist People's Freedom League (AFPFL) and allies win 200 out of 239 seats.

1952   September 1: Shan States placed under martial law.

1956   April 27: Second general election; AFPFL wins 173 seats, National Unity Front, 48 seats.

1958   June: AFPFL irrevocably split into "Stable" and "Clean" factions. **October 28:** U Nu hands power to Caretaker Government headed by General Ne Win.

1960   January 28: Treaty and border agreement between Burma and China signed. **February:** Third general election; U Nu's "Clean" AFPFL faction wins solid victory. **April 4:** U Nu forms new government, ending Caretaker Government period.

1961   January 24: Shan leaders in Taunggyi pass resolution calling for enhanced federalism. **August 26:** Buddhism adopted as state religion of Burma; measure alienates Christians, other minorities.

1962   February 25: Federal Seminar in Rangoon begins.

BURMA SOCIALIST PROGRAMME PARTY PERIOD (1962–1988)

1962   March 2: Ne Win leads coup d'état; 1947 constitution suspended, parliament dissolved (March 3). **March 9:** Revolutionary Council vests Ne Win with full governmental powers. **April 3:** "Burmese Way to Socialism" ideology published. **July 4:** Burma Socialist Programme Party (BSPP) established. **July 7:** Troops fire on demonstrators at Rangoon University. **July 8:** Rangoon University Student Union building demolished by military; universities closed.

1962–late 1960s   Nationalization of foreign and domestic companies; private media, private schools, etc., closed or placed under state control.

1963   February 8: Pragmatist Brigadier Aung Gyi dismissed from Revolutionary Council.

1964   March 28: Law to Protect National Solidarity makes BSPP sole political party. **May 17:** First demonetization.

1967   June: Anti-Chinese riots in Rangoon grow out of Mao badge incidents; crisis in Sino-Burmese relations.

1968   January 1: Communist Party of Burma base established on China border in Shan State; commanded by Naw Seng, it has full Chinese backing.

1969   August 29: Former Prime Minister U Nu establishes Parliamentary Democracy Party in exile.

1971   June28–July 11 First BSPP Congress held; Twenty-Year Plan unveiled.

1974   January 3: Constitution establishing the Socialist Republic of the Union of Burma promulgated, following popular referendum. **May–June:** Labor strikes due to shortages of food and other necessities.

December 5–11: U Thant incident; troops seize Rangoon University campus, many students killed, arrested.

1976 **July:** Discovery of plot by young military officers to overthrow Ne Win socialist regime.

mid-1978 Rohingya refugees, numbering 200,000–300,000, flee to Bangladesh to escape persecution in Arakan State.

1980 **May 24–27:** Congregation of the Sangha convened, recognizes state supervision of Buddhist monks; State Council declares general amnesty.

October 1982 Pyithu Hluttaw passes discriminatory new citizenship law.

1985 **November 3:** Second demonetization, of K100 notes.

1987 **August 10:** In a radio speech, Ne Win admits that serious mistakes were made during his years in power. **September 5:** Third demonetization; unlike previous two, without compensation, causing great hardship for Burmese of all classes. **December 11:** United Nations approves "Least Developed Country" status for Burma.

POPULAR MOVEMENT OF 1988

1988 **March 12–18:** Student demonstrations, harshly suppressed by Riot Police, following March 12 teashop incident, including March 16 White Bridge Incident, in which almost 300 students are reportedly killed by Riot Police. **June:** New student demonstrations in Rangoon (Myeinigone incident, June 21); unrest spreads to Pegu, Prome, and Moulmein. **June 8:** Aung Gyi's open letter to Ne Win on political, economic crisis. **July 23–25:** Extraordinary Congress of BSPP; Ne Win proposes multiparty system, resigns as BSPP chairman. **July 26–27:** Sein Lwin designated new BSPP chairman and president of Burma. **August 8:** The "Four Eights" movement to topple Sein Lwin begins; huge demonstrations; hundreds shot by army August 8–11 in Rangoon, Sagaing, and other cities. **August 12:** Sein Lwin resigns. **August 19:** Dr. Maung Maung appointed BSPP chairman and Burma's president. **August 26:** Aung San Suu Kyi makes speech at Shwe Dagon Pagoda, describes "second struggle for national independence." **September 17:** Trade Ministry Incident.

STATE LAW AND ORDER
RESTORATION COUNCIL (1988–1997)

1988   September 18: State Law and Order Restoration Council (SLORC) seizes power; Army methodically snuffs out opposition in late September, early October. **September 24:** National League for Democracy (NLD) founded by Aung San Suu Kyi, Tin U, and Aung Gyi.

1989   March–April: Mutiny within ethnic ranks of Communist Party of Burma results in retirement of top leaders and the party's breakup.. **July 20:** SLORC places Aung San Suu Kyi and Tin U under house arrest (Tin U later sentenced to jail).

1989–1997   Cease-fires concluded by SLORC and 22 major and minor ethnic armed groups, the largest of which is the United Wa State Army.

1990   May 27: General Election; NLD wins 392 out of 485 Pyithu Hluttaw seats contested. **July 27:** SLORC issues "Announcement No. 1/90" asserting its supreme power and barring NLD from forming a government. **Summer:** "Overturning the Offering Bowl" protest by Buddhist monks against SLORC, spreads from Mandalay to other cities; suppressed by autumn. **December 18:** National Coalition Government of the Union of Burma proclaimed at Manerplaw.

1991   October 14: Announcement that Aung San Suu Kyi has been awarded Nobel Peace Prize.

1992   April: Number of Rohingya refugees in Bangladesh fleeing persecution in Burma reaches 250,000. **April 23:** Senior General Saw Maung retires as SLORC chairman; succeeded by Than Shwe.

1993   January 9: National Convention convened for first time in Rangoon to draft outline for new constitution.

1994   Buddha Tooth Relic from China tours Burma for 45 days. **February 24:** Kachin Independence Army/Organization signs cease-fire with SLORC.

1995   January 26: Karen National Union forces abandon Manerplaw, which falls to Burmese army on January 27. **July 10:** Aung San Suu Kyi released from house arrest, recommences political activities, including holding public forums in front of her house on University Avenue, Rangoon. **November 28:** Boycott of National Convention announced by NLD.

1996   January 6: Khun Sa formally surrenders to the SLORC; Mong Tai Army disbanded; former warlord retires to Rangoon, engages in business; Burma is the world's largest producer of opiates. Massive relocation of people in central Shan State by army begins, affecting 300,000 by 1998. **November 9:** Attack on motorcade of Aung San Suu Kyi in Rangoon by pro-regime mob. **December:** Students demonstrate in Rangoon; 600 students and others arrested; Daw Suu Kyi's house blockaded.

1997   July 23: Burma formally admitted to the Association of Southeast Asian Nations (ASEAN).

STATE PEACE AND DEVELOPMENT COUNCIL (1997–)

1997   November 15: Reorganization of SLORC as State Peace and Development Council (SPDC); corrupt generals purged, but Than Shwe, Maung Aye, and Khin Nyunt remain top leaders.

1998   September 16: NLD establishes Committee Representing the People's Parliament (CRPP); confrontation between NLD and SPDC intensifies.

1999   April: SPDC-sponsored replacement of *hti* on summit of Shwedagon Pagoda, Rangoon.

2000   September: Aung San Suu Kyi placed under house arrest after attempting to leave Rangoon by train for Mandalay.

October 2000–May 2002   Secret talks between Aung San Suu Kyi and SPDC, brokered by Malaysia's Razali Ismail, raise hopes of reconciliation.

2002   March: Discovery of "coup plot" involving grandsons and son-in-law of Ne Win; Ne Win family including daughter Sanda Win, placed under arrest. **May 6:** Daw Suu Kyi released from house arrest; between then and May 2003 makes eight trips upcountry to meet with NLD local branches. **December 5:** Death of Ne Win, little or no coverage in official press; no state funeral.

2003   May 30: Pro-regime mob attacks Aung San Suu Kyi and her NLD supporters during upcountry trip, in Sagaing Division ("Black Friday" incident); many believed killed; she is placed under house arrest for third time after being imprisoned; the dialogue process is at an end.

2004   May 17: National Convention reconvenes. **October 18:** Khin Nyunt, prime minister (since 2003) and head of Military Intelligence, is arrested, accused of corruption and trying to split the armed forces; his MI subordinates also arrested or retired; "hard liner" General Soe Win becomes new prime minister.

2005   Growing movement within ASEAN to persuade Burma to relinquish chairmanship of ASEAN when its turn comes in 2006. **February 17:** National Convention reconvened, but adjourned on March 31. **March 27:** Senior General Than Shwe calls for "fully institutionalized discipline" at 60th anniversary celebration of Armed Forces Day. **May 7:** Three bomb blasts at crowded shopping centers in Rangoon kill and injure large number of bystanders (official figure of 11 fatalities and 160 wounded considered underestimations); SPDC accuses foreign-based opposition groups, but identity of the perpetrators remains unclear as of summer 2005. **July 22:** Khin Nyunt sentenced to 44 years in jail, suspended. **July 26:** Burma announces it will forgo 2006 chairmanship of ASEAN. **November 6:** Relocation of civil servants from Rangoon to new capital near Pyinmana, southern Mandalay Division, commences.

Introduction

When Burma (Myanmar) achieved independence from British colonial rule in 1948, many observers viewed it—with its high standards of education and abundant natural resources—as one of the Asian countries most likely to achieve economic development and modernization. However, even before General Ne Win imposed military rule in March 1962, Burma was afflicted by domestic insurgency, political factionalism, and foreign threats along its borders, especially with China. By 1988, formerly poor countries, such as Indonesia and South Korea, enjoyed impressive economic growth, industrialization, and the emergence of educated middle classes who supported greater political openness. But in September of that year, Burma's State Law and Order Restoration Council carried out a violent reimposition of military rule, killing or injuring thousands of demonstrators who marched in the streets of its cities and arresting many others. Although the new junta scrapped the post-1962 socialist system and encouraged foreign private investment, the economy remains in a state of disarray.

To use a cliché, Burma is a country of paradoxes, which are not confined to the contrast between the country's abundant land and natural resources and its present status as one of Asia's poorest countries. Human relations among the Burmese, and between Burmese and foreigners, are characterized by gentleness, grace, and an unwillingness to provoke conflict. For the great majority of Burmese, Theravada Buddhism provides a moral compass and a means of understanding and coping with the world. The country boasts many accomplishments in art, architecture, music, and literature. But the poorly educated military elite rules Burma almost literally at gunpoint, caring little for the people's welfare, and carrying out, or allowing, a large array of human rights abuses. Though official histories celebrate patriotic struggles against the British colonialists and the Japanese occupation, the military has reconstructed a genuinely "colonial" state in which the great majority of people are disenfranchised, and many if not most Burmese view the regime as illegitimate.

LOCATION, TOPOGRAPHY, AND CLIMATE

Burma is the westernmost country in Mainland Southeast Asia, bounded on the west and northwest by India and Bangladesh, on the north and northeast by the People's Republic of China, and on the east and southeast by Laos and Thailand. To the southwest and south, Burma has an extensive seacoast, formed by the Bay of Bengal, the Gulf of Martaban (Mottama), and the Andaman Sea. Altogether, its land boundaries are 6,285 kilometers (3,906 miles) in length, the longest being with China and Thailand (2,227 kilometers/1,384 miles and 2,098 kilometers/1,304 miles, respectively); the border with Laos, 235 kilometers (146 miles) is formed by the deepwater channel of the Mekong River. India's border with Burma is 1,453 kilometers (903 miles) in length, while the Bangladesh–Burma border is 272 kilometers (169 miles) long. The country's coastline, extending from the mouth of the Naaf River in Arakan (Rakhine) State in the northwest to Kawthaung (formerly known as Victoria Point) in the south, is 2,228 kilometers (1,385 miles) in length. There are many coastal islands, including Ramree Island (Yanbye Kyun) off the Arakan coast and the Mergui (Myeik) Archipelago.

The Union of Burma (Union of Myanmar) is the second largest country in the Southeast Asian region (the Republic of Indonesia being the largest), with an area of 676,581 square kilometers (261,228 square miles), including inland bodies of water as well as land. It is approximately the same size as the U.S. state of Texas and extends 2,052 kilometers (1,275 miles) in a north-south direction from several hundred miles north of the Tropic of Cancer to the Isthmus of Kra in the south (more than 18 degrees 59 minutes of latitude).

In terms of physical environment, Burma can be divided into three zones, which have had distinct impacts on the human societies living within them: the *coastal region*, including the deltas of the Irrawaddy (Ayeyarwady), Sittang (Sittoung), and Salween (Thanlwin) Rivers and what is now Arakan (Rakhine) State; a *central plain*, bisected by the Irrawaddy River (which is Southeast Asia's second longest river); and *upland and mountainous areas,* which form the country's borders with India, China, Laos, and Thailand. The coastal and river delta regions, endowed with fertile and well-watered soils where paddy rice can be cultivated, have been home to organized states established since the early first millennium CE by Mons and Arakanese (Rakhines). The central plain was the original homeland of the Burmans (Bamars), the largest ethnic group in the country, who had expanded out from this region, which includes Pagan (Bagan), Mandalay, and most other Burman royal capitals, to impose permanent control over the Irrawaddy Delta and Arakan by the late 18th century. The upland and mountainous areas have been home to a large number of ethnic minority groups who, with the exception of the Shans (Tais) in eastern Burma, did not establish organized states or adopt Indo-Buddhist civilization, as had the Burmans, Mons, and Arakanese. Many upland minority groups living in the more remote areas were not brought under central government control until the late 19th or early 20th centuries, during the British colonial period; the remotest areas, such as the Wa region on the Burma–China border, remain effectively outside of central government control even today.

Although Burmese states have had difficulty exerting their authority over the upland peoples, the "horseshoe" of mountains and hills where they live—which include the eastern spur of the Himalayas and the Chin Hills—have isolated and protected the country from domination and cultural assimilation by powerful neighboring states, especially those based in China or the Indian subcontinent. When the British subjugated Burma in three wars during the 19th century, their route of conquest was not across the mountains from northeastern India, but by sea to Rangoon (Yangon), where they established the center of their colonial administration in 1852, and north along the Irrawaddy River to the last royal capital at Mandalay, which fell to British forces in 1885. In a similar manner, the Arakan (Rakhine) Yoma (Arakan Mountain Range) protected the independent kingdom of Arakan from Burmese encroachments until the late 18th century.

Burma's climate is dominated by the seasonal monsoons, and most parts of the country, with the exception of the extreme north and south, have three recognizable seasons: a hot, dry season, from March to May; a rainy season from May or June to October; and a cool, dry season from November to February. The rainy season is vital for agriculture (in terms of gross domestic product and labor force, the most important sector in the economy), since irrigated fields are not extensive and most crops are rain-fed. Because of the "rain shadow" formed by the Arakan Yoma, the Dry Zone in the central Irrawaddy Valley (the Burman heartland) has semidesert conditions. Traveling overland from Rangoon to Mandalay, one encounters prosperous villages with abundant harvests of rice, vegetables, and fruit in the south (since colonial times known as "Lower Burma"), while outside of irrigated districts most settlements in the arid central part of the country ("Upper Burma") are significantly poorer, dependent on harvests of peanuts, sesame seeds, sugar palm, and other dry climate crops.

NATURAL RESOURCES

As mentioned, Burma is richly endowed with natural resources. Apart from rice (Burma was the world's largest exporter of rice before World War II), they include petroleum, natural gas, tin, silver, lead, gold, and some of the world's largest, though rapidly diminishing, tropical forests, from which teak (*tectona grandis*) and other hardwoods are extracted. Fabled "pigeon blood" rubies are mined at Mogok in Mandalay Division, and the Hpakant mine in Kachin State yields the world's highest-quality jade, which is especially valued in neighboring China. Since 1988, when the State Law and Order Restoration Council seized power and established an "open" economy, the military government and its business associates have generated large revenues from the export of raw materials, especially natural gas from offshore wells, forest products, and seafood. Until recently, however, probably the largest generator of hard currency was the export of opium and heroin from the "Golden Triangle" region of eastern Shan State to neighboring countries, though it is unclear what role the military government has played in this.

ADMINISTRATION

Burma is divided into 14 regional jurisdictions, seven divisions, and seven states: Rangoon (Yangon), Pegu (Bago), Irrawaddy (Ayeyarwady), Magwe (Magway), Mandalay, Sagaing, and Tenasserim (Tanintharyi) Divisions; and Arakan (Rakhine), Chin, Karen (Kayin), Kayah (Karenni), Mon, Shan, and Kachin States. States and divisions are divided into townships (324 in number), and townships into (rural) village tracts and (urban) wards. These institutions existed during the 1962–1988 Ne Win period, but the State Peace and Development Council (SPDC), the present military government, has reintroduced another level of administration, the district (between the state/division and township levels), to strengthen central control. Districts, which played an important role in colonial-era administration, will probably be formalized in the new constitution that is being drafted under SPDC auspices by the National Convention, along with provisions for "autonomous regions" of some sort in ethnic minority areas. On all administrative levels except the lowest, Peace and Development Councils headed by military officers exercise executive authority, an arrangement that will continue until the much-promised transition to constitutional government is completed.

POPULATION, ETHNICITY, AND SOCIETY

No official census has been undertaken since 1983, when the population was enumerated at 35.3 million. During the opening years of the 21st century, the total population is estimated at between 48 and 50 million, though the U.S. government provided a much lower estimate of only 42.5 million in July 2003 (*CIA World Factbook*). Estimates of annual population growth also vary widely, from 0.52 percent to 1.7 percent. Only about a quarter of the population lives in urban areas, reflecting the relatively undeveloped industrial economy. But the former capital and largest city, Rangoon, had between 4.5 and 5 million people in 2005, making it a good example of a Southeast Asian–style "primate city": not only the largest city by far in terms of population, but also the undisputed center of political, administrative, and economic power. The second largest city is Mandalay, with an estimated population of 600,000–800,000. Burma's average population density, estimated by the government in 2000 at 74 persons per square kilometer (191 persons per square mile), is not especially high, and is exceeded by Vietnam, Indonesia, and Thailand.

The ancestors of the modern Burmese came from various parts of what are now western/southwestern China and Tibet over the past two and a half millennia, to be joined by migrants from the Indian subcontinent and points west in recent centuries, especially during the British colonial era. Most of the indigenous peoples, including the Burmans (Bamars), Karens (Kayins), Kachins, and Chins, speak Tibeto-Burman languages, though there are significant communities of Tai-Kadai language speakers (the Shans or Tai) and groups who speak languages related to the Austroasiatic or Mon-Khmer group (such as Mons, Palaungs, and Was). Altogether, more than 100 indigenous languages are spoken in the country. Since colonial times, English has also been widely used, and Chinese is spoken in areas near the China–Burma border.

Although Burma is one of Southeast Asia's most ethnically diverse countries, ethnic identity before the colonial era was not clearly defined or conceptualized. In dynastic times, the most salient social differences were between "civilized" lowlanders, such as the Burmans, Arakanese, Mons, and Shans, who cultivated paddy rice, lived in dynastic states, and shared a common Indo-Buddhist civilization (as reflected, for example, in written scripts and literatures derived from India, the popularity of the Jataka or birth-tales, Indian concepts of monarchy, and the high social status of the Buddhist monkhood or Sangha), and the preliterate upland peoples who lived in much simpler societies, practiced swidden (slash-and-burn) agriculture, and were usually animists (though lowlanders, through *nat* worship, also practiced forms of animism in tandem with Buddhism). For example, the Shans (Tai) of Keng Tung, an Indo-Buddhist state established in the late 13th century, looked upon the non-Buddhist Akha or Kaw, who lived in the surrounding hills, as dangerous and uncivilized outsiders.

For reasons of administration and control as well as a zeal for scientific classification, the British colonialists in the 19th century promoted the image of Burma as a medley of diverse, colorful "races" who were described in loving detail (languages, customs, dress, physical appearance) by observers such as James George Scott. But the idea that the colonialists used rigid ethnic labels and ethnic minority nationalism to "divide and rule" a previously homogeneous (and harmonious) Burmese or Myanmar nation—a common assertion of the present military government—is at best an oversimplification. By the late 18th century, after the Konbaung Dynasty was founded, genuinely ethnic antagonisms had become quite intense, especially between the Burmans and Mons in Lower Burma, and between the Burmans and Arakanese in Arakan, conquered by the former in 1784–1785.

The enforcement of rigid ethnic boundaries has also remained very much a fact of life in independent Burma, as reflected in a discriminatory Citizenship Law enacted by the Ne Win government in 1982 that made Burmese nationals of "nonindigenous" ancestry (mostly descendants of Indian, Chinese, and European migrants) second-class citizens, and by the fact that all Burmese are required to carry identification cards that disclose both their ethnic and religious identities. Official depictions of ethnic diversity focus on "exotic" dress, dance, and artifacts (much like the British colonialists), while giving the minorities little space in which to develop their own languages, cultures, and identities.

Because ethnic identification is not a "racial" (genetic) phenomenon, but one dependent on self-definitions of culture, shared history, language, and social-political environment, defining Burma's contemporary ethnic situation is difficult. According to the 1983 census, there were 135 distinct ethnic groups in the country; some observers have suggested that this figure is more fancy than fact (1 + 3 + 5 adds up to 9, a numerologically auspicious number for Burma's former dictator, Ne Win). The Burmans (Bamars), the largest group, are estimated to constitute two-thirds of the population (about 33 million out of 50 million), but this probably includes many persons of Mon, Karen (Kayin), and other ancestry who have assimilated to the mainstream Burman language, customs, and culture, and most important, to Burmese Buddhism. According to Karen National Union sources, the Karen population, including related groups (such as the Padaungs and the Karennis), totals approximately 7 million, but Martin Smith writes that in the late 1980s the Burma Socialist Programme Party government estimated them at only 2 million; a "neutral" figure would probably be around 3 or 4 million Karens and related groups. According to Smith's estimates, found in his *Burma: Insurgency and the Politics of Ethnicity*, other major groups include the Shans and Mons, with around 4 million each; the Arakanese (Rakhines), with 2.5 million; the Chins with 2 or 3 million; the Kachins at 1.5 million; the Palaung and Wa, 1 to 2 million; and the Muslim Rohingyas of Arakan State, 1 to 2 million. Some ethnic groups are very small, such as the Mokens and Tarons, numbering only a few hundred or a few thousand.

In terms of the distribution of wealth, income, and influence, Burma is one of Southeast Asia's most unequal societies, and people on the lower rungs of the social ladder, especially ethnic minorities living in the border areas, have among the lowest standards of living in Southeast Asia. Although the Ne Win or Burma Socialist Programme Party government (1962–1988) achieved some success in improving standards of health and education for the population as a whole, at least in the coastal/river delta and central plain regions where Burmans and other lowland groups lived, overall living standards declined in comparison with the parliamentary era (1948–1962). Post-1988 military regimes (the State Law and Order Restoration Council, and after 1997, the State Peace and Development Council) have promoted a ruthless brand of state capitalism that has undercut social welfare infrastructure. The single largest item of government expenditure is defense, more than 40 percent of total spending, while the SPDC has spent little on health and education and has been slow to respond to social emergencies such as heroin addiction and the rapid spread of AIDS. Hospitals are often so poorly supplied that patients have to buy their own medicines on the black market. Because food is increasingly expensive in an inflationary economy, malnutrition is widespread, especially among children in poorer communities.

Although the military regime has made repeated verbal commitments to liberalize the domestic agricultural market, state procurement of rice and other staples from farmers has depressed rural standards of living, because official prices are artificially low. The military regime fears a repetition of the urban uprisings of 1988, which were in part inspired by inflation and food shortages, and has tried to ensure steady supplies of relatively cheap necessities for city dwellers. There has been some migration of unemployed or underemployed men and women from rural to urban areas, especially Rangoon, but their economic prospects in the city are limited because of stagnant foreign investment, international sanctions, and the lack of a consistent rule of law, which makes doing business highly risky for Burmese and foreigners alike. An important post-1988 migration pattern has been the influx of Han Chinese from neighboring Yunnan Province and elsewhere in China. In Upper Burma (the central plain) and in the areas on or near the Burma–China border, the new Chinese immigrants are increasingly important demographically as well as economically, as reflected in common Burmese complaints that Mandalay, the old royal capital and Buddhist center, has become one big "Chinatown." In this as in other areas, there are no reliable figures, but recent Chinese migrants in Burma probably number at least several tens and perhaps hundreds of thousands.

SOCIAL STRATIFICATION

As in other countries, social stratification in Burma is complex, but a few generalizations can be made. First, because top-ranking officers in the Tatmadaw (Burmese armed forces), including members of the SPDC junta, wield immense personal power and influence, they have substantial "private" control over economic resources, in large measure through the awarding of contracts and licenses; the generals stand in a patron–client relationship with the wealthiest business people, including black marketers and those persons, known euphemistically as "Wa-Kokang entrepreneurs," who have made fortunes in the international drug trade. In a pattern that goes back at least to the Ne Win era (despite the pre-1988 government's commitment to "socialist democracy"), relations between military officers on all levels and black-market businesspeople have been close and symbiotic. Partial liberalization of the economy since 1988 has also fostered the emergence of a small but growing middle class in urban areas, though because of the lack of the rule of law they, too, are dependent on military patronage and often suffer when military patrons fall into disfavor. Because of the chronic weakness of the *kyat*, Burma's currency, people with regular access to hard currencies, especially U.S. dollars, enjoy great economic advantages.

For the lower classes, especially in rural regions where Burmans predominate, a military career offers some opportunity for social mobility because Tatmadaw personnel have access to special stores, living quarters, schools, hospitals, and other facilities. The ranks of the armed forces have been expanded from 186,000 in 1988 to more than 400,000 in the early 21st century, meaning that there is greater need for new recruits. Another path of opportunity for a poor young man is to become a Buddhist monk, the Sangha (congregation of monks) being the most highly regarded group in Burmese society. Buddhists, who form around 89 percent of Burma's population, give generous offerings to the monks. Although monks are not allowed in principle to own property or handle money, *dana* (charitable donations to monks, or for pagoda projects) is believed to comprise a significant percentage of the nation's surplus wealth. Foreign visitors are often amazed at the magnificent gold adornments of pagodas and monasteries, while secular buildings and the houses of ordinary laypeople are usually simple and unadorned

People at the bottom of the social ladder, who have little or no social capital (connections to powerful or influential persons, especially the military), include not only border-area ethnic minority villagers (though ethnic armed insurgencies have their own, often quite wealthy, elites, especially in drug-producing areas), many of whom have become "internal refugees," but also villagers in the poorer areas of the Dry Zone (prime recruiting ground for the Tatmadaw), and the urban unemployed or underemployed, such as day laborers, street vendors, and pedicab ("sidecar") drivers. Among the poorest people are those who were forcibly relocated after 1988 from the city centers of Rangoon and Mandalay to remote "new towns" on the outskirts, where employment opportunities are minimal.

British colonial observers often claimed that Burmese women enjoyed freedom and social status approaching equality to men to an even greater degree than that of their European counterparts, but women outside of the wealthiest classes today are an especially vulnerable group. Poor women sometimes face horrifying choices, between letting their children starve or a life of prostitution. Some women become *silashin*, Buddhist devotees (sometimes described as Buddhist "nuns") and find refuge in a life devoted to spiritual ends.

RELIGIOUS LIFE

Theravada Buddhism remains at the core of Burma's national identity. Since the SLORC was established in September 1988, the new military government has made generous donations to members of the Sangha and sponsored ambitious pagoda construction projects, including replacement in 1999 of the *hti* (umbrella, or finial) on top of the Shwe Dagon Pagoda, Burma's holiest Buddhist site. Despite the restiveness and occasional political activism of younger monks, the junta has largely succeeded in co-opting older or senior monks and uses pagoda projects as a means of asserting its legitimacy. For example, at the new White Stone Buddha complex in Insein Township, Rangoon, where a huge, 500-ton marble Buddha image is located, there are large color pictures showing the top SPDC generals venerating the image.

But contemporary Burmese Buddhism is highly diverse and embraces many seemingly contradictory practices. Some Burmese undergo intensive meditation regimes (*vipassana* or insight meditation) at centers in Rangoon and elsewhere, which were founded by such teachers as the Mahasi Sayadaw or U Ba Khin, or have personal spiritual advisors to help them along the most austere paths to Enlightenment. Others, laypeople as well as monks, study the Pali Canon, and in a few cases even commit the entire body of scripture to memory (a project that can take up to 10 years). Yet Buddhism also merges with supernaturalism: astrology, alchemy, numerology, the study of omens, *yedaya* (preventive magic), *nat* (spirit) worship, and other phenomena regarded as outside of orthodox Buddhist teachings. Supernatural practices seem to reflect the atmosphere of fear and insecurity that pervades social life, for the military and business elites as well as ordinary people.

Religious minorities are marginalized. This is especially true of Muslims, most of whom are descendants of South Asian immigrants who arrived in the country during the British period. There are tight restrictions on Muslim religious activities, especially in Arakan State, and post-1962 governments have apparently been involved in, or have encouraged, their persecution; for example, twice, in 1978 and 1991–1992, 200,000 to 300,000 Muslim Rohingyas fled to neighboring Bangladesh to escape army persecution in Arakan. Conditions for Burmese Christians, such as the large community of Karen Baptists who live in Rangoon, are generally better; for example, they are allowed to maintain some links to Christian churches outside the country. In many ethnic minority areas, especially where Karens, Kachins, and Chins live, the church, brought by missionaries in the 19th century, remains the core of educational, social, and spiritual life. But Christian activities are also limited by the state, which despite the lack of a constitutional provision making Buddhism the official religion has tended to act on the old notion "to be Burmese is to be Buddhist." In other words, non-Buddhists are a "Them" juxtaposed to a Buddhist "Us."

HISTORICAL DEVELOPMENT

As mentioned, the peoples of Burma are descendants of migrants who came from other parts of the Asian continent. This occurred during a formative period lasting from around the last few centuries BCE to the early second millennium CE, though the migration has continued up to the present, as the settlement of Han Chinese in Upper Burma after 1988 attests. The first organized states in the early centuries CE, borrowing from Indo-Buddhist civilization, emerged in the coastal and river delta region, among the Mons and the Arakanese, who benefited from regional trade networks linking different communities along the Indian Ocean littoral. The Pyus, a people who entered the central plain at an indeterminate time, had dynastic states, a sophisticated material culture, and the practice of Buddhism and Hindu cults by the time Chinese records describe their state at Sri Ksetra (Thayekkhitaya, near modern Prome) in the seventh century. The Pyus were displaced, and probably absorbed, by the Burmans, who built a wall around the town of Pagan (Bagan) in 849 CE.

Dynastic Burma

From a Burman perspective, the country's history as a nation began with the reign of King Anawrahta (r. 1044–1077), founder of the Pagan (Bagan) Dynasty (1044–ca. 1325). He unified Upper and Lower Burma with the conquest of the Mon kingdom of Thaton in 1057 and brought its king, Manuha (described by some Burmese today as the country's "first political prisoner"); his family; and thousands of Mon monks, scholars, and artisans back to his royal capital. The Mons were to the Burmans what the Greeks were to the Romans, transmitters of a more sophisticated civilization, but the single greatest contribution of Anawrahta to Burma's evolving statehood was his recognition of Theravada Buddhism as the official religion, suppressing or subordinating other cults and establishing a close, symbiotic relationship between state and Sangha that continues, in much altered form, today. For this he depended on Mon monks, especially the revered Shin Arahan, for guidance. Physically, the most enduring legacy of the reign of Anawrahta and his successors are the several thousand pagodas, *pahto* (temples), and monasteries spread out across the Pagan plain—among the most impressive being the Ananda Temple, built by Kyanzittha (r. 1084–1113), and the Shwezigon Pagoda, built by Anawrahta and completed by Kyanzittha—which are recognized along with the Angkor ruins in Cambodia and the Borobudur temple in Java as the most outstanding monuments in the Southeast Asia region.

By the early 14th century, the Pagan monarchy had come to an end, its decline impelled in part by the Mongol invasion of 1287. Centuries of unrest and confusion followed in Upper Burma, though a new Burman royal capital was established at Ava (Inwa) in 1364. For the Mons in Lower Burma and the Arakanese, however, the 14th, 15th, and 16th centuries were a golden age, as witnessed by the reigns of King Razadarit (r. 1385–1423), Queen Shinsawbu (r. 1453–1472), and King Dhammazedi (r. 1472–1492) at Hanthawaddy (modern-day Pegu [Bago]), the last two being devout Buddhists who donated generously to the Shwe Dagon Pagoda; and King Min Bin (r. 1531–1553) at Mrauk-U, a cosmopolitan city that Portuguese voyagers described in glowing terms. Min Bin and his successors were perhaps unique among Burmese rulers in making full use of naval power, expanding Arakan's domains to include parts of present-day Bangladesh. North of the now-abandoned Arakanese capital is a complex of temples and pagodas, most notably the Shittaung (Sittaung) Temple, built in a style quite distinct from those of the Irrawaddy Valley.

During the reigns of Kings Tabinshwehti (r. 1531–1550) and Bayinnaung (r. 1551–1581), the country was united under a new Burman royal house, the Toungoo Dynasty (1486–1752), which traced its origins to the town of the same name in the Sittang (Sittoung) River Valley. Bayinnaung was the consummate conqueror king, imposing his authority over the Shan States; the rival Siamese kingdom of Ayuthaya, whose capital he captured in the 1560s; and Laos. Upper and Lower Burma were united after Bayinnaung captured Ava in 1555, and the Toungoo Dynasty monarchs established their seat of power at the old Mon city of Hanthawaddy (Pegu), which became renowned among Southeast Asian capitals for its wealth and power. But Bayinnaung's death in 1581 signaled the dynasty's decline, and by century's end Lower Burma was in a state of turmoil due to invasions by the Arakanese and Siamese and civil war.

However, the Toungoo Dynasty, restored, persisted until the mid-18th century. A fateful development was the decision of King Thalun (r. 1629–1648) to move the capital from Pegu back to Ava in the central plain in 1635; its inland location cut off the Burman power center from seaborne foreign trade and cosmopolitan influences, encouraging an isolationist worldview that was especially strong during the subsequent Konbaung Dynasty (1752–1885).

The Konbaung Dynasty was the third high tide of Burman imperial expansion. Alaungpaya, its founder (r. 1752–1760), ruthlessly crushed Mon and other rebel movements in Lower Burma and led an unsuccessful invasion of Siam; his son Hsinbyushin (r. 1763–1776) captured and pillaged Ayuthaya in 1767 and waged a successful campaign against Chinese attempts to impose suzerainty in the Shan States in 1766–1769; another of Alaungpaya's sons, Bodawpaya (r. 1782–1819), conquered the hitherto independent kingdom of Arakan in 1784–1785, launched numerous unsuccessful invasions of Siam, and promoted land surveys and expansion of irrigation in his kingdom. In his last years, however, he seems to have been afflicted with megalomania, as reflected in his construction of the massive Pagoda at Mingun on the Irrawaddy River (if completed, it would have been 170 meters high) and his claims to be a "Future Buddha," which the Sangha refused to recognize.

The Colonial Period

The British colonial occupation of Burma was accomplished in three operations during the 19th century: the so-called First, Second, and Third Anglo-Burmese Wars in 1824–1826, 1852, and 1885, respectively. British motivations for the occupation included the need to defend imperial possessions in India (the best defense being expansion, in the imperial mindset), first, from Burmese expansionism into what are now northeastern India—Assam and Manipur—and Bangladesh (the 1824–1826 war), and later from (perceived) French encroachments in Upper Burma (the 1885 war); the lure of Burma's abundant natural resources, especially minerals and forest products, and schemes to open up a southwest trade route from Burma into China's Yunnan Province that never came to fruition; and the alleged intransigence of the Konbaung kings, though King Mindon (r. 1853–1878), the most enlightened of his line, attempted, like his counterpart Mongkut in Siam, to promote friendly relations with Britain and modest internal reforms. On the eve of the third war, the British press portrayed Thibaw, dynastic Burma's last king (r. 1878–1885), as a liquor-sodden, Oriental Caligula. In fact, he was a weak and indecisive monarch, manipulated by his determined wife and only queen, Supayalat, and shortsighted court factions.

Only the 1824–1826 operation was a war in the genuine sense, involving combat between British and Burmese forces in northeastern India and a British expeditionary force, which landed at Rangoon, fought numerous engagements in and around the city, and pushed its way up to Yandabo on the Irrawaddy River before imposing a treaty on King Bagyidaw (r. 1819–1837), who ceded Arakan and Tenasserim (Tanintharyi) to British control and recognized the states of northeastern India as lying within the British sphere of influence. The 1852 war, sparked by a minor dispute over indemnities and alleged mistreatment of British merchants, was a model episode of "gunboat diplomacy" that led to the annexation of Lower Burma, including Rangoon. This left the Konbaung kingdom as a rump, consisting of Upper Burma with loose control over border area tributaries. The 1885 war, whose immediate cause was a commercial dispute over forestry leases, reflected the British assumption that Burma's independence was a fiction, and that full colonial occupation was both progressive and inevitable.

However, the fall of Mandalay in November 1885 and the British decision to abolish the monarchy stirred countrywide resistance. During 1885–1890, the British had to call in extra troops from India to carry out what became known as the "Pacification of Burma," a classic colonial war fought against rural guerrillas, often led by a *minlaung*, or pretender-king, who wished to restore the old dynasty or establish a new one. The British also imposed control over the upland ethnic minority areas, a more gradual process that continued into the early 20th century. For example, the Chin Hills were not fully under British control until after the 1917–1919 Anglo-Chin War.

The British colonial occupation transformed Burmese society, though the impact of the transformation differed according to region and ethnic/social group. Most fundamentally, the country was integrated into a globalized economic system that the British themselves dominated during the 19th and early 20th centuries. After Lower Burma was annexed in 1852, they encouraged Burmese migration from still-independent Upper Burma in order to develop an economy based on the cultivation and commercial export of rice. The settlement of the Irrawaddy Delta and the area around Rangoon, which had been depopulated by wars between Burmans and Mons in the previous century, was similar, in many ways, to the opening up of the American and Canadian West at roughly the same time: The government offered inducements to farmers and their families, built infrastructure for irrigation and transportation, and established a business-friendly legal regime that benefited large companies such as the Irrawaddy Flotilla and Steel Brothers and Company. By the close of the 19th century, this policy was a resounding success. Facilitated by advances in steamship technology and the opening of the Suez Canal in 1869, shipments of Burmese rice reached global markets, and the country became the world's largest exporter of this staple, a status it enjoyed until World War II. As long as land remained plentiful and rice prices relatively high, Burmese farmers benefited, and a modest consumer economy developed in Lower Burma's villages.

Other natural resources were thoroughly exploited. The British established a strict system of forest conservation that prevented reserves of teak and other tropical hardwoods from being depleted, a model for forestry in other countries. But forestry was dominated by large, foreign-owned firms that had exclusive rights to exploit leaseholds from the government. Oil had been extracted from wells in central Burma since at least Konbaung times, but the British-owned Burmah Oil Company built modern wells at Yenangyaung (Yaynangyoung) and Chauk, and a refinery at Syriam (Thanlyin) near Rangoon. The Namtu-Bawdwin mines in the Shan States, operated by the Burma Corporation, were the world's largest source of lead, and one of the world's largest sources of silver, before World War II. Other profitable natural resources exported from Burma included tin, rubber, and gemstones.

Thus, Burma developed into a classic colonial economy based on the export of raw materials, with only very modest industry and most manufactured goods being imported. This was also an economy dominated by foreigners. At its apex stood large, British- (or Scottish-) owned companies, such as the Irrawaddy Flotilla; while foreign Asians, mostly Indian but also Chinese, dominated its lower rungs as shopkeepers, craftsmen, laborers, and—perhaps most important—moneylenders, who provided Burmese farmers with the credit they needed to carry them through to harvest time. Most prominent among the moneylenders were the Chettiars from South India, who, as economic conditions deteriorated during the early 20th century, were bitterly resented by rural people.

Rangoon, the provincial capital, was a symbol of the economic and ethnic contradictions of colonial society. In 1941, it had a population of half a million, and because of the colonial export trade was one of the most modern cities in Asia, though without the industrialism of Tokyo, Osaka, or Shanghai. But more than two-thirds of its population was non-Burmese, most of these being immigrants from British India (which also included modern Pakistan and Bangladesh), with smaller numbers of Chinese, Europeans, Eurasians (Anglo-Indians or Anglo-Burmese), Sephardic Jews, and Armenians. A majority of middle- and lower-level civil servants, police, and professionals (physicians, engineers, accountants) were Indians, and the central business district fronted by the Rangoon River was dominated demographically by foreign Asians. Throughout Lower Burma, Indian immigrants, including agricultural laborers who could be paid the cheapest of wages, were a growing percentage of the population, since migration from their South Asian homelands—which shared with Burma a common political jurisdiction as part of British India—was not only administratively unimpeded but also encouraged by business interests.

This was what John S. Furnivall, a perceptive British observer of prewar Burma, called the "plural society"—an arrangement in which ethnic groups, both foreign and indigenous, not only carefully preserved their cultural, linguistic and religious identities (usually living in separate neighborhoods), but also interacted primarily in the marketplace and found themselves locked into an ethnically defined economic division of labor. In Burma, the pluralistic society tended to marginalize the indigenous peoples, especially the Buddhist Burmese. As economic conditions deteriorated in the early 20th century (reflected in falling prices for paddy rice paid to farmers and a high rate of foreclosure due to their inability to repay debts to moneylenders), the division of labor created clear economic winners and losers, who were ethnically defined. Naturally, a feeling of common citizenship or sense of identification with a national as opposed to an ethnic community was nonexistent. Conflict was inevitable.

The plural society problem was eventually "solved" at great human and economic cost through the mass overland evacuations of Indians at the beginning of World War II and the nationalizations of the Burma Socialist Programme Party era (1962–1988), which bankrupted many of the remaining South Asians and forced them to return to their ancestral homelands. Following the anti-Chinese riots of June 1967, many Chinese also left the country. By the early 1970s, the foreign Asian population had dwindled in Rangoon and other parts of Lower Burma.

However, geography, prejudice, and colonial policy conspired to create another problem that proved insurmountable after the country achieved independence in 1948: the deep political, social, and psychological rift between the peoples of the lowland areas, the coast, and central plain, which as mentioned were sites of Indo-Buddhist states since the early centuries CE, and the peoples of the upland and mountainous border areas, where social systems and religious institutions were less sophisticated and a subsistence economy prevailed. Colonial administrators institutionalized and perpetuated this division by placing the lowlands ("Burma Proper") and uplands (the "Frontier Areas," about 40–45 percent of Burma's total land area) under different systems of administration, though both were under the authority of the British governor.

"Burma Proper" had a rationalized system of direct rule (as described below), which reflected its economic importance to the British and its integration into the global system; in the "Frontier Areas" was a system of indirect rule in which local rulers—Shan *sawbwas*, Kachin *duwas*, Chin *ram-uk*—were confirmed in their authority through treaties with the British government. These "feudal" elites enjoyed considerable autonomy, though British officials promoted law and order and kept a sharp eye out for foreign interlopers. With the exception of the Namtu-Bawdwin mines near Lashio in the Shan States, the Frontier Areas were economically undeveloped, and there was little or no infrastructure. The biggest cash crop was opium, grown and exported from the small state of Kokang on the China–Burma border. Educational and health facilities were poor, though Christian missionaries did much-needed work in this area, along with spreading the gospel among animist tribespeople.

Upland minority peoples had few opportunities to associate with their fellow colonial subjects in the lowland areas, intensifying problems of communication and trust, the seriousness of which the British did not fully appreciate until after World War II. However, as mentioned, the alleged British policy of "divide and rule" has to be seen in a broader historical context: though conceived differently in different eras, inter-ethnic hostilities were nothing new at the time of the 1826 Treaty of Yandabo. In the words of an Arakanese writer, "the horse [of ethnic animosity] was saddled and ready; all the British had to do was ride it."

The colonial armed forces were small, just a few thousand soldiers after World War I, but the great majority of them were border area people, especially Chins and Kachins, as well as Karens. Given their history of insurrection, Burmans were not considered trustworthy as soldiers. Karen–Burman relations, characterized by mutual suspicion if not hostility, posed special problems for national integration. Large numbers of them lived in the Irrawaddy Delta and Rangoon as well as in the remoter Burma–Thailand border region, and a vigorous ethnic consciousness emerged, with British encouragement, especially after the establishment of the Karen National Association by Christian leaders in 1881 (though only a minority of Karens were, and are, Christians; the others are Buddhists and animists). Of all the minority peoples, the Karens developed the strongest sense of their separate nationhood under British rule, as expressed in Sir San Crombie Po's classic *Burma and the Karens* (1928); they also had the greatest apprehensions about what their future would be in a postcolonial, Burman-dominated state.

Administratively, Burma was a province of British India, which created further problems becausee conditions in the country were different from the caste-ridden subcontinent, and Indian laws and administrative practices were not always appropriate. In the lowland areas under the old kings, hereditary *myothugyi* ("circle chiefs") based in regional towns but with authority over adjoining villages played an important role in mediating between the central authorities and village communities, especially in matters of labor service and taxation. But the British abolished their posts in the late 1880s, regarding the *myothugyi* as untrustworthy, and redesigned local and regional administration in conformity with a rationalized, hierarchical model that often did not win the allegiance or cooperation of local people.

There was a strong feeling among many Burmans that the British government, having sent King Thibaw into exile, was illegitimate. The self-government measures that the British introduced before World War II—the "dyarchy" reforms of 1923 and the Government of Burma Act of 1935, implemented in 1937—were generally met with indifference, skepticism, or hostility, as reflected in low voting rates for the legislative assembly and a vocal noncooperation movement. Constitutional reforms were not an expression of the popular will, but the result of decisions made in distant London that had little positive impact on people's everyday economic condition. Business interests remained dominant in the reformed legislatures.

Burmese (or Burman) nationalism evolved steadily during the first three decades of the 20th century. Early movements focused on defense of the Buddhist religion, which was widely believed to be imperiled by the lack of state support (the colonial government was secular); official tolerance, though not active promotion of, Christian missionary activities; and the decline in popularity of traditional monastery schools (*kyaung*), as more and more Burmese, especially in the urban and upper strata, sought a modern education for their children. A Young Men's Buddhist Association (YMBA) was established in Arakan in 1902, and there was a branch in Rangoon four years later. Modeled on the YMCA, the YMBA soon spread nationwide and attracted reform-minded laypeople.

The "shoe controversy"—the refusal of some European visitors to take off their footwear while visiting pagoda precincts, seen by Burmese Buddhists as a sign of disrespect—became a nationwide issue backed by the YMBA in 1916, and a learned monk, the Ledi Sayadaw, published an influential essay, *On the Impropriety of Wearing Shoes on Pagoda Platforms*. Public pressure finally forced the British to allow trustees to bar shoe-wearing visitors from entering pagoda premises. One of the most prominent early political figures was U Ottama, an Arakanese Buddhist monk who believed colonial rule had led to Burma's moral decline, and inspired thousands of young "political *pongyis* (monks)" in monasteries around the country. Their noisy demonstrations of opposition to the British presence were described rather unsympathetically by the writer George Orwell in his famous essay, "Shooting an Elephant." U Ottama and U Wisara, another prominent monk activist, spent much of the 1920s and 1930s in jail, and the latter died on a hunger strike there in 1929.

Buddhism's—or rather, traditional, monastery-based Buddhism's—potential for inspiring nationalist resistance, however, was limited, because most of the senior monks were intensely conservative, and the younger ones, the political *pongyis*, remained largely outside of the new class of urban-based, secular-oriented intellectuals who increasingly took the initiative in political movements. In December 1920, college students conducted a strike in protest against the implementation of the Rangoon University Act, which established an elitist, British-style degree-granting institution designed to produce graduates who would enter the civil service and professions. Although the strike failed, the students and their sympathizers established "national schools" around the country that taught a Burmese curriculum; their most famous alumnus was independence leader Aung San, who studied at a national school in Yenangyaung (Yaynangyoung). It was these college and high school student activists, rather than mainstream politicians, who played a major role in confronting colonial rule and developing a tradition of revolutionary nationalism during the late 1930s.

The year 1930 was an important turning point for several reasons. First, communal violence between Burmese and Indians broke out in Rangoon in May, with hundreds of fatalities, most of them Indians. The British authorities were unprepared for the mob attacks, which raged unchecked for two days. The incident revealed the depth of the ethnic/communal divide, made worse by deteriorating economic conditions, and there were further outbreaks of communal violence throughout the 1930s. In the wake of the 1930 riots, urban intellectuals established the Dobama Asiayone ("We Burmans Association"), which became the most important political organization before World War II. Shaped by a surprising assortment of worldviews and ideologies, including Marxism-Leninism, Fabian socialism, Gandhism, and fascism, the Dobama Asiayone, also known as the Thakin Party, became increasingly militant and played a prominent role in the Oilfield Workers' Strike of 1938. A third important development was the revolt led by Saya San, a native physician and former Buddhist monk, which broke out in Tharrawaddy District north of Rangoon in December but soon spread to both Upper and Lower Burma. Though it was largely suppressed by the British the following year (Saya San was captured in the Shan States, and executed in November 1931), his tattooed peasant soldiers won the admiration of the people, even if their worldview was judged too traditionalist by Burmese with a modern education.

Students again became prominent in the nationalist movement when radical leaders were elected to the Rangoon University Students' Union (RUSU) in 1935. Maung Nu (later U Nu) became its president and Aung San a member of RUSU's executive committee and editor of its magazine, *Oway*. The two were expelled from the university in early 1936 because of the publication in *Oway* of an article deemed offensive by the school authorities. Following a strike by students during

February–May of that year, they were reinstated, and they then established a nationwide student organization known as the All Burma Students' Union (ABSU). This brought the young leaders to national prominence. In 1937–1938, both Nu and Aung San became members of the Dobama Asiayone, and the latter, serving as secretary general of the Thakin Party, joined with the Sinyetha Party of Dr. Ba Maw, a former prime minister and prominent mainstream politician, to form the Freedom Bloc after the outbreak of the war in Europe. The Freedom Bloc demanded self-rule, but the Churchill government, preoccupied with the threat of Nazi Germany, refused in any way to accommodate Burmese national aspirations.

The Japanese Occupation, 1941–1945

World War II and the 1942–1945 Japanese occupation were formative historical experiences, which transformed the country almost as fundamentally as the colonial occupation. First, the war provided Burmese (or Burman) nationalism with an epic myth: Aung San's secret departure from the country with a fellow Thakin in August 1940, his contact with Japanese agents in the Chinese port city of Amoy (Xiamen), and his fateful journey to Tokyo, where he agreed, with many misgivings, to cooperate with the Japanese military in exchange for their backing of the independence movement. With the support of Colonel Suzuki Keiji, head of the clandestine Minami Kikan (Minami Organ), he returned to Burma and recruited members of the Thakin Party to be smuggled out of the country. These men, along with Aung San and his original companion in Amoy, were the Thirty Comrades, who received military training from the Minami Kikan on the island of Hainan and formed the nucleus of the Burma Independence Army (BIA), which was established in Bangkok on December 28, 1941, after the outbreak of the Pacific War on December 8. The BIA, whose commander was Suzuki (who assumed the *nom de guerre* Bo Mogyo, the "Commander Thunderbolt" of Burmese legend), served as an auxiliary to the Japanese Army when it invaded Burma at the end of 1941. Poorly organized, composed of thousands of inexperienced young nationalists who joined its ranks and not a few village bullies, it could claim little credit for defeating the British. But its psychological impact on the Burmese was immense: For the first time since 1885, there was a *Burman* army commanded by heroic young patriots. As the Japanese invasion progressed, the BIA also established provisional administrations in liberated areas. Official historiography in Burma dates the history of the Tatmadaw, the present-day armed forces, from the BIA's establishment.

The principal Japanese objective in occupying Burma was to cut off the Burma Road, which was the sole route by means of which the British and Americans provided material support for Chiang Kai-shek (Jiang Jyeshi) at his wartime capital of Chungking (Chongqing); they hoped the cut-off would force Chiang to accept a resolution of the "China Incident" (the Sino-Japanese War) favorable to themselves. The Japanese war effort also required the raw materials that Burma could supply, especially rice and petroleum. The invasion began from bases in Thailand, formally Japan's ally, in December 1941, and the entire country, with the exception of the most remote Frontier Areas, was occupied by mid-1942; Rangoon fell in March, Mandalay in May, and Lashio, the northernmost point of rail links with the port of Rangoon and the starting point of the Burma Road to the Chinese border, in the same month. British commander General William Slim ordered a strategic retreat into India; the spectacle of the British giving way before the Japanese onslaught did little for the colonial rulers' prestige, but it kept Slim's forces largely intact for the reoccupation of Burma in 1944–1945.

Although Suzuki, a Lawrence of Arabia–type figure, was sympathetic to the Thirty Comrades' longing for independence, the regular Japanese military had other ideas: Burma was of value only insofar as it could be exploited for raw materials and manpower and could be used as a jumping-off point for an invasion of India. When Moulmein (Mawlamyine) fell in early 1942, the Japanese established a military administration that would administer all occupied areas, rather than granting the country immediate independence. This was the first of many disappointments for the Thakins, most of whom had leftist sympathies and were unenthusiastic about collaborating with "fascist Japan." By 1944, a small circle of Thakins, including Aung San and Than Tun (who later led the Communist Party of Burma), had established the underground Anti-Fascist Organization to plan an uprising against the Japanese in coordination with Allied operations.

The military administration ran the country until August 1, 1943, when Premier Tojo Hideki proclaimed Burma's independence as a member of the Greater East Asia Co-Prosperity Sphere (*Dai Tōa Kyōei Ken*). Dr. Ba Maw was appointed *Nain-ngandaw Adipadi* (head of state) in a regime that he described as "totalitarian" in nature. But Burma's independence was fictional, and the more arrogant Japanese officers treated its highest officials, including Ba Maw and Foreign Minister Thakin Nu, with barely disguised contempt.

But under both the military administration and Ba Maw's "independent" state, space was opened up within which Burmese could organize socially, politically, and even militarily. Japanese-sponsored groups, such as the East Asia Youth League and civil defense groups established by Ba Maw provided valuable leadership and organizational experience for young nationalists, but the most important institution to grow out of the Japanese occupation was the army. The BIA was dissolved in July 1942 and replaced by a smaller but more rationally structured Burma Defence Army (BDA), whose commander was Aung San. Following independence in 1943, the BDA was transformed into the Burma National Army (BNA). Aung San became a member of Ba Maw's cabinet as war minister, and Ne Win was appointed BNA commander. An officers' training school was established at Mingaladon, north of Rangoon, and a number of promising young men were sent off to Japan for training in military academies.

For the Burmans, wartime memories of the Japanese were not as bitter as in many neighboring countries, but the *Kempeitai*, the military police, carried out a reign of terror, arresting, torturing, and killing suspected communists or Allied agents. An estimated 100,000 Asians, including Burmese, died as forced laborers during construction of the notorious Thai–Burma Railway. The war also had an immense impact on the ethnic minorities, especially the Karens. During the opening months of the war, Karen soldiers fought alongside the British; after their defeat, they were demobilized. Returning to their homes in the Irrawaddy Delta, they became involved in armed clashes with BIA men, which led to a race war: Hundreds of villages were burned, and Karens, including women and children, were massacred, especially in Myaungmya (Myoungmya) district. The experience taught the Karens never to trust the Burmans, although both Aung San and Ba Maw tried to improve relations. There was also mob violence in early 1942 between Buddhist Arakanese and Muslims in Arakan. In the Frontier Areas, Kachin, Chin, Naga, and other "hill tribe" soldiers fought on the

British side, and the isolation of their homelands was lost forever; after the war, some of these veterans, especially Kachins, began armed resistance against the central government.

Following the disastrous Japanese Imphal Campaign into northeastern India in March–June 1944, which bled their forces white, the Allies began their offensives into northwestern and central Burma. On March 27, 1945, Aung San ordered the BNA to rise up against the Japanese— a pivotal event in official historiography that is now commemorated as Armed Forces Day (or Resistance Day). For the Tatmadaw, it is a matter of great pride that its earliest recruits fought not only the "British colonialists," but also the "Japanese fascists." By May 1945, the Allies had recaptured Rangoon, and Japanese forces were in full retreat toward the Thai border.

The Achievement of Independence, 1945–1948

Although the British had retaken Burma, the climate of opinion in the country at war's end, especially among the politically mobilized Burmans, was such that the colonial *status quo ante* could never be restored. But if the initial Japanese victory had shattered the myth of European invincibility and drawn down the curtain on Burma's colonial era, the war also left the country in a terrible shambles. During their retreat from the country in 1942, the British carried out a "policy of denial," destroying vital infrastructure, such as the Syriam oil refinery and most Irrawaddy Flotilla riverboats. The economy was further devastated during the 1944–1945 Allied offensives, the largest land operations in the Pacific War. Wartime communal violence had inflamed ethnic hostilities, especially among the Karens, whose most prominent leaders were dead set against any political arrangement that included integration with Burma. Pocket armies sprang up everywhere, and communist guerrillas were numerous and well organized. Both in central Burma and the Frontier Areas, it was men with guns, rather than officials or politicians, who determined the country's future. Had the war never taken place, or if the Japanese had not occupied the country, that future would most certainly have been more benign.

The prewar political establishment had been largely discredited (including Ba Maw, who was briefly imprisoned by the Allies in Tokyo), and the country's fate was increasingly caught up with the career of Aung San, who as commander of the Patriotic Burmese Forces (PBF), as the BNA was renamed after it joined with Allied forces in fighting the Japanese, enjoyed immense popularity. Only 30 years old at war's end, Aung San was considered a collaborationist by some British officials but had made a very positive impression on field commanders (including General Slim) and Lord Louis Mountbatten, head of the South-East Asia Command, who at a September 1945 conference at Kandy, Sri Lanka, offered him command of the postwar Burma Army. He declined, saying he intended to devote himself to politics. Aung San was president of the country's most popular and effective political organization, the Anti-Fascist People's Freedom League (AFPFL), which had grown out of the wartime Anti-Fascist Organization. It was a broad united front that included communist and noncommunist labor unions, peasant associations, women's and youth groups, and ethnic organizations representing Arakanese, Karens, and Shans, with a total membership of around 200,000. In December 1945, the AFPFL established its own paramilitary force, the People's Volunteer Organization (PVO), composed largely of BNA and PBF veterans.

Between late 1945 and early 1947, Burma was on the verge of civil war. The prewar British governor, Reginald Dorman-Smith, reassumed his post; he regarded Aung San as untrustworthy and sought to reinstate the old politicians, especially U Saw, a personal friend, brought back from East Africa, where he had been interned for attempting to make contact with the Japanese in 1941 (a fact of some relevance to British charges that Aung San had been a traitor). But Dorman-Smith was replaced by Hubert Rance, a military officer close to Mountbatten who was willing to take a more flexible approach to the AFPFL. In London, a new Labour government, headed by Clement Attlee, was committed to decolonization. Aung San, moreover, had serious disputes with the communists, which led to their expulsion from the League in 1946; as the Cold War heated up, his newly apparent anticommunist credentials enhanced his credibility as a leader in the eyes of the West. In December 1946, Attlee invited a Burmese delegation, headed by Aung San, to come to London to negotiate a final political settlement. On January 27, 1947, the Aung San–Attlee Agreement was signed, committing the parties to full independence for Burma within a year, national elections within four months, and British economic aid. When Constituent Assembly elections were held in April 1947, the AFPFL won 173 out of 182 seats contested, outside of those reserved for ethnic minorities. The London agreement also called for integration of the Frontier Areas with Burma Proper, which proved to be an intractable, "no-win" issue. A Karen Goodwill Mission had gone to London in 1946 to argue for an independent "Karen country," including large areas of Pegu and Tenasserim Divisions, but it was ignored by the Clement Attlee government. H. N. C. Stevenson, director of the Frontier Areas Administration, proposed an arrangement, the United Frontier Union, through which the border peoples would be included in a single administrative entity, separate from Burma Proper and under some form of British tutelage. This the AFPFL adamantly opposed. For Burman nationalists, the integration of Burma Proper and the minority peoples, an end to "divide and rule," was a non-negotiable demand; because of the impending independence of India, London did not have the Indian Army at its disposal to handle civil unrest and was in no position to disagree.

Fortunately, Aung San, essentially a modern-minded man who, unlike many of his military successors, had no feelings of nostalgia for old Burman conqueror-kings, was willing to be open-minded in responding to the concerns of Frontier Area communities. At a conference held at Panglong in Shan State on February 7–12, 1947, he and Shan, Kachin, and Chin leaders reached a consensus on guarantees of equality and full citizen rights for Frontier Area peoples, including the principle that "if Burma receives one *kyat*, you will also get one *kyat*"—referring to past economic neglect of the upland areas. These commitments were embodied in the 1947 Constitution, which established a semifederal system with special ethnic minority states. But the most important Karen organization, the Karen National Union, adopted a policy of determined noncooperation with the AFPFL, and smaller border area groups, such as the Was and Karennis, had not been represented at Panglong.

On the morning of July 19, 1947, gunmen acting on the orders of U Saw entered the Secretariat Building in downtown Rangoon and assassinated Aung San and members of his cabinet, the Executive Council, an event observed in Burma today as Martyrs' Day. This irrational act (U Saw had apparently convinced himself that with Aung San dead, the British would appoint him head of the interim government, enabling him to achieve his ambition of becoming prime minister) was a terrible national tragedy, reflecting the violence that had become endemic in the country during and after the war and removing the one Burman leader who had won the trust of the minorities. Aung San's words—"It will not be feasible for us to set up a Unitary State. We must set up a Union with properly regulated provisions as should be made to safeguard the rights of the National Minorities. We must take care that 'United we stand' not 'United we fall'."—proved prophetic as the country settled into a tragic pattern of military-promoted Burman chauvinism and border area insurgency, especially after 1962.

After the assassination, Governor Rance appointed U Nu as Aung San's successor. (U Saw and his accomplices were arrested, tried, and executed the following year.) When Burma became independent from British rule on January 4, 1948, U Nu became the country's first prime minister.

The Parliamentary Period, 1948–1962

Almost immediately following independence, U Nu's government was beset by "multicolored" insurgencies: On March 28, the mainstream of the Communist Party of Burma (CPB), led by Thakin Than Tun and known as the "White Flags," went underground (Thakin Soe's "Red Flag" communists had started their revolutionary struggle in 1946, based in the Arakan Yoma and the Irrawaddy Delta); they were joined by the "White Band" faction of the People's Volunteer Organization in late July. Communists and their sympathizers occupied key points in the Pegu Yoma and the Sittang Valley, and party cadres began land redistribution at Pyinmana in what is now Mandalay Division. The government's already-desperate situation worsened when Karen units of the Burma Army, who along with the Kachin units had been indispensable in fighting the communists, mutinied in January 1949; bitter fighting broke out between the rump of the armed forces still loyal to U Nu and the Karen National Defence Organization (KNDO) at Insein, just north of Rangoon, and combined CPB and KNDO forces captured Mandalay in March. These were the days of the "six-mile U Nu government," when the central authorities controlled little territory outside of central Rangoon. The Karen National Union, bitter over the Attlee government's desertion of them in 1947, had not succeeded in getting satisfactory terms on a separate state from U Nu's government and was willing to carve it out by force.

In mid-1949, the tide began to turn in favor of the government as rebel-held cities and towns in central Burma, including Mandalay, were recaptured. The following year, the army captured the Karen "capital" at Toungoo, and the KNDO was driven across the Salween River to its east bank. But the "multicolored insurgencies" left an indelible mark on Burmese politics. Following the KNU/KNDO uprising in January 1949, armed forces commander General Smith Dun and fellow Karen officers were obliged to retire; most Karen and other ethnic minority troops had gone over to the rebels. The great majority of officers and men who remained loyal to the government were Burmans, commanded by General Ne Win, Smith Dun's successor. Thus, the mixed, multiethnic army established by the British in 1945 was in rather short order replaced by a monoethnic, Burman one, especially on the command level. Moreover, Ne Win mobilized Burman *sitwundan*, local militias or territorial armies, to fight the rebels in central Burma and to defend the capital.

During the 1950s, Ne Win and his fellow officers carried out both "Burmanization" of the Tatmadaw and its development as an autonomous political force. Because Prime Minister U Nu depended on the army for his government's survival, he was in no position to curb its growing power as a "state within a state." This was especially true after the country faced a new crisis: the 1950 incursion of Kuomintang (Guomindang) troops into the hills around Keng Tung in Shan State where, with American aid, they attempted to carry out military operations against the Chinese Communists in Yunnan Province. By 1953, they and their Shan auxiliaries numbered 12,000 and had become deeply involved in the local opium trade. Shan State, which had largely escaped the devastation of war in 1941–1945, became Burma's major battlefield. More than 80 percent of government troops were sent to fight there, and Shan civilians suffered from harsh army pacification measures.

During 1948–1958, Burma had parliamentary government. In the elections of 1951–1952 and 1956, the Anti-Fascist People's Freedom League won solid majorities. Democratic freedoms, including freedom of the press (there were 56 newspapers, in Burmese and other languages), were largely respected, despite the countrywide insurrections. Under the 1947 Constitution, ethnic minority states for the Kachins, Shans, Karennis, and (after 1952) Karens had their own legislatures, but relations between the states and the central government were "federal in theory but unitary in practice." By the late 1950s, movements for a more genuine federal system emerged among Shan and other minority leaders.

U Nu was a socialist, though not a Marxist, and the economy was a mixed one, including state-owned enterprises and private firms, though the principal foreign-owned firms, such as Burmah Oil and Steel Brothers, were obliged to enter into joint ventures with the government. Land reform was carried out in rural areas, and large, absentee-owned estates were declared illegal. The prime minister's foreign policy was based on the principles of neutrality and nonalignment: Burma was the first noncommunist state to recognize the People's Republic of China in 1949, but it also had amicable relations with Western countries and Japan, though U.S. support for the Kuomintang intruders in Shan State caused a crisis in Rangoon–Washington relations. Burma received significant amounts of official development assistance (ODA), especially from Japan in the form of war reparations, but also from Western countries and the Soviet Union.

The failure of democracy in Burma following its brief flourishing in the 1950s is often attributed to the overweening ambition of Ne Win, who, assisted by able advisors, such as Brigadier Aung Gyi, transformed the Tatmadaw into a modern armed force, promoted strong "nation-building" consciousness among its officers (despite the army's politically neutral image), and presided over the emergence of a military-owned economic empire, the Defence Services Institute, which provided it with ample funds outside of official budgets. Long before Ne Win's coup d'état in March 1962, the top ranks of the army were controlled by his cronies—especially those who had served under him in the Fourth Burma Rifles. Organizationally, the Tatmadaw was also becoming increasingly independent of civilian control.

But a stronger and more stable parliamentary government might have been able to keep the army in its place. As things were, the Burmese political class was afflicted with corruption and factionalism. In early 1958, the AFPFL split into two factions: the "Clean AFPFL" loyal to U Nu, and the larger "Stable AFPFL," which supported Socialist Party leaders U Ba Swe and U Kyaw Nyein. Both factions had armed supporters outside the regular army: The Stable AFPFL commanded the allegiance of the Auxiliary Union Military Police, a paramilitary force, and the "peace guerrillas" of the All-Burma Peasants' Organization were loyal to an associate of U Nu. The 1958 factional split caused a crisis on the local and national levels, because local political bosses and their armed followers were aligned with one group or another. Burma seemed again to be veering toward civil war.

On October 28, 1958, U Nu proposed in parliament that General Ne Win be asked to head a "Caretaker Government," which would hold general elections in six months after restoring stability. Ne Win arrested politicians, stepped up the suppression of insurgencies, evicted urban squatters to remote "new towns," and promoted efficiency in the civil service. Middle-class Burmese were in some measure relieved by Ne Win's determination to impose stability in a top-down manner. But from the perspective of history, the Caretaker Government period, which was extended beyond the original six months in order to complete its tasks, was a dress rehearsal not only for the Revolutionary Council established by Ne Win in March 1962, but for the State Law and Order Restoration Council (SLORC), which seized power in September 1988. The Defence Services Institute expanded its control over vital economic sectors. Military officers were seconded to the civil service, where they wielded considerable power, although they were not professionally qualified. The Tatmadaw established a nationwide, local-level civic organization, the National Solidarity Association, which anticipated the mass organizations of the Burma Socialist Programme Party era (1962–1988) and the post-1988 SLORC's Union Solidarity and Development Association (USDA).

The promised election was held in February 1960, and U Nu's "Clean" faction won a landslide victory. Forming a new government in April, he reorganized his followers as the Pyidaungsu (Union) Party. Many voters had been won over by his promise to make Buddhism the state religion. That issue, and the issue of federalism, were major preoccupations during his two years in power. In his later years, U Nu had become a devout Buddhist, and sponsored the Sixth Great Buddhist Council during 1954–1956 to celebrate the 2,500-year anniversary of Gotama Buddha's attainment of *nibbana* (*nirvana*). But his proposed constitutional amendment to give the religion official status opened a Pandora's box of problems: Because it was widely popular among ordinary Burmese, the more militant members of the *Sangha* wanted to use it to curb Muslim and Christian religious activities, which the tolerant U Nu resisted. Ethnic minority leaders, especially among the Kachins, most of whom were Christian, were deeply troubled, worried that the end of Burma's commitment to secularism would marginalize their communities. However, the amendment was passed on August 26, 1961.

The First Military Government, 1962–1988

As mentioned, Tatmadaw operations in Shan State against the Kuomintang had caused great hardship for local people. The traditional rulers, the *sawbwas*, had been powerless to stop the worst army abuses even before they formally relinquished their traditional authority in 1959. Shan disaffection with the army and the central government was growing, and in November of the same year, Shan rebels captured the garrison town of Tangyan. Independent Burma's first president, Sao Shwe Taik, former *sawbwa* of the western Shan State of Yawnghwe, brought together Shan and other ethnic minority leaders at Taunggyi in June 1961 to propose constitutional changes to give the states greater autonomy. Out of this grew the Federal Movement, an essentially elite-centered and moderate initiative that U Nu recognized by sponsoring a Nationalities' Seminar in Rangoon to discuss constitutional proposals in February 1962. The Seminar was still in progress when, on March 2, 1962, Tatmadaw units seized strategic positions in the capital; arrested U Nu, other politicians, and minority leaders attending the seminar; and proclaimed a Revolutionary Council (RC) under the chairmanship of General Ne Win. The 1947 Constitution was suspended and parliament dissolved. Burma's short experiment with parliamentary government was over.

Ne Win framed his reasons for overthrowing U Nu's government in terms of the extreme demands of the Federal Movement (though, in fact, as mentioned, it called for only moderate constitutional change) and the turmoil caused by the prime minister's amendment making Buddhism the state religion. It was claimed these phenomena imperiled national unity, a persistent theme in the legitimizing of Burmese military regimes in later years. But he and his fellow officers, men of brigadier or colonel rank who formed the 17-member Revolutionary Council (RC), also had ambitions to remake Burmese society: to replace "parliamentary democracy" with "socialist democracy." In "The Burmese Way to Socialism," a policy statement published by the RC on April 3, 1962, they expressed their commitment to building a socialist economy in which there would be scientific planning to fully utilize "all the national productive forces" and an end to "the exploitation of man by man." "Socialist democracy" referred to the creation of a workers' state in which "mass and class organizations" would uphold the new political order; the debt to the Soviet model was evident, though it was only in February 1963, when Brigadier Aung Gyi, considered an economic pragmatist, was removed from the RC, that it became apparent that this model would be rigidly applied.

On July 4, 1962, the RC established its own party, the Burma Socialist Programme Party (BSPP, or *Lanzin* Party), which became the only legal political party in March 1964 following decree of the Law to Protect National Solidarity. Over the next few years, Ne Win's martial law government devoted considerable resources to "party building," converting the BSPP from a small elite group, a "cadre party," into a "mass party" with hundreds of thousands of full and candidate party members, which held its first Congress in June–July 1971.

The highest ranks of the BSPP were filled with military officers, active or retired, and the military also controlled the public administration through the Security and Administration Committees (SACs), which replaced regional (state and division) and local administrative bodies that had functioned under the 1947 Constitution. At the apex of this military-controlled hierarchy was the Central Security and Administration Committee in Rangoon, directly responsible to the RC. During the BSPP era, administration came increasingly into the hands of untrained and often poorly educated Tatmadaw men rather than professionally trained civil servants or technocrats, with disastrous consequences for the quality of governance. This was a continuation of the trend initiated during the Caretaker Government period.

Although Ne Win's "revolution" was built upon a Soviet-style power structure, it lacked the totalitarian aspirations of Stalin, Mao Zedong, or Pol Pot: to fundamentally transform society. No attempt was made to collectivize agriculture, which in the history of both Russia and China had caused the most violent "class struggle," with millions of deaths. All land in principle was owned by the state, but family farmers were allowed to retain and cultivate their plots (though low state prices, especially for rice, depressed rural standards of living and created a flourishing black market). Ne Win attempted to assert state control over the sometimes unruly Sangha, but unlike Stalin or Mao, he was not antireligious; by the 1980s, he had fitted himself into the role of a traditional pagoda-building king, sponsoring construction of the Maha Wizaya Pagoda, adjacent to the Shwe Dagon in Rangoon. Thus, Burma was spared a "cultural revolution" aimed at destroying its traditional values and cultural heritage. Furthermore, Ne Win did not attempt to create a personality cult centered on himself, like Mao or North Korea's Kim Il Sung, though his rule was highly personal and often arbitrary, misinformed, and swayed by bad temper and astrological predictions. The official ideology was considerably expanded through publication in 1963 of a long treatise, *The System of Correlation of Man and His Environment*, which was socialist but non-Marxist, with Buddhist metaphysical elements and a dash of humanism as expressed in the aphorism, "man matters most."

But dissent was systematically repressed. The state took over control of the media, and private newspapers, like *The Nation*, were closed down. All books and magazines were subject to censorship by the Press Scrutiny Board (PSB), which, according to 1975 guidelines, prohibited publication of items deemed "harmful to national solidarity and unity." This forced publishers to exercise self-censorship, which had a suffocating effect on Burmese literature. In late April 1965, 92 Buddhist monks were arrested for opposing a government plan to establish a nationwide *Sangha* organization and issue identity cards for monks. But outside of military operations against ethnic and communist insurgents, the state took its harshest measures against student activists. On July 7, 1962, University of Rangoon students demonstrated over campus issues, and Tatmadaw troops were ordered to fire on them point-blank; according to official figures, 15 students were killed, though the actual number may have been in the hundreds. Early in the morning on the following day, troops blew up the historic Rangoon University Students Union building, allegedly on orders from Ne Win.

The mid- and late 1960s witnessed a wave of nationalizations affecting enterprises large and small, domestic and foreign. In October 1963, the RC decreed the Enterprises Nationalization Law, which gave the government the authority to take over any company. By the end of the decade, some 15,000 enterprises had passed from private to state hands, including those owned by South Asian businesspeople, tens of thousands of whom were bankrupted and forced to leave the country, causing a brief diplomatic crisis with India. The anti-Chinese riots of June 1967 drove out many overseas Chinese entrepreneurs. Thus, the economic history of post-1962 Burma resembled that of Uganda, where the dictator Idi Amin expelled the Indian business class, rather than Thailand, Indonesia, or Malaysia, where nonindigenous Asians contributed tremendously to economic growth. The lively shops and bazaars that typify Southeast Asian commercial spaces were not entirely eliminated; but in the "official" economy, retail trade was dominated by branches of the state-owned People's Stores Corporation, which became synonymous for poor service and empty shelves. By 1970, Rangoon, once one of Southeast Asia's most sophisticated cities, had become dreary and threadbare.

Socialist policy emphasized import substitution—the development of a domestic industrial economy to overcome the contradictions of colonial dependency—including the operation of a steel mill, but in 1971 the first congress of the ruling party adopted a comprehensive "Long Term and Short Term Economic Policies of the BSPP" that outlined a 20-year plan and shifted emphasis from industry to the export of agricultural commodities, a wise move because this was still Burma's strongest sector. Yet agriculture was afflicted by low state prices for staple goods, an inefficient, state-run distribution system, and the vagaries of the yearly monsoon cycle. Farmers sought to boost their sagging incomes by holding back as much of their harvest as possible and selling it on the black market. Consumers, especially in urban areas, began experiencing food shortages for the first time in the country's modern history. These shortages, coupled with inflation that reflected growing economic irrationalities, led to urban unrest, beginning in 1967 with the anti-Chinese riots.

Economic reform, frequently promised by Ne Win, amounted to little more than tinkering because he and his military colleagues refused to abandon the belief that state initiatives rather than market forces should determine the economy's direction. Although introduction of high-yield varieties of rice in the mid-1970s was the major factor in impressive economic growth at that time, such growth could not be sustained. At all times, the black market overshadowed the official economy in dynamism and sometimes size. It took various forms: Apart from the underground trade in rice and other necessities, military officers and BSPP cadres, having privileged access to goods at low "official" prices, sold them at a huge profit to black market entrepreneurs, supplementing their meager salaries. There was also large-scale trade on the country's borders, especially with Thailand. Karen and Mon insurgents controlled border trading posts, especially at Three Pagodas Pass, where consumer goods destined for the domestic market entered and raw materials from Burma were exported. A profitable economy based on the export of opiates took root in Shan and Kachin States, involving a bewildering array of shady characters, from local warlords such as Olive Yang, "war lady" of Kokang, and the Shan-Chinese Khun Sa, to Kuomintang veterans who had forsaken the fight against communism in the search for quick profits, and an international network of drug dealers who imported the drugs from the "Golden Triangle" to Thailand and beyond.

By the late 1970s, Burma had partially modified its policy of economic self-reliance and was receiving hundreds of millions of U.S. dollars in the form of ODA, mostly from Japan and West Germany but also from other Western countries and multilateral lenders such as the Asian Development Bank. Much of this aid was predicated on promises of economic reform that failed to materialize. Ne Win accepted such aid, mostly in the form of concessional loans, reluctantly, but apparently thought it a relatively risk-free source of investment that would keep his regime afloat.

During 1962–1988, Burma's foreign policy remained committed to nonalignment and promoting friendly relations, if possible, with all countries. The single greatest diplomatic crisis came in the aftermath of the 1967 anti-Chinese riots. Beijing, radicalized by the Cultural Revolution and indignant over the death of a Chinese embassy official at the hands of a Rangoon mob, recalled its ambassador. The Chinese media called for the overthrow of Ne Win's "fascist" regime. In January 1968, several hundred troops of the Communist Party of Burma, led by Kachin commander Naw Seng, crossed the border and established a "liberated area" in northeastern Shan State, which soon became the center of the largest, best-equipped, and best-organized insurgency fighting the central government. Generously backed by China, the CPB's People's Army had as many as 15,000 mostly ethnic minority soldiers and occupied extensive territories, including the opium-rich Wa states and Kokang. Although Rangoon–Beijing relations were normalized by 1971, the CPB's northeastern command remained a thorn in the side of the Burmese government until its collapse in 1989.

A second theme of Ne Win's foreign policy was isolationism. Cultural and educational relations with Western countries were severed, including student and faculty exchanges under the U.S. Fulbright Program; the educational curriculum on all levels was "Burmanized" (meaning that learning English was downgraded); and foreign missionaries were expelled, their schools taken over by the state. Foreign scholars and tourists were kept out, though the government introduced a seven-day tourist visa in 1970 to generate foreign exchange. Burma showed no interest in joining the Association of Southeast Asian Nations (ASEAN), founded in 1967, because most of its member nations had Western military bases on their soil. Relations with Thailand were strained because the anticommunist Thai government, suspicious of the socialist regime in Rangoon, tolerated the presence of Karen, Mon, and other insurgents on its side of the poorly defined border.

In 1963, Ne Win invited representatives of insurgent groups to come to Rangoon for negotiations, but the peace talks failed. By the early 1980s, over 20 major communist, ethnic nationalist, and warlord armed groups operated in what had been the Frontier Areas during the colonial era. Communist bases in central Burma had been shut down by the Tatmadaw by the mid-1970s, but the "liberated area" along the China border remained intact despite repeated army campaigns, in which government troops suffered heavy casualties and often fought with weapons inferior to those of the communists. The most important noncommunist, ethnic nationalist groups (whose objectives were independence, or at least autonomy, for their people) were the Karen National Union, New Mon State Party, Karenni National Progress Party, and Kachin Independence Organization/Army, whose "liberated areas" were also extensive. Smaller groups claimed to represent the aspirations of the Shans, Nagas, Chins, Pa-Os, and other groups. Warlord armies could be defined as those who had no political aims, despite often impressive titles, and whose leaders sought to enrich themselves through the opium trade. These included remnants of the Chinese Irregular Forces (the Kuomintang); troops loyal to Lo Hsing-han, nicknamed "king of the Golden Triangle"; and the Shan United Army (later the Mong Tai Army), commanded by Khun Sa, who inherited the title from Lo after the latter was arrested and imprisoned in 1973. Between government-controlled areas in the coastal and central plain areas (the colonial-era "Burma Proper") and insurgent-controlled territories in the old Frontier Areas, existed a rough equilibrium; the Tatmadaw was not strong or well-equipped enough to defeat the armed groups, but the latter repeatedly failed to form a strong united front and had no reach inside central Burma. During the massive prodemocracy movement of 1988, the insurgents were bystanders to momentous events that changed Burma's history.

On January 3, 1974, a new constitution was promulgated, establishing the Socialist Republic of the Union of Burma, a highly centralized, BSPP-dominated state that remained committed to "socialist democracy" and established a system of People's Councils on the state/division and local levels, which were chosen in Soviet-style, rubber-stamp elections. During the mid-1970s, however, Ne Win's government faced some of its worst crises: labor strikes in May–June 1974, caused in large part to food shortages; the U Thant Incident of December 1974, which marked a revival in student and monk activism that was brutally suppressed by the army; and a coup d'état attempt by young officers intent on overthrowing the socialist system in 1976. There were also extensive purges of the BSPP hierarchy. In May 1983, the powerful head of military intelligence, Tin Oo, considered Ne Win's possible successor, was cashiered and arrested.

Ne Win, 70 years old in 1981, retired as president of Burma in that year but retained the post of BSPP chairman. The power structure that he had built up, centered on his loyal subordinates in the Tatmadaw, had never been characterized by commitment or effectiveness, and the "Old Man" (as he was widely known) increasingly devoted himself to *yedaya* (magic to avoid misfortune), pagoda-building, and thoughts of his impending mortality. A new economic crisis loomed in the mid-1980s, marked by recurrent food shortages, rampant inflation, and foreign debts that could not be serviced. Burma's leader admitted in August 1987 that serious policy mistakes had been made, hinting that genuine reform might be in order. But the following month he decreed demonetization of the country's currency without compensation in order to strike a mortal blow at "economic insurgents" (the black market); in fact, ordinary Burmese of all classes suffered because they kept much of their savings in cash rather than in bank accounts. The demonetization measure sparked the first student demonstrations since the 1970s and opened the way for the heroic but tragically thwarted popular movement of 1988.

1988: People's Power and the SLORC

The year 1988 represents a turning point in Burma's modern history, for several reasons. First, it was—initially for student activists but then for a growing proportion, possibly a majority, of the general population in central Burma—a dramatic reenactment of the "revolutionary nationalism" of the 1930s. The students and their supporters designated themselves Aung San's spiritual heirs, and the fortuitous appearance of Aung San Suu Kyi on the scene in summer 1988 galvanized their commitment to what she called "the second struggle for national independence," this time against the much-hated Ne Win regime. Second, it brought about the demise of Burmese-style socialism, though not the end of military rule. On September 18, a new martial law regime, the State Law and Order Restoration Council (SLORC), seized power and initiated significant changes in policy: promotion of private foreign investment and economic liberalization, abandonment of neutrality through cultivation of close ties with the People's Republic of China, and the signing of cease-fires with ethnic and former communist armed groups that radically changed conditions in many of the border areas, especially in northeastern Shan State. Third, in the new post–Cold War world, the political crisis in this formerly isolated and obscure country attracted sustained international attention, in large measure because of the international stature of Aung San Suu Kyi, winner of the 1991 Nobel Peace Prize.

Against a background of growing economic insecurity, made worse by the September 1987 demonetization, the popular uprising of 1988 began with a small incident: a March 12 brawl in a teashop in Insein Township, Rangoon, between Rangoon Institute of Technology (RIT) students and local youths. According to the most widely accepted account, one of the youths injured a student and was arrested but was later released because his father was a member of the local People's Council. On the next day was a protest march by several hundred RIT students. Riot Police (*Lon Htein*) shot and killed several of them, including Maung Phone Maw, who became a student martyr comparable to Bo Aung Gyaw, mortally injured by British colonial police in a December 1938 demonstration. The protest soon spread to other campuses, and on March 16 about a thousand students began a march from the Main Campus of Rangoon University to RIT; however, they were surrounded by Riot Police and Tatmadaw troops near the White Bridge, an embankment on the west shore of Inya Lake. The Riot Police attacked, and as many as 300 students were killed, including many drowned in the lake. Hundreds of other demonstrators were jailed, to face torture and abuse. Demonstrations continued on March 18 in downtown Rangoon.

The government's response to the unrest seems almost to have been calculated to inflame popular rage. It is difficult to comprehend why, facing protests that were sometimes unruly but in general peaceful, the Riot Police and later the Tatmadaw consistently employed lethal force, often firing point-blank into crowds. The students were for the most part the sons and daughters of the middle class and the elite, including military families. Their supporters among the townspeople of Rangoon and other cities were mostly Burmans or Burmese lowlanders, who shared with the army and BSPP leadership the same ethnic and religious identities. Poor training and a rigid command structure may be partial explanations. But more fundamentally, the lack of restraint with which the authorities crushed the protests showed that Burma's basic political problem was not its plurality of ethnic and religious groups who endangered national unity, for they were not significantly involved in the events of 1988, but a leadership that was radically out of touch with its people and a state that refused to share power or concede political space to any social group outside itself. In a very real sense, the State waged war against Society in 1988.

Moreover, the quality of governance was affected by the intensely hierarchical and centralized nature of state power since 1962: The BSPP state depended on Ne Win's personal brand of leadership rather than coherent policies in order to operate. The well-worn principle of *lu kaun, lu taw* ("good people before smart people") meant that the "Old Man," fearing challenges to his own authority, consistently chose mediocre but loyal subordinates for leadership positions, such as post-1981 President San Yu. Talented men, such as the pragmatist Brigadier Aung Gyi or the reform-minded defense minister, Tin U, were purged. Moreover, to protect themselves from his hot-tempered wrath and possible demotion, Ne Win's subordinates brought him only good news about conditions inside the country. Thus Ne Win, who, like France's King Louis XIV, could truthfully say *"l'état, c'est moi"* ("I am the state"), governed in a manner that was affected not only by his erratic temper but also by profound ignorance of real conditions. Though the March violence reflected a major national crisis, Ne Win went on his customary vacation in Europe on April 11, not returning until May 26.

The 1988 uprising was a battle for information as well as control of the streets of Rangoon and other cities. On March 17, 1988, the government established a committee to carry out an inquiry into the initial shootings of RIT students, but when its report was published in May, citizens considered it a whitewash. The state media, including the newspaper *Loketha Pyithu Nezin* (*Working People's Daily*) and the Burma Broadcasting Service, made no mention of the killings. Ordinary Burmese people relied on three sources for uncensored information: foreign radio broadcasts, especially the Burmese service of the British Broadcasting Corporation (BBC); hushed conversations in tea shops, a traditional source of unauthorized information; and letters written by Aung Gyi to Ne Win, especially one in June 1988 describing in detail the events of March, including the White Bridge incident, which were photocopied and widely distributed. Foreign broadcasts, including those from the BBC, Voice of America, and All India Radio, became so popular that after the SLORC seized power, it published a book, *Skyful of Lies*, that accused the overseas media of trying to destroy national unity. As the disparity between official and nonofficial sources of information grew, public trust in the government evaporated. When a bloody clash broke out near Rangoon's Myeinigone Market on June 21, townspeople joined with student activists in fighting the Riot Police—a significant turning point.

The Extraordinary Congress of the BSPP, convened on July 23, 1988, was an opportunity for the leadership to show its willingness to compromise with popular sentiment. Ne Win proposed holding a referendum on whether a multiparty system should replace the one-party state, but the party delegates turned it down in favor of an economic reform program. In his long and rambling speech on July 23, the BSPP chairman made an unveiled threat that further inflamed popular sentiment: "If in future there are mob disturbances, if the army shoots, it hits—there is no firing into the air to scare." On July 26, the party central committee, undoubtedly with Ne Win's approval, chose as Ne Win's successor as BSPP chairman Sein Lwin, a loyal crony who had earned the nickname "Butcher of Rangoon" because of his command of the Riot Police during the March and June incidents. On the following day, Sein Lwin was also designated Burma's president by the *Pyithu Hluttaw* (or People's Assembly).

His promotion to the country's two top posts surprised and enraged the people. Student activists declared that a general strike would be held on August 8, 1988, the "four eights," a date with numerological significance connected to the collapse of royal dynasties. At eight o'clock in the morning of the designated day, hundreds of thousands of people marched to city centers in Rangoon, Mandalay, Sagaing, and elsewhere, carrying banners and portraits of Aung San and calling for Sein Lwin's resignation. Because martial law had been declared in Rangoon, the Tatmadaw took over responsibility for public order from the Riot Police. The demonstrations began in a carnival atmosphere, as groups of citizens from practically every city neighborhood in Rangoon participated. But the army began shooting at the amassed demonstrators late on the evening of the eighth, in front of the Sule Pagoda and town hall, and the bloodshed continued until August 12, when Sein Lwin resigned.

Aung San Suu Kyi, Aung San's 43-year-old daughter, had lived abroad for many years but had returned to Burma in early 1988 to take care of her ailing mother. She assumed a leading role in the national crisis after giving a speech on the western slope of the Shwe Dagon Pagoda hill on August 26, attended by hundreds of thousands of Rangoon citizens. Daw Suu Kyi's rapid rise to a preeminent position inside the opposition reflected both the continued appeal of her father and the lack of viable alternatives among the pre-1962 political establishment, including former prime minister U Nu, who had hopes, ultimately thwarted, of making a comeback. Only Daw Suu Kyi and some student activist leaders, especially Min Ko Naing, had sustained popular appeal.

During August and the first half of September, conditions throughout central Burma were extremely unsettled. Demonstrations continued in urban areas, public services ground to a halt, and foreign embassies urged their nationals to evacuate. On August 19, Dr. Maung Maung was appointed BSPP chairman and Burma's president. At a second Extraordinary BSPP Congress held on September 10, he promised the adoption of a multiparty democratic system to replace the one-party state. Two days later, Aung San Suu Kyi, Tin U (the former defense minister with a reputation as a reformist), and Aung Gyi formed a coalition, advocating the establishment of an interim government. This later became the National League for Democracy.

In the late afternoon of September 18, the State Law and Order Restoration Council, a junta composed of 19 officers of general, brigadier, and colonel rank headed by defense minister General Saw Maung, seized power. This action was often described as a "coup d'état" like Ne Win's original coup in March 1962, but this was not entirely accurate. After martial law was suspended in Rangoon on August 24, troops were withdrawn from the city, and the government maintained a low profile. Conditions inside the capital city were chaotic—government *agents provocateurs* carried out sabotage, and neighborhoods barricaded themselves and established self-defense committees—but this was also a time of unprecedented freedom during which a large number of uncensored street publications appeared, new democratic organizations were established, and the fragile beginnings of a new civil society could be seen. While this was going on, Ne Win and his subordinates made plans to recapture power. Thus, the establishment of the SLORC was not the coercive replacement of one government by another but the rescue of the old military power structure, the "army state," by a younger generation of hard-line generals. Although the details of the planning for the SLORC are unclear, it had Ne Win's blessing.

Burma under the SLORC and SPDC

The SLORC imposed order with ruthless efficiency. It is estimated that at least 1,000 Rangoon demonstrators lost their lives in the days following its inception. Government institutions as defined by the 1974 Constitution, including the People's Assembly (*Pyithu Hluttaw*) and regional and local bodies, were dissolved and replaced by state/division and township Law and Order Restoration Committees (LORCs) headed by and composed of military officers, analogous to the RC-era SACs. Regime spokesmen described the junta as a temporary government that would oversee the transition from "socialist democracy" to "multiparty democracy," just as the Revolutionary Council had managed the transition from "parliamentary democracy" to "socialist democracy." Given the longevity of the RC, almost 12 years, there was no reason to believe the SLORC was in any hurry to establish a new democratic, civilian government. But one of the few nonmilitary institutions allowed to survive the imposition of a martial law regime was the oddly named Elections Commission for Holding Democratic Multi-party General Elections. In its first decree on September 18, the SLORC announced its determination to hold successful elections. A day later, the 1964 Law to

Safeguard National Solidarity, which recognized the BSPP as the only political party, was repealed, and on September 27 the Political Party Registration Law was enacted, establishing the legal framework through which new parties could be organized. By mid-1989, some 233 parties had been established. Most of these were small and often whimsical groups, such as the Ever-Green Young Men's Association; however, the National League for Democracy (NLD) drew supporters because of the popularity of Aung San Suu Kyi, and the National Unity Party (NUP), the reorganized Burma Socialist Programme Party, still had considerable funds and a network of cadres left over from before the SLORC takeover. When the general election was held on May 27, 1990, only 93 parties participated, the rest having been "deregistered" by the Election Commission.

For the SLORC, the election was to serve the function of enhancing its legitimacy. Saw Maung and his fellow generals probably expected either that the voters, intimidated by armed force, would support the NUP, or that seats in the new Pyithu Hluttaw would be divided among a large number of small parties. In either case, the elected representatives would offer proof of Burma's democratic credentials without constituting an effective opposition. Because the military regime had been criticized for its human rights abuses by Western governments, which cut off flows of ODA, successful completion of the balloting could result in such aid flows being restored, a major incentive for the cash-starved regime. Indeed, after the junta announced a schedule for the election in early 1989, the Japanese government formally recognized the SLORC and restarted a portion of its massive official development assistance program that had been suspended the previous year.

The actual results of the May 27 election, which most observers agree was free and fair, apparently came as a great surprise to the junta: The NLD won 59.9 percent of the vote and 392 of 485 single-seat constituencies contested, despite the fact that Daw Suu Kyi was under house arrest and barred from running in a constituency. Three ethnic minority parties, the Shan Nationalities League for Democracy, the Arakan Democracy League, and the Mon National Democratic Front, won 23, 11, and 5 seats, respectively. The "progovernment" NUP won only 21.2 percent of the vote and 10 seats. However, the SLORC was not entirely unprepared for this outcome. In the run-up to the election, regime spokesmen had adopted an ambiguous stance toward the election's actual purpose: Was it to choose members of the People's Assembly, who would form a government? Or would the elected representatives play some role in drafting a new constitution? By the summer of 1990, it had become apparent that the first option was out of the question. In July, the junta issued SLORC Announcement No. 1/90, which asserted that a civilian government could not be established until a new constitution was drafted, and that the martial law regime exercised exclusively the powers of government. In 1992, the SLORC established a constitutional drafting body, the National Convention, which met for the first time in January 1993. Since then, it has convened intermittently; because it had not completed a constitutional draft by mid-2005 indicates that the junta, now known as the State Peace and Development Council (SPDC), has judged that the time is not ripe for a political transition.

Aung San Suu Kyi was placed under house arrest by the junta on July 20, 1989; released in July 1995 (a period of confinement just under six years); confined again between September 2000 and May 2002; and began her third term of house arrest following the "Black Friday" incident of May 30, 2003, in which she and her supporters were attacked by proregime mobs in Sagaing Division, an incident that aroused international condemnation and resulted in severe economic sanctions on the part of the United States. Although foreign parties, particularly Malaysia, attempted to initiate dialogue between Daw Suu Kyi and the junta, their efforts failed to bear fruit. When free from confinement in 1995–2000 and 2002–2003, Daw Suu Kyi valiantly attempted to rejuvenate her party and the democratic spirit that had been expressed in May 1990. But the sheer dead weight of military coercion blocked any sort of progress; in 2005, the NLD was desperately struggling for survival, and a peaceful settlement of the country's political crisis remained beyond reach. The National Convention reconvened in May 2004 to draft a constitution that would enshrine military domination of the political system. Neither the NLD nor the second-largest opposition party, the Shan Nationalities League for Democracy, attended the convention.

The internal dynamics of the post-1988 junta remain largely opaque. Burma watchers have detected personal and worldview differences between the top military figures. SLORC/SPDC chairman Senior General Than Shwe (who replaced the erratic Saw Maung in April 1992) and vice-chairman General Maung Aye, both part of the regular combat army, are considered conservative, hard line in dealing with the opposition, and tending toward isolationism; while SLORC/SPDC Secretary-1 Lieutenant General Khin Nyunt, director of military intelligence (a former Ne Win protégé who was appointed to this post in 1984) was more flexible, interested in promoting ties with foreign countries and taking a more accommodating (or perhaps more manipulative) approach toward the NLD. But Khin Nyunt was arrested in October 2004, charged with corruption and attempting to split the Tatmadaw, and was sentenced to 44 years in jail, suspended. His military intelligence subordinates were also arrested or forced into retirement.

What seems apparent is that the junta has achieved "system maintenance"; that is, individual generals have been removed, but the unity of the Tatmadaw top command has been preserved, and Than Shwe, an uncharismatic, frequently underestimated figure, has managed to consolidate personal control at the top, becoming Ne Win's successor as "Number One." In November 1997, the SLORC was reorganized as the State Peace and Development Council (SPDC). Although Than Shwe, Maung Aye, and Khin Nyunt retained their positions, other SLORC generals were retired, including those who had garnered a reputation for corruption. Through its control of a "state capitalist" economy, especially the sale of natural resources, such as natural gas, to neighboring countries, the SPDC and the Tatmadaw officer corps have evolved into a *rentier* class that, in contrast to the pre-1988 Tatmadaw, enjoys little esteem among the general population but is more deeply entrenched in power than ever before.

SLORC/SPDC policies could be characterized as combining the authoritarian proclivities of the Ne Win era—suppression of opposition, rigid censorship, and control of information—with controlled globalization, in a manner similar to that of Burma's huge northern neighbor, China. The government has encouraged foreign tourism, including the construction of international class hotels and promotion of "Visit Myanmar [Burma] Year" in 1996–1997; foreign private investment has been welcomed with the decree of a post-1988 legal regime facilitating the participation of wholly owned foreign enterprises and foreign–local joint ventures in the economy; Burma joined the Association of Southeast Asian Nations in July 1997; there are plans to connect Burma to the Asian Highway, linking the country overland with Thailand, Indochina, and India; and Burma is part of the Great Mekong Subregion development project that is being promoted by the Asian Development Bank. Most rural areas in Burma remain largely unaffected by globalization, but Rangoon and other urban areas increasingly resemble the commercialized urban spaces found in Bangkok, Singapore, or Ho Chi Minh City.

After 1988, SLORC Secretary-1 Khin Nyunt established close and friendly ties with the People's Republic of China. Many observers argue that without China's economic, military, and diplomatic support (including the sale of weapons), the junta would have had a much more difficult time resisting Western sanctions or, conversely, that had China exerted pressure on the junta to liberalize, it would have done so. Some have accused China of turning Burma into an economic "neo-colony," where the pattern of the import of manufactured goods and export of raw materials has been reinstated on a large scale. But the SPDC has succeeded in promoting amicable relations with all its neighbors: India, Bangladesh, Thailand, and other members of ASEAN. In 1988, the Indian government was strongly critical of the SLORC's human rights abuses, but in more recent years ties have greatly improved, including cooperation in suppressing insurgents and building highways and other infrastructure in the India–Burma border area. Compared to the Ne Win era, the region where Burma is located is increasingly stable, prosperous, and economically integrated. This has benefited the SPDC, if not necessarily Burma's people.

The situation in Burma's former Frontier Areas was radically transformed by Khin Nyunt's policy of signing cease-fires with armed groups, beginning with the ethnic components of the Communist Party of Burma after its breakup in 1989. By 1997, cease-fires had been signed with 22 major and minor groups, including the Kachin Independence Organization and Khun Sa's drug-financed Mong Tai Army. This enabled the Tatmadaw to undermine the Democratic Alliance of Burma, a post-1988 united front of ethnic and Burmese student groups, and focus its armed might on the holdouts, especially the Karen National Union, resulting in the fall of KNU headquarters at Manerplaw in January 1995. Enjoying substantial autonomy, the United Wa State Army had emerged as the most powerful cease-fire group by the mid-1990s, and was exporting massive amounts of opiates and amphetamines to Thailand and China from processing centers in Shan State. For a time, Burma had the dubious distinction of being the world's largest single source of opiates, although it was surpassed by Afghanistan after the fall of the Taliban regime in 2001.

In early November 2005, the State Peace and Development Council began relocating civil servants to a heavily fortified compound located outside of Pyinmana, in southern Mandalay Division, a site that would replace Rangoon not only as military headquarters of the Tatmadaw but also as a new national capital (reportedly to be named *Nay Pyi Daw*, or "place of the king"). The move astounded both Burmese and overseas observers, who speculated that astrology and other occult arts must have played a role in the decision because Senior General Than Shwe is extremely superstitious. It is also likely that the generals' desire to insulate themselves from potential urban unrest like that of 1988 and to isolate themselves from the outside world (foreign diplomats were left in the dark about the decision) was also an important factor. However, whether "Nay Pyi Daw" will fully replace Rangoon as the country's administrative center remained unclear at the close of 2005.

Burma remains a country in crisis. Although a few prosper from state capitalism, the majority of the population face untamed inflation and economic uncertainty; social problems such as widespread malnutrition, drugs, and AIDS remain largely unaddressed; hundreds of thousands of Burmese are refugees in neighboring countries or are internally displaced; the country's political future remains unclear; and the democratic opposition faces harsher-than-ever suppression. Despite its leaders' commitment to "national unity," Burma is a deeply divided society, over which a history of war, colonial occupation, and ethnic antagonism casts a long, dark shadow.

The Dictionary

ADAPTATION OF EXPRESSIONS LAW (1989). In June 1989, the **State Law and Order Restoration Council** decreed the Adaptation of Expressions Law, which changed the official foreign language name of the country from "the Union of Burma" to "the Union of Myanma," or, more commonly in English, "Myanmar," and also changed many place names to a new romanized form closer to the **Burmese (Myanmar) language** pronunciation than terms originally used during the British colonial period. The military government justified the country name change on the grounds that "Burma" (*Bama* in Burmese) refers only to the **Burman (Bamar)** ethnic group, while "Myanmar" (*Myanma*) refers to the citizens of the country regardless of ethnic affiliation (e.g., the difference between "England" and "Britain"). In fact, this is untrue: both *Bama* and *Myanma* refer to the same thing, the country of the Burmans, though the former is more commonly found in conversation and the latter in more formal, literary contexts. Though the words have different nuances, they are used interchangeably by Burmese people in everyday communication. "Myanmar" has been adopted as the official country name by the **United Nations** and most Asian governments, but the governments of the **United States** and some European countries continue to use "Burma." Since 1989, preference for one or the other has to some extent expressed approval or disapproval of the post-1988 military government, which causes difficulties for those wishing to be politically neutral. To avoid making a political statement, a few writers use the cumbersome "Burma (Myanmar)," or vice versa.

Many towns and cities located on the coast had colonial-era English names based on nonstandard pronunciations of Burmese words by foreigners, which the Adaptation of Expressions Law changed to something closer to the Burmese original. The old name of **Rangoon** reflected the **Arakanese** pronunciation of "Yangon," which is now its official foreign language name. Other examples include **Pegu** (now "Bago"), **Moulmein** (now "Mawlamyine"), **Bassein** (now "Pathein"), and **Tavoy** (now "Dawei"). Because their transliteration into English more closely approximated the Burmese original, many towns in **Upper Burma**, such as **Mandalay**, **Sagaing**, and **Meiktila**, have the same romanizations under the pre- and post-1989 systems. However, **Ava** became "Inwa," **Pagan** became "Bagan," and **Magwe** became "Magway." The **Irrawaddy**, **Salween**, and **Sittang Rivers** became, respectively, "Ayeyarwady," "Thanlwin," and "Sittoung." Many of the post-1989 spellings of places in ethnic minority regions, especially **Shan State**, have no meaning in the local language, for example, the new rendering of **Keng Tung**, "Kyaing Tong." The new place names have caused considerable confusion, and many supporters of the movement for democracy refuse to use them. The law also changed the official foreign language name of the Burman and **Karen** ethnic nationalities, to "Bamar" and "Kayin," respectively. **Arakan** and **Karenni** have also disappeared from the official list of ethnic names, now replaced by "Rakhine" and "Kayah" (though both of these terms were also used before 1989). *See also* "Old and New Country and Place Names" in the frontmatter.

ADMINISTRATION AND SOCIETY, PRECOLONIAL BURMA. Before the British colonial period, Burma was an absolute monarchy, the king's authority legitimized by the myth of the **Maha Thamada** and his possession of superior merit, accumulated over many lifetimes (thus he was often referred to as *Hpaya laung*, or "future Buddha"). Residing at "the center of the universe" in the royal palace, he was both ceremonial ruler and power-holder. In a pattern established by the late **Toungoo Dynasty**, the king was advised by the **Hluttaw**, or Council of State, and the Byedaik, or Privy Council. The former was responsible for the executive and judicial functions of the state and the provincial administration, while the latter took care of the management of the royal court and liaison between the monarch and central government bodies.

On the regional level, the realm was divided into districts or *myo* (a word that also referred to provincial urban centers), encompassing what later was known as **Upper** and **Lower Burma**. Each *myo* was under the control of an appointed governor and a *myosa* (*myoza*, "district eater"), a member of the royal family or nobility whose income, as the name indicates, came from extracting resources from his or her jurisdiction rather than from a fixed salary. Local authorities known as *myothugyi*, whose posts were usually hereditary, acted as intermediaries between the governor and *myosa* on the one hand and the common people on the other, playing an important role in mitigating the most extreme royal demands on the villagers in the form of **rice**, silver, **forced labor**, and military service. In traditional Burmese political culture, the king and his officials were not—like the emperor and elite scholar-officials of Confucian China—regarded (ideally) as benevolent protectors of the people. Instead, the ruler (*min*) was described, along with fire, flood, personal enemies, and thieves, as being one of the "five dangerous things to be avoided." Oppressive kings like **Bodawpaya** drained the country of manpower and resources on expensive public works projects (including the massive **pagoda** at **Mingun**) and military campaigns against neighboring states, especially Siam, while weak monarchs like **Thibaw** allowed their realm to collapse into lawlessness. Rarely was a king both strong and moderate in his demands, though King **Mindon** approached this ideal. Palace politics was extremely unstable and at times violent, especially after a king died, and a succession struggle ensued among his many male progeny, that is, his sons by his numerous royal wives.

The society of the valley and delta of the **Irrawaddy (Ayeyarwady) River**, the Burmese heartland, was divided into four general strata: the *min-myo* (rulers), the *ponna-myo* (Brahmins, or ritualists versed in the Hindu Vedas), *thuhtay-myo* (bankers and rich merchants), and *sinyetha-myo* (the "poor people," or commoners). Modeled roughly on the caste system of India (the four *varna*), membership in these groups was hereditary and could be changed only by the king's decree. Another important division in precolonial Burmese society was between *ahmudan*, "royal service subjects"—members of descent groups who supplied the royal house with goods and services, including military officers and men, craftspeople, and palace servants—and *athi*, general subjects who paid taxes to the king. The *ahmudan* lived in discrete settlements outside the regular administration and were considered more prestigious than the *athi* because of their close association with the palace. A final social division existed between free people and slaves (*kyun*), who usually were dependent on a certain individual (e.g., debt slaves) or foreign prisoners of war, but who could belong to any of the four social strata mentioned above, with the exception of the royal family. By the end of the 18th century, a large number of foreigners had been forcibly relocated to Upper Burma, including Arakanese, Siamese, and people from **Manipur**, contributing to ethnic heterogeneity.

In precolonial Burma, "ethnic" consciousness in the modern sense did not exist, though antagonisms between **Burmans (Bamars)** and **Mons** intensified in Lower Burma after the mid-18th century: Burman rulers tended to view their Mon subjects as disloyal and all too eager to cooperate with archenemy Siam. But there was a strong consciousness of the differences between the cultures and lifestyles of lowlanders, such as the Burmans, Mons, and **Arakanese (Rakhines)**, who shared a common Indo-Buddhist civilization, and upland groups, such as the **Karens (Kayins)** and **Chins**, who were animist and lived in scattered communities without organized states. The traditional rulers of the **Shans (Tai)**, the *sawbwa*, had tributary relations with the Burmese king, and Shan princesses frequently married into the royal family. However, Burmese control over the **Shan States** was minimal and over the Chins, **Kachins**, and **Nagas**, it was practically nonexistent.

Nationhood—the concept of a fixed land area and population having a "national" identity—emerged in Burma during the British colonial period. During the dynastic period, the power of the state "radiated" outward from the royal capital, reaching to more distant regions (the mountainous areas) when the king was strong and contracting to close around the capital when his power and authority were weak. Thus, national **boundaries** were an idea introduced by the Western colonialists and employed after Burma became part of the community of independent nations after 1948.

ADMINISTRATION OF BURMA, BRITISH COLONIAL PERIOD. Following the formal annexation of **Upper Burma** in January 1886, Upper and **Lower Burma** were administered as a Province of the British Indian Empire. The country was subject to essentially the same laws and procedures as the Subcontinent, though the people, their customs, and their physical environments were quite different. The system was highly centralized and bureaucratized in **Burma Proper** (Upper and Lower Burma, also known after 1935 as "Ministerial Burma"). In 1897, the post of lieutenant governor of the province was established. Following the **dyarchy** reforms of 1923, Burma became a governor's province. Wielding executive authority and advised by a legislative council, the governor was answerable to the Viceroy of India.

The idea of establishing indirect rule in Burma Proper, employing a relative of King **Thibaw** as puppet monarch, was discarded early on because a suitable royal candidate could not be found. The Upper Burma Village Regulation (1887) and the Burma Village Act (1889) led to the abolition of the *myothugi*, district chiefs under the precolonial system who had enjoyed considerable autonomy and popular support. They were replaced by village headmen who were mere functionaries of the colonial state. Governmental legitimacy and social stability suffered.

The civil service bureaucracy was divided into two sections: the elite Indian Civil Service (ICS), who until the 1920s were entirely British, and the Provincial Civil Service, who included Burmese and **Anglo-Burmese**. By the beginning of the 20th century, specialized departments of the provincial government dealing with such matters as health, sanitation, education, veterinary science, agriculture, fisheries, etc., proliferated. Their specialized officials, responsible to departmental secretaries, operated independently of the local authorities and were coordinated by the Secretariat in **Rangoon (Yangon)**. In April 1937, Burma became a Crown Colony, whose governor was responsible directly to the British government in London.

Burma Proper contained eight (later seven) divisions: **Arakan, Irrawaddy, Magwe, Mandalay, Meiktila, Pegu, Sagaing,** and **Tenasserim**. These were subdivided into **districts**, subdivisions, **townships**, and village tracts. Administratively, the district (two or three per division) was the "pivot" of regional-local administration, supervised by deputy commissioners who had wide-ranging responsibilities.

Although constitutional reforms allowed for a measure of self-government during the 1920s and 1930s in "Ministerial Burma," the governor retained ultimate authority in vital areas such as defense and finances. He was also directly responsible for what became known as the **Frontier Areas**, where ethnic minorities, the so-called hill tribes, lived. Unlike Burma Proper, the Frontier Areas were allowed considerable autonomy in local administration, and rulers, such as the Shan *sawbwas* and Kachin *duwas*, retained their authority, if not their power. Several grades of "chiefs" were recognized by the British and were supervised by British residents. The five small **Karenni states** were not formally a part of British India but were in a "subordinate alliance" with the British government.

Because of the administrative separation of "Burma Proper" and the Frontier Areas, the country was never governed as a single unit during the colonial period, which had serious implications for **national unity** after independence in 1948. *See also* ADMINISTRATION AND SOCIETY, PRECOLONIAL BURMA; GOVERNMENT OF BURMA ACT; SHAN STATES.

ADMINISTRATION OF BURMA, BURMA SOCIALIST PROGRAMME PARTY ERA (1962–1988). Following the establishment of the **Revolutionary Council** by **Ne Win** in March 1962, state, division, and local administration became the responsibility of a hierarchy of **Security and Administration Committees (SAC)**, which on the national level were controlled by a Security and Administration Council Central Committee, directly answerable to the Revolutionary Council. Chairmen of the SACs on all levels were military officers.

Following implementation of the **Constitution of 1974**, the SACs were replaced by state/division, **township**, and ward/village tract **People's Councils**, whose members were elected by popular vote from a list approved by the **Burma Socialist Programme Party**. In principle, the People's Councils had responsibility for administration on the regional or local level, but in fact they exercised little autonomy. Military officers continued to play a dominant role in administration, while the influence of professionally trained civil servants, many of whom were forced to retire after 1962, declined. The abolition of the Secretariat in 1972 also diminished the influence of civilian civil servants. In addition, the administrative system was uniform for the whole country; no attempt was made to accommodate the special circumstances of the ethnic minority states. *See also* PYITHU HLUTTAW; STATE COUNCIL.

ADMINISTRATION OF BURMA, STATE LAW AND ORDER RESTORATION COUNCIL/STATE PEACE AND DEVELOPMENT COUNCIL ERA (1988–). After the **State Law and Order Restoration Council (SLORC)** was established on September 18, 1988, Burma's administrative system came under the control of a martial law regime. The **Constitution of 1974** was suspended and **People's Councils** and the **Burma Socialist Programme Party** were abolished. The situation was similar to the suspension of the **Constitution of 1947** following establishment of the **Revolutionary Council** in March 1962. On the national level, the chairman of the SLORC (known as the **State Peace and Development Council [SPDC]** after 1997) served concurrently as prime minister and head of the government's functionally specific, cabinet-level agencies (although a military leader different from the chairman of the SPDC, Senior General **Than Shwe**, was appointed prime minister in 2003).

On the regional and local levels, **state, division, township**, and ward/village tract "Law and Order Restoration Councils (LORCs)" composed of military officers directed governmental functions. With the reorganization of the SLORC as the SPDC in November 1997, the names of these bodies were changed to state/division, township, and ward/village tract "Peace and Development Councils." According to some observers, the original three-tiered structure of regional and local administration has been modified with the insertion of an additional level, "Township Circle" or **district** PDCs, between the state/division and township levels. Military control is pervasive, and there is some evidence that the authority of the central government has been weakened by the augmented powers of generals in charge of the **Regional Military Commands**. In addition, **cease-fire groups** in the ethnic minority areas often enjoy significant autonomy, including their own armed forces.

AGRICULTURE. Blessed with a warm climate and an abundance of land, Burma traditionally has been a country where no one starved.

Before World War II, it was the world's leading exporter of **rice**. Agriculture remains the most important sector in the Burmese economy, employing 63 percent of the labor force and producing 57 percent of the Gross Domestic Product (2000 figures). Agricultural products still predominate among Burma's exports, despite the increasing importance of energy exports. Most Burmese farmers are smallholders, their croplands averaging no more than two hectares (five acres). Three types of cultivated land are found: well-watered alluvial lowlands, located in and around the deltas of the **Irrawaddy (Ayeyarwady)**, **Sittang (Sittoung)**, and **Salween (Thanlwin) Rivers** and in coastal areas of **Arakan State**, where paddy **rice** is grown; the **Dry Zone** of central Burma along the upper reaches of the Irrawaddy, where water is insufficient for wet-rice cultivation (outside of irrigated areas, such as **Kyaukse**) and crops, such as oil seeds (sunflower and sesame), beans and pulses, sugar palms, maize, ground nuts (peanuts), and cotton are grown; and upland areas, especially near the borders with Thailand, China, and India, where ethnic minorities practice shifting cultivation (*taung-ya* or hill-clearing, though the **Shans** are cultivators of paddy rice). In upland areas, hillside vegetation is cleared, usually by burning, to prepare relatively poor soils for the cultivation of dry rice, buckwheat, or maize in a cycle of subsistence farming that is repeated every few years. In Shan and **Kachin States**, the most important agricultural export has been raw and processed **opium**, though cultivation and export of opiates have declined in recent years because of drug-eradication policies. Tropical and subtropical fruits are grown throughout the country. The pungent-smelling durian is perhaps the most widely esteemed, though strawberries grown around **Maymyo (Pyin Oo Lwin)** are also popular.

Burma's agricultural potential is huge because much arable land remains undeveloped or underutilized. The introduction of high-yield varieties of rice and other crops in the mid-1970s increased production, but the increases were not sustained during the 1980s because of the essentially coercive nature of the **Whole Township Extension Program** and insufficient inputs, such as fertilizers, pesticides, and farm mechanization (water buffalo or cattle are still widely used for plowing). Coercive state procurement of rice and other crops at artificially low prices has not given farmers incentives to be productive. Moreover, only about 13 percent of total arable land is irrigated, though the **State Peace and Development Council** has carried out a crash program in dam construction. Agriculture in nonirrigated areas is dependent upon the seasonal monsoon, making it hostage to periodic flooding and drought. To increase agricultural exports and earn hard currency, the military regime has promoted expansion of arable land, double cropping, and the development of large-scale "agribusinesses."

In the early 21st century, Burma faces an increasingly serious food security problem because of deforestation (causing floods and soil erosion), degradation of soils (partly because of double cropping and lack of fertilizers), and a chronically inefficient distribution system left over from the **Burma Socialist Programme Party** era. In contrast to the abundant past, malnutrition in both urban and rural areas is now widespread, especially among children. *See also* ECONOMY AND ECONOMIC POLICY, BURMA SOCIALIST PROGRAMME PARTY ERA; ECONOMY AND ECONOMIC POLICY, STATE LAW AND ORDER RESTORATION COUNCIL/STATE PEACE AND DEVELOPMENT COUNCIL ERA; HEALTH.

AID, FOREIGN (OFFICIAL DEVELOPMENT ASSISTANCE). After Burma became independent in 1948, it accepted aid from both Western and socialist nations, reflecting its policy of nonaligned neutrality. This included P.L. 480 grants from the **United States; Japanese** war reparations (which were not strictly aid, but constituted the largest early source of development assistance, a total of US$250 million between 1955 and 1965 and an additional US$140 million in "quasi-reparations" that were paid out until the early 1970s); assistance from the People's Republic of **China** and **India;** and loans and grants from **Russia** (the Soviet Union) and its Eastern European allies, including such projects as construction of **Rangoon (Yangon) Institute of Technology** and the Inya Lake Hotel. Aid flows were affected by political developments: In 1953, the government of U **Nu** terminated an aid agreement with the **United States** because of the Central Intelligence Agency's involvement with **Kuomintang (Guomindang)** forces in **Shan State;** in 1967, Beijing halted aid following **Anti-Chinese Riots.**

After **Ne Win** established the **Revolutionary Council** in 1962, aid was drastically reduced, with the important exception of Japanese war reparations and **United Nations** programs. However, the failure of socialist self-reliance to promote economic development led to a change in the regime's attitude toward foreign aid in the 1970s, at a time when it was promoting limited economic reform. In 1976, a donors' consortium, the **Burma Aid Group**, was established, consisting of Japan, the World Bank, the Asian Development Bank, West **Germany**, France, Great **Britain**, the United States, and others. Allocations from major donor countries increased greatly in the late 1970s, with Japan and West Germany the largest and second-largest bilateral (nation-to-nation) donors, respectively. Their assistance was mostly in the form of concessional loans denominated in yen and deutschmarks. Washington provided support for the Ne Win regime's drug-eradication program, selling Burma helicopters to be used to interdict cross-border drug trafficking. Total bilateral and multilateral aid allocations grew from US$22.9 million in 1970 to US$450.6 in 1988. But foreign debt piled up, reaching US$4.5–5 billion in the late 1980s; the government, unable to meet debt service obligations, sought and received Least Developed Country status from the United Nations in 1987.

In the wake of 1988's **Democracy Summer**, major donors halted flows of aid to protest human rights violations, and these **sanctions** remained in place through the early 21st century, due in part to the refusal of the **State Law and Order Restoration Council/State Peace and Development Council** to recognize the results of the **General Election of May 27, 1990**. After establishing formal diplomatic ties with the new military regime in February 1989, however, Japan resumed some aid projects and offered the SLORC debt relief grants. Western nations have given grants for humanitarian purposes, and China has emerged as an increasingly important aid donor. But in contrast to the 1976–1988 period, when the Ne Win regime became heavily dependent on official development assistance to fund internal investment, the post-1988 military regime's principal source of hard currency has been the sale of natural resources to neighboring countries and inflows of foreign private **investment**. *See also* ECONOMY AND ECONOMIC POLICY, BURMA SOCIALIST PROGRAMME PARTY ERA; ECONOMY AND ECONOMIC POLICY, STATE LAW AND ORDER RESTORATION COUNCIL/STATE PEACE AND DEVELOPMENT COUNCIL ERA.

AIDS IN BURMA. Burma has one of the highest instances of acquired immunity deficiency syndrome (AIDS) in Southeast Asia. Unsafe sexual practices (prophylactics are scarce and expensive, and sex education almost nonexistent) and the widespread use of **heroin** injected with unsanitary needles have resulted in an explosion of cases, as many as 600,000 AIDS/HIV-positive persons in 2005. The **State Peace and Development Council** has generally been slow in adopting effective countermeasures. However, several **nongovernmental organizations (NGOs)** have begun to address the problem.

AIDS is closely tied to poverty. Among the major spreaders of the AIDS virus are truck drivers who patronize sex workers while on the road. In the past, prostitutes were rare outside the big cities, but village women have entered the trade in increasing numbers because of the stagnating rural economy, meaning that truck drivers have greater access to sex workers. Because the SPDC invests very little in public health, treatment is almost nonexistent. The poor state of AIDS awareness has hastened its spread far beyond the world of drug addicts and brothels; for example, razors used to shave the heads of young monks during the ceremonies associated with *shinbyu* are sometimes infected, making them HIV-positive. Critics of **sanctions** claim that trade embargoes against Burmese exports (mostly garments destined for the **United States**) have put tens of thousands of factory women out of work, driving them into the sex industry and worsening the AIDS epidemic. *See also* HEALTH; HUMAN RIGHTS IN BURMA; WOMEN IN BURMESE SOCIETY.

AIR FORCE (TATMADAW LEI). One of the three services of the **Tatmadaw**, its commander in chief is a (three-star) lieutenant general and member of the **State Peace and Development Council**. Although compared to the **Army** it is small in terms of personnel, budget allocations, and political influence, the Air Force has experienced a major expansion in terms of personnel (15,000 in 2000, up from 7,500 in the mid-1980s), aircraft (including modern, though not state-of-the-art, interceptors and fighter-bombers), and other equipment since the **State Law and Order Restoration Council** was established in 1988. New aircraft have been procured mostly from the People's Republic of **China**, but also from **Russia** and Yugoslavia. Historically, the Air Force's mission has been support of Army ground operations, especially against ethnic minority and communist insurgents, but acquisition of modern jet fighters, including Russian-built Mig-29s, significantly increases its range of operation. Major air bases are located at **Mingaladon, Meiktila,** Shante (in **Mandalay Division), Myitkyina,** Hmawbi, **Toungoo (Taungoo),** and Namsang (in central **Shan State).**

AIR TRANSPORT, CIVIL. Before World War II, Imperial Airways of Britain offered service to **Sittwe (Sittway,** then known as Akyab) in present-day **Arakan (Rakhine) State** and **Rangoon (Yangon),** landing at the aerodrome at **Mingaladon,** which served then (as now) as the country's major international facility; competitor KLM Royal Dutch Airways also connected Rangoon with Europe, Singapore, and the Netherlands East Indies metropolis of Batavia (now Jakarta, Indonesia). For a brief period, the **Irrawaddy Flotilla Company** operated domestic air service between Rangoon, **Mandalay,** and other points in central and southern Burma.

After Burma became independent in 1948, the Union of Burma Air Transport Board was established, which became Union of Burma Airways (UBA) the next year. Following the **Karen (Kayin)** uprising of January 1949, domestic air links between the capital and beleaguered upcountry towns became vital for the survival of Prime Minister U **Nu**'s government, and UBA chartered a number of overseas private airlines to fly troops and supplies. Among these was Hong Kong's Cathay Pacific, which, in the words of one chronicler, was "something of a buccaneering outfit." After the government regained control of most of the central part of the country in 1950, contracts with foreign charter airlines were ended, and UBA expanded its service; by 1953, UBA's DC-3 aircraft were flying between Rangoon and 35 domestic destinations, including **Keng Tung** and **Myitkyina** in remote **Shan** and **Kachin States.**

In the mid-1950s, Mingaladon airport's newly completed, air-conditioned terminal building and 2,470-meter (8,100-foot)-long runway were among the best in Asia; the airport was included on east-west routes by major international airlines, including British Overseas Airways Corporation (BOAC), KLM, and Pan American Airways. But these airlines dropped their services during the **Ne Win** era (1962–1988), reflecting the country's isolation and economic stagnation. UBA flew domestic and international routes with Fokker F-27 and F-28 aircraft and chartered a Boeing 727 for international service in 1969, part of a **tourism** promotion policy. By the early 1990s, UBA, renamed Myanma Airways, flew aging aircraft that were so crash-prone that foreign governments advised their citizens not to use the airline.

The **State Law and Order Restoration Council**'s economic liberalization policies and the **"Visit Myanmar Year"** campaign in 1996–1997 led to the establishment of new airlines that were joint ventures with foreign companies: Myanmar Airways International, Air Mandalay, and Yangon Airways. The last two were designed to carry tourists to such popular domestic destinations as Mandalay, **Inle (Inlay) Lake**, and **Pagan (Bagan)**, using French-built 66-seat ATR-72 turboprops. A number of regional airlines fly into Rangoon, including Thai International, Malaysia Airlines, Air China, Biman Bangladesh, and Silk Air (Singapore).

In 2002, Burma had 80 airports, of which only eight had paved runways; only two airports had runways over 3,047 meters (10,055 feet) long. Thirty-four airports had runways under 914 meters (3,016 feet) long. Once one of Asia's most modern facilities, Mingaladon Airport is now obsolete, and its runway cannot take wide-bodied aircraft, such as Boeing 747s. In the late 1990s, the Japanese government gave "humanitarian aid" to modernize it, apparently fearing a crash by All Nippon Airways, which briefly offered a Kansai (Osaka)-Rangoon flight. A second airport serving Rangoon is planned near **Pegu (Bago)**, though it apparently remains in the planning stage. A new international airport at Mandalay was completed at a cost of US$3.15 billion in 2000. Its runway, at 4,242 meters (14,000 feet), is said to be the longest in Southeast Asia and is capable of accommodating wide-bodied aircraft. *See also* AIR FORCE (TATMADAW LEI); RAIL TRANSPORT; ROAD TRANSPORT; WATER TRANSPORT.

AKHAS. An ethnic nationality who live in **Shan State**, in the **Keng Tung (Kengtung)** region east of the **Salween (Thanlwin) River**. Known also as *Kaw* or *Ekaw*, they speak a Tibeto-Burman language and are also found in northern Thailand, Laos, and China's Yunnan Province, their place of origin. Living in settlements above 3,500 feet, they practice slash-and-burn agriculture on the hillsides, including cultivation of **opium** poppies. Most Akhas are animist, though some have been converted to Christianity by **missionaries**. Their lands were incorporated into the Northeastern Command of the **Communist Party of Burma (CPB)**, but after the 1989 CPB mutiny, Akha contingents have served in the **National Democratic Alliance Army— Eastern Shan State**, a drug-financed armed group.

ALAUNGPAYA, KING (r. 1752–1760). Founding king of the **Konbaung Dynasty**, he was a local leader at Moksobomyo, north of **Ava (Inwa)**, which he made into a fortified capital and renamed **Shwebo**. In 1752, **Binnya Dala**, the ruler of the **Mon** state of **Hanthawaddy**, captured Ava, but Alaungpaya (as he styled himself after proclaiming himself king, meaning "embryo Buddha") recaptured it the following year and led an armed expedition down the **Irrawaddy (Ayeyarwady) River** into **Lower Burma**, capturing **Dagon**, which he renamed **Rangoon (Yangon)**, meaning "end of strife," in 1755, **Syriam (Thanlyin)** in 1756, and Pegu in 1757. With Pegu's fall, Binnya Dala was deposed and the history of independent Mon states ended. Alaungpaya attacked the small but troublesome state of **Manipur** in northeastern India, dealt harshly with Mon uprisings in Lower Burma, and launched an unsuccessful invasion of Siam (**Thailand**) by way of **Tenasserim (Tanintharyi)** in 1760. On this expedition, he died of disease or injury.

An exemplar of warlike **Burman** values, historians believe that Alaungpaya's reign marked the beginning of polarization between the Burmans and the ethnic minorities, especially the rebellious Mons. Earlier kings, such as **Bayinnaung**, were great admirers of Mon culture. Lower Burma was largely depopulated by Alaungpaya's campaigns.

ALCHEMY. The "science" of magically transforming substances, the precursor of modern chemistry, which probably had its origins in ancient Egypt; distinct alchemical traditions emerged among the Greeks and Romans, Arabs, Indians, and Chinese. In Burma, metallurgy for magical purposes (*aggiya*, "work with fire") sought a "philosopher's stone" that would free the possessor from old age and death, circumventing the cycle of death and rebirth (*samsara*) that **Buddhism** declares is the fate of all living things. *Zawgyi* (alchemists) claimed that by extending life they would be able to encounter in person the Future Buddha, who will appear 5,000 years after the death of Gotama **Buddha**, enabling them to pass directly into *nibbana*. One of the most famous legendary alchemists was the "Goat-Bull Monk," who, having blinded himself, used the philosopher's stone he concocted to replace his sightless eyes with one eye each from a goat and a bull, bought at a butcher's shop. His image is found at the **Shwe Dagon Pagoda**. *Zawgyi* traditionally have been popular figures in Burmese drama, often depicted as pitiful or comic rather than heroic figures. Though strong in body and endowed with strong desires, they cannot have congress with women because the odor of meat-eating human beings is overpowering, and they must content themselves with the company of nonhuman "fruit maidens," which grow on extremely rare trees in the Himalayas. This legend may have been antimagical propaganda circulated by orthodox Buddhists. It also reflects the ancient belief that immortal beings are tragically denied the consolation of human companionship and love. *See also* DHAMMAZEDI; WEIKZA.

ALL BURMA FEDERATION OF STUDENT UNIONS (ABFSU). Growing out of the tradition of student political activism established by the **Rangoon University Students Union** and **All Burma Students Union** of the 1930s, the ABFSU first came to prominence when its leader, **Min Ko Naing**, called for a general strike on August 8, 1988, the **Four Eights (8.8.88) Movement**. It was formally established at a student conference on August 28, 1988, with Min Ko Naing as chairman and Moe Thee Zun as general secretary, bringing together student unions from a large number of universities and high schools. At that time, the ABFSU claimed a membership of 50,000. Following the seizure of power by the **State Law and Order Restoration Council (SLORC)**, the leaders of the student movement decided to divide it into three parts: a legal political party, the **Democratic Party for a New Society (DPNS)**; an armed movement, which became the **All Burma Students' Democratic Front (ABSDF)**; and the ABFSU, chaired by Min Ko Naing, which worked underground. The effectiveness of the student union movement, however, was hindered by the arrest of many of its leaders and members, including Min Ko Naing in 1989 (he was released in 2004). SLORC's tactics included dividing the movement against itself; closing down university campuses throughout most of the 1990s; and, perhaps most effectively, relocating universities in remote areas and keeping them under tight surveillance. *See also* STUDENTS, HISTORICAL ROLE OF.

ALL BURMA STUDENTS' DEMOCRATIC FRONT (ABSDF). Following the power seizure by the **State Law and Order Restoration Council** on September 18, 1988, thousands of students and other oppositionists fled central Burma for the border areas. By 1989, they totalled as many as 10,000 persons. On November 1, 1988, several student groups, affiliated with the **All Burma Federation of Student Unions**, held the first congress of the ABSDF in territory controlled by the **Karen National Union (KNU)** near the border with **Thailand**. The front, which claimed as many as 5,000 "student-soldiers" in 1990, was a founding member of the **Democratic Alliance of Burma (DAB)**, whose chairman was KNU leader Bo **Mya**. Its first chairman was Htun Aung Gyaw, but at the ABSDF second congress in 1991 it broke into two factions, led by Dr. Naing Aung and Moe Thee Zun. These were later reconciled, and the ABSDF chairman in 2005 was Than Khe.

The ABSDF's survival depended on good relations with the KNU, which in the early years supplied it with food, shelter, and a limited number of arms. The front suffered from not only factional divisions but also the hard living conditions in the jungle, which caused many to leave its ranks and go to **Thailand** or other foreign countries. It also suffered a serious reverse when the **Tatmadaw** captured the KNU headquarters at **Manerplaw** in January 1995 (its headquarters at Dawn Gwin were located nearby). Although its original purpose was to carry out armed struggle against the military regime, the ABSDF has branched out into health, educational, and community development programs. It has attempted to organize grassroots activities inside Burma and also functions as a provider of information to the outside world on the Burmese political situation. Perhaps its greatest historical significance has been its promotion of a united front between **Burman (Bamar)** and ethnic minority oppositionists. With a primarily Burman membership, it has lived, worked, and fought side by side with minorities, especially the **Karens (Kayins)**. *See also* NATIONAL COALITION GOVERNMENT OF THE UNION OF BURMA; STUDENTS, HISTORICAL ROLE OF.

ALL BURMA STUDENTS UNION (ABSU). Known by the acronym *Ba Ka Tha* in the **Burmese (Myanmar) language**, the ABSU was established at a nationwide students' conference on May 8, 1936. Its original leaders included Ko **Aung San**; it participated in the massive demonstrations of 1938–1939 organized by the **Dobama Asiayone** and was a member of the **Freedom Bloc** united front headed by **Ba Maw** and Aung San before **World War II**. It played a prominent though not unchallenged role in student political activism during the parliamentary period (1948–1962), was suppressed by the **Ne Win** regime, and came into prominence again during the nationwide demonstrations of 1988. *See also* ALL BURMA FEDERATION OF STUDENT UNIONS; STUDENTS, HISTORICAL ROLE OF.

ALL BURMA YOUNG MONKS UNION (ABYMU). Established on November 27, 1988, the ABYMU became a member of the **Democratic Alliance of Burma (DAB)** and supports its program of resisting the post-1988 military regime, though "within the bounds of Buddhist practices"; that is, it does not take part in armed struggle. In its publicity, it has drawn attention to the **State Law and Order Restoration Council/State Peace and Development Council**'s arrest of dissident members of the **Sangha** and the council's attempts to use **Buddhism** to secure its hold on power.

ALL RAMANYA MON ASSOCIATION (ARMA). Established in August 1939 in **Rangoon (Yangon)**, near the **Shwe Dagon Pagoda**, ARMA was a nonpolitical organization whose goal was the preservation of **Mon** language, culture, and identity. Largely inactive during **World War II**, after the war the Association published Mon language textbooks and a journal, *The Mon Bulletin*. Although it was basically apolitical, some ARMA members supported the **Anti-Fascist People's Freedom League**, while others wanted to make common cause with other minority groups, especially the **Karens (Kayins)**. *See also* NEW MON STATE PARTY.

AMARAPURA. Meaning "city of the Immortals," Amarapura is located 11 kilometers southwest of **Mandalay**, in **Mandalay Division**. King **Bodawpaya** of the **Konbaung Dynasty** made it his royal capital in 1783, reportedly because the bloody purges carried out in association with his rise to power left the old capital, **Ava (Inwa)**, infested with wrathful *nats*; the capital was located at Ava from 1823 to 1837, but was reestablished at Amarapura from 1841 to 1857, before King **Mindon** moved it to its final location, Mandalay. Also known as Taungmyo ("Southern City"), Amarapura has retained little of its past glory but is now the center of the Burmese silk weaving industry.

AMPHETAMINES (ATS). Or metamphetamines. Known as *yaa baa* ("crazy medicine") in the Thai language, a flood of amphetamine-type stimulants (ATS) or "speed" pills have entered Thailand from Burma's **Shan State** since the mid-1990s, to an extent eclipsing the traditional but declining production and export of **opium**. Total production is estimated at 800 million tablets, most of which are produced in territory controlled by the **United Wa State Army**. In contrast to opium suppression measures taken by the **State Peace and Development Council**, the military regime has done little to deal with the problem of amphetamines, which is creating major social and health problems not only in Thailand but in other Asian countries, including Burma itself. *See also* DRUG ECONOMY; HEROIN.

ANADE (AH-NAR-DE). A social value that many Burmese believe is unique to their culture, though equivalents are found in other Asian societies. It involves very strong inhibitions against asserting oneself in human relations, described as shyness, embarrassment, or awkwardness. This is coupled with a strong sense of consideration for the feelings of others and a desire not to cause them to feel psychological distress or unease. For example, *anade* may inhibit a student from asking questions of a teacher, even if he or she does not understand a lecture, because this would trouble a social superior; a Burmese person may go to great effort or expense to show a guest some sight of interest, such as a **pagoda**, that he or she has seen many times but to put the guest's heart at rest about obligations accrued will claim that this is also the first time he or she has seen it. A person may hesitate to tell family members that he or she is seriously ill, for fear of causing them worry and distress.

Anade is not supposed to be typical of relations between close friends, who can afford to be frank with each other, or in situations where the agent sees himself or herself as superior to others, for example, a colonial-era civil servant interacting with villagers, a **Tatmadaw** officer dealing with civilians, or perhaps a **Burman (Bamar)** among ethnic minorities. In such cases, bullying often occurs, given the strong sense of hierarchy and inequality that pervades social relations. Many observers of the contemporary Burmese scene claim that *anade* inhibits the development of democracy and a civil society because it makes it difficult for people to discuss things frankly or debate issues. Such frankness or directness is regarded as aggression.

Non-Burmese dealing with Burmese often find it difficult to get at the truth of a matter because the latter may feel reluctant to divulge bad or unsettling news that could be distressful to the hearer, even if in the long run it would be in his or her interest to know about it.

It is probably necessary to distinguish between *anade* and mere survival tactics, or passivity in the face of danger. For, example, during the **Ne Win** period (1962–1988), his subordinates were very careful to give him nothing but good news, for example, about the performance of the socialist economy. Because the hot-tempered dictator's word was law, he would readily punish subordinates who displeased him, with no hope for reprieve. *See also HPOUN.*

ANANDA PAHTO (ANANDA TEMPLE). One of the principal **Buddhist** monuments (*pahto*) of **Pagan (Bagan)**, believed to have been built in the early 12th century by King **Kyanzittha** (r. 1084–1112). A square, terraced building with entrances on each side and narrow, vaulted interior passages, its highest elevation, a gilded *hti*, is 51 meters. At the center of the interior are standing images of the four historical Buddhas, including Gotama **Buddha**, before which life-sized statues of Kyanzittha and **Shin Arahan**, the king's Buddhist teacher, kneel. The Ananda is richly decorated with bas reliefs and terra cotta tiles depicting the **Jatakas**, or birth-tales of the Buddha. *See also* ARCHITECTURE, RELIGIOUS; PAGAN DYNASTY; SHWEZIGON PAGODA.

ANAUKPETLUN, KING (r. 1605–1628). Monarch of the **Toungoo Dynasty**, who succeeded in reasserting control over **Upper** and **Lower Burma** following the collapse of royal power at the end of the 16th century. In 1613, he captured **Syriam (Thanlyin)** and executed the Portuguese soldier of fortune **Felipe de Brito**, who had carved out his own kingdom in that part of the country in an alliance with a **Mon** prince. Anaukpetlun also waged war aggressively with **Thailand** (Siam), capturing Chiang Mai and turning it into a Burmese province in 1615.

ANAWRAHTA, KING (r. 1044–1077). Also known as *Aniruddha*, the **Burman (Bamar)** founding king of the **Pagan (Bagan) Dynasty** and the first unifier of **Upper Burma** and **Lower Burma**. He established what is sometimes called the "First Burmese (Myanmar) Empire." Conquering the Mon city-state of **Thaton** in 1057, he brought its ruler, Manuha (or Makuta) and 30,000 of his subjects back to **Pagan (Bagan)**. This resulted in a transformation of the culture of the unsophisticated and warlike Burmans, who were deeply influenced by the older and more refined art, literature, and manners of the **Mons**. In effect, the Mons were intermediaries who brought the Burmans into the mainstream of Indo-Buddhist civilization. The earliest monuments at Pagan are of Mon design, and the Burmans adapted the Mon writing system to their own language. But the most important development of Anawrahta's reign was his recognition of Theravada **Buddhism** as the state religion, largely through the influence of a Mon monk, **Shin Arahan**. Among the booty brought back from Thaton were copies of the Pali **Tipitaka**. Anawrahta curbed, but did not eliminate, Mahayana influences, and established the pantheon of 37 *nats*, enshrined at the **Shwezigon Pagoda**, who were an important though subordinate feature of later Burmese religious life. His realm apparently included most of modern Burma, including parts of **Arakan, Tenasserim (Tanintharyi)**, and possibly **Shan State**. Some historians believe he blocked the westward expansion of the Khmer Angkor Empire, ruled by Suryavarman I, and had close relations with the Sinhalese ruler of Sri Lanka, a coreligionist. *See also* KYANZITTHA, KING; MANUHA TEMPLE.

ANGLO-BURMESE. Also known as Anglo-Burmans or Eurasians, the children of mixed European and Burmese parentage played a prominent role in colonial society. Colonial Burma was an intensely race-conscious society, and Anglo-Burmese, along with Anglo-Indians (children of mixed European-Indian parentage) occupied an ambiguous position. Although they were never fully accepted in either indigenous or European society, the British considered them more trustworthy than the indigenous ethnic groups, especially the **Burmans (Bamars)**. The Anglo-Burmese found employment in the civil service (working on the railroads, port authority, and schools), the police, and the **colonial armed forces**, as well as in private business. Because of this, the Burmese often resented them, especially after nationalist sentiment intensified in the 1920s and 1930s. Usually the term "Anglo-Burmese" was used synonymously with "Eurasian" to refer not only to persons of partial British ancestry but also to the children of Burmese and continental European (especially Portuguese), North American, Australian, and possibly also Middle Eastern (**Armenian**) parents. Most Anglo-Burmese were Christians and were educated at schools run by **missionaries**. They possessed their own culture and ways of life, reflecting British values, and are best understood not as a "race" (or "mixed race") but as a distinct ethnic group.

The history of Anglo-Burmese/Eurasians goes back at least to the **Bayingyi**, Portuguese followers of **Felipe de Brito** who were resettled near **Shwebo** in **Upper Burma** in the early 17th century. Before the **Third Anglo-Burmese War** and the fall of the **Konbaung Dynasty**, a special official, the *kalawun*, was responsible for resident Europeans, Eurasians, and Indians (*kala* originally referring in the **Burmese [Myanmar] language** to persons from the Indian subcontinent). Colonization brought large numbers of British male soldiers, officials, and merchants, many of whom had relationships with Burmese women, although such contacts were officially discouraged. This policy was in contrast to the Netherlands East Indies (now Indonesia), where there was a centuries-long tradition of intermarriage between Europeans and locals (though the Dutch, for status reasons, also preferred "pure" European spouses). This created a lamentable double standard. European women in Burma were few, especially up-country. Brief liaisons with local women, or the keeping of Burmese mistresses, was tolerated, while lawful matrimony with a Burmese woman often subjected a European and his children to both social and official opprobrium. Gordon Luce, an eminent scholar of early Burma, had a Burmese wife, and was criticized by the governor himself, Reginald Craddock, for being "pro-Burman" (that is, liking the Burmese better than his own race). Because of this double standard, European men frequently abandoned their Burmese consorts and Eurasian children, leaving them destitute and at the mercy of a society that despised them. Some of the most vivid descriptions of the Anglo-Burmese plight are found in **George Orwell**'s *Burmese Days*. However, toward the close of the colonial era, the prejudice against interracial marriage seems to have diminished.

In the 1930s, the Eurasian population of Burma, including Anglo-Burmese, Anglo-Indians, and others, was 110,000 (out of a total of 17 million). The 1931 census of **Rangoon (Yangon)** counted 9,878 Anglo-Indians, an official category that included Anglo-Burmese, out of a total population of 400,415; this was more than double the 1901 figure, 4,674 out of a total of 248,060. Special seats were allocated for Anglo-Indians/Anglo-Burmese in the legislatures established by the **dyarchy** reforms of 1923 and the **Government of Burma Act** of 1935.

When the Japanese invaded Burma in late 1941, many Anglo-Burmese left the country, often going on foot over the mountains to India and suffering great hardship. Those who remained frequently attempted to pass as Burmese. As Burma approached independence after **World War II**, the Anglo-Burmese community faced a difficult choice: whether to throw in their lot with the new nation, necessary for surviving in a Burmese- or Burman-dominated society, or leave their homeland of many generations. Independence leader **Aung San** stressed that they must "prove their allegiance by actions and not by words," reflecting the nationalist belief that they had been "disloyal" in the past. They continued to play an important role in national life during the period when U **Nu** was prime minister (1948–1962), but the establishment of a military regime by **Ne Win** in 1962 led to their exclusion from the civil service and the higher ranks of the **Tatmadaw**. They were denied full citizenship rights under the **Citizenship Law** of 1982 because their ancestors had arrived in Burma after the **First Anglo-Burmese War** (1824–1826). Despite such barriers, a handful of Anglo-Burmese achieved prominence after 1962, including an Anglo-**Shan**, Brigadier Tommy Clift, who served in the original **Revolutionary Council;** June Rose Bellamy (Yadana Natmai), the child of an Australian and a Konbaung princess who became Ne Win's wife; and Brigadier David Abel, who served as minister of economic planning under the **State Law and Order Restoration Council (SLORC).** However, the SLORC and the **State Peace and Development Council** perpetrated crude slanders against **Aung San Suu Kyi**, accusing her of being a "race-traitor" because she had married an Englishman, Dr. Michael Aris.

Many Anglo-Burmese emigrated to the United Kingdom, Australia, and other countries, the community in western Australia being especially prominent. Because of their fluency in English and their cultural orientation to the West, Anglo-Burmese have found it relatively easy to assimilate to British and Australian society.

ANGLO-BURMESE WAR, FIRST (1824–1826). War between Burma and British India broke out on two fronts in January 1824: Cachar in northeastern **India** and the border between Burmese-ruled **Arakan (Rhakine)** and British Bengal. The latter had been the site of border clashes and insurgent activity by Arakanese rebels since King **Bodawpaya** conquered and sacked the kingdom of Arakan in 1784. The Burmese commander, **Maha Bandula**, adopted an aggressive policy of catching the British in a double pincer movement, planning to invade Bengal from Arakan while a second force would enter British Indian territory from the northeastern hills; his goal was apparently the conquest of Bengal. But Maha Bandula's strategy was thwarted by an unexpected British landing at **Rangoon (Yangon)** on May 10, 1824. Forced to return home from Arakan, he attempted to blockade the British in Rangoon, but was killed in battle in April 1825 at Danubyu (now in **Irrawaddy [Ayeyarwady] Division**). The British expeditionary force moved north along the **Irrawaddy (Ayeyarwady) River**, capturing **Prome (Pyay)** and coming within 64 kilometers of the royal capital at **Ava (Inwa)**. His capital endangered, King Bagyidaw (r. 1819–1838) was obliged to sign the Treaty of Yandabo on February 24, 1826; it provided for cession of the territories of **Arakan** and **Tenasserim (Tanintharyi)** to the British, recognition of British dominance over the small states of northeastern India (including Cachar, Assam, and **Manipur**), a million-pound indemnity, and the establishment of diplomatic relations between Ava and Calcutta. When the indemnity was paid in full, British forces quit Rangoon, in December 1826.

The war was a classic instance of the clash between two expanding empires. Though the Burmese fought with great courage in defense of their homeland, British superiority in technology and organization prevailed, though at a high price, because 15,000 out of a total force of 40,000 British Indian troops died, mostly from disease and lack of adequate supplies. The war marked a shift in Burma's relations with Britain from the offensive to the defensive. But with the exception of King **Mindon** (r. 1853–1878), Burmese monarchs failed to find a way of dealing effectively with the people they dismissively called the *Kalapyu* ("white Indians"). The **Second** and **Third Anglo-Burmese Wars** were examples of gunboat diplomacy rather than protracted wars and resulted in Burma's complete colonization.

ANGLO-BURMESE WAR, SECOND (1852). What began as a series of legal and commercial disputes between British India and Burma ended in the annexation of **Lower Burma.** Following the fining of two British sea captains for various offenses by the Burmese governor of **Rangoon (Yangon)** and the captains' request that Calcutta enforce compensation, Lord Dalhousie, the Indian governor-general, sent a naval force to Rangoon demanding the sum, a little less than £2,000, and removal of the Rangoon governor. Intent on war and expansion of British rule, Dalhousie issued a further, stiffer ultimatum (including an indemnity of the equivalent of £100,000), and sent an expeditionary force to Rangoon in April 1852. The Burmese response was incoherent, and the invading force speedily gained control of most of Lower Burma, which was declared the British Indian Province of **Pegu (Bago)** on December 20, 1852. In 1863, this territory was amalgamated with **Arakan** and **Tenasserim (Tanintharyi),** which had been annexed during the **First Anglo-Burmese War.**

The war marked a turning point in the country's colonization. The Burmese kingdom was deprived of some of its richest provinces, where the British developed a flourishing export economy based on **rice.** Rangoon, later independent Burma's capital, became the colony's economic and administrative center. The moderate King **Mindon** (r. 1853–1878) tried to negotiate the return of Lower Burma, but without success. Unlike the first war, the second one was not concluded with a treaty, and Anglo-Burmese relations were highly unstable. *See also* ANGLO-BURMESE WAR, THIRD.

ANGLO-BURMESE WAR, THIRD (1885). As in the **Second Anglo-Burmese War**, the immediate cause of the third war was a relatively minor dispute, the decision of the Burmese government to impose a fine on a British firm, the Bombay Burmah Trading Company (BBTC), for illegal extraction of **teak** from royal forests near **Toungoo (Taungoo)**. In addition, against the background of Anglo-French rivalry following establishment of the latter's interests in Indochina, the attempt of King **Thibaw** (r. 1878–1885) to cultivate close ties with Paris to counterbalance the British proved dangerously provocative (there were rumors that if the BBTC's forestry lease was terminated, it would be given to a French company). His rule was undermined by incompetence and factionalism, and his powerful Queen **Supayalat**, backed by a reactionary court faction, demanded a hard line against the British. The fact that the British envoy to the court at **Mandalay** had been recalled (in 1879) made negotiation over the dispute nearly impossible, while the rumors of expanding French influence grew thicker on the ground in the royal city and in **Rangoon (Yangon)**.

On October 22, 1885, the Viceroy of India, Lord Dufferin, sent an ultimatum to Thibaw demanding settlement of the commercial dispute, further trade privileges for the British, reestablishment of diplomatic relations, and British control of Burma's foreign relations, a measure that, if accepted, would have meant an end to the country's independence. On November 9, Thibaw issued an ambiguous reply. It was interpreted as a refusal, and a British expeditionary force was ordered to move up the **Irrawaddy (Ayeyarwady) River** from **Lower Burma** on November 14. It captured Mandalay two weeks later, after minimal Burmese resistance. Thibaw and Supayalat were sent into exile in India, to the distress of their subjects. On January 1, 1886, the annexation of **Upper Burma** was proclaimed, and subsequently all of Burma was made a province of the British Indian Empire. Although the Third Anglo-Burmese War was little more than "gunboat (or riverboat) diplomacy," British troops were tied down for years afterwards, suppressing guerrilla resistance both in what became known as **Burma Proper** and the **Frontier Areas**. *See also*

ADMINISTRATION OF BURMA, BRITISH COLONIAL PE-
RIOD; PACIFICATION OF BURMA.

ANGLO-CHIN WAR (1917–1919). A major event in the history of
Burma's **Chins**, sparked by the refusal of many young Chin men, especially those belonging to tribes living around **Haka (Hakha)**, to
obey British orders to make themselves available for combat and
non-combat service in connection with World War I. At the time, as
many as one million men from India and Burma were serving in
France and Middle Eastern combat zones. A major reason for the
Chins' rebellion was their belief that once separated from their land,
they would not be protected by their local guardian deities (*Khua-
hrum*). Following the rebels' unsuccessful attempt to capture Haka,
British forces carried out systematic and sometimes brutal pacification of villages in the rebel areas, which in many ways resembled the
"**Four Cuts**" policy of the **Tatmadaw**. In 1919, when the rebellion
was suppressed, rebel leaders were tried, imprisoned, and in three
cases, sentenced to death. However, the Anglo-Chin War marked an
important turning point in relations between the Chins and the colonial government: To gain local support, the British recognized the authority of the traditional *Ram-uk* (chiefs), which had been nullified
by the 1896 Chin Hills Regulations; recruited Chins to serve in the
colonial army; and made schools established by Christian **missionaries** part of the colonial education system. These changes, coupled
with the influence of thousands of young Chins who did serve in Europe, resulted in a social transformation of East **Chinram**, including
a rapid increase in converts to Christianity. During **World War II**,
Chin soldiers played a major role in British campaigns against the
Japanese. *See also* STEVENSON, H. N. C.

ANTI-CHINESE RIOTS (JUNE 22–29, 1967). Popular resentment
against **black market** entrepreneurs of Chinese ancestry became strong
in the 1960s as such necessities as **rice** were increasingly in short supply because of rigid socialist policies. Moreover, in 1967 officials at
the Chinese embassy in **Rangoon (Yangon)** began encouraging pro-
Beijing local Chinese to express their support for the Great Proletarian
Cultural Revolution, including the wearing of red armbands and Mao
Zedong badges by Chinese students in state-run Burmese schools. This

was seen as an affront to Burma's national sovereignty, and badge-wearing was prohibited by the authorities on June 19, 1967. Two thousand Chinese students held demonstrations in protest and were attacked by local Burmese in what was probably the worst racial violence since the 1930s. Mobs wrecked Chinese-owned shops and houses in downtown Rangoon and killed around 50 people (official figure; the Chinese government said that several hundred were killed). The Chinese embassy was attacked on June 29, and one official was killed by a Burmese intruder.

The **Ne Win** regime proclaimed martial law but failed to apologize for the incidents, causing what was probably the greatest diplomatic crisis in Burma's post-independence history. The killer of the Chinese official was only punished for criminal trespass on embassy property. Not only did the Beijing government withdraw its ambassador, suspend **foreign aid** programs, and begin broadcasting propaganda calling for the overthrow of "fascist dictator" Ne Win, but it also established a powerful **Communist Party of Burma** base along the China–Burma border in **Shan State**. The CPB's "Northeastern Command" soon became the strongest and best-organized insurgency fighting the central government. There is evidence that the Ne Win regime encouraged anti-Chinese violence in order to find an outlet for the people's growing economic discontent, but if this is true, China exacted a heavy price. *See also* CHINA, PEOPLE'S REPUBLIC, RELATIONS WITH.

ANTI-FASCIST ORGANIZATION (AFO). Term used by the British to refer to underground networks of **Thakins**, young military officers and members of the **Communist Party of Burma** who prepared for an uprising against the Japanese, working closely with **Force 136**. Prominent AFO leaders were **Aung San**, Thakin **Than Tun**, and Thakin **Soe**. Operating between August 1944 and May 1945, the AFO was the precursor of the **Anti-Fascist People's Freedom League** (AFPFL). *See also* BURMA NATIONAL ARMY; MOUNTBATTEN, LORD LOUIS; THEIN PE MYINT, THAKIN; WORLD WAR II IN BURMA (MILITARY OPERATIONS).

ANTI-FASCIST PEOPLE'S FREEDOM LEAGUE (AFPFL). Established in August 1944 during the **Japanese Occupation**, by **Aung**

San and **Than Tun**, and known to the British as the **Anti-Fascist Organization**, its founding charter outlined its goals as ridding the country of the "fascist Japanese" and winning independence. At the end of the war, it emerged as the most powerful political organization in Burma, successfully negotiating with the British to achieve independence and governing the country during the tumultuous period from 1948 to 1958. Both its popular appeal and its ultimate weakness derived from its structure; it was not a single party but a united front organization consisting of groups with diverse agendas, of which the **Socialist Party** and its affiliated Burma Trade Union Congress and All Burma Peasants' Organization were the most important. Other component groups included the Burma Muslim Congress, the Karen National Congress, the United Hill Peoples' Congress, the All-Burma Women's Freedom League, the Youth League, and the All Burma Teachers' organization. The **People's Volunteer Organization** (**PVO**) was the League's paramilitary unit, made up of veterans of the **Patriotic Burmese Forces/Burma National Army**. The **Communist Party of Burma** was expelled from the AFPFL in October 1946. The League won a decisive victory in the April 1947 elections to the Constituent Assembly, the interim legislature charged with drafting the **Constitution of 1947**, gaining 171 of 182 noncommunal seats contested. Aung San was president of the AFPFL until his assassination on July 19, 1947, when U **Nu** assumed the post and became independent Burma's first prime minister.

In the 1951 general election, held over seven months because insurgencies made polling in some areas difficult, the AFPFL won 200 out of 239 seats contested. In the April 1956 general election, Burma's second, the AFPFL and its allies won 173 seats (the AFPFL alone won 155), still a solid majority, though a stronger opposition had emerged in the form of the **National Unity Front**.

The League's lack of internal coherence created serious problems, especially as the Socialist Party under **Ba Swe** and Kyaw Nyein grew stronger and threatened to break away, leaving the AFPFL a powerless rump. Through their intolerance and dogmatism, the socialists made many enemies, especially among the ethnic minorities. The Auxiliary Union Military Police functioned as their private army. In June 1958, the League split into two rival factions, the "Clean AFPFL" led by U Nu and the "Stable AFPFL" under Ba Swe and Kyaw

Nyein. Because the split threatened to make Burma ungovernable, U Nu requested that General **Ne Win**, who as commander in chief of the **Tatmadaw** had cultivated an image of responsible neutrality, establish a **Caretaker Government**. When general elections were held in February 1960, U Nu's faction, later renamed the **Pyidaungsu Party**, was returned to power, defeating the AFPFL-Stable.

ANTI-INDIAN RIOTS (1930, 1938). When Indian dockworkers in **Rangoon (Yangon)** went on strike in 1930, their employers hired Burmese to replace them; as soon as the strike was settled in May, the Indians were rehired, the Burmese discharged, and fighting broke out between the two groups of workers, which soon turned into mob violence in which hundreds of Indians, including women and children, were killed. The British authorities were overwhelmed by the scale of the riots, which raged unchecked for two days. In July 1938, U **Saw** and politically active members of the **Sangha** denounced a book written by an Indian Muslim that allegedly disparaged the **Buddhist** religion, leading to further anti-Indian riots and almost 200 more people killed. Both incidents showed the fragility of Burma's colonial-era **plural society**. *See also* INDIANS IN BURMA.

ANTI-SEPARATION LEAGUE. Also known as the Anti-Separationist League, an organization established in July 1932 to bring together all those groups who opposed Burma's constitutional separation from India. Dr. **Ba Maw**, an influential figure in the League, advocated temporary federation with India as a step before attainment of full independence. *See also* GOVERNMENT OF BURMA ACT.

ANYEINT (ANYEINT PWE). A kind of traditional performance combining instrumental music, song, dance, and comedy routines. It has been compared to vaudeville. Originally confined to the royal court, the demise of the **Konbaung Dynasty** in 1885 led to its widespread adoption as popular entertainment. *Anyeint* troupes contain about 10 or 12 members, both male and female. During the colonial, U **Nu**, and **Ne Win** periods, it was not uncommon for such troupes to include comedians who made members of the political elite into figures of harmless fun. However, political satire in any form has been prohibited by the **State Law and Order Restoration Council/State Peace and Development Council**, as reflected in their arrest of the **Moustache Brothers** in 1996. *See also PWE.*

ARAKAN LEAGUE FOR DEMOCRACY (ALD). Established by Dr. Saw Mra Aung and U Oo Tha Tun following the 1988 prodemocracy movement, the ALD won 11 out of 26 constituencies contested in **Arakan (Rakhine) State** in the **General Election of May 27, 1990.** This made it, in terms of seats won, the third most successful party in the election, behind the **National League for Democracy** (392 seats) and the **Shan Nationalities League for Democracy** (23 seats).

ARAKAN NATIONAL CONGRESS (ANC). Established in 1938 to promote the interests of the **Arakanese (Rakhines)**, it held its first convention in 1940. After **World War II, Aung San** persuaded U Aung Zan Wai and other leaders to dissolve the ANC and join the **Anti-Fascist People's Freedom League** as individuals rather than as members of an AFPFL united front group. Meanwhile, U Seinda, a militant Arakanese leader and member of the **Sangha,** began resistance against the central government in 1946 with the goal of establishing an independent Arakan.

ARAKAN (RAKHINE, RAKHAING). A series of independent kingdoms that flourished from around the fourth century CE, when an urban center was established at Dhanyawadi, until 1784–1785, when Arakan was conquered by the **Burman (Bamar)** King **Bodawpaya.** Located in a coastal and riverine region largely coterminous with modern **Arakan (Rakhine) State**, the Arakanese enjoyed abundant supplies of water, rich harvests of **rice**, and close land and sea communications with the Indian subcontinent. After Dhanyawadi's fall, new capitals and states were established at Vesali (sixth to tenth centuries CE), and other locations on or near the Le-Mro River.

The original Arakanese were probably from India, but the eighth- and ninth-century migration of Tibeto-Burman peoples created a population linguistically and culturally closely related to the Burmans. Arakan was one of the first areas in Southeast Asia to receive Indian civilization and the Buddhist religion, and its importance to

Buddhism is reflected in the legend of the **Maha Muni Image**, which Bodawpaya, like his predecessor King **Arawrahta**, longed to capture. Although Islamic influences were strong, the Arakan kingdoms were Buddhist, and a number of distinctive **pagodas** and temples are located there, including the **Shitthaung (Sittaung) temple.** These are comparable in historical and artistic importance to those found at **Pagan (Bagan).**

Arakan's golden age was the early centuries of the **Mrauk-U (Mrohaung, Myohaung)** period (1433–1784), when the capital of Mrauk-U was a center of free trade and a formidable naval power in the Bay of Bengal. In the 16th and 17th centuries, Portuguese mercenaries helped Mrauk-U control the regional slave trade and occupy the eastern part of Bengal. At the end of the 16th century, an Arakanese force invaded **Lower Burma**, capturing the capital city of **Pegu (Bago).** For a brief time, Mrauk-U's authority extended along the coast from Dhaka (Dacca) in modern Bangladesh to **Moulmein (Mawlamyine)** in present-day **Mon State.** During the late 17th and 18th centuries, however, the country was weakened by repeated civil wars and the growing power of the Mughal Empire in India and the Burmans. In October–December 1784, Mrauk-U fell quickly to a Burman occupying force, which took the Maha Muni Image, the royal family, and 20,000 Arakanese subjects back to Bodawpaya's capital of **Amarapura.** Arakanese resistance against the Burmans continued until the British captured it during the **First Anglo-Burmese War** of 1824–1826. *See also* ARAKANESE; MIN BIN, KING.

ARAKAN (RAKHINE) STATE. One of Burma's 14 **states** and **divisions**, it has an area of 36,778 square kilometres (14,200 square miles) and a population estimated at 2.7 million in 2000 (1983 census figure: 2,045,559). Ethnically, the majority of the population are **Arakanese (Rakhines)**, who are **Buddhists** and share strong cultural and linguistic affinities with the **Burmans (Bamars)**, though **Arakan (Rakhine)** was an independent state until subjugated by King **Bodawpaya** in 1784. However, there is a large minority of **Rohingyas**, who are Muslim, as well as **Chins** and Burmans. The state capital is **Sittwe (Sittway**, known during the British colonial period as Akyab). Recognized as a state by the **Constitution of 1974**, it contains five **districts** (Sittwe, Maungdaw, Buthitaung, Kyaukpyu, and Sandoway [Thandwe]), subdivided into 17 **townships**. Arakan State is elongated, extending in a northwest-southeast direction. To the northwest it shares a short international boundary with Bangladesh, defined by the Naaf River. **Chin State** lies to the north, **Magwe (Magway)** and **Pegu (Bago) Divisions** to the east, and **Irrawaddy (Ayeyarwady) Division** to the southeast and south. The Arakan coast, fronting the Bay of Bengal, is fringed with islands, of which the largest are Ramree (Yanbye) and Cheduba (Man-aung). The **Arakan Yoma** separates the state from central Burma. The state's major river, the Kaladan, reaches the sea at Sittwe.

The state is a major grower of **rice**, and the abundance of paddy explains the rise of early kingdoms in the region. Fishing and fisheries are also economically important. Abundant natural gas resources are found in Burmese territorial waters off the coast, in the Bay of Bengal. *See also* MAHA MUNI BUDDHA IMAGE; MIN BIN, KING; MRAUK-U.

ARAKAN (RAKHINE) YOMA. A mountain range (*yoma* in the **Burmese [Myanmar] language**) running in a north-south direction, which lies between the valley of the **Irrawaddy (Ayeyarwady) River** and the **Arakan (Rakhine)** coastal plain. In the north, it joins the Chin Hills, while the southernmost extension is Cape Negrais in what is now **Irrawaddy (Ayeyarwady) Division**. The highest elevations are 1,500–2,000 meters (4,921–6,562 feet). The mountains effectively isolate central Burma from the Bay of Bengal littoral, though there are several passes, of which the An, Gwa, and Taungup are the most important. After **World War II**, the Arakan Yoma was home to several insurgent movements, including the "Red Flag" faction of the **Communist Party of Burma**, led by **Thakin Soe** until his capture in 1970.

ARAKANESE (RAKHAING, RAKHINES). One of the major ethnic minorities of Burma, their homeland is **Arakan (Rakhine) State**, bordering **Bangladesh** on the Bay of Bengal. Independent kingdoms based on the Indian model existed in this region between the fourth century CE and its occupation by King **Bodawpaya** in 1784. The Arakanese, like the **Burmans**, speak a Tibeto-Burman language, and probably migrated into modern Burma from Inner Asia around the same time, the eighth and ninth centuries CE. Some linguists suggest that Arakanese is similar to archaic Burmese. Most Arakanese are **Buddhists**, though there is a Muslim minority, commonly called **Rohingyas**, and Muslim influences from the Indian subcontinent have historically been strong. According to the 1983 census, the last taken, the Arakanese comprised 4.5 percent of Burma's population. *See also* ARAKAN (RAKHINE); MRAUK-U.

ARCHITECTURE, MODERN. The history of modern architecture in Burma can be said to have begun after the British occupied **Rangoon (Yangon)** in 1852, following the **Second Anglo-Burmese War**, and built a new city based on Western and British Indian design. A rectangular, east-west grid of streets that became Rangoon's central business district and the location for many government buildings was laid out around the **Sule Pagoda**. In contrast with **traditional architecture**, the British made extensive use of brick and masonry, although many colonial-era houses were made of **teak**. The most common type of European residence in suburban or rural areas was the bungalow, a British Indian design, with a single storey, veranda, and low-pitched roof.

Although generally fireproof, the larger colonial buildings built of brick or stone were not really suited for the tropical climate, providing poor ventilation. Many of the most prominent—including the Strand Hotel, Secretariat (now Ministers' Building), Rangoon General Hospital, and Port Authority building in central Rangoon— reflected Victorian or Edwardian rather than indigenous design, but Rangoon's central railway station and the Municipal Corporation (City Hall), designed by U Tin in the early 20th century, used Burmese motifs, especially the traditional *pyat-that* or tiered roof. In densely populated downtown areas, such as those of Rangoon and **Moulmein (Mawlamyine)**, the typical building was a three- or four-story row house with a shop on the ground floor and dwellings above, usually with a stucco façade, much like shop houses found in **Singapore** or Malaya. In hill stations, such as **Maymyo (Pyin Oo Lwin)** and **Kalaw**, guest houses, "chummeries" (bachelor quarters for British company employees), and other buildings were faithfully designed to evoke, for Europeans fleeing the lowland hot season, the atmosphere of "home." An outstanding example is Maymyo's mock-Scottish Candacraig (Thiri Myaing) Hotel.

Functional, "international" design was used in many post-independence buildings, including the terminal of **Mingaladon** International Airport and newer buildings on the Main Campus of **Rangoon (Yangon) University**, such as the university library. However, the socialist era of **Ne Win** (1962–1988) saw little new construction, especially in urban areas, and existing buildings were poorly maintained. One of the best examples of socialist-era architecture is the huge building housing the now inoperative **Pyithu Hluttaw**, west of Rangoon's People's Park.

Following the establishment of the **State Law and Order Restoration Council (SLORC)** in September 1988 and the opening of the economy to **foreign investment**, the architecture of urban areas, especially Rangoon and **Mandalay**, was transformed. During the 1990s, new hotels, office buildings, and shopping centers sprang up, very similar in functional, profit-oriented design to those found in cities like Bangkok or Singapore. A few (e.g., the Kandawgyi Palace Hotel) made effective use of traditional materials and motifs. Post-1988 government buildings, such as the new National Museum and Defense Services Museum, tend to be utilitarian. In suburban areas of Rangoon and other cities, the design of housing developments for the wealthy are similar to those found in other parts of Southeast Asia or even Southern California.

The **Yangon City Development Committee** maintains a list of 189 historic sites that cannot be demolished, but the profit motive has resulted in the tearing down of many others, especially in the old downtown area. In Mandalay, the colonial-era *zeigyo* (open air market) was demolished and replaced by a three-story enclosed structure of Chinese design. The *haw* of the *sawbwa* of **Keng Tung**, inspired by traditional **Shan** and Indian Muslim designs, was the most remarkable example of modern Shan palace design until the SLORC demolished it in 1991, replacing it with a tourist hotel. *See also* AR-CHITECTURE, RELIGIOUS; ARCHITECTURE, TRADITIONAL.

ARCHITECTURE, RELIGIOUS. The most striking feature of the human landscape in both urban and rural Burma is the abundance of religious buildings, which reflects the importance of **Buddhism** in

Burmese life. Although some of these structures, such as the monuments at **Sri Ksetra (Thayakhittaya)** and **Pagan (Bagan)**, are very old, construction and renovation of religious buildings continue to be major activities today. Indeed, investment of scarce resources in such projects has increased since the **State Law and Order Restoration Council (SLORC)** assumed power in 1988.

Generally speaking, religious architecture in Burma includes three types of structures: **pagodas**, temples (*pahto*), and monastery buildings (*kyaung*). The pagoda contains a chamber housing relics associated with Gotama **Buddha** and is surmounted by a *stupa*, or spire, often with a *hti* ("umbrella") at its apex. Most pagodas are solid structures, but some, such as the Botataung and **Maha Vizaya** Pagodas in **Rangoon (Yangon)**, are hollow. The platforms of major pagodas, such as the **Shwe Dagon**, are filled with elaborate and impressive shrines, pavilions, and *tazaung* (devotional halls), funded by prominent donors. Covered stairways with shop arcades often lead to the pagoda platform. Many of these adjacent buildings are adorned with elaborate tiered roofs, known as *pyat-that,* which vary in number but are always uneven.

Pahto, of which the most important examples are found at Pagan, are hollow and built to resemble caves, containing one or more Buddha images. Within their dark interiors, the atmosphere is not unlike early Romanesque churches. Pagodas and *pahto* are generally built of brick or stone, and there are regional variations in design, for example, among those found at Pagan, **Lower Burma** (including Rangoon, **Pegu [Bago]** and **Prome [Pyay]**), **Shan State**, and **Arakan (Rakhine) State**. Huge statues of the Reclining Buddha represent a special category of religious site, the most prominent of which are the Shwethalyaung in Pegu and the Chaukhtatgyi in Rangoon. In Burmese, pagodas, *pahto,* and Buddha images are frequently referred to as *paya*.

Monasteries, where members of the **Sangha** live and carry out their religious devotions, traditionally were made of wood. Among the best remaining examples of this type are the Shwenandaw Monastery in **Mandalay** and the Bagaya Monastery in **Ava (Inwa)**. During the British colonial period, Western design was often incorporated in wooden or masonry monastery buildings and *thein* (ordination halls), good examples of which can be found in Rangoon and

Sagaing. The Kaba Aye Pagoda, constructed in Rangoon by the government of U **Nu** in 1952, employs rather modern motifs.

After 1988, the SLORC (after 1997 known as the **State Peace and Development Council**) sponsored a large number of religious building projects, including the Buddha Tooth Relic Pagoda, Theravada Buddhist International Missionary University, and White Stone Buddha complex in the northern part of Rangoon. It has also carried out renovation of the Shwe Dagon Pagoda, particularly replacement of the *hti* in 1999. Smaller pagodas, monasteries, and other religious buildings have also been constructed by private persons with state encouragement. The new structures often incorporate traditional design with modern construction methods and materials. *See also* ANANDA PAHTO; ARCHITECTURE, MODERN; ARCHITECTURE, TRADITIONAL; MAHA MUNI BUDDHA IMAGE; MRAUK-U; SALAY; SHITTAUNG TEMPLE; SHWEMAWDAW PAGODA; SHWESANDAW PAGODA; SHWEZIGON PAGODA; SULE PAGODA.

ARCHITECTURE, TRADITIONAL. Although Burma is best known for its **religious architecture**, the country has a long tradition of secular architecture, including both royal palaces and what is often known as "vernacular architecture," that is, architecture of the common people. Because both royal and common dwelling structures were built of wood or thatch, they were not especially durable because of the tropical climate and the frequent outbreak of fires, which often devastated (and continue to devastate) residential areas. Most of the older surviving structures, including Buddhist monasteries, date from the 19th century. Nothing remains of the old royal palace at **Pagan (Bagan)**. Except for its extensive brick wall and gateways surmounted by tiered roofs, **Mandalay Palace** was destroyed during **World War II**.

Royal palaces, constructed mostly of **teak**, were immense complexes built according to a strict design that reflected Indian concepts of the structure of the universe; at their center was a multitiered roof tower (*pyat-that*), representing Mount Meru or the "center of the universe," below which the principal royal throne was placed. Both palace buildings and the houses of commoners were raised above the ground, supported by pillars or (in the case of humbler dwellings) stilts, a design found throughout Southeast Asia. A house thus raised was protected from flood and unwanted intruders. The simplest sort of village house, also found in the poorer, outlying districts of large cities like **Rangoon (Yangon)** and **Mandalay**, is made of thatch, woven grass, and bamboo, and is often shielded from the hot sun by large trees. The ground floor is used for storage, while the living space is on the floor above. The spare design of well-maintained thatch houses rivals the traditional Japanese house in its beauty and simplicity. More substantial dwellings are made of wood, often elaborately carved and joined together. Sometimes several wooden houses are grouped together on a single large platform. Before the British colonial period, strict sumptuary laws governed the design of the houses of commoners and court officials. They were forbidden in any way to imitate the style of the royal palace.

Zayat (rest houses), also made of wood with high roofs, are a common architectural form. Many are found near important Buddhist sites, such as the **Shwe Dagon Pagoda** and **Mandalay Hill**. *See also* ARCHITECTURE, MODERN.

ARIS, MICHAEL (1946–1999). Scholar of Tibetan studies and Oxford University professor, he married **Aung San Suu Kyi** in 1972 and, after she became prominent in the 1988 prodemocracy movement, played an important role in conveying her messages to the outside world and editing her collection of writings, *Freedom from Fear*. He had few opportunities to meet her after 1988, however, and the **State Peace and Development Council (SPDC)** turned down his request for a visa to see her in **Rangoon (Yangon)** when he was dying of cancer. According to reliable accounts, even telephone communication between the two was cut off by the SPDC. He passed away on March 27, 1999. Daw Suu Kyi's marriage to Dr. Aris provided the military junta with a pretext to brand her as a *bogadaw* (an old term meaning the Burmese wife of a British colonial official) and an "axe-handle" of Western neocolonialists, using racist images in the *New Light of Myanmar* and other media outlets that were astonishing for their crudity.

ARMED FORCES, BURMA (MYANMAR). *See* ARMY; TATMADAW; TATMADAW, HISTORY OF.

ARMED FORCES, COLONIAL. The major characteristics of the armed forces in Burma under British colonial rule were their relatively small size, reflecting dependence in emergencies on the British Indian Army; preference shown to ethnic minorities, especially **Karens (Kayins)**, **Chins**, and **Kachins**, in recruitment; and their organization into ethnically defined "class battalions." Few **Burmans (Bamars)** served in the ranks; according to official statistics for 1931, there were only 472 "Burmans" out of a total of 3,837 men, and this category also included **Mons** and **Shans**. Because the principal role of the colonial forces was to enforce internal security, the British were reluctant to encourage participation by Burmans because they were regarded as potentially disloyal, an assumption bolstered by the student strike of 1920 and the **Saya San Rebellion**. Official histories of the **Tatmadaw** brand the colonial armed forces as "mercenaries," while the units that grew out of the predominantly Burman **Burma Independence Army** were "patriotic soldiers."

ARMED FORCES DAY (MARCH 27). A major national holiday, perhaps Burma's most important secular observance, commemorating the uprising of the **Burma National Army** led by **Aung San** against the Japanese on March 27, 1945. Originally the anniversary was known as Resistance Day, and the name change to Armed Forces Day has been criticized by some Burmese because the **Tatmadaw's** history began in December 1941, when the **Burma Independence Army** was established, rather than March 1945, and because the military regime has changed the holiday's meaning, from a celebration of the popular uprising against fascism in 1945 to one glorifying the Tatmadaw's role in defending national sovereignty. Official celebrations in **Rangoon (Yangon)** included a parade to Resistance Park and a speech by the chairman of the **State Peace and Development Council**, Senior General **Than Shwe**. Neither was accessible to the general public, as had been the case at Resistance Day celebrations in the past.

ARMENIANS IN BURMA. Armenia is an ancient country located north of Iran that has the distinction of being the first to adopt Christianity as its national religion. Adept in trade, Armenian merchants did business in the Middle East, Central Asia, India, and points east.

There was a small but prosperous Armenian community in **Rangoon (Yangon)** following its establishment by King **Alaungpaya** in 1755, and they constructed their own church around 1766. Under British rule, they remained prominent in the expatriate business community, especially the Sarkies brothers, who opened the Strand, Rangoon's premier hotel, in 1901. However, their numbers remained small, according to the official Rangoon census: 252 in 1921, and 136 ten years later. War, independence, and nationalization under the **Ne Win** regime further reduced their numbers. See also JEWS IN BURMA.

ARMY (TATMADAW KYI). The largest of the **Tatmadaw**'s three services. Its commander in chief is a full general (in 2005, General **Maung Aye**, who also serves as vice chairman of the **State Peace and Development Council**). Since 1988, when its personnel numbered approximately 170,000 and its order of battle included weapon systems dating back to World War II, the Army has experienced a dramatic expansion in terms of men and women under arms (an estimated 400,000 by the end of the 1990s) and equipment, mostly imported from the **People's Republic of China, Singapore**, and Pakistan. In 2000, the Army contained 437 infantry battalions (including 266 light infantry battalions, which serve as a mobile force) and an enhanced number of armored, artillery, engineer, signal, military intelligence, transport, and medical units using modern, though not state-of-the-art, equipment.

Although the Army is far better funded and equipped than before 1988, harsh command practices (which some observers suggest were inherited from the Japanese Imperial Army), poor training, inadequate logistics (in some areas, Army units must grow their own crops or confiscate them from local, usually ethnic minority, residents), and the forceful recruitment of child soldiers has severely damaged morale. Moreover, officers, who before 1988 cultivated close ties with their men in combat against ethnic and communist insurgents, now devote themselves to making money through graft and control of military-owned enterprises. Nevertheless, the Army has evolved into one of the most formidable land forces in Southeast Asia, with enhanced "force projection" not only internally, but also along the borders with **Thailand, Bangladesh**, and **India**. See also TATMADAW, HISTORY OF.

ARTS AND CRAFTS, TRADITIONAL. Although sharing affinities with the arts and crafts of neighboring countries, Burmese textiles, tapestries, wood carving, pottery, and sculpture have evolved their own distinct styles. Cotton and silk *longyis* and other garments are woven by hand in various parts of the country, such as **Arakan (Rakhine) State, Amarapura**, and the **Inle Lake** region, and have attractive and sophisticated patterns; the intricate *acheik* patterns of Arakan are very popular among those who can afford them. *Kalagas* or tapestries, produced chiefly in **Mandalay**, have intricate appliqué designs. Burmese wood carving, traditionally used for the decoration of royal palaces and **Buddhist** monasteries, has enjoyed something of a revival because of a construction boom in international hotels in the 1990s, not only in **Rangoon (Yangon)** and **Mandalay**, but also in **tourist** sites, such as **Pagan (Bagan)**. The most characteristic form of Burmese pottery is rather plain, used for practical purposes, such as the water jars that householders place by the side of the road for the benefit of passers-by; most of these are produced at Twante, near Rangoon. The carving of Buddha images from marble is done in Mandalay; the stone is quarried in nearby Sagyin district. The largest marble Buddha image, weighing over 500 tons, is located at the White Stone Buddha complex in Rangoon's **Insein Township.** Colorful parasols are made in **Bassein (Pathein)**. Of all traditional arts, the making of **lacquerware**, especially in the Pagan region, is arguably the most developed, with a tremendous diversity of designs and shapes.

The post-1988 military regime's encouragement of tourism has benefited traditional craftspeople; quality has improved since the years of socialist isolation (1962–1988), and tourists find lacquerware, *kalagas,* and silk fabrics especially attractive.

ASSOCIATION OF SOUTHEAST ASIAN NATIONS (ASEAN) AND BURMA. When ASEAN was established in 1967, the original founding member-states—**Thailand, Singapore, Malaysia, Indonesia**, and the Philippines—had pro-Western governments and close security ties with the **United States** and **Britain**, including American and British military bases on their soil. Because of Burma's commitment to nonalignment and **Ne Win**'s deep suspicion of foreign countries, the **Burma Socialist Programme Party** regime kept aloof from the regional association. After socialist isolationism was abandoned in 1988, however, the **State Law and Order Restoration Council (SLORC)** expressed interest in joining, though ASEAN's decision to admit it was highly controversial. Because of the SLORC's **human rights** abuses and its refusal to recognize the results of the **General Election of May 27, 1990**, the governments of the United States and some European countries opposed Burma's ASEAN membership, even though they themselves were not members. Within ASEAN, Malaysia under Prime Minister Mahathir Mohammad was the SLORC's strongest backer, while the relatively liberal governments of Thailand and the Philippines expressed doubts about the regime's readiness to play a constructive role in the association. In the end, SLORC's supporters won the day and the country, along with Laos, officially became a member on July 23, 1997, at the ASEAN Foreign Ministers' meeting in Kuala Lumpur.

For ASEAN, the perceived advantages of Burma's membership were largely economic (potential markets and the country's rich natural resources), but also included security factors (the need to counterbalance **China**'s growing influence inside the country) and the desire of ASEAN member states to assert their independence in the face of not-so-subtle pressure from Washington. Also, some ASEAN leaders hoped that Burma's regional integration would promote, through "constructive engagement," the country's economic and political liberalization.

One of ASEAN's fundamental principles is noninterference in the internal affairs of member states, but Burma's continuing political and human rights problems, including the **"Black Friday" Incident** of May 30, 2003, have made the country, in the words of one journalist, ASEAN's "problem child." Immediately following the incident, ASEAN leaders called for the release of **Aung San Suu Kyi** from detention, and Prime Minister Mahathir, quite uncharacteristically, even suggested that Burma might have to be expelled from the group. In the months that followed, ASEAN did nothing to follow through on its criticism of the **State Peace and Development Council (SPDC)**, although there was a movement within the group, supported by Western countries, to deny the SPDC the regional chairmanship of ASEAN when its turn comes around in 2006. In fact, the SPDC relinquished the chairmanship in favor of the Philippines in July 2005.

ASTROLOGY. The "science of the stars," originally brought from **India**, continues to have a strong grip on the minds of many Burmese. Traditionally, the exact moment of a person's birth becomes the basis for a horoscope (*sada* in the **Burmese [Myanmar] language**), which is drawn up by an astrologer and serves as a lifelong guide to prudent behavior. Inscribed on a palm leaf, the *sada* is filled with complicated symbols and figures and is often destroyed when the bearer dies. Depending upon which day of the week he or she was born, a person is believed to be under the influence of the planet corresponding to that day (e.g., Mars is the planet for Tuesday). The Burmese believe in nine planets, eight of which have astrological influence that can be either favorable or unfavorable, depending on the relationship with one's birth-planet and a number of other complicated factors. **Pagoda** platforms, most famously the **Shwe Dagon Pagoda** in **Rangoon (Yangon)**, have separate shrines at the cardinal points of the compass for each of the eight planets and birth-days. Thus, astrology has connections with **Buddhism**. Those most addicted to astrology will undertake no major enterprise, such as going on a journey, concluding a business deal, or getting married, without getting an astrologer to examine their horoscopes to find an auspicious day. Following astrological advice, people often change their names to avoid misfortune.

The exact time and date of Burma's independence from Britain, the early morning of January 4, 1948, was determined by astrological calculations. **Ne Win** was famous for his belief in astrology as well as other occult arts, such as *yedaya* and **numerology**. The interior ceiling of the **Maha Vizaya Pagoda**, built largely through his sponsorship in the 1980s, contains astrological symbols, and journalists report that his astrologers used a planetarium located near the Shwe Dagon Pagoda and donated by the Japanese government (for educational purposes) to chart the movements of the planets. Though educated Burmese generally disparage it as unscientific, astrology remains important in the lives of ordinary people and many members of the military elite. This can be explained as part of a pervasive atmosphere of insecurity: the lack of a rule of law, which encourages governmental abuses of power; the **State Peace and Development Council**'s fears about popular unrest; worsening economic conditions; lack of social welfare facilities to deal with sickness or loss of income; and the declining quality of **education** for most Burmese. *See also* NAMES, BURMESE; WEEK, BURMESE.

AUNG, BOHMU (1910–2004). *Nom de guerre* of one of the **Thirty Comrades**, originally known as Thakin Saw Hlaing. He served in the **Burma Independence Army** during **World War II** and held prominent positions in the **Anti-Fascist People's Freedom League** and the governments of Prime Minister U **Nu** after independence. Jailed by **Ne Win** following the March 1962 coup d'état, he later went into exile and became head of the northwestern command of the **Parliamentary Democracy Party**, U Nu's Thailand-based insurgency, returning to Burma in 1980 after Ne Win declared an amnesty. During 1988's **Democracy Summer**, he was a member of U Nu's "parallel government" and later became the leader of a group of "veteran politicians" who advocated dialogue between the **State Law and Order Restoration Council/State Peace and Development Council** and the **National League for Democracy**. His death in November 2004 left only two surviving members of the Thirty Comrades.

AUNG GYAW, BO (?–1938). Student at Judson College, **Rangoon (Yangon) University**, who died of wounds inflicted by British military police during a demonstration in downtown **Rangoon (Yangon)** on December 20, 1938. His body was brought to the **Rangoon University Students Union (RUSU)**, where it lay in state for three days, and then to Kyandaw Cemetery, where on December 27, his funeral, according to press accounts, drew as many as 300,000 people. A monument to Bo Aung Gyaw built next to the RUSU building still stands, although the building itself was demolished in July 1962. His counterpart as student martyr in the massive demonstrations of 1988 was **Maung Phone Maw**.

AUNG GYI, BRIGADIER (1919–). Close associate of **Ne Win** who became a prominent opposition figure during 1988. He served in the **Burma Defence Army/Burma National Army** during **World War II** and, after the war, in the **Fourth Burma Rifles** commanded by Ne Win. He was an important figure in the **Caretaker Government** of 1958–1960 and a member of the **Revolutionary Council** following the March 2, 1962 coup d'état. Aung Gyi was forced off the Council on February 8, 1963, however, following disagreements with doctrinaire socialists **Tin Pe** and U **Ba Nyein** over economic policy. He advocated pragmatic policies with a role for foreign investment, while his opponents adopted an Eastern European model, with disastrous consequences during the 1960s and 1970s. Although he was jailed from 1965 to 1968 and in 1973–1974, he grew wealthy operating a chain of cake shops.

His four open letters to Ne Win on economic policy, politics, and **human rights** violations had a great impact on the emerging popular protests of 1988, and he was jailed once again from July 29 to August 25 of that year. Joining in the *Aung-Suu-Tin* coalition with Daw **Aung San Suu Kyi** and U **Tin U**, he became president of the **National League for Democracy (NLD)** after the September 18 power seizure by the **State Law and Order Restoration Council (SLORC)** but left the NLD after making accusations that Daw Suu Kyi was influenced by elements of the **Communist Party of Burma**. Never completely trusted by students and other oppositionists, he was quickly eclipsed as a prodemocracy leader by **Aung San**'s daughter. In the **General Election of May 27, 1990**, his party, the Union Nationals Democracy Party, won a single seat. *See also* AUNG GYI, LETTERS OF; DEFENCE SERVICES INSTITUTE; DEMOCRACY SUMMER.

AUNG GYI, LETTERS OF (1987–1988). Four letters written by retired Brigadier **Aung Gyi**, an original member of the **Revolutionary Council**, to **Burma Socialist Programme Party (BSPP)** Chairman **Ne Win** in July 1987 and March, May, and June 1988. They had a tremendous impact on public opinion because of his outspoken criticism of the BSPP regime. The first two dealt largely with economic reform, the third discussed his and Ne Win's role in Burmese history, and the fourth and most influential, dated June 8, described the brutality of the **Riot Police (*Lon Htein*)**, including a detailed description of the March 16, 1988 **White Bridge Incident**. Aung Gyi attempted to persuade Ne Win, to whom he was deeply loyal, to repudiate hard-liners such as **Sein Lwin** and their **human rights** abuses. The letters, especially the one from June 8, were photocopied and circulated widely among the public. *See also* DEMOCRACY SUMMER.

AUNG SAN, ASSASSINATION OF. Around 10:30 A.M. on Saturday, July 19, 1947, four men armed with automatic weapons entered an upper-floor room of the Secretariat building (now the Ministers' Building) in downtown **Rangoon (Yangon)**, where **Aung San** was holding a meeting of the Executive Council, Burma's interim government before independence. They killed Aung San, six other members of the Council, and two others, a crime that, from the perspective of Burma's subsequent history, was a major national tragedy. The country's most able political leader lost his life at the age of 32. The gunmen were followers of U **Saw**, a political rival, who, according to some accounts, wanted revenge after having been wounded in an assassination attempt that he believed was carried out on Aung San's orders. But at the trial of U Saw and his followers, it was revealed that he had ordered the killing of the entire Executive Council in the mistaken hope that, with Aung San and his colleagues out of the way, the British would appoint him independent Burma's first prime minister. **Thakin Nu** was another intended victim, but he was not in the Secretariat at the time of the attack.

Like the assassination of U.S. President John F. Kennedy, the assassination of Aung San is surrounded by some controversy. Elements in the British army came under suspicion when it was discovered that U Saw was deeply involved in an arms-procurement conspiracy with a Captain David Vivian and other officers. Some Burmese suggest that **Ne Win** instigated the plot, using U Saw and his henchmen. But the evidence is scanty and contradictory. July 19 is commemorated annually as Martyrs' Day, though its importance has been deemphasized since the **State Law and Order Restoration Council (SLORC)** came to power in 1988. *See also* AUNG SAN, LEGACY OF.

AUNG SAN, BOGYOKE (1915–1947). Modern Burma's most important political figure, who played the principal role in winning independence from Britain after **World War II**. Burmese people often refer to him as *bogyoke* (commander in chief) because he is credited with establishing Burma's **Tatmadaw** (armed forces) during the war. Born in Natmauk, **Magwe (Magway) Division**, on February 13, 1915, he was an excellent student and attended the **National School** in **Yenangyaung (Yaynangyoung)** on a scholarship. There, he began to take an intense interest in politics. In 1932, he entered **Rangoon (Yangon) University** and during the 1935–1936 academic year became editor of *Oway*, the magazine of the **Rangoon University Students' Union (RUSU)**. Refusing to disclose the name of the writer of an article deemed highly offensive by the university authorities, he and RUSU President **Nu** were expelled, an action that sparked the student strike of February–May 1936. The strike made him a figure of national political prominence, and he became a founder and secretary of the **All Burma Students' Union (ABSU)** at its first conference in 1937 and a prominent member of the Thakin **Kodaw Hmaing** faction of the **Dobama Asiayone** the following year. As secretary general of the **Freedom Bloc** in 1939–1940, he worked closely with **Dr. Ba Maw** in a nationalist united front and also served as secretary general of the newly established **Communist Party of Burma.**

Aung San left Burma in August 1940 to secure foreign backing for the independence struggle. He was contacted by a Japanese agent in Amoy (Xiamen), China, and brought to Tokyo where, with considerable misgivings, he agreed to work with Colonel **Suzuki Keiji** to establish a Burmese armed force that would assist in the Japanese defeat of the British in Burma and, Aung San hoped, the establishment of an independent nation. Returning to Burma to recruit the **Thirty Comrades**, he became their leader when they received Japanese military training on the island of Hainan in 1941 and was senior staff officer in the **Burma Independence Army**, established in December 1941 under Colonel Suzuki's command. Aung San served as commander of the **Burma Defence Army** in 1942–1943 and minister of defense when the country became nominally independent in August 1943. From the very beginning, however, he had no illusions about the Japanese occupation, and together with Thakin **Soe**, Thakin **Than Tun**, and others established the **Anti-Fascist Organization (AFO)** in August 1944. On March 27, 1945, a date commemorated as Resistance Day or **Armed Forces Day**, he ordered the **Burma National Army (BNA)** to rise up against the Japanese.

Though some British regarded him as a traitor, Aung San won the trust of **Lord Louis Mountbatten**, who regarded cooperation with his army, renamed the **Patriotic Burmese Forces**, as essential for Allied war aims. Leaving the military to pursue a political career, he became president of the **Anti-Fascist People's Freedom League** and between 1945 and 1947 used his immense popularity to bring the British to the negotiating table on the issue of independence. The **Aung San–Attlee Agreement** was achieved in January 1947 after Aung San journeyed to London to negotiate with British Prime Minister Clement Attlee. Winning the support of ethnic minority leaders at the **Panglong Conference** in February, Aung San cleared the way for the creation of the Union of Burma's semifederal constitutional order. He would have become the new nation's first prime minister, but he was assassinated along with members of his cabinet by gunmen loyal to a political rival, U **Saw**, on July 19, 1947, a day commemorated as Martyrs' Day. *See also* AUNG SAN, ASSASSINATION OF; AUNG SAN, LEGACY OF; STUDENTS, HISTORICAL ROLE OF.

AUNG SAN, LEGACY OF. **Aung San**'s legacy has been contested by successive Burmese governments, ethnic minorities, and the democratic opposition, especially after 1988. Following his rise to national prominence during the 1936 student strike, he became a man of action, a military as well as political leader, rather than a man of ideas. Yet he had a strongly modernist vision of the nation, as reflected in his commitment to the separation of **religion** and state, an opinion he held as early as his secondary school days. He was also opposed to the restoration of the monarchy in a postcolonial Burma. Like his nationalist student comrades, he embraced socialism as the antidote for colonial economic exploitation, and he was one of the founding members of the **Communist Party of Burma**, serving as its secretary general in 1939–1940. He broke with the communists in 1946, however, and his successors, U **Nu** and **Ne Win**, espoused non-Marxist forms of socialism. Some scholars argue that Buddhist and other traditional influences on his thinking have been greatly underestimated, but he is largely remembered as the founder of a modern army and state.

Ethnic minority leaders remember him fondly as the one **Burman (Bamar)** leader who treated them as equals in nation-building, at the February 1947 **Panglong Conference**. Unlike his successors, he did not propose the use of **Buddhism** or Burman ethnic identity as the basis for national unity. Especially during the Ne Win period (1962–1988), Aung

San was revered as the "father" of the **Tatmadaw**, while Ne Win was its "stepfather." Portraits of him, usually in uniform, were prominent in government offices and on the nation's paper currency. His short life was a major theme in the country's history textbooks. On the 35th anniversary of Martyrs' Day in 1982, the state media described him as the "fourth unifier" of Burma, following the old kings **Anawrahta, Bayinnaung,** and **Alaungpaya.**

When student activists and citizens carried his portrait in the streets of **Rangoon (Yangon)** and other cities during the massive demonstrations of 1988, he became a symbol of Burma's democratic aspirations, especially after his daughter, **Aung San Suu Kyi,** emerged as the most prominent leader of the post-1988 opposition movement. In several highly controversial statements, Aung San Suu Kyi indicated that Ne Win had betrayed Aung San's vision of the Tatmadaw as an army serving the people. As the **State Law and Order Restoration Council (SLORC)** consolidated its power in the early 1990s, it consciously downgraded Aung San's historical significance, while at the same time exalting the nation-building achievements of the old kings, especially Bayinnaung, whose royal palace at **Pegu (Bago)** was reconstructed. Portraits of Aung San largely disappeared from the nation's currency after 1988, and Aung San Suu Kyi, the most potent living symbol of Aung San's legacy, has been kept for considerable periods under house arrest. *See also* AUNG SAN, ASSASSINATION OF; STUDENTS, HISTORICAL ROLE OF.

AUNG SAN SUU KYI, DAW (1945–). Daughter of **Aung San,** Aung San Suu Kyi is one of the founders of the **National League for Democracy (NLD)** and the most prominent leader of the post-1988 democracy movement. Born in **Rangoon (Yangon)** on June 19, 1945, she was the second of three children of Aung San and his wife Daw **Khin Kyi.** She was only two when her father was assassinated on July 19, 1947. After her mother was appointed Burma's ambassador to India in 1961, she lived most of her life abroad, until 1988. She obtained a degree in philosophy, politics, and economics from Oxford University; worked for the United Nations in New York; and married a British scholar of Tibet, **Michael Aris,** in 1972. Subsequently, they lived in Bhutan, London, Oxford (where Dr. Aris was a fellow at St. John's College), and India, and Daw Suu Kyi spent some months in

1985–1986 at Kyoto University doing research on her father's wartime relations with the Japanese. Her life, including raising two sons, was very private; during this time, she did not become actively involved in her country's politics.

The illness of her mother brought her to Rangoon in April 1988, but she refrained from playing a role in the momentous events of that year until August 15, when she sent a letter to the government urging political compromise and deploring the use of arms by the **Tatmadaw** against peaceful demonstrators. On August 26, she made her first major political speech at the western entrance to the **Shwe Dagon Pagoda**, an event that drew hundreds of thousands of Rangoon citizens. Her eloquence and her resemblance to her father in both words and appearance made her instantly popular. Rivals, such as **Aung Gyi**, dismissed her as a neophyte and influenced by underground communists. But in her role as secretary general of the NLD, campaigning up and down the country during late 1988 and early 1989, she was largely responsible for winning the popular support reflected in the party's landslide victory in the **General Election of May 27, 1990**, despite the fact that she was barred from running for a seat in the **Pyithu Hluttaw** and placed under house arrest in July 1989. Frank in her speech and courageous to the point of death (once facing down armed soldiers during a NLD campaign trip), she had become a leader in her own right, quite apart from her connection with the universally respected Aung San.

She remained confined at her residence on University Avenue under house arrest for just under six years, from July 20, 1989 to July 10, 1995, largely cut off from the outside world (except for a radio) and from her family, and suffered some physical hardship. Much of the time she spent in reading and meditation. In 1991, she was awarded the Nobel Peace Prize in recognition of her nonviolent struggle for democracy. The regime's decision to release her on July 10, 1995, seems to have been based in part on the belief that six years of house arrest had marginalized her. But the popularity of "public forums" that she held outside her residence (until they were closed down in November 1996) and the universal respect she commanded both at home and abroad showed that she was a more formidable opponent of the **State Law and Order Restoration Council (SLORC)** than ever.

The period from November 1995, when she withdrew the National League for Democracy from the **National Convention** constitution-drafting process, branding it undemocratic, to a second term of house arrest beginning in September 2000, was a time of tense and confrontational relations with the SLORC (renamed the **State Peace and Development Council [SPDC]** in late 1997). She aroused the generals' ire by supporting the imposition of economic **sanctions** by Western countries and the continued freeze on overseas development assistance to the SLORC/SPDC, and urged an international boycott of "**Visit Myanmar Year**," the regime's campaign in 1996–1997 to raise revenue through **tourism**. The regime responded by calling her an "axe handle" (tool) of foreign, neocolonial powers, a traitor to her race for marrying an Englishman, and a power-hungry witch, as depicted in childishly tasteless cartoons in the state-run *New Light of Myanmar (Myanmar Alin)* newspaper in the late 1990s. All this abuse did little to undermine the esteem in which she was held by her compatriots and abroad, though some critics argued, not always with disinterested motives, that she was too confrontational and unschooled in Burmese cultural values.

Her second term of house arrest—arising from her insistence on visiting NLD offices outside Rangoon, which the regime wished to prevent—lasted from September 2000 until May 6, 2002. In January 2001, the special envoy of the United Nations Secretary-General to Burma, Razali Ismail, announced that Daw Suu Kyi and the SPDC had begun secret talks, aimed at confidence building, as the preliminary step toward reaching a peaceful political accommodation. After her release, she was given unprecedented freedom to travel around the country and meet with local NLD members, and she seemed to have toned down her criticism of the SPDC. At the end of 2002, however, there was no indication that the military regime was willing to undertake serious political dialogue with her. Following the "**Black Friday**" **Incident** of May 30, 2003, in which she and her supporters were attacked by pro-junta mobs in **Sagaing Division**, Aung San Suu Kyi was imprisoned and then placed under a third term of house arrest. *See also* AUNG SAN SUU KYI, IDEAS OF; AUNG SAN SUU KYI, SYMBOLISM OF.

AUNG SAN SUU KYI, IDEAS OF. Receiving a Western education at elite institutions, such as Oxford University, moving among cosmopolitan circles as an adult yet strongly committed to preserving her Burmese and Buddhist heritage, **Aung San Suu Kyi** has indicated, in her essay "Intellectual Life in Burma and India under Colonialism," her adherence to a model of modernization in which a synthesis of Eastern and Western values on the intellectual and spiritual levels precedes the more conventional modernization of the economic or technical variety. This synthesis was practiced by leading figures of the late 18th- and 19th-century "Hindu Renaissance," whom she describes in her essay, contrasting the highly developed nature of Indian social and political reform movements during the colonial era with the relative lack of development of their counterparts in Burma. In this and other essays, compiled in the anthology *Freedom from Fear and Other Writings*, she emphasizes the universal validity of both **Buddhist** and Western democratic ideas, arguing for their compatibility and denying the legitimacy of the kind of cultural relativism that is often used to legitimize authoritarian regimes. Major influences on her ideas have included not only her father **Aung San**, whose career she researched before 1988, but also Mahatma Gandhi and Dr. Martin Luther King Jr., who both saw resistance against oppression in spiritual as well as political terms and employed nonviolent methods of opposition.

AUNG SAN SUU KYI, SYMBOLISM OF. Although an able and committed political leader in her own right, **Aung San Suu Kyi** has also become a symbol, embodying the traditions, aspirations, and assumptions of her Burmese and foreign supporters. In Burma, where political authority is traditionally defined in terms of charismatic and sometimes magical personal characteristics, politics after 1988 has often been described in terms of a battle of wills between Aung San Suu Kyi and the **State Law and Order Restoration Council (SLORC)/State Peace and Development Council (SPDC)** leadership. In such a scenario, political ideas and institutions often seem irrelevant. During her 1989–1995 term of house arrest, she was sometimes referred to as "the Goddess (*Nat-Thami*) of University Avenue," and supernatural signs occurring after the **General Election of May 27, 1990**, allegedly included the swelling of the left-hand side of the chests of Buddha images, indicated that a woman would become Burma's ruler (since the left-hand side of the body is traditionally the side of the mother). Above all, in a land where family relations are all-important, her tie to her father **Aung San** gave her unparalleled authority as an oppositionist. Thus, she was cast by some Burmese in the role of a *minlaung*, a pretender to the throne or monarch-to-be.

In the West, both governments and individuals have lauded her as a living testament to the universal relevance of **human rights** and democracy, at a time when these values are being challenged by more particularistic "Asian values." Her emphasis on the spiritual aspects of democratization and her synthesis of democratic and **Buddhist** values have also given her a symbolic appeal overseas similar to that of Mahatma Gandhi during India's struggle for independence.

AUNG SAN–ATTLEE AGREEMENT (JANUARY 27, 1947). On December 20, 1946, Britain's Labour prime minister, Clement Attlee, invited Burma's Executive Council to send a delegation to London to discuss the process through which the country would achieve independence. **Aung San** led the six-man delegation, which included Thakins Mya and **Ba Pe** of the **Anti-Fascist People's Freedom League (AFPFL)**, **Ba Sein**, U Saw, and U Tin Tut, a distinguished civil servant. They arrived in London on January 9, 1947, and after generally cordial negotiations signed the agreement on the 27th. It determined that the Executive Council would enjoy the status of an interim government similar to that of India, that the British government would consult it on matters of defense and foreign affairs and recognize its command of Burmese **armed forces**, and that an election for a constituent assembly would be held in April 1947. On the delicate issue of the relationship between **Burma Proper** (Ministerial Burma) and the **Frontier Areas**, the agreement affirmed the principle of their unification and provided for the establishment of a **Frontier Areas Committee of Enquiry (FACE)** to ascertain the opinions of the ethnic minority peoples on this matter. The success of the negotiations was due largely to Attlee's support of the AFPFL's demand for unification of the two areas, while his opponents in Parliament saw this as a betrayal of the ethnic minorities, especially the **Karens (Kayins)**, who had stood by **Britain** in the war and wanted either continued British rule or their own independent state. U Saw and Ba Sein refused to sign the agreement, saying that it did not determine the date for independence, a tactic meant to undermine Aung San's leadership. *See also* KAREN GOODWILL MISSION; KAREN NATIONAL UNION; PANGLONG CONFERENCE.

AUNG SHWE, U. A leader of the **National League for Democracy (NLD)**, who served as the party's acting chairman after the imprisonment of U **Kyi Maung** in September 1990. He joined the **Burma Independence Army** in 1942 and after independence rose to the rank of brigadier, though he was obliged to leave the military in 1962 and served in a number of ambassadorships, including Australia, Egypt, and France, before retiring in 1975. After the NLD was established in September 1988, he served as a member of its executive committee along with other veteran military officers, U **Kyi Maung** and U **Lwin**. Following Kyi Maung's arrest, Aung Shwe played the leading role in ensuring the NLD's survival until Daw **Aung San Suu Kyi** was released from house arrest in July 1995.

AUSTRALIA, RELATIONS WITH. Although Australia suspended **foreign aid** after the **SLORC** seized power in September 1988, Canberra's perception of the importance of maintaining friendly ties with neighboring Asian countries contributed to relations based largely on "constructive engagement," in contrast to the policies of the **United States** and some members of the **European Union**. Beginning in 2000, the Australian government funded seminars on **human rights** for Burmese civil servants, although Daw **Aung San Suu Kyi** was sceptical about the usefulness of this program. *See also* BRITAIN, RELATIONS WITH; NORDIC COUNTRIES AND BURMA.

AVA (INWA). Meaning "mouth of the river" (*in-wa*), Ava began its history as a royal capital during the reign of King Thadominbya (1364–1368) and remained the capital of **Burman (Bamar)** kingdoms until the early **Toungoo Dynasty**. King **Thalun** returned the capital from **Pegu (Bago)** to Ava in 1635, where it remained until 1752, when it was laid waste by **Mon** rebels. It was the **Konbaung Dynasty** royal capital from 1765 to 1783, during the reigns of Kings **Hsinbyushin** (r. 1763–1776), Singu Min (r. 1776–1781), and Maung Maung (r. 1781), but King **Bodawpaya** moved the capital to **Amarapura** in 1783. Between 1823 and 1837, Ava served as the capital again, but an **earthquake** damaged it in 1837, and King Tharawaddy (r. 1838–1846) moved the capital back to Amarapura. Ava is located on the eastern bank of the **Irrawaddy (Ayeyarwady) River** southwest of **Mandalay**, where the Irrawaddy is joined by the smaller Myitnge River, and close to the irrigated rice fields of **Kyaukse**. Little of its past glory remains. Timbers from the Ava palace were used in the 19th century to build U Bein's bridge, the longest **teak** bridge in the world (1.2 kilometers), in neighboring Amarapura. Other sites include the Ava Bridge, built by the British in 1934, which was until the 1990s the only bridge spanning the Irrawaddy River; and the Ok Kyaung, a wooden monastery built by Me Nu, King Bagyidaw's chief queen. During the 19th century, the term "Ava" was often synonymous with **Upper Burma**. *See also* AVA (INWA) PERIOD.

AVA (INWA) PERIOD (1364–1555). Following the collapse of the **Pagan (Bagan) Dynasty** at the beginning of the 14th century, central or **Upper Burma** was in a state of great upheaval as **Shans (Tai)** from what are now Yunnan Province in China and Burma's **Shan State** invaded the valleys of the **Irrawaddy (Ayeyarwady)** and **Chindwin (Chindwinn) Rivers**. Between 1298 and 1364, they established royal capitals at Myinsaing, Pinya, and **Sagaing**. In 1364, the **Burman (Bamar)** King Thadominbya (r. 1364–1368) established a new capital at **Ava (Inwa)**, southwest of modern **Mandalay** on the east bank of the Irrawaddy. A canal was dug to make the city a more easily defensible island, and its proximity to the irrigated **rice** fields of **Kyaukse** gave it a great economic advantage. Thadominbya's successors emphasized their connections with the long-departed greatness of Pagan.

Although kings ruled at Ava for almost two centuries (until 1555, when the city was conquered by King **Bayinnaung**), the period is generally regarded as a tumultuous interregnum between the collapse of the "First Burman Empire" at **Pagan (Bagan)** and the establishment of the "Second Burman Empire" by the rulers of the **Toungoo Dynasty**. During this period, no ruler succeeded in unifying the entire country. In **Lower Burma**, the **Mon** dynasty established by **Wareru** enjoyed a golden age in the 15th century, **Arakan (Rakhine)** reached its pinnacle under King **Min Bin** in the 16th century, while **Toungoo** emerged as an independent Burman power center. The warlike Shans remained a constant threat to Ava, as did repeated interventions by the Chinese across the **Salween (Thanlwin) River** during the Yuan and early Ming dynasties. In 1527, Ava fell to Thohanbwa, a Shan *sawbwa*, who wreaked great devastation and is remembered by Burmans today as a kind of Attila the Hun. He and other Shans ruled there until 1555.

– B –

BA KHIN, U (1898–1971). A prominent teacher of *vipassana* (insight) **meditation**, he was not, like the **Mahasi Sayadaw**, a member of the **Sangha** but a layperson. After graduating from St. Paul's College in **Rangoon (Yangon)** in 1914, he worked for the *Thuriya* (*The Sun*) newspaper for a few years and then joined the civil service as a low-level clerk. Working his way up through the ranks of the Office of the Auditor General of the British colonial government, he became a special supervisor after the **Government of Burma Act** was implemented in 1937. It was around this time that he became interested in **Buddhism**, reading the works of the **Ledi Sayadaw** and becoming a member of several Buddhist devotional and discussion groups. He sought guidance from respected meditation teachers, perfected his *vipassana* techniques, and taught them to others, including members of the wartime Burmese government such as Foreign Minister U **Nu**. When Burma became independent in 1948, he was appointed the nation's first accountant-general, at the same time continuing his spiritual activities. He established the Accountant-General Vipassana Association in 1952. This became the nucleus of the International Meditation Centre in Rangoon, which specializes in teaching *vipassana* to foreign devotees. Though not a monk, his rapid progress in mastering meditation techniques and passing them on to others made him one of postwar Burma's most respected public figures.

BA MAW, DR. (1893–1977). Prewar prime minister and head of state of "independent" Burma during **World War II**. Educated at Rangoon College (later **Rangoon [Yangon] University**), Cambridge University, Grey's Inn, and the University of Bordeaux in France, where he completed a doctorate, he opened a legal practice in **Rangoon (Yangon)** in 1924 and first came to prominence as a defense lawyer for rebel leader **Saya San** in 1931. The following year, he began his political career as a leader of the **Anti-Separation League**, and in 1936 he founded his own party, the **Sinyetha** (Proletarian or Poor Man's) **Party**. In 1937, he became the first prime minister under the **Government of Burma Act**, but his government fell in February 1939. In October of that year, he became president of the **Freedom Bloc** (in Burmese, *Htwet Yat Gaing*, or "Association of the Way Out"), a nationalist alliance of the Sinyetha Party, the **Dobama Asiayone**, and the **All Burma Students' Union**. Secretary general of the Bloc was Thakin **Aung San**, with whom he had a close if not necessarily smooth working relationship during the war.

Before he was tried and imprisoned by the British for sedition (August 1940–April 1942), Ba Maw met Japanese diplomats and secret agents in the hope that Tokyo would aid the struggle for independence, facilitating Aung San's departure from Burma and contact with Colonel **Suzuki Keiji**. After the Japanese Army occupied Burma, the Military Administration (*Gunseikanbu*) designated him head of the Burmese Executive Administration. When Burma's "independence" under Japanese rule was proclaimed on August 1, 1943, he became head of state (*Nain-ngandaw Adipadi*). Seeking to impose "totalitarian" rule under the slogan "One blood, one voice, one leader," he established a single state party, the Dobama Sinyetha Asiayone (later known as the *Maha Bama* Party) in 1942, and mass organizations of workers (the *Chwe Tat* or "Sweat Army"), civil servants, and ordinary citizens. Viewed by many of the **Thakins** as a Japanese puppet, he was in fact so jealous of his independence that a clique in the Japanese army arranged an unsuccessful assassination attempt against him in February 1944. At the end of the war, he escaped to Japan and was imprisoned at Sugamo Prison in Tokyo before being allowed to return home in 1946. Although he reassumed leadership of the Maha Bama Party, his wartime association with the Japanese discredited him in Burmese eyes, and he never again played a major political role. In 1966, he was imprisoned for a time by the **Ne Win** regime.

Ba Maw's *Breakthrough in Burma: Memoirs of a Revolution, 1939–1946* is a well-written and authoritative, though not unbiased, account of this historically important period. *See also* JAPANESE OCCUPATION; MINAMI KIKAN; THIRTY COMRADES.

BA NYEIN, U (1914–). Civilian economist, advisor to Brigadier **Tin Pe**, and a theorist behind the "**Burmese Road to Socialism**," appointed to the **Revolutionary Council** in 1971. The following year, he became minister of cooperatives. His influence over policy began to decline by the mid-1970s, however. Amid growing demands for some kind of reform, he was obliged to resign from the central committee of the **Burma Socialist Programme Party** at its Third Congress in February 1977.

BA PE, U (1883–?). A prominent figure in the early 20th-century history of Burmese nationalism, Ba Pe was a founding member of the **Young Men's Buddhist Association** in 1906 and also established *Thuriya (The Sun)*, one of the most important **Burmese (Myanmar) language** newspapers during the British colonial period, in 1911. After the split in the **General Council of Burmese Associations** in 1922, he became leader of the "Twenty-One Party," which advocated cooperation with the colonial authorities in carrying out the **dyarchy** reforms. Though he served as legislator and cabinet minister in a number of governments during the 1930s, his popularity declined as a new generation of nationalists came on the scene. Yet in the words of historian U Maung Maung, "[I]t can truly be said that Burmese politics was fathered by U Ba Pe . . . ."

BA SEIN, THAKIN (1910–1964). President of the **Rangoon University Students Union** in 1930–1931 and chairman of the **Dobama Asiayone** in 1935–1936, he broke away from the mainstream *Dobama* in 1938 along with Thakin Tun Oke to form what became known as the Ba Sein-Tun Oke faction of the party. He served in the wartime government of Dr. **Ba Maw** but because of his political intrigues was sent by the Japanese to Java, Indonesia. Returning after the war, he was favored by British governor Reginald Dorman-Smith and became a member of his executive council. Accompanying **Aung San** and other leaders to London, he refused to sign the January 27, 1947 **Aung San–Attlee Agreement** and served a brief prison sentence in 1947–1948 for his alleged connection with the **Aung San's assassination**.

BA SWE, U (1915–1987). A leading politician and one of the founders of the **Socialist Party of Burma** at the end of **World War II**, becoming its president in 1947. From 1947 to 1952, he was secretary general of the **Anti-Fascist People's Freedom League (AFPFL)** and in 1956–1957 served as prime minister of the Union of Burma. Following the split in the AFPFL in March 1958, he and U Kyaw Nyein became leaders of the "Stable" faction, in opposition to U **Nu**'s "Clean" faction.

BA THEIN TIN, THAKIN (1914–). Member of the **Communist Party of Burma (CPB)** from its inception in 1939, he went underground with the mainstream faction, led by Thakin **Than Tun**, in March 1948. Described by one observer as "*de facto* leader of the CPB" from the mid-1960s, he did not formally become chairman of the party until the assassination of Thakin Zin in 1975. Following the mutiny of ethnic minority troops and the CPB's breakup in April 1989, he fled from the CPB's former headquarters at Panghsang, **Shan State**, into China, where he remains in retirement. *See also* CEASE-FIRES.

BA U GYI, SAW (1905–1950). Charismatic **Karen (Kayin)** leader who founded the **Karen National Union (KNU)**. Born to a wealthy family in **Bassein (Pathein)** in the delta of the **Irrawaddy (Ayeyarwady) River** in 1905, he was a **Rangoon (Yangon) University** graduate and studied and practiced law in Britain and Burma. After **World War II** he advocated a separate Karen State in the British Commonwealth and led the KNU uprising in January 1949. On August 12 of the following year he was killed by government troops led by Major **Sein Lwin**. The **Tatmadaw** displayed his bullet-shattered body in **Moulmein (Mawlamyine)** and then dropped it in the sea to deprive his Karen followers of a martyr's gravesite, but he remains one of the best-known leaders of the Karen resistance, which has continued for almost six decades. *See also* MYA, BO; WORLD WAR II, ETHNIC MINORITIES IN.

BANGLADESH, RELATIONS WITH. Bangladesh became independent of Pakistan in December 1971. **Arakan (Rakhine)** and **Chin States** form Burma's border with that country. In 1978 approximately 200,000 (some sources say 300,000) Muslims from Arakan, known as **Rohingyas**, fled across the border, escaping abuses at the hands of the **Tatmadaw**. Although most of them were successfully repatriated (partly because the **Ne Win** regime feared an international Islamic backlash), a second **refugee** crisis occurred in 1991–1992, involving as many as 280,000 persons, and in this case repatriation proceeded more slowly. However, by the early 21st century, relations between the two countries, both members of **BIMSTEC**, were amicable, as reflected in the March 2003 state visit of the Bangladeshi prime minister to **Rangoon (Yangon)**. *See also* INDIA, RELATIONS WITH; MUSLIMS IN BURMA.

BAO YOUXIANG. Though not as notorious as **Lo Hsing-han** or **Khun Sa**, "Kings of the Golden Triangle" during the **Ne Win** and early **State Law and Order Restoration Council (SLORC)** periods, at the beginning of the 21st century Bao is Burma's richest and most powerful "drug warlord," commanding the 20,000-strong **United Wa State Army (UWSA)**. His background is obscure: born in the late 1940s or early 1950s to a local chief in the northern **Wa** district, he fought in the ranks of the People's Army of the **Communist Party of Burma (CPB)** until the CPB broke up in 1989; thereafter, he headed the UWSA, signed a **cease-fire** with the SLORC, and expanded the group's trade in **opium**, **heroin**, and **amphetamines**. He has declared that he will make the areas under UWSA control "opium free" by 2005, famously promising that "if we have any more opium here after 2005, you can come and chop my head off."

BASSEIN (PATHEIN). The capital of **Irrawaddy (Ayeyarwady) Division**, located in the delta of the **Irrawaddy (Ayeyarwady) River**. With an estimated population of 182,496 in 1996, it is one of Burma's largest cities. Bassein is an important seaport and a center for the milling and distribution of **rice**. It is well known for its fragrant rice and the manufacture of colorful umbrellas and parasols (*hti*). The city's name may derive from *Pathi*, meaning "Muslim" in the **Burmese (Myanmar) language**, signifying the importance of Arab and Indian traders in its early history.

BAYINGYI. Derived from *feringhi*, a term widely used in India and the Malay world to refer to white Europeans, especially the Portuguese, this **Burmese (Myanmar) language** term refers to the followers of **Felipe de Brito**, who were captured after the fall of **Syriam**

(Thanlyin) in 1613 and exiled to villages near **Shwebo** in **Upper Burma**, where they formed a separate community who continued to adhere to the Catholic faith. Some served in Burmese armies as artillerymen. Reportedly some inhabitants of Bayingyi villages still have fair hair, though they have long intermarried with local Burmese.

BAYINNAUNG, KING (r. 1551–1581). One of Burma's most renowned kings, the third monarch of the **Toungoo (Taungoo) Dynasty**, succeeding his brother-in-law **Tabinshwehti** following the latter's assassination. Crushing **Mon** resistance and capturing **Hanthawaddy** (modern **Pegu [Bago]**) in 1551, he made it his royal capital, and in the following years campaigned in the north, capturing **Ava (Inwa)** from the **Shans** in 1555 and subjugating the **Shan States**. This enabled him to assert suzerainty over Chiang Mai (Lan Na) and brought him into confrontation with the states of Luang Prabang and Vientiane (in modern Laos), with whom he fought inconclusively until the end of his reign. Like Tabinshwehti, he made ample use of Portuguese mercenaries and firearms.

His greatest military achievement was the capture of Ayuthaya, the Siamese capital, in 1564. The Siamese royal family was taken to Burma as hostages, but a Mon revolt in **Lower Burma** made it necessary for Bayinnaung to return home. He recaptured Ayuthaya from rebels in 1569, pillaging it completely, and Siam became Bayinnaung's vassal state. By the mid-1580s, however, it had regained its independence under the "Black Prince," Pra Naret.

Cruel in war, Bayinnaung was a model **Buddhist** monarch, building **pagodas**, donating a *hti* to the **Shwe Dagon Pagoda**, and securing what was claimed to be a **Buddha tooth relic** from Sri Lanka. He prohibited animal sacrifices by **Muslims** and devotees of the *nats*, which were offensive to Buddhists. His capital at **Pegu (Bago)** was one of the richest cities in Southeast Asia. But endless warfare exhausted his subjects, and his successor, Nanda Bayin (r. 1581–1599), was unable to sustain his father's imperial expansion.

The **State Law and Order Restoration Council/State Peace and Development Council** has made the warrior king one of its principal national heroes. In the early 1990s, the military regime built a concrete replica of his Kanbawzathadi Palace at Pegu, and it has provocatively put up statues of the monarch at the borders with **Thailand**. The military regime's use of Bayinnaung asserts the **Tatmadaw**'s historical role in carrying on his work of hard-fisted nation-building and also deemphasizes the pre-1988 pantheon of modern heroes, especially **Aung San**, whose daughter, **Aung San Suu Kyi**, leads the prodemocracy movement.

BETEL CHEWING. What is commonly called "betel chewing" involves mastication of a nut from the areca palm (*Areca cathechu*), which is sliced or chopped up and wrapped artfully with a bit of liquefied lime in a betel leaf, which comes from a vine (*Piper betel*) related to pepper. Sometimes other ingredients, such as tobacco or spices, are added. Mildly stimulating, betel chewing, a custom they share with many other peoples in Southeast and South Asia, has been practiced by the peoples of Burma since before the beginning of recorded history. Chewing the betel quid produces copious, red-colored juice mixed with saliva, which is expectorated. Teeth stained red-black by habitual betel chewing were traditionally thought to be a mark of beauty.

Betel chewing is heavily laden with cultural and religious symbolism. Burmese **women** customarily offered a betel quid to their lovers; monks used it to increase their concentration; and Burmese kings and high officials possessed beautifully crafted implements for preparing, storing, and offering betel quids, whose design was regulated by strict sumptuary laws. High-quality betel boxes were often made of lacquer or silver.

In recent years, the chewing of betel quids has declined in popularity, especially in cities. The sidewalks of **Rangoon (Yangon)** are no longer as heavily streaked with blood-red juice as they were a couple of decades ago. The **State Law and Order Restoration Council** sought to discourage betel chewing on grounds of health and appearance. Among those people who can afford it, it has been largely supplanted by other, probably less healthy diversions, such as smoking Western-style cigarettes or drinking imported whiskey.

BHAMO. A town in **Kachin State**, located on the banks of the **Irrawaddy (Ayeyarwady) River**, south of the state capital of **Myitkyina**. Bhamo is the highest navigable point on the Irrawaddy, and in the past was an important trade center linking China and **Upper Burma**.

BILU. Also known as a *yaksha*, in Burmese art and mythology, an ogre or demon. Such fearsome creatures figure prominently in the **Jataka Tales** and are common artistic motifs at **Buddhist** sites, such as **pagodas** and temples, where their images serve symbolically as guardians. *Bilus* are supposed to have an appetite for human flesh, and Bilu Gyun ("Ogre Island"), in **Mon State** adjacent to **Moulmein (Mawlamyine)**, may have acquired its name because cannibals inhabited the place in antiquity. In modern history, perhaps the most famous reference to these ogres was made by a **Shan** delegate to the **Panglong Conference**, referring to **Aung San**: "here at Panglong the Burmese *bilu* unmasked himself, and the Shans, **Kachins** and **Chins** found him not to be the *bilu* they were wont to regard him but a human being as themselves, who regarded them as equals and colleagues."

BIMSTEC. The acronym for "**Bangladesh-India**-Myanmar-Sri Lanka-**Thailand** Economic Cooperation," a regional group established in June 1997; Burma became a full member in December of that year. The goals of the group include economic, educational, and technical cooperation, and each member state is given an area of special responsibility (Burma's is the energy sector). In 2004, the group, including new members Nepal and Bhutan, signed an agreement paving the way for a free trade agreement over the next 15 years. Burma's inclusion in the group reflects the **State Peace and Development Council**'s desire to diversify its economic ties, implying its concern not to become economically too dependent on the **People's Republic of China**. *See also* ASSOCIATION OF SOUTHEAST ASIAN NATIONS (ASEAN) AND BURMA.

BINNYA DALA (BANNYA DALA, r. 1747–1757). The last king of the **Mons**, who succeeded **Smim Htaw Buddhaketi** in a 1747 palace coup. In 1752, his forces captured **Ava (Inwa)**, extinguishing the Burman **Toungoo (Taungoo) Dynasty**, but **Alaungpaya** recaptured Ava the following year, and carried the war back from **Upper** to **Lower Burma**. In May 1757, Binnya Dala's capital of **Hanthawaddy** (modern **Pegu [Bago]**) fell to Alaungpaya with great bloodshed. This marked the end of a long history of independent Mon states. Following repeated uprisings by the Mons in Lower Burma and Burman fears that they would ally with Siam (**Thailand**), Alaungpaya's son **Hsinbyushin** executed the captive Binnya Dala in 1774. *See also* KONBAUNG DYNASTY.

"BLACK FRIDAY" INCIDENT (MAY 30, 2003). While returning from a visit to **Kachin State**, Daw **Aung San Suu Kyi** and members of her **National League for Democracy (NLD)** were attacked by a large gang of men armed with bamboo staves and other crude weapons near the town of Budalin in **Sagaing Division**. The assailants were believed to be members of the progovernment **Union Solidarity and Development Association (USDA)**, and the violence left as many as 70 or 80 persons dead (the official figure was four). Daw Suu Kyi was taken into "protective custody," and by fall of 2003 was back under house arrest. U **Tin U** and other party leaders accompanying her were also detained. The **State Peace and Development Council (SPDC)** claimed that the May 30 incident had been provoked by overzealous members of the NLD, but most observers believe it was a move by the SPDC to crush the opposition party after Daw Suu Kyi's trips to different parts of the country following her May 2002 release from house arrest showed that she still enjoyed tremendous grassroots support. In the wake of the incident, the authorities closed down many NLD branch offices and detained more party members.

In terms of political dynamics within the SPDC junta, "Black Friday" seemed to reflect the ascendancy of Senior General **Than Shwe** over "moderates" led by SPDC Secretary-1 **Khin Nyunt** (who was in fact purged in October 2004). The incident had major international repercussions. The **United States** passed new **sanctions**, **Japan** temporarily halted new **aid**, and even the **Association of Southeast Asian Nations** broke with precedent to criticize the SPDC's hard line. **Malaysia**'s Prime Minister Mahathir Mohamed even suggested that ASEAN might have to expel Burma from membership. The proposal of Prime Minister Thaksin Shinawatra of **Thailand** that Burma follow a "road map" toward democratization was met with widespread skepticism. *See also* STATE PEACE AND DEVELOPMENT COUNCIL, INTERNAL DYNAMICS.

BLACK MARKET. Market-driven commercial activity occurring outside the state-controlled economy of the **Burma Socialist Programme Party (BSPP)** period (1962–1988), which **Ne Win** labeled "economic insurgency" and tried to cripple with **demonetization** and other measures. Probably its most important dimension was illegal trade in **rice** and other agricultural products, since much higher prices were offered to farmers on the black market than by the state agricultural marketing board. So much rice flowed onto the black market that even in years of good harvests it was often scarce in urban government stores; when harvests were poor due to drought or flooding, urban residents were desperately short of rice and other foodstuffs, which contributed to social unrest, especially in the mid-1970s and in 1988. Another form of black market activity was the illegal sale of goods by military officers, who had privileged access to government warehouses, to *hmaung-kho* (black market entrepreneurs), which earned huge profits for both parties. Economic ties between top military officers (or their wives, who often had a keen business sense) and the *hmaung-kho* were so widespread that when U **Tin U** and **"MI" Tin Oo** were arrested on charges of dealing on the black market, observers knew this was just a pretext to eliminate potential challengers to Ne Win's power monopoly. The illegal export of agricultural products and import of manufactured products across Burma's borders by ethnic minority insurgents was probably larger than official external trade, even when the **opium** trade is not included. According to economist Mya Maung, the black market constituted two-thirds of all domestic and external trade during the 1962–1988 period.

Because the socialist system was corrupt and inefficient, it was impossible for most people to survive on a day-to-day basis without the black market; an estimated 90 percent made use of it. Since government budgets were severely limited, BSPP and state officials depended on contributions from *hmaung-kho* to perform their official duties, offering them legal protection in return. Wealthy *hmaung-kho* also contributed generously to **pagoda** building, offerings to members of the **Sangha**, and traditional festivals. By the 1980s, they may have numbered as many as several hundred thousand. Many observers believe that Ne Win's demonetization of September 1987, which choked off black market activity and imposed widespread hardship, was the major factor in the nationwide unrest and antigovernment movements of 1988.

In principle, the black market no longer exists, since the **State Law and Order Restoration Council** decreed the end of the socialist system in 1988. However, laws relating to business are applied inconsistently, private businesses are still barred from some sectors (such as **gemstones** and **oil and natural gas**), and the present military regime continues to view business people as motivated by an evil profit motive. Thus crackdowns, especially on currency traders, are frequent. *See also* AGRICULTURE; CURRENCY AND EXCHANGE RATES; ECONOMY AND ECONOMIC POLICY, BURMA SOCIALIST PROGRAMME PARTY ERA.

BO. Literally "lieutenant" in the **Burmese (Myanmar) language**, it refers more generally to a military officer or commander. Just before **World War II**, the **Thirty Comrades** used the title to refer to themselves, along with a *nom de guerre* (e.g., Bo **Let Ya**). *Bo* was also used to refer to the commanders of local armies, or local political bosses. *Bogyoke*, meaning "major general," refers to the army's commander in chief but historically has been used to refer to two men, Bogyoke **Aung San**, founder of the **Tatmadaw**, and Bogyoke **Ne Win**, his successor. *See also* TATMADAW, HISTORY OF.

BO BO AUNG. The most prominent **weikza**, or occult master, who was said to have acquired supernatural powers through the use of magic letters (Burmese "runes"). According to popular belief, his boyhood companion, who became King **Bodawpaya** (r. 1782–1819), feared Bo Bo Aung's powers and tried to have him executed. In captivity, the *weikza* challenged the king to a test: Drawing the o-shaped Burmese letter *wa* on a wall of the palace, he asked him to erase it. The king failed to do so, and the letter multiplied magically until thousands of *wa*s covered the wall. Bo Bo Aung's occult prowess allegedly caused the king to retire and become a recluse. He is also believed to have rescued Setkya Min, son of King Bagyidaw (r. 1819–1838), from a royal purge, taking him to a safe place where he could prepare to become a future king and drive the British from **Lower Burma**.

Dr. **Ba Maw** used the Bo Bo Aung legend to gain popular support for his **Freedom Bloc** between 1939 and 1941, a time when the movement for independence from colonial rule was gaining strength, and a song about the occult master was popular. Ba Maw writes in his autobiography, *Breakthrough in Burma*, that worshippers at the **Maha Muni Image** in **Mandalay** claimed to have seen Bo Bo Aung's *wa* letter reflected on the gilded body of the Buddha image, a sign that the *weikza* would deliver Burma from her travails.

BO MOGYO. The Burmese name ("Commander Thunderbolt") assumed by Colonel **Suzuki Keiji** after he became commander of the **Burma Independence Army**. It was apparently suggested to him by **Aung San**. For ordinary Burmese, it had tremendous resonance because a prophecy stated that just as a hunter (**Alaungpaya**, founder of the last royal dynasty) had been struck down by an "umbrella rod" (symbolizing the British), so the umbrella rod would be shattered by a thunderbolt. There were other stories that Suzuki was a descendant of the Myingun Prince, who fled Burma after the **Third Anglo-Burmese War**. Suzuki promoted his "Burmese" persona by habitually appearing at public functions in indigenous formal dress. *See also* JAPANESE OCCUPATION; THIRTY COMRADES.

BODAWPAYA, KING (r. 1781–1819). Sixth monarch of the **Konbaung Dynasty**, he was the third and last of **Alaungpaya**'s sons to occupy the throne and was one of Burma's most prominent kings. He is also known as *Badon Min*. During his reign, Burma enjoyed, for the last time, a period of military expansion. His coming to power resulted in a bloody purge of his rivals, and he quit the *nat*-infested capital of **Ava (Inwa)**, building a new one at **Amarapura**. Crushing a revolt by the **Mons** in 1783, he invaded and occupied the Kingdom of **Arakan** in 1784, depriving it of its centuries-long independence and the sacred **Maha Muni Image**, which was brought back by his army along with 20,000 prisoners to Amarapura by way of the **Arakan Yoma** and the **Irrawaddy (Ayeyarwady) River**. He attempted unsuccessfully to subjugate the newly established Chakri Dynasty in Siam (**Thailand**) and allowed the East India Company to base residents at **Rangoon (Yangon)**. However, he was basically uninterested in pursuing amicable relations with the British, who were increasingly bothered by his arrogance as well as his intervention in northeastern **India** (Assam).

Bodawpaya's domestic policies combined practical and religious themes. He initiated a thorough survey of his realm's land and population for tax purposes (the "Burmese Domesday Book") and promoted public works, especially irrigation. He sought to purify the *Sangha*, backing orthodoxy, and sponsored the establishment of the conservative Amarapura Sect in Sri Lanka. If completed, his **pagoda** at **Mingun** would have been the tallest in the world, at 170 meters. He attempted unsuccessfully to get the *Sangha* to recognize him as a Future Buddha.

Bodawpaya's incessant demands for manpower for public works and military expeditions imposed terrible hardship on the population, especially in Arakan, which fanned insurgency that was a contributing cause of the **First Anglo-Burmese War**. Although a tyrant, he was the classical **Burman** ruler, in the words of one observer, "a masterful man who never hesitated to punish."

BOGYOKE YWA. "Generals' village" in the **Burmese (Myanmar)** language, referring to neighborhoods, chiefly in **Rangoon (Yangon)**, where top-ranking **Tatmadaw** officers, including members of the **State Peace and Development Council (SPDC)**, live with their families. At present there are six or seven of these in Burma's capital, including parts of Bahan Township, south of **Inya Lake**, and near Eight Mile Junction in Mayangone Township, north of the lake, where SPDC Chairman Senior General **Than Shwe** resided until the nation's capital was moved to a site near **Pyinmana** in 2005. "Generals' villages" have special privileges: Residences are spacious and comfortable, residents can buy high-quality foodstuffs from mobile vans at subsidized prices, electricity is provided 24 hours a day (part of the **"VIP Grid"**), and security is tight. These super-elite neighborhoods go back at least to the **Ne Win** era (1962–1988). As generals grow old or fall from favor, they often sell their homes in the *Bogyoke Ywa* to rich businesspeople, including drug-dealing entrepreneurs from the **Kokang** or **Wa** areas of **Shan State**. *See also* TATMADAW AND BURMESE (MYANMAR) SOCIETY.

BORDER AREA DEVELOPMENT. A policy adopted by the **State Law and Order Restoration Council (SLORC)** in 1989 after the military government negotiated **cease-fires** with breakaway ethnic components of the **Communist Party of Burma**. The cease-fire groups, of which the largest is the **United Wa State Army (UWSA)**, requested economic assistance from the government, and a "Central Committee for the Development of Border Area and National Races" was established to this end in May 1989. In September 1992, a cabinet-level agency, the Ministry for Progress of Border Areas and National Races, was established. In 1994 the SLORC published a "Border Areas Development Master Plan," which set targets for a three-year (1993–1994 to 1995–1996) and two four-year (1996–1997 to 1999–2000 and 2000–2001 to 2003–2004) plans. Border Area Development was the responsibility of Lieutenant-General **Khin Nyunt** and the **Military Intelligence** network he commanded. Within the top ranks of the **Tatmadaw**, this situation generated some friction because regular Army commanders resented the "soft" line Khin Nyunt took toward the cease-fire ethnic armed groups, many of whom had engaged the Burmese army in pitched battles before 1989. Following the purge of Khin Nyunt in October 2004, the future of Border Area Development is unclear.

The Border Areas (largely coterminous with the colonial-era **Frontier Areas**, but also including parts of **Tenasserim [Tanintharyi] Division** and **Mon State**) have been divided into 19 regions:

Kachin Special Region No. 1	**Padaung** Region
Kachin Special Region No. 2	**Kayah** Region
Kokang Region	**Kayin (Karen)** Region
Wa Region	**Mon** Region
Mawpha Region	Tanintharyi (Tenasserim) Region
Kachin Northeast Region	**Rakhine (Arakan) Region**
Keng Tung (Kyaingtong) Region	**Chin** Region
Shan Region	Kabaw Valley Region, and
Palaung Region	**Naga** Region
Pa-O Region	

Apart from economic development, including exploitation of natural resources and the construction of roads and bridges, a major goal of border area development has been eradication of **opium** poppy cultivation, especially in the Wa and Kokang regions of northeastern **Shan State** near the border with China. **Foreign aid** from the **United Nations, Japan, South Korea**, and other sources has been used for these projects, including Japanese support for opium crop substitution in Kokang. Critics of the **State Peace and Development Council (SPDC)** say that Border Area Development is largely "window dressing," designed to improve the government's global image, but some observers believe the programs are having a major impact in areas that, before the 1990s, had known nothing but war for decades. *See also* STATE PEACE AND DEVELOPMENT COUNCIL, INTERNAL DYNAMICS.

BOUNDARIES, INTERNATIONAL. Before the imposition of British colonial rule, Burmese kingdoms did not have fixed boundaries; rather, they extended their power and influence in a circle (*mandala*) radiating outward from the royal capital, its perimeter determined by the fluid dynamics of power politics and war between competing states as well as the quality and quantity of human and material resources at the ruler's disposal. Thus, at certain times during the **Toungoo** and **Konbaung Dynasties**, the Burmese realm included much of modern Siam (**Thailand**), Laos, and northeastern India, while after the **Second Anglo-Burmese War** it encompassed only **Upper Burma** and, loosely, certain ethnic minority areas, such as the **Shan States**.

In the late 19th and early 20th centuries, the British made treaties with neighboring states that fixed, at least roughly, the international boundaries of modern Burma. Following the **Government of Burma Act (1935)**, neighboring jurisdictions in British India were separated from Burma by an international boundary. After the country became independent in 1948, the governments of U **Nu** and **Ne Win** and the post-1988 military regime concluded further territorial and boundary agreements. At present, Burma's land boundaries total 6,285 kilometers (3,906 miles) in length: 2,227 kilometers (1,384 miles) with the People's Republic of **China**, 2,098 kilometers (1,304 miles) with Thailand, 1,453 kilometers (903 miles) with **India**, 235 kilometers (146 miles) with Laos (the entire boundary constituting the mid-channel of the **Mekong River**), and 272 kilometers (169 miles) with **Bangladesh**.

Sea boundaries totaling 2,228 kilometers (1,385 miles) front the Bay of Bengal, the Gulf of **Martaban (Mottama)**, and the Andaman Sea, with territorial jurisdiction extending 12 miles from shore and an exclusive economic zone (EEZ) of 200 nautical miles beyond the territorial waters. Such demarcation is important, given the large quantities of natural gas found within the EEZs, exploited after 1988 with the participation of foreign oil companies.

Until recently, both Burma's land and sea boundaries have been poorly defended: insurgents, especially those belonging to the **Communist Party of Burma**, the **Kachin Independence Army/Organization (KIA/KIO)**, the **Karen National Union**, and the **Mong Tai Army**, controlled much of the China–Burma and Thai–Burma border area, gaining major financial support from the **black market** and **opium** trade. The Bangladesh–Burma border was unsettled because of the determination of the Ne Win and **State Law and Order Restoration Council** regimes to expel Muslim **Rohingyas** from **Arakan (Rakhine) State** and the operations of Muslim guerrillas, known as *mujahadin*. The India–Burma border was destabilized by **Chin** and **Naga** insurgents, who passed freely between both countries. Burma's waters were regularly infiltrated by foreign vessels, especially Thai fishermen poaching the country's rich marine resources.

After 1988, **cease-fires** with ethnic minority armed groups and **Border Area Development** programs increased the central government's leverage along the country's boundaries, though areas along the China–Burma border under the control of the **United Wa State Army** remain closed to the **Tatmadaw**. Purchases of naval vessels and patrol boats since 1988 have enabled the government to more adequately defend its sea boundaries. The **State Peace and Development Council**'s policy of achieving friendly and cooperative relations with all neighboring states has also played a major role in stabilizing its international boundaries.

BRANG SENG, MARAN (1931–1994). Leader of the **Kachin** armed resistance against the central government, considered one of the ablest ethnic opposition figures before his death in 1994. He graduated from **Rangoon (Yangon) University** in 1954 and became headmaster of the Kachin Baptist High School in **Myitkyina** in 1957. In 1963, he joined the newly founded **Kachin Independence Army/ Organization (KIA/KIO)** and rose quickly to positions of responsibility, including leadership of KIO delegations to the People's Republic of **China** in 1967, 1968, and 1979. Becoming commander of the KIA and chairman of the KIO in 1975–1976, he worked hard to promote cooperation among ethnic nationalist armed groups and the **Communist Party of Burma (CPB)** and was chosen vice chairman of the **Democratic Alliance of Burma** in November 1988. His death by stroke in August 1994, after the KIA/KIO had signed a **cease-fire** with the **State Law and Order Restoration Council (SLORC)**, was a serious blow to the Kachin community and the ethnic nationalist movement in general. He was succeeded as KIO chairman by Zau Mai.

BRITAIN, RELATIONS WITH. Although Britain was Burma's colonial ruler and presided over the introduction of Western influences in many areas of life, including widespread use of the English language, post-independence ties have not been as close as in the case of many other former British colonies, because Burma elected to remain outside the British Commonwealth of Nations and the country became isolated after **Ne Win** established the **Revolutionary Council** in 1962. Britain provided military assistance under the 1947 Bo **Let Ya**–Freeman Defence Agreement, but it was abrogated in 1954. Colonial-era British firms, such as the Bombay Burma Trading Company, the **Irrawaddy Flotilla**, and Burma Oil, were nationalized. Other countries, especially **Japan** and West **Germany**, surpassed Britain in the amount of **foreign aid** given, especially during the 1970s and 1980s. After the **State Law and Order Restoration Council (SLORC)** seized power in September 1988, aid from Britain was suspended, except for humanitarian purposes, and successive governments in London have condemned the post-1988 regime's violations of **human rights**. During and since the **Democracy Summer** in 1988, the Burmese-language service of the public British Broadcasting Corporation (BBC) has provided radio listeners within the country with a much-needed alternative to the official **mass media**.

BRITO, FELIPE DE (?–1613). During the 16th and early 17th centuries, Portuguese soldiers of fortune played an important role in the turbulent history of the times as mercenaries of Burmese rulers, especially **Tabinshwehti** and **Bayinnaung**. De Brito, who served the king of **Arakan** during his invasion of **Lower Burma** in 1599, gained control of the port of **Syriam (Thanlyin)** and attempted to establish his own independent realm. He initially enjoyed friendly relations with the **Mons**, who offered to recognize him as king, and defeated attacks by the Arakanese war fleet and the **Burmans** at **Toungoo (Taungoo)**. But his arrogant behavior, which included the plunder of Buddhist **pagodas** and plans to convert the population to Christianity, made him many enemies. After de Brito captured and pillaged Toungoo, King **Anaukpetlun** laid siege to Syriam and occupied it in early 1613. De Brito was executed by impalement, most of his officers were also killed, and other Portuguese prisoners were taken to **Upper Burma**, where they served in the king's army as musketeers, retained their Catholic faith, and formed their own distinct community, known as **Bayingyi** (*feringhi*). *See also* TOUNGOO DYNASTY.

BUDDHA, GOTAMA (BCE 563–483). Also Gautama Buddha, the founder of **Buddhism**. Born into a wealthy and prominent family in the north Indian state of Sakka (Sakya), Siddhartha Gotama renounced the world and achieved Enlightenment (*bodhi*, thus his name, the Enlightened One) through meditation. He devoted the last 40 years of his life to preaching and established the monastic order, or **Sangha**. At his death, he passed into *nibbana* (nirvana), freeing himself from *samsara*, or the cycle of rebirth. Theravada Buddhists believe that Buddha was a man, not a divine being, and upon entering *nibbana* no longer exists in the ordinary sense. Thus, he cannot intercede on behalf of believers or answer their prayers. All that remains are his teachings (*dhamma*), which the Sangha preserves and propagates. However, there is also a long-established belief among Buddhists that veneration of the Buddha's personal possessions and bodily relics (for example, **Buddha tooth relics**) brings the devotee a deeper comprehension of the *dhamma*. Such relics have been housed in **pagodas**, of which the most famous in Burma is the **Shwe Dagon Pagoda** in **Rangoon (Yangon)**.

Through the ages, there have been many, perhaps numberless, Buddhas, each preaching the same doctrine. Gotama Buddha was the 25th of 26 to appear in the present "world cycle" (*kappa*); the last Buddha of the cycle, Metteya (Maitreya), will appear 5,000 years after the death of Gotama. There are two kinds of Buddhas: "private Buddhas," including *arahants*, who achieve *nibbana* on their own but do not teach the *dhamma,* and "perfect Buddhas," such as Gotama, who do teach *dhamma.* The latter are considered superior. The **Jataka**, or "birth-tales," recount episodes in Gotama Buddha's former lives and are a formative influence on Burmese **literature**, drama, and art, as well as religion.

BUDDHA TOOTH RELICS. When Gotama **Buddha** died and passed into *nibbana*, parts of his body, especially his teeth and bones, were regarded as holy relics, a belief similar to the veneration of Christian saints' remains in Catholic countries. In the 16th century, the king of Kandy in Sri Lanka was the proud possessor of one of four Buddha tooth relics said to be extant. A devout Buddhist, King **Bayinnaung** sent special offerings to the Kandy tooth, including brooms made from his hair and that of his chief queen. When the Portuguese captured the tooth in 1561, bringing it back to their colony of Goa in western India, the Burmese king offered them a royal ransom in exchange. The Portuguese civil authorities were happy to convey the tooth to Bayinnaung's capital of **Pegu (Bago)**, but the archbishop of Goa intervened and demanded that it be destroyed. As horrified Burmese envoys looked on, the tooth was ground to dust and cast into a river (though according to legend, it magically reconstituted itself and returned to Kandy, where it remains today). Some years later, Bayinnaung accepted a tooth relic from the king of Colombo, which was placed in Pegu's Mahazedi **Pagoda** but later moved to the **Kaunghmudaw Pagoda** in **Sagaing**.

Tooth relics were also brought to China and venerated at the Tang Dynasty (618–906 CE) capital of Chang-an. At the beginning of the 20th century, one was discovered at a Buddhist monastery near Beijing. Though the People's Republic of **China** is a communist regime that disparages religion as "superstition," it has used this tooth relic as a means of promoting friendship with Buddhist communities in neighboring countries. In the 1950s, the relic was sent to Burma as part of the **Sixth Great Buddhist Council** sponsored by Prime Minister U Nu; in 1994, it was sent again to Burma, where it stayed for 45 days amid great pomp and ceremony, reflecting close ties between China and the **State Law and Order Restoration Council.** Two replicas of the relic were made, one of which is kept at **Mandalay**, the other at the "Tooth Relic Pagoda," located north of **Inya Lake** in

Rangoon (Yangon). The pagoda is frequently visited by members of the **State Peace and Development Council,** including its chairman, Senior General **Than Shwe.** The histories of the Sri Lankan and Chinese tooth relics in relation to Burma show how politics, diplomacy, and religion have been complexly intertwined.

BUDDHISM. Established by **Gotama Buddha,** it is the religion of between 85 to 90 percent of Burma's people. Burmese Buddhism, like that of Thailand, Sri Lanka, and Cambodia, is of the Theravada stream, although before the establishment of the **Pagan (Bagan) Dynasty** in the 11th century CE, the practice of Mahayana Buddhism was also widespread. Burmese legends tell of the Buddha's visit to Burma during his lifetime, but the religion probably did not enter the country until the early centuries CE. Buddhist centers were located at Dhanyawadi and Vesali in **Arakan (Rakhine)** around the fourth to eighth centuries CE, and at **Mon** states established in **Lower Burma** around the same time. Both areas had close trade and cultural ties with the Indian subcontinent. The **Pyus** and the **Burmans** adopted the religion after their migration from Inner Asia. King **Anawrahta** of Pagan, advised by the Mon monk **Shin Arahan,** made Theravada Buddhism the official religion of his unified realm and established patterns of state–**Sangha** relations that persist in modified form to this day.

In Burma's multiethnic society, the overwhelming majority of Burmans, Mons, and **Shans,** as well as many **Karens (Kayins),** are adherents of Buddhism. The fact that elites of the Karens and other "hill tribe" minorities, such as the **Kachins** and **Karennis (Kayahs),** are Christian, and most persons of Indian ancestry are Hindu or Muslim, has tended to keep these minorities out of the national mainstream, where the dominant idea is that "to be Burmese is to be Buddhist."

In Burma, Buddhist thought, life-cycle events, and daily practice are tremendously complex, including the paying of homage to members of the Sangha, Buddha images, and **pagodas;** giving monks food or other offerings; the performance of other meritorious deeds, such as building pagodas, liberating animals, and sponsoring *shinbyu* ceremonies; and undergoing strict **meditation** regimes. Members of the Sangha, who in the late 1980s numbered around 300,000, are expected to observe the 227 rules of the *vinaya,* while laypeople have a less-strict code based on the five or ten precepts (*sila*). Although the Buddha himself is not considered a god, Burmese Buddhism coexists with a pantheon of gods or *nats*, local and brought from India, who are often seen as divine protectors of the religion.

The Buddha's teachings can be summarized as emphasizing impermanence, suffering as the basic quality of life, and non-self, that is, the lack of an immortal soul. The basic principles are summed up in the Four Noble Truths and the Eightfold Path of Righteousness that Gotama Buddha taught. Escape from *samsara* and the attainment of *nibbana* are considered the supreme goods. Most ordinary Buddhists hope that by accumulating merit (*kutho*) through performance of good deeds, they can achieve a rebirth on a plane higher than their present one, or at least avoid the torments of hell. Connected with Buddhism, though not doctrinally consistent with it, are certain magical practices, such as *yedaya*, that can be used as protection against ill fortune.

BURMA AID GROUP. Also known as the Aid Burma Consultative Group, a consortium of national and multilateral donors of **foreign aid** established in 1976 to coordinate official development assistance, mostly in the form of concessionary loans, to the **Ne Win** regime. Its members included **Japan** (the single largest donor), the World Bank, the Asian Development Bank, West **Germany**, France, **Britain, Australia**, the **United States**, and the **United Nations**. Largely in response to Ne Win's promise to implement market-oriented economic reform, the Group oversaw the disbursement of hundreds of millions of U.S. dollars annually during the late 1970s and early 1980s, though it seems to have become largely inoperative by 1988, when most aid funds were cut off for political and **human rights** reasons. *See also* ECONOMY AND ECONOMIC POLICY, BURMA SOCIALIST PROGRAMME PARTY ERA.

BURMA ARMY. The armed forces established by **Lord Louis Mountbatten**, Supreme Allied Commander, South East Asia, following the September 1945 **Kandy Conference** between himself, other British officials, and leaders of the **Patriotic Burmese Forces (PBF)** and the **Anti-Fascist People's Freedom League (AFPFL)**. Until independence in January 1948, it was part of British Commonwealth forces, and its commander was a British major general, assisted by Bo **Let Ya** and **Smith Dun**, who both held the rank of deputy inspector general. It consisted of three battalions of PBF men, **Burman** veterans of the **Burma National Army** who had risen against the Japanese on March 27, 1945, and seven "class battalions" (units specified by ethnicity) comprising **Karens (Kayins)**, **Chins**, **Kachins**, and the small number of Burmans who had served in the prewar **colonial armed forces**. Naval and air force units were also established. During the communist and ethnic minority rebellions of 1948–1949, the majority of its men defected to the insurgent side, but the **Fourth Burma Rifles** commanded by **Ne Win** and other mostly Burman units remained loyal to the central government. They formed the core of the modern **Tatmadaw**. *See also* AUNG SAN; BURMA INDEPENDENCE ARMY; PEOPLE'S VOLUNTEER ORGANIZATION; TATMADAW, HISTORY OF; WORLD WAR II IN BURMA (MILITARY OPERATIONS).

BURMA DEFENCE ARMY (BDA). The Burmese armed force that replaced the **Burma Independence Army (BIA)**. Formally established on August 26, 1942, its recruits were taken chiefly from among BIA veterans. With **Aung San** serving as commander in chief, the BDA consisted initially of three 1,000-man battalions, based at **Pyinmana** in the central part of the country. Japanese military advisors on all levels kept a close eye on its operations. An officers' training school was established at the former British military cantonment of **Mingaladon**, north of **Rangoon (Yangon)**, and the most promising graduates were sent to military academies in Japan for further study. Like the BIA, the overwhelming majority of its officers and men were **Burmans**. *See also* BURMA NATIONAL ARMY; JAPANESE OCCUPATION; TATMADAW, HISTORY OF.

BURMA INDEPENDENCE ARMY (BIA). Established by the **Minami Kikan** in Bangkok on December 28, 1941, the BIA was Burma's first postcolonial armed force, the predecessor of the independence-era **Tatmadaw**. Commanded by General **Suzuki Keiji**, with **Aung San** serving as senior staff officer, its officers included both Japanese members of the Minami Kikan and members of the **Thirty Comrades**. BIA units accompanied the Japanese Fifteenth Army in the invasion of Burma, and a significant engagement against the British was fought at Shwedaung, near **Prome (Pyay)**, in March 1942. But its military role was less significant than its symbolic one. For the ethnic majority **Burmans**, its appearance alongside the Japanese, who claimed to be fighting for the liberation of Asia, marked the end of a bitter era of colonial humiliation at the hands of the British. However, Japanese unwillingness to grant immediate independence after the city of **Moulmein (Mawlamyine)** was captured in January 1942 was a cause of great disillusionment among BIA officers.

Thousands of young village men joined its ranks (reliable estimates of its size vary from 15,000 to 23,000), and the BIA set up provisional governments in various parts of the country during the chaotic months of early 1942. Like the Tatmadaw and unlike the colonial-era army, the great majority of BIA recruits were Burman, with little or no ethnic minority representation. Because of their lack of discipline and poor quality (many BIA men were little better than gangsters), law and order collapsed in many areas it occupied. At **Myaungmya**, in the Delta of the **Irrawaddy (Ayeyarwady) River**, a race war broke out between Burman BIA men and Delta **Karens**, with both sides responsible for massacres. On July 24, 1942, the Japanese Military Administration (*Gunseikanbu*) dissolved the overlarge BIA and replaced it with a smaller and better-organized **Burma Defence Army**. In the words of Dr. **Ba Maw**, the BIA was a "spontaneous race explosion at a very confused, desperate, and violently racial moment in the struggle of a people to recover what they had lost or lacked for centuries" (*Breakthrough in Burma*, 217). *See also* BURMA NATIONAL ARMY; JAPANESE OCCUPATION; MYAUNGMYA MASSACRES; TATMADAW, HISTORY OF; WORLD WAR II IN BURMA (MILITARY OPERATIONS).

BURMA NATIONAL ARMY (BNA). Armed force established in August 1943, after Burma received nominal independence from Japan's premier, Tojo Hideki. The BNA's commander was Bo **Ne Win**, while **Aung San** served as minister of defense in Dr. **Ba Maw**'s cabinet. The BNA was essentially the reorganized **Burma Defence Army** and had a strength of approximately 15,000 men in late 1944. On March 17, 1945, Aung San presided over a ceremony in **Rangoon (Yangon)**

marking the BNA's departure for the front, and 10 days later, on March 27 (commemorated now as **Armed Forces Day**), the army began attacking Japanese units, largely through guerrilla operations. **Lord Louis Mountbatten**, Commander for South-East Asia, recognized the BNA as part of the Allied war effort, designating them the **Patriotic Burmese Forces**. *See also* ANTI-FASCIST ORGANIZATION; FORCE 136; JAPANESE OCCUPATION; WORLD WAR II IN BURMA (MILITARY OPERATIONS).

BURMA PROPER. This term has several meanings. Historically, it refers to those parts of British Burma that were directly ruled by colonial officials and administratively divided into **divisions** and **districts**. They roughly coincided with **Lower** and **Upper Burma**, if the ethnic minority regions of the latter, annexed and pacified during and after 1885–1890, are excluded. After the **Government of Burma Act (1935)** was implemented, it was included within "Ministerial Burma," while the "Excluded Areas," comprising parts of the **Frontier Areas**, were administered separately by the London-appointed governor. Burma Proper also corresponds to the divisions of independent Burma after 1948, as opposed to the **states**. Ethnographically and geographically, the term refers to the central plain and delta of the **Irrawaddy (Ayeyarwady) River**, where the **Burmans** and smaller numbers of **Mons, Karens (Kayins)**, and other minorities live; in other words, lowland areas of the country where the people adopted Indo-Buddhist civilization and established sophisticated polities in precolonial times.

BURMA RESEARCH SOCIETY. Established by **John S. Furnivall** in 1909 and holding its first meeting the following year, the society's goal was to promote scientific and cultural studies on the country. It sponsored seminars and conferences and published *The Journal of the Burma Research Society*, which contained articles in both the **Burmese (Myanmar) language** and English and was the principal scholarly publication in Burma until **Ne Win** closed down the Society in 1980, claiming it was an unneeded relic of British colonialism.

BURMA ROAD. Constructed between 1937 and 1939, the Burma Road was the main route along which Western countries supplied the

Chiang Kai-shek (Jiang Jyeshi) government in Chongqing (Chungking) with weapons and materiel during **China**'s war with Japan. An engineering marvel, it wound through steep mountainous terrain, from the railhead at **Lashio, Shan State**, to the Chinese border at Wanting (Wanding), and continued on to Kunming, capital of Yunnan Province. Thence another road carried supplies to Chongqing. Its importance grew after Japanese forces occupied most of China's east coast ports and closed down an alternate supply route from northern Vietnam (French Indochina) in September 1940. Between 1938 and 1940, the volume of supplies brought up by road or rail from the port of **Rangoon (Yangon)** grew from 2,000 to 10,000 tons a month. Tokyo saw closure of the road as essential to a speedy resolution of the "China Incident," and, when diplomatic pressure on Britain failed, sought a military solution. Neglected after the war, the Burma Road was reconstructed when the **State Law and Order Restoration Council** established close relations with China in 1989, largely for purposes of overland trade. *See also* JAPANESE OCCUPATION; LEDO ROAD; MINAMI KIKAN; SUZUKI KEIJI, COLONEL; WORLD WAR II IN BURMA.

BURMA SOCIALIST PROGRAMME PARTY (BSPP). Between 1964 and 1988, the BSPP (in Burmese, *Myanma Sosialit Lanzin Pati*, or *Ma-Sa-La*) was Burma's only legal political party. Established by the **Revolutionary Council** on July 4, 1962, it espoused a socialist ideology (the **"Burmese Road to Socialism"**) and operated according to the principles of a Marxist–Leninist revolutionary party. Parallel party and state organizations existed on all levels of the administration, from the center to "cells" on the ward or village tract level, and decision making was based on "democratic centralism," meaning that power was exercised from the top down, requiring the absolute obedience of lower-level party members. A March 1964 law made the BSPP the country's sole political organization, with a revolutionary mission of transforming society in accordance with socialist (but not communist) principles.

Between 1962 and 1971, the BSPP evolved from a "cadre party" with only a handful of elite members, most of whom were also members of the Revolutionary Council, into a "mass party," holding its First Congress in June–July 1971. At that time, it had 344,226 full and candidate members. By early 1981, membership had expanded to 1.5 million. **Tatmadaw** personnel and most civil servants were expected to join the party. But widespread corruption and abuses of power led to the purge of over 150,000 of the party rank and file during the mid-1970s.

Policy making was in the hands of a Central Executive Committee, chosen from among the Central Committee, which itself was selected by Party Congresses. The party's leader and chairman from 1962 to 1988 was **Ne Win**. More than two-thirds of all top party officials were military officers.

The BSPP's status as Burma's sole political organization was reaffirmed in the **Constitution of 1974**, which stated that the "working people" of Burma must "faithfully follow the leadership" of the party and that it "is the sole political party and shall lead the State." For example, the BSPP nominated candidates for the **Pyithu Hluttaw**, or People's Assembly, and **People's Councils** on the state/division, township, and ward/village tract levels.

At the **BSPP Extraordinary Congress of July 23–25, 1988**, Ne Win retired and was succeeded by **Sein Lwin**. Although Ne Win's proposal to hold a referendum on establishing a multiparty political system was turned down by the congress, **Dr. Maung Maung**, Sein Lwin's successor as state president and BSPP leader, presided over a second **BSPP Extraordinary Congress on September 10, 1988**, at which the holding of a multiparty democratic election was promised. The BSPP's demise was imminent. On September 16, members of the Tatmadaw and the civil service were "permitted to resign" from it. On September 26, 1988, eight days after the power seizure by the **State Law and Order Restoration Council**, the BSPP transformed itself into a "democratic" party with a new name, the **National Unity Party**.

To generate popular support, the BSPP established **mass organizations**, of which the most important were the Lanzin youth group and Workers' and Peasants Associations. Each had millions of members and resembled the **Union Solidarity and Development Association** established in 1993. Party managers, or cadres, were trained at the Central School of Political Science at **Mingaladon**, in northern **Rangoon (Yangon)**. *See also* ADMINISTRATION, BURMA SOCIALIST PROGRAMME PARTY ERA.

BURMA SOCIALIST PROGRAMME PARTY, EXTRAORDI-NARY CONGRESS (JULY 23–25, 1988). Sometimes referred to as the "Emergency Congress." In the face of rising popular opposition, **Burma Socialist Programme Party (BSPP)** Chairman **Ne Win** convened the congress a year earlier than scheduled to propose radical changes: the retirement of himself, party vice chairman (and president) **San Yu**, BSPP joint secretary general **Sein Lwin**, and three other top leaders; the holding of a popular referendum on whether the BSPP one-party system should be maintained, or scrapped in favor of a multiparty "democratic" system; and implementation of fundamental economic reforms (including foreign private investment). In his opening speech, Ne Win also gave his prophetic warning: "when the Army shoots, it shoots to hit; it does not fire into the air to scare." The congress concluded that while Ne Win and San Yu could retire, the other leaders should remain at their posts, and it rejected Ne Win's proposal of a referendum, citing economic rather than political reform as the first priority. On September 26, the BSPP Central Committee chose Sein Lwin as its new chairman, and on the 27th the **Pyithu Hluttaw** designated him president of the Socialist Union of the Republic of Burma. The much-hated Sein Lwin's assumption of power incited the massive protests of the **Four Eights Movement.** *See also* DEMOCRACY SUMMER.

BURMA SOCIALIST PROGRAMME PARTY, EXTRAORDI-NARY CONGRESS (SEPTEMBER 10, 1988). The second such congress of the **Burma Socialist Programme Party (BSPP)** during 1988, sometimes referred to as an "Emergency Congress," at which President and Party Chairman Dr. **Maung Maung** promised that a "free and fair" multiparty democratic election would be held in the near future. He confessed that the BSPP had become corrupt and complacent under a one-party system. *See also* BURMA SOCIALIST PROGRAMME PARTY, EXTRAORDINARY CONGRESS (JULY 23–25, 1988); DEMOCRACY SUMMER.

BURMANS (BAMARS). Burma's largest ethnic group, after whom the country is named. During the British colonial period, it was common to use "Burman" and "Burmese" interchangeably; more recently, "Burman" has been used to refer to the ethnic group, while

"Burmese" applies to nationals of Burma, regardless of ethnicity. "Burman" and "Burmese" are both English renditions of the **Burmese (Myanmar) language** term *Bama*, the colloquial name for the people (*Myanma* is the literary or formal term, with essentially the same meaning). When the **State Law and Order Restoration Council (SLORC)** decreed the **Adaptation of Expressions Law** in 1989, the official name of the group was changed to "Bamar," while the meaning of the term "Myanma"/"Myanmar" was changed to refer not to the majority ethnic group but to all nationals of the country, in other words, to be synonymous with "Burmese."

In the 1983 census, the last taken, Burmans numbered 23.5 million (69 percent of a total population of 35.3 million). The "heartland" of the Burmans, where they migrated in the early centuries CE from eastern Tibet or southwestern China, encompasses what are now **Mandalay, Magwe (Magway)**, and southern **Sagaing Divisions** (often referred to as **Upper Burma**). They also form the majority of the population of **Lower Burma**, where they have intermarried extensively with other groups, particularly the **Mons, Arakanese (Rakhines)**, and **Karens (Kayins)**. The "purity" of the Burmans of Upper Burma is something of a myth, because over the centuries, they have intermarried with the **Pyus**, who have now disappeared, and prisoners of war brought to the royal capital from Siam, **Arakan (Rakhine)**, Laos, **Manipur**, and Portugal (the **Bayingyi**). Given the large number of recent **Chinese** migrants in Mandalay and northern Burma, the "foreign" element in the Burman gene pool continues to be significant.

The first important Burman state was established at **Pagan (Bagan)**, on the banks of the **Irrawaddy (Ayeyarwady) River**, in the ninth century. Raised in a harsh, semidesert environment, the Burmans were a warlike people who carried out repeated military campaigns until put on the defensive during the **First Anglo-Burmese War**. The more dynamic kings of the **Bagan, Toungoo**, and **Konbaung Dynasties** conquered and controlled neighboring states in Lower Burma, **Arakan**, northeastern India, Laos, and Siam, imposing limited authority over border area peoples, such as the **Shans (Tai)** and Karens.

The Burmese language is the most widely spoken of the Tibeto–Burman language group, which also includes the languages of the

Arakanese, **Tavoyans**, **Kachins**, Karens, **Chins**, and **Nagas**. Burman self-identification focuses on language, customs, distinct artistic and musical motifs, and a shared history. But above all, it is connected with **Buddhism**. Ethnic/national identity is often summarized in the saying, "to be Burman/Burmese is to be Buddhist," and Burman converts to other religions, such as Christianity or Islam, are often considered marginal to mainstream society.

Successive Burman states, from the Pagan Dynasty to the **State Peace and Development Council (SPDC)**, have actively promoted the Buddhist religion, making generous offerings to the **Sangha**, promoting religious orthodoxy, and building **pagodas**. Aspects of Indo-Buddhist civilization were transmitted to them by the Mons, especially after the conquest of **Thaton** in Lower Burma in 1057 by King **Anawrahta**, though they have also been influenced by Buddhist trends in Sri Lanka. In the early 20th century, Burman/Burmese nationalism began with groups who sought to defend the Buddhist religion from the corrosion of modernity and foreign rule, such as the **Young Men's Buddhist Association**. However, the cult of the **Thirty-seven Nats** constitutes another aspect of a distinctively Burman religious life.

Although Pagan was the first of several important Burman urban centers where kingly power was established, most Burmans traditionally have lived in rural communities, economically dependent on the cultivation of wetland **rice** or other lowland crops. The focus of village life is the pagoda and the Buddhist monastery (*kyaung*), which also provided village children in the past with a basic **education**. Compared to their eastern neighbors, the Siamese (Thais), the Burmans had limited commercial and other relations with the outside world before the colonial era, fostering an isolationist outlook that continues to be expressed today in the antiforeign sentiments of the SPDC. In one form or another, post-independence governments—headed by U **Nu**, **Ne Win**, the SLORC, and the SPDC—have promoted the cultural "Burmanization" (Myanmarization) of other ethnic groups. *See also* BURMA PROPER; DRY ZONE; ERA, BURMESE; FAMILY SYSTEM, BURMESE; NAMES, BURMESE; TATMADAW AND BURMESE (MYANMAR) SOCIETY; WOMEN IN BURMESE SOCIETY.

BURMESE (MYANMAR) LANGUAGE. Used by the ethnic majority **Burmans (Bamars)** and members of other ethnic groups who have been assimilated into the mainstream culture and society, Burmese (Myanmar) is Burma's official language. About 40 million people speak it, 30 million speaking it as their first language. Burmese is a member of the Sino-Tibetan language group, subgroup Tibeto-Burman, and, like related languages, is monosyllabic and tonal.

Modern-spoken Burmese uses three tones: creaky high tone, high tone, and low tone. Different tones convey different meanings to the same combination of consonants and vowels; for example, *kyaung* in different tones can mean "cat" or "monastery/school." In addition, syllables are sometimes "stopped" or "weak," and the proper pronunciation of Burmese cannot ignore these distinctions. Sentence structure is S-O-V (subject-object-verb), in contrast to English, which is S-V-O (subject-verb-object). Nouns are frequently modified by particles that function like prepositions in English; for example, *Yangoun-go* means "to Rangoon." Although linguists believe they are not related, Burmese and Japanese have striking resemblances in terms of grammatical structure (such as the use of particles), which has been a great benefit to post-1988 Burmese exiles struggling to make a living in Japan.

Standard Burmese is based on the dialect spoken in **Rangoon (Yangon)** and **Mandalay**; **Arakanese** and Tavoyan (the language of the people of **Tavoy [Dawei]**) are closely related variations. Written (literary) and spoken (vernacular) Burmese are quite different, which (along with politics) is the source of the post-1989 controversy over whether "Burma" (*Bama*) or "Myanmar" (*Myanma*) is the proper name of the country: The former is colloquial, the latter literary, and both mean essentially the same thing.

The writing system is derived from the old Devanagari script of India, which was introduced to the Burmans by the **Mons**. It has 33 consonants (some of which are used only to transliterate **Pali** words) and 12 vowels. The Rajakumar inscription, found at **Pagan (Bagan)** and dated from 1112 CE, is the earliest known example of written Burmese, and also includes inscriptions in Mon, **Pyu**, and Pali. The round-shaped letters of Burmese are very appealing to look at and very difficult for foreigners to tell apart.

Many Pali words have entered the Burmese language, not only to signify religious and philosophical concepts connected with **Buddhism**, but also to provide formal vocabulary for increasingly complex and sophisticated precolonial societies, much as Latin and Greek enriched English and other Germanic languages. During and after the British colonial era, Burmese absorbed many English words; for example, *pati* means "(political) party," *democrati* means "democracy," and *saika* (**"sidecar"**) refers to a bicycle-like trishaw still widely used in urban and rural areas.

Colonial-era nationalists feared that Burmese was being relegated to the status of a "kitchen language" because elites preferred to use English. During the 1920s, they established **National Schools** to promote the instruction of the national language; the **Dobama Asiayone** also promoted the national language in the following decade. During the **Ne Win** era (1962–1988), the teaching of English (and indigenous minority languages) was deemphasized in favor of Burmese on all levels of the state-run system of **education**; to some extent, the policy in relation to English has been reversed since the **State Law and Order Restoration Council** took power in 1988. At the beginning of the 21st century, the Burmese language is increasingly influenced by the forces of "globalization." *See also* LANGUAGES OF BURMA; MON LANGUAGE; SHAN LANGUAGE.

"BURMESE ROAD TO SOCIALISM." The ideology of Burma's ruling party, the **Burma Socialist Programme Party (BSPP)**, during the **Revolutionary Council** (1962–1974) and Socialist Republic of the Union of Burma (1974–1988) periods. It is embodied in two documents, "The Burmese Road to Socialism" published by the Revolutionary Council on April 30, 1962, and *The System of Correlation of Man and His Environment: the Philosophy of the Burma Socialist Programme Party,* published in January 1963.

"The Burmese Road to Socialism" was a relatively short statement of the alleged inadequacies of parliamentary democracy and the new regime's commitment to establishing "socialist democracy" and a just social order. *The System of Correlation* was a longer and more ambitious attempt to synthesize **Buddhist**, Marxist, and non-Marxist socialist ideas. Although the latter employed much of the terminology of Marxism-Leninism, it rejected "vulgar materialism" and asserted the importance of such "psychical principles" as morality and self-reflection in the building of an ideal socialist society. Eschewing dogmatism, it admitted the need to constantly reevaluate and amend the state's revolutionary ideology. These two documents owed much to the socialist beliefs of Burma's leaders during the struggle for independence from colonial rule. Though they made room for traditional Buddhist values within a modernist, socialist context, they had little appeal among intellectuals or the general public during the BSPP period.

BUTTERFLY SPIRIT. *Leikpya* in the **Burmese (Myanmar) language**, the widely held belief that the soul of a human being can leave his or her body during sleep, and that its departure at death is permanent. Animist in origin, the notion of the butterfly spirit is reconciled with **Buddhism** in the idea that the *leikpya* released at death enters a new body in the process of *samsara*, the cycle of rebirth; in other cases, when a normal process of rebirth is hindered, it may animate a *nat*. Illness is sometimes explained as the *leikpya's* failure to return to the body, requiring special rituals.

– C –

CALENDAR, BURMESE. The Burmese calendar consists of twelve 28-day lunar months, and begins with **Thingyan** in early or mid-April. Because of the disparity between the lunar calendar and the rotation of the earth around the sun, an extra month, known as "second Waso," is added every few years. The months are, in order: Tagu, Kasone, Nayone, Waso, Wagaung, Tawthalin, Thadingyut, Tazaungmone, Nadaw, Pyatho, Tabodwei, and Tabaung. The full moon is a time for **pagoda** festivals, such as the festival at the **Shwe Dagon Pagoda** during Tabaung (mid-February to mid-March). In addition, other festivals are held each month throughout the year, such as the Festival of Lights at the end of Lent, during Thadingyut (mid-September to mid-October). Burmese newspapers and official documents are usually dated using this calendar, though the Western date may also be included.

Some of the ethnic minorities have their own calendars; for example, the **Karen (Kayin)** New Year falls in December. *See also* ERA, BURMESE; WEEK, BURMESE.

CARETAKER GOVERNMENT (1958–1960). A military-controlled government that assumed power on October 28, 1958, following the political confusion that resulted from the split of the **Anti-Fascist People's Freedom League (AFPFL)** into "Clean" and "Stable" factions earlier in the year. Prime Minister U **Nu** introduced a motion in parliament that General Ne Win, commander of the **Tatmadaw**, be offered the prime ministership for a six-month period to restore stability and create suitable conditions for holding a general election. Parliament subsequently extended his term for a longer period.

Ne Win ordered the arrest of many politicians and took a hard line toward insurgents in the countryside. The power of civilian authorities on all levels of administration was drastically weakened, as military officers were placed in control of central and **state/division** government agencies. The army-owned **Defence Services Institute**, managed by the capable Brigadier **Aung Gyi**, expanded rapidly, taking over state-owned and even private enterprises. In **Shan State**, the hereditary rulers, *sawbwa*, relinquished the powers they had enjoyed under British rule. Throughout the country, the Tatmadaw established branches of the National Solidarity Association to promote security and social welfare.

Although the restoration of law and order and greater government efficiency were widely appreciated, the Caretaker Government was much resented by poor people in **Rangoon (Yangon)**, more than 170,000 of whom were victims of **forced relocation** to satellite towns. Many ethnic minority communities also feared and hated the military. The general elections held in February 1960 resulted in a victory for U Nu's **Pyidaungsu (Union) Party**, as the AFPFL Clean faction was later renamed, despite widespread army backing for the AFPFL Stable faction. Power was transferred without incident to the new government in April 1960. Many observers view the Caretaker Government as a dress rehearsal not only for the **Revolutionary Council** established in March 1962, but also for the September 1988 **State Law and Order Restoration Council (SLORC)**, because the latter depicted itself as a transitional administration and also promised to hold a election, which took place on May 27, 1990, with unexpected results. The **Union Solidarity and Development Association**, founded by the SLORC in the early 1990s, bears a strong resemblance to the National Solidarity Association. *See also* OKKALAPA, NORTH AND SOUTH; THAKETA.

CARTOONS, POLITICAL. The history of political cartoons in Burma goes back to the early 20th century, when they satirized British colonial rule. Most of the earliest cartoonists were Europeans, whose work appeared in English-language papers such as the *Rangoon Times*. Ba Gale was probably the first Burmese to become a full-time professional cartoonist, publishing his work in the *Times* and the Burmese-language paper, *Thuriya (The Sun)*. One of his most famous pieces, published abroad, lampooned the European obsession with Mahatma Gandhi's loincloth, which the Indian nationalist leader wore when visiting London in 1933. A famous cartoon for *Thuriya* made fun of subservient Burmese who, wishing to please overweight British visitors who were loath to doff their shoes in holy places, carried them around on their backs on the platform of the **Shwe Dagon Pagoda**. After independence in 1948, Ba Gyan became prominent for his cartoons. But the art of the political cartoon languished after **Ne Win**'s military takeover in March 1962.

During **Democracy Summer**, political cartoons again flourished, especially in unofficial "street publications," often depicting Ne Win and his cronies as horned demons. Since 1988, both the **State Law and Order Restoration Council/State Peace and Development Council** and the democratic opposition have used cartoons to make their point. The SLORC/SPDC cartoons, appearing in the *New Light of Myanmar (Myanmar Alin)*, are often crude, for example, 1999 cartoons depicting Daw **Aung San Suu Kyi** as a power-hungry, gap-toothed old hag. On the opposition side, cartoonists in exile. such as "Mr. Burma" and "Green November," have drawn humorous takes on the grim realities of life under military rule.

CEASE-FIRE GROUPS. Between 1989 and the late 1990s, 22 major and minor ethnic armed groups signed **cease-fires** with the **State Law and Order Restoration Council/State Peace and Development Council**:

Myanmar National Democratic Alliance Army (MNDAA, 1989)
United Wa State Army (UWSA, 1989)
National Democratic Alliance Army (NDAA, 1989)
Shan State Army-North (1989)
New Democratic Army-Kachin (NDA-K, 1989)

Kachin Defence Army (former **KIA** Fourth Brigade, 1991)
Pa-O National Organization (1991)
Palaung State Liberation Party (1991)
Kayan National Guard (1992)
Kachin Independence Army (KIA, 1994)
Karenni Nationalities People's Liberation Front (1994)
Kayan New Land Army (1994)
Shan State Nationalities Liberation Organization (1994)
New Mon State Party (1995)
Democratic Karen Buddhist Army (DKBA, breakaway **Karen National Union** group, 1995)
Mongko Peace Land Force (**Kokang** breakaway group, 1995)
Shan State National Army (1995)
Mong Tai Army (MTA, 1996)
Karenni National Defence Army (1996)
Karen Peace Force (former Karen National Union battalion, 1997)
Communist Party of Burma (**Arakan State**, 1997)
KNU 2d Brigade Special Region Group—**Toungoo** (1997)

Although many of these armed groups were members of the **Democratic Alliance of Burma**, the cease-fires undermined a united front among the ethnic minorities and opened their territories to closer economic and other connections with **Rangoon (Yangon)** and foreign countries. As of early 2005, groups that had not yet signed cease-fires were the Karen National Union, the **Shan State Army-South**, the **Chin National Front**, the Arakan Rohingya National Organization (ARNO), and the **Karenni National Progressive Party**, which agreed to a cease-fire in 1995 that subsequently broke down. Following the purge of **Khin Nyunt** in October 2004, there was evidence that other groups might withdraw from cease-fire arrangements. *See also* BORDER AREA DEVELOPMENT.

CEASE-FIRES (1989–). An important development in relations between the central government and ethnic minority armed groups in the Border Areas occurred in 1989 with the signing of cease-fire agreements between the **State Law and Order Restoration Council (SLORC)** and four ethnic components of the former **Communist Party of Burma (CPB)**, which had split in the spring of that year. The cease-fires, which were tentative arrangements rather than permanent treaties, gave government recognition to the **United Wa State Army**, the **Myanmar National Democratic Alliance Army**, the **National Democratic Alliance Army-East Shan State**, and the **New Democratic Army**, which with the exception of the last were based in **Shan State**. Between 1989 and 1997, cease-fires were concluded with about 18 other major and minor groups, including the **Kachin Independence Organization/Army**, the **New Mon State Party**, the **Democratic Karen Buddhist Army**, and the **Mong Tai Army** of **Khun Sa** (the latter breaking up into smaller groups). In exchange for cooperating with, or at least not resisting, the **Tatmadaw**, the SLORC recognized the armed groups' freedom to control their own territory, keep their arms, and engage in business, including the lucrative trade in **opium** and other narcotics. Some **cease-fire groups**, especially the United Wa State Army, have become extremely powerful and control extensive territory and drug-related business enterprises.

The SLORC adopted the cease-fire strategy, which resembles the **Ka Kwe Ye** policy of the early 1960s, to prevent the emergence of a strong ethnic minority alliance; neutralize the effectiveness of **Burman (Bamar)** "student armies," such as the **All Burma Students' Democratic Front**, which cooperate closely with the minorities; and put increased pressure on recalcitrant groups, such as the **Karen National Union**, that still have not signed a cease-fire. The cease-fires also opened up money pipelines to **Rangoon (Yangon)**, especially after retired drug warlords Khun Sa and **Lo Hsing-han** settled in the capital and invested in business conglomerates. SLORC Secretary-1 **Khin Nyunt**, head of **Military Intelligence**, negotiated the cease-fires and remained responsible for **border area development**, an important factor in his struggle with factional rivals within the **State Peace and Development Council**. The future of the cease-fires was cast into doubt, however, when Khin Nyunt was ousted as prime minister and arrested in October 2004. *See also* DEMOCRATIC ALLIANCE OF BURMA; STATE PEACE AND DEVELOPMENT COUNCIL, INTERNAL DYNAMICS.

CHETTIARS. Or Chettyars, a caste of moneylenders from southern India (present-day Tamil Nadu State) who migrated to Burma in the late 19th century in large numbers and provided loans to Burmese farmers at high interest rates. When prices in the export-oriented **rice** economy deteriorated in the early 20th century, the large number of foreclosures meant that by 1936 about 25 percent of the crop land in major rice-growing districts of **Lower Burma** was in Chettiar hands. Naturally they were highly resented by the farmers, especially as the ranks of landless laborers swelled in the 1920s and 1930s, and rural sentiment against the Chettiars was a major factor in the 1930 **Saya San Rebellion**. Following the Japanese invasion of Burma in 1941–1942, most Chettiars returned to India. After 1945, they failed to regain their former economic influence. *See also* INDIANS IN BURMA.

CHIN NATIONAL FRONT (CNF). An ethnic minority movement claiming to represent the interests of the **Chins**, established in 1985. Its armed contingent, the Chin National Army (CNA), was organized in the wake of the 1988 prodemocracy movement, and about 100 CNA soldiers were trained by the **Kachin Independence Organization/ Army**. In 1989 the CNF/CNA became a member of the **Democratic Alliance of Burma**, but it has suffered from factional splits. As of 2004 it had not signed a **cease-fire** with the **State Peace and Development Council**.

CHIN STATE. One of Burma's 14 **states** and **divisions**, with an area of 36,019 square kilometers (13,907 square miles), and an estimated population in 2000 of 480,000 (1983 census figure: 368,949). The state capital is **Haka (Hakha)** (formerly, the capital was Falam). Chin State contains two districts (Falam and Mindat), subdivided into nine **townships**. The topography is characterized by rugged hills and deep valleys, and its highest point is Kaw Nu M'htung, which has two peaks over 10,000 feet high. Two important rivers, even though they are not navigable, are the Manipur and the Kaladan. Chin State is bounded on the east by **Sagaing** and **Magwe (Magway) Divisions** and on the south by **Arakan (Rakhine) State**. To the west, it has a long border with India and a shorter one with Bangladesh, which have been the sites of some insurgent activity.

Ethnically, the **Chins**, who are subdivided into six major tribal groups and a much larger number of tribal and linguistic subgroups, are the majority, although there are some **Burmans (Bamars)** and **Nagas**; **Arakanese (Rakhines)** live in the southern part of the state. Croplands are not extensive because of the mountainous landscape, and shifting cultivation (*taungya*) is widespread. The region is heavily forested. The transportation and communication infra structure is poorly developed. Between independence in 1948 and implementation of the **Constitution of 1974**, Chin State was known as the Chin Special Division.

CHINA AND BURMA (HISTORICAL RELATIONS). Although southwestern China and Tibet are believed to be the original homelands of most of the present-day inhabitants of Burma, China's impact on the development of Burmese civilization since antiquity has been less important than that of **India**. However, Chinese expansionism has frequently threatened the independence of Burmese states. The non-Han Chinese state of **Nan Chao**, located in what is now Yunnan Province, extended its power into the valley of the **Irrawaddy River** and waged war with the **Pyus** in the eighth and ninth centuries CE. Only with Nan Chao's decline in power were the **Burmans** able to establish a strong state at **Pagan (Bagan)**, in the midninth century. In 1253, the Mongol emperor Khubilai Khan conquered Yunnan. Mongol forays hastened the end of the **Pagan Dynasty** in the late 13th century. Even today, Chinese people are called *taiyoke*, meaning "Turk," in the **Burmese (Myanmar) language**, referring to Khubilai's Central Asian–Muslim soldiers.

In the 17th century, a Manchu (Ch'ing, Qing) army attempting to capture Yong Li, a Ming Dynasty prince, penetrated Burma as far south as **Sagaing**. Between 1766 and 1769, King **Hsinbyushin** successfully fought a series of battles against the Ch'ing that were caused by disputes over control of the eastern **Shan States**. A Chinese punitive force led by a son-in-law of the emperor approached the Burmese capital of **Ava (Inwa)** but was defeated, and Hsinbyushin's military commander, Maha Thiha Thura, agreed to the Treaty of Kaungton in 1770. The treaty, a face-saving measure for the humiliated Manchus, committed the Burmese king to sending tribute missions to Beijing every 10 years in recognition of the superior status of the Chinese emperor. Thereafter, the China–Burma border region became stable. Following the formal British annexation of **Up-**

per **Burma** in 1886, Britain and China signed a border treaty that later was significantly revised with the signing of a new border demarcation agreement by the independent Union of Burma and the **People's Republic of China** in 1961.

During World War II, Chinese Nationalist (**Kuomintang/ Guomindang**) troops participated in Allied operations against the Japanese. Since the People's Republic of China was established in 1949, the incursion of Kuomintang irregulars into the Shan States, and Beijing's support for a **Communist Party of Burma** base along the border following the **Anti-Chinese Riots** of June 1967, have contributed greatly to Burma's instability and provide a major rationalization for the perpetuation of military dictatorship. *See also* BURMA ROAD; CHINESE IN BURMA; KENG TUNG; KOKANG; LEDO ROAD; OPIUM; SINO-BURMESE; WAS.

CHINA, PEOPLE'S REPUBLIC OF (PRC), RELATIONS WITH. The Union of Burma was the first noncommunist state to extend diplomatic recognition to the People's Republic of China (on December 17, 1949), and it supported Beijing's claim to China's seat in the **United Nations**. Prime Minister U **Nu** and China's premier, Zhou En-lai, agreed to abide by the "five principles of peaceful coexistence," which included noninterference in each other's domestic affairs. Both countries saw the presence of **Kuomintang (Guomindang)** forces in **Shan State**, backed by the **U.S.** Central Intelligence Agency, as a threat to their sovereignty. However, illegal Chinese immigrants in Burma, the presence of exiled members of the **Communist Party of Burma (CPB)** on Chinese soil, and the complex issue of border demarcation were potentially divisive issues. Border issues were resolved with the ratification of a treaty in January 1961, in which China and Burma exchanged small parcels of land in **Shan** and **Kachin States** and China relinquished claims to larger areas. Beijing began supplying Burma with **foreign aid**, and a joint Chinese–Burmese military operation was carried out against the Kuomintang irregulars in early 1961.

Thus, relations were cordial, characterized by Zhou En-lai and **Ne Win**, who himself was **Sino-Burmese**, as ties between *pauk paw*, "distant cousins." But **anti-Chinese riots** in June 1967 constituted the greatest diplomatic crisis in independent Burma's short history.

As a result of Burmese mob attacks on the Chinese embassy in **Rangoon (Yangon)** and the killing of an embassy official, the Chinese ambassador was recalled, foreign aid was suspended, and Chinese propaganda called for the overthrow of the "fascist dictator" Ne Win. With Chinese logistical support, the CPB established a strong base along the China–Burma border in Shan State that soon became the most powerful and best-organized antigovernment insurgency. Although Beijing's support for the CPB diminished during the 1980s, it continued under the pretext of "fraternal party relations" between Chinese and Burmese communists—even after state-to-state relations were normalized in the early 1970s.

The seizure of power by the **State Law and Order Restoration Council (SLORC)** in September 1988 signaled a new era of much closer relations. Desperate for external props, the new military regime legalized China–Burma border trade, and in October 1989, sent a top-level delegation headed by Lieutenant General **Than Shwe** to Beijing to meet with Chinese leaders. Thereafter, China sold Burma more than US$2 billion in weapons, including tanks, patrol boats, and fighter jets; modernized Burmese naval installations located on the Indian Ocean; and provided training for **Tatmadaw** personnel. It has also played an important role in encouraging **cease-fires** between the SLORC and ethnic armed groups near the border (the dissolution of the CPB in early 1989 removed a major irritant in Beijing–Rangoon relations). Buttressed by state and private interests in neighboring Yunnan Province, the Chinese economic presence increased dramatically in the 1990s, not only along the border but also in **Mandalay** and other parts of **Upper Burma**, where a large but unspecified number of new Chinese residents have settled. Many Chinese immigrants purchased the identification cards of deceased Burmese, allowing them to live freely in the country.

After 1988, China exercised virtually unchallenged economic influence in the country, supplanting **Japan**, which before 1988 enjoyed a privileged position because of its close historical ties with Burmese leaders and foreign aid. Modernization of the naval base and schemes to open a transportation corridor between Yunnan Province to the Indian Ocean by way of **Arakan (Rakhine) State** have been cause for concern in **India**, China's regional rival.

For China, the relationship is not without problems. The powerful **United Wa State Army (UWSA)** threatens peace along the border; moreover, **opium**, **heroin**, and other narcotics produced by the UWSA and other armed groups in the **Wa** and **Kokang** districts of Shan State flow into China, creating major drug abuse and crime problems, especially in Yunnan.

Beijing and Rangoon's authoritarian leaders have similar worldviews, especially concerning the defense of national sovereignty, though some Tatmadaw officers resented **Khin Nyunt**, the principal backer of close bilateral relations, for selling out the country's independence to Beijing; this was apparently the motive for an assassination plot against him in 1992. It is unclear whether the purge of Khin Nyunt in October 2004 has had a significant impact on Beijing–Rangoon relations, but Chinese moral and material support has been a key factor in the **State Peace and Development Council**'s ability to ignore international criticism and Western **sanctions**. *See also* CHINA AND BURMA (HISTORICAL RELATIONS).

CHINDITS. Military group organized by Brigadier Orde Wingate, a master of unconventional warfare. The Chindits went behind enemy lines in Burma during **World War II**, coordinated their operations by radio, and were supplied by air drops flying out of India. There were two Chindit operations: "Longcloth" (February 1943) and "Thursday" (March 1944), the latter employing gliders landing troops at jungle airstrips. Although their effectiveness in destroying Japanese installations was limited and casualties were high, the Chindits provided a much-needed boost in morale to the Allies, especially in 1943, and showed how infantry and air operations could be coordinated through the effective management of radio-relayed information. The name is derived from the *chinthe*, a mythological Burmese beast resembling a lion that guards temples and **pagodas**. *See also* JAPANESE OCCUPATION; MERRILL'S MARAUDERS.

CHINDWIN (CHINDWINN) RIVER. One of Burma's largest river systems, with a length of 800 kilometers. It rises in the Kumon Mountains of **Kachin State** and flows through the **Naga** Hills **(Sagaing Division)** to join the **Irrawaddy (Ayeyarwady) River**

north of **Pagan (Bagan)**. The Burmese name, meaning "hole (or cave) of the **Chins**," indicates that the Chindwin river valley may once have been inhabited by the Chins, although it does not pass through present-day **Chin State**. The lower reaches of the Chindwin are navigable, but only during the monsoon season.

CHINESE IN BURMA. People of Chinese ancestry have lived in Burma for many centuries. In the British colonial era, they could be divided into two groups: Overseas Chinese, whose roots were in southern China (principally Fujian and Guangdong Provinces), who either came to Burma directly or previously lived in other parts of Southeast Asia (especially other British colonies, such as the Straits Settlements and Malaya); and migrants from Yunnan Province, which became part of the Chinese empire in the 13th century. The former tended to congregate in urban areas of **Lower Burma**, and the latter in **Upper Burma**, including parts of the **Frontier Areas** close to the Chinese border. **Kokang** Chinese had their own autonomous state, located east of the **Salween (Thanlwin) River** in **Shan State**, while the **Panthays**, Muslims from Yunnan, were active as traders and mule drivers on China–Burma trade routes. Both groups have played an important role in the shipment of **opium** to neighboring countries.

"Chinatowns" emerged in metropolitan areas of colonial Burma, especially **Rangoon (Yangon)**, **Mandalay**, and **Moulmein (Mawlamyine)**. In Rangoon, Chinese gold shops are still conspicuous west of Shwe Dagon Pagoda Road in the old downtown business district. According to the 1931 census, Chinese comprised 7.9 percent of the city's population, far outnumbered by Indians or South Asians (54.9 percent). In the country as a whole, they numbered 194,000 in 1931 (1.3 percent of the population).

Despite the popular stereotype of the Chinese as rich businessmen (many were in fact quite poor), Burmese relations with them were generally better than with Indians, not only because they were less numerous but also because they assimilated more easily into the Burmese population; Burmese people often referred to the Chinese as *pauk paw* ("distant cousins"). A number of Burma's most prominent figures have been **Sino-Burmese**, of mixed Chinese–Burmese ancestry, including General **Ne Win**. But many Chinese left Burma following the June 1967 **Anti-Chinese Riots**, and those who remained took care to downplay their Chinese identity.

After the **State Law and Order Restoration Council** seized power in September 1988, ties with the **People's Republic of China** became close, and large-scale immigration of Chinese people occurred. The widespread practice of selling the identity cards of deceased Burmese to Chinese immigrants made it possible for them to integrate—administratively though not culturally—into Burmese society. Because there are no accurate census figures, the number of new Chinese residents is not known, but it is believed that they comprise around 30 percent of the population of Mandalay. An article in the Hong Kong–based *Asiaweek* magazine in 1999 reported that hundreds of thousands of Chinese may have entered the country following flooding in southern China. According to a Thai observer quoted in that article, the inflow has "chang[ed] the whole demographic balance in north Burma," and local resentment of the new immigrants is growing because they control much of the economy, especially in Upper Burma. For example, in Mandalay they have raised property values in the city center, forcing the former Burmese residents to move to cheaper, outlying areas.

Burma has also served as a way station for Chinese wishing to immigrate to the United States. After paying an exorbitant fee to be smuggled out of China (as much as US$30,000), they pass through Burma to Thailand, whence they go by sea to North America. *See also* CHINA AND BURMA (HISTORICAL RELATIONS); INDIANS IN BURMA; PLURAL SOCIETY; POPULATION.

CHINRAM. The "land of the **Chins**," a term used by members of that ethnic nationality to refer to their homeland, located in the mountainous border area between western Burma, northeastern India, and eastern Bangladesh. It includes **Chin State** ("East Chinram"), Mizoram State in India ("West Chinram"), and upland areas east of the port city of Chittagong in Bangladesh. Some writers (e.g., Lian Sakhong in *In Search of Chin Identity*) also use Chinram to refer to the ancient homeland of the Chins in the valley of the **Chindwin (Chindwinn) River**, *Chindwin* meaning, in the **Burmese (Myanmar) language**, "hole [cave] of the Chins."

CHINS. One of Burma's major ethnic minorities, most of whom live in **Chin State** on the country's mountainous western border with **India** and **Bangladesh**, though smaller numbers are found in **Arakan State** and **Magwe (Magway) Division**. Census data are unreliable, but they are believed to comprise about 2 percent of the population. They are also found in India's Mizoram and Manipur States and in upland areas east of the port city of Chittagong in Bangladesh. Taken together, their homelands are often referred to as **Chinram**. The Burmese Chins are divided into many local groups and speak 44 mutually unintelligible but related languages, which are part of the Tibeto-Burman group, like the **Burmese (Myanmar) language**. The large number of languages among them (more than one-third of Burma's total of 107 recognized languages) is explained by a Chin legend resembling the story of the Tower of Babel. Although American Baptist **missionaries** working among the Chins in the late 19th and early 20th centuries standardized the different languages so that textbooks and translations of the Bible could be distributed, no single standard language was adopted such as the one promoted by missionaries among the **Kachins**. This has been an impediment to Chin unity. However, the missionaries did devise a written script for the languages, based on the Roman alphabet.

There are six major Chin tribal groups: Asho, Cho/Sho, Khuami, Laimi, Mizo, and Zomi. Chin legends claim a common origin for the people and an ancestral homeland in the valley of the **Chindwin (Chindwinn) River** (*Chindwin* meaning, in Burmese, the "hole [cave] of the Chins), from which the **Shans** drove them into the western hills around the 13th to 14th centuries. The origin of the name *Chin* is in dispute; it seems to derive from the Burmese language, meaning "friend," although some scholars in the colonial era thought it was derived from the Chinese *jen*, "man." They are known as *Kuki* by the Bengalis and Assamese, and in referring to themselves traditionally used some variation on the term *Zo*, which is said to mean "uncivilized."

Before they were "pacified" by the British and proselytized by Baptist missionaries, the Chins lived in isolated and mutually exclusive tribal groups governed by *Ram-uk*, or chiefs. Their society was hierarchical, with noble, commoner, and slave strata. The chiefs were not only rulers, owners and distributors of crop land, and commanders in war, but also high priests who offered sacrifices to the *Khua-hrum*, or guardian deities. The Chins frequently raided Burma or Bengal in search of slaves, which led to confrontations with the British, who in 1871 began sending military expeditions into Chin territory. By 1896, they had largely succeeded in imposing control, and implemented the Chin Hills Regulations as a means of governing them. But a major uprising, the **Anglo–Chin War** (1917–1919), occurred, and after this war the Chin Hills Regulations were reformed to make British rule more acceptable, one of the most important measures being to restore the *ram-uk* to their traditional authority. Many Chins were recruited into the colonial armed forces, and the Chin Levies fought alongside the British against the Japanese in **World War II**.

Traditionally, the Chins were animists, but by the end of the 20th century as many as 80 percent of them were Christians, mostly Baptists (some sources give a lower percentage). Conversion brought not only a change in old beliefs (though some aspects of the old religion could be reconciled with Christianity, such as belief in an afterlife and Supreme God), but also a social revolution, as tribal society broke down and was replaced by communities of worshippers, presided over by new elites of preachers in churches and teachers in missionary schools, a process that continued up to and even during World War II, when much of Chin State was a battleground.

The economy of Chin communities has traditionally been based on swidden (slash-and-burn) **agriculture** in upland areas. The old religion was closely tied to the indigenous economy and social system because sacrifices of cattle and other livestock were seen as necessary to appease the guardian deities and to celebrate major events, such as a wedding or a successful hunt. Only nobles and chiefs could afford such ritual sacrifices, so the old religion confirmed social and economic inequalities.

Apart from trade and slave -raiding, the Chin tribes were largely isolated from the outside world until the late 19th century, and their relations with the **Burmans (Bamars)** were relatively amicable. The **Panglong Conference** of February 1947 cleared the way for establishment of a "Chin Special Division" under the **Constitution of 1947** (it became Chin State in 1974). Compared to the **Karens (Kayins)**, **Mons**, and Kachins, the Chins have lacked a strong ethnic nationalist insurgency, although the **Chin National**

Front, established in 1985, has not signed a **cease-fire** with the **State Peace and Development Council**. Many Chin men have served in the rank and file of the **Tatmadaw**.

CHINTHE. A mythological beast resembling a lion that guards Buddhist **pagodas** and temples in Burma. *Chinthes* are usually located at the entrance, in pairs, such as the ones that guard the southern entrance to the **Shwe Dagon Pagoda**.

CHRISTIANITY. *See* MISSIONARIES, CHRISTIAN.

CITIZENSHIP LAW (1982). In October 1982, the **Pyithu Hluttaw** passed a Citizenship Law that distinguished among three types of Burmese citizen: full, associate, and naturalized. Those persons whose ancestors resided in Burma (in the law's wording) "anterior to B.E. 1185, 1823 A.D." were recognized as full citizens, while associate citizens were the descendants of people who arrived in Burma after that date. The measure appears to have been directed at persons of **Indian** (South Asian) ancestry who settled in Burma during the British colonial period. The law gave the **State Council** the authority to determine which ethnic groups had "national" (full citizen) status. The ethnic identity of individuals was determined by a "Central Body" whose head was the Minister of Home Affairs, with appeal to the Council of Ministers. Ethnicity, along with religion, is included in each Burmese citizen's national identity card.

The law implied that full political rights, including the right to hold state or **Burma Socialist Programme Party** offices, were conferred only on full citizens of indigenous ancestry, disenfranchising Burmese of South Asian, **Chinese**, or other descent. Interestingly, Article 15(a) stated that a citizen would not automatically lose his or her citizenship by marrying a foreigner, meaning that charges by **State Law and Order Restoration Council** spokesmen that **Aung San Suu Kyi,** by marrying British citizen **Michael Aris,** was no longer a Burmese national, were groundless. *See also* HUMAN RIGHTS IN BURMA; ROHINGYAS.

CLIMATE. Burma is located in tropical rather than equatorial Southeast Asia, and most parts of the country experience three distinct seasons that are determined by the monsoons. The southwest monsoon, bringing warm and wet winds from the Indian Ocean, reaches the country in mid-May or June, creating a rainy season that usually lasts until October. This is vital for **agriculture** because most croplands are rain-fed. The northeast monsoon, bringing cooler and dry winds from the Asian continent, dominates weather patterns during the cool-dry season of November to February. A hot, dry season prevails from March to May. The hottest month, April, witnesses the **Thingyan** New Year's celebrations. In **Rangoon (Yangon)** and other parts of **Lower Burma**, rain is abundant but falls mostly during May–September. In the **Dry Zone** of central Burma, rainfall is scarce throughout the year; around **Pagan (Bagan)**, semidesert conditions prevail. Higher elevations on the **Shan Plateau** and other upland regions along the border with China, India, and Thailand enjoy cooler climates, and the highest mountains in the north, such as **Hkakabo Razi**, are snow-capped.

The monsoons not only determine the times of year that **rice** is planted and harvested, but also festivals associated with **Buddhism** and even the patterns of warfare. Offensives carried out by the **Tatmadaw** against ethnic minority insurgents such as the **Karen National Union** have usually reached their peak during the dry seasons; the coming of the rains halts, or slows down, military operations.

COLLIS, MAURICE (1889–1973). A British writer, raised in Ireland, he entered the Indian Civil Service in 1912 and served in Burma. Upon retiring, he devoted himself to a literary career. His books include accounts of his personal experiences in the country, such as *Into Hidden Burma* and *Trials in Burma;* histories and biographies, such as *The Land of the Great Image*, about the **Maha Muni Buddha Image** in **Arakan (Rakhine)**; travelogues (*Lords of the Sunset*, about the **Shan States**); and historical such romances as *She was a Queen*, about a **Pagan Dynasty** royal figure. *Trials in Burma*, describing his years as a magistrate in **Rangoon (Yangon)**, is interesting for his critical description of British racial attitudes toward the Burmese and other Asians. *See also* ORWELL, GEORGE.

COMMITTEE REPRESENTING THE PEOPLE'S PARLIAMENT (CRPP). In June 1998, the leadership of the **National League**

for **Democracy (NLD)** set a deadline of August 21, 1998, for the **State Peace and Development Council (SPDC)** to recognize the results of the **General Election of May 27, 1990**, and allow a government to be formed. When this went unheeded, the NLD, backed by 251 elected representatives, appointed a 10-member Committee Representing the People's Parliament on September 16. The CRPP's function is to work "on behalf of the Parliament until a parliamentary session attended by all the elected representatives is convened." It has declared null and void laws decreed by the SPDC and its predecessor, the **State Law and Order Restoration Council**, as well as certain pre-1988 laws deemed repressive. The CRPP also established 10 subcommittees dealing with such areas as economics, ethnic nationalities, and foreign affairs. The SPDC, viewing the creation and actions of the CRPP as a provocation, increased its pressure on the NLD, including detention of CRPP president Saw Mra Aung. In 2002, the CRPP's membership was expanded to 13, adding three representatives of ethnic minority opposition parties.

COMMUNIST PARTY OF BURMA (CPB). Sometimes known as the Burma Communist Party (BCP), one of the major revolutionary movements in Southeast Asia during the Cold War; it broke apart in 1989. Although communist parties were established in India, China, and Japan during the 1920s, an indigenous communist movement was established in **Rangoon (Yangon)** only on the eve of World War II, on August 15, 1939, by a group of **Thakins**, including **Aung San**, Hla Pe (Bo **Let Ya**), and **Thein Pe Myint**. The most important postwar communist leaders, Thakin **Soe** and Thakin **Than Tun**, did not attend the initial meeting but joined soon afterward. The first communist cell opposed British imperialism, but in July 1941 Thakins Soe and Than Tun, imprisoned at **Insein Jail**, issued a manifesto calling for alliance with the British against Japanese fascism. After the Japanese invasion began in December 1941, Thakins **Thein Pe Myint** and Tin Shwe went to India, and during the war they worked with the British **Force 136** to organize underground resistance. The CPB was a founding member of the **Anti-Fascist People's Freedom League (AFPFL)**, and in the last months of the war, as many as 30,000 communist guerrillas fought the Japanese.

In the postwar period, communists were divided on the issue of whether to cooperate with the largely nationalist AFPFL, led by Aung San, or begin revolutionary struggle. Thakin Soe broke with the CPB mainstream to start an insurgency in February 1946, known as the "Red Flag" Communists, in the **Arakan (Rakhine) Yoma** and the delta of the **Irrawaddy (Ayeyarwady) River**. In October of that year, the CPB was expelled from the AFPFL. On March 28, 1948,Thakin Than Tun's mainstream group, the "White Flag" Communists, began an uprising against the central government in the countryside.

From 1948 to 1950, the communists, along with ethnic insurgents, posed a serious threat to the government of Prime Minister U **Nu**, but thereafter they suffered military reverses that shrank the size of their liberated areas. The White Flag Communists, based primarily in the **Pegu (Bago) Yoma**, were not entirely suppressed by the **Tatmadaw** until 1975, when communist leaders Thakins Zin and Chit were killed. The CPB's headquarters were officially moved from the Pegu Yoma to Panghsang, on the Burma–China border. During the 1960s, the communist movement was seriously weakened by Chinese Cultural Revolution-style purges designed to get rid of "revisionists"; leading communists, such as Goshal, Yebaw Htay, and Bo Yan Aung (one of the **Thirty Comrades**), were executed.

A major turning point in the CPB's history was the establishment of the "Northeastern Command" along the China–Burma border in Shan State in January 1968. This was generously backed by the **People's Republic of China** after **anti-Chinese riots** broke out in Rangoon in June 1967. The CPB's People's Army, equipped with Chinese arms and advised by Chinese cadres, became the strongest insurgency opposing the Ne Win government, numbering as many as 15,000 men by the early 1980s, mostly ethnic minority soldiers, two-thirds of whom were **Wa**. Increasingly they became involved in the **opium** economy in the Burma–China border area. Decreasing Chinese support during the 1980s and ethnic minority soldiers' resentment of the **Burman (Bamar)** communist leadership were contributing factors in the March–April 1989 mutiny that led to the retirement of chairman Thakin **Ba Thein Tin** and other leaders to China and the breakup of the People's Army into four new ethnic-based forces, of which the largest and most powerful was the **United Wa State**

Army. During 1989, these forces signed **cease-fires** with the **State Law and Order Restoration Council** regime, and the history of the Communist Party of Burma was effectively over.

Although its revolution failed, the CPB had a tremendous impact on Burmese politics. The authoritarian nature of the regime established by General **Ne Win** in 1962 and the Tatmadaw's monopolization of political power were justified largely in terms of the communist threat, especially after China began giving the CPB a large amount of aid after 1967. In the 1950s and early 1960s, many university **students** were attracted to communism, and Ne Win suppressed them harshly. By the early 1980s, however, communist influence in central Burma was virtually nonexistent. Communism had little or no impact on the events of **Democracy Summer** in 1988. But the **State Law and Order Restoration Council (SLORC)** continued to employ the communist threat to legitimize its hard-line policies. In 1989, SLORC Secretary-1 **Khin Nyunt** published a lengthy tract, *Burma Communist Party's Conspiracy to Take Over State Power*, claiming that student oppositionists were manipulated by a communist "underground." **Aung Gyi** claimed that Daw **Aung San Suu Kyi** was influenced by communist members of her **National League for Democracy**.

CONGREGATION OF THE SANGHA (1980). In full, the Congregation of the Sangha of All Orders for Purification, Perpetuation and Propagation of the Sasana (Buddhist religion), held under the auspices of the **Ne Win** government on May 24–27, 1980. The purpose of the assembly was to ensure religious orthodoxy and state supervision of the **Sangha.** This was accomplished through the establishment of a nationwide hierarchy of monks' committees on the national, **state/division**, **township**, and ward/village tract levels, similar to the structure of the **Burma Socialist Programme Party** and the state under the **Constitution of 1974**. The Congregation brought together 1,219 monk representatives, who ratified rules relating to the organization and management of the Sangha, including the requirement that all monks carry identification cards. They also chose central governing bodies, including the 33-member State Sangha Maha Nayaka Committee. By the end of 1981, Sangha Nayaka Committee members had been elected on the three lower levels. Coordination with state agencies, for example, the Ministry of Home and Religious Affairs, was tight. Although the Sangha was expected to govern itself and discipline errant monks, it enjoyed little or no autonomy. The new rules ratified by the Congregation prohibited the establishment of new sects (*gaing*) outside of the nine already in existence. By ensuring that the Sangha was controlled by conservative senior monks, the new system established by the Congregation minimized monk political activism. This was reflected in the ease with which the **Overturning the Offering Bowl** movement in late 1990 was suppressed by the **State Law and Order Restoration Council**. A second Sangha Congregation was held in May 1985.

CONSTITUTION OF 1947. Approved by the Constituent Assembly on September 24, 1947, the 1947 Constitution served as the basic law of the Union of Burma when it became independent on January 4, 1948. It created a system that one of the drafters described as "federal in theory and unitary in practice." The three ethnic minority states: were **Kachin**, **Kayah (Karenni)**, and **Shan** (the last formerly the Federated Shan States and Wa States; a fourth state, **Karen State**, was added by amendment in 1951), and Chin Special Division (later **Chin State**). What in colonial times had been **Burma Proper** was composed of **divisions**. Among the divisions, the governmental system was unitary, but the minority states and Chin Special Division were granted limited autonomy, including their own assemblies, whose elected members served concurrently in the Union Parliament. The Union government, headed by a prime minister in the manner of Westminster, reserved portfolios for Shan, Kayah, Karen, and Chin affairs; the ministers served concurrently as heads of state in their respective jurisdictions. Most controversially, Shan and Karenni States were guaranteed the right to secede from the Union 10 years after promulgation of the Constitution. The head of state was the president of the Union of Burma, who served for a five-year term. The Union Parliament was bicameral, composed of a Chamber of Deputies and a Chamber of Nationalities.

The 1947 Constitution was in effect from January 4, 1948, until March 2, 1962, when General **Ne Win** established the **Revolutionary Council (RC)** and closed down parliamentary political institutions. However, it was not abolished but remained operative in areas not affected by decrees issued by the RC. Following a December 1973 referendum, the **Constitution of 1974** established the Socialist Republic of the Union of Burma. The status of the 1947 Constitution (and its 1974 successor) remain ambiguous: in June 1989, a spokesman for the **State Law and Order Restoration Council** suggested that representatives elected in "multiparty democratic general election" scheduled for May 1990 could choose which constitution to use as the country's basic law or draft a new one.

CONSTITUTION OF 1974. Independent Burma's second constitution, which enshrined the principles of socialism and revolutionary one-party rule. Its preamble states: "We, the working people, firmly resolve that we shall . . . faithfully follow the leadership of the **Burma Socialist Programme Party**." When it was promulgated on January 3, 1974, the martial law **Revolutionary Council** was disbanded. The new basic law replaced the bicameral national legislature with a unicameral **Pyithu Hluttaw** ("People's Assembly"), the "highest organ of State power" (Article 41); elected legislatures known as **People's Councils** were also established on the **state/division, township**, and ward/village tract levels. Although elections on all levels were held every four years, the BSPP chose the candidates, and voters merely approved them. In practice, the Pyithu Hluttaw served as a rubber stamp for decisions made by the BSPP leadership, meeting briefly each year in March and October. Executive power was in the hands of two organs: the **State Council**, which ran the government when the legislature was not in session, and the Council of Ministers, which operated as a cabinet with functionally specific portfolios and was the highest administrative body. The chairman of the State Council was president of the Socialist Republic of the Union of Burma (**Ne Win**, 1974–1980; **San Yu**, 1981–1988).

The 1974 Constitution established **Mon, Arakan**, and **Chin States**, in addition to the older **Shan, Kachin, Karen**, and **Karenni (Kayah) States**; in addition, seven divisions were created: **Rangoon (Yangon), Irrawaddy (Ayeyarwady), Pegu (Bago), Magwe (Magway), Sagaing, Mandalay**, and **Tenasserim (Tanintharyi)**. However, in this highly centralized governmental system, there were no differences in administration between the states and the divisions and no concession to autonomy for the ethnic minorities. Operating on the assumption that Burma was basically a homogeneous country, the constitution did not recognize the country's ethnic diversity, although Article 8 prohibited "the exploitation . . . of one national race by another," and Article 152 recognized the **Burmese (Myanmar) language** as the national language but conceded that "**languages** of the other national races may also be taught."

Between 1971 and 1973 the Revolutionary Council carried out extensive "consultations" with people in all walks of life on the nature of the new constitution, and it was ratified in a nationwide referendum held December 15–31, 1973. Ninety percent of eligible voters who participated gave their support to the new basic law. If the Constitution of 1947 drew much of its inspiration from Westminster, with adaptations to local conditions, the 1974 Constitution was modeled on those of the Soviet Union and Eastern Europe, not only concerning one-party rule but also in viewing elections not as exercises of popular sovereignty but rather as ritualistic reaffirmations of state power.

COUP D'ETAT ATTEMPT (JULY 1976). Led by Captain Ohn Kyaw Myint, a group of younger captains and majors plotted the overthrow of President **Ne Win**, General **San Yu**, and Colonel **Tin Oo** (head of **Military Intelligence**), but they were arrested in July 1976. Put on trial in the fall, Ohn Kyaw Myint was sentenced to death and his fellow conspirators to terms in prison. Former Defense Minister **Tin U** was also tried and sentenced to a seven-year jail term for having known about the plot but failing to report it to the authorities. The young officers admired Tin U's reformist tendencies and wished to change Burma's one-party regime and socialist economic system. Following the coup attempt, promotions in the **Tatmadaw** were increasingly based on loyalty to Ne Win rather than talent.

COUP D'ETAT ATTEMPT (MARCH 2002). On March 7, 2002, the son-in-law of **Ne Win**, Aye Zaw Win, and his three grandsons, Aye Ne Win, Kyaw Ne Win, and Zwe Ne Win, were arrested on charges of plotting the overthrow of the **State Peace and Development Council (SPDC)**. According to the government, they were attempting to win over the troops who guarded Ne Win's residence on the shores of **Inya Lake** with expensive presents and special privileges, anticipating that they could form the vanguard of a coup attempt. The plot apparently also included Ne Win's influential daughter, **Sanda Win**, but she was not charged, instead being placed under house arrest. Official accounts are somewhat bizarre: the plotters consulted a practitioner of **astrology** to ensure the coup's success; they possessed images of the three top SPDC generals, which they apparently planned to use as "voodoo dolls"; and they were hoping to establish a new dynasty, complete with a family seal modeled on those of European royalty. The four plotters were put on trial for high treason and sentenced to death in September; their December 2002 appeal was turned down, but it is likely that the death sentences will be commuted to life imprisonment.

If this was a genuine attempted coup d'état, it was extraordinarily clumsy, and posed no real threat to the SPDC. Its relationship to **SPDC internal dynamics** is unclear, though a number of high-ranking military officers were purged in connection with it. Many observers believe that Aye Zaw Win and his sons, who were universally disliked, had become so greedy and lawless that some pretext was needed to get rid of them. Kyaw Ne Win had become notorious as leader of the "Scorpions," a criminal gang that terrorized Rangoon residents. Ne Win, whose reputation was sullied by the incident, passed away on December 5, 2002, marking the end of an era.

CROMBIE PO, SAN (?–1946). Karen (Kayin) leader, best known for his 1928 *Burma and the Karens*. After a medical education in the **United States**, he returned to Burma in 1894 and worked as a civil servant until 1902. Appointed a member of Burma's Legislative Council in 1915, he emerged as the principal spokesmen for the Karens in negotiations over future constitutional arrangements, including a legally recognized special status for the community in the legislature. He was a strong advocate of a "Karen country," separate from Burma and under British protection. Karens consider him to be a major figure in their modern history, and his book was reprinted in 2001. *See also* BA U GYI, SAW; KAREN GOODWILL MISSION (1946); KAREN NATIONAL UNION.

CURRENCY AND EXCHANGE RATES. Burma's independence-era currency is the *kyat*. Because of poor economic conditions during the **Burma Socialist Programme Party** era (1962–1988), the state enforced an official exchange rate of around K6 to one U.S. dollar to prevent its depreciation, with penalties for those dealing in currency on the **black market**. Confidence in the *kyat* was undermined by three **demonetizations**, in 1964, 1985, and 1987, designed to cripple "economic insurgency." During this period, U.S. dollars were used in many facilities, such as hotels and stores for foreign **tourists**. After the **State Law and Order Restoration Council** seized power in September 1988, currency exchange was in practice liberalized, with free-market *kyats* readily available on the streets of **Rangoon (Yangon)** and other major cities. Post-1988 Burma has had three parallel *kyat*-dollar exchange rates: the official rate (around K5.5–6.5 to the dollar); the free-market rate, which fluctuates widely in response to economic conditions (falling from K60 = US$1.00 in 1989 to over K1,000 = US$1.00 in 2005); and a special rate used by the government for payment of customs by foreigners, usually between the official and free-market rates. Although international economists have criticized the multiple exchange rates as an irrational impediment to trade and investment, members of the military elite and black-market entrepreneurs can manipulate them to acquire huge profits. For example, they can use the official rate to change *kyats* into dollars to buy expensive foreign consumer goods or do business abroad, while ordinary Burmese must use the free-market rate. But when the value of the *kyat* falls precipitously on the free market, the **State Peace and Development Council** often arrests currency dealers, accusing them of greedy speculation.

Burma also has had three different currencies in circulation: *kyat* banknotes, U.S. dollars ("greenbacks"), and Foreign Exchange Certificates (FECs), which were denominated in dollars and were supposed to be equal in value to them, though in recent years their value in relation to the greenback (i.e., the number of *kyat* they can be exchanged for) has declined. Upon entering Burma, tourists were required to purchase $200–300 worth of FECs in dollars or a hard currency equivalent, but this practice was abolished in 2003, and the FECs themselves had largely fallen out of circulation by 2005. **Sanctions** implemented by the **U.S.** government in 2003 deprived Burmese businesses of easy access to dollars, and there was speculation at the time that another hard currency, for example euros, might be used as a substitute. But as of 2005, greenbacks still functioned as the hard currency of choice. However, Chinese and Thai currencies are widely used in some border areas, such as **Kokang** in **Shan State**. The continued fall of the *kyat* on the free market reflects not only economic ills but also the government's policy of printing money to cover budget deficits. Given paper money's ephemeral value, people have followed the traditional practice of keeping their assets in gold or gemstones; gold shops in Rangoon's Chinatown do a flourishing business. Those who can afford to hoard greenbacks or other hard currency, or invest in real estate (luxury condominiums are popular) and durable goods such as imported automobiles, which can be hired out and provide a steady source of income. The weakness of the *kyat* and its unpredictable exchange rate fluctuations contribute greatly to daily economic insecurity for all but the wealthiest and best connected. *See also* ECONOMY AND ECONOMIC POLICY, STATE LAW AND ORDER RESTORATION COUNCIL/STATE PEACE AND DEVELOPMENT COUNCIL ERA.

– D –

DAGON. Also *Lagon* or *Lagun*, a **Mon** settlement established around the end of the first millennium CE at Singuttara Hill, site of the **Shwe Dagon Pagoda** (known in the **Mon language** as the **Kyaik** Lagun). Never a Mon royal city, its significance was primarily religious. **Alaungpaya** captured it in 1755, renaming it *Yangoun*, meaning "end of strife." Its political and economic importance dates from its occupation by the British in 1852, following the **Second Anglo-Burmese War**. *See also* RANGOON (YANGON).

DAGON UNIVERSITY. Established in the mid-1990s, after the **State Law and Order Restoration Council** seized power, Dagon University, located in the **new town** of East Dagon Township within the city limits of **Rangoon (Yangon)**, is a major new institution of higher education with an extensive campus and projected enrollment of 60,000. It is an example of the military regime's establishment of colleges and universities far from the city center to prevent **students** from freely associating with townspeople and becoming involved in political activism, as they did in 1988. *See also* EDUCATION, HIGHER.

DANA. "Giving" or "charity" in the **Pali** and **Burmese (Myanmar) languages**, the principal means through which laypeople can acquire merit (*kutho*) in Burmese **Buddhism**. *Dana* includes offering food, monastic robes, or other goods to members of the **Sangha**; constructing or contributing to the construction or renovation of monasteries and **pagodas**; and sponsoring ceremonies connected with **Buddhism**, such as *shinbyu*. Since 1988, the **State Law and Order Restoration Council/State Peace and Development Council** has embarked on ambitious pagoda building and other Buddhist projects that enable laypeople to make generous donations, for example, replacing the *hti* at the top of the **Shwe Dagon Pagoda** in 1999, an unprecedented merit-making opportunity. Burmese people often say: "*dana* is good for the next life, and for political connections in this life as well." Wealthy businesspeople, including those who have made their fortunes in the **opium** trade, give large donations in order to win the favor of the authorities and purchase respectability. Lists of donors are displayed prominently at pagoda sites, and the military government annually bestows special titles on people whose *dana* has been especially generous. Visitors to Burma are often impressed by the grandeur of its religious buildings, although it is one of Southeast Asia's poorest countries. There are no reliable figures on the percentage of GDP devoted to *dana*, but it must be high.

DAWNA RANGE. A mountain range located in eastern Burma, forming the border between **Karen (Kayin) State** and **Thailand**. Its highest point is Mularit Peak (2,080 meters or 6,824 feet). The Dawna Range has been the site of major clashes between the **Tatmadaw** and insurgent armed groups, especially the **Karen National Union**, for many decades. *See also* BOUNDARIES, INTERNATIONAL.

DEFENCE SERVICES ACADEMY (DSA). Established in 1955 as a university-level military academy. It is similar to West Point or Sandhurst, offering a four-year course and graduating officers who receive commissions in the three services of the **Tatmadaw**. The DSA is located in **Maymyo (Pyin Oo Lwin)**, and since the establishment of the **State Peace and Development Council** in 1997, it has had an expanded enrollment of 1,500. Although the focus is on military science, academic and technical courses are also offered, and the DSA has been significantly upgraded in terms of curriculum and facilities since 1988. DSA graduates are considered better educated than their counterparts from the **Officers' Training School**. But rivalries between officers from the two institutions, who comprise the armed forces high command, have not undermined the basic unity and coherence of the **Tatmadaw**.

DEFENCE SERVICES COMPOUND (DSC). Headquarters of the Ministry of Defence and the **Tatmadaw**, located in central **Rangoon (Yangon)**. It is an extensive area, bounded on the east by Zoological Garden Road and on the west by Shwe Dagon Pagoda Road, just north of the city center. Since the disturbances of 1988, it has been fortified by a red brick wall and blockhouses with gun slits, as well as a barbed wire fence. Closed to the public, the compound reportedly contains not only Ministry of Defence offices but also an artificial lake, club house, and 18-hole golf course. However, some headquarters functions have been transferred in recent years to a new Tatmadaw complex at Eight Mile Junction, north of **Inya Lake**. *See also* PYINMANA.

DEFENCE SERVICES INSTITUTE (DSI). Established in 1951 as a military-managed organization originally meant to provide **Tatmadaw** personnel with reasonably priced consumer goods. It established "DSA shops" throughout the country, but during the **Caretaker Government** period (1958–1960), it became the largest economic entity in Burma, controlling 14 enterprises involved in shipping, construction, financial services, trade, **tourism**, food processing, and other sectors. Although nationalized in 1963, it represented the Tatmadaw's determination to control the **economy** and was the prototype for the military-owned **Union of Myanmar Economic Holdings, Ltd.**, postsocialist Burma's largest conglomerate.

DEMOCRACY SUMMER (1988). A series of events between July and September 1988 that constitute the largest popular uprising in Burma's modern history. In her speech of August 26, 1988, at the

Shwe Dagon Pagoda, Daw Aung San Suu Kyi called this uprising the "second struggle for national independence." Following the Burma Socialist Programme Party Extraordinary Congress, which convened on July 23 and resulted in Ne Win's retirement and the selection of Sein Lwin, the "Butcher of Rangoon" (for his role in the suppression of March and June demonstrations), as his successor, student activists led by Min Ko Naing proclaimed the Four Eights Movement of August 8, a general strike aimed at forcing Sein Lwin to resign. Hundreds of thousands of ordinary townspeople participated, in Rangoon (Yangon) and elsewhere. Sein Lwin stepped down on August 12, but only after hundreds of demonstrators had been killed or wounded by the Tatmadaw in Rangoon, Sagaing, and other cities.

After the authorities lifted martial law on August 24, the army was withdrawn from Rangoon, and for a few weeks its citizens enjoyed unprecedented freedom. The media were not censored; "strike centers" were set up both in the capital and around the country (in 200 of 314 townships); and new political leaders, of whom the most important was Daw Suu Kyi, became prominent. After President Maung Maung promised on September 10 that multiparty elections would be held, Daw Suu Kyi, U Tin U, and Aung Gyi established a coalition calling for an interim government (it later became the National League for Democracy). But popular rage against suspected government informers, actions by regime *agents provocateurs*, and an economy in chaos contributed to an atmosphere of fear and suspicion. On September 18 the State Law and Order Restoration Council (SLORC) seized power, killing hundreds more demonstrators and shutting down Democracy Summer. The total number of fatalities from July to September 1988 is unknown, since the authorities made no effort to identify the dead or return the remains to their families. However, it is estimated to have been at least several thousand. Thousands more were held in prison or fled to neighboring countries.

Although most of the events of Democracy Summer occurred in Rangoon, there were massive demonstrations in urban centers around the country. Mandalay was for a brief period governed by a committee of young monks, students, and workers. However, rural and ethnic minority areas were largely unaffected. Despite SLORC claims to the contrary, the **Communist Party of Burma**, based along the Burma–China border, had little or no role in the uprising. Democracy Summer focused international attention on Burma, a previously obscure country, and initiated a movement both inside the country and abroad to replace military rule with some form of democracy. But unlike Presidents Ferdinand Marcos in the Philippines and Suharto in Indonesia, overthrown by popular movements in 1986 and 1998, the post-1988 military regime has been ruthlessly successful in blocking political change. *See also* ALL BURMA FEDERATION OF STUDENT UNIONS; GENERAL ELECTION OF MAY 27, 1990; OKKALAPA, NORTH AND SOUTH; RANGOON GENERAL HOSPITAL INCIDENT; SAGAING MASSACRE; TATMADAW AND BURMESE SOCIETY; THAKETA; TRADE MINISTRY INCIDENT; WHITE BRIDGE INCIDENT.

DEMOCRATIC ALLIANCE OF BURMA (DAB). A multiethnic united front established in the border areas in November 1988, following the seizure of power by the **State Law and Order Restoration Council (SLORC)**. Bo **Mya**, leader of the **Karen National Union**, became its chairman. The DAB initially included all the major insurgencies, with the important exceptions of the **Communist Party of Burma** and **Khun Sa**'s drug-dealing **Mong Tai Army**. They included the **All Burma Students' Democratic Front**, the **All Burma Young Monks Union**, the **Democratic Party for a New Society**, the **Kachin Independence Organization**, the Karen National Union, the **New Mon State Party**, and 17 other groups. The alliance was celebrated as an unprecedented example of **Burman** and ethnic minority oppositionists working together. However, the DAB had little influence in central Burma, failing to coordinate its activities with those of the **National League for Democracy**, and it was greatly weakened by the defection of insurgent groups, which signed **ceasefires** with the SLORC beginning in 1989. *See also* UNITED FRONTS, BORDER AREAS.

DEMOCRATIC KAREN BUDDHIST ARMY (DKBA). A progovernment group composed of defectors from the **Karen National Union (KNU)** and founded by U Thuzana, a pro-**State Law and Order Restoration Council** Buddhist monk, in late 1994. Since then, it has cooperated closely with the **Tatmadaw** in fighting the KNU along the Thai–Burma border and has also attacked pro-KNU **Karen (Kayin)** villagers, forcing them to flee to Thailand. Its estimated strength is around 1,500–2,500 armed men, and its headquarters, Myaing Gyi Ngu (Khaw Taw in the Karen language), is located near **Pa-an (Hpa-an)**, the capital of **Karen (Kayin) State**. Without the cooperation of the DKBA, the Tatmadaw possibly would not have been able to capture **Manerplaw** in January 1995 because the splinter group provided vital intelligence. The DKBA, whose members often wear distinctive yellow headbands, has become heavily involved in business, especially logging. *See also* GOD'S ARMY.

DEMOCRATIC PARTY FOR A NEW SOCIETY (DPNS). Part of the **student** movement that emerged during 1988, established as a legal political party on October 14, 1988, after the **State Law and Order Restoration Council (SLORC)** seized power. In 1988–1989, the DPNS organized branches in 250 of Burma's **townships** and claimed a membership of 250,000. Seeking support from students and young people, it did not put up its own candidates for the **General Election of May 27, 1990**, but rather backed the **National League for Democracy**. The SLORC arrested most of its leaders; since the early 1990s, its activities have been concentrated in the border areas. It is a member of the **Democratic Alliance of Burma**. *See also* ALL BURMA FEDERATION OF STUDENT UNIONS.

DEMONETIZATION (1964, 1985, 1987). An order of the government that revokes the legal tender status of currency notes, rendering them worthless. Burma under General **Ne Win** experienced three demonetizations: in May 1964, November 1985, and September 1987. They were designed to cripple "economic insurgency" (the **black market**), but the first two demonetizations offered limited compensation to persons who surrendered old banknotes. The 1987 order did not, wiping out as much as 80 percent of the country's savings because most people hoarded cash, reluctant to put their funds in the unreliable state banking system. The government replaced currency notes in denominations of 25, 35, and 75 *kyats* with oddly numbered notes of 45 and 90 *kyats*, reflecting Ne Win's preference for the auspicious number nine. In response, **student** demonstrations broke out, the first since the mid-1970s. Most observers believe the 1987 demonetization contributed substantially to the transformation of antigovernment sentiment into a nationwide opposition movement in 1988. Since the establishment of the **State Law and Order Restoration Council**, periodic fears of a new demonetization have added uncertainty to unsettled economic conditions. Those who can afford it keep their wealth in gold, jewelry, U.S. dollars, or capital-generating possessions such as automobiles. *See also* ECONOMY AND ECONOMIC POLICY, BURMA SOCIALIST PROGRAMME PARTY ERA; ECONOMY AND ECONOMIC POLICY, STATE LAW AND ORDER RESTORATION COUNCIL/STATE PEACE AND DEVELOPMENT COUNCIL ERA; NUMEROLOGY.

DHAMMA. The **Pali** counterpart of the Sanskrit *Dharma*, meaning "law" or "moral law," and in the Buddhist context, the teachings of Gotama **Buddha** as found in the **Tipitaka**. *Dhamma* is one of the "Three Gems" of **Buddhism**, in which the believer takes refuge, the others being the Buddha and the **Sangha**.

DHAMMAZEDI, KING (r. 1472–1492). Son-in-law of Queen **Shinsawbu** (r. 1453–1472), and her successor as ruler of **Hanthawaddy** (modern **Pegu [Bago]**). One of Burma's most prominent **Mon** kings, he originally was a member of the **Sangha**, who aided Shinsawbu in her flight from **Ava (Inwa)**. While king, he gained a reputation for just rule and religious devotion, donating gold for gilding the **stupa** of the **Shwe Dagon Pagoda**, sponsoring the compilation of one of the major Mon *Dhammathats* or law codes, and presiding over a reform of the Mon Sangha, which was brought in line with the severe disciplines of Sinhalese (Sri Lankan) Buddhism. In 1485, he commissioned the engraving of stone tablets, known as the *Kyaik Lagun* inscriptions, which are kept at the Shwe Dagon. They give the legendary account of the founding of the pagoda and valuable details on the monarchs of the Mon dynasty established by **Wareru** in the late 13th century. Other inscriptions attributed to him are found at the Kalyani *Thein* (ordination hall), near Pegu. According to legend, Dhammazedi was skilled in the use of "runes" (magical letters) and **alchemy**. *See also* RAZADARIT.

DIRECTORATE OF DEFENSE SERVICES INTELLIGENCE (DDSI). Also known as the Military Intelligence Service (MIS), the DDSI was Burma's most powerful and pervasive intelligence agency before the purge of its director, Lieutenant General **Khin Nyunt**, in October 2004. Established during the **Burma Socialist Programme Party** era (1962–1988), it controlled **Military Intelligence** units within the three services of the **Tatmadaw** as well as special units under its own command, which after 1992 reported directly to DDSI headquarters rather than through the regular armed services chain of command. The headquarters was divided into nine bureaus with functional jurisdiction over counterterrorism, antinarcotics operations, foreign intelligence operations, etc. In the **Burmese (Myanmar) language**, DDSI was known as the *Tatmadaw Htauk Hlan-ye Hyun-kyar Yehmu Youn*. With Khin Nyunt's ouster in 2004, DDSI's powers have been significantly curbed. *See also* MILITARY INTELLIGENCE; MILITARY INTELLIGENCE, ORGANIZATION OF.

DISTRICTS. During the British colonial period, the district was the "pivot" of regional administration, the responsibility of deputy commissioners who had wide-ranging authority. But the district was not included in the four-level administrative structure defined by the **Constitution of 1974**: the national level, the **state/division** level, the **township** level, and the ward/village tract level.

The **State Peace and Development Council**, however, has reintroduced the districts, intermediate between the states/divisions and the townships, a measure that will probably be formalized by the introduction of a new constitution. The measure has apparently been adopted to strengthen central government control over the localities. District-level Peace and Development Councils are the responsibility of a **Tatmadaw** officer of lieutenant-colonel rank. Burma, at present, is divided into 62 districts, further subdivided into 324 townships. *See also* ADMINISTRATION OF BURMA, BRITISH COLONIAL PERIOD; ADMINISTRATION OF BURMA, STATE LAW AND ORDER RESTORATION COUNCIL/STATE PEACE AND DEVELOPMENT COUNCIL ERA.

DIVISIONS. *Taing* (plural: *taing-myar*) in the **Burmese (Myanmar) language**; refers to the major unit of territorial administration below the national level and above the **district** and **township** levels. There are seven divisions: **Bago (Pegu), Irrawaddy (Ayeyarwady), Magwe (Magway), Mandalay, Rangoon (Yangon), Sagaing,** and **Tenasserim (Tanintharyi).** At present, each division has a "Peace and Development Council" composed of **Tatmadaw** officers, under the command of the **State Peace and Development Council.** Under the **Constitution of 1947,** they were included in a unitary form of government and were equivalent to the colonial-era **Burma Proper.** The **states,** corresponding roughly to the **Frontier Areas,** had quasi-federal powers, but the distinction between divisions and states (which also number seven) became administratively and politically irrelevant after the **Constitution of 1974** was adopted.

DOBAMA ASIAYONE (WE BURMANS ASSOCIATION). Also known as the **Thakin** Party, the most important political organization demanding independence from British colonial rule before **World War II.** It was established following the **Anti-Indian Riots** of May 1930 by young urban intellectuals, including graduates of **Rangoon (Yangon) University.** Members addressed each other as *thakin,* meaning "master," a term (like *sahib,* used in British-ruled India) that had customarily been employed by Burmese in everyday communications to address the British. Their use of the term to refer to themselves was subversive to British authority, but many older, conservative Burmese thought it inappropriate because the young "Thakins" were generally obscure and of low social status.

Ideologically, the Dobama Asiayone is described by historians as "modernist," but also eclectic, drawing on divergent ideologies popular in Asia and Europe during the 1930s: the ideas of the Indian National Congress, the Fascism–Nazism of Benito Mussolini and Adolph Hitler, Japanese "Pan-Asianism," Sun Yat-sen's *San Min Chu-I* (Three Principles of the People), revolutionary Marxism-Leninism, and non-Marxist "Fabian" socialism. In Dr. **Ba Maw**'s words, "[M]ost of those who accepted [revolutionary ideas] did not care much whether the ideas were black or red or yellow, whether they were from Russia or Germany or China or Japan. It was enough that they promised something new and were on their side, as against the colonial rulers, and held out a future that would be totally their own" (*Breakthrough in Burma,* 1968). Along with many other Burmese, the Thakins admired the courage of those who participated in the 1930 **Saya San Rebellion**, but they were not attracted to Saya San's use of traditional **Burman (Bamar)** royal symbolism and had no intention of supporting the reestablishment of a Burmese monarchy.

In 1931, the Dobama Asiayone organized a paramilitary wing, the *Dobama Let-yone Tat* (Our Burmans Army of Braves), a widespread practice among political groups at the time (even the **Rangoon University Student Union** had such a wing), demonstrating that the Thakins had little enthusiasm for Gandhi's principle of nonviolent resistance. Their demonstrations during the 1930s tended to be rowdy attacks on established authority, especially old-line politicians who cooperated with British colonial rule. Vehemently opposed to the **Government of Burma Act**, they set up their own party, the *Komin Kochin Aphwe* ("One's own King, One's own Kind Association"), to contest the parliamentary elections held following implementation of the new constitution. Three of its candidates were elected, largely for the purpose of disrupting parliamentary proceedings.

In the late 1930s, prominent **student** activists, including **Aung San** and **Nu**, joined the Dobama Asiayone, which played a prominent role in the **Oil Field Workers' Strike** of 1938. In that same year, the organization split into two factions, headed by Thakin Thein Maung and Thakin **Ba Sein**. The two factions are often described as different in ideology: Thein Maung's, which included Thakins Aung San and Nu, was "left wing," while Ba Sein's was "right-wing" (the latter included Thakin Shu Maung, later known as **Ne Win**). The split, however, had more to do with personalities and power politics than with political philosophies. A party executive meeting in June 1938 at the **Shwe Dagon Pagoda** almost ended in a violent confrontation. The Thakins' mentor, Thakin **Kodaw Hmaing**, sought to reconcile the two groups, but was unsuccessful. In 1939, the Dobama Asiayone joined Dr. Ba Maw's **Sinyetha Party** in the **Freedom Bloc**, and the two groups were merged into the Dobama Sinyetha Asiayone during the **Japanese Occupation**. Though factionalism and ideological vagueness undermined its effectiveness, all of Burma's leaders before 1988 — Aung San, U Nu, and Ne Win — came from its ranks.

DOCTOR CYNTHIA (CYNTHIA MAUNG, 1959–). A physician who has earned international recognition for her medical work along the Thai–Burma border. Born into a **Karen (Kayin)** family in **Moul-mein (Mawlamyine)**, she attended medical school in **Rangoon (Yangon)** and after graduating worked in a hospital in Rangoon's **North Okkalapa** Township, where she witnessed **Tatmadaw** shootings of demonstrators in 1988. She then went to the border and established a clinic near **Mae Sot-Myawaddy**, which cares for an estimated 30,000 patients a year, mostly **refugees** and Burmese workers resident in the area. She has also started a "backpack medics" course to bring basic medical care to remote villages inside Burma. In 2002, Dr. Cynthia won the Ramon Magsaysay Award for Community Leadership.

DRUG ECONOMY. After 1949, when the **People's Republic of China** began suppressing the cultivation and sale of **opium** within its borders, Burma emerged as one of the world's largest exporters of opiates (opium and **heroin**) to neighboring countries and world markets. Although Burma's opium exports are now (2005) surpassed by those of Afghanistan, the country remains a major exporter of **amphetamines**, especially to **Thailand**, where the drugs, known as *yaa baa* ("crazy medicine"), have become a huge social problem affecting people of all classes. The development of the drug economy can be explained in terms of the conjunction of four factors: physical, social, political-military, and international. The physical factor is the presence of extensive upland areas, largely coterminous with the colonial-era **Frontier Areas**, where soils are poor, water is often insufficient, and agricultural yields are low. For farmers to generate income to survive, the most suitable crop is opium poppies (*papaver somniferum*), which require little care and can be grown in mountainous fields. The social factor is that the upland area peoples, members of ethnic minorities such as the **Was, Kokang** Chinese, **Shans, Kachins,** and **Akhas**, have been isolated from the lowland areas of **Burma Proper** not only physically (by lack of good roads and other infrastructure) but also culturally, remaining mostly outside the **Buddhist** Burmese mainstream. The political–military factor is the emergence of communist, ethnic nationalist, and warlord groups, which have alternately fought and coexisted with the central government in **Rangoon (Yangon)** since the 1950s and have taxed or controlled the drug trade as their major source of revenue. Finally, the international factor is both the existence of well-developed drug-trading networks connecting Burma's upland areas with markets outside the country and strong demand for opiates and other narcotics in markets as distant as North America and Australia.

The **State Peace and Development Council** has committed itself to drug eradication by the year 2014, but many observers are skeptical because drug-generated funds, in "laundered" form, are a large and probably indispensable component of Burma's present economy. For example, hundreds of millions of dollars in such funds have been invested in real estate in Rangoon and **Mandalay**. Moreover, opium-suppression schemes—especially in Kokang—have had negative consequences for cultivators, who have no alternate crops and have been suddenly deprived of income, leading to widespread malnutrition. As the experience of Thailand shows, effective drug suppression requires time, investment (especially in infrastructure and substitute crops), and patience. *See also* BAO YOUXIANG; BORDER AREA DEVELOPMENT; CEASE-FIRE GROUPS; CEASE-FIRES; COMMUNIST PARTY OF BURMA; KA KWE YE; KHUN SA; KUOMINTANG (GUOMINDANG); LO HSING-HAN; MONG TAI ARMY; MYANMAR NATIONAL DEMOCRATIC ALLIANCE ARMY/PARTY; NATIONAL DEMOCRATIC ALLIANCE ARMY—EASTERN SHAN STATE; NEW DEMOCRATIC ARMY; PHEUNG KYA-SHIN; UNITED WA STATE ARMY.

DRY ZONE. That part of central Burma located within a "rain shadow" formed by the **Arakan Yoma** mountain range, which prevents the area from receiving the rains of the southwest monsoon. As a result, rainfall is extremely scarce: about 12.7 centimeters (cm) at **Pagan (Bagan)** and 83.8 cm at **Mandalay**, compared to 292.1 cm in the delta of the **Irrawaddy [Ayeyarwady] River**. Paddy **rice** cultivation in the Dry Zone is impossible without irrigation. Major crops in the area include oil seeds (sunflower and sesame), cotton, and groundnuts. This harsh environment, semidesert in places and described in the old chronicles as the "parched land," has traditionally been the homeland of the **Burmans (Bamars)** and the site of their royal capitals, beginning with Pagan in the ninth century and ending with Mandalay between 1857 and 1885. *See also* AGRICULTURE; CLIMATE.

DUWA. In traditional **Kachin** society, the chief, who exercised authority over at least a few villages and, in some cases, as many as one hundred. The status was hereditary, being passed from the father to the youngest son within chiefly lineages. The *duwa* imposed labor service duties on his villagers and had the right to the best portions of animals offered up for sacrifice to the spirits. But he was expected to sponsor costly festivals, *manao*, on special occasions. Usually, the chief exercised his authority with the assistance of a council of elders. The British colonial government ruled the Kachin Hills, part of the **Frontier Areas**, indirectly, recognizing the authority of the *duwa*. Under the *gumlao* system, some Kachin communities did not recognize hereditary chiefs but had a more democratic form of authority exercised by local councils.

DYARCHY. "Dual rule" or "dual government"; refers to the establishment of a new constitutional system in Burma in 1923 following the general contours of the Montagu–Chelmsford reforms in India. Limited governmental responsibilities were transferred to local nationals while the governor retained control over more vital jurisdictions. It provided for a Legislative Council of 103 members: 58 elected by popular vote from geographical constituencies, 15 elected from communal constituencies (**Chinese, Indians, Karens [Kayins]**, Anglo-Indians [including **Anglo-Burmese**]), and 23 nominated ex officio (by virtue of their holding administrative offices) by the governor. Its powers were enhanced compared to the original Legislative Council established in 1897. Under the dyarchy system, the executive function of government was the responsibility of the Executive Council, consisting of the governor; two ministers in charge of "reserved subjects," such as police, finance, labor, and irrigation, who were under the governor's authority; and two ministers responsible for "transferred subjects," such as forestry, education, and health, who were chosen by the Legislative Council. The governor was solely responsible for administration of the **Frontier Areas** and could veto legislation passed by the Council. Still other areas of responsibility, such as foreign relations, currency, and the civil service, remained under the control of the Indian government in New Delhi and the Secretary of State for India in London. Implementation of the new system aroused the opposition of the **General Council of Burmese Associ-**

ations (GCBA), although a GCBA faction, the Twenty-One Party, chose to cooperate. Turnout for Legislative Council elections held in 1922, 1925, and 1928 was low. The system was changed with the **Government of Burma Act** of 1935, although in that system the governor still retained control over the most important areas of responsibility.

– E –

EAR BORING. *Natwin* in the **Burmese (Myanmar) language**, a rite of passage for a young girl in which her ear lobe is pierced with a (golden) needle; it usually takes place at the same time as the *shinbyu* ceremony for her brother, cousin, or other male relative. Unlike *shinbyu*, it has no formal connection with **Buddhism**, and the ceremony earns no merit (*kutho*) for sponsors, but the girl, like her brother, is dressed in royal regalia.

EARTHQUAKES IN BURMA. Burma is located in a seismically active region, and earthquakes occasionally cause great damage and loss of life. In 1930, a large earthquake destroyed the **Shwemawdaw Pagoda** in **Pegu (Bago)**, causing many deaths. A 1975 earthquake damaged temples and pagodas at **Pagan (Bagan)**. Given the flimsiness of much of the new construction in **Rangoon (Yangon), Mandalay**, and other towns since 1988, there are fears that a large quake could cause many fatalities in urban areas. On December 26, 2004, an earthquake of over 9.0 magnitude occurred where the Burma Plate is undercut by the Indian Plate in the Indian Ocean, close to western Sumatra in **Indonesia**, causing massive tsunamis (sea waves). An estimated 226,000 people died or are missing in Indonesia, Sri Lanka, India, Thailand, Malaysia, and other countries. Several hundred Burmese workers resident in southern Thailand are believed to have died. In Burma itself, the **State Peace and Development Council** has released very little information about casualties or the extent of damage. According to the Myanmar Red Cross, 86 people died in **Irrawaddy (Ayeyarwady)** and **Tenasserim (Tanintharyi) Divisions** and **Arakan (Rakhine) State**. Investigations by the **United Nations** confirmed that, compared to neighboring countries, the number of deaths was small, and probably did not greatly exceed official figures, but that some 30,000 people were in need of emergency aid.

EAST ASIA YOUTH LEAGUE. A mass organization established by the Japanese Military Administration (*Gunseikanbu*) in June 1942, with as many as 65,000 members by late 1944. Many of its initial recruits were veterans of the **Burma Independence Army.** The League had a nationwide network of several hundred branches and promoted sports, social welfare, and civic activities. Because it enjoyed greater autonomy than other wartime groups, the League became an important vehicle for mobilizing young people for the independence struggle. The central leadership espoused cooperation with the Japanese, but local League members often had close ties to the **Communist Party of Burma.** See also JAPANESE OCCUPATION.

ECONOMY AND ECONOMIC POLICY, BURMA SOCIALIST PROGRAMME PARTY ERA (1962–1988). Following the coup d'état of March 2, 1962, which put the **Revolutionary Council (RC)** in power, Burma's new leader, General **Ne Win**, promised to get the country moving along the **"Burmese Road to Socialism,"** with the goal of eliminating economic exploitation. Brigadier **Aung Gyi**, who had argued for a moderate policy, including mixed public–private ownership and a role for private foreign investment, was purged from the RC in February 1963, and economic policy came under the control of Brigadier **Tin Pe** and U **Ba Nyein**, both doctrinaire, Eastern European–style socialists. They promoted nationalization of large and small enterprises, about 15,000 in all; Soviet-style industrialization; and elimination of foreign participation in the economy, which included not only nationalization of foreign-owned firms, such as the Burmah Oil Company, but also the economic disenfranchisement of Burmese citizens of **Indian** (South Asian) and **Chinese** ancestry, most of whom were forced to leave the country after their property was expropriated. State corporations were established to control all economic sectors, including the People's Store Corporation, a retail network that was responsible for making goods available to consumers. Most managers of these corporations were military officers. By the late 1960s, the inefficient and corrupt socialist system had caused substantial declines in living standards, especially in urban areas. Throughout the country, economic growth lagged behind population growth.

Unlike the Soviet and Chinese Communist regimes, the RC did not ban private use of agricultural land (although the state asserted ownership of all land and abolished tenancy, meaning that farmers did not have property rights in land) or establish collective farms. The state-run Agricultural Corporation determined which crops farmers had to plant and bought their **rice** and other crops at artificially low prices. Cultivators preferred to sell their crops at much higher prices on the **black market**, meaning that rice delivered to the People's Stores or Cooperatives was scarce at the best of times and of inferior quality. In times of flood or drought, severe rice shortages caused social and political unrest, especially in the mid-1970s.

Following the publication of "The Long-Term and Short-Term Economic Policies of the BSPP" at the first Congress of the Burma Socialist Programme Party in June–July 1971, socialist policies were modified to some extent: A realistic 20-year economic plan was drawn up, industrialization was abandoned in favor of development of the agricultural sector, and socialist self-sufficiency was repudiated. However, the plan's ultimate goal was to increase, rather than decrease, state control over the economy. Engagement with donors of **foreign aid**—especially **Japan**, West **Germany**, and multilateral agencies, such as the World Bank and the Asian Development Bank—increased. By the 1980s, official development assistance (ODA) was vital for the regime's economic survival. By the end of the decade, the country's burden of foreign debt—incurred through ODA loans—approached US$5.0 billion, mostly denominated in Japanese yen and German deutschmarks. But the Ne Win regime never carried out the liberalizing reforms that had been promised to international lenders, and its 1987 application to the **United Nations** for Least Developed Country status, to shield it from international creditors, was testimony to the ultimate failure of Burmese socialism.

Despite improvements in **agriculture** following the adoption of high-yield varieties of **rice** in the late 1970s, the economy never achieved sustained growth, and Burma suffered a new economic crisis in the late 1980s, including inflation and shortages of rice, made worse by the ill-advised **demonetization** of September 1987. In 1988, the BSPP regime collapsed, and with it the "**Burmese Road to Socialism**."

See also CURRENCY AND EXCHANGE RATES; ECONOMY AND ECONOMIC POLICY, STATE LAW AND ORDER RESTORATION COUNCIL/STATE PEACE AND DEVELOPMENT COUNCIL ERA; INVESTMENT, FOREIGN; LABOR STRIKES; WHOLE TOWN-SHIP EXTENSION PROGRAM.

ECONOMY AND ECONOMIC POLICY, STATE LAW AND OR-DER RESTORATION COUNCIL/STATE PEACE AND DE-VELOPMENT COUNCIL ERA (1988–). The **Burma Socialist Programme Party Extraordinary Congress,** held in July 1988, determined that the socialist economic policy that had been in force since 1962 would be scrapped. In November 1988, after the **State Law and Order Restoration Council (SLORC)** assumed power, it decreed a Union of Burma [Myanmar] Foreign Investment Law, which allowed foreign companies to establish branches, wholly owned subsidiaries, and joint ventures with domestic firms in Burma. Cross-border trade with **China** was also legalized. By the mid-1990s, private **foreign investment,** particularly from neighboring countries (such as **Singapore, Malaysia,** and **Thailand**) and Western countries (such as the **United States** and France), was substantial, and **Chinese** businesspeople wielded considerable economic influence, especially in **Kachin** and **Shan States** and **Mandalay.** Military-owned conglomerates, such as **Union of Myanmar Economic Holdings, Ltd.** and the Myanmar Economic Corporation, played a dominant role in the postsocialist economy.

Privately owned banks were permitted to exist for the first time since 1962, and some of these new financial institutions allegedly have links to drug-dealing warlord armies in the border areas. The extent to which the postsocialist economy is dependent on infusions of cash from the production and export of **opium** and other drugs is a matter of intense speculation. Drug exports earn groups, such as the **United Wa State Army,** hundreds of millions of U.S. dollars in revenues, some of which is apparently used for construction of condominiums, luxury hotels, and other projects in **Rangoon (Yangon),** Mandalay, and other central Burma cities.

Although the SLORC/SPDC hoped to emulate the successes of postsocialist China and Vietnam and transform Burma into a newly industrializing economy, Burma's foreign investment was in steep decline by the late 1990s because of a complicated system of exchange rates for its **currency**, the *kyat*, lack of the rule of law in business dealings, widespread corruption, poor infrastructure, and Western **sanctions**. The Asian financial crisis of 1997 also had an impact. Despite its oft-stated commitment to liberalizing agricultural trade, the state continues to procure **rice** harvests from farmers at artificially low prices at the beginning of the 21st century, causing considerable rural hardship (in 2003, the SPDC decreed an end to state procurement; it is unclear whether this has actually happened). There is little evidence that the **State Peace and Development Council** listens to the advice of qualified economic planners, and policy decisions are made on an unpredictable, ad hoc basis. SPDC chairman **Than Shwe** apparently wishes to return Burma to a modified form of economic autarky, such as existed before 1988, while, before his purge in October 2004, Prime Minister **Khin Nyunt** wanted continued economic internationalization. Close economic ties with Asian countries are likely to intensify, especially in the face of stiffening Western sanctions.

For ordinary Burmese people, conditions are probably harsher than they were under socialism, because of periodic shortages of necessities, high rates of inflation, and deteriorating **health** services. Malnutrition is widespread among poorer people in both urban and rural areas, and many children cannot afford to attend school. For lack of other opportunities, many poor women enter the **sex industry**, not only in Rangoon but also in provincial towns. The constant need to give bribes to military and government officials imposes great hardship, not only for businesspeople but also for ordinary citizens. An affluent few with the right connections and access to hard currency have been able to prosper, and Southern California–style "gated communities" with luxury housing have sprung up on the outskirts of Rangoon. As gaps between rich and poor widen, the economy of postsocialist Burma, like that of post-Soviet Russia, is in a state of chaotic transition, and it is unclear whether it will be able to achieve stability and sustained growth. *See also* AGRICULTURE; ECONOMY AND ECONOMIC POLICY, BURMA SOCIALIST PROGRAMME PARTY ERA.

EDUCATION. Like other Asian peoples, the Burmese have high esteem for education and educated persons. Books are customarily treated with care (e.g., they should not be placed on the ground), and the term *saya (hsaya)*, meaning "teacher" in the **Burmese (Myanmar) language**, conveys great respect. Before the colonial era, members of the **Sangha** were the chief custodians of knowledge, and **Buddhist** monasteries operated what amounted to a public school system, giving village boys and girls elementary lessons in literacy, arithmetic, and the basic principles of the religion. Scholarly monks were versed in **Pali**, much as clerics in medieval Europe knew Latin and Greek. Colonial-era European observers were impressed by the high literacy rates of the Burmese compared to the peoples of India, despite the complexities of the writing system.

During the colonial period, education was revolutionized, as the British introduced secular and scientific curricula. On the elite level, English supplanted Burmese as the language of instruction. Many Burmese who could afford it sent their children to **missionary** institutions such as the Methodist High School in **Rangoon (Yangon)**. Among ordinary people "vernacular schools," which gave instruction in Burmese or minority languages, drew pupils away from the monasteries, resulting in a decline in the Sangha's social prestige. The monks were unwilling to teach modern subjects like geography or sciences, perhaps because these subjects contradicted traditional cosmologies. A much smaller number of "Anglo-vernacular schools" taught primarily in Burmese, with some courses in English, while "European Code" schools such as those run by the missionaries taught in English, with Burmese usually offered as a second language.

Following the **student** strike in protest against the act creating **Rangoon (Yangon) University** in 1920, activists established a system of nongovernment **National Schools** offering a curriculum emphasizing Burmese language, patriotism, and the Buddhist religion. They were viewed by the colonial authorities with great suspicion. **Aung San** graduated from the national high school in **Yenangyaung (Yaynangyoung)** before entering Rangoon University.

In the **Frontier Areas** inhabited by ethnic minorities, Christian missionaries promoted their own educational revolution, establishing schools and nurturing an educated Christian elite among the **Karens (Kayins)**, **Chins**, **Kachins**, and other groups, for whom a community without both a church and a school was unthinkable. Such education opened up new worlds for previously isolated and often illiterate "hill tribes." Nonindigenous Asian groups, such as the **Chinese** and **Indians**, also had their own schools until the early 1960s.

Although the **Burma Socialist Programme Party** regime (1962–1988) was committed to expanding education and promoting nationwide literacy, it sought to impose a homogeneous educational system in which there was no place for the cultivation of ethnic or religious minority identities. All schools were nationalized. Burmese, rather than minority languages or English, was the primary medium of instruction; this caused a decline in Burma's previously high quality of English-language knowledge that hampered communications with the outside world. Missionary schools were shut down, their foreign teachers sent home. Against a background of economic stagnation, the quality of education overall deteriorated. The inadequacies of the education system were reflected in the fact that in Rangoon alone, 1,264 private schools in the early 1980s offered supplementary lessons to students, compared with 113 state-run high schools and 140 state-run middle schools. A common complaint at the time (and thereafter) was that middle and high school teachers took "side jobs" at the private schools to earn extra money and often had little time or energy for their ordinary students.

After the **State Law and Order Restoration Council** seized power in September 1988, the situation further deteriorated. Government allocations for education declined, as scarce funds were allocated for rising military expenditures; within Asia, Burma is one of the countries spending the lowest percentage of its GDP on education (1.4 percent in 2003). According to official statistics, in 1994–1995 there were 35,856 primary schools employing 169,748 teachers and educating 5,711,202 students, 2,058 middle schools with 53,859 teachers and 1,390,065 students, and 858 high schools with 18,045 teachers and 389,438 students. UNICEF estimated in 1995 that literacy had fallen to 55 percent of the population (compared to a figure of 82 percent for males and 71 percent for females reported in the 1983 census, the last taken). Dropout rates are high because parents cannot afford to keep their children in school, a situation that is worse in rural than urban areas, and worst in ethnic majority areas near the country's borders. UNESCO reports that 45 percent of Burmese children fail to complete primary education.

Many if not most teachers, whose salaries cannot cover living expenses, continue to supplement their income by tutoring students on a private basis, either individually or in private cram schools. Fulltime private schools, including those attached to Buddhist monasteries, are emerging as alternatives to the public system for people who can afford them. Also, vocationally oriented schools teaching computer science, business, and foreign languages are becoming popular in Rangoon and other cities, though these are essentially money-making ventures.

Universal education has been the key to the social and economic development of most Asian countries, and Burma's lack of progress in this area bodes ill for its future. *See also* EDUCATION, HIGHER.

EDUCATION, HIGHER. Before the establishment of **Rangoon (Yangon) University (RU)** by the British colonial authorities in 1920, students could only pursue higher education at Rangoon College and Judson College (the latter being a Baptist missionary institution) and sit for examinations conferring degrees from the University of Calcutta. The establishment of an autonomous, degree-granting institution in Rangoon had long been advocated by local leaders. It constituted a turning point in Burma's modern political as well as educational history, since RU **students** were in the forefront of political activism during the late 1930s when the movement for full independence began to take shape. At that time, RU had a coeducational student body of around 1,700 and four faculties: University College, Judson College, Teachers' Training College, and Medical College. There were also postgraduate (M.A.) courses in law and engineering. In 1925, the University of **Mandalay** was established.

It was widely believed that a major drawback of the colonial university system was its elitism and emphasis on the liberal arts, which were primarily designed to train civil servants, while practical subjects were generally neglected. Plans by Burmese activists to establish a "national university" teaching a Burmese curriculum were never realized.

During the parliamentary era (1948–1962), university students remained politically active, including supporters of the **Communist Party of Burma**, and academic freedom and the autonomy of universities were generally respected. Many students were educated at universities in the West and Japan, and foreign scholars lectured at RU and other institutions. During the **Burma Socialist Programme Party** era (1962–1988), the regime cut international educational ties and exercised tight control over students and faculties, substantially reorganizing the universities. In contrast to the colonial era, university admissions policy channeled the brightest students into practical fields; those who scored highest on the entrance examination could enter the Institute of Medicine or **Rangoon (Yangon) Institute of Technology**. Those with lower grades studied economics or education; the lowest scorers could only attend what was known after 1964 as Rangoon Arts and Sciences University, which offered liberal arts courses. The number of students grew from 19,855 to 97,757 between 1961 and 1978, but deteriorating economic conditions meant that they had poor job prospects after graduation, regardless of their major. Some graduates became trishaw drivers. Economic discontent contributed greatly to the student activism that brought about the mass demonstrations of 1988.

Until 1965, Rangoon University taught most of its courses in English, but the "New University Education Law" decreed by the **Revolutionary Council** created a curriculum in which the Burmese language predominated. By the early 1980s, however, the authorities had recognized the negative impact this had on higher education; even the state-run *Working People's Daily* newspaper stated in an article on July 4, 1982 that "over-zealous and short-sighted people in power demonstrated their false sense of patriotism by de-emphasizing the teaching of English in the basic education system . . . the importance of English as the key to the realm of higher learning was ignored."

After the **State Law and Order Restoration Council (SLORC)** seized power in September 1988, it sought to prevent a replay of **Democracy Summer** by keeping campuses closed most of the time until 2001. Over the longer term, its strategy has been to keep campuses in central **Rangoon (Yangon)** largely inoperative and to establish new institutions, such as **Dagon University** and the Institute of Economics at Ywathargyi, which are located so far from the city center that students have little opportunity to mingle with the urban population. In addition, the **State Peace and Development Council**

(SPDC) has established a number of distance education or correspondence courses, which keep students away from campuses and apparently have quite large enrollments. Both strategies have been implemented at the cost of educational quality, not to mention comfort and affordability for the students.

A special feature of post-1988 higher education is the importance of special universities for members of the **Tatmadaw** and their families, which are much better funded and equipped than those for civilians. These include not only the old **Defence Services Academy**, but also the Defence Services Institute of Medicine, the Defence Services Institute of Nursing, the Defence Services Technological Academy, and the Defence Services Technical Colleges. In addition, elite-track technical courses are offered by the Maritime University, under the Ministry of Transportation, and by the Aerospace Engineering University, under the Ministry of Science and Technology, both established in 2002.

According to official statistics, Burma in 1994–1995 had six universities and 62 other institutions of higher education, including teacher training colleges. Altogether they enrolled 313,477 students (universities: 62,098). In addition, a growing number of Burmese students, including both prodemocracy and ethnic minority exiles and nonpolitical students from wealthy or well-connected families, study abroad. *See also* JULY 7, 1962 INCIDENT; NATIONAL SCHOOLS; RANGOON UNIVERSITY STUDENT UNION; U THANT INCIDENT.

ELEPHANTS, WHITE. Elephants have played an important role in Burmese history, as beasts of burden (most famously, in the extraction of **teak**) and as mounts for battle used by kings and commanders. But the white elephant has special significance as the expression of the power and authority (*hpoun*) of the old kings, a belief that the Burmese shared with the Indians, Siamese, and Cambodians. A white elephant figures in the birth legend of Gotama **Buddha**. Possession of these animals, whose physical identification is subject to exacting criteria, enhanced the ruler's prestige and signified the prosperity of his realm. Both **Tabinshwehti** and **Bayinnaung** demanded white elephants from the king of Siam (**Thailand**), and when the latter refused, used this as a pretext for war. When Bayinnaung conquered

Siam and brought some of the animals back to Burma, he bestowed upon himself the title **Hsinbyushin** ("Lord of the White Elephant"), which is also the name of a prominent **Konbaung Dynasty** ruler. In 2001–2002, the **State Peace and Development Council (SPDC)** captured three white elephants in **Arakan State**. They are kept in a special compound in **Insein** Township, **Rangoon (Yangon)**, where the public can view them under tight security. Naming one of them "royal elephant that bestows grace upon the nation," the military regime claims that they are a sign of SPDC legitimacy and portents of prosperity. Modern-minded critics who point out that possession of white elephants has nothing to do with economic development have found themselves in trouble with the authorities.

ERA, BURMESE. The Burmese era began in 638 CE, when the **Pyu** ruled at **Sri Ksetra (Thayakhittaya)**, so the Burmese equivalent of 2005 CE is 1366–1367. The new year begins in April, with **Thingyan**. The year 1300 (1938) witnessed massive demonstrations against the British colonial rule, and the Burmese consider it significant that **Democracy Summer** occurred exactly 50 years later, in 1350 (1988). The Buddhist era, which began in 543 BCE, is also used (e.g., 2005 was 2548), as well as the Western system. *See also* CALENDAR, BURMESE.

ETHNIC POLITICAL PARTIES. Following promulgation of the 1988 **Political Party Registration Law** by the **State Law and Order Restoration Council**, parties were established that claimed to represent ethnic minority communities and contested the **General Election of May 27, 1990**. Among the most important were the **Shan Nationalities League for Democracy (SNLD)**, which won 23 **Pyithu Hluttaw** seats out of the 57 it contested (the second largest total after the **National League for Democracy**, which won 392 seats); the **Arakan League for Democracy**, which won 11 out of the 26 seats it contested; and the Mon National Democratic Front, which won 5 out of the 20 seats contested. Sixteen other ethnic parties won between one and three seats. In 2005, only the SNLD and seven much smaller parties, including three that won no seats in 1990, were still in existence, the others having been "deregistered" by the government. *See also* UNITED NATIONALITIES LEAGUE FOR DEMOCRACY.

EUROPEAN UNION (EU), RELATIONS WITH. The 25 member countries of the European Union pursue their own foreign policies, and among those that have significant relations with Burma, some are strongly critical of the **State Peace and Development Council (SPDC)** (Great **Britain** and the **Nordic countries**), while others favor "constructive engagement" (France and **Germany**). For example, while the British government formally requested in July 2003 that a major domestic firm, British American Tobacco (BAT), close down its operations in the country, France has established a significant economic presence, including the sale of ATR-72 jet-prop aircraft to local airlines and the participation of the state-owned oil company Total in the **Yadana Pipeline Project.**

However, the EU adopted a "common position" toward Burma in October 1996 that included a ban on visits to EU member countries by high-ranking officials of the SPDC (then known as the **State Law and Order Restoration Council**) and the **Tatmadaw**, and a suspension of visits by high-level European officials to Burma. Although (as of 2005) the common position remains in force, in June 1999 an EU delegation went to **Rangoon (Yangon)** to talk with SPDC leaders and **Aung San Suu Kyi** in the hopes of promoting political dialogue. Aside from halting **foreign aid** (outside of humanitarian grants) to Burma in 1988, a 1990 arms embargo, and the exclusion of Burmese exports from the Generalized System of Preferences (GSP) in 1996, the EU has not adopted comprehensive economic **sanctions** like those enacted by the **United States** in 1997 and 2003. After Burma became a member of the **Association of Southeast Asian Nations** in 1997, the EU expressed reluctance to participate in Asia–Europe Meetings (ASEM) if a SPDC delegate also attended, while ASEAN, **Japan**, **China**, and **South Korea** wished Burma to be included. However, in 2005, there was evidence that the EU as a whole was adopting a policy more amenable to "constructive engagement" with the junta.

– F –

FAMILY SYSTEM, BURMESE. In contrast to the family and kinship systems of neighboring China and India, the predominant family system in Burma is nuclear rather than extended, with two or three generations living together in one household (parents, dependent children, sometimes one or more grandparents), and is bilateral rather than patrilineal, meaning that descent is through both the maternal and paternal lines. Many observers have noted that Burmese family life has more in common with that found in Europe and America rather than in other parts of Asia.

A major consequence of this is that **women** enjoy considerable freedom in relation to their husbands and in-laws, although they must show them deference (the husband is traditionally referred to as *ein oo nat*, the "guardian spirit of the house"). Ideally, a newly married couple will live on their own, but they may live with either the husband's or the wife's parents if it is convenient or economical—there is no strong expectation, as in China, that they remain part of the paternal household. Although the family is nuclear in structure, ties with aunts, uncles, cousins, and other more distant kin are usually strong because of the need for mutual aid, which is as important in a big city like **Rangoon (Yangon)** as it is in a small village. Wealthy people are expected to assist their poorer relations; for example, they may employ young female relatives as servants and arrange suitable marriages for them. For most Burmese in the early 21st century, the family system provides psychological and material support in what is often a harsh and unforgiving environment, where social services are practically nonexistent.

FEDERAL MOVEMENT (1961–1962). A movement organized by leaders of the ethnic minorities, especially the **Shans (Tai)**, to amend the **Constitution of 1947** to make it more genuinely federal in character. In **Shan State**, support for the movement was inspired not only by shortcomings in the constitution but also by the harsh treatment local populations received at the hands of the **Tatmadaw** following the **Kuomintang (Guomindang)** intrusions of the early 1950s. The principal leader of the movement was Sao **Shwe Taik**, who had been Burma's president from 1948 to 1952.

In January 1961, 33 Shan leaders met at the state capital, **Taunggyi**, and formed a Constitutional Revision Steering Committee. On June 8–16, 1961, a Constitutional Conference was held in the same city, attended by 226 delegates, including not only Shan but **Karen,**

Kachin, and **Chin** representatives. Their proposals included reconstruction of the Union of Burma as a group of "co-equal" states; making **Burma Proper** a single state, separate from the central (federal) government; giving the two chambers of Parliament equal powers, so that the Chamber of Nationalities could better serve ethnic minority state interests; and the establishment of stronger and more autonomous state governments. Prime Minister **U Nu** was receptive to their proposals and invited ethnic minority leaders to a "Federal Seminar" in **Rangoon (Yangon)** in February 1962. While the talks were underway, General **Ne Win** seized power on March 2, 1962, and closed down parliamentary government. U Nu and ethnic leaders, including Sao Shwe Taik, were imprisoned. Brigadier **Aung Gyi**, a member of the original **Revolutionary Council**, stated that "we had economic, religious and political crises with the issue of federalism as the most important reason for the coup." Undoubtedly, stronger state governments in the ethnic areas, a key federal proposal, would have challenged the Tatmadaw's growing appetite for power.

FORCE 136. The Far Eastern branch of the British Special Operations Executive (SOE). Its mission in Burma and other parts of Southeast Asia was to organize local resistance against the Japanese during World War II. Largely through the work of Major **Hugh Seagrim**, it organized **Karen (Kayin)** guerrillas in the hill country east of the **Sittang (Sittoung) River**; and, with the cooperation of **Communist Party of Burma** operatives, especially **Thein Pe Myint**, made contact with the underground **Anti-Fascist Organization** among the **Burmans (Bamars)**. Force 136 made extensive use of "Jedburgh Teams," consisting of two British officers and a wireless operator who were parachuted behind enemy lines. The effectiveness of Karen guerrillas during the 1945 Allied thrust into Burma and the uprising of the **Burma National Army** against the Japanese on March 27 were vindications of Force 136's underground activities, which were regarded with some skepticism by other elements of the British government and army. *See also* ARMED FORCES DAY; AUNG SAN; JAPANESE OCCUPATION.

FORCED LABOR. In precolonial Burma, commoners performed compulsory labor service or *corvée* as a form of taxation, much as they did in other Asian countries and in many parts of Europe before the French Revolution. Often, such exactions were highly oppressive, such as during the reign of King **Bodawpaya** (r. 1782–1819), who used *corvée* labor on ambitious public projects in **Upper Burma**, including construction of a huge **pagoda** at **Mingun**. The British imposed some labor service obligations (the Village and Towns Acts of 1907–1908, although these required the payment of a wage), and the Japanese used hundreds of thousands of Burmese and other Asian *romusha* ("labor service workers") on construction of the **Thai–Burma Railway** (the "Death Railway") and other war-related projects between 1942 and 1945. After independence in 1948, the **Tatmadaw** used forced labor in counterinsurgency operations, and following the establishment of the **Caretaker Government** in October 1958 and the **State Law and Order Restoration Council (SLORC)** in September 1988, the new military authorities drafted residents of **Rangoon** (**Yangon**) to clean up the city.

Forced labor—state- or military-imposed labor without any form of compensation—has become especially prevalent since 1988, in contravention of a 1930 resolution by the International Labour Organization (ILO) that categorically bans its use. It generally occurs in two contexts: in connection with Tatmadaw counterinsurgency operations in ethnic minority regions, especially in contested areas of **Shan, Mon, Karen** (**Kayin**), and **Kayah** (**Karenni**) **States**; and in infrastructure projects unrelated, or indirectly related, to the war against ethnic armed groups. The first is generally more onerous: Minority villagers are rounded up to serve as military porters, often under very dangerous conditions, and are sometimes used as "human mine sweepers" or "human shields" in operations against insurgents. The death rate is high, **women** porters are often sexually abused, and families suffer economically because able-bodied people taken away for porterage, often for very long periods of time, are unavailable for farming.

Since 1988, the government has promoted the construction of new highways, bridges, and dams, routinely using forced labor. Some projects, such as the railway between Ye and **Tavoy (Dawei)**, described as a second "Death Railway," and the **Yadana Pipeline Project**, built with **foreign investment**, have exacted a high cost in worker fatalities, while others, such as forcing residents of **Mandalay** to clean up the moat around **Mandalay Palace** in preparation for **"Visit Myanmar Year"** in the mid-1990s, imposed great hardship and inconvenience especially on elderly citizens, who were not exempted from labor service. Prisoners, including political prisoners, have also been used on forced labor details. In addition, local people living around military bases have been obliged to provide uncompensated services for army "income generation projects," such as logging and shrimp cultivation. When workers are needed, local military authorities send orders to village headmen demanding a certain number, often enclosing a bullet to show what will happen if the order is not followed. Individuals often can pay the military to purchase an exemption, although the amount is usually more than the average person can afford.

On July 2, 1998, the ILO published a report, *Forced Labour in Myanmar (Burma),* drawn from extensive eyewitness accounts that told of severe abuses nationwide. Faced with the prospect of **sanctions** by ILO member countries, which were recommended by its Governing Body in November 2000, the **State Peace and Development Council (SPDC)** allowed a high-level inspection team of ILO experts in September–October 2001 to visit sites freely. They reported that although the situation had improved since 1998 in connection with civilian infrastructure projects, military bases continued to use forced labor. Its use in insurgent-contested areas, which are usually remote and difficult to inspect, continues to be widespread. To monitor the SPDC's promise to abolish the practice, an ILO liaison office was established in Rangoon.

In the past, the SPDC has argued that "contributions" of labor by the people were a part of Burmese tradition. But state-imposed forced labor must be distinguished from community-based projects, such as the construction of pagodas by villagers, where the donation of labor is voluntary or at most a matter of social pressure. Since 1988, however, some Tatmadaw-sponsored pagoda projects have also used forced labor. *See also* HUMAN RIGHTS IN BURMA; UNITED NATIONS IN BURMA.

FORCED RELOCATION (INTERNAL DISPLACEMENT). The prevalence of forced relocation of urban and rural residents in Burma since 1988 reflects both the strategic and economic priorities of the **State Law and Order Restoration Council (SLORC;** after 1997 known as the **State Peace and Development Council**) and the lack of firm legal guarantees of property rights. In precolonial times, Burma's land was considered the property of the king, and post-independence constitutions have asserted that land rights rest ultimately with the state. The most extensive forced relocations have occurred in ethnic minority areas, in connection with the **Tatmadaw**'s counterinsurgency operations. In the mid-1990s, at least 300,000 persons in eight townships in central **Shan State** were forced to leave their villages and resettle in military-controlled sites that resembled the "strategic hamlets" of the Vietnam War. This policy was an application of the "**Four Cuts**," designed to eliminate popular bases of support for insurgents, in this case the **Shan State Army**. Relocation of villagers on a large scale has also occurred in **Karen (Kayin)**, **Kayah (Karenni)**, **Mon**, and **Arakan (Rakhine) States**.

Urban forced relocation, involving mostly **Burmans**, can be traced back to the **Caretaker Government** of 1958–1960, which moved some 170,000 squatters and other poor people out of central **Rangoon (Yangon)** to new townships in **Thaketa** and **North** and **South Okkalapa**. After the SLORC seized power, several hundred thousand people (no exact figure is available) were moved from downtown Rangoon to other **new towns**, such as North and South Dagon and Hlaing Thayar, located beyond the old city limits. Most, though not all, of these moves were involuntary. The government took the measure to ensure that popular uprisings like **Democracy Summer** would not recur, since not only squatters but communities where protesters were sheltered, including people living in substantial housing, were singled out for relocation. In another case of relocation, the Main Campus of **Rangoon (Yangon) University**, a center of protest in 1988, has been largely closed down, and most undergraduates pursue their studies at distant outlying campuses, such as **Dagon University**, a policy designed to keep concentrations of **students** distant from city residents.

Construction of new highways and other facilities under the sponsorship of the **Yangon City Development Committee** has resulted in additional relocations; as highways are widened and improved, adjacent houses are torn down and replaced with multistory structures. City residents living on prime land slated for development by private but junta-connected firms have little or no legal recourse to prevent destruction of their neighborhoods. Similar situations exist in other large urban areas, such as **Mandalay**, and in smaller communities such as the village located within the ruins of **Pagan (Bagan)**, which was closed down by the authorities in 1990, its residents forced to move to an undeveloped area, to improve access to the archeological area.

Victims of forced relocation often find that the areas to which they have been moved lack such basic amenities as water, suitable croplands, and transportation. In minority regions like Shan State, people who leave resettlement areas to retrieve food stored in their old villages have sometimes been shot by the army, which regards areas cleared of inhabitants as free-fire zones. The exact number of internally displaced people is not known, but it has been estimated by international agencies at from 600,000 to one million. Because of the lack of physical and economic security, many become **refugees** in neighboring countries. *See also* HUMAN RIGHTS IN BURMA.

FOREIGN RELATIONS. After Burma became an independent state in January 1948, the government of Prime Minister U **Nu** adopted a foreign policy based on the principles of neutralism and nonalignment, a trend that became more pronounced as the Cold War intensified in the 1950s, and the Burmese prime minister joined other Asian and African leaders at the 1955 Bandung Conference in **Indonesia**. Participants at the conference sought a "third way" between the type of communist revolution promoted by **Russia** (the Soviet Union) and the People's Republic of **China** and the "Free World" capitalism of the former imperial powers and the **United States**. U Nu had especially close ties to another prominent nonaligned leader, Prime Minister Jawaharlal Nehru of **India**, but also promoted friendly relations with anticommunist **Thailand**. One of Burma's earliest diplomatic crises involved **Kuomintang (Guomindang)** troops from China, who, with U.S. backing, attempted to establish anticommunist bases in **Shan State** in the 1950s. Although this caused serious problems in relations with Washington, Burma accepted **foreign aid** from Western countries, **Japan** (in the form of war reparations), and the Soviet Union.

When parliamentary government was ended by General **Ne Win** in March 1962, the commitment to "positive neutrality" and nonalignment continued, but Ne Win added another theme: isolationism. Foreign firms were nationalized; trade with foreign countries declined steeply (except through the **black market**) because of the socialist commitment to economic autarky; South Asian (Indian and Pakistani) businesspeople were forced out of the country; cultural ties, including academic exchanges, with foreign countries were cut; and tourists were prohibited from entering the country until 1970, when a week-long visa was granted to generate foreign exchange. The **Anti-Chinese Riots** of June 1967 led to a diplomatic crisis with Beijing. The following year, the Chinese supported the establishment of a powerful **Communist Party of Burma (CPB)** base along the China–Shan State border that offered stiff resistance to central government troops until the CPB broke up in early 1989. During the late 1970s and 1980s, Ne Win's personal style of diplomacy seemed to gravitate toward the West, as his regime accepted hundreds of millions of dollars in **foreign aid** from West **Germany**, Great **Britain**, and above all Japan, which had close ties to the United States. There was some resumption of cultural and other exchanges, although the Ne Win government remained basically very suspicious of foreigners.

The power seizure by the **State Law and Order Restoration Council (SLORC)** in September 1988 changed Burma's foreign relations in fundamental ways: a new military-owned, state capitalist economy supplanted socialism, and the SLORC actively sought foreign private investment; relations with China grew close, particularly after the collapse of the CPB; and because of the new military regime's violations of **human rights**, relations with the United States and the **European Union** deteriorated sharply, with Western governments imposing limited economic and other **sanctions**. Many observers believe that the post-1988 regime has effectively abandoned neutrality because of its close ties with China, whose support in the military, economic, and diplomatic spheres has allowed it to turn a deaf ear to criticism from the West. Burma's achievement of membership in the **Association of Southeast Asian Nations (ASEAN)** in July 1997 marked a major break with the isolationism of the pre-1988 era, and relations have also improved with South Asian neighbors India and **Bangladesh**. In sum, the leaders of the **State Peace and Development Council** (as the SLORC was renamed in 1997) have exhibited considerable pragmatism and flexibility in their relations with other Asian states, in sharp contrast to the political hard line taken inside the country against domestic opposition. *See also* AUSTRALIA, RELATIONS WITH; BOUNDARIES, INTERNATIONAL; BRITAIN, RELATIONS WITH; CHINA AND BURMA (HISTORICAL RELATIONS); GERMANY, FEDERAL REPUBLIC, RELATIONS WITH; GREATER MEKONG SUBREGION; INVESTMENT, FOREIGN; KOREA, NORTH, RELATIONS WITH; KOREA, SOUTH, RELATIONS WITH; MALAYSIA, RELATIONS WITH; NORDIC COUNTRIES AND BURMA; SANCTIONS; SINGAPORE, RELATIONS WITH; THAILAND (SIAM) AND BURMA; THAILAND, RELATIONS WITH; UNITED NATIONS IN BURMA.

FORESTS AND FORESTRY IN BURMA. Burma is blessed with rich forest resources. However, since 1988 the irresponsible exploitation of forests both by pro- and antigovernment groups has caused rapid deforestation—as much as 1.4 percent annually during the 1990s. It is estimated that at independence in 1948, forests covered 70 percent of Burma's land area, and that currently there is only 41–42 percent forest cover (27.2 million hectares), still one of the highest in Southeast Asia.

Seventy-five percent of Burma's forests are tropical; the other 25 percent, located in northern areas, are temperate. Historically and commercially, the most important tree species is **teak** (*Tectona grandis*; *kyun* in Burmese); Burma possesses about 70 percent of the world's teak reserves. During the dynastic period, teak was a royal monopoly, and both British colonial and independent Burmese governments claimed teak forests as state property, meaning that the state has the authority to control logging, usually carried out on a concessionary basis by private firms. Teak has been used for construction of royal palaces, Buddhist monasteries, traditional and Western-style houses, furniture, and ships. Because of its high quality, there is considerable international demand at present for teak furniture, flooring, and decks for ships, a major reason for Burma's alarming deforestation. Other important hardwoods are *pyinkado* or Burmese ironwood (*Xylia dolabriformis*), used for bridges, docks, and railroad ties, and *padauk* (*Pterocarpus macrocarpus*), used for bullock carts, boats, and housing. *In* (*Dipterocarpus tuberculatus*), a tree yielding an inferior type of wood, has been widely used for building low-cost houses, carts, and boats. Resin from the *thitsi* tree is used in traditional **lacquerware**.

When the British annexed **Tenasserim** (**Tanintharyi**) and **Moulmein** (**Mawlamyine**) following the **First Anglo-Burmese War**, they allowed unregulated exploitation, which within decades stripped these areas of most of their forest cover. Hardwoods were used primarily for ship construction. In 1856, following the annexation of **Lower Burma**, the colonial government established the Forest Department, which enforced strict conservation of teak and other trees. The Brandis Selection System (named for the official, Dietrich Brandis, who was the Forest Department's first director and initiated scientific logging in Burma) guaranteed sustainable exploitation by determining that only trees with a girth of at least 6.5 to 7.6 feet could be felled. Logging became a principal source of revenue for the Province of Burma. On the eve of **World War II** (1939–1940), British Burma produced 447,000 tons of timber, an amount unsurpassed in the postwar era. Yet colonial-era forests remained largely intact. Colonial-era loggers used elephants to move the logs to rivers, where they were floated in huge rafts down to sawmills. The most valuable forests were found in the teak-rich **Pegu Yoma** uplands of central Burma.

After independence in 1948, forest conservation was hampered by political instability and insurgency. Central governments attempted to enforce modified versions of the Brandis Selection System, but border area insurgents, especially the **Karen National Union**, controlled extensive forest lands and made money from sale of hardwoods to neighboring countries, especially **Thailand**.

After it seized power on September 18, 1988, the **State Law and Order Restoration Council (SLORC)** found itself desperately short of hard currency. Following a state visit by Thai army commander Chaovalit Yongchaiyudh in December, SLORC concluded five-year concessionary agreements with 42 Thai firms to exploit forests inside the Burmese border. Clear cutting became rampant as the licensees sought to make as quick a profit as possible. Although these concessions were shut down in 1993, unregulated export of Burmese hardwoods into Thailand continues. At the beginning of the 21st century, it is surpassed in scale by logging operations along the Burma–China border involving local businesspeople and armed groups that have signed **cease-fires** with the central government. Despite passing a Forest Law in 1992, the post-1988 military regime has been unable or unwilling to slow the pace of deforestation, and many observers fear that hardwood forests will disappear within a generation.

"FOUR CUTS" (*PYAT LEI PYAT*). An integrated counterinsurgency strategy adopted by the **Tatmadaw** in the late 1960s to deny ("cut") food, funds, information, and recruits to ethnic minority or communist insurgents. The "Four Cuts" resembles the British "new villages" program used during Malaya's Emergency (1948–1960) and the "strategic hamlets" program carried out by U.S. forces in South Vietnam. The countryside was divided into three zones: black (where insurgents exercise control), brown (disputed by insurgent and government forces), and white (insurgent-free). Villagers in black or brown areas were forcibly relocated to "strategic villages," and the adjoining territory was turned into a "free-fire zone" where the Army could with impunity eliminate anyone suspected of being an insurgent, including villagers in search of food stored in their evacuated settlements. Although the **cease-fires** initiated in 1989 ended Tatmadaw counteinsurgency operations in many ethnic minority areas, the "Four Cuts" are practiced in areas where resistance against the central government continues. In the mid-1990s, for example, an estimated 300,000 people in central **Shan State** were forcibly relocated to new settlements in order to uproot popular support for the **Shan State Army**. See also FORCED RELOCATION; HUMAN RIGHTS IN BURMA.

FOUR EIGHTS (8.8.88) MOVEMENT. The general strike that began early on the morning of August 8, 1988, seeking to force the resignation of **Sein Lwin** as chairman of the **Burma Socialist Programme Party** and president of Burma. Organized by **student** activists, it involved hundreds of thousands of ordinary citizens in street demonstrations in **Rangoon (Yangon)** and other cities. The demonstrators were peaceful and well disciplined but nevertheless were fired upon by the **Tatmadaw** in central Rangoon (near the **Sule Pagoda** and Town Hall) shortly before midnight. The choice of that date reflected the belief that eight is an inauspicious number for rulers; in the "three eights" year of the **Burmese Era** (888; 1526–1527 CE), **Ava (Inwa)** fell to the **Shan (Tai)** usurper, Thohanbwa, beginning an era of anarchy and destruction. *See also* ALL BURMA FEDERATION OF STUDENT UNIONS; DEMOCRACY SUMMER; MIN KO NAING.

FOURTH BURMA RIFLES (4th BURIFS). One of three Burma Rifles (Burif) battalions established following the September 1945 **Kandy Conference** between **Aung San** and Lord **Louis Mountbatten**, which was entirely composed of **Burman (Bamar)** soldiers from the former **Patriotic Burmese Forces**. The battalion was placed under the command of **Ne Win**. During the **Communist Party of Burma** and **Karen (Kayin)** uprisings of 1948–1949, it was one of the few military units to remain loyal to the government of Prime Minister U **Nu**. Some of Ne Win's Fourth Burma Rifles subordinates became prominent in the 1958–1962 **Caretaker Government** and the military regime he established in March 1962, including **Sein Lwin**, **Aung Gyi**, and **Tin Pe**. *See also* BURMA ARMY.

FREEDOM BLOC. Known in the **Burmese (Myanmar) language** as the *Htwet Yat Gaing*, "Association of the Way Out"; established in October 1939 as an alliance of the **Sinyetha Party**, the **Dobama Asiayone**, and the **All Burma Students Union**. It asserted Burma's right to self-government. By 1941, most of its leaders were in jail or underground. Its president was **Ba Maw** and its secretary-general was **Aung San**.

FRONTIER AREAS. Historically, those areas of Burma outside of **Burma Proper** where the British colonial government allowed local rulers, such as the *sawbwas* of the **Shans** and the **Karenni**, considerable autonomy under the surveillance of British residents. In 1922, the Burma Frontier Service was established, separate from the officials who administered Burma Proper. Following implementation of the **Government of Burma Act (1935)**, the Frontier Areas were divided into Excluded and Partially Excluded Areas (or "Part I" and "Part II" areas). The former remained entirely outside the authority of the elected legislature, being the responsibility of the governor, while the latter were the responsibility of the legislature and, in some cases, could elect representatives. Geographically and ethnically, "Frontier Areas" refers to the upland and mountainous areas surrounding the central lowlands, bordering **India, China, Thailand**, and Laos, which are inhabited by ethnic minorities, such as the Shans, **Chins, Kachins**, and Karennis. Comprising about 40–45 percent of the land area of modern Burma, the Frontier Areas included the **Shan States** and **Wa** districts, the Karenni states, the **Karen** hills, the **Arakan** Hill Tracts, the Chin Hills, the Kachin Hills, the **Naga** Hills, and a number of smaller jurisdictions.

Burmese nationalists have accused the British colonialists of separating the country into Burma Proper and Frontier Areas, zones that had little opportunity for political association, in order to "divide and rule." The British claimed that the Frontier Areas, lacking modern economic or social development, required a period of special tutelage before achieving equal status and integration with Burma Proper. *See also* AUNG SAN–ATTLEE AGREEMENT; PANGLONG CONFERENCE.

FRONTIER AREAS COMMITTEE OF ENQUIRY (FACE). One of the conditions outlined in the **Aung San–Attlee Agreement** of January 1947 was the establishment of a commission that would investigate the sentiments of a broad spectrum of peoples in the **Frontier Areas** concerning integration with **Burma Proper**, which, it was hoped, could be achieved with "the free consent of the inhabitants of those areas." During March–April 1947, the eight-man committee, chaired by Colonel D. R. Rhees-Williams, solicited opinions from many different ethnic minority groups, including those who had not participated in the February 1947 **Panglong Conference.** They included the remote **Wa**, whose leaders reportedly said they had no opinion on constitutional issues "because we are a wild people." Though a wide variety of opinions were expressed to FACE, there was general agreement among the minorities that they should enjoy autonomy and equal rights with the people of Burma Proper; but **Karen (Kayin)** leaders were bitterly suspicious of **Burman (Bamar)** intentions and demanded special concessions. The FACE Report, presented to the British and Burma governments in June 1947, included recommendations on state autonomy, representation of the Frontier Areas in the Constituent Assembly, and which territories should be recognized as part of the states, which part of "Ministerial Burma." *See also* CONSTITU-TION OF 1947.

FURNIVALL, JOHN S. (1878–1960). British official and scholar who served in Burma as a member of the Indian Civil Service from 1902 to 1923 and founded the **Burma Research Society** in 1909 and the Burma Book Club in 1928. He is best known for describing the social and economic impact of colonial rule in terms of the **plural society**, a critique of laissez faire capitalism in a multiethnic society that after World War II was widely accepted as the definitive analysis of the Western imperial legacy in Southeast Asia and other parts of the Third World. He argued that although foreign rule and economic development had made Burma prosperous, this prosperity benefited foreign rather than indigenous communities: "[U]nder Burmese rule the Burman was a poor man in a poor country; now [1948] he is a poor man in a comparatively rich country."

His books include *An Introduction to the Political Economy of Burma* (1931), which was long used as a textbook at the **University of Rangoon (Yangon)**; *The Fashioning of Leviathan: The Beginnings of British Rule in Burma* (1939); and *Colonial Policy and Practice: A Comparative Study of Burma and Netherlands India* (1948), in which he most fully elaborated the plural society concept. From 1935 to 1941, he was a lecturer at Cambridge University, and also served as advisor to Prime Minister U **Nu** from 1948 to 1960.

– G –

GALON. Also known as the *Garuda*, a bird from Indian mythology, the mount of the Hindu god Vishnu, which is found in numerous motifs throughout Southeast Asia (e.g., an eagle-like *garuda* is the national symbol of the Republic of **Indonesia**). It is depicted as immensely powerful, often shown trampling on **nagas** or snakes, its mortal enemy. *Galon* symbolism was adopted by participants in the **Saya San Rebellion** in 1930–1931, and the *Galon Tat* was the paramilitary wing of the Myochit or Patriot Party of U **Saw** before **World War II**. *See also HONGSA*; PEACOCK.

GANDHI HALL DECLARATION. On July 27–28, 1990, the Central Executive Committee of the **National League for Democracy** convened a meeting of representatives elected in the **General Election of May 27, 1990,** at Gandhi Hall in downtown **Rangoon (Yangon)** and issued a declaration calling on the **State Law and Order Restoration Council** to allow the new members of parliament to form a government; release Daw **Aung San Suu Kyi, U Tin U,** and other political prisoners from detention; and suspend laws and decrees that restricted civil liberties.

GEMSTONES. Burma is renowned for its gemstones, especially "pigeon blood rubies," which for centuries have been mined at **Mogok (Mogoke)** in what is now **Mandalay Division.** Before the British colonial period, the mining of rubies at Mogok, Sagyin (near **Mandalay**), and Nanyarzeik (in **Kachin State**) was a royal monopoly. Sapphires are also found in these places. **Hpakant** in Kachin State produces the world's finest jadeite, highly valued in China, and pearls are found in the **Mergui Archipelago.** Amber, of a fine variety known as "Burmite," has been mined in the **Hukawng Valley** of Kachin State.

Under both the **Ne Win** regime and the **State Law and Order Restoration Council (SLORC)/State Peace and Development Council (SPDC),** gemstones have remained a government monopoly, controlled by the Myanmar Gems Enterprise, which holds annual emporia for international buyers each year in March, an important source of foreign exchange. Like Burma's old kings, the post-1988 military regime believes that the possession of extraordinary gemstones is an auspicious sign, an indicator of legitimacy. In 1990, the SLORC announced that it had successfully recovered a huge, 496-carat ruby that had been mined at Mogok; then taken by **black market** entrepreneurs across the border to Bangkok but recaptured by **Military Intelligence** agents. The stone was dubbed the "*Nawata* (SLORC) Ruby" in the state-controlled media. In 1991 a special postage stamp was issued to commemorate it. *See also* MINERAL RESOURCES.

GENERAL COUNCIL OF BURMESE ASSOCIATIONS (GCBA). Growing out of the General Council of Buddhist Associations, the peak organization of the **Young Men's Buddhist Association (YMBA)**, the GCBA substituted "Burmese" for "Buddhist" in its English name at its March 1920 national conference in order to have a wider popular appeal. It was the major vehicle of Burmese nationalism before the **Saya San (Hsaya San) Rebellion** of 1930–1932 and, unlike the YMBA, was a political rather than a cultural-religious organization. Adopting the methods of the Indian National Congress, it led a boycott of the election of Burmese members to the Indian legislature in 1920 and also opposed the government act that established **Rangoon (Yangon) University** as a degree-granting institution. It had a network of 12,000 local branches in **Lower** and **Upper Burma**; worked closely with "political *pongyis*," including U **Ottama**; and played a major role in the **national schools** movement after the university boycott. During the 1920s, however, it was weakened by factionalism and power politics. It split in 1922 over the issue of whether to support or oppose **dyarchy** reforms, with the "Twenty-One Party" (21 members of the GCBA) participating in the 1923 dyarchy elections, while the "Hlaing-Pu-Gyaw GCBA" boycotted them. In 1924, a further split occurred over the issue of noncooperation in tax payment. The following year, the U Soe Thein faction, also known as the "Pongyis' GCBA," broke away from the mainstream GCBA, proposing a harder line, on against cooperation with the British. By the late 1920s, the GCBA had been largely discredited. In the years before **World War II**, many of its original leaders collaborated closely with the colonial state. *See also* DOBAMA ASIAYONE; GENERAL COUNCIL OF SANGHA SAMMEGGI (GCSS).

GENERAL COUNCIL OF SANGHA SAMMEGGI (GCSS). Established by "political *pongyis*" as a national organization in 1920 in opposition to British colonial rule (*sammeggi* means "united" or "unity"). Working closely with the **General Council of Burmese Associations (GCBA)**, its protests against the authorities were highly effective because **Buddhist** monasteries (*kyaung*) were found in every Burmese village; activist monks (*dhammakatika*) preaching on political themes had growing influence during a time of hardship in rural Burma (despite the disapproval of many senior **sayadaws**, who believed monks should avoid politics); and young monks, having renounced family ties, made ideal "shock troops" for demonstrations.

The monks established thousands of *wunthanu athin* in rural villages. However, government crackdowns and the GCSS's own factionalism, which paralleled that of the GCBA, had undermined its credibility by the 1930s. *See also* OTTAMA, U; WISARA, U.

GENERAL ELECTION OF MAY 27, 1990. On September 10, 1988, the **Burma Socialist Programme Party (BSPP)** held its second **Extraordinary Congress**, at which it promised to hold a multiparty general election. After the **State Law and Order Restoration Council (SLORC)** was established on September 18, the new military junta included the holding of a general election as one of its "four tasks," indicating that it would transfer power to a duly elected government once social stability had been reestablished and the election properly carried out. Election management became the responsibility of a body redundantly named the "Elections Commission for Holding Democratic Multi-Party General Elections," given legal status on September 21. A **Political Party Registration Law** decreed by the SLORC a week later created the framework within which parties running in the election could be organized. Having lost its status as the only legal political party, the BSPP reorganized itself as the **National Unity Party (NUP)**. The **National League for Democracy (NLD)** soon emerged as the most popular new party. Altogether, more than 230 parties were established, mostly small organizations with only a handful of members. Most of these were "deregistered" by the Commission, and only 93 parties actually contested the election.

In February 1989, the SLORC announced that the election would be held within 14 months of the issuance of a **Pyithu Hluttaw Election Law**, which was decreed on May 31, 1989. Single-member election constituencies were described as being the same as those of the **Pyithu Hluttaw**, or BSPP-era People's Assembly. In November 1989, the exact date of the election, May 27, 1990, was announced in the state media.

Observers doubted that the election would be fair, given the National Unity Party's superior resources (as the former BSPP) and the SLORC's initial refusal to allow outside monitoring in any form. Moreover, **Aung San Suu Kyi**, who was under house arrest, was barred from running for a seat in a **Rangoon (Yangon)** constituency. The choice of the date, the 27th of the month, seemed to reflect retired leader **Ne Win**'s preoccupation with his lucky number, nine (2 + 7 = 9). The election went smoothly, however, observed by representatives of the different parties, diplomats, and foreign journalists. The results—a substantial victory for the NLD, which won 59.9 percent of the popular vote and 392 (81 percent) of the 485 contested seats—indicate that the SLORC had made little or no effort to interfere with the process. The Election Commission publicly reported results for 485 constituencies in full detail (due to local conditions, seven constituencies out of a total of 492 did not choose representatives). Other winning parties were the **Shan Nationalities League for Democracy** (23 seats), the **Arakan (Rakhine) League for Democracy** (11 seats), the NUP (10 seats), and the Mon National Democratic Front (5 seats). The participation rate, 72.6 percent, was the highest in Burma's short history of elections (two million votes were declared invalid and not included in the official results).

The SLORC apparently held the election in the belief that either the National Unity Party would win a majority or that a number of small, weak parties would form a coalition that the regime could easily manipulate. That the result was quite different, even though NLD leaders Aung San Suu Kyi and **Tin U** were under house arrest, suggests that **Military Intelligence** had underestimated the depth of popular dissatisfaction. Constituencies with large military populations, such as **Mingaladon Township** in northern Rangoon, returned NLD candidates, showing wide support for the opposition party among the armed forces rank and file.

However, on July 27, 1990, the military regime issued **SLORC Announcement 1/90**, declaring that a civilian government could not be established until a new constitution was drafted. In the July 28, 1990, **Gandhi Hall Declaration**, the NLD called for a speedy transfer of power.

GERMANY, FEDERAL REPUBLIC OF, RELATIONS WITH. Imperial, Weimar, and Nazi Germany had few significant contacts with Burma other than commercial ties, but after the country became independent in 1948, West Germany played an important, though still little understood, role involving General **Ne Win**. In 1955, a company owned by the West German state, Fritz Werner, was invited by the

Union of Burma government to assist in the establishment of an indigenous armaments industry, to provide the **Tatmadaw** with small arms, ammunition, and explosives. A number of Tatmadaw personnel were trained by the company in Germany, and between 1962 and 1988 Ne Win visited Germany every year as a personal guest of the company, on what one German scholar calls "a mixture of private holidays and business trips" (his last trip there was in May 1988). Fritz Werner arranged for the construction of Union of Burma Five Star Line ships in Bremen and Hamburg and established one of the very few joint ventures in socialist Burma, Myanma Fritz Werner, for the purpose of promoting industry.

Political relations between the two countries during this time were also friendly, as reflected in an official visit by Germany's President Richard von Weizsächer to Burma in February 1986. Between 1970 and 1988, Germany was consistently the second-largest donor of **foreign aid** to the Ne Win government (after **Japan**), mostly in the form of concessional loans, which during the economic crisis of the late 1980s left the country with a huge, unpayable debt in deutschmarks (and yen). The flow of official development assistance funds from Bonn to **Rangoon (Yangon)** increased significantly in the late 1970s, reaching a high of US$75 million in 1983. German policy makers thought Burma an appropriate destination for aid because it represented a "third way" in economic systems, between Western capitalism and Soviet-style communism. Aid was halted, however, after the **State Law and Order Restoration Council** seized power in September 1988. *See also* EUROPEAN UNION, RELATIONS WITH.

GLASS PALACE CHRONICLES (HMANNAN YAZAWIN). Compiled in 1829 by order of King Bagyidaw (r. 1819–1838), a history of Burma (or more precisely, the kingdoms established in the central valley of the **Irrawaddy [Ayeyarwady] River**) from its legendary origins to the **Konbaung Dynasty**. It was so named because the committee of "learned Brahmins, learned monks and learned ministers" who were appointed to compose it worked in a pavilion decorated with glass mosaic located within the palace compound at **Ava (Inwa)**. The *Chronicles* trace the origins of the Konbaung royal family to the kingdom of Tagaung in **Upper Burma**, whose founder was a prince of Sakya in northern India, the country where **Gotama Bud-**

dha was born. Direct descent from the **Maha Thamada**, the first king, was also claimed. The *Glass Palace Chronicles* were not intended to present an objective view of history, but rather to glorify the dynasty established by **Alaungpaya** (r. 1752–1760), who, however, seems to have been of rather humble origin.

GOD'S ARMY. In the Sgaw Karen language, *K'sa Do Yuah Thu'Mu* ("The Great Lord's Army"), a small **Karen (Kayin)** armed group that defected from the **Karen National Union** in 1996–1997 and was headed by nine-year-old twin boys, Johnny and Luther Htoo. God's Army was an example of the kind of millenarian religion, featuring Messiah-like saviors, which has frequently emerged among the Karens. Johnny and Luther's followers believed that they had supernatural powers, including invulnerability to **Tatmadaw** bullets and the command of "invisible armies" containing hundreds of thousands of "angel warriors." Like the **Democratic Karen Buddhist Army**, God's Army was an expression of Karen disillusionment with the KNU's mainline Christian leadership. It also reflected the chaotic conditions along the Thai–Burma border after the fall of **Manerplaw**. The group was allegedly connected with a hostage-taking incident at a hospital in Ratchaburi, Thailand, in 2000, in which one hostage and the 10 hostage takers were killed. The short history of God's Army came to an end in January 2001 when Johnny and Luther surrendered to Thai authorities and were tearfully reunited with their mother.

GOLF. Introduced to Burma during the British colonial period, the game of golf is not only recreation but also an occasion for wealthy and powerful members of society, especially high-ranking **Tatmadaw** officers and their business partners, to develop profitable relationships. Although **Ne Win** isolated the country from most foreign influences, he loved golf and frequently traveled from his heavily guarded compound on the shores of **Inya Lake** to one of the few operating golf courses in **Rangoon (Yangon)**. During the **Burma Socialist Programme Party** period (1962–1988), local state and party officials sometimes sponsored the construction of golf courses in their jurisdictions to give themselves a place where they could entertain and influence higher officials. After the **State Law and Order**

Restoration Council opened the country to foreign economic influences in 1988, golf assumed even greater importance, as military officers and local businesspeople made joint venture deals with foreign partners. Many golf courses are military owned. Lavish courses, such as the Pun Hlaing Golf Estate in Rangoon's Hlaing Thayar Township or the Hanthawaddy Golf and Country Club near **Pegu (Bago)**, have been designed to meet international standards.

GOVERNMENT OF BURMA ACT (1935). A law in effect between April 1, 1937, and the **Japanese occupation** that separated Burma administratively and politically from **India** and placed it under the executive authority of a governor directly responsible to London, rather than to the Viceroy of India. Although the governor exercised control over matters relating to defense, foreign affairs, finances, and the "Excluded Areas," which formed a major portion of the **Frontier Areas**. In other matters, he was obliged to act in accordance with the decisions of the cabinet, headed by a prime minister, who was chosen by Parliament. The Parliament was bicameral, consisting of a 36-seat Senate and a 132-member House of Representatives. Dr. **Ba Maw** became the first prime minister under the new system after a general election was held in 1936; his leadership was constrained, however, not only by the governor's reserved powers but also by business and communal interests in the legislature. Many Burmese political leaders opposed the 1935 act; by separating Burma from India, it seemed to deprive the country of the constitutional advances being accomplished on the Subcontinent. *See also* DYARCHY.

GREAT BUDDHIST COUNCIL, FIFTH (1871). A meeting of members of the **Sangha**, sponsored by King **Mindon** (r. 1853–1878), at **Mandalay** to produce an authoritative version of the **Tipitaka**, or **Buddhist** scriptures. In connection with this event, the king also donated a *hti* to the **Shwe Dagon Pagoda** in **Rangoon (Yangon)**. The Council recited and corrected the scriptures, which were carved on stone stelae and housed on the grounds of the **Kuthodaw Pagoda**. *See also* GREAT BUDDHIST COUNCIL, SIXTH; NU, U.

GREAT BUDDHIST COUNCIL, SIXTH. Following the precedent set by King **Mindon** (r. 1853–1878), Prime Minister U **Nu** convened the Sixth Great Buddhist Council in May 1954 to produce an authoritative **Burmese language** translation of the scriptures, or **Tipitaka**, from the **Pali** original. Held at the Maha Pasana Guha, an artificial cave built on the grounds of the Kaba Aye (World Peace) **Pagoda** in **Rangoon** (**Yangon**), it brought together learned members of the **Sangha** and completed its task by 1956. The Council, which is also known as the Sixth Buddhist Synod, coincided with the 2,500th anniversary of the attainment of *nibbana* by **Gotama Buddha**. *See also* GREAT BUDDHIST COUNCIL, FIFTH.

GREATER MEKONG SUBREGION (GMS). A scheme promoted by the Asian Development Bank (ADB) to develop infrastructure, including roads, waterways, and electric power generation, to achieve the economic integration of countries connected by the **Mekong River**. Six countries fall within the GMS: Burma, Cambodia, **China** (Yunnan Province), Laos, **Thailand**, and Vietnam. One of the planned initiatives of the GMS is the "East-West Economic Corridor," which would be an overland route connecting the Andaman and the South China Seas, running from Burma by way of Thailand and Laos to Vietnam. Through the GMS regional context, the Asian Development Bank has been giving modest amounts of official development assistance to Burma, despite the fact that some countries on the ADB's governing board have imposed formal or informal **sanctions** on the **State Peace and Development Council**. *See also* AID, FOREIGN.

– H –

HAKA (HAKHA). The capital of **Chin State**, with a population estimated at 15,496 in 1996. Located in the central part of the state, it was the homeland of the Haka or Lai tribe of the **Chins**, served as a center of administration for the southern Chin Hills during the British colonial period, and was where American Baptist **missionaries** established their headquarters in 1899. The former capital of Chin State was Falam, located to the north.

HANTHAWADDY (HONGSAWADDY). The most important city-state established by the **Mons**, ca. 825 CE, and now known as **Pegu**

(**Bago**), on the river of the same name. According to legend, Gotama **Buddha** on his travels in the area saw two Brahminy ducks (*hongsa* in the **Mon Language**) perched on a rock, the male supporting the female, and prophesized that this would be the site of a great nation. The Hinthagone **Pagoda** marks the spot. Hanthawaddy's golden age was in the 15th century, when it was the capital of a powerful Mon state, and again in the 16th century, when the **Burman (Bamar)** rulers **Tabinshwehti** and **Bayinnaung** made it the capital of a unified Burma. According to 16th-century European witnesses, it was one of the richest ports in Southeast Asia, a rival of Malacca and Ayuthaya. But **Alaungpaya** sacked the city in 1757, and it declined in importance, not only because of the war and the depopulation of **Lower Burma** but also the progressive silting of the Pegu River. *See also* BINNYA DALA; DHAMMAZEDI; KYAIK; RAZADARIT; SHINSAWBU; SHWEMAWDAW PAGODA; SMIM DAW BUDDHAKETI.

HAW. The residence of a *sawbwa* (*sao-pha*), a traditional **Shan (Tai)** ruler. In the smaller of the **Shan States**, these were often rather simple wooden structures, but others were quite elaborate, made of teak and modeled on the **Mandalay Palace**, with a central spire or *pyatthat* elevated above the central throne room. During the British colonial period, some of the wealthier *sawbwas*, such as the rulers of **Keng Tung, Hsipaw**, and **Yawnghwe**, built palaces that combined traditional, Western, and Indian designs. To the distress of the Shan people, the Keng Tung *haw* was demolished in 1991 by the **State Law and Order Restoration Council** to make may for a tourist hotel. Other *haw*, like the one in Yawnghwe, remain in a state of neglect. *See also* ARCHITECTURE, TRADITIONAL.

HEALTH. Burma, like neighboring Asian countries, has a sophisticated tradition of indigenous medicine, and many long-established customs, such as frequent bathing and a diet rich in fruits and vegetables, are healthful. But the history of modern public health services began during the British colonial period. After independence, the governments of U **Nu** and **Ne Win** invested significant resources in health facilities in accordance with the socialist principle that they should be available to all. From 1962 to 1988, when the **Burma Socialist Programme Party (BSPP)** was in power, the number of trained physicians, nurses, and midwives increased 300 to 500 percent, and the number of hospitals almost doubled. Medical care was free in principle, although of a rather low standard. Since the **State Law and Order Restoration Council (SLORC)** seized power in September 1988, both the quality and availability of health care for the great majority of Burmese people has declined dramatically. This is because smaller percentages of government budgets are allocated to health compared to the BSPP years (while military-related spending has grown dramatically), and because the old system of public hospitals and clinics has been allowed to deteriorate. Since 1988, people with money have patronized expensive, private sector hospitals, and **Tatmadaw** personnel have their own relatively well-equipped system of hospitals and clinics.

Three other factors have also had a negative impact on health standards: the growing expense of food, including **rice**, which has led to widespread malnutrition among poor people, especially children; the Tatmadaw's stepped-up pacification of ethnic minority areas, where people are often subjected to **forced relocation** and **forced labor**; and growth in the **sex industry** and the use of **heroin**, which have created an epidemic of **AIDS**. According to a 2000 report by the World Health Organization (WHO), Burma ranked 139 out of 191 countries listed in terms of the population's overall health. Life expectancy at birth for both sexes, 55.8 years, is low by regional standards (Thailand's is 71.2 years), while rates of infant, child, and childbirth death are high. There are grave shortages of physicians, nurses, and equipment at most hospitals, and patients often have to buy their own medicines on the **black market**.

At present, malaria surpasses even AIDS as a serious public health threat, not only because of inadequate facilities, but because treatment-resistant strains of the mosquito-borne parasite have emerged, especially in the mountainous region along the Thai–Burma border. **Refugees** and forcibly relocated persons in the border areas, including many **Karens (Kayins)**, **Karennis**, and **Shans**, are especially vulnerable. In Burma, most cases of malaria (according to one source, 85 percent) are of the potentially lethal *P. falciparum* variety. Tuberculosis is also widespread, according to WHO statistics reported in 2002, causing 85,000 new cases and 20,000 deaths a year. Other widespread diseases include dengue fever, dysentery, and hepatitis.

Since 1991, a number of international **nongovernmental organizations** have worked in Burma's health sector, though under restrictive conditions imposed by the military regime. Because of the country's many health emergencies, the issue of humanitarian aid has become controversial. Some groups, such as the **National Coalition Government of the Union of Burma** and ALTSEAN-Burma, argue that humanitarian aid should not be given unless it is in consultation with the **National League for Democracy** and without **State Peace and Development Council (SPDC)** involvement; aid given in border areas should be strictly monitored by independent observers. Critics of this position, such as the International Crisis Group, say that the health crisis is too serious for aid to be subject to "political" conditions, and that it should be given even through SPDC-controlled channels. *See also* EDUCATION; POPULATION.

HEARN KHAM, SAO NANG (1915–2003). *Mahadevi* (chief queen) of the **Shan State** of **Yawnghwe**, prominent member of parliament, and leader of a **Shan (Tai)** insurgent movement during the 1960s. The daughter of the formidable **Khunsang Ton-Huung** of Hsenwi, she married Sao **Shwe Taik**, *Sawbwa* of Yawnghwe, in 1937 and was Burma's first lady when her husband served as president of the Union from 1948 to 1952. As a member of parliament during the mid-1950s, she strongly advocated Shan interests. She was overseas when **Ne Win** seized power and closed down parliamentary government on March 2, 1962, and imprisoned her husband. She returned to Burma following his death in November 1962, and the following year escaped with her five children to Thailand, where she became chairperson of the War Council of the original Shan State Army. She held that post until 1969, when she emigrated to Canada.

HEROIN. A narcotic derived and refined from the latex of the **opium** poppy (*Papaver somniferum*). Its various grades, usually injected into the bloodstream with a needle, are much stronger and more addictive than opium, which is usually smoked. Not only are large amounts of heroin refined in laboratories inside Burma and exported to foreign countries, but heroin addiction has also become a serious domestic problem. Although some heroin abuse was recorded in Burma's larger cities during the **Ne Win** era (1962–1988), it expanded rapidly after the **State Law and Order Restoration Council (SLORC)** seized power in 1988 because of greater availability, the result in large measure of **cease-fires** negotiated between the SLORC and drug-dealing armed groups, especially the **United Wa State Army.** While rumors that **Military Intelligence** encouraged heroin use among college students in order to demoralize them are unsubstantiated, addiction rates have been high among unemployed youth and students left idle by the closure of universities during the 1990s. Addiction is also widespread among miners, especially at the **Hpakant** mine in **Kachin State**, where jadeite is extracted. The United Nations Drug Control Program estimates that there are a half million opium, heroin, and synthetic drug addicts in Burma. Because the needles used to inject heroin are reused, often many times, under very unsanitary conditions, heroin addiction has been the major factor in the rapid spread of **AIDS**. *See also* AMPHETAMINES.

HKAKABO RAZI. Burma's highest mountain, at 5,887 meters (19,309 feet); also the highest mountain in Southeast Asia. An extension of the eastern Himalaya range, it is located near the northern tip of **Kachin State**, overlooking the borders with China and India. Other high peaks in this region are Gamlang Razi, at 5,837 meters (19,144 feet); Dindaw Razi, at 5,466 meters (17,927 feet); and Sheankala Razi, at 5,000 meters (16,399 feet). Hkakabo Razi was known as the "Putao Knot" during the British colonial period, but it was little explored (**James G. Scott** does not mention it in his 1906 *Burma: A Handbook of Practical Information*). It was not climbed until September 1996, by a Burmese–Japanese team. All the higher mountains in this region are snow covered all year-round.

HLUTTAW. The Council of State in precolonial Burma, a major governmental institution during the later **Toungoo** and **Konbaung Dynasties**. It consisted of four *wungyi* ("great burden bearers"), senior ministers of state who together were responsible for the kingdom's administration and also tried important legal cases. *See also* ADMINISTRATION AND SOCIETY, PRECOLONIAL BURMA.

HONGSA. The **Mon Language** name of the Brahminy Duck or Golden Sheldrake, known as *hamsa* in **Pali** and *hintha* in the

Burmese Language. Much as the **peacock** is the symbol of the **Burmans**, the Brahminy Duck is the symbol of the **Mons**, associated with the legendary founding of the city of **Hanthawaddy** (modern-day **Pegu [Bago]**). The bird is esteemed for having only one mate during its lifetime. In **Lower Burma**, where many **pagodas** such as the **Shwe Dagon** were built by the Mons, the *hongsa* is a common motif, often depicted atop "prayer posts."

HPAKANT. The world's major source of the high-quality jadeite, the blue-green stone that has been esteemed in China for millennia. The open-pit mines at Hpakant, located west of the state capital of **Myitkyina** in **Kachin State**, produce a grade of jadeite considered superior in quality even to stones found in China itself. Few foreigners have seen the mine; **gemstones** are a state monopoly, and access is tightly controlled by the **Tatmadaw**. As many as half a million desperately poor miners work there under harsh conditions, drawn by the hope of making their fortune. Described by one journalist as "Burma's black heart," Hpakant's mostly male population suffers high rates of **heroin** addiction and **AIDS**.

HPOUN. Sometimes *hpon* or *pon*, an important concept in Burmese social and political life that is frequently translated as "glory" but more accurately means the possession of powerbecause of the accumulation of merit (*kutho*) in past lives. Although a person with *hpoun* may act in violent or immoral ways, this is not seen as delegitimizing his power, since it has already been "earned" in previous existences. Thus, power, or the holding of it, is equivalent to authority. This concept supports a conservative, hierarchical society in which opposition to abuses of power rarely occurs. **Ne Win**'s success in holding onto power from 1962 to 1988 despite economic stagnation, ethnic minority insurgency, and his regime's violations of **human rights**, was sometimes explained in terms of his possession of abundant *hpoun*. Males are said to possess special *hpoun*, which may be damaged if they find themselves in a subordinate position to a **woman**. In part, this explains the antipathy of the **State Peace and Development Council** to Daw **Aung San Suu Kyi**.

Victory in battle, no matter how cruelly the defeated are treated, capture of sacred objects, such as the **Maha Muni Image**, or possession of sacred **white elephants** were traditionally viewed as signs of *hpoun* in rulers. Defeat, assassination, or some other calamity was a sign that the ruler's store of merit had been exhausted. Many observers see the hierarchy and inequality inherent in the concept of *hpoun* as a major obstacle to the development of democratic values in contemporary Burma. However, true members of the **Sangha** possess abundant *hpoun* (thus, they are known as *hpoungyi* or *pongyi*, "great glory") and dedicate themselves to a blameless spiritual life. Moreover, the ideal ruler, as defined by the Buddhist Ten Duties of the King, was expected to rule justly and compassionately, like the Indian Emperor Asoka (268–233 BCE).

HSENWI. One of the major **Shan States**, bordered on the north by China's Yunnan Province, on the east by **Kokang**, and on the south and west by the Shan states of **Hsipaw**, Mongmit, and South Hsenwi. In the 1950s, it covered an area of 16,685 square kilometers (6,442 square miles) and had a population of 240,000, including **Shans (Tai)**, **Kachins**, and other ethnic minority groups. The major town is **Lashio**, the railhead for the **Burma Road** during **World War II**. In the late 1880s, the British recognized **Khunsang Ton-huung** as (North) Hsenwi's *sawbwa*, while giving South Hsenwi to his rival Sao Mong, son of the old *sawbwa* of Hsenwi, who had attempted to overthrow Ton-huung with the aid of the Burmese.

HSINBYUSHIN, KING (r. 1763–1776). Third king of the **Konbaung Dynasty** and son of its founder, **Alaungpaya**. His reign was marked by military aggression and many victories, including capturing and pillaging the Siamese capital of Ayuthaya in March 1767. Its complete destruction (the ruins of its temples and palaces can still be seen today) inspired a Siamese chronicler to write that, "the King of **Hanthawaddy** [**Bayinnaung**] waged war like a monarch; the King of **Ava** [Hsinbyushin] like a robber." Prior to this conquest, he had subjugated Chiang Mai and Vientiane (Laos). But his expansion into the **Shan States** aroused **China**, which launched four unsuccessful punitive campaigns against him between 1766 and 1769, including one led by a son-in-law of the Chinese emperor that got within 48 kilometers (30 miles) of **Ava (Inwa)** before being routed. Hsinbyushin's commander, General Maha Thiha Thura, signed a treaty with the Chinese in 1770 at Kaungton that stabilized relations but angered the king, who wanted the Chinese force exterminated. He invaded the small state of **Manipur** in northeastern **India**, placing his nominee on the throne, but the war in Siam (**Thailand**) was going badly, and the **Mons** staged uprisings in **Lower Burma**. Siam, which grew powerful under the Chakri Dynasty established in 1782, was never again conquered by the Burmese. *See also* KENG TUNG.

HSIPAW (THIBAW). One of the most important of the old **Shan States**, located in the northern part of modern **Shan State**, near **Lashio**. It comprised 11,891 square kilometers (4,591 square miles), and because of its geographic proximity to **Upper Burma** was deeply influenced by Burmese culture. Its *sawbwas* were tributaries of the **Toungoo** and **Konbaung Dynasties**. Well endowed with natural resources, it was one of the few Shan States to be opened to rail transportation during the colonial period, including the Goktheik Viaduct, which, when it was built over 100 years ago by American engineers, was the world's second-highest railway bridge. An important aspect of local commerce was the trade in tea, grown by upland **Palaungs**. The Bawgyo **Pagoda**, located near Hsipaw town, is one of the most important Buddhist sites in Shan State. The last *sawbwa* of Hsipaw, the Western-educated Sao Kya Hseng, was an outspoken critic of **Tatmadaw** abuses in his state, and he disappeared after **Ne Win** closed down parliamentary government in March 1962. Inge Sargent, an Austrian national who was the Hsipaw *Mahadevi* (the *sawbwa's* chief queen), wrote about her experiences in Hsipaw in *Twilight over Burma: My Life as a Shan Princess*.

HTI. "Umbrella" in Burmese, referring to parasols and rain umbrellas. The town of **Bassein (Pathein)** is famous for umbrellas, including waterproofed saffron-colored ones used by Buddhist monks. In precolonial Burma, umbrellas were also a sign of status, the nine-tiered white umbrella being used exclusively by the king, while other colors and sizes were reserved for high ministers, lower-ranking officials, and commoners according to a precise set of sumptuary laws. *Hti* also refers to the finial that adorns **pagodas**, which resembles the royal umbrella and—in the case of the more famous pagodas, such as the **Shwe Dagon**—is richly adorned with gold, jewels, small Buddha images, and thousands of small bells that make an agreeable sound when the wind blows. Burmese monarchs frequently donated *hti* to prominent pagodas; the *hti* were installed with great ceremony and celebration when a pagoda was newly built or renovated. *See also* SHWE DAGON PAGODA, ARCHITECTURE AND LAYOUT; SHWE DAGON PAGODA, POLITICAL SIGNIFICANCE OF.

HUKAWNG VALLEY. A lowland area, comprising approximately 20,720 square kilometers (8,000 square miles), located in northern **Kachin State**. The name derives from *ju-kawng*, meaning "cremation grounds" in the Jinghpaw **Kachin** language, referring to the place where the bodies of **Shans** slain by Kachins were burned. During **World War II**, it earned the epithet "Valley of Death" because many people perished there while trying to reach India to escape the invading Japanese. Since the 1960s, it has been under the control of the **Kachin Independence Army/Organization**, though decreasingly so since the KIA signed a **cease-fire** with the **State Law and Order Restoration Council** in 1994. The Hukawng Valley has deposits of amber and gold, which are being extensively worked by prospectors, and large forests, which are being rapidly depleted. Recently, the Forest Department of the central government established a wildlife sanctuary in the valley that covers its entire extent and makes the Hukawng Valley the world's largest tiger reserve.

HUMAN RIGHTS IN BURMA. Although violations of basic human rights were widespread during the **Ne Win** era (1962–1988), especially in ethnic minority areas, such as **Karen (Kayin)** and **Shan States**, human rights in Burma did not become an issue of major international concern until 1988, when the **State Law and Order Restoration Council** seized power and suppressed the popular movements of **Democracy Summer** with great brutality. Monitoring by the **UN** High Commission for Human Rights, government agencies, such as the **U.S.** Department of State, international **nongovernmental organizations**, such as Amnesty International and Human Rights Watch, and Burmese groups, such as the Shan Human Rights Foundation and the Karen Human Rights Group, has revealed systematic abuse in practically every category of the 1949 Universal Declaration of Human Rights. The **State Peace and Development**

Council (SPDC) has one of the poorest records on rights worldwide, reflecting the absence of a consistent and fair rule of law and the junta's conviction that **national unity** can only be achieved through force.

The SPDC uses an array of laws, such as the 1950 Emergency Provisions Act, the Unlawful Associations Act, and the Law to Safeguard the State from the Dangers of Those Desiring to Cause Subversive Acts, to detain and imprison nonviolent oppositionists, especially members of the **National League for Democracy (NLD)**. Once in jail, political prisoners, who are estimated to number around 1,600, are frequently subjected to torture and solitary confinement and receive little or no medical care. Many have died in prison. Often, those who are detained for long periods of time are not even formally charged or tried before a judge (most famously Daw **Aung San Suu Kyi**, who had been put under house arrest three times as of 2005). Political prisoners sometimes have their sentences arbitrarily extended while in jail. Outside of jail, dissidents are frequently bullied or attacked by members of the progovernment **Union Solidarity and Development Association**, who were involved in the **"Black Friday" Incident** of May 30, 2003. The SPDC has resorted to a wide variety of obstructive tactics to prevent the NLD and other moderate groups from engaging in ordinary political activities.

All publications are censored by the **Press Scrutiny Board**, and comments critical of the government are harshly punished, for example, the imprisonment of the comedian **Zargana** and the **Moustache Brothers** for satirical remarks made at the junta's expense. **Information technology** is carefully controlled, and Burma is one of the few Asian countries where access to the Internet is not widely available because of government restrictions. **Military Intelligence** informers keep a close watch on the population, especially university students, who were the core of the Democracy Summer protests, a system that creates widespread social distrust and alienation. The military has defrocked and imprisoned members of the **Sangha** who oppose them, contrary to Buddhist principles, which state that monks can only be expelled from the Order by their superiors. It has also ruled that members of the NLD and other political parties cannot be ordained as monks.

Official discrimination against members of ethnic and religious minorities has been a part of Burmese life since at least the Ne Win era, including indigenous groups, such as the **Karens (Kayins)**, **Karenni**, **Shans**, **Chins**, and **Kachins**, as well as descendants of people who came from the Indian Subcontinent during the British colonial period, most of whom are Muslim, Christian, or Hindu. A **Citizenship Law** passed in 1982 distinguishes among three unequal classes of citizens, with only the first group (descendants of people resident in Burma before the **First Anglo-Burmese War**) entitled to full privileges. Each Burmese citizen is required to carry a national identity card, which states his or her ethnicity and religion. Because these cards are necessary to secure permission to travel, conduct business, and perform other important tasks, ethnic and (especially) religious minorities are vulnerable to unfair treatment by government officials. The activities of non-Buddhist religious communities, especially Muslims of South Asian descent and ethnic minority Christians in the border areas, are tightly restricted (e.g., Muslims cannot construct new mosques, while old ones are sometimes demolished). In 1978 and again in late 1991, 200,000–300,000 Muslim **Rohingyas**, residents of **Arakan State**, were forced to flee to **Bangladesh** because of **Tatmadaw** persecution.

Crimes against **women** by the military are widespread, especially in ethnic minority areas, such as **Shan State**, and appear to be systematic, despite heated denials by the SPDC. In insurgent controlled or contested areas, soldiers frequently subject village women to violent sexual abuse, and the arbitrary killing of men, women, and children is not uncommon. Life has become so difficult for minority communities that hundreds of thousands of **refugees** have fled to **Thailand** and other neighboring countries, where they struggle to survive in refugee camps or as illegal aliens.

"Welfare rights" are largely ignored, as the government allocates at least 45 percent of total spending to the military while neglecting **education** and **health**. The quality of hospitals, clinics, and schools has declined since the end of Ne Win socialism in 1988. Between 1962 and 1988, a minimum, though not necessarily high, standard of public education and health care were available to all. Now only those who can pay have access to adequate schools or health care. The government has not adopted a comprehensive strategy to combat the spread of **AIDS**, and hospitalized patients often have to buy their own medicine on the black market. Ninety-eight percent of schoolchildren drop out before finishing high school. Universities have been closed for long periods since 1988; when open, they operate under heavy restrictions. Lack of rational economic planning on the part of the government keeps both rural and urban populations desperately poor in an inflationary economy, spawning social problems such as the entry of poor women into the domestic and international **sex industry** and a flourishing **drug economy.**

Forced labor and **forced relocation** affect millions of Burmese, including both **Burmans** and ethnic minorities. The use of child soldiers in the Tatmadaw is also widespread, and insurgents recruit them as well.

The SPDC's reaction to international criticism of its human rights record has been to deny the allegations or argue that some practices, such as forced labor (described as labor contributions), are a part of Burma's traditions. At times, the government has shown some responsiveness to outside criticism, such as negotiating with the International Labour Organization over the issue of forced labor in 2000–2002, and allowing the International Committee of the Red Cross to visit political prisoners since 1999. The government of **Australia** has sent experts to train Burmese officials in human rights awareness. Since 1988, there has been little evidence that such concessions represent a significant change in junta attitudes about basic human rights. *See also* INSEIN JAIL; MIN KO NAING; TATMADAW AND BURMESE SOCIETY.

– I –

IMPHAL CAMPAIGN (MARCH–JUNE 1944). An offensive into northeastern India (now Manipur and Nagaland States) carried out by the Japanese Fifteenth Army under the command of Lieutenant-General Mutaguchi Renya. Its purpose was to cut off India–China supply routes, occupy the Imphal Plain, and inspire an uprising of Indian patriots against British colonialism. For this purpose, the attacking force included the Indian National Army, numbering 40,000, commanded by Subhas Chandra Bose. Intense fighting took place, especially around Imphal and Kohima, and conditions were made hellish by the monsoon rains and mountainous topography. But the British lines, supplied by airdrops, held. The Fifteenth Army was forced to retreat out of India and across the **Chindwin (Chindwinn) River** in June–July. The failure of the campaign, which cost the Japanese as many as 80,000 casualties, opened the way for Allied reoccupation of Burma the following year. In the words of Christopher Bayly, "[T]he Japanese army thrown against Imphal and Kohima was a kind of mass suicide squad. When it was defeated by the vastly increased firepower of the British and Indian armies and American air power, it was cast aside and abandoned by its commanders" (*Forgotten Armies*, 2004, 388). *See also* WORLD WAR II IN BURMA (MILITARY OPERATIONS).

INDAWGYI LAKE. Located in western **Kachin State**; the largest lake in Burma, with an area of 210 square kilometeres (81 square miles). To the northeast the Indaw River flows out of it to join the Mogaung River.

INDIA AND BURMA. The civilization of India has profoundly influenced the development of the cultures and societies of Southeast Asia, the region's "Indianization" having begun more than two millennia ago. The Indian impact was especially strong in lowland areas, where an agricultural economy based on **rice** emerged, and where such powerful, organized states as Angkor in Cambodia; Ayuthaya in Siam (**Thailand**); and **Pagan (Bagan)**, **Hanthawaddy**, and **Arakan (Rakhine)** in Burma were established. Although Theravada **Buddhism** was the most important element in Indian civilization adopted by early Burmese states, they also adopted classical Indian political ideas, law, sciences, medicine, literature, writing systems, **architecture**, and visual and **performing arts**, in order to enhance their power and prestige. Although there are no indigenous Burmese Hindus (as distinguished from Hindus of Indian ancestry), and Burma did not adopt the Indian caste system, Hindu influences on Burmese Buddhism have been significant. Many of Burma's most important *nats* are Hindu gods, such as **Thagya Min**, the divine protector of the Buddhist religion, and Thurathadi (Saraswati), goddess of learning. **Pali**, the sacred language of Theravada Buddhism, is an Indian language and has had a deep impact on the **Burmese (Myanmar) language**.

The **Arakan (Rakhine) Yoma** poses a formidable barrier to land communication between central Burma and the Indian Subcontinent, but seaborne trade and migration from South Asia helped bring Buddhism and Indian civilization to Burmese shores. The **Mons**, who established organized states in **Lower Burma** in the early centuries CE, played an indispensable role in transmitting Indian civilization to the **Burmans**. A key player in this process was the founder of the **Pagan (Bagan) Dynasty**, King **Anawrahta** (r. 1044–1077), who brought Mon monks, scholars, and artisans from Lower Burma to his capital at Pagan.

In later centuries, kingdoms in Sri Lanka, sharing with Burma a strong adherence to Theravada Buddhism, probably had a greater impact on Burma than the Subcontinent. Following the **Third Anglo-Burmese War**, however, Lower and **Upper Burma** became a province of the British Indian empire, governed by the Viceroy in Calcutta. The struggle for home rule and independence of the Indian National Congress had a major influence on nationalist movements in Burma, which was less modernized socially and politically than India in the early twentieth century, but Mahatma Gandhi's principle of nonviolent struggle (*satyagraha*) was not popular with members of the **Dobama Asiayone**, the most important prewar nationalist group. *See also* INDIA, RELATIONS WITH.

INDIA, RELATIONS WITH. Independence leader **Aung San** and Prime Minister U **Nu** were close to India's prime minister, Jawaharlal Nehru, sharing the common experience of struggle against British colonial rule. Nehru's and U Nu's governments also shared a commitment to nonalignment in foreign policy and moderate socialism. The Burma–India border was relatively unproblematic, and a joint boundary commission was established only in 1967; by 1976, most of the 1,600-kilometer-long, mountainous border had been demarcated.

When **Ne Win** seized power in March 1962, relations were strained because the **Burma Socialist Programme Party (BSPP)** regime's nationalization and **demonetization** policies appeared to target Indian businesspeople. The latter petitioned the Indian government for help, but New Delhi ascertained that because the BSPP policies affected all people resident in Burma and not just Indians, it could not interfere. Approximately 300,000 South Asians (including both Indians and Pakistanis) were repatriated between 1963 and 1967; Burma offered them some compensation in the early 1970s. U Nu's residence in India from 1974 to 1980 caused additional tensions because the former prime minister had led a Thailand-based antigovernment insurgency.

Following **Democracy Summer** and the seizure of power by the **State Law and Order Restoration Council** in September 1988, India was the only Asian country that was outspokenly supportive of the prodemocracy movement. Along with the British Broadcasting Corporation and the Voice of America, All India Radio (AIR) provided listeners in Burma with crucial information on the domestic political situation. When two Burmese students hijacked a **Rangoon (Yangon)**-bound Thai airliner to Calcutta in late 1990, Indian officials treated them leniently, releasing them on bail.

By 1991–1992, however, New Delhi's policy had begun to change, as reflected in the halting of critical AIR broadcasts. Although the Indian government continued to give moral support to the prodemocracy movement (**Aung San Suu Kyi** was awarded the prestigious Jawaharlal Nehru Award for International Understanding in 1995), trade ties with Burma were promoted, and high-level meetings of Indian and Burmese officials became more frequent, including a visit by General **Maung Aye**, second most powerful figure in the **State Peace and Development Council**, in November 2000. Three factors account for India's growing reliance on constructive engagement. First, New Delhi feared that **China** was gaining too much influence over the SLORC. Indian leaders were alarmed at the volume of Chinese military aid to the **Tatmadaw**, including modernization of naval bases fronting the Andaman Sea and the Gulf of Bengal. Plans announced by Beijing in 1997 to construct a new transportation corridor from Yunnan Province by way of the **Irrawaddy (Ayeyarwady) River** to Kyaukpyu in **Arakan (Rakhine) State** were another source of concern, though these plans have yet to be put in action. From New Delhi's perspective, it seems that China has been using Burma to challenge India's mastery of the Indian Ocean.

Second, insurgents belonging to the **National Socialist Council of Nagaland (NSCN)** had long used Burmese soil as a sanctuary in their attacks on Indian security forces, while the **Chin National**

Front, which has not signed a **cease-fire** with the SPDC, has bases in India's Mizoram State, where the local people are ethnically the same as the **Chins**. Agreements between the Indian and Burmese militaries have enabled them to carry out joint operations against these groups and to more effectively halt the flow of Burmese drugs across the Indian border. To develop the border area, India has given aid to construct infrastructure, such as an Indo-Myanmar Friendship Road connecting **Chin State** with Moreh in Mizoram.

Third, India now has substantial economic interests in Burma. Two-way trade in 1997–1998 totaled US$264.7 million. Principal Burmese exports to India are beans, pulses, and wood products, while Burma imports manufactured goods, such as iron and steel, pharmaceuticals, and chemicals. Trade also flourishes at the border. In 2004, it was announced that a natural gas field, the "Shwe [Gold] Prospect" in the Bay of Bengal off **Arakan State**, which is being developed by South Korean and Indian oil firms in cooperation with the Myanmar Oil and Gas Enterprise, would start production in 2009, providing India with natural gas piped either through Arakan to Assam or by way of **Bangladesh** to West Bengal. The Shwe Prospect will provide much-needed energy for India's rapid industrialization and earn the SPDC between US$800 million and US$3 billion in profits each year. India and Burma are both members of the **BIMSTEC** ("Bangladesh, India, Myanmar, Sri Lanka and Thai Economic Cooperation) group. *See also* INDIA AND BURMA.

INDIANS IN BURMA. During the British colonial era, the Indian population of Burma ("Indian" in this context refers to South Asians, persons from what are now **India, Bangladesh**, and Pakistan) increased rapidly because to British encouragement of immigration to provide cheap labor for the modern colonial economy and Indians' perception that the country was a land of opportunity, where they could escape the crushing poverty of home. Even after the **Government of Burma Act** was implemented in 1937, separating Burma from India, there were no effective curbs on Indian immigration until the eve of **World War II**. According to the 1931 census, Indians numbered more than one million, mostly in **Lower Burma**, and comprised 7 percent of the country's total population. **Rangoon (Yangon)** was primarily a South Asian city: 54.9 percent of its people came from the Subcontinent, outnumbering **Chinese** and Europeans, not to mention indigenous Burmese (33.1 percent).

Known as *kala* to the Burmese, a word with negative connotations, Burma's Indian population reflected the diversity of the Subcontinent: among them were impoverished Tamil and Oriya laborers, who worked on farms and factories, as coolies on the dockyards and sweepers in the city streets; Bengalis, many of whom were lower-level civil servants or professionals; Chittagongians, who came over to **Arakan (Rakhine)** from what is now Bangladesh; Sikhs and Gurkhas (the latter from Nepal), who served as soldiers or policemen; and South Indian **Chettiars**, a wealthy money-lending class who provided Burmese farmers with credit. Relations between Burmese and Indians were generally hostile, not only because of the latter's large numbers and cultural and religious differences (most Indians were Hindu or Muslim), but also because poor Burmese competed with Indians for jobs during the 1930s. The Chettiars were intensely disliked, especially after bad economic conditions led to foreclosures of family farms and they became major absentee landowners. Burmese nationalists feared that the unrestricted flow of Indian immigrants would result in the extinction of their race, and opposed marriages between Burmese women and Hindu or Muslim men more vehemently than those with Chinese or Europeans. Bloody **anti-Indian riots** broke out in Rangoon in 1930 and 1938.

When the Japanese invaded and occupied Burma in 1941–1942, as many as 600,000 Indians escaped overland and by sea to British territory, apparently fearing massacres at the hands of the Burmese; of these, 80,000 are estimated to have died, including those who attempted to reach Bengal or Assam State by way of the **Arakan (Rakhine) Yoma** or the mountain ranges separating Burma from northeastern India. After **Ne Win** established the **Revolutionary Council**, he enacted socialist policies that targeted businesspeople of South Asian origin, forcing the repatriation of as many as 300,000 of them to India and Pakistan between 1963 and 1967. By 1983, when the last official census was held, the South Asian population was much diminished: Indians, Chinese, and other persons of nonindigenous ancestry altogether comprised only 7.4 percent of Rangoon's population.

Despite Burmese–Indian antagonisms, some Indians, such as U Raschid, played an important role in the nationalist movement, and many nationalists were influenced by the ideas of Mahatma Gandhi and the Indian National Congress. *See also* CHINESE IN BURMA; INDIA, RELATIONS WITH; MUSLIMS IN BURMA; PLURAL SOCIETY.

INDONESIA, RELATIONS WITH. Although there have been business and investment connections between Indonesia and Burma since the establishment of the latter's postsocialist economy in 1988–1989, arguably the most important impact of bilateral ties has been political: the **State Law and Order Restoration Council/State Peace and Development Council**'s attempt to adopt a version of President Soeharto's doctrine of *dwi fungsi* ("two functions"), vesting the military with a social/political development role, as well as a national defense role. This is reflected in the principles adopted by the **National Convention**, including granting the **Tatmadaw** a given number of seats in the national legislature under a new constitution. Although the fall of Soeharto in May 1998 meant the end of *dwi fungsi* in its home country, the concept remains important in the SPDC's plans for a future political system. The government of post-Soeharto Indonesia, Southeast Asia's largest country and a fellow member of the **Association of Southeast Asian Nations,** has occasionally criticized the SPDC, especially over the issue of the house arrest of **Aung San Suu Kyi,** but its basic policy remains noninterference in the domestic affairs of fellow ASEAN members.

INFORMATION TECHNOLOGY (IT) IN BURMA. The seizure of power by the **State Law and Order Restoration Council (SLORC)** in September 1988 occurred on the eve of the "revolution" in information technology that made the Internet and electronic mail available around the world. By the mid-1990s, "cyberactivism," organized by Burmese exiles and their supporters in North America, Europe, and Asia, played an indispensable role in promoting cooperation among widely disbursed Burmese democracy groups, as well as informing the general public and policy makers about Burma issues. Although in the early 1990s exile groups produced and distributed a wide variety of hardcopy newsletters, such as *Burma Issues,* by the end of the decade most of these groups were online.

In 1993, an American student based in **Thailand** started *BurmaNet,* placing articles from the *Bangkok Post* and *Nation* on the Internet; these two Thai newspapers provided the most reliable English-language information about Burma. *BurmaNet* grew rapidly and was joined by *The Irrawaddy*, a hardcopy magazine also based in Thailand that began providing an extensive online edition. At the beginning of the 21st century, both of these online services and several others provide information on a daily basis about the latest developments inside the country, as reflected in their coverage of the **"Black Friday" Incident** of May 30, 2003. Cybercampaigns have also been organized by the Free Burma Coalition and other groups to support the Massachusetts Selective Purchasing Law and boycotts of companies, such as Pepsi Cola, that have done business with the post-1988 military regime. In the late 1990s, the **State Peace and Development Council** began to sponsor its own website ("Myanmar.com"), which now includes an online edition of the slick *Myanmar Times and Business Review*.

Fearful that a flood of electronically delivered information could cause unrest, the SLORC in September 1996 decreed the "Computer Science Development Law," which imposes heavy penalties (7 to 15 years' imprisonment and fines) on persons who operate a computer without obtaining a license from the Ministry of Communications, Posts and Telegraphs. It prohibits the use of computers to "undermine State Security," and established a "Myanmar Computer Science Development Council," chaired by SLORC Secretary-1 Lieutenant General **Khin Nyunt**, to oversee the IT sector.

Although the law is concerned specifically with computers, harsh punishments have been dealt out for the use of lower-tech information devices as well. In 1996, the authorities arrested James Leander Nichols, honorary consul for Norway and Denmark in **Rangoon (Yangon)** and a close friend of Daw **Aung San Suu Kyi** and her family, for illegal possession of two fax machines and a telephone switchboard. Sentenced to three years in prison with hard labor, he died at **Insein Jail** under mysterious circumstances.

Burma was one of the few Asian countries where e-mail and the Internet were not widely available, but in 2001 the SPDC allowed limited access. All Internet and e-mail transmissions pass through government-controlled servers, which block sensitive sites. In 2002, the regime, in cooperation with private computer firms, established an Information and Communications Technology (ICT) Park on what had been the Hlaing Campus of **Rangoon (Yangon) University**, and opened a second ICT park at the Yadanabon Market in **Mandalay**. Like many authoritarian states, the SPDC would like to reap the economic benefits of IT while avoiding the political risks. *See also* HUMAN RIGHTS IN BURMA.

INLE LAKE. Located in western **Shan State**, home to the **Intha** people and since British colonial days one of Burma's major tourist attractions. Inle Lake extends in a north-south direction, is approximately 17–18 kilometers long and 5–6 kilometers wide, and is at an elevation of 875 meters above sea level. Its shores and islands are densely populated, with about 150,000 people living there, and the area is a major producer of **rice**, vegetables, and fruit. Many crops are grown on "floating islands," which are masses of soil tied together with strands of water hyacinth. It is also a major center for silk weaving, comparable to **Amarapura**. The major town is **Yawnghwe (Nyaungshwe)**, the capital of one of the old **Shan States**. Best known to tourists for its "leg rowers," fishermen who use one leg to row their narrow wooden boats while dropping their conical nets over the fish below, Inle Lake is also the location of the **Phaung Daw U Paya**, an important **Shan (Tai)** Buddhist site.

INSEIN JAIL. Burma's largest prison, located in **Insein Township** in the northern part of **Rangoon (Yangon)**, near the Hlaing River. Built by the British in 1887, the extensive main prison is an octagonal structure with cell blocks radiating out from the center and surrounded by two brick walls. Before **World War II,** the British used it to confine leaders of the independence struggle, including Thakin **Than Tun**. Political prisoners continued to be housed there after the country became independent in 1948. Their numbers increased significantly during the **Ne Win** era (1962–1988), especially following the labor strike and U **Thant Incident** of 1974. A riot that broke out under mysterious circumstances in August 1988 led to the escape of many common criminals from the jail (and from eight other prisons around the country). The escapees roamed the city streets, sowing an atmosphere of fear and panic among ordinary citizens. This gave rise to suspicions that the breakouts had been arranged by the government to create the atmosphere for a military power seizure.

At present, Insein Jail has about 9,000–10,000 prisoners in the main and attached facilities. Of these, an estimated 1,600 are political prisoners. Although political prisoners received lenient treatment during the British and U **Nu** periods, since 1962 they have been singled out for harsh treatment, including torture, denial of adequate medical treatment, and solitary confinement. They often endure violence at the hands of ordinary criminals, including gangsters who serve in powerful "trusty" positions. Prominent oppositionists who have been confined there since 1988 include U **Tin U**, U **Kyi Maung**, and **Min Ko Naing**. Following the "**Black Friday**" Incident of May 30, 2003, **Aung San Suu Kyi** may have been confined there briefly. Other jails where political prisoners have been kept under severe conditions include those at Thayet and Tharrawaddy. *See also* HUMAN RIGHTS IN BURMA.

INSEIN TOWNSHIP. A township located in north **Rangoon (Yangon)**, its western border formed by the Hlaing River. An estimated 57 percent of its population of 250,000 are **Karen (Kayin)**, making this the largest concentration of Karens inside Burma's largest city and former capital (the name *Insein* itself is believed to be of Karen rather than Burmese origin). Because a majority of the resident Karens are Christian, the area is known for its many churches and "Seminary Hill," where three theological schools are located, including the Karen Baptist Theological Seminary. (There were reports in 2005 that the seminaries were being relocated to a remote location.) Insein is also the site of the notorious **Insein Jail**. In 1949, bitter fighting between **Karen National Union** forces and central government troops occurred in the township, and **Rangoon (Yangon) Institute of Technology** on Insein Road was the site of the initial student activism in 1988. *See also* MISSIONARIES, CHRISTIAN; TEA SHOP INCIDENT.

INTERNAL UNITY ADVISORY BOARD (IUAB). Established in 1968 by **Ne Win** to draw up plans for Burma's future political system; consisted of 33 veteran political and ethnic minority leaders, who were ordered to submit their recommendations by May 31, 1969. The majority favored a return to the **Constitution of 1947**, with amendments and retention of the semifederal system; a minority called for a "national unity congress" (presumably to draft a new constitution) and establishment of a one-party socialist state. Former prime minister U **Nu** submitted his own recommendations: Because the March 1962 coup d'état that ended parliamentary government was illegal, the old parliament should be reconvened, and U Nu as prime minister would formally transfer power to Ne Win. U Nu also called for restoration of democratic freedoms. His proposals were rejected, and he left the country, assuming leadership of a Thailand-based antigovernment insurgency. *See also* PARLIAMENTARY DEMOCRACY PARTY.

INTHAS. An ethnic minority group who lives on or around **Inle Lake**, in **Yawnghwe (Nyaungshwe)**, one of the old **Shan States**. Their name means "sons [children] of the lake." Known for their industriousness, they are skilled fishermen, weavers of silk, and farmers, constructing "floating islands" of soil tied together with water hyacinth strands, which are used to grow crops on the lake's surface. According to a widely accepted account, the Inthas came from **Tavoy (Dawei)** in what is now **Tenasserim (Tanintharyi) Division**, in the 14th century, their reputation for hard work recommending them to the local *sawbwa,* who encouraged their migration from the south. They speak a distinct dialect of the **Burmese (Myanmar) language**, and are devout **Buddhists**.

INVESTMENT, FOREIGN. Although a state-owned West **German** company, Fritz Werner, began operating inside Burma in the 1950s, manufacturing small arms for the **Tatmadaw**, and Japanese oil companies were involved in exploration in the Andaman Sea in the 1980s, there was no significant foreign private investment in the country during the **Burma Socialist Programme Party** period (1962–1988). In November 1988, the **State Law and Order Restoration Council**, following the precedents of **China** and Vietnam, decreed the "Union of Burma Foreign Investment Law," which granted foreign firms the right to establish branches, wholly owned subsidiaries, and joint ventures with state-owned or private Burmese firms. By 1998, more than US$6.8 billion in foreign investments had been committed, although the amount actually disbursed was much lower. The largest amounts were in the **oil and natural gas**, manufacturing, **tourism**, real estate, and mining sectors. However, by the late 1990s, investment had slackened because of the 1997 Asian financial crisis, Western **sanctions**, and political-economic uncertainty inside the country. The major sources of investment capital in the late 1990s were, in descending order of magnitude: **Singapore** (US$1.49 billion), **Britain** (US$1.35 billion), **Thailand** (US$1.24 billion), **Malaysia** (US$587 million), the **United States** (US$582 million), France (US$470 million), the Netherlands (US$238 million), **Indonesia** (US$236 million), and **Japan** (US$219 million). The largest single investment was the US$1.2 billion **Yadana Pipeline Project**, a French–American–Thai joint venture with the Myanmar Oil and Gas Enterprise to supply Thailand with natural gas. Investment statistics for 2003–2004 reveal commitments by **South Korea** ($34.9 million), Britain ($27 million), Thailand ($22 million), Hong Kong ($3 million), China ($2.8 million), and Canada ($1.5 million). Statistics on real Chinese investment since 1988 may be understated. *See also* ECONOMY AND ECONOMIC POLICY, STATE LAW AND ORDER RESTORATION COUNCIL/STATE PEACE AND DEVELOPMENT COUNCIL ERA.

INYA LAKE. Known during British colonial times as Victoria Lake, Inya Lake is a large body of water located in the north-central part of **Rangoon (Yangon)**, bounded on the east by Kaba Aye Pagoda Road and on the west by Pyay (Prome) Road. The Main Campus of **Rangoon (Yangon) University** lies to the lake's southwest, and on the shores of the lake are residences of prominent people, including Daw **Aung San Suu Kyi** and—before the **coup d'état attempt** of March 2002—the family of Burma's deceased ruler, **Ne Win**.

IRRAWADDY (AYEYARWADY) DIVISION. One of Burma's 14 **states** and **divisions**, with an area of 35,139 square kilometres (13,567 square miles) and an estimated population in 2000 of 6.8 million (1983 census figure: 4,994,061). The divisional capital is **Bassein (Pathein)**, and the division is divided into five **districts** (Bassein, Henzada [Hinthada], Ma-U-Bin, Myaungmya [Myoungmya], and Pyapon) and 26 **townships**. It is bounded on the north by **Pegu (Bago) Division**, on the northwest by **Arakan (Rakhine) State**, and on the east by **Rangoon (Yangon) Division**. The coastal region is formed by the delta of the **Irrawaddy (Ayeyarwady) River**.

The mostly flat land is formed by alluvium from the Irrawaddy River. Well watered and fertile, it is a major producer of **rice**; pulses, beans, oil seeds, and groundnuts are also grown. Fresh and marine water fisheries, mangrove forests, and jute are economically important. Irrawaddy Division is a major source of *ngapi*, a paste made from fish or shrimp that is a staple of the Burmese diet. Ethnically, **Burmans (Bamars)** form the majority of Irrawaddy Division's population, although there is also a large population of **Karens (Kayins)**, who are known as "Delta Karens," and smaller groups of **Arakanese (Rakhines), Chins**, and people of **Indian** and **Chinese** ancestry. Ancestors of the Delta Karens migrated from their native hills along the Thai–Burma border to what is now Irrawaddy Division in the 19th century, after the British opened up the land for rice cultivation. Although many Karens assimilated to Burmese culture, language, and religion, the Delta Karens, especially the Christians among them, played a leading role in developing Karen identity and "nationhood" during the late 19th and early 20th centuries. After Burma became independent, Irrawaddy Division was a site of the 1949 **Karen National Union** insurgency.

IRRAWADDY (AYEYARWADY) RIVER. Burma's largest river system; bisects the country in a north-south direction, linking **Upper** and **Lower Burma**. Its headwaters (the confluence of two smaller rivers) rise just north of **Myitkyina** in **Kachin State**, and it is navigable year round for a length of 1,448 kilometers (905 miles) between **Bhamo** and the sea. Over the centuries, the Irrawaddy has been the single most important geographic factor in central Burma's political, cultural, and economic integration: With the exception of **Pegu (Bago)**, all of Burma's major historical capitals have been located on or near it, including **Mandalay, Pagan, Ava (Inwa), Amarapura**, and **Sagaing. Rangoon (Yangon)** is connected to it by the Twante Canal. Even after the introduction of rail, air, and highway transport during the British colonial period, it has been the country's main commercial artery. In the early 20th century, the **Irrawaddy Flotilla Corporation** operated the world's largest fleet of riverboats and carried nine million passengers a year. The first bridge to span the river was the Ava Bridge, built by the British in 1934 but heavily damaged during **World War II**; the **Chinese** built a second bridge near **Prome (Pyay)** in 1998. With Chinese assistance, the river is being deepened with dredges, making it part of a new transportation system reaching from Yunnan Province to the Bay of Bengal (including a highway connecting a port on the river with the coast of **Arakan [Rakhine] State**). Just upriver from Pagan the Irrawaddy is joined by **Chindwin (Chindwinn) River**; to the south, the Irrawaddy Delta, which empties into the Andaman Sea, is large and fertile, providing an ideal environment for the cultivation of paddy **rice**. *See also* MEKONG RIVER; SALWEEN (THANLWIN) RIVER; SITTANG (SITTOUNG) RIVER.

IRRAWADDY FLOTILLA COMPANY. Established in 1865 as a public corporation. By the 1930s, the Scottish-owned Irrawaddy Flotilla Company operated the world's largest fleet of river boats, including 270 steamboats and 380 barges and "flats" on the **Irrawaddy (Ayeyarwady)** and other rivers in British Burma. Its "mail boats" were over 300 feet (100 meters) long and could hold more passengers than the R.M.S *Titanic*, most of these taking third class accommodation on the deck. Although the steamer captains were British, most of the crew were Chittagongians, from what is now **Bangladesh**. For a short period of time, the Irrawaddy Flotilla also operated a small airline that flew between **Rangoon (Yangon), Mandalay**, the oil fields in what is now **Magwe Division, Tavoy (Dawei)**, and **Mergui (Myeik)**. Enjoying privileged access to the colonial government, it operated a virtual monopoly that put many Burmese river boat operators out of business. The glory days of the Flotilla ended with **World War II**, when the British destroyed most of its boats and barges to prevent their falling into the hands of the Japanese. *See also* AIR TRANSPORT; WATER TRANSPORT.

– J –

JAPAN, RELATIONS WITH. Before **World War II**, Japan had rather small-scale trade and cultural relations with Burma. On the eve of the war, such prominent politicians as U **Saw** and **Ba Maw** cultivated friendly ties with Japanese diplomats and undercover agents as a means of gaining external support for the struggle against British colonialism, and the **Minami Kikan** gave military training to the **Thirty Comrades** led by **Aung San** in 1941; Colonel **Suzuki Keiji** established the **Burma Independence Army** as Burma's first postcolonial armed force in December of that year. The **Japanese occupation** from 1942 to 1945 transformed the country. The land was devastated in some of the largest land battles of the war; relations between the **Burmans** and the ethnic minorities, especially the **Karens**, became hostile because the latter remained largely loyal to the British; and the armed forces became a permanent fixture in postwar Burmese politics. As former Prime Minister **Khin Nyunt** once said, "[O]ur **Tatmadaw** was made in Japan." The occupation also gave Aung San and other nationalists the opportunity to organize in both a political and military way to successfully oppose reestablishment of a postwar British colonial regime. In that sense, Japan contributed significantly to Burma's independence in 1948, although Japanese rule, including the depredations of the *Kempeitai* (military police) and the death of as many as 50,000 Burmese laborers (*romusha*) on the **Thai–Burma Railway**, left many bitter memories.

After 1954, when the Union of Burma and Japan signed a treaty normalizing diplomatic relations, Japan's influence in the country was economic rather than military. Between that year and 1988, it was the country's largest donor of **foreign aid**, initially in the form of war reparations, totaling US$390 million. By the mid-1980s, Tokyo was disbursing hundreds of millions of U.S. dollars in aid annually, mostly in the form of concessional loans, for such projects as airport modernization, industrialization, infrastructure, electric power generation, and hospital construction. Major Japanese general trading companies (*sōgō shōsha*), such as Mitsubishi Shoji and Mitsui Bussan, maintained offices in **Rangoon (Yangon)**, not only to procure goods for official development assistance contracts awarded by the Japanese government, but also in the hope that the socialist economy of this resource-rich country would be liberalized. But when the socialist system was scrapped after the **State Law and Order Restoration Council** seized power in September 1988, bilateral relations entered a new and uncertain period.

The Japanese government froze its aid allocations for political, **human rights**, and financial reasons in late 1988, although it formally recognized the SLORC regime in February of the following year and allowed the resumption of some aid projects. Pressured by its major ally, the **United States**, Japan was reluctant to undertake full-scale economic engagement (that is, new large-scale aid), especially after the SLORC's house arrest of **Aung San Suu Kyi** in 1989 and its refusal to transfer power after the **General Election of May 27, 1990** aroused strong criticism from Washington and other Western governments. However, Japan did not enact **sanctions** against the regime, refraining from funding new aid projects but allowing old ones to continue on a case-by-case basis. After 1988, Tokyo also forgave much of Burma's yen-denominated debt through debt-relief grants. Inside Japan, many critics saw their government's Burma policy as ambiguous and opportunistic, but foreign ministry spokesmen claimed that although Japan and the United States shared the same goal, Burma's democratization, the means were different, that is, Japan was pursuing a "sunshine policy" rather than sanctions and harsh criticism. However, Japan's Burma policy was frequently difficult to decipher; for example, funds for modernization of Rangoon's **Mingaladon** Airport were disbursed under the inappropriate and confusing category "humanitarian aid" in the late 1990s.

China has gained influence in the country at Japan's expense since 1988. Presently, Japanese leaders emphasize the importance of deepening ties with the **Association of Southeast Asian Nations (ASEAN)** as a way of counteracting Beijing's growing influence in Southeast Asia as a whole; since Burma joined ASEAN in 1997, Tokyo's Burma policy has taken a regional, ASEAN perspective (for example, Khin Nyunt was invited to attend the Japan–ASEAN Summit in Tokyo in 2003 in his capacity as prime minister). With its rich natural resources, the country remains important to Japan's economic strategies.

Japanese often claim that Burma is the "friendliest country in Asia toward Japan" because of wartime experiences, a common religion (**Buddhism**), and shared values. Takeyama Michio's novel, *Harp of Burma*, a perennial best seller, is a sentimental story about Japanese soldiers' wartime sacrifices, and war veterans have visited the country regularly to collect the remains and pray over the graves of their fallen comrades. **Aung San Suu Kyi** studied at Kyoto University during the mid-1980s. Since 1988, 10,000 Burmese exiles, many of whom are active in the prodemocracy movement with the support of sympathetic Japanese citizens, have established residence in Japan. *See also* JAPANESE OCCUPATION: TATMADAW, HISTORY OF; WORLD WAR II IN BURMA (MILITARY OPERATIONS).

JAPANESE OCCUPATION (1941–1945). The Japanese invasion and occupation of Burma was motivated initially by the need to cut off the **Burma Road**, through which the **United States** and **Britain** provided supplies to the Chiang Kai-shek (Jiang Jyeshi) government in Chungking (Chongqing). Acquisition of the country's rich natural resources, especially **rice** and petroleum, was another major objective (though Allied submarines crippled the export of vital materiel to other parts of the Japanese Empire between 1942 and 1945). Burma was also used as a base from which to launch an invasion of northeastern India in March–June 1944, the **Imphal Campaign**.

Wartime administration of the country can be divided into three periods: January–May 1942, a chaotic time when the Japanese army successfully drove the British out of the country and local government in many areas was controlled by the **Burma Independence Army**; June 1942–July 1943, when the Japanese Military Administration (*Gunseikanbu*) exercised full governmental authority; and August 1943–August 1945, when Tokyo granted Burma nominal independence within the "Greater East Asia Co-Prosperity Sphere." However, Dr. **Ba Maw**'s government had little freedom to exercise its authority because the Japanese commander of the Burma Area Army remained effectively in control.

Burma was transformed by the occupation. The British defeat in 1942 shattered the myth of European superiority, making it impossible for them to reimpose the colonial system after the war. Old elites, including Burmese civil servants and politicians, were swept aside. The prewar **plural society** broke down after as many as 600,000 **Indians**, Anglo-Indians, and **Anglo-Burmese** fled Burma by land and sea for the Subcontinent in early 1942. Many did not return after the war. Though largely powerless, Ba Maw's "independent" state asserted a Burmese, or **Burman (Bamar)**, national identity, and promoted "totalitarian" mobilization of the previously apathetic population through party and mass organizations.

However, the most important consequence of the occupation was establishment of a Burman-officered and manned army (known as the **Burma National Army** after August 1943), the direct predecessor of the **Tatmadaw**, which viewed itself not only as the defender of national unity and independence but also as a revolutionary force deeply involved in politics. Thanks in large measure to his prominent role in the activities of the Japanese-organized **Thirty Comrades** and the wartime army, **Ne Win** was able to become commander of Burma's armed forces after the **Karen (Kayin)** uprising in 1949. The **Thakins** were disillusioned with Japanese intentions after it became clear that Tokyo would not grant Burma immediate independence in 1942. By 1944, they had organized an underground **Anti-Fascist Organization**, and on March 27, 1945, now celebrated as **Armed Forces Day**, **Aung San** ordered the Burma National Army to rise up against the Japanese. Postwar Burmese historiography emphasizes Aung San's leadership of the struggle against both the "imperialist British" and the "fascist Japanese." However, the post-1988 military regime, the **State Peace and Development Council**, has emphasized Japan's positive contributions to Burma's independence, largely to secure Tokyo's financial support.

Burma's abundance of rice prevented the terrible famines that afflicted Indochina and Java during the war, though the country's infrastructure was devastated and the presence of over 300,000 Japanese troops on Burmese soil imposed a heavy economic burden. The *Kempeitai* (Japanese military police), perpetually on the lookout for Allied spies and communist agents, was universally feared and hated. Outrages against local **women** by Japanese troops were not uncommon, despite the "import" of large numbers of Korean, Chinese, and other "comfort women" for the troops' recreation (a small number of Burmese women were also forced into this role). But the large-scale atrocities that characterized the Japanese occupation of other Southeast Asian countries and China did not, for the most part, occur. Japanese troops were instructed to regard the Burmese as their allies and friends, in stark contrast to the situation in wartime China. When they undertook their desperate retreat to the Thai border in 1945, many Japanese soldiers were aided by Burmese villagers, who gave them food, medicine, and shelter. Memories of Burmese kindness provided a firm foundation for the postwar Burma–Japan relationship. Postwar Burmese governments have also assisted Japanese veterans' groups in locating the graves of their fallen comrades, who numbered as many as 190,000.

However, approximately 50,000 Burmese laborers, members of Ba Maw's "Sweat Army," died under extremely harsh conditions, especially during construction of the **Thai–Burma Railroad**. Communal violence between Burmans and Karens in early 1942, especially in **Myaungmya (Myoungmya)**, and the fact that most of the ethnic minority "hill tribes" remained loyal to the British during the war, created intense ethnic minority distrust of the Burmans, with negative postwar consequences. The inflow of arms and armed men between 1941 and 1945, both in **Burma Proper** and the **Frontier Areas**, created a vicious cycle of civil war and political violence that continues to this day. *See also* JAPAN, RELATIONS WITH; MINAMI KIKAN; PATRIOTIC BURMESE FORCES; SUZUKI KEIJI, COLONEL; THAI–BURMA RAILWAY; WORLD WAR II IN BURMA (MILITARY OPERATIONS).

JATAKA TALES. Part of the canon of sacred **Buddhist** literature, stories of **Gotama Buddha**'s previous incarnations, in human or animal form, numbering 550 and composed between the third century BCE and the fifth century CE. Their setting is commonly northern **India**, especially Varanasi (Benares), and each tale has a moral message (e.g., "associate with the wise and good"). In Burma, the Jataka tales have been a major inspiration for the traditional performing and visual arts and form an important part in education at village monastery-schools. Holy sites, such as **pagodas**, are often decorated with illustrations of the Jataka Tales, and traditional marionette performances during *pwe* reenact them.

JEWS IN BURMA. A small Jewish community has lived in Burma since at least the British colonial period, and probably before, mostly in **Rangoon (Yangon)**. In the 1931 city census, Rangoon's Jewish population was recorded at 1,069 (out of a total of more than 400,000).The city's only Jewish place of worship, the Musmeah Yeshua Synagogue on 26th Street, was first built in 1854 and reconstructed on a larger scale in 1896. Most of its congregation were Sephardic Jews from the Middle East and India, but they have dwindled in number since **World War II**, many emigrating to Israel. In 2004, the congregation was composed of only eight families. *See also* ARMENIANS IN BURMA.

JUDSON, ADONIRAM (1788–1850). An early American Protestant missionary, originally a Congregationalist but affiliated with the Baptist Church before arriving in Burma in 1815. His efforts to convert Burmese Buddhists were largely unsuccessful, and the Burmese authorities imprisoned him under harsh conditions during the **First Anglo-Burmese War**. At war's end, he moved to **Moulmein (Mawlamyine)** and began preaching to **Karens (Kayins)**, achieving much greater success. Fluent in the **Burmese (Myanmar) language**, he translated the Bible into Burmese, composed a Burmese grammar, and wrote Burmese English/English Burmese dictionaries. He was commemorated by the name of Judson College, which was a constituent college of **Rangoon (Yangon) University**. *See also* MISSIONARIES, CHRISTIAN.

JULY 7, 1962 INCIDENT. Following the establishment of the **Revolutionary Council (RC)** by General **Ne Win** on March 2, 1962, the government imposed tight regulations on university campuses, which had been hotbeds of antigovernment activism. A dispute over campus curfews, in which a student was injured, led to a large demonstration on July 7 at **Rangoon (Yangon) University**. When the police failed to control the students, the authorities called in a **Tatmadaw** regiment, commanded by **Sein Lwin** and composed of ethnic minority **Chins**, who could be expected to show little sympathy for the mostly **Burman (Bamar)** demonstrators. The soldiers opened fire on the students, a shocking and totally unexpected act. According to official figures, there were 15 fatalities, although the actual figure may have been as high as several hundred. In the early morning of July 8, the **Rangoon University Student Union** building was blown up, allegedly on orders from Ne Win, although he accused RC member **Aung Gyi** of the act.

"JUMPING CAT MONASTERY." **Buddhist** monks at the Nga Phe Kyaung monastery on the shores of **Inle Lake** in **Shan State** trained cats to jump through hoops to wile away quiet days. This has become a popular attraction for foreign **tourists**, although the 150-year-old monastery also has a collection of interesting **Buddha** images and is an excellent example of Shan wooden **religious architecture**. That the performing cats are named after Hollywood movie stars—Leonardo di Caprio, Demi Moore, Brad Pitt—shows the steady progress of globalization in Burma.

– K –

KA KWE YE (KAR KWE YE, KKY). Because the **Ne Win** regime lacked sufficient military and economic resources to control border areas, it began recognizing local warlord groups as *Ka Kwe Ye*, "home guard" or "self-defense" forces, in 1963. In a classic "divide and rule" policy, the regime expected KKY forces to assist in its fight against communist and ethnic insurgents. In return, they were free to engage in the **opium** trade. The policy went a long way toward fragmenting opposition to the central government in **Shan State**. The two "kings of the Golden Triangle," **Lo Hsing-han** and **Khun Sa**, both became prominent as KKY commanders in the early 1960s. More than 50 groups had been organized as KKY by the late 1960s, but in 1973 the Ne Win regime declared them illegal. The **cease-fires** initiated by the **State Law and Order Restoration Council** with ethnic armed groups beginning in 1989 resemble the KKY arrangements, since the cease-fire groups have also been able to conduct private business. In both cases, government recognition of the legal status of armed groups has led to a major expansion in the **drug economy**.

KACHIN INDEPENDENCE ARMY/ORGANIZATION (KIA/KIO). Before it signed a **cease-fire** with the **State Law and Order Restoration Council** in 1994, the Kachin Independence Army was one of the best-organized and most-effective border area insurgencies, with "liberated areas" encompassing much of central and eastern **Kachin State** and a portion of northern **Shan State**, as much as 40,000 square kilometers. It had an armed strength in the early 1990s of 6,000 guerrillas. The Kachin Independence Organization is its political arm.

A handful of **World War II** veterans established the KIA/KIO in February 1961 near **Lashio**. The new army's goal was to create an independent "Kachinland," reflecting disillusionment with the U **Nu** government's neglect of the **Kachins**, his plan to cede portions of Kachin State to the **People's Republic of China**, and his determination to make **Buddhism** the state religion (most Kachin leaders were Christian). Its most effective leader was **Brang Seng**, a **Rangoon (Yangon) University** graduate and former headmaster of a Baptist mission school in **Myitkyina**, who went underground with the KIO in 1963 and served as its chairman from 1975 until his death in 1994. In contrast to the chaotic insurgent and drug warlord situation in Shan

State, the KIA/KIO succeeded in presenting the Ne Win regime with a united front, bringing together the **Jinghpaw** and smaller Kachin groups, such as the Lashi, **Lisu**, and Maru. Sales of **opium** and jade funded its operations, though not on the scale of groups in Shan State. Its relations with other armed groups and neighboring countries was characterized by pragmatism: It both fought and negotiated with the **Communist Party of Burma**, joined the National Democratic Front alliance of 11 armed groups, and received limited support from the government of **India**.

The motivation for the 1994 cease-fire, which came after a 1991 agreement made by the Kachin Defense Army (formerly the fourth brigade of the KIA), was a longing for peace after over three decades of fighting and the belief that the political situation inside of Burma was changing, that the KIA/KIO could play a constructive role in bringing about a comprehensive reconciliation involving the ethnic groups, the Burmese opposition, and the post-1988 military regime. Since then it has been relatively successful in promoting development within its territories, including the running of Kachin language-medium schools, a Teachers Training College, and hospitals, and the completion of infrastructure projects, such as roads, bridges, and hydroelectric plants. Its post-1994 achievements as a de facto "federal" government are in large measure due to strong community organization, though KIA/KIO chairman Zau Mai, who succeeded Brang Seng in 1994, was forced from power in 2001 because of widespread discontent with his top-down leadership and the alleged corruption of family members. After the cease-fire, the **State Peace and Development Council** gained control of the lucrative jadeite mines at **Hpakant**, leaving the KIA/KIO short of revenues. It has turned to selling timber to China, causing significant deforestation in the Kachin State–China border area. *See also* NAW SENG.

KACHIN STATE. One of Burma's 14 **states** and **divisions**, with an area of 89,042 square kilometers (34,379 square miles) and an estimated population in 2000 of 1.27 million (1983 census figure: 904,794). The state capital is **Myitkyina**. Kachin State contains three **districts** (Myitkyina, Bhamo, and Putao), subdivided into 18 **townships**. The topography is rugged, with several mountain ranges and Burma's highest peak, **Hkakabo Razi** (5,887 meters or 19,315 feet). The highest peaks in northern Kachin State are snow covered. Lowland areas include the

Hukawng Valley and the plains around the towns of Putao, Myitkyina, and Bhamo. The state contains the headwaters of the Irrawaddy (Ayeyarwady) River, which is navigable up to Bhamo, and Indawgyi Lake, Burma's largest. To the south, Kachin State is bounded by Shan State, and on the west by Sagaing Division. It also has a long eastern border with the People's Republic of China and a shorter western one with India.

Ethnically, the population includes the many subgroups of the Kachin ethnic group, especially the Jingpaws, as well as Shans (Tai) and Burmans (Bamars). Until the early 1990s, when a cease-fire was signed with the State Law and Order Restoration Council, much of the state's territory was controlled by the Kachin Independence Army, one of the best-organized antigovernment insurgencies. The rough terrain limits agricultural potential, except in the plains, but Kachin State is richly endowed with forests (though massive export of logs to China is causing serious deforestation) and has large deposits of jadeite (jade), especially at Hpakant, which finds ready markets in China and among Chinese communities in Southeast Asia. Other exploitable minerals include amber, gold, and iron. Small amounts of opium have been cultivated in Kachin State.

KACHINS. One of Burma's major ethnic groups, numbering 465,484 in the last official census taken in 1983 (1.4 percent of the total population). At the end of the 20th century, the Kachin population was estimated at around one million. Most live in Kachin State or the northern part of Shan State, although there are smaller Kachin communities in China's Yunnan Province and India's Assam and Arunachal Pradesh States. *Kachin* is a Burmese term, used in Western languages to refer to six groups speaking Tibeto-Burman languages: the Jinghpaw, Rawang, Lisu, Lashi, Maru, and Atsi (Azi). The Jingpaw or Jinghpaw (known as *Jingpo* in China and *Singpho* in India) are the largest and most influential group; most of the leadership of the Kachin Independence Army/Organization (KIA/KIO) are Jingpaws, and their language serves as the Kachin lingua franca. The KIO commonly refers to the Kachin people as *Wunpawng* ("core" or "center"), an ethnically neutral term.

Although historical records are practically nonexistent, it is believed that the Kachins migrated from eastern Tibet or southwestern China, sharing a common origin with the Burmans (Bamars), Karens

(**Kayins**), **Chins**, and **Nagas**. Their legendary homeland is referred to as *Majoi Shingra Bum*, "naturally flat mountain," possibly the Tibetan plateau. As mentioned, they speak languages belonging to the Tibeto-Burman group, although these are mutually unintelligible. Their homeland within Burma is the "triangle" formed by the two major tributaries of the **Irrawaddy (Ayeyarwady) River**, the Mali Hka, and the N'Mai Hka Rivers, north of **Myitkyina**, the present capital of Kachin State. A warlike people, they spread from the triangle to the **Hukawng Valley** and areas to the south, displacing earlier **Shan (Tai)** inhabitants. They were completely independent of Burman power centers and stoutly resisted the imposition of British colonial rule. The triangle—the cradle of traditional Kachin culture and religion—was not completely "pacified" by the British until just before **World War II**. However, Kachins were recruited for the colonial army and fought bravely against the Japanese, preventing their advance north of Sumprabum. Putao (Fort Hertz) in northern Kachin State was one of the few areas in Burma where the British flag flew before the successful Allied offensives of 1944–1945. Major campaigns were fought in the Kachin country, especially around Myitkyina.

Living among some of the highest mountains in Burma, Kachins traditionally have been practitioners of swidden or slash-and-burn **agriculture**, which in some cases has caused deforestation of upland areas (though worse damage has been done by commercial overexploitation of **forests** since the 1994 **cease-fire** of the Kachin Independence Army/Organization). In recent times, some Kachins have settled in lowland areas, growing wetland **rice**. The cultivation of **opium** is also widespread, though not as extensive as in the **Wa** and **Kokang** regions of Shan State. **Heroin** addiction has become a serious problem in some parts of Kachin State.

Unlike the Burmans, the Kachins trace descent through the male line rather than bilaterally, and they are one of the few indigenous groups in Burma to use family names. Descent is carefully recorded, and the five major descent groups (sibs) are the Marip, Lahtaw, Lahpai, N'hkum, and Maran. Among chiefs is an elaborate system of exogamy that determines which descent groups will exchange brides and grooms. The *manao*, the traditional Kachin festival, was (and remains) an important part of public life, hosted by chiefs and involving dances, feasting, and sacrifices to the Kachin gods or spirits. *Manao* posts are erected at the festivals and painted in colorful designs. Kachin women are skilled weavers, and many of their patterns have enjoyed great popularity in other parts of Burma.

Anthropologists, most notably Edmund Leach (in *Political Systems of Highland Burma*), have described in detail two contrasting social systems within Kachin society: the *gumsa*, a hierarchical system in which hereditary chiefs (*duwa*) exercised authority over village communities, possibly influenced by Shan political institutions (the *sawbwa*); and the *gumlao*, a more horizontal or egalitarian system in which authority was exercised by a local council. The British suppressed the *gumlao* because they were associated with rebellion against authority. The colonizers also outlawed the practice of slavery, which was widespread in Kachin society before the early 20th century.

Like other upland, Tibeto-Burman groups (such as the Chins), the Kachins believed in a single creator God (*Karai Kasang*), and below him a host of often malevolent spirits similar to the Burmese *nats*. Very few Kachins became Buddhists. Christian **missionaries**, especially those associated with the American Baptist church, began evangelizing in the mid- and late 19th century. The Swedish-American Baptist missionary Ola Hanson, who worked among Kachins between 1890 and 1929, played a major role not only in converting the people to Christianity but also in developing the Kachin language, giving it a written script and translating the entire Bible into Jingpaw Kachin (using the term *Karai Kasang* for God). The written language, using Roman rather than Burmese letters, has been instrumental in promoting literacy and ethnic consciousness among the Kachins. Although exact figures on the number of Christians among the Kachins are not available, they are estimated to comprise over 90 percent of the population, with Baptists and Catholics being the largest groups. Christian churches and schools have become major institutions in Kachin life. Since all three Kachin armed groups—the KIO/KIA, the Kachin Defence Army, and the New Democratic Army-Kachin—signed cease-fires with the **State Law and Order Restoration Council** in the 1990s, Kachin communities have enjoyed peace for the first time since the KIO/KIA revolt broke out in the early 1960s, but the price has been environmental spoilage and social problems caused by rampant commercialization and the increased influence of the central government, including the **State**

Peace and Development Council's efforts to promote **Buddhism** among Christians and animists.

KADUS. One of Burma's smaller ethnic minority groups, who live in and around Katha **district** in **Sagaing Division**. Speaking a Tibeto-Burman language, they cultivate **rice** on irrigated terraces and have become largely assimilated to **Burman (Bamar)** culture, including **Buddhism**. Traditionally, many of them work as *ouzi* (elephant drivers) in the forests of **Upper Burma**.

KALAW. Located in **Shan State** on the edge of the Shan Plateau, Kalaw, like **Maymyo (Pyin Oo Lwin)**, was a popular "hill station" during the British colonial period for Europeans seeking respite from Burma's hot season. Its population of approximately 20,000 includes **Indians** and Nepali Gurkhas, as well as **Burmans (Bamars)** and **Shans**. It is located near **Inle Lake** and the Pindaya Caves, popular **tourist** destinations.

KAMMA. Kan in the **Burmese (Myanmar) language**, known as *karma* in English, which means (voluntary) action. A basic doctrine of **Buddhism**, which states that all voluntary actions accumulate merit or demerit (*kutho*, *akutho*) according to their moral status. These are the cause of good or ill fortune in future lives, that is, misfortune for evil deeds, good fortune for good ones. Burmese people often say that a person's good or ill fortune is the "fruit" of good or bad *kamma* from a previous existence. For example, a person who cannot free himself or herself from poverty is considered to have been stingy in a prior life. In everyday life, *kan/kamma* is often merely synonymous with "luck." Moreover, Burmese people do not equate all ill fortune with bad *kamma* and often attempt to avoid it through use of magical practices, such as *yedaya*. *See also* ASTROLOGY.

KANDAWGYI LAKE. Known during the British colonial period as the Royal Lakes, a body of water located just north of the downtown district of **Rangoon (Yangon)** and east of the **Shwe Dagon Pagoda**. The British built their Boating Club there; at present, the lake is the site of traditional Burmese regattas sponsored by the government.

KANDY CONFERENCE (1945). Meeting held September 6–7, 1945, at the headquarters of **Lord Louis Mountbatten**, Supreme Allied Commander, South East Asia, in Kandy, Ceylon (Sri Lanka), attended by himself, **General William Slim**, other top-ranking British military and civilian officials, and leaders of the **Patriotic Burmese Forces (PBF)** and **Anti-Fascist People's Freedom League**, including **Aung San** and Thakin **Than Tun**. The purpose of the conference was to decide the future of the PBF and its integration into a new **Burma Army** under British command. According to the agreement between Aung San and Mountbatten published on September 7, the PBF contingent was to consist of at least 5,200 men and 200 officers, amalgamated with **Karen (Kayin)**, **Kachin**, and **Chin** troops who had fought with the British during the war. Infantry forces were to be "class battalions" (ethnically defined), while other units were to be "mixed." Colonial officials close to the governor, Reginald Dorman-Smith, opposed establishment of the army before the prewar civilian government reassumed authority, but Mountbatten overruled them after hearing the views of the Burmese delegation. The Supreme Commander offered Aung San a commission in the new army, but he refused, citing his determination to enter political life. *See also* TATMADAW, HISTORY OF.

KAREN GOODWILL MISSION (1946). A four-man delegation, consisting of **Karen (Kayin)** lawyers Saw **Ba U Gyi**, Saw Tha Din, Sidney Loo Nee, and Saw Po Chit, who went to London in August 1946 to express to the British government their community's opposition to being included in an independent state dominated by **Burmans (Bamars)**. Although they received a sympathetic hearing from **Frontier Areas** administrator **H. N. C. Stevenson**, the policy of Prime Minister Clement Attlee was integration of the Frontier Areas with **Burma Proper**, as reflected in the January 1947 **Aung San–Attlee Agreement**. Thus, the mission ended in December without achieving its purpose. *See also* KAREN NATIONAL UNION.

KAREN NATIONAL ASSOCIATION (KNA). Considered by many historians to have been the first genuine political association established in British-ruled India (the Indian National Congress was first convened in 1885), the KNA was founded in 1881 by Christian **Karens (Kayins)**. Its leaders, of whom the most prominent were San

Crombie Po and Sydney Loo Nee, hoped to use the KNA to advance the interests of their community within the British Empire. When the Montagu-Chelmsford hearings on political reform for India were held in 1917, the KNA opposed the aspirations of the **Young Men's Buddhist Association** by arguing that the Province of Burma, because of its ethnic diversity, was not ready for self-government. The KNA lobbied for special communal representation for the Karens in the colonial legislature, and by the late 1920s had begun to advocate a separate "Karen country," to be located in what is now **Tenasserim (Tanintharyi) Division**, which would be under British rule in a decentralized Burmese federation of nationalities. Dominated by Western-educated Christians, it was only in 1939 that the KNA established a parallel association for Karen Buddhists, who in fact were a majority within the Karen community. *See also* KAREN NATIONAL UNION (KNU).

KAREN NATIONAL LIBERATION ARMY (KNLA). Since 1975, the armed force of the reunited **Karen National Union (KNU)**, under the command of Bo **Mya**. With a current strength of 2,000–3,000 armed men and women, it operates in the Thai–Burma border area, although its base at **Manerplaw** was captured by the **Tatmadaw** in 1995.

KAREN NATIONAL UNION (KNU). At the beginning of the 21st century, the oldest and strongest ethnic minority organization opposing the **Burman (Bamar)**-dominated central government. It was established on February 5, 1947, as a successor to the **Karen National Association**, with Saw **Ba U Gyi** serving as its first president. The KNU reflected Karen disaffection over the failure of the August 1946 **Karen Goodwill Mission** to London to convince the government of Clement Attlee to recognize the establishment of a Karen state within the British Commonwealth but separate from the Union of Burma, and the signing of the January 1947 **Aung San–Attlee Agreement**. Consisting of Karen veterans of **World War II**, the KNU's armed branch, the Karen Nation Defence Organization (KNDO), was established in July 1947. The KNU refused to recognize Burma's independence on January 4, 1948, insisting on its demand for an independent **Kawthoolay** (Karen Free State) that would have included what are now **Irrawaddy (Ayeyarwady)** and **Tenasserim (Tanintharyi) Divisions**, as well as other territories in **Lower**

Burma. In the words of a KNU publication: "[I]t is extremely difficult for the Karens and the Burmans, two peoples with diametrically opposite views, outlooks, attitudes and mentalities, to yoke together." Memories of wartime atrocities, including the **Myaungmya (Myoungmya) Massacres**, were still fresh in Karen minds.

Following the March 1948 uprising of the **Communist Party of Burma (CPB)**, Karen officers and men in the **Burma Army** and the Union Military Police remained loyal to the government of Prime Minister U **Nu**, but there were violent incidents in which Burman *sitwundan* units attacked and killed Karen civilians, threatening a renewal of the racial violence of **World War II**. In January 1949, the KNU went underground, and KNDO units seized control of Insein (now **Insein Township**) north of **Rangoon (Yangon)** and **Toungoo (Taungoo)** in **Pegu (Bago) Division**. Burma fell more deeply into civil war. Karens who formed the backbone of the Burmese armed forces deserted to join the uprising and were supported by the commander of the 1st **Kachin** Rifles, **Naw Seng**, who captured **Mandalay** in March 1949. By May of that year, most of central Burma and what is now **Arakan (Rakhine) State** were in ethnic and communist insurgent hands, and U Nu's government was called the "six-mile Rangoon government" because its control barely extended beyond the capital. However, the "multicolored insurgency" was undermined by ideological incompatibility and lack of coordination, and the tide had turned in favor of the central government by early 1950. The KNU and its armed force, the KNDO, were driven from central Burma into the upland areas near the **Salween (Thanlwin) River** and the Thai–Burma border. Although sporadic unrest occurred in Karen communities in the delta of the **Irrawaddy (Ayeyarwady) River** until the early 1990s, the Karen hill country has remained the heartland of the KNU insurgency up to the early 21st century, a period of over five and a half decades.

One of the most important consequences of the KNU uprising was the "Burmanization" of the **Tatmadaw**. Burma Army ranks left empty by mutinous Karen and other ethnic minority soldiers were filled, on both the officer and enlisted levels, with Burman members of the *sitwundan* (although **Chin** soldiers remained largely loyal to the central government). The Karen general **Smith Dun** was replaced as commander of the armed forces by **Ne Win**.

During the 1950s and 1960s, the KNU underwent factional divisions, largely along communist and anticommunist lines. A Marxist-oriented Karen National United Party (KNUP) was established with its own armed force, the Karen (or Kawthoolei) People's Liberation Army (KPLA), which increasingly adopted Maoist-style guerrilla tactics. The KNUP and a second group, the Karen Revolutionary Council (KRC), participated in **peace talks** with the Ne Win regime in 1963, but only the KRC, led by the antileftist Saw Hunter Thamwe, agreed to lay down their arms. By the late 1960s, the left-leaning KNUP and the Karen National United Front (KNUF), founded and led by Saw Bo **Mya**, were the major components and rivals within the Karen insurgency. In 1975–1976, the two factions were reunited as the Karen National Union under Bo Mya, who rejected Marxism in favor of a nationalist, anticommunist stance and purged leftists from the movement.

The KNU maintained a large administrative network in its liberated areas along the border between Burma and **Thailand**. Economically, it depended on the exploitation of extensive stands of **teak**, logs being exported to Thailand, and control of the **black market** trade between the two countries, consisting of consumer and manufactured goods brought in over the border from Thailand in exchange for Burmese raw materials. The major outlet for trade was **Three Pagodas Pass**, controlled and sometimes contested by the KNU and the **New Mon State Party**. The KNU refrained from participating in the profitable trade in **opium** and other narcotics, because of both the convictions of its leaders and the historical unfamiliarity of the Karens with the drug. By the early 1980s, the KNU's armed force, the **Karen National Liberation Army (KNLA)**, had a well-trained and equipped force of between 5,000 and 8,000 men, second only to the People's Army of the CPB, which had 8,000–15,000 men under arms. The KNU became a member of the National Democratic Front in 1976, and of the **Democratic Alliance of Burma** in 1988.

The KNU and other ethnic minority armed groups did not participate in the **Democracy Summer** movement of 1988, but after Burman **student** activists, who established the **All Burma Students Democratic Front**, left central Burma for the border areas, they were included in the DAB united front under Bo Mya's leadership and assisted by the KNLA, which gave them training and some arms. Because the KNU's headquarters at **Manerplaw**, established in 1975, was also a focal point for other ethnic minority and Burman opposition groups, including the **National Coalition Government of the Union of Burma (NCGUB)**, the Tatmadaw made it the target of concerted dry-season offensives, especially during 1992 and 1995. The latter offensive succeeded in capturing Manerplaw and another base, Kawmoorah, dealing the KNU/KNLA a serious blow. An important factor in their success was the defection of the **Democratic Buddhist Karen Army (DKBA)** from the KNU. The increasingly cooperative attitude of the Thai government toward the **State Law and Order Restoration Council** in the early 1990s also denied KNLA soldiers sanctuary on Thai soil. Manerplaw's fall resulted in an increased number of Karen **refugees** fleeing to KNU-affiliated camps in Thailand, and left those remaining behind vulnerable to systematic **human rights** abuses by the Tatmadaw. As of 2005, the KNU, led formally since 2000 by Saw Ba Thin, had not signed a **cease-fire** with the **State Peace and Development Council**. Despite the growing receptiveness of Bo Mya, still the KNU's de facto leader, to a negotiated end to the war, the central government remained unwilling in early 2005 to make concessions that the Karen movement would find acceptable.

KAREN (KAYIN) STATE. One of Burma's 14 **states** and **divisions**, with an area of 30,383 square kilometers (11,731 square miles) and a population estimated at 1.49 million in 2000 (1983 census figure: 1,055,359). Ethnically, the majority of the population belongs to **Karen (Kayin)** groups. Until the mid-1990s, much of the state was under the control of the insurgent **Karen National Union (KNU)**, which maintained strongholds along the border with **Thailand**. The state capital is **Pa-an (Hpa-an)**. Established in 1951, Karen State contains three **districts** (Pa-an, Myawaddy, and Kawkareik), subdivided into seven **townships**.

The topography is generally rugged. Mountains, such as the **Dawna Range**, run from the northwest to the southeast of the state and have traditionally provided refuge for insurgents. Being elongated, Karen State shares a boundary with **Mon State** to the west and southwest, **Pegu (Bago) Division)** to the west and northwest, **Mandalay Division** and **Shan State** to the north, and **Kayah State** to the northeast. It also shares a long international border with Thailand to the east, southeast, and south. The **Salween (Thanlwin) River** bisects the state before entering Mon State and emptying into the Gulf of **Martaban (Mottama)**.

Forestry is economically important, though stands of valuable hardwoods, such as **teak**, have been seriously depleted since 1988, when the **State Law and Order Restoration Council** gave logging concessions to firms from Thailand, which often practiced clear-cutting. Once controlled by insurgent groups (such as the KNU and the **New Mon State Party**), border trading posts (such as **Three Pagodas Pass** and **Mae Sot-Myawaddy**) played an important role in Burma's **black market**, drawing in imports from foreign countries in exchange for Burmese raw materials, such as forest products, **rice**, and livestock. There are plans to open the "Asian Highway" through Mae Sot in Thailand's Tak Province into Burma by way of Myawaddy, which would link **Rangoon (Yangon)** with Bangkok.

KARENNI NATIONAL PROGRESSIVE PARTY (KNPP). An ethnic minority armed group that operates along the Burma–Thai border in **Kayah (Karenni) State**. Its stated purpose is to defend the independence of the **Karenni States**, recognized by the British in 1875, from Burmese intrusion, although its leaders claim that they will support their inclusion in Burma under a democratic and federal scheme, reflecting the spirit of the agreement made at the 1947 **Panglong Conference** between **Aung San** and ethnic leaders. Established in 1957, the KNPP has split into several factions. One of these, the originally pro-**Communist Party of Burma** Karenni Nationalities Peoples Liberation Front, signed a **cease-fire** with the **State Law and Order Restoration Council** in 1994. In the following year, the KNPP also signed a cease-fire, but it broke down, and there have also been armed clashes between the KNPP and the smaller KNPLF.

KARENNI STATES. Comprising what is now **Kayah (Karenni) State**, they were five principalities under the authority of **Karenni (Kayah)** rulers who entered into a "subordinate alliance with the British government" outside of the sovereignty of British India in 1875. This arrangement, which recognized the states as essentially independent, was reluctantly recognized by the government of King **Mindon**. They were administered as part of the Southern **Shan States** with an administrative headquarters at **Loikaw**. The Karenni States were Bawlake, Kyebogyi, Kantharawaddy, Nawngpalai, and Nammekon.

KARENNIS (KAYAHS). An ethnic minority nationality who live largely in **Kayah (Karenni) State** and are closely related linguistically and culturally to the **Karens (Kayins)**. In the **Burmese (Myanmar) language**, *Karenni* means "Red Karens," referring to their dress. However, they generally consider themselves to be a separate group. According to official census figures, they numbered 141,028 in 1983. Because of fighting and **"Four Cuts"** pacification along the border, many Karennis have become internally displaced persons or **refugees** in Thailand. *See also* KARENNI NATIONAL PROGRESSIVE PARTY (KNPP); KARENNI STATES.

KARENS (KAYINS). One of Burma's major ethnic groups, considered the third largest after the **Burmans (Bamars)** and **Shans (Tai)**. In the last official census, taken in 1983, they numbered 2,122,825 — 6.2 percent of Burma's total population at the time (35.3 million). According to U.S. government statistics, they comprised 7 percent of a population of 42.5 million in 2003, or about 3 million (*CIA World Factbook*, 2003). The **Karen National Union** claims that the "Karen nation" has a population of seven million. Given the long interval since the 1983 census, the dispersed nature of the Karen population, and the difficulty in some cases of defining ethnic boundaries between them and other groups, only an estimate of the Karen population is possible; between three and four million is likely. A smaller number of Karens, about 200,000, live in neighboring **Thailand**.

The Karens speak closely related languages belonging to the Tibeto-Burman group. According to their own folklore, they entered Burma after crossing a "river of running sands," which some observers have identified with the Gobi Desert in Mongolia. Some Christian **missionaries** claimed they were part of the Ten Lost Tribes of Israel, citing their belief in a Creator God, *Ywa*, resembling the Old Testament *Yahweh*. But linguistic and other evidence suggests that the original Karens entered Burma from southwestern China at around the same time as the **Pyus** and **Burmans (Bamars)**, in the early centuries CE. The Karen bronze drum, called a "frog drum" because of the ornamentation on its outer edge, resembles the Dong Son drum of northern Vietnam, dated to the fourth century BCE. Frog drums are precious possessions of Karen communities, and one appears in the Karen national flag.

Today, Karen populations are widely distributed. They inhabit a belt of upland and mountainous territory forming the border between Burma and Thailand, including southern **Shan State, Kayah (Karenni) State, Karen (Kayin) State, Mon State,** and **Tenasserim (Tanintharyi) Division,** as well as parts of **Pegu (Bago) Division,** especially around **Toungoo (Taungoo).** In upland areas, they have traditionally practiced swidden or slash-and-burn **agriculture,** similar to other "hill tribes." Large numbers of Karens also live in the delta of the **Irrawaddy (Ayeyarwady) River,** where they practice the cultivation of wetland **rice** and have largely assimilated with adjacent Burman or **Mon** populations. Karen communities are found in and around **Bassein (Pathein),** Pyapon, and Henzada (Hinthada), in **Irrawaddy (Ayeyarwady) Division.** There is also a substantial population of Karens in **Rangoon (Yangon),** especially **Insein Township.**

Anthropologists generally divide the Karens into four major subgroups: Sgaw, Pwo, **Pa-O,** and **Karenni (Kayah).** According to Karen mytho-history, the Sgaw and Pwo were rival groups, and the former were generally identified as highlanders, while the latter were plains dwellers. They speak different **languages** (or dialects), and the Christian leadership of the **Karen National Union** has recognized Sgaw as the basis for the standard Karen language, used in administration, publications, and their education system. However, the Sgaw-Pwo distinction does not appear to be especially significant within the Karen community today. The Karenni and Pa-O are generally considered, and consider themselves, to be separate ethnic groups.

Because the most prominent members of the Karen community have been Christians, it is often assumed that most Karens are adherents. In fact, Christians (mostly Baptists, but also including Seventh Day Adventists and other denominations) are usually estimated at around 25 percent of the total Karen population. Before **World War II,** the British colonial government estimated that two-thirds of all Sgaw Karens and 93 percent of Pwo Karens were Buddhist. A substantial number of Karens are animists, especially in the highlands. Cults founded by charismatic individuals who pose as saviors, promising to deliver the Karens into a Promised Land, have been quite common, for example, the tragic-comic **God's Army,** led by twin boys Luther and Johnny Htoo, which operated along the Thai–Burma border in the late 1990s.

Before modern times, the Karens, unlike the Mons, **Arakanese (Rakhines)**, and **Shans (Tai)**, did not have a state of their own. However, unlike the **Chins** and the **Kachins**, they were not so remote from lowland power centers that they enjoyed the freedom guaranteed by isolation. Thus, they have suffered a long history of oppression at the hands of the Mons, Shans, and especially Burmans, particularly during the **Konbaung Dynasty**. Karen spokesmen claim that the name of the town of **Meiktila** in central Burma actually comes from the Sgaw Karen *meh ti lawn*, meaning "falling tears" because of the Burmans forced Karen slaves to dig an artificial lake there. Because they were not (at the time) Buddhists or participants in Indo-Buddhist civilization like the Shans, Mons, or Arakanese, the Burmans tended to look down on the Karens as the "cattle of the hills."

During the British colonial period, the once-oppressed Karens enjoyed the benefits of being regarded by the colonizers as trustworthy allies. Missionaries provided them with a written language (based on Burmese script) and a Western-style education at mission schools, including Judson College (nicknamed "Karen College"), which after 1920 was part of **Rangoon (Yangon) University**. Many Karens became missionary teachers and preachers, serving not only their own community but also other groups (such as the **Kachins** and **Chins**). The British favored them with entry into the police, civil service, and army. Many Karen women worked in the nursing profession. In the British-operated forest reserves, Karen *ouzis* (elephant trainers and tenders) and foresters were indispensable for the extraction of **teak**.

Often, Karen loyalty to the British made them objects of resentment in the eyes of the Burmans because they fought alongside the colonizers in the **Anglo-Burmese Wars** and also helped suppress the **Saya San (Hsaya San) Rebellion** of 1930–1932. During World War II, elements of the **Burma Independence Army** massacred hundreds of Karen villagers at **Myaungmya (Myoungmya)** and other localities in the Irrawaddy Delta, incidents that made the Karens deeply suspicious of any Burman-dominated government. Remaining loyal to the British, Karen guerrillas working with **Force 136** played an important role in the Allied liberation of Burma from the Japanese in 1944–1945.

Karen nationalism was fostered by community leaders with the active encouragement of missionaries and colonial officials. Missionaries founded Burma's first newspaper, *The Morning Star (Sah Muh Taw)*, published in Karen at **Tavoy (Dawei)**, in 1843; it continued operating up until World War II. In 1881, the **Karen National Association** was established, considered by some historians to be the first genuine political organization in British India. Before the outbreak of war in 1941, Karen and Burman/Burmese nationalism evolved in fundamentally different directions: The former wanted continued close association with **Britain**, while the latter, by the late 1930s, demanded full independence. Few Karens participated in the **student** strikes at Rangoon University that attracted so many Burmans/Burmese in 1920 and the late 1930s. After the war, the most important Karen group was the Karen National Union (KNU), established in 1947, which commenced an armed struggle against the central government in early 1949 with the goal of creating a Karen country independent of the Union of Burma. At the beginning of the 21st century, the KNU is the only major ethnic minority armed group that has not signed a **cease-fire** with the **State Peace and Development Council**, although negotiations between the armed group and the military regime have commenced. *See also* BA U GYI, SAW; BO MYA; HUMAN RIGHTS IN BURMA; JUDSON, ADONIRAM; MYAUNGMYA (MYOUNGMYA) MASSACRES; SEAGRIM, HUGH; SMITH DUN, GENERAL.

KAUNGHMUDAW PAGODA. A **pagoda** located near **Sagaing**, built in the early 17th century and reaching 46 meters (150 feet) in height. Its distinct shape, rounded rather than bell-shaped like most Burmese pagodas, is said to represent the well-shaped breast of a Burmese queen. *See also* ARCHITECTURE, RELIGIOUS; BUDDHA TOOTH RELICS; STUPA.

KAWTHOOLAY. Or *Kawthulay*, the country of the **Karens (Kayins)**. The name literally means the "flowery land," or "black land" (the latter referring to land that must be fought over). It denotes the territory claimed by the **Karen National Union** when it initiated an uprising against the Burmese central government in 1949, located around the present Thai–Burma border. However, the **Revolutionary Council**

also used the term to refer to **Karen (Kayin) State** from 1964 to 1974.

KAYAH (KARENNI) STATE. One of Burma's 14 **states** and **divisions**, with an area of 11,733 square kilometers (4,530 square miles), making it the smallest state and the second smallest of Burma's regional jurisdictions. The population was estimated at 266,000 in 2000 (1983 census figure: 168,429). The state capital is **Loikaw**. Kayah State contains two **districts** (Loikaw and Bawlake [Bawlakhe]), subdivided into seven **townships**. Topographically, the state is part of the Shan Plateau, and the **Salween (Thanlwin) River** bisects it in a roughly north-south direction. Ethnically diverse, it is home to **Karennis (Kayahs)**, **Burmans (Bamars)**, **Karens (Kayins)**, and **Shans**.

During the British colonial era, Kayah State's territory comprised five **Karenni states**—Kantarawadi, Bawlake, Kyebogyi, Nawngpalai, and Nammekon—which in 1875 entered into a "subordinate alliance" with the British Indian government. These states were not considered part of Burma, but independent, and their entry into the Union of Burma was only recognized with the agreement signed at the **Panglong Conference** of 1947. The **Constitution of 1947** guaranteed it the right of secession after 10 years. Originally known as "Karenni State," the present name was adopted in 1951.

Kayah State is bordered on the north and northwest by **Shan State**, on the west by **Karen (Kayin) State**, and on the east by Thailand. It is well endowed with **forest** resources, and tin and tungsten are mined at Mawchi. The Baluchaung hydroelectric plant, built with Japanese war reparations, provides **Rangoon (Yangon)** with electric power, although it is in poor repair, resulting in periodic blackouts. *See also* KARENNI NATIONAL PROGRESSIVE PARTY; KARENNI STATES.

KENG TUNG (KYAINGTONG). Also Kengtung, the largest of the old **Shan States**, located east of the **Salween (Thanlwin) River** and encompassing approximately 31,100 square kilometers (12,000 square miles) before the autonomy of its *sawbwa* was relinquished in 1959. The name also refers to the city that was the *sawbwa's* royal capital, the site of his *haw* or palace, which is now the most important town in eastern **Shan State**. Home of the *Tai Khun*, a branch of the **Shan** (**Tai**) ethnic group, Keng Tung traces its origins to the late 13th century, when the fortified city (*möng* in the **Shan language**) was established by a Tai ruler related to the royal family of Chiang Mai. The original inhabitants of the Keng Tung area were apparently **Wa**, although the most numerous "hill tribe" people are **Akha**.

In the late 1760s, conflicting claims of suzerainty over Keng Tung were among the causes of a war between King **Hsinbyushin** and the Manchu Ch'ing (Qing) Dynasty. The city has long been an important waystation in the trade between **China** and **Thailand**. A 19th-century British account tells of an annual traffic of 8,000 mules bringing Chinese goods by way of Keng Tung to Chiang Mai. During the British colonial period the *sawbwa* of Keng Tung, like his counterparts in other Shan States, enjoyed considerable autonomy. During **World War II**, the Japanese transferred suzerainty over Keng Tung and another Shan State, Mongpan, to Thailand.

After Burma became independent in 1948, Keng Tung suffered heavily from war, insurgency, and, after 1988, the full impact of military rule. In the early 1990s, the **State Law and Order Restoration Council** opened an overland route for foreign travelers from Mae Sai on the Thai–Burma border to Keng Tung, and the city is likely to play an important role in the development of highway links connecting eastern and northern Shan State with Thailand and China. The headquarters of the Triangle **Regional Military Command** of the **Tatmadaw** is located there, and the Keng Tung area is subject to heavy cultural "Burmanization."

Among Keng Tung's monuments are the **Wat Zom Kham**, which according to legend dates from the lifetime of Gotama **Buddha** and is said to contain six of his hairs, the Naung Tung Lake in the center of town, and the old city gate (the city was originally surrounded by a wall). Keng Tung is famous for its **lacquerware**. Over the protests of local people, the ornate *haw* or palace of the *sawbwa* was torn down by the military regime in 1991 and replaced by a **tourist** hotel.

KHANTI, U (U KHAN DEE, ?–1949). The famous "Hermit of **Mandalay Hill**," who devoted his life to restoring Buddhist sites in and around **Mandalay** and other parts of Burma. After spending 12 years as a member of the **Sangha**, he was invited by the **Kinwun Mingyi**, at the time an advisor to the British, to collect donations for the restoration of the temples on Mandalay Hill. He also collected donations to build a reliquary on the hill to house relics of Gotama **Buddha** that had been discovered in Peshawar (in present-day Pakistan) and donated by the British government to Burma. His zealous construction efforts, spanning four decades, won him renown among Buddhists worldwide, and many admirers claimed he had supernatural powers.

KHIN KYI, DAW (1912–1988). Wife and widow of **Aung San** and mother of **Aung San Suu Kyi**. A nurse, she tended to Aung San during an illness and married him in 1942, bearing him two sons and a daughter. She was a prominent member of the All Burma Women's Freedom League and the **Anti-Fascist People's Freedom League**, and served as director of social welfare in the government headed by U **Nu**. From 1960 to 1967, she was Burma's ambassador to India, the first Burmese woman to serve in an ambassadorial post. A strict mother, she had a formidable influence on her daughter, inculcating in her respect for traditional values.

Daw Khin Kyi's illness brought her daughter to **Rangoon (Yangon)** in 1988. After she died on December 27 of that year, hundreds of thousands of people attended her funeral, including Western ambassadors.

KHIN NYUNT (1939–). From 1988 to 2003, first secretary (Secretary-1) of the **State Peace and Development Council (SPDC**, known before November 1997 as the **State Law and Order Restoration Council**, or **SLORC**) and director general of **Military Intelligence** (**MI**, also known as the Military Intelligence Service or the **Directorate of Defence Services Intelligence, DDSI**), one of the most powerful figures in the military junta established on September 18, 1988. After studying at **Rangoon (Yangon) University**, he completed the course at the **Officers' Training School** (25th batch) and received a commission in 1960. He was tactical operations commander of the 44th **Light Infantry Division** when, following the October 1983 **Rangoon Incident**, in which four members of the South Korean cabinet and other officials were killed in a North Korean bomb blast, **Ne Win** ordered him to carry out a thorough reorganization of Military Intelligence. In 1984, he was appointed director of MI/DDSI.

Although Khin Nyunt was appointed Secretary-1 of the SLORC on September 18, 1988, and continued to hold this post when the junta was reorganized as the SPDC in November 1997, attaining the rank of lieutenant-general, he was relieved of this post on August 25, 2003, and appointed prime minister. Most observers saw this as a demotion, placing him outside the junta inner circle. Previously, he had been the SPDC's third-highest-ranking officer, below Chairman Senior General **Than Shwe** and Vice Chairman General **Maung Aye**.

A protégé of the late leader **Ne Win**, Khin Nyunt was considered better educated and more sophisticated than his fellow generals in the junta and had a reputation for hard work and an austere lifestyle. His command of Military Intelligence and a vast amount of potentially incriminating data on his fellow officers and civilians made him universally feared and disliked, although his intelligence apparatus apparently failed to forecast the landslide victory of the **National League for Democracy** in the **General Election of May 27, 1990**.

During the 1990s, foreign observers recognized Khin Nyunt as head of a "Military Intelligence faction" inside the junta that was more receptive to economic reform and opening to the outside world than conservative officers belonging to a rival "Regular Army faction," headed by General Maung Aye. Some argued that he was more willing than other generals to negotiate a political settlement with **Aung San Suu Kyi**. He promoted close and friendly ties with the **People's Republic of China (PRC)**, which apparently motivated some officers to attempt to assassinate him in 1992 for selling out the country's independence. His role in brokering **cease-fire** agreements with ethnic minority armed groups beginning in 1989 gave him considerable influence in Burma's border areas, especially among components of the former **Communist Party of Burma**, and he was prominent in the state-run media as head of numerous committees involved with **education**, public service, and other matters. A conspicuous promoter of state-sponsored **Buddhism**, he served in 1998–1999 as patron of the committee responsible for renovating the **Shwe Dagon Pagoda**, replacing the *hti* (umbrella) that had been donated to the pagoda in the 19th century by King **Mindon**.

On October 18, 2004, Khin Nyunt was arrested in Rangoon on charges of corruption and attempting to split the armed forces. According to General **Thura Shwe Mahn**, his actions "could have led to the disintegration of the **Tatmadaw** and posed extreme danger for the country." He was dismissed from his post as prime minister (his successor was **Soe Win**) and placed under house arrest. Hundreds of his subordinates in Military Intelligence were arrested, and many others linked to MI were retired or transferred to other posts. In 2005 Khin Nyunt was placed on trial inside **Insein Jail** and given a 44-year jail sentence, suspended. It is believed he will be kept under house arrest. *See also* BORDER AREA DEVELOPMENT; STATE PEACE AND DEVELOPMENT COUNCIL, INTERNAL DYNAMICS.

KHUN SA (CHANG CHI-FU, 1934–). Born in Loimaw, northern **Shan State** to a Chinese father and a **Shan** mother, Chang first became prominent as the commander of the Loimaw **Ka Kwe Ye** in 1963. He soon became a powerful figure in the **opium** trade but was defeated in a Burma–Thailand–Laos border area "opium war" by **Kuomintang (Guomindang)** rivals and was arrested and jailed by the **Ne Win** regime in 1969. His loyal supporters captured Soviet physicians as hostages in **Taunggyi**, Shan State, and used them to negotiate his release from prison in 1974. Using the Shan name Khun Sa ("prince of prosperity"), he rebuilt his power base along the Thai–Burma border and became **Lo Hsing-han**'s successor as "king of the Golden Triangle." By the early 1990s, his **Mong Tai Army** (**MTA**, an amalgamation of smaller armed groups) was one of Burma's most powerful border area insurgencies, and the government of the **United States** demanded Khun Sa's extradition from Burma as a drug trafficker. Khun Sa posed as a Shan patriot, but his sincerity was doubted even before he signed a **cease-fire** with the **State Law and Order Restoration Council** in January 1996. The subsequent dismantling of the MTA altered the balance of power in central Shan State, enabling the **Tatmadaw** to carry out harsh pacification of the region, including the **forced relocation** of as many as 300,000 Shans. Khun Sa retired to **Rangoon (Yangon)**, where he manages several lucrative businesses. *See also* DRUG ECONOMY.

KHUNSANG TON-HUUNG (?–1917). A prominent **Shan (Tai)** leader of the late 19th century, considered a folk hero. He defeated Burmese and Shan forces sent against him by the Burmese king at **Mandalay** in the 1870s. after the British asserted their authority over the **Shan**

States, he became the *sawbwa* of North **Hsenwi**, with their backing. Although a commoner by origin who engaged in the salt trade, the British favored him over a royal rival to the Hsenwi throne because of his courage and initiative. His daughter, Sao Nang **Hearn Kham**, married Sao **Shwe Taik** in 1937 and was a prominent Shan patriot.

KINWUN MINGYI (1821–1908). Also known as U Kaung or U Kyin, a **Konbaung Dynasty** court official who served as a senior minister under Kings **Mindon** (r. 1853–1878) and **Thibaw** (r. 1878–1885). Widely described as a reformer, he led two delegations to Europe, in 1872 and 1874. Although he had an audience with Queen Victoria in 1872, he failed to impress upon the British government Burma's status as a fully independent state, but did conclude commercial treaties with France and Italy that subsequently aroused British suspicions about alliances with rival European states. With the accession of Thibaw and the growing power of his queen, **Supayalat**, the Kinwun Mingyi lost influence at court but served until the British capture of Mandalay in the **Third Anglo-Burmese War**. In 1897, he was appointed an advisor to the lieutenant governor of British Burma.

KODAW HMAING, THAKIN (1875–1964). Burma's premier nationalist writer. He received a traditional monastic education and is said to have witnessed British troops taking King **Thibaw** and Queen **Supayalat** off to exile in India at the end of the **Third Anglo-Burmese War** while living at a monastery in **Mandalay**. He began a journalistic career in 1894 when he became editor of *Myanma Nezin* (*Myanma Daily*) in **Moulmein (Mawlamyine)** and served as editor of *Thuriya (The Sun)*, one of the major **Burmese (Myanmar)** language newspapers established during the colonial period, between its inception in 1911 and 1921. He also became a professor at the "National University" established as part of the **National Schools** movement in 1921, but subsequently returned to journalism. During the late 1930s, he was mentor and leader of the mainstream faction of the **Dobama Asiayone**. Despite his traditional upbringing and strong Buddhist beliefs, he seems to have been very receptive to the left-wing ideas of the young **Thakins**, including **Aung San**; in reaction to this, a right-wing **Ba Sein**-Tun Oke faction broke away from the mainstream Dobama in 1939.

Kodaw Hmaing's best-known writings are his *tikas* (long essays or commentaries), which criticized British rule and those Burmese politicians who cooperated with it. In *Boh Tika* ("On Europeans"), published in 1913, he criticized those Burmese women who married foreign men out of economic necessity. In *Thakin Tika*, written in 1935, he proclaimed his support for the Dobama Asiayone. *See also* LITERATURE, BURMESE (MODERN).

KOKANG. A region of northeastern **Shan State**, east of the **Salween (Thanlwin) River** and adjacent to the border with China, which since the 17th century has been populated by **Chinese** who had been loyal to the Ming Dynasty and opposed the Manchu conquest of their country. For most of its history, Kokang was an autonomous state, ruled by the Yang family, the Yang patriarch assuming the title of *heng*, or ruler. Kokang came under British jurisdiction following the Anglo-Chinese Treaty of 1897 but was so remote from the center of colonial power that its autonomy was largely unimpaired. During **World War II**, the Yang *heng* supported Allied operations against the Japanese, and in 1947, on the eve of Burma's independence, was recognized by the British as a *sawbwa*.

Kokang is a poor, mountainous area, where soils are poor; for generations, the most important crop has been **opium**. After **Kuomintang (Guomindang)** irregulars from Yunnan Province entered Shan State in 1950, Kokang farmers began cultivating opium poppies in large quantities for export. Olive Yang (Yang Jinxiu), who was de facto ruler of Kokang from 1960 to 1962, allied herself with the Kuomintang to bring opium to the border with Thailand and international markets. Another important figure in the drug economy of Kokang was **Lo Hsing-han**, who served under Olive Yang, later cooperated with the **Ne Win** government as commander of a **Ka Kwe Ye** militia, and earned a reputation as "king of the Golden Triangle" before being jailed and sentenced to death in Burma in the mid-1970s (he was released in a 1980 amnesty). After Olive Yang was arrested by the government in 1963, her brother, Jimmy Yang (Yang Zhensheng), organized the insurgent Kokang Revolutionary Force.

Between 1968 and 1989, Kokang was under the control of the **Communist Party of Burma (CPB)**, but in early 1989 Kokang troops, along with those in other communist-dominated areas, mutinied against the CPB leadership; under **Pheung Kya-shin** (Peng Jia-sheng) and his brother Pheung Kya-fu (Peng Jiafu) they established a new armed force, the **Myanmar National Democratic Alliance Army (MDNAA)**, which signed a **cease-fire** with the **State Law and Order Restoration Council (SLORC)**. Lo Hsing-han served as go-between, facilitating negotiations between the Pheung brothers and SLORC Secretary-1 **Khin Nyunt**. The agreement enabled the MNDAA to expand opium and **heroin** production and export, although the Kokang armed force's activities in this area were surpassed by the **United Wa State Army** in the neighboring **Wa** districts and along the Thai–Burma border during the 1990s. Opium eradication policies of the **State Peace and Development Council** have encountered some success in Kokang because divisions within the Kokang leadership make it easier for the military regime to exert pressure. *See also* PANTHAYS.

KONBAUNG DYNASTY (1752–1885). Sometimes called the "Third Burmese (Myanmar) Empire" because, like the **Pagan (Bagan)** and **Toungoo (Taungoo) Dynasties**, it unified the country. Established by **Alaungpaya** in 1752, it enjoyed a period of military expansion during the reigns of **Hsinbyushin** (r. 1763–1776) and **Bodawpaya** (r. 1782–1819): The former conquered Siam (1767) and defeated a Chinese invasion, while the latter subjugated **Arakan (Rakhine)**. But their successors were defeated by the British during the **First, Second**, and **Third Anglo-Burmese Wars**. Although King **Mindon** (r. 1853–1878) implemented limited reforms and sought peaceful relations with the British, the Konbaung Dynasty was extinguished when his successor, **Thibaw** (r. 1878–1885), was forced to abdicate by the British and was exiled to India following British capture of the royal city of **Mandalay** in November 1885.

Monarchs of the Konbaung Dynasty	Year of Accession
Alaungpaya	1752
Naungdawgyi	1760
Hsinbyushin	1763
Singu Min	1776
Maung Maung	1781
Bodawpaya	1781 (or 1782)

Bagyidaw	1819
Tharrawaddy	1838
Pagan Min	1846
Mindon Min	1853
Thibaw	1878 (to 1885)

Source: D. G. E. Hall, *A History of South-East Asia*. London: Macmillan, 1964.

KOREA, DEMOCRATIC PEOPLE'S REPUBLIC OF (NORTH KOREA), RELATIONS WITH. Following the **Rangoon Incident** of October 9, 1983, diplomatic ties between Burma and North Korea were severed by the **Ne Win** regime and have not been formally restored. However, there are reliable reports that Pyongyang has supplied the **State Peace and Development Council (SPDC)** with small arms ammunition, 130mm field guns, and shipboard surface-to-surface missiles. International suspicions about more ambitious arms deals have been aroused by the frequency with which North Korean freighters visit Burmese ports and the presence of North Korean technicians in the country, including those spotted at the Monkey Point naval installation in **Rangoon (Yangon)**. In late 2003, the *Far Eastern Economic Review* published a report that the SPDC was thinking of acquiring a nuclear reactor from Pyongyang, and there has been further speculation that it wishes to purchase a North Korean–made submarine for its navy. Given the junta's seemingly insatiable appetite for arms and North Korea's position as a major arms exporter, a substantial community of interests seems to exist between the two pariah states. *See also* KOREA, REPUBLIC OF (SOUTH KOREA), RELATIONS WITH.

KOREA, REPUBLIC OF (SOUTH KOREA), RELATIONS WITH. Soon after the **State Law and Order Restoration Council** seized power and initiated an "open economy" policy in 1988–1989, Daewoo, a South Korea *chaebol* (business conglomerate), established a presence in Burma, especially in the electronics sector. Other major firms, such as Hyundai and Lucky-Goldstar, have also become involved in projects during the 1990s and early 21st century, and Korean private **foreign investment** totaled about US$100 million. The largest single project, development of an extensive natural gas field in the Bay of Bengal off the coast of **Arakan (Rakhine) State**, involves the participation of Daewoo International in exploration. Although Korean president Kim Dae-jung, a veteran of human rights struggles in his own country, expressed solidarity with **Aung San Suu Kyi** while in office (1998–2003), the relationship between Seoul and **Rangoon (Yangon)** remains primarily economic in nature. The South Korean government supplies Burma with some **foreign aid** and technical training. *See also* OIL AND GAS IN BURMA; RANGOON INCIDENT.

KOYIN. Or *kouyin*, a novice member of the **Sangha**, who has not been ordained. Traditionally, most Burmese boys spend at least a short time in a monastery as a *koyin*, following an elaborate *shinbyu* ceremony, the most important rite of passage for Burmese **Buddhist** males.

KUOMINTANG (KMT, ALSO GUOMINDANG). Following the communist victory in China's civil war and the 1949 establishment of the **People's Republic of China**, about 2,000 Nationalist Chinese (Kuomintang) troops crossed over into **Shan State** from Yunnan Province and established bases from which Chiang Kai-shek (Jiang Jyeshi) could open a "second front" against the communists (the first front being on Taiwan). Aided by the **U.S.** government, the Kuomintang irregulars scored no victories against the People's Liberation Army in Yunnan, but their "secret war" against Beijing threatened Burma's sovereignty, especially when it became clear that the KMT was seeking alliances with local ethnic insurgents, such as the **Karen National Union**. During the mid-1950s, most units of the **Tatmadaw** were committed to fighting the Kuomintang intruders, and joint operations with the People's Liberation Army were carried out in 1961. Many KMT soldiers were forced to relocate to northern **Thailand**. To raise funds, the KMT became deeply involved in the **opium** trade and established mutually profitable working relationships with Shan State warlords, especially the Yang family, the rulers of **Kokang**.

KUTHO **(MERIT).** In **Buddhism**, the idea that the performance of voluntary good works will ensure a fortunate rebirth, perhaps as a wealthy, powerful, or talented male. There are three ways in which merit can be accumulated: through adherence to moral principles (*sila*), such as refraining from drunkenness, illicit sexual practices, or killing; through the practice of meditation; and through charitable donations (*dana*) to monks or religious institutions. The last is most common among ordinary Burmese Buddhists, and includes giving food and other offerings to monks, sponsoring a *shinbyu* or ordination ceremony for a boy, and building or repairing a **pagoda**. Construction of a new pagoda is believed by many Burmese to be the most effective way to accumulate merit, though usually only the rich and powerful can sponsor it. Propagating Buddhist teachings is also a major source of *kutho*. Merit can be shared with or transferred to others (including possibly the deceased). The doing of bad deeds accumulates *akutho* (demerit), with negative consequences for rebirth. *See also* KAMMA.

KUTHODAW PAGODA. A **pagoda**, built in the style of the **Shwezigon** in **Pagan (Bagan)**, constructed by King **Mindon** in **Mandalay**. The building itself is not especially significant, but on the pagoda grounds are 729 marble stelae carved with the entire **Tipitaka**, or **Buddhist** scriptures, often called "the biggest book in the world." Each stele is covered by its own **stupa**. The king commissioned them after completion of the **Fifth Great Buddhist Council** in 1874. *See also* NU, U; GREAT BUDDHIST COUNCIL, SIXTH.

KYAIK. A word for **pagoda** or Buddhist holy site in the **Mon language** (equivalent to *paya* in Burmese), used in the names of some pagodas in **Lower Burma**, where **Mon** kingdoms ruled before the mid-18th century. They include **Kyaiktiyo** in **Mon State** and Kyaik Pun in **Pegu (Bago)**. Though less commonly used today than their **Burmese (Myanmar) language** names, Kyaik Dagon/Kyaik Lagun is the Mon name of the **Shwe Dagon Pagoda**, Kyaik Athok that of the **Sule Pagoda**, and Kyaik Mawdaw that of the **Shwemawdaw**.

KYAIKTIYO PAGODA. A major site of **Buddhist** pilgrimage, the **stupa** is only 7.3 meters (23.7 feet) high, built on a boulder that hangs precariously on a cliff in **Mon State**. According to legend, the boulder, which is covered by gold leaf, is secured to the cliff by a hair of Gotama **Buddha**, deposited there by a hermit. The site is associated with a legendary visit by the Buddha to Burma, and the **pagoda** includes the boulder in which the hair was placed, which was allegedly lifted up to the edge of the cliff by **Thagya Min**, king of the gods. In the Buddhist cycle of legends, the Kyaiktiyo is closely associated with the **Shwe Dagon Pagoda** in **Rangoon (Yangon)**. Because of its religious importance, the **State Peace and Development Council** sponsored extensive renovations of the site in 2001. *See also* ARCHITECTURE, RELIGIOUS.

KYANZITTHA, KING (r. 1084–1112). Third king of the **Pagan (Bagan) Dynasty** and son of its founder, **Anawrahta**. Best known for building the **Ananda Pahto** (Ananda Temple), he promoted the commingling of **Burmans** and **Mons**, marrying his daughter to the great-grandson of Manuha, Mon king of **Thaton**, and proclaiming their child rather than his own son the legitimate successor (King Alaungsithu, r. 1112–1165). Under Kyanzittha, the spectacular monument building at **Pagan (Bagan)** really began. *See also* MANUHA TEMPLE.

KYAUKSE. Located south of **Mandalay** in **Mandalay Division**, the site of a large irrigation complex that has played an indispensable economic role in the development of organized states in **Upper Burma**. Because rainfall is scarce year-round compared to other parts of Burma, the surpluses of **rice** necessary to support complex and densely populated societies can only be grown if fields are irrigated. At the end of the **Konbaung Dynasty** in the late 19th century, irrigated rice fields around Kyaukse totaled 100,000 acres. Their origin is unclear. The irrigation complex was in existence before the **Pagan Dynasty**, whose kings often used prisoners of war to maintain the tanks and canals. The fields were extended by both Pagan and post-Pagan Dynasty rulers, who had the grain brought by barge up the Zawgyi and Myitnge Rivers to the **Irrawaddy (Ayeyarwady) River** and then on to the royal capital. Other irrigation works are located at **Meiktila**, Yamethin, and Minbu. Because Kyaukse is the birthplace of Senior General **Than Shwe**, chairman of the **State Peace and Development Council**, it has benefited in recent years from special government-funded projects, especially in **agriculture**.

KYI MAUNG, U (1919–2004). A leader of the **National League for Democracy (NLD)**, who served as the party's vice chairman. Educated at **Rangoon University**, he took part in the anticolonial struggle and joined the **Burma Independence Army** in 1941; between 1943 and 1945, he underwent military training in Japan. Although he was a member of the **Revolutionary Council** of General **Ne Win**, he fell out with the new regime, was forced to retire from the military, and was jailed; he was imprisoned a second time in 1988. But in the months before the **General Election of May 27, 1990**, when **Aung San Suu Kyi** and U **Tin U** were under house arrest, he played a leading role in the NLD's election victory, only to be imprisoned in September 1990. His retirement from politics and the NLD in 1997 is said to have been caused by disagreements with Daw Suu Kyi.

– L –

LABOR STRIKES (1974). The inefficiencies and corruption of the socialist **economy** caused inflation and shortages of necessities in the early 1970s, and poor weather conditions in 1974 made shortages of **rice** still more severe. On May 13, 1974, a strike at a railroad yard near **Mandalay** broke out; the workers demanded higher rice rations. The strike spread to factories in Mandalay and **Meiktila**, to oil field workers at Chauk and **Yenangyaung (Yaynangyoung)**, site of the famous 1938 **oil field workers' strike** against the Burmah Oil Company, and to **Arakan (Rakhine) State**. By early June, more than 40 factories in **Rangoon (Yangon)** were closed down. In one incident at the railroad yard in **Insein**, strikers forced the release of workers arrested by the authorities. When strikers in Rangoon began making political demands, calling for the restoration of parliamentary democracy, the **Tatmadaw** cracked down. The official casualty figure was 22 dead, but the actual figure may have been in the hundreds. Like the **U Thant Incident**, the labor strikes were a massive expression of discontent with the **Ne Win** regime, and anticipated the **Democracy Summer** of 1988.

LACQUERWARE. One of Burma's most distinctive arts. Lacquerware items are usually fashioned of coiled bamboo strips, upon which as many as seven successive coats of sap or resin (*thit si* in Burmese) from a large tree (species *Gluta usitata*) are applied. These trees grow in the wild and are not damaged by the process of extracting sap (the resin is quite different from Western lacquers derived from insects, resembling those used in China and Japan). The items are frequently engraved in delicate and complicated patterns, using several colors (usually red, yellow, and/or green, on a black or red background). After each layer of resin is applied, the wares are placed for an extended time in a cool cellar for drying. The highest-quality pieces are so supple that they can be bent without causing damage to either the lacquer coating or the bamboo frame, and can take as long as six months to make. Black, high-gloss items, upon which gold leaf has been applied to form patterns or pictures, are known as *shwe zawa*. Important centers of lacquerware production are the **Pagan (Bagan)** area in **Mandalay Division** and **Shan State**, especially **Keng Tung**.

Despite the growing popularity of Western-style utensils, lacquerware is an indispensable part of Burmese daily life, in the form of cups, trays and plates, tiffin boxes, sets of containers holding the ingredients for **betel chewing**, decorative plaques, **Buddha** images, and *hsun ok*, elaborate, covered offering bowls used to carry donations for members of the **Sangha**. The history of Burmese lacquerware is unclear, but the art is possibly derived from **China**, and the more-sophisticated techniques, used for making the multicolored, engraved items (known as *yun* in Burmese), may have been brought in recent centuries from northern **Thailand**. During the **Burma Socialist Programme Party** era (1962–1988), the quality of wares declined because of the lack of resources, but in recent years there has been an effort to improve it, making better-quality items for the **tourist** and international markets.

LAHUS. An ethnic minority nationality who speak **languages** belonging to the Tibeto-Burman group and live between the **Salween (Thanlwin)** and **Mekong Rivers** in **Shan State**, around **Keng Tung**. Linguistically the Lahus are closely related to the **Akhas** and **Lisus**. Ethnologists divide them into several subgroups: the *Lahu Na* (Black Lahu), *Lahu Nyi* (Southern Lahu), and *Lahu Shi* (Yellow Lahu). Lahus live not only in Burma but also in China's Yunnan Province, northern Thailand (the *Lahu Shehleh*), and Laos. Traditionally, Lahu village communities have been located on hillsides at elevations of 1,300 meters (4,000 feet) or more, and they practice slash-and-burn (swidden) **agriculture**. Lahu men have a reputation as skilled hunters. Village communities tend to be strongly self-sufficient. Their religion is animist, though apparently influenced by (Tibetan) **Buddhism**. By 1950, American Baptist **missionaries** in Burma claimed 28,000 Lahu converts.

An armed group, the Lahu National United Party/Lahu State Army, fought against the central government after 1973 but surrendered in 1984. The Lahu National Organization/Army, established in 1985, is based along the Thai–Burma border near Mae Hong Son and cooperates with **Karenni (Kayah)** insurgents.

LANGUAGES OF BURMA. According to one estimate, Burma has 107 "living languages." Most of Burma's indigenous languages belong to the Tibeto-Burman subgroup of Sino-Tibetan languages. They include not only the **Burmese (Myanmar) language**, which is the most widely spoken, but also the languages of the **Akhas, Chins, Kachins, Karens (Kayins), Lahus**, and **Nagas**. The prevalence of this language subgroup indicates that the origin of most of the present inhabitants of Burma was Tibet or southwestern China. The major non-Tibeto-Burman languages include the **Shan language**, which belongs to the Tai-Kadai group, bearing close affinities to the language of **Thailand**, and the languages of the **Mons, Palaung,** and **Wa**, which are Mon-Khmer (Austroasiatic), sharing a common origin with Cambodian (Khmer). The **Moken** speak an Austronesian language, related to Malay. Among nonindigenous languages, English and Chinese are widely used, the latter being important in the China–Burma border areas. Although **Pali** is not a vernacular, its role as the sacred language of Theravada **Buddhism** gives it an incomparable importance in Burmese life. *See also* MON LANGUAGE.

LASHIO. A major town in northern **Shan State**, with an estimated population of over 110,000 in 1996. It serves as the terminus for the railroad line running south/southwest to **Mandalay** and **Rangoon (Yangon)**, and before **World War II** linked Burma's capital by rail with the **Burma Road**, which enabled the Allies to ship weapons and supplies overland to Chiang Kai-shek (Jiang Jyeshi) at his wartime capital of Chungking (Chongqing). The Japanese capture of Lashio in May 1942 cut off the Burma Road. Before the signing of **cease-fires** with ethnic minority armed groups, Lashio, close to the **Chinese** border, was strategically sensitive, and off limits to foreign visitors.

LAW IN BURMA (PRECOLONIAL AND MODERN). During their colonial occupation of Burma, the British claimed that they were bringing the blessings of the rule of law to the country, but Burma already had well-established legal institutions going back at least to the **Pagan (Bagan) Dynasty**. In Thant Myint-U's words, "the Irrawaddy basin possesses one of the oldest legal traditions in the world" (*The Making of Modern Burma*, Cambridge: Cambridge University, 2001, p. 87). The model for Burmese law was the legal code of Manu, the original lawgiver in the Hindu Indian tradition, but the major legal writings, *Dhammathat* (*Dharmasastra* in Sanskrit), were compilations of customary law and precedent that reflected conditions in Burmese society. Some 36 Dhammathats were compiled between the first millennium CE and the 19th century, of which 26 were produced during the **Konbaung Dynasty**, which seems to have been a golden age for Burmese law.

In addition, Burma seems to have been the only Asian country in which a class of professional lawyers or legal representatives (*shay nay*) was recognized. Trained as apprentices by experienced lawyers, they accepted private clients and argued their cases before royal judges. Civil law (*lawka wut*) was distinguished from criminal law (*raza-wut*, dealing with violations of the "king's peace"); there were sophisticated rules of evidence; and witnesses were required to swear an oath, perjury being threatened with terrible punishments (in the next life, if not in this). Lawyers wore special dress in court, collected standardized fees (plus a percentage of the value of the issue under judgment), and lived in a special quarter of town.

During the Konbaung Dynasty, the *myowun* heard criminal cases, and *tayathugyi* presided over civil cases in provincial administrative centers; in the royal capital, the **Hluttaw** functioned as the court of final appeal. Although bloody executions were common during times of struggle over royal succession (e.g., when King **Thibaw** succeeded King **Mindon** in 1878), **Buddhist** precepts precluded capital punishment on other occasions. Sometimes members of the **Sangha** intervened to save someone from execution.

British annexation of Burma during the 19th century led to the imposition of a foreign legal model, and Burmese customary law was restricted to three "native law zones": religion, marriage, and succession (inheritance), which became known as "Burmese Buddhist law" or *"Dhammathat* law." By the early 20th century, a class of British-educated Burmese attorneys, nicknamed the "barristocrats" because of their prestige and high social position, had become prominent in political as well as legal life. They included **Ba Maw**, his brother Ba Han, Sydney Loo Nee, and Mya Bu, the latter serving as prime minister in the wartime, pro-Japanese government of Ba Maw. Under British rule, the Burmese became a litigious people, freely resorting to the courts to solve all manner of disputes.

The British-style legal system, including the tradition of the independence of the judiciary, remained largely intact during the period when U **Nu** was prime minister. However, after **Ne Win** established the **Revolutionary Council** in March 1962, it was steadily undermined. On the advice of Dr. **Maung Maung**, who was the most influential legal expert during the Ne Win period (1962–1988), the entire legal system was reformed in 1972, creating a system of socialist legality in which the courts were subordinate to the **Burma Socialist Programme Party (BSPP)**, the revolutionary vanguard party. The judiciary consisted of People's Courts, whose officials were not legal professionals (though they accepted the nonbinding advice of such professionals) but were lay judges chosen by the BSPP. On the central government level, the judiciary was controlled by the Council of People's Justices. Lawyers became People's Attorneys, paid by the state and under the control of the Council of People's Attorneys, operating "law offices" on the **state/division** and **township** levels. Both Councils were responsible to the **State Council** and the **Pyithu Hluttaw**.

After the **State Law and Order Restoration Council (SLORC)** was established in September 1988, the **Constitution of 1974**, which defined the structure of the judicial system, became inoperative, and the SLORC junta ruled by means of decrees. According to **SLORC Announcement No. 1/90**, it exercised exclusive judicial power. If natural law concepts—that independent jurists could arrive at proper decisions through the exercise of reason and impartiality—were reflected in both the dynastic and British legal traditions, after 1962, and especially after 1988, a crude legal positivism was exercised; that is, in John Austin's words, law was quite literally the "command of the sovereign." *See also* MAHA THAMADA.

LEDI SAYADAW (1846–1923). A prominent member of the **Sangha**, who after the **Third Anglo-Burmese War** and the fall of **Mandalay** in 1885 established a monastery near Monywa in what is now **Sagaing Division**, later traveling to different parts of the country to promote **Buddhism**. He taught and wrote extensively on the **Pali** Canon and *vipassana* (insight) **meditation**, some of his works being translated into English. He is most famous, however, for publishing an essay, "On the Impropriety of Wearing Shoes on Pagoda Platforms," which supported the campaign by the **Young Men's Buddhist Association** after 1916 to ban this practice, mostly by Western **tourists** visiting the **Shwe Dagon Pagoda** and other holy sights. *See also* "SHOE QUESTION."

LEDO ROAD. A 1,079-mile-long strategic route that started from Ledo in northeastern India and intersected the **Burma Road** at the Burma–China border, which the Japanese cut off in 1942. It passed through what is now **Kachin State**. Constructed by 35,000 Burmese, Indian, and Chinese laborers and 15,000 U.S. Army personnel (most of whom were Afro-Americans) under terrible conditions, it was completed by January 1945 and made overland supply of Nationalist China from India possible. It was also known as the "Stilwell Road." *See also* MERRILL'S MARAUDERS; WORLD WAR II IN BURMA (MILITARY OPERATIONS).

LET YA, BO (1911–1978). *Nom de guerre* of Thakin Hla Pe, member of the **Dobama Asiayone** who became one of the **Thirty Comrades**. In 1947, he negotiated a defense agreement with the British, the "Let Ya-Freeman Agreement," which was included in the October 1947 **Nu–Attlee Agreement**. After Burma's independence in 1948, he went into private business, but then joined former Prime Minister U Nu's **Parliamentary Democracy Party** in the late 1960s and served as commander of its armed units in the Thai–Burma border area. He was killed in an engagement with **Karen (Kayin)** insurgents on November 29, 1978.

LIGHT INFANTRY DIVISIONS (LID). Elite units of the Burmese **Army** designed for mobile operations. The first Light Infantry Division, the 77th LID, was established in 1966 to fight the forces of the **Communist Party of Burma** in the **Pegu (Bago) Yoma** region. During **Democracy Summer**, the 22d and 33d LIDs were deployed in **Rangoon (Yangon)** to suppress antigovernment demonstrations. At the beginning of the 21st century, the Army contained 10 LIDs, including the 11th LID, based at Htaukkyan, north of Rangoon, which can be used to contain unrest in the former capital. LIDs are under the control of the Ministry of Defense rather than the Army's **Regional Military Command** structure.

LIMBIN CONFEDERACY. An alliance of *sawbwas* of the **Shan States**, established in 1883, initially to oppose King **Thibaw**. It backed the accession to the throne of the Limbin Prince, a member of the Konbaung royal family, in the hope that he would recognize the autonomy of the Shan States and abolish the oppressive *thathameda* (household) tax. When the British removed Thibaw from the throne at the end of 1885, the Confederacy, whose stoutest supporters included the rulers of Lawksawk, Mongnai, and Mongpawn, became an anti-British movement, which attempted to win the support of Sao On, *sawbwa* of **Yawnghwe**, who chose instead to side with the British. There ensued what amounted to a civil war between the Confederacy and pro-British *sawbwas*. In May 1887, the Limbin Prince surrendered to **James G. Scott**, British administrator for the Shan States, and went into exile in India. *See also* PACIFICATION OF BURMA.

LISUS. An ethnic minority nationality who speak **languages** belonging to the Tibeto-Burman group and live in **Shan State**, with smaller concentrations in **Kachin State**, around Bhamo and **Myitkyina**. Linguistically, the Lisus are closely related to the **Akhas** and **Lahus**. The "Black" Lisus, traditionally known for their independence from any kind of central control, live mostly in China's Yunnan Province, while "Tame" Lisus, who have adopted aspects of Chinese culture, live in northern Shan State. A small number have settled in the northernmost parts of Thailand. Traditionally, Lisu village communities are found in upland areas and practice slash-and-burn (swidden) **agriculture**. Many cultivate poppies and trade in **opium**. They are animists, with a belief in multiple, often malevolent, spirits, and also practice a form of ancestor worship.

LITERATURE, BURMESE (DYNASTIC PERIOD). Burmese literature during the dynastic period—from the early **Pagan Dynasty** until the end of the **Konbaung Dynasty**—was characterized by strongly religious themes relating to **Buddhism**, an emphasis on the idealized achievements of kings, and the development of sophisticated forms of verse. Fictional works in prose, novels, and short stories did not appear until the British colonial period. Literature surviving from the early centuries is found on stone inscriptions (*Kyauk-sa*), the earliest being the Rajkumar or Myazeidi Inscription of 1113, carved on a four-faced stele with passages in the **Burmese (Myanmar) language**, **Pali**, the **Mon language**, and the language of the **Pyus**. Its subject matter is devoted to the Buddhist good works of members of the royal family. The earliest extant Burmese verse is also found on a stone inscription dating from 1374, but it is dedicatory or panegyric rather than lyrical in nature.

The use of palm leaves (*pei-za*) inscribed with a stylus and paper folded into a book, accordion-style (*parabaik*), dates at least to the Pagan period, but no manuscripts from that time have survived. The earliest extant literature in this form comes from the **Ava (Inwa) Period** (1364–1555): a palm leaf manuscript titled the *Yakhaing Minthami* (Princess of **Arakan**), dated to 1455. Most authors during the Ava Period were members of the **Sangha**, men who had spent many years in Buddhist monasteries, and their themes with few exceptions remained religious and royal. Probably the greatest of the monk-poets was Shin Rathtathara (1468–1530), who wrote on the competing attractions of the worldly and monastic life. Distinct verse-forms emerged: the *eigyin* (historical ballads, e.g., the *Yakhaing Minthami*, above), *mawgun* (odes in praise of royal personages), and *pyo* (verses based on the **Jatakas**, or birth-tales of the **Buddha**, a medium in which Rathtathara excelled).

A fourth verse form, *yadu,* were short poems, one to three stanzas long, on a wider variety of themes, including nature, romantic love, and the experiences of soldiers in war. During the **Toungoo Dynasty** (1555–1752), *yadu* poetry flourished, the most renowned poets being Nawaday the Elder (1545–1600) and Prince Nat Shin-naung (1578–1619). The early 18th-century writer Padei-tha-ya-za (1633–1754) composed *pyo* on nonreligious themes and also wrote about the common people. After the conquest of Ayuthaya, the capital of Siam, by King **Hsinbyushin** in 1767, Burmese literature was strongly influenced by Siamese *(Yodaya)* styles. During the 19th century, new literary forms emerged, including the *yagan,* a long narrative poem, and the *pya-zat,* or drama. Important writers included U Sa (1766–1853), Letwet Thondara, the Hlaing Princess, and the dramatist U Ponnya (1812–1867). During the late Konbaung period, dramas were extremely popular, and printed plays became bestsellers, in some sense anticipating the novels and short stories of the colonial and postcolonial eras. Between 1875 and 1900, 400 *pya-zat* were written and published.

Historical literature was in the form of *thamaing,* the histories of **pagodas,** monasteries, or local districts, and *yazawin,* or royal chronicles *(rajavamsa* in Pali). U Kala (1678–1738) produced the *Maha Yazawin-gyi* (the Great Chronicle) in 1724, covering the period from the legendary beginning of the Burmese kingdom until 1711. King Bagyidaw commissioned a group of scholars to compile an official history, the *Hman-nan Yazawin-daw-gyi* (**Glass Palace Chronicle**) between 1829 and 1832, based largely on U Kala's work. A supplement to this was commissioned by King **Mindon** but not published until 1899. *See also* LITERATURE, BURMESE (MODERN).

LITERATURE, BURMESE (MODERN). Because of Western influences, Burmese literature had undergone great changes by the beginning of the 20th century. One was the appearance of the novel. In the **Burmese (Myanmar) language,** "novel" is translated as *ka-la-paw wut-htu,* "the day's narrative," as contrasted with the traditional *Hpaya-haw wut-htu,* "narrative preached by the **Buddha.**" The first Burmese novel was James Hla Gyaw's *Maung Yin Maung Ma Meh Ma Wut-htu (The Story of Master Yin Maung and Miss Meh Ma),* published in 1904. It was an adaptation of Alexandre Dumas's *The Count of*

Monte Cristo, set in **Upper Burma**. A popular adventure story, it inspired many imitators despite the disapproval of the older generation, including conservative members of the **Sangha**.

By the second and third decades of the 20th century, social themes, often critical of colonialism, became prominent in popular literary works. Two novels by U Latt, *Zabebin* and *Shwepiso*, appearing from 1912 to 1914, expressed concern about the loss of traditional Burmese values under colonial rule; U Maung Gyi wrote novels in the 1920s about past Burmese heroes, *Nat Shin-naung* and *Tabinshwehti*; and U Lun (later known as Thakin **Kodaw Hmaing**) wrote *tikas* (long essays) on the evils of British rule, for example, the *Boh Tika* ("On Europeans"), which advised against Burmese **women** marrying foreigners, an issue adopted by the **Young Men's Buddhist Association**. **Thein Pe Myint** became controversial because of his 1936 novel *Tet Pongyi* (*Modern Monk*), which exposed the corruption of the contemporary Sangha; P. Monin wrote novels about the common people; and Dagon Khin Khin Lay, the first woman novelist, wrote short stories and historical novels. In 1933–1934, two *Khitsan* ("Testing the Times"), anthologies of short stories and poems, were published by students of the first Burmese professor of English at **Rangoon (Yangon) University**, U Pe Maung Tin. The *Khitsan* expressed distinctly modern styles and themes; one of the most prominent writers involved in the *Khitsan* movement was Zawgyi, a poet and literary critic who espoused revolutionary and nationalist themes.

The chaos of **World War II** made it difficult for Burmese writers to perfect their craft, although Thein Pe Myint's experiences provided material for his popular nonfiction *Sit Ah Twin Kha Ye The* (*Wartime Traveller*). In 1947, on the eve of independence, the government established the Burma Translation Society, later known as the *Sarpay Beikman* (House of Literature), which awarded prizes to talented writers. The first prize was given in 1948 to Min Aung for *Mo Auk Myebin* (*The Earth under the Sky*). Prime Minister U **Nu** was a writer of not inconsiderable talent, publishing his memoirs, *Nga Hnit Yathi* (*Five Years*), and a play. During the parliamentary period (1948–1962), the government promoted a national literature but did not impose tight controls on writers.

Postwar literature was influenced by Soviet as well as British and American models, and there was a renewed emphasis on depicting the hardships of ordinary people; an example of this genre was Maung Htin's *Nga Ba (The Peasant)*. Ludu U Hla, a prolific leftist writer, produced *Hlaing chaine-hte-ga-nhet-myar (The Caged Ones)*, an account of his four years in jail in the 1950s, which told the life stories of fellow prisoners. Maung Ne Win's *Lu Pyi Hmar Ah Ne Ye Like Pa (Courage to Live in This Human World)*, published in 1960, described the desperate poverty of a young woman whose husband must go far away to earn a living. One of the most important postwar woman writers was Gyanegaw Ma Ma Lay, whose *Mon-ywei Mahu (Not out of Hate)* told the tragic story of a traditional Burmese young woman and her unhappy—and ultimately fatal—marriage to a Westernized Burmese man. It is one of the few Burmese novels translated into English.

Taya (Star) Magazine, established by the left-wing writer Dagon Taya, was highly influential in literary circles. Beginning in the 1920s and 1930s, monthly literary magazines such as *Dagon* and *Gandalawka (The World of Books)* played an indispensable role in promoting vernacular literature. Along with *Taya*, their most important postwar counterparts included *Shumawa, Thwei-thauk,* and *Myawaddy*.

During the **Burma Socialist Programme Party** era (1962–1988), the state viewed writers as "mental workers" who had to contribute to the building of socialism. The **Ne Win** regime established an "Organization Committee for the Federation of Literary Workers" in 1965; many of its members were later purged. The preferred genre was a Burmese version of Soviet-style "socialist realism," and literary output was severely censored by the **Press Scrutiny Board**. Few high-quality novels were produced because authors were reluctant to submit a long work, to which they would have devoted much time, to the Board's ambiguous and unpredictable criteria. However, the monthly literary magazines published many short stories because the costs of having a shorter work "inked out" were much lower for both writers and the handful of private publishers, for whom publishing a long novel was a risky investment. Because of Burma's economic stagnation during this time, there were frequent shortages of paper for printing and other materials. Typewriters were generally unavailable at state stores, and **black market** prices for them were prohibitive. Burmese publishers in 1971 turned out a total of 2,106 titles; this number had fallen to 584 titles by 1976.

After the **State Law and Order Restoration Council** seized power in 1988, the severe and arbitrary censorship regime under the Press Scrutiny Board continued, and a number of writers, including the distinguished poet Tin Moe, have since been jailed or have left the country. Few observers of the Burmese literary scene believe that quality literature can be produced under these circumstances, although the volume of publications has grown compared to the Ne Win period. *See also* LITERATURE, BURMESE (DYNASTIC PERIOD); MASS MEDIA IN BURMA.

LO HSING-HAN (LUO XINGHAN, 1934–). Born in **Kokang** in northeastern **Shan State**, Lo Hsing-han served in forces commanded by the ruling Yang family before defecting to the **Ne Win** government in 1963 and becoming leader of a **Ka Kwe Ye** militia force. By the early 1970s, Lo had earned the title "king of the Golden Triangle" for his prominent role in the lucrative export of **opium** and **heroin** to Thailand and international markets. When the government issued an order disbanding the Ka Kwe Ye militias in 1973 he went underground, but he was arrested in Thailand and extradited to Burma, where he was sentenced to death in 1976. Released from jail in a 1980 amnesty, Lo cooperated with the government as leader of the Shan State Volunteer Force. When the **Communist Party of Burma (CPB)** broke up in early 1989, he played a crucial role in negotiating **cease-fires** between the **State Law and Order Restoration Council** and ethnic components of the CPB. Retiring to **Rangoon (Yangon)**, he established postsocialist Burma's largest business conglomerate, Asia World, which has made substantial investments in real estate, **tourism**, and transportation and seems to have received "laundered" funds from the flourishing drug economy. One of its enterprises is a toll road connecting opium-growing areas in **Shan State** with the Chinese border. Asia World's managing director is Lo Hsing-han's son, Steven Law, who has close ties with Singaporean and Malaysian business people. *See also* KHUN SA.

LOIKAW. The capital of **Kayah State**; its population was estimated at 48,017 in 1996. Located at an elevation of 1,200 meters, it remains largely off-limits to visitors. Nearby is the Baluchaung Hydroelectric plant, built with Japanese war reparations, which provides Burma with much of its electric power.

LONGYI. The distinctive lower garment worn by Burmese, which resembles the wraparound Malay *sarong*. Male *longyis*, known as *pasoe*, are usually subdued in color, often with a checked pattern (such as the **Kachin**-style *longyi*, which became associated with political activism during 1988), and the male wearer traditionally ties it in front. Women's *longyis*, known as *thamein* (or *htamein*), are more colorful, often skillfully woven (hand-woven *longyis* from **Arakan [Rakhine]** and **Inle Lake** are especially prized), and are tied at the side. Although *sarong*-type garments have been traditionally used through Southeast and South Asia, Burma is one of the very few countries where the majority of the people continue to wear them in preference to Western-style skirts or trousers; in fact, the term "men in trousers" is synonymous with the **Tatmadaw**.

Upper garments for Burmese men include the traditional jacket, the *tai bon*, which is collarless and usually reddish-brown or tan in color. For everyday wear, a Western-style shirt or T-shirt often suffices. The traditional women's blouse, the *ingyi*, is usually plain, light-colored, and with long sleeves; Western-style blouses and T-shirts are also popular. For formal occasions, men often wear the *gaung baung*, a turbanlike head covering.

Despite the country's traditional conservatism in dress, in part a consequence of its isolation from the outside world, Western clothes have become steadily more popular among the younger generation since 1988, especially in large cities like **Rangoon (Yangon)** and **Mandalay**. Models, movie stars, and rock groups are often the vanguard in this trend. The popularity of Western-style dress, although it is usually more modest than that found in neighboring countries, dismays the older generation. In mid-2004, university authorities established student dress codes, which mandate that students wear traditional *longyi* on campuses.

LOWER BURMA. A term first used by the British in the 19th century to refer to those territories annexed following the **First** and **Second Anglo-Burmese Wars** (1824–1826, 1852), in contrast to **Upper**

Burma, which was ruled by the **Konbaung Dynasty** until the **Third Anglo-Burmese War** (1885). Lower Burma was frequently also referred to as "**Pegu**," the region's most prominent city until **Rangoon (Yangon)** became Burma's colonial capital; after the 1852 war, it included **Arakan (Rakhine)**, **Tenasserim (Tanintharyi)**, the **Irrawaddy (Ayeyarwady) River** Delta, and most of what are now **Mon State** and **Pegu (Bago) Division**. The terms Lower and Upper Burma are still often used because the areas they denote retain a strong regional distinctiveness. Historically, Lower Burma, home of the **Mons**, has been a sea-girt, well-watered area where international trade and **rice** cultivation have been highly developed since antiquity. During the colonial period, it was characterized by ethnic diversity and cosmopolitanism, including a large population of migrants from **India**, in contrast to Upper Burma, which was more isolated and ethnically homogeneous. Both regions constituted **Burma Proper**, in contrast to the **Frontier Areas**. *See also* ADMINISTRATION OF BURMA, BRITISH COLONIAL PERIOD.

"LUKAUN LUTAW." In the **Burmese (Myanmar) language**, "good men before smart men," referring to **Ne Win**'s preference for promoting loyal cronies rather than talented persons to high positions, a practice that has continued under the **State Peace and Development Council**. *Lukaun lutaw* is considered a major reason for the poor quality of economic planning during the **Burma Socialist Programme Party** era, and why the **economy** remains in a state of crisis today.

LWIN, U. A leader of the **National League for Democracy (NLD)** and a member of its executive committee. Along with U **Tin U**, U **Kyi Maung**, and U **Aung Shwe**, he was a veteran military officer, who joined the **Burma Independence Army** in 1942 and was sent to undergo military training in Japan. Between 1962 and 1988, he served in various posts in the military and the government under **Ne Win** before retiring from the **State Council** in 1980. He joined the NLD at its inception in 1988 and became its secretary in 1992; at present, he plays the important role of spokesman for the party to foreign diplomats and journalists at a time when its top leaders are again under house arrest.

– M –

MAE SOT-MYAWADDY. Mae Sot, located in **Thailand**'s Tak Province, and Myawaddy, in Burma's **Karen (Kayin) State**, are separated by the Moei River. The former is often known as "little Burma" because as many as 100,000 Burmese **refugees** live and work in and around the town, in factories, construction sites, and brothels. Economic distress has brought them not only from nearby Karen and **Mon States**, but also from central Burma. Abuse of Burmese illegal workers in Mae Sot, including those in the **sex industry**, is regularly reported by international **human rights** organizations. A **Karen (Kayin)** physician, **Doctor Cynthia (Maung)**, has established a major hospital and clinic at Mae Sot, which serves border area people.

Mae Sot and Myawaddy lie along one of the projected routes of the 141,204-kilometer-long "Asian Highway" network; the highway is planned to run from the two towns through **Pagan (Bagan)** in **Mandalay Division** to Tamu on the Indian border. In 1997, a "Thailand–Burma Friendship Bridge" was completed, opening up cross-border road traffic and greatly stimulating trade.

MAGWE (MAGWAY). The capital of **Magwe (Magway) Division**, with a population estimated at 71,450 in 1996. It is located on the east bank of the **Irrawaddy (Ayeyarwady) River**, astride river, rail, and road connections linking **Mandalay** and **Pagan (Bagan)** in the north with **Prome (Pyay)** and **Rangoon (Yangon)** to the south.

MAGWE (MAGWAY) DIVISION. One of Burma's 14 **states** and **divisions**, with an area of 44,820 square kilometers (17,305 square miles) and an estimated population in 2000 of 4.55 million (1983 census figure: 3,243,166). The divisional capital is **Magwe (Magway)**, and the division has five **districts** (Magwe, Minbu, Thayet, Gangaw, and Pakkoku) and 25 **townships**. It is bounded on the north by **Sagaing Division**, on the northwest by **Chin State**, on the southwest by **Arakan (Rakhine) State**, on the south by **Pegu (Bago) Division**, and on the east by **Mandalay Division**.

Located in the **Dry Zone**, a "rain shadow" formed by the **Arakan (Rakhine) Yoma**, Magwe Division receives scant rainfall compared to areas to the south, although as much as half a million acres of cropland are devoted to the cultivation of **rice**. It is Burma's largest producer of millet and groundnuts (peanuts), and the country's second largest producer of sesame seeds, cotton, pulses, and beans. The landscape is rolling or flat and gives the impression of desert or savannah, the horizon interrupted by clumps of shaggy sugar palms. Bisected by the **Irrawaddy (Ayeyarwady) River**, Magwe Division is a major link in north–south water, road, and rail transportation.

Yenaungyaung (Yaynangyoung) and Chauk have been important for the production of **oil** since before the British colonial era. Industries include petroleum refineries, rice mills, cotton mills, fertilizer and cement plants, and factories for producing machinery and consumer goods. **Forestry** is economically important, with reforestation projects being implemented. Part of the **Burman (Bamar)** heartland (**Upper Burma**), Magwe Division is rather homogeneous ethnically and includes the town of Natmauk, the birthplace of independence hero **Aung San**. Beikthano (the "City of Vishnu"), a **Pyu** site, is located southeast of Magwe, and **Sale (Salay)**, located southwest of Chauk, contains interesting but little-investigated monuments dating from the late **Pagan (Bagan) Dynasty**.

MAHA BANDULA (ca. 1780–1825). General who fought the British during the **First Anglo-Burmese War**. Born near Monywa in what is now **Sagaing Division**, he served both Kings **Bodawpaya** and Bagyidaw. A renowned commander, he was Bagyidaw's viceroy in Assam after the country was occupied by Burmese troops and planned to subjugate not only the small states of northeastern India but also British Bengal. Launching an attack on Bengal from Burmese-occupied **Arakan (Rakhine)** when war was declared on March 5, 1824, Maha Bandula was forced to withdraw to **Lower Burma** after a British expeditionary force landed at **Rangoon (Yangon)** in May. He fought pitched engagements against the British in and around Rangoon, but in April 1825 he was killed during a battle at Danubyu, a stockade located northwest of the city. Among Burmese, Maha Bandula's name is synonymous with impetuous courage.

MAHA MUNI BUDDHA IMAGE. The most important Buddha image in Burma, located in a temple complex just south of the center of

Mandalay. Maha Muni means "great sage," and according to legend, a king of **Arakan (Rakhine)** commissioned it during the lifetime of Gotama **Buddha**, who "breathed life upon it," giving it special powers. Archeological evidence suggests it was one of the earliest representations of Buddha, created in the early centuries CE. The Maha Muni image served as the protector of the Arakan Kingdom until King **Bodawpaya** brought it to his capital in central Burma following his subjugation of Arakan in 1784–1785. The image is approximately four meters (13 feet) high and adorned with a crown in the manner of a "universal monarch"; generations of devotees have covered it with so much gold leaf that its original shape has been distorted. Only the Maha Muni image's face is shiny and smooth. Burmese people refer to it as *paya*, the word also used to designate a **pagoda**, but which in the broadest sense means any person or object worthy of devotion or veneration.

MAHA THAMADA (MAHA THAMMADA). In Indo-Buddhist and Burmese tradition, the first king. At the beginning of the world epoch, human beings were naturally good, like the inhabitants of the Garden of Eden, but over time they became greedy, lustful, and corrupted, and constantly quarreled. Recognizing this, they elected a wise man to rule over them and make the laws. He was the "Great Chosen One" (*Maha Thamada*). Scholars have compared this myth with the Western concept of the social contract and James Madison's belief, expressed in *The Federalist Papers*, that "if men were angels, no government would be necessary." On an ideological level, it provided incumbent rulers with legitimacy, especially because Burmese kings claimed descent from the *Maha Thamada*, although royal succession was dynastic or through force majeure rather than by election. *See also* ADMINISTRATION AND SOCIETY, PRECOLONIAL BURMA.

MAHA VIZAYA PAGODA. Often called "**Ne Win**'s pagoda" because of his role in sponsoring its construction, the Maha Vizaya ("Great Victory") Pagoda is located adjacent to the southern entrance to the **Shwe Dagon Pagoda** in **Rangoon (Yangon)**. Dedicated in 1980 to commemorate the establishment of a state-controlled Supreme Sangha Council, it enshrines relics donated by the King of Nepal and unlike most pagodas is hollow. Its inner chamber is lavishly decorated and contains many symbols related to **astrology**.

MAHASI SAYADAW (1904–1982). A prominent member of the **Sangha**, who perfected a method of **meditation** that has attracted large numbers of Burmese and foreign practitioners. Born in the village of Seikkhun near **Shwebo** in what is now **Sagaing Division**, he entered the monkhood at the age of 6; at 12 was ordained as a novice (*samanera*); at 19, he decided to devote his life to religion and received ordination as a monk (*bhikkhu*). While at monasteries in **Moulmein** (**Mawlamyine**) and **Thaton**, he carried out intensive study of the **Pali** Canon in order to understand the principles of *satipatthana-vipassana* (insight-awareness) meditation. He taught them to his first disciples in his hometown of Seikkhun in 1938. During **World War II**, he remained in Seikkhun (residing at the Mahasi Monastery, thus his title), taught meditation techniques, and wrote a *Manual of Vipassana Meditation*. In November 1949, Prime Minister U **Nu** invited him to teach at the *Sasana Yeiktha* (Buddhist or Meditation Center) in **Rangoon** (**Yangon**). He played a prominent role in the **Sixth Great Buddhist Council**, convened by the prime minister between 1954 and 1956, and headed missions to promote Theravada **Buddhism** and *vipassana* meditation methods in **Japan**, Sri Lanka, **Indonesia**, and Western countries. Through his efforts and those of his disciples, meditation centers based on his teachings were established not only in Burma but also in **Thailand**, Sri Lanka, and elsewhere. Aside from teaching, the Mahasi Sayadaw was a prolific translator and writer on Buddhist subjects. *See also* BA KHIN, U.

MALAYSIA, RELATIONS WITH. After the **State Law and Order Restoration Council** seized power in September 1988, Malaysia's prime minister, Mahathir bin Mohammad, promoted close bilateral relations, including substantial **foreign investment** (US$600 million by the end of the 1990s) and trade, sponsorship of Burma's successful 1997 bid to join the **Association of Southeast Asian Nations** (**ASEAN**), and strong criticism of Western countries for allegedly interfering in Burma's and the Association's internal affairs by opposing the country's ASEAN membership. Critical of Western **sanctions**, Mahathir argued that "constructive engagement" was more effective in encouraging democratic change. His close associate, diplomat Razali Ismail (formally acting under the authority of **United Nations** Secretary General Kofi Annan) traveled many times to **Rangoon (Yangon)** between 2000 and 2003 to promote dialogue between Daw **Aung San Suu Kyi** and the military regime. However, the "**Black Friday**" Incident of May 30, 2003, caused even the Malaysian prime minister to criticize the regime for its intransigence. In June 2005, on the occasion of the 60th birthday of Daw Suu Kyi, Mahathir called on the **State Peace and Development Council (SPDC)** to release her from house arrest. It is unclear how Malaysia's Burma policy has changed under his successor, Abdullah Ahmad Badawi, but Anwar Ibrahim, a prominent opposition leader who was jailed by Mahathir in 1998 but later released, has called for a tougher policy toward the military regime.

One delicate issue in the bilateral relationship has been the SPDC's treatment of Burma's Muslim minority, especially **Rohingyas**, an estimated 10,000 of whom have become **refugees** in Malaysia. *See also* MUSLIMS IN BURMA; SINGAPORE, RELATIONS WITH.

MANDALAY. Capital of **Mandalay Division** and Burma's second largest city, located on the east bank of the **Irrawaddy (Ayeyarwady) River** in **Upper Burma**. Its population was 533,000 at the time of the 1983 census, and at the beginning of the 21st century was estimated at between 600,000 and 800,000. Between 1857 and 1885, it served as Burma's last royal capital, having been constructed by order of King **Mindon** on a site that, according to legend, had been favored by Gotama **Buddha** as the place where a great city would be built 2,400 years after the founding of the Buddhist religion.

Mandalay's most notable landmark is the moated wall that surrounds the place where the **Mandalay Palace** stood until it was destroyed during **World War II**. The city also contains important Buddhist sites, such as **Mandalay Hill**, the **Maha Muni Buddha Image**, and the **Kuthodaw Pagoda**. Because of its status as a former royal capital, Mandalay is a center for traditional Burmese arts, culture, and religious life.

Massive demonstrations occurred in Mandalay in 1988, and a "strike committee" in which monks played a prominent role briefly governed the city during **Democracy Summer**. In the summer of 1990, senior monks at Mandalay monasteries began a boycott of the **Tatmadaw**, known as **Overturning the Offering Bowl**, which spread to other parts of the country.

Economic liberalization has transformed the city since 1988. Both the *zeigyo*, the old central market, and the colonial-era railway station have been replaced by multistoried modern structures, several international class hotels have been built with foreign investment, and **Chinese** businesspeople have bought up property in the city center, causing land prices to rise, forcing many of the original Burmese residents to relocate to outlying districts. A new $3.15 billion international airport has been constructed south of the city by a Thai construction company, with facilities to handle wide-bodied jets and a capacity of three million passengers annually.

Mandalay's economic ties with **China**, especially Yunnan Province, strengthened after 1988, and a large though unspecified number of Yunnanese and other Chinese have settled in the city, often purchasing Burmese identity cards. Chinese-owned businesses are so numerous that local Burmese often call central Mandalay "Chinatown."

MANDALAY DIVISION. One of Burma's 14 **states** and **divisions**, with an area of 37,946 square kilometers (14,651 square miles) and an estimated population in 2000 of 6.76 million (1983 census figure: 4,577,762). The divisional capital is **Mandalay**, which was Burma's last royal capital and is the country's second largest city. Mandalay Division comprises seven **districts** (Mandalay, **Maymyo [Pyin-Oo-Lwin]**, **Kyaukse**, Myingyan, Nyaung-U, Yamethin, and **Meiktila**) and 31 **townships**. Located in the **Dry Zone**, a "rain shadow" formed by the **Arakan (Rakhine) Yoma**, it receives scant rainfall compared to areas to the south. To alleviate water shortages, the **State Peace and Development Council (SPDC)** has built numerous dams and irrigation networks. The land is generally low-lying, although the division includes the foothills of the Shan Plateau (it is bordered by **Shan State** to the east), the northern part of the **Pegu (Bago) Yoma**, and isolated high points, such as **Mandalay Hill** and the volcanic Mount **Popa**. The **Irrawaddy (Ayeyarwady) River** runs along part of its western border with **Magwe (Magway) Division**, and tributaries of the **Sittang (Sittoung) River** flow south from the division. Elongated in a north–south direction, its northern arm includes **Mogok (Mogoke)**, a famous center of ruby mining. Major crops include **rice**, millet, groundnuts, oil seeds (sesame and sunflower), pulses, beans, toddy (sugar) palm, and cotton. Mandalay Division has significant industry, including factories for the production of such consumer goods as textiles, soft drinks, and canned goods, and the **rail transport** workshops at Myitnge. Since the 1990s, industrial estates have been established in Mandalay city. **Forestry** is also economically important, and the town of Kyaukpadaung is a hub for highway transportation.

Located in the **Burman (Bamar)** heartland **(Upper Burma)**, Mandalay Division is the site of many of the country's old royal capitals: Mandalay, **Pagan (Bagan)** in Nyaung-U District, **Ava (Inwa)**, and **Amarapura**. Even after the British shifted the center of political and economic power to **Rangoon (Yangon)**, these towns have remained important as places where traditional art, culture, and manners are preserved. For example, Amarapura is a center for traditional silk weaving, and marble Buddha images are carved at Sagyin outside of Mandalay. Most of the population are Burmans, though there are smaller numbers of **Shans** and other indigenous ethnic minorities, and an undetermined (though probably large) population of migrants from the **People's Republic of China**. In 2005, the SPDC announced that a new national capital would be built at **Pyinmana**, in the southern part of Mandalay Division, and relocation of personnel commenced in November of that year.   .

MANDALAY HILL. Rising 236 meters above **Mandalay** to the northeast of **Mandalay Palace**, the hill is associated with a legend in which Gotama **Buddha**, standing at the summit, prophesied that a great city would be built on the plain below, 24 centuries after the establishment of **Buddhism**. A standing Buddha image, pointing toward the city, represents this episode (Mandalay was in fact established by King **Mindon** as his capital, construction being completed in 1857). A number of Buddhist sites are on the hill, the construction of which was sponsored by a prominent hermit, U **Khanti**. Fighting between Allied and Japanese forces occurred on Mandalay Hill in 1945.

MANDALAY PALACE. Completed by King **Mindon** in 1857, the Mandalay Palace's layout was similar to that of the previous royal residence at **Amarapura**. It was surrounded by a moat and an eight-meter-(26-foot)-high square wall made of brick, each side of which is about two kilometers long. Twelve gates piercing the wall are topped with wooden tiered-roof structures or spires (*pyatthat* in the **Burmese [Myanmar] language**). The wall and moat remain intact today. The interior buildings were made of **teak**, including the royal palace itself, the hall where the **Hluttaw** met, and religious buildings. The palace design reflected the Indo-Buddhist concept that the king's abode was the "center of the cosmos," and a seven-tiered *pyatthat* was built over the central throne room, representing Mount Meru. During Mindon's reign, as many as 5,000 persons lived within the palace precincts.

Following the **Third Anglo-Burmese War**, the British took over the palace, renaming it Fort Dufferin. The queen's reception room was used for a time as a British social club. During **World War II**, Japanese forces made it their headquarters, and most of the buildings were burned down in Allied bombings in 1945. The **State Law and Order Restoration Council** built reproductions of some of them in the 1990s and cleaned up the moat, a massive task, using **forced labor**.

MANERPLAW. Meaning "Field of Victory," Manerplaw was established as the headquarters of the **Karen National Union (KNU)** and its armed force, the **Karen National Liberation Army (KNLA)**, in 1975. It was located in what seemed to be an impregnable position: To the east was the Moei River, which formed the border with **Thailand**, while to the west was the **Salween (Thanlwin) River**, and to the south and west, the **Dawna Range**. Manerplaw became the headquarters of the National Democratic Front (NDF), an alliance of noncommunist ethnic minority armed groups, in 1976, and of the **Democratic Alliance of Burma** in 1988. It was also the site where the **National Coalition Government of the Union of Burma** was proclaimed in December 1990.

Given its location just inside the Burmese border and its status as the "capital" of the ethnic minority and **Burman (Bamar)** opposition, Manerplaw became the objective of a massive offensive by the

Tatmadaw in 1992; it failed but left the KNLA gravely weakened. A second offensive in 1995, designated Operation *Pyi Zanh* ("Hero of the People"), captured Manerplaw on January 27. A second major Karen base at Kawmoorah, 80 kilometers southeast of Manerplaw, fell on February 21. Major factors in the operation's success were the Tatmadaw's superior intelligence and the active assistance of the **Democratic Karen Buddhist Army (DKBA)**, which had defected from the KNU in December 1994.

MANIPUR. Formerly an independent kingdom, located in what is now Manipur State, **India**, to the west of Burma's **Chin State**. It was sometimes a vassal state of Burma, but in the mid-18th century Manipuri cavalry staged crippling raids into **Upper Burma**, almost capturing **Ava (Inwa)** in 1749. A decade later, **Alaungpaya** subjugated it; thereafter, Manipuri Brahmin practitioners of **astrology**, taken prisoner by the king, served in the Burmese palace. During the **First Anglo-Burmese War**, it fell under British control. Manipur was the site of the **Imphal Campaign**, one of the major battles of **World War II**.

MANUHA TEMPLE. **Buddhist** monument at **Pagan (Bagan)**, built around 1059 by Manuha, the **Mon** king of **Thaton** who was taken captive by **Anawrahta**, founder of the **Pagan Dynasty**. Often considered "Burma's first political prisoner," Manuha was treated disrespectfully by his captor but allowed to build the temple, the design of which allegedly shows his displeasure at losing his freedom. The building is small and rather unimpressive, and three seated and one reclining Buddha images are too large for the narrow, claustrophobic chambers in which they are housed, where they look distinctly uncomfortable. *See also* ARCHITECTURE, RELIGIOUS; PAGAN DYNASTY.

MARTABAN (MOTTAMA). Located at the mouth of the **Salween (Thanlwin) River** across from **Moulmein (Mawlamyine)** in **Mon State**, fronting the Gulf of Martaban, Martaban is the site of a port and **Mon** kingdom, established by **Wareru** in the late thirteenth century. The Portuguese briefly established a presence there in the sixteenth century.

MASS MEDIA IN BURMA. Mass media include both print (newspapers and magazines) and broadcast (radio and television) outlets for information and entertainment. Under British rule, Burma had a number of vernacular newspapers, of which the most notable were *Thuriya* (*The Sun*) and *Myanma Alin* (*New Light of Myanmar*). During the parliamentary period (1948–1962), there were as many as 56 different newspapers, published not only in the **Burmese (Myanmar) language**, but also in the English, Chinese, and Indian languages. After **Ne Win** established the **Revolutionary Council** in March 1962, most of these were closed down, and the **Press Scrutiny Board (PSB)**, which remains operative today, imposed draconian censorship on the few publications that were allowed to continue. In 1966, the regime issued a decree stating that newspapers could be published only in Burmese and English.

The Ne Win regime's principal press organ was the *Loketha Pyithu Nezin* (*Working People's Daily*), which was published in both languages, a newspaper that can be compared to the *Renmin Ribao* (*People's Daily*) in Mao Zedong–era China for its heavy propagandistic content. Radio and television (the latter introduced to Burma in 1980) were under the control of the state-owned Burma Broadcasting Service (BBS).

During 1988, foreign radio stations, such as the Voice of America, All India Radio, and especially the British Broadcasting Corporation (BBC) played an indispensable role in providing Burmese listeners with credible information at a time when the state media tried to conceal events, such as the **White Bridge Incident.** After coming to power in September 1988, the **State Law and Order Restoration Council (SLORC)** accused these stations of serving as instruments of neocolonial powers wishing to undermine **national unity**, as expressed in a regime publication, *Sky Full of Lies.* In the early 21st century, the BBC, Radio Free Asia, and the Voice of Democratic Burma remain important sources of information for listeners inside the country, and some observers credit their impact on Burmese people's awareness of current events as more crucial than that of **information technology**, such as the Internet, which the **State Peace and Development Council (SPDC)** monitors and controls tightly.

The SLORC's postsocialist "open economy" policies helped foster a more diverse though still compliant media scene in the 1990s. Renamed *Myanma Alin* (**New Light of Myanmar**) in 1993, the *Working People's Daily* remains the official mouthpiece, controlled by the Ministry of Information. A handful of other newspapers are allowed to publish, including *Kyemon (Mirror Daily)*, *City News*, and *Yadanabon*. In 2000, the *Myanmar Times and Business Review* was inaugurated; this weekly, published both in English and Burmese and edited by an Australian journalist, has an appealing format and interesting stories, although it was reportedly established with the assistance of **Military Intelligence** and does not publish articles critical of the SPDC. There reportedly were plans to make the *Myanmar Times* a daily paper, but its future was uncertain after **Khin Nyunt**'s purge in October 2004.

In recent years, some 50 private weekly and monthly magazines have been established, among them "lifestyle" and business magazines that cater to affluent urban audiences who are influenced by global trends. A streetside newsstand in **Rangoon (Yangon)** might sell *Eleven* (sports), *Dana,* and *Myanmar Dana* (business), *Image* and *Idea* (ladies' fashion magazines), and even *Golf*. Like the *Myanmar Times*, they are glossy; *Image*, for example, looks like a Burmese-language version of *Cosmopolitan*, though more modest in content. A reader can even purchase *News Update*, which deals with world affairs (though apparently not relating to Burmese politics). All these publications remain subject to heavy censorship by the PSB. When officials find offending articles, they order them inked over or torn out of the magazines.

Myanmar Radio and Television (MRTV), the former BBS, manages several TV channels, including one that broadcasts in English, while the **Tatmadaw** has its own channel, Myawaddy TV. Programs focus on official visits by SPDC leaders to different parts of the country or overseas and are so dull that viewers look forward to seeing the commercials, which feature popular film stars or models. Imported Chinese and South Korean television dramas also have many viewers. Those tired of domestic fare can, if they can afford it, place a satellite dish on the roof of their residence, though this is technically illegal without a special permit from the government. The **Yangon City Development Committee** has established a new radio station,

City FM, which is popular with younger people in **Rangoon (Yangon)**. Despite the growing diversity of Burma's media, the people remain starved for reliable news. Within the relatively safe confines of their homes, listening to the BBC Burmese Service has become a valued daily routine. *See also* MOTION PICTURES IN BURMA.

MASS ORGANIZATIONS, BURMA SOCIALIST PROGRAMME PARTY ERA (1962–1988). In the one-party state that evolved after the **Burma Socialist Programme Party** was established by **Ne Win** in 1962, "mass and class organizations" played a role in "agitating and organizing the people into appreciating and accepting the Party's policies and decisions and to induce wide mass participation in the national development projects" (*Working People's Daily*, December 20, 1982). These included youth-oriented groups aimed at different ages (Lanzin, Shaysaung, and Teza Youths), Workers' Asiayone (Workers' Associations), Peasants' Asiayone (Peasants' Associations), and groups of war veterans and "literary workers." In the case of the larger groups, members numbered in the millions (7.8 million in the Peasants' Associations in 1982), but the rapid collapse of these mass organizations following the prodemocracy demonstrations of 1988 indicates that, at best, the population regarded them with indifference. The post-1988 equivalent is the **Union Solidarity and Development Association**, which also has many millions of members.

MAUNG AYE, GENERAL (1940–). Vice chairman of the **State Peace and Development Council (SPDC)**, he graduated with the first class of the **Defence Services Academy** in 1959. During the 1980s, he served as head of **Regional Military Commands** and became deputy commander in chief of the **Tatmadaw** in 1993 and vice chairman of the **State Law and Order Restoration Council** in 1994, holding the same position under the SPDC when it was established in 1997. Compared to the relatively "moderate" **Khin Nyunt**, he is considered a hard-liner, but in the opening years of the 21st century, he appeared to be losing influence because he was not especially close to SPDC Chairman **Than Shwe**. It is unclear whether the purge of Khin Nyunt in October 2004 has resulted in an enhancement of his power and influence within the junta. *See also* STATE PEACE AND DEVELOPMENT COUNCIL, INTERNAL DYNAMICS.

MAUNG MAUNG, DR. (1924–1994). The only intellectual known to have been close to General **Ne Win** during his long military and political career, Dr. Maung Maung served briefly in 1988 as chairman of the **Burma Socialist Programme Party** and president of Burma. He was in the **Burma Defence Army/Burma National Army** during **World War II**. After the war, he studied at Mandalay College and **Rangoon (Yangon) University**. He pursued his studies abroad at Lincoln's Inn, London, the University of Utrecht, and Yale University, earning doctorates at the latter two institutions. In the mid-1950s, he established the *Guardian* magazine and newspaper. After Ne Win's coup d'état in March 1962, Dr. Maung Maung was appointed Chief Justice and was one of the main authors of the **Constitution of 1974**. After **Sein Lwin**'s resignation as head of the party and state in the face of popular indignation, Maung Maung assumed these posts, on August 19, 1988. He enjoyed little credibility among the populace, however, being nicknamed "the Puppet." On September 10, he announced to the second **BSPP Extraordinary Congress** that multiparty democratic elections would be held in the near future. After the **State Law and Order Restoration Council** assumed power on September 18, he retired from public life.

Dr. Maung Maung wrote a number of books on Burmese history and law, including *Burma and General Ne Win* and *The 1988 Uprising in Burma,* which are well-written apologies for Ne Win and his regime. *See also* DEMOCRACY SUMMER; FOUR EIGHTS MOVEMENT.

MAUNG PHONE MAW (1965–1988). Student at **Rangoon (Yangon) Institute of Technology** who was shot and killed by the **Riot Police (Lon Htein)** during a demonstration on March 13, 1988, following the **Tea Shop Incident**. An official Inquiry Commission reported in May 1988 that he and another student (Soe Naing) died of multiple gunshot wounds. As the first student victim of 1988, he has been compared to Bo **Aung Gyaw**, a **Rangoon (Yangon) University** student killed by British colonial police in December 1938. The anniversary of his death on March 13 is commemorated by oppositionists as "Burma Human Rights Day." *See also* MIN KO NAING.

MAYMYO (PYIN OO LWIN, PYIN U LWIN). Located in **Mandalay Division** on the edge of the Shan Plateau, Maymyo, named after a British officer who participated in the **Pacification of Burma**, was the summer capital of the British governor and other officials during the colonial period and was also popular with other Europeans seeking respite from the hot weather. At an elevation of over 1,000 meters (3,250 feet), it is noted for its fresh, cool air, pine trees, strawberries, and old buildings designed to remind Europeans of "home," such as the Candacraig Hotel. It is also the location of the **Defence Services Academy** and a new university for **Tatmadaw** personnel specializing in technology. There are large populations of Indians and Nepali Gurkhas, whose forebears came during the colonial period. *See also* KALAW.

MEDITATION. Meditation is central to the serious practice of **Buddhism**; Gotama **Buddha** attributed his enlightenment to meditation techniques. Simply described, it involves two stages: the achievement of tranquility (*samatha*) through proper concentration, calming the mind's restlessness; and the achievement of insight (*vipassana*), through which a person can fully comprehend the truths of Buddhism, including impermanence and non-self (*anatta*). Burmese Buddhists believe that their country is home to advanced and scripturally authentic meditation techniques. After World War II, Burmese meditation teachers, especially the **Mahasi Sayadaw** and U **Ba Khin**, attracted disciples both from inside and outside the country and established meditation centers that continue to be popular today. Many of Burma's political leaders, such as Prime Minister U **Nu**, practiced meditation; during her term of house arrest from 1989 to 1995, Daw **Aung San Suu Kyi** also meditated, though without benefit of a teacher.

MEIKTILA. A city in **Mandalay Division**, with a population estimated at 127,837 in 1996. Known for its lake and a large **air force (Tatmadaw lei)** base, its location at the intersection of the east-west Bagan-Taunggyi road and the north-south **Rangoon (Yangon)-Mandalay** road makes it an important commercial center in **Upper Burma**. It was the site of a major battle between Allied and Japanese forces during **World War II**.

MEKONG RIVER. The largest river system in Southeast Asia, with a length of 4,200 kilometers, the Mekong rises in southwestern **China** (Tibet) and flows through or along the borders of all mainland Southeast Asian countries: Vietnam, Laos, **Thailand**, Cambodia, and Burma. It forms Burma's eastern border with Laos. Comprehensive economic development plans for the **Greater Mekong Subregion** promoted by the Asian Development Bank include Burma, and ambitious projects to facilitate riverine communications and integrate the economies of southwestern China and the five Southeast Asian countries will have a major impact on what are now some of Burma's remotest areas in eastern **Shan State**.

MERGUI (MYEIK, BEIK). Fronting the Andaman Sea, Mergui is located in south-central **Tenasserim (Tanintharyi) Division** and had an estimated population of 100,000 in 1996. Because of its good harbor, the town has had a long history as a trade center, serving the northeastern littoral of the Indian Ocean. For much of this time, it was under the control of Siam rather than Burma. During the seventeenth century. an Englishman, Samuel White, served as its harbormaster, and the tomb of his wife Mary, who died in 1682, can still be seen. His adventures are described in a book by **Maurice Collis**, *Siamese White*. Since 1988, Mergui, known for its attractive traditional and colonial architecture, has experienced significant economic growth through the export of seafood products to Thailand. *See also* MERGUI ARCHIPELAGO.

MERGUI (MYEIK, BEIK) ARCHIPELAGO. An island group found along the eastern shore of the Andaman Sea, which, according to British colonial geographers, contains 804 islands, extending roughly from **Mergui (Myeik, Beik)** in **Tenasserim (Tanintharyi) Division** in the north to the Thai–Burma border (Kawthaung, Victoria Point) in the south. The largest island is King Island (Kadan Kyun), opposite Mergui, and others include St. Matthew, Domel, and Kisseraing Islands. The archipelago is home to the **Moken**, "Sea Gypsies." Although ecotourism taking advantage of the beautiful marine environment is being developed, the islands remain largely isolated from the outside world. Some have limestone caves where swiftlets build their nests, which are gathered and used for "bird's nest soup," a Chinese delicacy that can fetch high prices in Hong Kong and Singapore. Pearls are found in offshore waters; the once-abundant marine life has been over-fished in recent years, often by fishermen using dynamite.

MERRILL'S MARAUDERS (5307 COMPOSITE UNIT). Informally named for their commander, Brigadier General Frank D. Merrill, this **World War II** American unit numbering 2,997 officers and men was organized as a counterpart to Brigadier Orde Wingate's **Chindits.** Under the command of General Joseph Stilwell, its objectives were to recapture northern Burma from the Japanese and clear the way for completion of the **Ledo Road.** In an operation code-named "Galahad," the Marauders marched overland from northeastern India into the **Hukawng Valley** (in present-day **Kachin State**) in February 1944, fought tenaciously against Japanese units alongside the 22d and 38th Chinese Divisions, and captured the vital airstrip at **Myitkyina** in May. Allied control of the airfield enabled them to fly more than 14,000 supply flights from India to China between May and October 1944. But the Japanese counterattacked, and the town of Myitkyina did not fall to the Allies until August. That same month, the Marauders, having suffered terrible casualties, were demobilized. *See also* BURMA ROAD.

MILITARY INTELLIGENCE (MI). The **State Peace and Development Council (SPDC)** has operated an extensive military intelligence apparatus that not only provided the **Tatmadaw** (armed forces) with reliable information on conventional national security matters—the task of military intelligence agencies in most countries—but also monitored the civilian population closely for signs of dissent, kept an eye on the Tatmadaw's own rank and file to detect disloyal elements, and carried out public relations activities in foreign countries to make the SPDC regime more acceptable in the eyes of the international community. Since 1989, it has also played a central role in negotiating **cease-fires** between the central government and ethnic minority armed groups. Burma's most powerful intelligence agency was the Directorate of **Defense Services Intelligence (DDSI)**, also known as the Military Intelligence Service (MIS), which was formally under the authority of the **National Intelligence Bureau** and the Ministry of Defence.

Most ordinary Burmese know Military Intelligence as "MI." Its network of informers in **tea shops**, on college campuses, and in local neighborhoods has been a part of daily life for many years. Foreign visitors have sometimes been shadowed by MI agents. Burmese living abroad have also been aware that MI *agents provocateurs* may be operating in their midst. MI has been widely criticized by international **human rights** organizations for some of the SPDC's worst abuses, including the torture and killing of detainees at interrogation centers, such as the DDSI's Ye Kyi Aing facility north of **Rangoon (Yangon)**.

When Burma became independent in 1948, Military Intelligence units were established to gather information on communist and ethnic minority insurgents. However, they were poorly organized and coordinated. During the **Caretaker Government** and **Burma Socialist Programme Party (BSPP)** periods (1958–1960, 1962–1988), MI was extensively reorganized, rationalized, and expanded, and became deeply involved in surveillance of the general population. Informers were recruited, especially among university students, using threats or bribes, a practice that continues today. In the aftermath of the **U Thant Incident** in 1974 and the massive popular demonstrations of 1988, MI informers helped put thousands of dissidents in jail.

Because MI officers were generally better educated than their counterparts in the regular army and operated with considerable autonomy, **Ne Win** perceived them as a threat to his own power base and ordered the purge of the powerful **"MI" Tin Oo** in mid-1983. That same year, Military Intelligence was reorganized to ensure tighter **State Council** and regular army control. This left the intelligence apparatus in some disarray, apparently making it possible for agents from **North Korea** to carry out a terrorist bombing of the Martyrs' Monument during a state visit of the South Korean cabinet on October 9, 1983, the **Rangoon Incident**. Ne Win charged Colonel **Khin Nyunt** with the task of rebuilding the MI apparatus, and he became its head in 1984.

During 1988, Khin Nyunt and his fellow intelligence officers seriously misread the depth of popular dissatisfaction, as demonstrated by the BSPP regime's inept and heavy-handed response to the demonstrations of **Democracy Summer**. A second intelligence failure was the landslide victory of the **National League for Democracy** in the **General Election of May 27, 1990**. However, after the **State Law and Order Restoration Council** was established in September 1988, MI underwent a major expansion in terms of manpower, equipment, and new technology (much of which was obtained from **China, Singapore**, and other countries). After 1992, its command structure operated independently of the regular Tatmadaw. At the beginning of the 21st century, it had the capability to carry out sophisticated HUMINT (Human Intelligence, e.g., agents, informers), SIGINT (Signals Intelligence, monitoring communications), and even IMINT ([overhead] Imagery Intelligence, using aircraft) operations against domestic and foreign targets.

Because the SLORC/SPDC enjoys little or no popular support, Military Intelligence became indispensable for keeping it in power. Not only the regime's "eyes and ears" but also its "brains," it informed the top junta leadership, who are largely uneducated and ignorant of the outside world, about the latest domestic and international developments, carrying out a function that in other political systems would be done by not only intelligence agencies but also political analysts, agencies of the executive and legislative branches of government, and independent **mass media**. However, the efficiency of its operations was hampered by the wide range of its responsibilities and the limited resources available to it.

On October 18, 2004, MI commander Khin Nyunt was arrested on charges of corruption and attempting to split the Tatmadaw. His sudden, though not entirely unexpected, fall from power left the intelligence apparatus in disarray because as many as 2,000 of his subordinates were also arrested or forced into retirement. The purge was motivated by intra-junta factional rivalries, and Khin Nyunt's rivals, including Generals **Maung Aye** and **Soe Win**, with the backing of Senior General **Than Shwe**, apparently believed Khin Nyunt was building a "junta within the junta," which endangered their own power base. One result of the dismantling of the MI apparatus was an amnesty extended to thousands of prisoners, but only a handful of these were political prisoners, and there was no evidence that the SPDC was softening its attitude toward **Aung San Suu Kyi** and her supporters.

On May 7, 2005, three bomb blasts at crowded shopping centers in Rangoon killed, according to official reports, 11 people, although the actual figure may have been much higher. In a sense, this was history repeating itself, for, like the October 1983 Rangoon Incident, it occurred at a time when the Military Intelligence apparatus was in disarray following its leader's arrest. However, unlike the 1983 bombings, it was unclear who the perpetrators were. The regime blamed foreign-based opposition groups, but some observers speculated that elements within the military, perhaps reacting to the purge of Khin Nyunt and his subordinates, may have been responsible. *See also* DIRECTORATE OF DEFENSE SERVICES INTELLIGENCE; MILITARY INTELLIGENCE, ORGANIZATION OF; NATIONAL INTELLIGENCE BUREAU; OFFICE OF STRATEGIC STUDIES.

MILITARY INTELLIGENCE (MI), ORGANIZATION OF. The organizational structure of **Military Intelligence** was established during the **Burma Socialist Programme Party** period (1962–1988), with some modifications after the **State Law and Order Restoration Council** came to power in September 1988. Stated briefly, the modifications restored much of the autonomy enjoyed by Military Intelligence agencies before the purge of **"MI" Tin Oo** in 1983. Before the purge of MI commander Lieutenant-General **Khin Nyunt** in October 2004, the **National Intelligence Bureau**, which was directly responsible to the **State Peace and Development Council (SPDC)**, oversaw all intelligence activities, including not only the **Directorate of Defense Services Intelligence** (DDSI, also known as the Military Intelligence Service, MIS), which was under the authority of the Ministry of Defence, but also intelligence agencies attached to the Ministries of Foreign Affairs, Home Affairs, National Planning and Economic Development, and Immigration and Population. However, the DDSI was the most powerful intelligence organ, carrying out the SPDC's most important information-gathering activities and exercising control over the civilian intelligence agencies. Its director, Khin Nyunt, was concurrently director general of the National Intelligence Bureau and (until 2003) Secretary-1 of the SPDC. Following his 2004 ouster, the National Intelligence Bureau was abolished.

All intelligence units attached to the three services of the **Tatmadaw** were subordinate to the DDSI, which also commanded its own hierarchy of special units (Military Intelligence companies) on the regional level. The number of these special units increased from

14 in 1989 to approximately 40 by 2000. They were concentrated in urban areas and in border regions adjacent to **China, India**, and **Bangladesh**. After 1992, they reported directly to the DDSI headquarters, rather than through the regular Tatmadaw chain of command. Some DDSI personnel were responsible for surveillance of the Tatmadaw rank and file, which, along with its independence from the regular chain of command, made the DDSI a focus of strong resentment on the part of the regular military.

In the mid-1990s, the **Office of Strategic Studies (OSS)** was established as a "think tank," with Khin Nyunt as its head. Although the DDSI's headquarters had been located in the heavily guarded **Defence Services Compound** in central **Rangoon (Yangon)**, it reportedly moved to a new location at Eight Mile Junction north of **Inya Lake**. DDSI had working relations with the governments of a number of SPDC-friendly countries, including China, **Singapore**, and possibly Israel. Since Khin Nyunt's purge, however, the MI apparatus has been in disarray, and it is unclear what will replace it as the "eyes and ears" of the SPDC.

MIN BIN, KING (r. 1531–1553). Also known as Man Pa, ruler of **Arakan (Rakhine)**, whose reign witnessed the country's emergence as a major power. He established close ties with the Portuguese and was able to take advantage of their superior shipbuilding techniques and firearms to fortify his capital, **Mrauk-U**, and build a strong navy that conducted both trade and piracy in the Bay of Bengal. Portuguese served as officers in Min Bin's army, which consisted of mercenaries from a number of European and Asian countries. Min Bin not only imposed Arakanese control over eastern Bengal, including the port of Chittagong, but also successfully repulsed an invasion by the Burman King **Tabinshwehti** in 1546–1547. He was the builder of one of Arakan's most important **Buddhist** monuments, the **Shitthaung (Sittaung)** temple.

MIN KO NAING (1962–). *Nom de guerre* of Paw Oo Htun, the most prominent **student** leader of the 1988 prodemocracy movement. It means "conqueror of kings." A zoology student at **Rangoon (Yangon) University**, he expressed his opposition to the government of **Ne Win** in the mid-1980s by organizing a *than gyat* or song-and-skit troupe during **Thingyan**, which satirized the regime and its corrupt practices. He gave a speech at the university's Main Campus on March 16, 1988, and participated in the demonstration that ended with the **White Bridge Incident**. A founder of the **All Burma Federation of Student Unions (ABFSU)**, he issued the proclamation announcing the **Four Eights Movement**, a general strike with the aim of forcing the resignation of **Sein Lwin** as president and chairman of the **Burma Socialist Programme Party**. Preferring to do political work in the capital rather than fleeing to the border after the **State Law and Order Restoration Council** seized power, Min Ko Naing was arrested on March 23, 1989, and sentenced to 20 years for subversion. Kept at **Insein Jail** under extremely harsh conditions, including torture and solitary confinement, he was later transferred to the prison in **Sittwe (Sittway)**, **Arakan (Rakhine) State**. Although his sentence was reduced to ten years in 1993, he remained in confinement, suffering poor health, until released following an amnesty that was proclaimed after the purge of Lieutenant General **Khin Nyunt** in October 2004. *See also* DEMOCRACY SUMMER.

MIN MAHAGIRI. Known as the "Lord of the Great Mountain," he is one of the principal gods included in the pantheon of **Thirty-seven Nats** established by King **Anawrahta**. According to legend, he was a blacksmith of great strength, whose powers were feared by the king of Tagaung. The king married the blacksmith's beautiful sister and then treacherously invited the brother to come to his court. The blacksmith was bound to a tree and burned to death. His sister, who is known as Taunggyi Shin, or more popularly "Lady Golden Face," threw herself on the pyre and perished with her brother. Their images are enshrined at Mount **Popa**. Min Mahagiri also serves as the *nat* protector of households, whose presence is symbolized by an unhusked coconut hung from a high pillar, to which family members give daily offerings.

MINAMI KIKAN (MINAMI ORGAN). Established on February 1, 1941, by the Imperial General Headquarters of the Japanese Army, the Minami Kikan was a clandestine organization designed to promote Japanese war aims in Burma. Named for its head, Colonel **Suzuki Keiji** (who collected information and contacts in Burma under the name "Minami Masuyo"; *minami* also means "south" in Japanese), it operated for the most part in **Thailand**, using a front organization, the "Southeast Asia Industrial Investigation Association," as a cover for its activities. Its headquarters were in Bangkok, and branches were located at Kachanaburi, Ranong, Chiang Mai, and Raheng. The Minami Kikan recruited the **Thirty Comrades**; arranged their secret departure from Burma; gave them military training at a facility, the "Sanya Peasants' Training Center," on Hainan island, **China**; and provided arms and logistical support for the **Burma Independence Army**, which was formally established on December 28, 1941, in Bangkok.

The Minami Kikan originally included both Japanese army and navy officers, but navy resentment of Colonel Suzuki's often highhanded manner led to their withdrawal from the organization. After Suzuki was transferred from Burma back to Japan in June 1942, the Minami Kikan became inoperative. After the war, members of the Minami Kikan maintained contact with Burmese ruling circles. In 1981, eight of them received decorations, the "Order of Aung San" (*Aung San Tagun*), from President **Ne Win**. *See also* AUNG SAN; JAPANESE OCCUPATION.

MINDON, KING (r. 1853–1878). Tenth and penultimate monarch of the **Konbaung Dynasty**, he seized the throne after his half brother, Pagan Min (r. 1846–1853), suffered the loss of **Lower Burma** in the **Second Anglo-Burmese War**. Like his contemporary, King Mongkut of Siam (**Thailand**), he spent most of his adult life as a member of the **Sangha** before becoming king, promoted limited reforms of his realm, and pursued amicable relations with the British, who threatened Burma's independence as never before. He moved the royal capital from **Amarapura** to a new city, **Mandalay**, building an extensive palace compound at the foot of **Mandalay Hill**. With the support of his most influential minister, the **Kinwun Mingyi**, he undertook modernization of the civil service, tax system, and currency. One of his sons, the Mekkara Prince, embarked on a modest program of industrialization, setting up textile and other factories. Telegraph lines were strung between his kingdom and British Burma. A devout **Buddhist**, he convened the **Fifth Great Buddhist Council** in 1871, which produced an authoritative version of the **Tipitaka**, or scriptures. These were engraved on stone stelae and placed in the **Kuthodaw Pagoda**.

Mindon failed to persuade the British to return Lower Burma to him, and they barred him from coming to **Rangoon (Yangon)** to donate a *hti* to the **Shwe Dagon Pagoda** in 1871, because that might be interpreted as acknowledging his continued authority in British-occupied territory. The loss of Lower Burma left his kingdom landlocked, cutting Mindon off from effective communications with the other European powers. The British regarded him as equivalent to the Indian *maharajas*, a tributary rather than the sovereign of an independent state; he was never allowed to negotiate directly with the government in London (as Siam's Mongkut did), but only with the Indian Viceroy. British insistence on "free trade" led to the abolition of old royal monopolies, for example, on **teak**. Anglo-French rivalry, growing British economic interests in **Upper Burma**, and chronic unrest both in central Burma and ethnic minority areas doomed his efforts to preserve his country's independence.

Although the **"shoe question"** increased Anglo-Burmese tensions, Mindon succeeded in keeping the peace even though rumors of French interests in Burma were rife. Because a coup d'état attempt in 1866 resulted in the assassination of the crown prince, there was a succession struggle following Mindon's death on October 1, 1878 that resulted in a less able monarch, **Thibaw**, ascending the throne. *See also* THIRD ANGLO-BURMESE WAR.

MINERAL RESOURCES. The production and export of non-hydrocarbon minerals has been important to the Burmese **economy** since precolonial times, though production after the British colonial era declined because of insurgency in mining areas, nationalization, and underinvestment. Significant deposits of tin and tungsten (wolfram) extend from **Shan State** to **Tenasserim (Tanintharyi) Division**, the Mawchi mine in **Kayah State** having once been the world's largest source of tungsten. Also, the Namtu (Bawdwin) mine in Shan State was one of the world's richest producers of lead, silver, copper, and zinc. High-quality jade, much prized in China, is produced at Hpakant in **Kachin State**. **Mogok**, northeast of **Mandalay**, is famed as the source of sapphires and famed "pigeon blood" rubies. Since 1988 and the end of the socialist system, there has been significant **foreign investment** in the mining sector. *See also* GEMSTONES; OIL AND NATURAL GAS.

MINGALADON (TOWNSHIP). Located in northern **Rangoon (Yangon)**, Mingaladon Township is the site of Rangoon's international airport, the country's largest (in terms of traffic). There are also extensive **Tatmadaw** installations, so that a significant percentage of the township's population is military personnel. Both the airport and the military "cantonments" date back to the British colonial period.

MINGUN. A town on the **Irrawaddy (Ayeyarwady) River**, upriver from **Mandalay**, best known for the Mingun **Pagoda**, built by King **Bodawpaya** (r. 1782–1819). Intended to be the world's tallest pagoda, with a height of 170 meters (553 feet), its construction, which involved thousands of slaves and prisoners of war, was halted at Bodawpaya's death in 1819, and an **earthquake** damaged it in 1838. The ruins, standing 50 meters (163 feet) high, are still impressive. A 90-ton bronze bell, commissioned by Bodawpaya in 1808, is the largest undamaged bell in the world.

MINKYINYO, KING (r. 1486–1531). Founder and first monarch of the **Toungoo (Taungoo) Dynasty**. His small state, **Toungoo (Taungoo)**, located in the valley of the **Sittang (Sittoung) River**, attracted many **Burman** chiefs following the occupation of **Ava (Inwa)** by the Shans in 1527. He planned to conquer the **Mon** state of **Hanthawaddy** (modern-day **Pegu [Bago]**) in **Lower Burma**, but died in 1531; his son, **Tabinshwehti**, completed the task. *See also* BAYINNAUNG.

MINLAUNG. In the **Burmese (Myanmar) language**, an "imminent king," a person destined (from the perspective of **Buddhism**, through his accumulation of superior merit or *kutho*) to become ruler of the country, overthrowing the reigning monarch. The emergence of a *minlaung* was believed to be accompanied by special omens and signs; in the months following the **General Election of May 27, 1990**, many Burmese believed that **Aung San Suu Kyi** had assumed this role.

MISSIONARIES, CHRISTIAN. The role of Christian missionaries in Burmese history is controversial. They are often depicted as accomplices of British colonial oppression and agents of cultural imperialism, robbing indigenous people of their "authentic" beliefs and ways of life, but other observers point to their vital role in promoting **health**, **education**, and literacy, and a new national identity for ethnic minority peoples, especially among the **Karens (Kayins)**, **Kachins**, and **Chins**.

The first Christian missionaries were Roman Catholic and accompanied the Portuguese when they established a presence in **Lower Burma** in the 16th and 17th centuries. The most prominent early convert was Nat Shin-naung, lord of **Toungoo (Taungoo)** and would-be king, who was also renowned as a poet. Outraged by his renunciation of **Buddhism** and the egregious behavior of **Felipe de Brito**, which included plundering the **Shwe Dagon Pagoda**, King **Anaukpetlun** of **Ava (Inwa)** captured Toungoo and **Syriam (Thanlyin)** in 1613 and subjected de Brito to a horrible execution. However, Christianity was not totally eradicated; throughout the 18th and early 19th centuries, Roman Catholic priests, most notably Father Vincentius Sangermano, carried out limited missionary work, and a large church was built by a wealthy **Armenian** family at Syriam around 1766.

Because the commercially oriented East India Company did not want missionaries working in the areas under its control, Protestant missionaries did not arrive in Burma until the early 19th century. The first were **Adoniram Judson** and his wife Ann, American Baptists, who landed at **Rangoon (Yangon)** in 1813 and tried, without much success, to proselytize Buddhist **Burmans (Bamars)**. But the Judsons, who relocated themselves in British-occupied territories after the **First Anglo-Burmese War**, won a large number of converts among the **Karens (Kayins)**. In the late 19th and early 20th centuries, the Baptists achieved even greater success among the **Kachins** and **Chins**. Other Christian denominations, including the Catholics, Presbyterians, Methodists, and Seventh-Day Adventists, have made many converts among the **Karennis (Kayah)**, **Padaungs**, and **Nagas**. Because large measure to the missionaries' work, some 4 percent of Burma's population is now Christian, of whom three-quarters are Baptists and most of the rest Roman Catholic.

The missionary experience in Burma generally conformed to a pattern found throughout the non-Western world: Adherents to "world religions," such as **Buddhism**, Islam, or Hinduism were generally satisfied with their own faiths and suspicious of the missionaries' intentions, while animists, living in localized, "tribal" societies, were often quite receptive, though their enthusiasm for Christianity is sometimes exaggerated by church historians (many Chins, for example, were outraged by Christian desecration of their ancient holy places). Not only could missionaries offer the "hill tribes" medical care, schooling, and other social services (which were not always appreciated), but the Christian religion as they preached it intersected in meaningful ways with traditional beliefs. For example, many of the hill tribe people believed in a Supreme God and an afterlife, and had a mytho-history sharing themes with the Bible (e.g., accounts of a great flood). Resentment of oppression at the hands of Buddhist Burmans led hill Karens to believe they would be liberated by white foreigners bringing a powerful sacred Book. Many missionaries actively promoted a "national identity" for minority peoples by devising writing systems, promoting language/dialect standardization, and making translations of the Bible and other books into indigenous **languages**. Missionary schools fostered a new elite of preachers and teachers, and Christian minority soldiers formed the backbone of the **colonial armed forces**, many of whom rebelled against the Burmese government after independence in 1948.

Conversions were often inspired by the courage and dedication of individual missionaries, who typically were few in number, short of resources, and frequently exposed to dangers in isolated "mission stations" in the hills. Although some worked closely with British colonial authorities, others, such as the Baptist Laura Carson among the Chins, were outspokenly critical of British "pacification" policies.

Burmans viewed the missionary construction of minority national identity as a "divide and rule" tactic. There was an element of truth to this; for example, during the **Third Anglo-Burmese War**, some foreign missionaries encouraged Karens to cooperate with the British in suppressing Burmese rebels. Moreover, the close connection between the Buddhist religion and national identity (*Buddha Bata Myanma Lu-myo*, "to be Burmese/Burman is to be Buddhist") among the Burmese meant that Christians were not viewed as genuine members of mainstream Burmese society, a sentiment that reaches back at least to the days of Nat Shin-naung in the 17th century and is also widespread today.

After **Ne Win** established the **Revolutionary Council** in March 1962, foreign missionaries were obliged to leave the country, and the schools they had established, such as the prestigious Methodist High School in Rangoon (one of its alumnae is **Aung San Suu Kyi**) were nationalized, a measure that robbed them of their religious character. Since 1988 the **State Law and Order Restoration Council/State Peace and Development Council** has aggressively promoted the Buddhist religion, including the sponsorship of **pagoda** construction nationwide. Sometimes Christians and other religious minorities are forced to contribute to these activities, while the building of new churches and the holding of Christian meetings are sharply circumscribed. The SPDC has been accused of carrying out systematic persecution of Christians and other religious minorities, and seems to have the attitude that Christians, because of their religion, are potentially subversive and disloyal elements.

MOGOK (MOGOKE). Located in the uplands of northern **Mandalay Division.** Mogok has for centuries been Burma's major producer of sapphires and world famous "pigeon blood" rubies. Because **gemstones** are a state monopoly, the extensive mines, both open pits and tunnels, are tightly controlled by the **Tatmadaw**, although foreign visitors have been allowed in recent years. Because of the uncertainties and sudden changes in fortune of the gem trade, the people of Mogok have a reputation for being especially devout **Buddhists**.

MOKENS (SALONS). An ethnic minority, one of the very few groups living in Burma who speak an Austronesian (Malayo-Polynesian) language. *Moken* or *Maw Ken* is the name they call themselves, while *Salon* or *Salone* is the **Burmese (Myanmar) language** name for them; the British referred to them as "Sea Gypsies." They live in the **Mergui Archipelago** in southern **Tenasserim (Tanintharyi) Division**, and are seminomadic boat dwellers, living on land only during the rainy season. Closely related groups live in southern Thailand and the west coast of Peninsular Malaysia. They are skilled boat makers, fishermen, and divers, and according to a legendary account sought refuge on the water to escape oppression at the hands of the Malays. According to **James G. Scott**, their traditional craft were dugouts that could be as long as 30 feet (10 meters) and had large sails made of palm fronds. The present population is not known but probably does not number more than a couple of thousand; the colonial census of 1891 recorded a population of 1,628. The scenic Mergui Archipelago is being opened to international **tourism**, which may have a negative impact on traditional lifestyles; for example, the government and private tourist agencies organized a commercialized "Salon Festival" in February 2004.

MON LANGUAGE. A member of the Austro-Asiatic group of **languages** widespread throughout Southeast Asia. Mon is closely related to Khmer (Cambodian) and thus is often referred to as a "Mon-Khmer language." Although there are about two million **Mons** in Burma today, many speak the **Burmese (Myanmar) language** rather than Mon. A literary language since the sixth century CE, its writing system is based on Indian scripts. Unlike Burmese, it does not have tones, and modern Mon has three dialects, centered on **Moulmein (Mawlamyine)-Martaban (Mottama)**, **Pegu (Bago)**, and Ye (Yay). Because of the "Burmanization" policies of the **State Peace and Development Council**, many Mon scholars fear the extinction of their language and its rich literary heritage. However, the school system administered by the **New Mon State Party** and monastery schools run by the Mon **Sangha** use Mon as the medium of instruction.

MON STATE. One of Burma's 14 **states** and **divisions**, with an area of 12,297 square kilometers (4,748 square miles) and a population estimated at 2.5 million in 2000 (1983 census figure: 1,680,157). Ethnically, the population is largely **Mon** and **Burman (Bamar)**, though there are also **Karens (Kayins)**, **Shans**, and others. The state capital is **Moulmein (Mawlamyine)**, Burma's third largest city (1996 estimated population: 299,085). It contains two **districts** (Moulmein and Thaton), subdivided into 10 **townships**. Mon State came into being with the implementation of the **Constitution of 1974**, which recognized the separation of Moulmein and Thaton districts from **Tenasserim (Tanintharyi) Division** and their amalgamation as a separate state.

The topography is hilly, except on the coast. Mon State is bounded by **Karen (Kayin) State** on the northeast and east and shares a short international boundary with **Thailand** to the southeast; to the northwest it touches **Pegu (Bago) Division**, and to the south, Tenasserim Division. On the west, Mon State's long seacoast is fringed with islands (the largest is Bilu Gyun, or "demons' island," near Moulmein) and fronts the Gulf of **Martaban (Mottama)**. At Moulmein, the **Salween (Thanlwin) River** runs into the sea.

Major agricultural products are **rice**, rubber, sugarcane, and tropical fruits, especially durians. Fisheries are also economically important. The towns of Moulmein, Thaton, and Martaban (Mottama) are important in the maritime history of Burma. In the northern part of the state, **Kyaiktiyo Pagoda** (the "Golden Rock") is one of the most important sites in Burmese **Buddhism**.

MONG TAI ARMY (MTA). In the **Shan language**, *Mong Tai* means "Shan State," thus "Shan State Army." Commanded by the drug-dealing warlord **Khun Sa**, it was one of the most powerful ethnic minority armed groups in the early 1990s, with a total armed strength of as many as 19,000 guerrillas. Although Khun Sa voiced his commitment to Shan patriotism, the MTA, with its power base primarily in central and southern **Shan State** and its headquarters at Homong near the border with **Thailand**, played a major role in the profitable export of **opium** and **heroin** to international markets. In January 1996, Khun Sa surrendered to the **State Law and Order Restoration Council**, which was a blow to **Shan (Tai)** nationalists, who saw his armed group as a means of defending the interests of their people. With its collapse, the **Tatmadaw** was able to gain effective control in much of central Shan State and carried out extensive **forced relocations**. The SLORC–MTA agreement was different from other post-1988 **cease-fires** because the armed group broke up rather than continuing an autonomous existence like the **Kachin Independence Organization** or the **United Wa State Army** (the increasingly powerful UWSA played an important role in SLORC's pre-1996 strategy of softening up the MTA). Composed of MTA veterans, the **Shan State Army (South)** continues to resist the **State Peace and Development Council** in central Shan State.

MONS. One of the major ethnic nationalities of Burma, distinguished by language, culture, and a history of organized states reaching back to the early centuries CE. The **Mon language** is related to Cambodian (Khmer), but the origin of the Mons is unclear. According to one theory, they came to Mainland Southeast Asia from India (*Talaing*, the Burmese term for them, is said to refer to southern India's Telingana region, though the Mons do not use this term as a self-reference, considering it derogatory). Another widely accepted theory says they came from the Yangtze River region of eastern China. They established kingdoms in **Lower Burma** (which they called *Ramanyadesa*), were avid sailors and traders, and were primarily responsible for introducing Indian civilization and Theravada **Buddhism** to what are now Burma and **Thailand**. The premier Mon city-state in Burma, **Hanthawaddy**, was established ca. 825 CE at what is now **Pegu (Bago)** and served as the capital of states ruled by both Mons and **Burmans** for more than nine centuries.

King **Anawrahta**, founder of the **Pagan (Bagan) Dynasty**, conquered the Mon state of **Thaton** in 1057, bringing its king, Manuha, and many thousands of Mon monks, craftsmen, and artists back to his capital in **Upper Burma**. This was the beginning of a period when Burman culture and national identity were deeply transformed—especially in the religious, literary, and artistic fields—by the Mons. Mon monks, such as Anawrahta's spiritual advisor, **Shin Arahan**, imposed strict Theravada orthodoxy; the early Buddhist monuments of **Pagan (Bagan)** were essentially of Mon design; and the Burmans adopted the Mon writing system. Following the collapse of the Pagan Dynasty, **Wareru** established a powerful Mon dynasty at Martaban in the late 13th century. In the 14th and 15th centuries, the Mon state of Hanthawaddy flourished, especially during the reigns of **Razadarit** (r. 1393–1423), **Shinsawbu** (r. 1453–1472), and **Dhammazedi** (r. 1472–1492). The three monarchs are best remembered as patrons of Buddhism and generous donors to the **Shwe Dagon** and **Shwemawdaw Pagodas**.

Although the Burman rulers **Tabinshwehti** (r. 1531–1550) and **Bayinnaung** (r. 1551–1581) subjugated Lower Burma in the 16th century, they made Hanthawaddy their capital, and highly esteemed Mon culture for its contributions to religion and the arts. But **Alaungpaya**, founder of the **Konbaung Dynasty**, reestablished Burman hegemony in Lower Burma following an uprising led by **Smim Daw Buddhaketi** between 1740 and 1747. He captured **Dagon** in 1755 and pillaged Hanthawaddy in 1757. By this time, antagonism between Burmans and Mons had become intense. With Hanthawaddy's fall, the history of independent Mon states came to an end, and the last Mon king, **Binnya Dala**, was executed by King **Hsinbyushin** in 1774.

During the 19th century, the British attempted to enlist the support of the Mons against the Burmans, but with less success than they had with the **Karens (Kayins)**. During the colonial period, the Mons were largely written off as a dying race and culture, but community leaders established the **All Ramanya Mon Association** in 1939 to promote cultural revitalization. Proponents of Mon identity have tended to define it in terms of ancestry rather than language, which a decreasing number of people speak. An estimated two to four million Mons live in Burma today, about 4 to 8 percent of the population, mostly in **Mon State** but also in adjoining **Tenasserim (Tanintharyi) Division** and **Karen (Kayin) State**. Most of the original Mon population of the **Irrawaddy (Ayeyarwady) River** Delta and Pegu Division fled to Thailand during the late 18th century or has been assimilated by the Burmans. With the exception of a few Christians, most Mons are Buddhists, and they also venerate spirits similar to the Burmese *nats*, known as *kalok*.

After Burma became independent in 1948, some Mon armed groups fought the central government, the most important being the **New Mon State Party (NMSP)**, established in 1958 and led by Nai Shwe Kyin. In 1995, the NMSP signed a **cease-fire** with the **State Law and Order Restoration Council**, but other armed groups, such as the Monland Restoration Army, continue insurgent activities. *See also* HONGSA; MANUHA TEMPLE.

MOTION PICTURES IN BURMA. The history of cinema in Burma goes back to 1920, when a home-produced silent film, *Myitta nit Thuyar* (*Love and Liquor*, described by *The Irrawaddy* magazine as "the first successful attempt at film-making by the Burmans under the directorship of Maung Ohn Maung") was shown at a **Rangoon (Yangon)** theater. The first talking film, *Ngwe Pay Lo Maya* (*It Can't Be Paid with Money*), premiered in 1932. Before World War II, a number of Burmese studios produced motion pictures for local audiences, although the colonial government sometimes banned films touching on controversial subjects (such as *Aung Thapyay*, which dealt with King **Thibaw** and his exile by the British). However, Thakin **Nu** co-produced a film about the student movement, *Boycotta*, which the government permitted to be shown; his comrade **Aung San** is said to have acted in some scenes. During **World War II** and the **Japanese Occupation**, a perennial foreign favorite with Rangoon audiences was *Gone with the Wind*.

After the war, Burmese cinema enjoyed a revival, with as many as 80 films being released annually from 1950 to 1960; many dealt with political themes, such as *Pa Le Myat Ye* (Tears of Pearls), with its theme of anti-imperialism. One of the most famous film stars was Naw Louisa Benson, a former "Miss Burma" who married a **Karen (Kayin)** guerrilla leader and assumed command of his men after he was assassinated in 1965; undoubtedly, she was Burma's most glamorous insurgent leader. Another popular film actress, Wa Wa Win Shwe, had a scandalous relationship with Olive Yang, the notorious "war-lady" of **Kokang**.

After **Ne Win** established the **Revolutionary Council** in March 1962, studios and movie theaters were nationalized, and Burmese cinema assumed a monochromatic socialist hue. With the seizure of power by the **State Law and Order Restoration Council** in 1988, the film industry was privatized, but it remains under the tight control of the Motion Picture and Video Censor Board. For example, films cannot be shot on college campuses because of the traditional association of **students** with political opposition, and a recent ruling by the Board forbids actresses to wear Western clothes, no matter how modest. According to the 1996 Motion Picture Law, the industry's purpose is "to consolidate the national unity, to give correct thoughts, and to promote sound knowledge; to help towards purifying the moral character; and to contribute to perpetuation of sovereignty and national peace and development."

Often, **Military Intelligence** or departments of the government subsidize productions, such as *Thu Kyun Ma Khan Byi* (*Never Shall We Be Enslaved*), a melodramatic film by Dr. Myo Thant Tin about patriotic resistance against the British at the time of the **Third Anglo-Burmese War**. Predictably, it won seven indigenous "academy awards" in 1996. **State Peace and Development Council** Secretary-1 **Khin Nyunt** played a guiding role in the film industry before his arrest in October 2004. It is through his encouragement that a film on **AIDS in Burma**, *Ngar Thutabar Yaukkyar Meinma* (*Men and Women Are Both Human*), was produced, distributed, and won seven "Oscars" in 2004.

Because of censorship and the lack of resources, most local films are dull, and there are few foreign alternatives. But watching movies is a popular pastime, and cinemas are almost always crowded because few other pastimes are available to people of modest means — even in a big city like Rangoon. Those who have access to satellite television (satellite dishes sprout in large numbers on top of Rangoon buildings) and videodiscs have a much wider variety of entertainment from which to choose. *See also* MASS MEDIA IN BURMA.

MOULMEIN (MAWLAMYINE, MAWLAMYAING). The capital of **Mon State**, located in the delta of the **Salween (Thanlwin) River**. With an estimated population of 299,085 in 1996, it is Burma's third or fourth largest city and one of the country's most important seaports. Most of the population is **Mon** or **Karen (Kayin)**. Between 1827 and 1852, it was the administrative center and most important city in British Burma, a major port for the export of **teak**, but thereafter its prominence was eclipsed by **Rangoon (Yangon)**. Offshore is Gaungse Kyun, or "Shampoo Island," which contains a spring from which water was drawn for the Burmese king's hair-washing ceremony during **Thingyan**. The city's many old colonial buildings attest to its cosmopolitan past.

MOUNTBATTEN, LORD LOUIS (1900–1979). Supreme Allied Commander, South East Asia Command, 1943–1946, Mountbatten carried out the Allied recapture of Burma from the Japanese. He is best remembered by the Burmese for recognizing **Aung San**'s March 27, 1945, uprising against the Japanese as a legitimate part of the Allied war effort (the rebels were designated the **Patriotic Burmese Forces**) and for playing a major role in a conciliatory British policy toward Aung San and the **Anti-Fascist People's Freedom League** in the months following the end of **World War II**. In 1946, he was given the title Viscount (later Earl) Mountbatten of Burma in honor of his wartime achievements. His assassination by Irish Republican Army terrorists in 1979 was widely mourned in Burma.

MOUSTACHE BROTHERS. A troupe of *anyeint* performers, based in **Mandalay**. Specializing in song and dance, skits, and especially comedy, their routines resemble old-fashioned vaudeville. In March 1996, troupe members Par Par Lay and Lu Zaw were sentenced to seven years' imprisonment for satirizing the **State Law and Order Restoration Council** at an Independence Day celebration at the house of Daw **Aung San Suu Kyi** in **Rangoon (Yangon)**. They were confined in a labor camp under harsh conditions in **Kachin State**, later transferred to other prisons, and released in July 2001. The Moustache Brothers continue to perform inside their house in Mandalay but are not allowed to perform outside. *See also* HUMAN RIGHTS IN BURMA; *PWE*; ZARGANA.

MRAUK-U (MROHAUNG, MYOHAUNG). Capital of the **Arakan (Rakhine)** kingdom between 1433 and 1784. During its golden age from the mid-16th to mid-17th centuries, it was a major power in the Bay of Bengal and a center of international trade. After the **First Anglo-Burmese War**, it was abandoned as an administrative center in favor of **Sittwe (Sittway)** and became overgrown by the jungle. Its **Buddhist** temples and **pagodas**, located mostly north of the ruins of the old royal palace, are of great archeological and artistic interest, comparable to **Pagan**. Mostly built of stone, their design reflects Indian Muslim influences and is quite different from the Buddhist monuments of **Lower** or **Upper Burma**. *See also* MIN BIN; SHIT-THAUNG TEMPLE.

MUSIC, TRADITIONAL AND MODERN. Although deeply influenced by Indian models, classical Burmese music received its inspiration from **Thailand** after Thai/Siamese musicians and performers were brought back to Burma following the capture of the Siamese capital, Ayuthaya, by the armies of King **Hsinbyushin** in 1767. Such musical genres are known by the Burmese as the *"Yodaya* (Ayuthaya) style,"* synonymous with refinement. In the traditional orchestra, containing seven to ten players, the most prominent instrument is the *saing waing*, a circle of finely tuned drums; accompanying instruments include the *kye waing* (brass gongs), the *saung gauq* (a harp with 13 strings), the *mi-gyaung* ("crocodile lute"), the *pattala* (xylophone), and the *hneh* (similar to an oboe). For foreign listeners who find Burmese instrumental music discordant, a more appealing genre may be solos on the "Burmese harp" (*saung gauq*), often performed by a woman, which are remarkable for their tranquil and meditative moods.

Western musical modes were introduced during the British colonial period, and a "pop" (popular) music scene has existed in **Rangoon (Yangon)** and other urban areas since at least the **Burma Socialist Programme Party** era (1962–1988), although **Ne Win** himself regarded Western-style music as a decadent influence. Under the **State Peace and Development Council**, globalization has encouraged one of Southeast Asia's liveliest rock music scenes, which includes local versions of "rap" and "hip-hop"; given political tensions and the regime's perennial fear of unrest, the SPDC's strategy has been to co-opt, rather than suppress, popular youth-oriented music groups like Iron Cross. But, as in other countries, rock music often serves as a barometer for the younger generation's frustrations and disillusionment. *See also* PERFORMING ARTS, TRADITIONAL.

MUSLIMS IN BURMA. Members of the Islamic community have lived in Burma since before the **Pagan Dynasty**, arriving by way of Indian Ocean trade routes and the Indian subcontinent. At the beginning of the 21st century, the Burmese government estimated that Muslims comprised 4 percent of the country's population, while other sources estimate it as high as 10 percent. As many as 1.5 million Burmese Muslims live abroad, primarily in Bangladesh, Pakistan, and the countries of the Middle East. A substantial number of these have fled persecution at the hands of the government, and **Rohingyas**, the most numerous refugee group, have been called the "new Palestinians."

There is considerable diversity among Burmese Muslims. The earliest wave of migrants included merchants and mercenary soldiers of Arab, Iranian, or Indian ancestry who arrived during the precolonial period. In royal capitals, such as **Ava (Inwa)**, **Amarapura**, and **Mandalay**, there were special quarters for Muslim merchants and craftsmen, and they were allowed by the king to build mosques for their community. Some Muslims achieved high office under the Burmese kings. There are also **Panthays**, descendants of **Chinese** Muslims who came from Yunnan Province during the 19th century and live for the most part in **Shan State**. During the colonial period, a third group of Muslims migrated from the Indian subcontinent, immigration being encouraged by the British for economic reasons. Many became merchants and civil servants, and **Rangoon (Yangon)** has extensive Muslim neighborhoods dating from this time. A fourth group, the largest, are the Rohingyas of **Arakan (Rakhine) State**, including both descendants of migrants from neighboring Bengal (now **Bangladesh**) and **Arakanese (Rakhine)** converts to Islam.

Because the ancestors of most Burmese Muslims were not resident in the country before the **First Anglo-Burmese War**, they are not considered "indigenous" and do not enjoy full rights under the **Citizenship Law** of 1982. *Zerbadi (Zerabadi)*, a term derived from Persian (*zir-bad*, "below the winds," i.e., Southeast Asia), is used to refer to the children of Muslims (usually Muslim men) and Burmese. Before **World War II**, such mixed marriages aroused the resentment of Burmese nationalists. Partly to better observe *sharia* (Islamic law) Muslims in Burma tend to live in segregated communities.

The Muslim community, especially the Rohingyas, have suffered systematic persecution at the hands of successive governments since **Ne Win** seized power in 1962, and their social position has deteriorated on a number of fronts. In contrast to the parliamentary government period (1948–1962), they hold no important political offices. Few if any Muslims are found in the higher ranks of the **Tatmadaw**. Like all Burmese, they are required to carry identification cards stating their religion, which leaves them vulnerable to official discrimination. In recent years, they have often not been allowed to build new mosques, or even repair old ones, and many mosques have been torn down by the authorities, especially in Arakan State. There is ample evidence to suggest that the **State Law and Order Restoration Council/State Peace and Development Council** has manipulated popular prejudices to incite mob violence against Muslim neighborhoods. It is also true, however, that such anti-Muslim prejudices are deeply rooted among Burmese **Buddhists**, including members of the **Sangha**, stimulated by everyday frictions between Muslims and non-Muslims in an environment of deepening poverty, as well as government-encouraged rumor-mongering. *See also* HUMAN RIGHTS IN BURMA.

MYA, BO (1927–). Also Saw Bo Mya, a prominent **Karen (Kayin)** insurgent leader, who has fought against the Burmese central government since the **Karen National Union (KNU)** uprising of January 1949. Unlike many leaders of the Karen community, he was born not in the delta of the **Irrawaddy (Ayeyarwady) River** but in the hilly Papun District, near the border with Thailand, and was an animist until his conversion to the Seventh-Day Adventist church in 1961. During **World War II**, he served as a policeman under the Japanese but also worked with **Force 136**. After the 1949 revolt against the government of U **Nu** began, Bo Mya commanded guerrillas in the **Dawna Range** and gained a strong economic base for his insurgency by operating "toll gates" for the cross-border trade near the town of **Mae Sot-Myawaddy** in Thailand's Tak Province; his army prospered as the **black market** absorbed imports from Thailand during the **Ne Win** era, but he did not engage in the trade in **opium** or other drugs.

Strongly anticommunist, he purged the mainstream Karen movement of leftists in the 1960s and became chairman of a reunified KNU in 1976, a post that he held until 2000, when Saw Ba Thin Sein replaced him. He was chairman of an ethnic minority **united front**, the National Democratic Front, between 1976 and 1987, and became the leader of the **Democratic Alliance of Burma** in November 1988. With only a grade-school education, he exhibited a toughness and determination lacking in many of the more educated, urbanized Karen leaders. But the low point of his long career came with the fall of the KNU headquarters at **Manerplaw** in 1995, which many blamed on his allegedly heavy-handed and inflexible leadership. The **Tatmadaw**'s success in capturing the base was caused in large measure to the defection from the KNU of the **Democratic Karen Buddhist Army**, whose members had become alienated from Bo Mya and other, mostly Christian, Karen leaders. On January 15, 2004, Bo Mya, as KNU vice chairman, went to **Rangoon (Yangon)** for talks with then Prime Minister **Khin Nyunt** on a **cease-fire** between the KNU and the **State Peace and Development Council**.

MYANMAR MATERNAL AND CHILD WELFARE ASSOCIATION (MMCWA). Established in 1991, a major GONGO ("government organized nongovernmental organization"), headed for a time by the wife of former Secretary-1 **Khin Nyunt**. Its leadership consists of the wives of high-ranking **Tatmadaw** officers, and membership nationwide is estimated at around 1.1 million "ordinary" and 340,000 "permanent" members. Like the **Union Solidarity and Development Association**, the MMCWA is designed to assert the government's control at the grassroots level, but some observers have credited it with raising ordinary **women**'s awareness of the dangers of **AIDS** and the **sex industry**. Other important GONGOs include the Myanmar Red Cross and the Myanmar Fire Brigade.

MYANMAR NATIONAL DEMOCRATIC ALLIANCE ARMY/ PARTY (MNDAA/MNDAP). A **cease-fire** armed group formed after the break-up of the **Communist Party of Burma** in 1989, which is based in the **Kokang** region of **Shan State**. Originally led by **Pheung Kya-shin** (Peng Jiasheng) and his brother Pheung Kya-fu (Peng Jiafu), the group lost power to another warlord, Yang Mo Lian, in the "**opium** war" of late 1992, but later regained control of Kokang and the MNDAA. It is one of the major drug-funded armed groups in Burma. *See also* UNITED WA STATE ARMY.

MYANMAR POLICE FORCE (MPF). Formerly known as the People's Police Force, the Myanmar Police Force was reorganized in 1995 and at the beginning of the 21st century consists of 72,000 personnel. Formally under the authority of the Ministry of Home Affairs, the MPF includes state and division police forces and nine "combat battalions," totaling 4,500 men, many of whom are based in and around **Rangoon (Yangon)**; these combat units are believed to have absorbed the old *Lon Htein* **(Riot Police)**, which achieved infamy after their brutal handling of demonstrations in Rangoon during March and June 1988. Though often commanded by retired army officers, the combat battalions, like other MPF units, are jurisdictionally independent of the **Tatmadaw** but serve as auxiliaries in internal security operations, especially in urban areas.

MYAUNGMYA (MYOUNGMYA) MASSACRES (1942). A township in the delta of the **Irrawaddy (Ayeyarwady) River**, in present-day **Irrawaddy (Ayeyarwady) Division**, and the site of ethnic violence between the **Burman (Bamar)** soldiers of the **Burma Independence**

Army **(BIA)** and the local **Karen (Kayin)** population, as well as a smaller number of Indians who fought alongside the latter. After the British retreated from **Lower Burma** in early 1942, many Karens in the Delta region, including those demobilized from British forces, remained loyal to them, and the assassination of a Japanese officer provoked an order from Colonel **Suzuki Keiji** to the BIA that all the inhabitants of two Karen villages (which had nothing to do with the assassination), including women and children, be massacred. The Karens, who had refused to surrender their British-issued weapons to the BIA, retaliated, and a race war began, with many innocent victims on both the Karen-Indian and Burman sides. The worst incidents were in and around Myaungmya, where an estimated 1,800 Karens were killed and 400 Karen villages destroyed. The massacres were stopped only when the regular Japanese army moved in to restore order. Dr. **Ba Maw** sought reconciliation between the races, establishing a "Karen Central Organisation" to promote this end, but Karen suspicion of the Burmans continued, leading to the 1949 **Karen National Union** uprising, which had as its goal the creation of an independent Karen state. *See also* JAPANESE OCCUPATION; WORLD WAR II, ETHNIC MINORITIES IN.

MYEINIGONE MARKET INCIDENT (JUNE 21, 1988). A major clash between **student** demonstrators and the authorities, which occurred near the Myeinigone (Myay Ni Gone) Market north of the **Shwe Dagon Pagoda** in **Rangoon (Yangon)**. Several thousand students began a march from the Main Campus of **Rangoon (Yangon) University** to the Institute of Medicine downtown along Prome (Pyay) Road, protesting the imprisonment of their comrades and the suspension of classes on university campuses. Surrounded and attacked by **Riot Police (*Lon Htein*)** and army troops, they escaped into narrow side streets, were sheltered by local residents, and fought back using *jinglees*, or homemade catapults that launched sharpened bicycle spokes, like primitive crossbows. At least 10 Riot Police died, and students suffered an estimated 100 casualties. In 1998, a decade after the clash, there were rumors that the Myeinigone area was infested with *nats*, the ghosts of protestors who had been killed. *See also* DEMOCRACY SUMMER.

MYITKYINA. The capital of **Kachin State**, with a population estimated at 73,554 in 1996. It is located in a valley along the upper reaches of the **Irrawaddy (Ayeyarwady) River**. It was the site of major battles between the Allies and Japanese during **World War II**, including operations carried out by **Merrill's Marauders**.

MYO. Meaning town, city, or an administrative jurisdiction in the **Burmese (Myanmar) language**, it originally referred to a fortified settlement with a wall, a permanent market (*zay*), and a shrine dedicated to the local spirit or *nat*. During the precolonial period, the *myoza*, or "town eater," was a member of the royal family or a high-ranking official to whom the king allocated the income of the *myo*, a kind of appanage. The *myothugyi*, or chief of the *myo*, was a member of the local gentry (not a clearly defined aristocratic class) whose post was generally hereditary, and who served as intermediary between the the *myo* and its adjacent villages and the royal court, for example, in negotiating taxation or "labor service." Deeming them untrustworthy, the British abolished the post of *myothugyi*, a measure that is said to have created major problems for their subsequent administration. *See also* ADMINISTRATION AND SOCIETY, PRE-COLONIAL BURMA; ADMINISTRATION OF BURMA, BRITISH COLONIAL PERIOD.

– N –

NAGA. A mythological serpent-dragon, originally an Indian motif but now widespread in Southeast Asia (e.g., carved in stone at Angkor Wat in Cambodia). *Nagas* figure prominently in the legends associated with Gotama **Buddha**, and a *nagayon* temple is one where a serpent, usually resembling a cobra, is depicted protecting a Buddha image with its hood, an outstanding example being the one built at **Pagan (Bagan)** by King **Kyanzittha**.

NAGANI BOOK CLUB. A publishing enterprise established in 1937 by Thakins **Nu, Than Tun**, and other members of the **Dobama Asiayone** to expose their compatriots to modern political and world affairs literature. During the British colonial period, few books were published in the **languages** of Burma, and most of them dealt with traditional subjects, such as **Buddhism**. The Nagani (Red Dragon)

Book Club published both original books and translated ones, numbering 71 titles, between 1938 and 1941. They dealt with Burmese politics; Soviet Russia; the Irish revolution; Chinese politics, including the works of Sun Yat-sen; Adolph Hitler; and other issues, including a translation of Dale Carnegie's *How to Win Friends and Influence People* by Thakin Nu. The club also held public lectures and published a journal and had a major influence on encouraging young Burmese to become politically active during and after **World War II**.

NAGAS. An ethnic nationality living in the mountainous region between the valley of the **Irrawaddy (Ayeyarwady) River** and the basin of the Brahmaputra River in northeastern **India**. The majority of Nagas live in India, but there is also a significant population located principally in **Sagaing Division**, and also in **Chin** and **Kachin States**, along the Burma–India border. Naga sources estimate the total population at 3.5 million. *Nagalim*, a term that the Nagas frequently use to refer to their homeland, encompasses parts of both India and Burma.

The Nagas speak Tibeto-Burman languages and are subdivided into 42 tribal groups. In broad contours, their history, beliefs, and customs resemble those of other Tibeto-Burman upland groups such as the **Chins** and the **Kachins**. They were never controlled by lowland **Burman (Bamar)** or Indian states, and adhered to animistic beliefs until a majority of Nagas were converted to **Christianity** in the late 19th and early 20th centuries. Living in mountainous areas, they traditionally practiced slash-and-burn or swidden **agriculture** and had no unifying political institutions above the village level. Intervillage raids, including head hunting, were frequent. The village center was the *morung* (men's association), which was decorated with human skulls, taken to enhance the fertility of Naga fields and as a proof of manhood by young warriors. The British colonial government imposed effective control over the Burmese Nagas only in 1940. Naga levies fought alongside the British during **World War II**. In part because of the activities of the Christian **missionaries**, the Nagas developed a strong national consciousness and demanded their own state on the eve of India's independence from Britain in 1947. The major armed group claiming to represent the Nagas is the **Na-**

tional Socialist Council of Nagaland (NSCN), which has operated primarily in India, but also in Burma.

NAMES, BURMESE. Burmese names usually consist of two or three monosyllables which, taken together, have a meaning; for example, **Khin Nyunt** can be a man or woman's name, meaning "the utmost of friendliness." Occasionally a name may be a single syllable, such as that of Burma's former prime minister, **Nu**, "gentle." Westerners often thought his name was "U Nu," but the first syllable is a respectful title (see below). Unlike East Asians or Westerners, Burmese do not have family names, and attempts to introduce them have not been successful. Nor do they have patronymics, like the "son/daughter of" forms found in Russian, Arabic, and other languages. Traditionally, the day of the eight-day **week** on which a person is born determines the letter with which his or her name begins, for example, the Burmese equivalent of "k/g" on Monday, and "m" or "b/p" on Thursday. Parents take special care to give a child an auspicious name, and the name may be changed in later life on the advice of a practitioner of **astrology**. However, neither men nor women change their names upon marrying.

Because of the lack of family names, there is often considerable confusion because so many people have the same given name, even taking into account the tonal differences of the **Burmese (Myanmar) language**. For example, there are three important **Tin Oo**'s (or **Tin U**'s) in modern Burmese history: a former director of **Military Intelligence**, a leader of the **National League for Democracy**, and a general who was second secretary (Secretary-2) of the **State Peace and Development Council** until his accidental death in 2001. People with the more common sort of names often append a clarifying prefix; for example, in daily conversation, people will distinguish between "Mandalay Maung Shwe" (Maung Shwe who comes from Mandalay) and "Tekatho [university] Maung Shwe" (Maung Shwe who attended/graduated from university). "Suu Kyi" is a common lady's name, but **Aung San Suu Kyi** could only be the daughter of Burma's independence leader. It is said that even Military Intelligence makes mistakes in identifying people because of the large number of commonly used names, although careful dossiers are kept on dissidents. Despite the end of British colonial rule, many Burmese take a Western given name to supplement their Burmese name, which is useful in dealing with foreigners. Christians often take a name from the Bible.

Apart from the names themselves, honorific forms of address are used to indicate a person's age and status. *U* ("uncle") and *Daw* ("aunt") are used to address adult men and women; *ko* is used for a young male, *ma* being the female equivalent; and *maung* for a boy, while *ma* is used for girls. *Saya*, meaning "teacher" (female: *sayama*), is used not only for educators, but also for physicians, writers, artists, bosses, or any person in a responsible position whose approval one seeks. Members of the **sangha**, or Buddhist monkhood, have special names and titles that must be used with care.

The minorities have their own terms of address. Among the **Shans**, *Sai* is the equivalent of *U*, *Nang* for *Daw*; among the **Mons**, *Nai* for *U* and *Mi* for *Daw* or *Ma*; and among the **Karens**, *Saw* for *U* and *Naw* for *Daw* or *Ma*. Most of Burma's ethnic minorities do not have family names; the **Kachins** are an exception.

NAN CHAO. During the Later Han Dynasty, in the second century CE, the Chinese gained control of what is now Yunnan Province. In the seventh century, a local state known as *Nan Chao* was established, which succeeded in wresting control of the region from the Chinese by the middle of the following century. Scholars originally believed the rulers of Nan Chao had a common origin with the **Shan (Tai)** of eastern Burma and other Tai groups, but most currently believe, on linguistic evidence, that they were people speaking a Tibeto-Burman language, possibly related to the Lolos of modern Yunnan. During the eighth and ninth centuries, Nan Chao was a militarily powerful state that exercised influence, if not control, over several areas of Mainland Southeast Asia, including the upper **Irrawaddy (Ayeyarwady) River** Valley. Its expansion had a major impact on the **Pyu** states of early Burma.

By the 10th century, however, Nan Chao's power had waned because of internal dissension, the rise of an independent Vietnam (Dai Viet), and other factors. It was no longer a major force in the politics and warfare of **Upper Burma** when in the mid-11th century King **Anawrahta** founded the **Pagan Dynasty**, whose nucleus was a settlement on the Irrawaddy River founded by the **Burmans (Bamars)** two centuries earlier. The role of Nan Chao in early Burmese history is not clearly understood, but it was probably of major importance, especially because the control of Yunnan by non-Chinese dynasties between the 8th and 13th centuries may have prevented Burma from undergoing Chinese cultural assimilation similar to that experienced by Vietnam. Burma remained firmly within the Indian sphere of civilization, as reflected in the central role of Theravada **Buddhism** in national identity. When Nan Chao's successor state was conquered by Khubilai Khan in the mid-13th century, the way was cleared for **China** to assume a more important, and at times threatening, role in Burmese affairs. *See also* PAGAN (BAGAN).

NARATHIHAPATE, KING (r. 1254–1287). The last major king of the **Pagan (Bagan) Dynasty.** He earned the inglorious title "the king who fled from the Chinese" following an invasion of Upper Burma by an army of Kubhilai Khan, Mongol emperor of **China**. Refusing to become Kubhilai's tributary, Narathihapate foolishly executed the Mongol ambassador, and was driven from **Pagan (Bagan)** by the Mongols in 1283, seeking refuge in the delta of the **Irrawaddy (Ayeyarwady) River**. In 1287, shorn of his realm, he was assassinated by one of his sons.

NATIONAL COALITION GOVERNMENT OF THE UNION OF BURMA (NCGUB). A major opposition organization, which describes itself as "constituted by elected members of parliament in exile." Following the victory of the **National League for Democracy (NLD)** in the **General Election of May 27, 1990**, members of parliament, including those from other parties, met and issued the July 28 **Gandhi Hall Declaration**, calling for a speedy transfer of power. This was in response to the **State Law and Order Restoration Council**'s issuance of **SLORC Announcement 1/90** on the previous day, declaring that only it had the right to exercise legislative, executive, and judicial authority. Subsequently, plans were made to arrange the convening of parliament in **Mandalay**, but a wave of arrests of key NLD leaders, including U **Kyi Maung**, persuaded NLD parliamentarians still at large to endorse a provisional government in Burma's border areas. Thus, the NCGUB was established on December 18, 1990, at **Manerplaw**, headquarters of both the **Karen**

National Union and Democratic Alliance of Burma, with Dr. Sein Win, a cousin of Daw Aung San Suu Kyi, serving as prime minister. In 2005, the NCGUB had its headquarters in Washington, D.C., and played a primarily formal and informational role, for example, publishing a *Human Rights Yearbook*. *See also* NATIONAL COUNCIL OF THE UNION OF BURMA.

NATIONAL CONVENTION (NC). The constitution-drafting body established by the State Law and Order Restoration Council (SLORC) in 1992. According to SLORC Announcement No. 1/90, a transfer of power from the military regime to a civilian government cannot occur until a new constitution is promulgated. The NC, consisting of 702 delegates, met in plenary session for the first time on January 9, 1993. Delegates included 99 members of political parties that had participated in the General Election of May 27, 1990, including the National League for Democracy, and appointed delegates drawn from six other groups: ethnic nationalities, peasants, workers, intellectuals, civil servants, and "other invitees." In November 1995, Aung San Suu Kyi withdrew members of the National League for Democracy from the NC, protesting its undemocratic procedures.

When Prime Minister Khin Nyunt announced a "road map" for democratization following the "Black Friday" Incident of May 30, 2003, one of the first goals was completion of the new constitution. On May 17, 2004, the NC reconvened near Hmawbi, outside of Rangoon (Yangon). Over 1,000 delegates attended, but there were doubts about whether it could draft a basic law that would be considered legitimate, not only because the National League for Democracy refused to participate (Daw Suu Kyi was again under house arrest), but also because six ethnic armed groups that had signed cease-fires with the post-1988 military regime, including the Kachin Independence Army/Organization and the New Mon State Party, recommended that the draft constitution be amended to reduce the Tatmadaw's role in politics, a proposal Khin Nyunt flatly rejected. Just as in the 1993–1996 period, no opposition party now has a role in the work of the organizing committee. Although the NC has published a detailed outline of a proposed new constitution, it had not produced a final constitutional draft as of mid-2005. Reasons for the delay seem to include a desire on the part of the military regime to postpone transition to a civilian government and difficulties in working out constitutional arrangements between the central government and armed ethnic minority groups living in the border areas. *See also* NATIONAL CONVENTION, CONSTITUTIONAL OUTLINE OF.

NATIONAL CONVENTION, CONSTITUTIONAL OUTLINE OF. In the mid-1990s, the **National Convention** published a detailed outline of a proposed constitution, though it has not issued the final draft. Its most fundamental characteristic is the dominant role that the **Tatmadaw** would continue to play in the new political system: one-quarter of all seats in the bicameral national legislature would be allocated to military personnel; the armed forces would continue to have a major role in national and regional administration, especially in relation to security matters; and would have a decisive say in choosing the Union president. The Tatmadaw would appoint the ministerial portfolios of defense, home affairs, and border security and be free of supervision or control by civilian officials. Martial law could be reimposed in times of national emergency, just as in 1988. The outline reflects the military regime's conviction that civilian politicians ought not to "meddle" in national politics; but it also owes much to the model of President Suharto's "New Order" in **Indonesia**, especially the guaranteed military seats in the law-making body and tight restrictions on political parties.

NATIONAL COUNCIL OF THE UNION OF BURMA (NCUB). Part of the Burmese government-in-exile, it is often confused with the **National Coalition Government of the Union of Burma (NCGUB)**. The NCUB in principle functions as a parliament-in-exile, composed of members of the **National League for Democracy—Liberated Areas (NLD—LA)**, the Members of Parliament Union (MPU), the **Democratic Alliance of Burma (DAB)**, and the National Democratic Front. The NCGUB is the "government" or "cabinet" of the NCUB, headed by the prime minister, Dr. Sein Win, and is "responsible" to it. The NCUB has drafted a constitution and advocates the initiation of a "tripartite dialogue" involving the ethnic nationalities, the democratic forces led by **Aung San Suu Kyi**, and the military government to achieve political reconciliation.

NATIONAL DEMOCRATIC ALLIANCE ARMY—EASTERN SHAN STATE (NDAA—ESS). A cease-fire armed group formed after the breakup of the **Communist Party of Burma** in 1989, which is based in **Shan State**, north of **Keng Tung**. With an armed strength of 3,500–4,000 men, it is considered a major player in the drug trade with China and other neighboring countries. *See also* UNITED WA STATE ARMY.

NATIONAL INTELLIGENCE BUREAU (NIB). An agency that oversaw the wide-ranging intelligence activities of the **State Peace and Development Council**, established during the **Burma Socialist Programme Party** era (1962–1988). Until it was abolished in October 2004, it coordinated the work of information-gathering agencies in the Ministries of Home Affairs, Foreign Affairs, National Planning and Economic Development, and Defence, though the Defence Ministry's **Directorate of Defence Services Intelligence (DDSI)** was the single most powerful intelligence organ. *See also* KHIN NYUNT; MILITARY INTELLIGENCE; MILITARY INTELLIGENCE, ORGANIZATION OF.

NATIONAL LEAGUE FOR DEMOCRACY (NLD). Burma's largest opposition party, winner of the **General Election of May 27, 1990**. The party traces its origins to the *Aung-Suu-Tin* coalition of opposition leaders, **Aung Gyi, Aung San Suu Kyi**, and **Tin U**, who joined forces on September 12, 1988. On September 24, 1988, in the wake of the power seizure by the **State Law and Order Restoration Council** and the establishment of a multiparty political system, they founded the NLD, with Aung Gyi serving as chairman, Tin U as vice chairman, and Aung San Suu Kyi as general secretary. Party leadership also included a 12-member central executive committee, composed of mostly conservative figures, including retired army officers, such as U **Aung Shwe**, U **Kyi Maung**, and U **Lwin**. At one time, the party claimed a membership of as many as two million, with branches nationwide.

From its inception, the NLD faced serious difficulties. On December 9, 1988, Aung Gyi and his supporters left the party, claiming that the **Communist Party of Burma** had infiltrated the NLD and that Aung San Suu Kyi was under its influence. On July 20, 1989, Daw Suu Kyi, who is the NLD's most popular figure, and party chairman

Tin U were placed under house arrest; the former was not released until July 10, 1995. Although the NLD, which campaigned under the symbol of the *kamauk* or farmer's bamboo hat, won almost 60 percent of the popular vote and over 80 percent of the seats contested in the May 1990 election, the SLORC did not allow it to form a government. Instead, the party has endured systematic repression at the hands of the authorities, including periodic arrest of most of its top leaders (including all but four members of the central executive committee by late 1990), detention or arrest of elected NLD parliamentarians, intimidation and arrest of local party branch leaders and members (many of whom were pressured to resign), and "mass" rallies, organized by the **Union Solidarity and Development Association**, demanding the party's dissolution. In the late 1990s, the **State Peace and Development Council (SPDC)** repeatedly prevented Daw Suu Kyi from visiting NLD branches outside **Rangoon (Yangon)**, and **Military Intelligence** kept careful watch on both Daw Suu Kyi's home on University Avenue and NLD headquarters on West Shwegondine Road in the capital city. Pressure on the party intensified further after it established the **Committee Representing the People's Parliament** on September 16, 1998, although as of mid-2005 the SPDC had not taken the final step of revoking the party's legal status. Hundreds of NLD leaders and members languish in jail, though others were released during a 2001–2002 "thaw" brokered by **United Nations** special envoy Razali Ismail.

Some observers have criticized Daw Suu Kyi and other NLD leaders for failing to develop coherent party policies, especially concerning relations between the **Burmans (Bamars)** and the ethnic minorities, and for being intolerant of dissent inside the party. However, it is evident that the SPDC has tried hard to divide the NLD from within, largely by discrediting Daw Suu Kyi, and has denied the party the freedom necessary to carry out normal activities.

Following her release from house arrest in May 2002, Daw Suu Kyi was able to visit party branches in various parts of the country, including **Shan State, Mandalay Division**, and **Arakan (Rakhine) State**. Most analysts considered the NLD's organizational structure moribund after more than a dozen years of persecution, although the sympathy and support of a "silent majority" of Burmese for the party remains potentially huge. *See also* "BLACK FRIDAY" INCIDENT;

NATIONAL LEAGUE FOR DEMOCRACY—LIBERATED AR-
EAS; NATIONAL COALITION GOVERNMENT OF THE UNION
OF BURMA.

**NATIONAL LEAGUE FOR DEMOCRACY—LIBERATED AR-
EAS (NLD—LA).** Established in February 1991 at **Manerplaw** in
Karen (Kayin) State; it represents the **National League for De-
mocracy** in the border areas and foreign countries.

NATIONAL SCHOOLS. Following the 1920 **student** boycott that opposed the act establishing **Rangoon (Yangon) University,** "national
schools" offering a curriculum emphasizing **Burmese (Myanmar)
language** and culture and **Buddhism** were established throughout
the country. A Council of National Education was set up in 1921,
which set standards and examinations for the schools. Between 1921
and 1923, the number of such schools increased rapidly, although a
controversy ensued between those schools that were willing to accept
government aid (subjecting them to a measure of government regulation) and those that rejected it. Many of the schools went bankrupt,
but those national schools that survived graduated many of the leaders of the independence struggle during the 1930s and 1940s, including **Aung San,** who attended a national high school in **Yenangyaung
(Yaynangyoung)** in what is now **Magwe (Magway) Division.**

A "national college," conceived as a patriotic alternative to Rangoon University with its British curriculum, was established in August 1921 at a Buddhist monastery in Bahan Township, **Rangoon
(Yangon).** Its faculty included the famous writer Thakin **Kodaw
Hmaing.** But it suffered from lack of funding, government displeasure, and factional splits within the main Burmese political organization, the **General Council of Burmese Associations,** and closed in
1923. *See also* EDUCATION; EDUCATION, HIGHER.

NATIONAL SOCIALIST COUNCIL OF NAGALAND (NSCN). Es-
tablished in 1980, the principal armed group claiming to represent the
Nagas. Its goal is to establish an independent Nagaland (*Nagalim*).
The movement divided into two factions in 1988, one headed by
Thuingaleng Muivah and Isaac Chishi Swu (NSCN-IM), the other
headed by SS Khaplang (NSCN-K). Both factions have engaged in

peace talks with the Indian government, the NSCN-IM more extensively. In the 1990s the NSCN-K established a "government-in-exile" in the Patkai Mountains in western **Sagaing Division**, but it was overrun by the **Tatmadaw** in 2003, reflecting increased cooperation between Burma and **India** in suppressing border area insurgents.

NATIONAL UNITY. Although **Aung San** recognized ethnic minority aspirations for administrative and cultural autonomy at the **Panglong Conference** of February 1947, in principle promoting "unity through diversity" and limited **federalism**, the government of General **Ne Win** (1962–1988), dominated by ethnic majority **Burmans**, imposed a concept of national unity based on linguistic and cultural "Burmanization," top-down **Tatmadaw** control of politics and the economy, and a worldview that stressed that differences between the various ethnic groups are trivial and were used as a "divide and rule" tactic by the British during the colonial period. Thus, successive military regimes have asserted the essential homogeneity of the Burmese people, an idea that can be traced back at least to the wartime "totalitarian" government of Dr. **Ba Maw**.

Both during the **Revolutionary Council** period (1962–1973) and after the **Constitution of 1974** was implemented, the ethnic minority states lost their special status, as defined in the **Constitution of 1947**. Legal expressions of ethnic minority identity were largely confined to national costumes and dance and the rituals of Union Day, February 12, which celebrates the Panglong accord. The **State Peace and Development Council** (SPDC) has committed itself to upholding the Tatmadaw's historical role of safeguarding national unity, which constitutes its principal claim to legitimacy. It sees foreign countries, especially in the West, as determined to reimpose colonial subjugation by dividing the peoples of Burma, and has attacked Daw **Aung San Suu Kyi** as an accomplice in this scheme because of her marriage to a British academic and the moral support she has received from Europe and North America. SPDC officials and their foreign supporters claim that if controls on the democratic opposition and the minorities are loosened, the country will "break apart," like Yugoslavia. However, **cease-fires** with certain minority armed groups have given some of them de facto autonomy. *See also* HUMAN RIGHTS IN BURMA; THREE MAIN NATIONAL CAUSES.

NATIONAL UNITY FRONT (NUF). Established in 1955 as a coalition of the Burma Workers' and Peasants' Party and other groups; functioned as the principal opposition to the **Anti-Fascist People's Freedom League (AFPFL)** in the general election of 1956, winning 47 parliamentary seats and 37 percent of the popular vote. When the AFPFL split in 1958, the NUF supported U **Nu**'s "Clean" faction. Most NUF leaders were jailed during the **Caretaker Government** period, and it failed to win any seats in the 1960 general election. However, some NUF leaders advised the **Revolutionary Council** after March 1962 and contributed to the **"Burmese Road to Socialism"** ideology. Like other political parties, it was banned by the Revolutionary Council in 1964.

NATIONAL UNITY PARTY (NUP). Name of the **Burma Socialist Programme Party (BSPP)** after it lost its status as the only legal political party and was reorganized as a "democratic" party on September 26, 1988. Although many observers believed it would do well in the **General Election of May 27, 1990** because of superior resources and connections, the NUP's leadership consisted of low-ranking cadres from the old BSPP, and the party was shunned by many voters because of its record of failure between 1962 and 1988. In the election, it won 21.2 percent of the popular vote and 10 seats. However, the NUP was included among parties represented on the **National Convention**, the constitution-drafting body convened in January 1993.

NAT-PWE. A festival in honor of the *nats* (spirits) of traditional Burmese **religion**. It involves their invocation, customarily through the playing of loud music, and has the object of securing their blessing. The spirit comes down to Earth and enters a *nat-gadaw* (*"nat* wife"), usually a male transvestite (less commonly nowadays a woman), whose role is similar to that of a shaman who enters an ecstatic trance. The *nat-gadaw* (or *nat-kadaw*) is said to be "elected" by a patron *nat* for a lifetime role as spiritual intermediary. While possessed by the *nat*, he or she dances and behaves outrageously, transgressing Burmese social norms. Ordinary persons are also sometimes possessed by *nats* at these festivals and have to undergo rites of exorcism. In contrast to the generally calm and gentle nature of Buddhist observances, *nat-pwe* are loud, dissolute, and sometimes violent.

Nat festivals are popular throughout Burma, sometimes held in conjunction with **shinbyu** ceremonies, showing the coexistence of nat worship and **Buddhism**. The biggest and most popular is held in summer at Taungbyone, just north of **Mandalay**, where thousands of devotees gather for six days of wild celebration. Mount **Popa** is also the site of *nat* festivals, in spring and winter. Like other aspects of *nat* worship, *nat-pwe* are tolerated in Buddhist Burma but are often avoided by respectable people, who find the wild atmosphere unsettling. *See also* PWE.

NATS. Sometimes *naq* or *na'*, spirits or gods, encompassing a wide variety of divine or supernatural beings in traditional Burmese religion. Although *nat* worship antedates the establishment of Theravada **Buddhism** as the state religion by King **Anawrahta** in the 11th century, and in some cases can be equated with animism, it has coexisted, though in a subordinate position, with Burma's dominant religion.

Nats include the following categories, which are not mutually exclusive: gods borrowed from Indian mythology, including **Thagya Min**, the king of the gods who is the protector of the Buddhist religion, and Thurathadi (Saraswati), goddess of learning, to whom students pray to pass examinations; spirits of nature, such as those inhabiting rivers, storms, and trees (especially banyan trees); spirits associated with human activities, such as the construction of houses or cultivation of **rice**; and spirit guardians of specific places or territories. In addition, the spirits of dead persons are often recognized as *nats*.

The pantheon of **Thirty-seven Nats** established by Anawrahta consists of legendary or historical figures, who usually met violent ("green") or tragic deaths, often at the hands of a king. Because of the nature of their demise, they could not be reincarnated and roamed the world at large, causing havoc. To appease them, the king instituted a state-supported cult that transformed them into protective deities. Their images were placed on the platform of the **Shwezigon Pagoda**. Their number, 36, reflected Hindu cosmology, to which Anawrahta added Thagya Min, to make 37. In this way, Anawrahta and his successors sought to keep *nat* worship under state control. Over time, the individual figures in the *nat* pantheon have changed, but the number has remained the same. Festivals (*nat-pwe*) are held in their honor, especially around **Pagan (Bagan)** and **Mandalay**. The most important center of *nat* worship is **Mount Popa**, in **Mandalay Division**. *Nat* shrines are found in villages, at the entrance to **pagodas**, and in Burmese households, where offerings are made to an unhusked coconut, which is hung in an elevated position and represents **Min Mahagiri**, one of the 37 nats who was especially esteemed by King **Kyanzittha**. Statues of *nats*, such as the Sule Nat at the **Sule Pagoda** in **Rangoon (Yangon)**, associated with the legendary founding of the **Shwe Dagon Pagoda**, are a prominent feature of Burmese religious art (though of less importance than Buddha images).

Belief in *nats* is fluid, like Western belief in ghosts, and many Burmese today still believe that the place where a person met a violent death is haunted by a dangerous *nat* who must be placated with offerings. In 1998, it was said that *nats* caused strange phenomena (the sounds of disembodied screams, the appearance of blood) near the Myeinigone Market in Rangoon, the site of a massacre of **student** demonstrators by the **Riot Police** in June 1988. *See also* MYEINIGONE MARKET INCIDENT.

NAVY (TATMADAW YAY). One of the three services of the **Tatmadaw**, its commander in chief is a (three-star) lieutenant general. Unlike some of its neighbors in Southeast Asia, Burma does not have a strong maritime tradition. Yet its long coastline and many islands make it vulnerable to piracy and poaching of marine resources by foreign parties. After 1988, the Navy expanded significantly in terms of personnel (16,000 by 2000, compared to 7,000 in 1988), equipment, mostly acquired from abroad (including Chinese- and Yugoslavian-made coastal patrol boats), and coastal bases, some of which were reportedly modernized in the 1990s with Chinese assistance. It has responsibility for defending both coastal and riverine areas, and during times of emergency the civilian Merchant Marine can be placed under naval (or military) command. But compared to the **Army**, its political influence, budgets, and manpower remain severely limited. Navy regional commands are located at **Rangoon (Yangon), Moulmein (Mawlamyine), Mergui (Myeik)**, Hainggyi Island, and **Sittwe (Sittway)**.

NAW SENG (1922–1972). A **Kachin** military commander who served with distinction in the Northern Kachin Levies during **World War II** and was twice decorated by the British. In 1946, he became a captain in the First Kachin Rifles and fought **Communist Party of Burma (CPB)** rebels in 1948, earning himself the reputation of being the "terror" of communists who had established a base at **Pyinmana** in southern **Mandalay Division**. In February 1949, however, he joined forces with the **Karen National Union** uprising against the government of Prime Minister U **Nu**, apparently because his harsh treatment of **Burman (Bamar)** communist rebels had aroused criticism in government circles and because he could not bear to fight against fellow Christian **Karens (Kayins)**. In March, his forces briefly occupied **Mandalay** and then moved south, hoping to assist KNU-affiliated Karen National Defence Organization troops fighting at Insein (now **Insein Township**) adjacent to **Rangoon (Yangon)**. They reached **Pegu (Bago)** but then retreated northward to **Shan State**. Naw Seng hoped to establish the independence of the Kachins from the Union of Burma, and his Pawngyawng National Defence Force (Pawngyawng being the name of the republic he wanted to establish), organized in November 1949, was the first Kachin antigovernment insurgency. In 1950, he crossed the border into China, where he remained until January 1968, when he returned to northern Shan State as head of the CPB's Northeastern Command. To his dismay, he had to fight not only the **Tatmadaw** but also the anticommunist **Kachin Independence Army**. He died in March 1972, reportedly having "fallen off his horse" (or a cliff), although the demise of this colorful and much-admired rebel leader might have been ordered by the CPB, who considered him too independent and an overly zealous Kachin patriot.

NE WIN (SHU MAUNG, 1911–2002). Wartime comrade of **Aung San**, commander in chief of Burma's armed forces from 1949 to 1972, and the country's leader during the **Caretaker Government** period (1958–1960) and the 26-year-long **Burma Socialist Programme Party** era (1962–1988). Born on March 14, 1911, in Paungdale, near **Prome (Pyay)** in what is now **Pegu (Bago) Division**, Shu Maung was of mixed Chinese–Burmese ancestry. Dropping out of **Rangoon (Yangon) University** in 1931, he joined the

Dobama Asiayone and was a member of its right-wing faction, led by **Ba Sein** and Tun Oke. Recruited as one of the **Thirty Comrades** by Aung San, the **Minami Kikan** placed him in command of a unit of the **Burma Independence Army (BIA)** responsible for sabotage behind enemy lines. Following the establishment of the BIA in December 1941, he adopted the *nom de guerre* Ne Win, meaning "the brightness of sun." When Japan granted Burma nominal independence in August 1943, he was appointed commander in chief of the **Burma National Army** and joined Defense Minister Aung San in resisting the Japanese after March 27, 1945.

Ne Win succeeded General **Smith Dun** as commander in chief of independent Burma's armed forces following the **Karen National Union** uprising in January 1949. Between 1949 and 1950, the rump of the **Tatmadaw** that he commanded, which remained loyal to the central government, proved indispensable in preventing the overthrow of Prime Minister U **Nu**'s government by ethnic minority and communist insurgents. Ne Win solidified his control over the Tatmadaw by forging close ties with subordinate officers and presided over the "Burmanization" of its top ranks. He placed loyal subordinates from his old regiment, the **Fourth Burma Rifles**, in positions of special responsibility. When the ruling united front, the **Anti-Fascist People's Freedom League**, split into two factions in 1958, parliament passed legislation enabling Ne Win to assume the prime ministership as head of the Caretaker Government, which remained in power from October 1958 to April 1960. This period proved to be a dress rehearsal for the military regime he established on March 2, 1962, overthrowing U Nu and establishing the **Revolutionary Council** with himself as chairman, a post he held until the Socialist Republic of the Union of Burma was established in 1974 and he became its president.

In July 1962, Ne Win established the Burma Socialist Programme Party (BSPP), which became the country's only legal party in 1964. He implemented Eastern European–style socialist policies (the **"Burmese Road to Socialism"**) and made military officers responsible for public administration and economic management. He is largely blamed for presiding over Burma's decline from being one of Southeast Asia's richest and most promising economies to being one of its poorest, and for having isolated the country culturally as well as economically from the international community. He resigned as president of the Socialist Republic of the Union of Burma in 1981 but remained chairman of the BSPP until retiring from that post on July 23, 1988. Though an adherent of non-Marxist socialism and advocate of the separation of **religion** and the state like Aung San, Ne Win's ruling style, dictatorial and personal in the classical Southeast Asian sense, belied his ambition to establish a modern "socialist democracy." Known by his people as "The Old Man" or "Number One," he often adopted the trappings of old Burman kings; regarded the nation's natural resources, especially **gemstones**, as his private property; and terrorized his subordinates with a violent temper. He was addicted to **numerology** and *yedaya* (occult practices), and had a scandalous private life. His style of diplomacy was largely based on personal ties rather than a coherent **foreign policy**, and he enjoyed close and mutually profitable relations with officials and private citizens in **Japan**, West **Germany**, and other countries. He ruthlessly suppressed all forms of dissent, especially **students** and ethnic minorities, and his **Military Intelligence** service, headed after 1983 by **Khin Nyunt**, kept a close eye on the population.

After his 1988 retirement, there was speculation that he continued to manipulate politics from behind the scenes. Although this might have been true in the initial years of the **State Law and Order Restoration Council** junta, by the mid-1990s, he largely devoted himself to **meditation** and other religious practices, holding a Buddhist ceremony with old BSPP comrades in attendance on his 90th birthday in 1999. The alleged involvement of his daughter **Sanda Win**, his son-in-law, and three grandsons in a **coup d'état attempt**, uncovered in March 2002, marked the eclipse of his prestige. When he died on December 5, 2002, there was no state funeral, and his passing was only briefly mentioned in the state-run media.

NE WIN, LEGACY OF. Although eulogized by his biographer, **Dr. Maung Maung**, for having almost single-handedly defended the country's **national unity** from communists, ethnic minority separatists, and street mobs, Ne Win's legacy is generally cast in highly negative terms. Continuities between the Ne Win era (1962–1988) and those of the **State Law and Order Restoration Council**

(SLORC, 1988–1997) and the **State Peace and Development Council (SPDC**, 1997–) include exclusive control of essential sectors of the economy by a **Tatmadaw** élite, either through state socialism or state capitalism, undermining competition and the ability of the economy to grow; a flourishing **black market**, including the **drug economy**; structural corruption; lack of the rule of law; routine abuses of power; an overly personal style of rule and concentration of power in a single "strongman" or group of "strongmen"; **Burman (Bamar)** chauvinism at the expense of non-Burman minorities; and Burma's continued cultural and social isolation despite the economic liberalization policies adopted in 1988 by the SLORC. Ne Win closed down Burma's civil society, and it has not been allowed to revive under his successors.

By being insulated from, or insulating himself from, dissenting or objective points of view and demanding unquestioning loyalty, Ne Win ensured mediocrity in personnel and policy making (reflected in the Burmese saying *lukaun lutaw*, "good people are better than smart people"), in contrast to his authoritarian counterparts in other Asian countries, such as Suharto in Indonesia and Park Chung-hee in South Korea, who gave foreign-educated economic planners (technocrats) considerable autonomy. Although in recent years the SPDC leadership has tried to distance itself from the Ne Win legacy, especially mistakes made in economic policy, their very similar worldviews and policies continue to hinder democratization and economic development.

NEW DEMOCRATIC ARMY (NDA). A **cease-fire** armed group formed after the breakup of the **Communist Party of Burma** in 1989, which is based in **Kachin State**. It contains only a few hundred armed men, and trades in **forest** products and **drugs** across the border with **China**.

NEW LIGHT OF MYANMAR (MYANMA ALIN). The official newspaper of the **State Peace and Development Council (SPDC)**, published by the Ministry of Information. Until a name change in 1993, it was known as the *Working People's Daily (Loketha Pyithu Nezin)*, established by the **Revolutionary Council** in 1963 with editions in both English and the **Burmese (Myanmar) language**. During the **Burma Socialist Programme Party** era (1962–1988), it was one of the few **mass media** outlets in Burma. *Myanma Alin*, named for a colonial-era vernacular publication, also has dual Burmese–English editions. Over the years, the newspaper's content has scarcely varied: Government slogans are run across the top of the front page, visits of high-ranking SPDC officials overseas or to various parts of the country are carefully noted, and there are feature articles on the military regime's latest political agenda, for example, in 2004, popular resistance to the U.S. occupation of Iraq, reflecting government hostility generated by Washington's **sanctions**. Its circulation (around 14,000) is limited, and its stodgy, socialist-era format contrasts starkly with a newer progovernment publication, the glossy *Myanmar Times and Business Review*.

NEW MON STATE PARTY (NMSP). Established in July 1958 by Nai **Shwe Kyin;** claims to represent the **Mons** and has operated in rural areas around **Moulmein (Mawlamyine)**, along the shore of the Andaman Sea and on the Thai–Burma border. Its armed force, swelled by **students** who went underground after the 1963 **peace talks**, was 1,000 in 1971 and around 1,500 in the late 1980s. The NMSP split into two factions, led by Nai Shwe Kyin and Nai Nol Lar, in 1981, but they were reunited in 1987. In 1990, the party claimed that it controlled four districts, around **Thaton, Moulmein (Mawlamyine), Tavoy (Dawei)**, and **Mergui (Myeik)**.

The New Mon State Party has been a member of the National Democratic Front and the **Democratic Alliance of Burma**. Its armed force is now known as the *Mon National Liberation Army*. The NMSP signed a **cease-fire** with the **State Law and Order Restoration Council** in June 1995, in part because of pressure from **Thailand** and because the fall of **Manerplaw** left it dangerously exposed to **Tatmadaw** attacks. As a **cease-fire group**, it enjoys only limited independence but continues in its efforts to promote the interests of the Mon community. A 2001 breakaway faction, the Hongsawatoi Restoration Party, has refused to recognize the cease-fire. When Nai Shwe Kyin died in March 2003, he was succeeded as NMSP president by Nai Htin. *See also* ALL RAMANYA MON ASSOCIATION (ARMA); THREE PAGODAS PASS.

NEW TOWNS (RANGOON). Although new towns or satellite towns (**Thaketa, North** and **South Okkalapa**) were established by the

Caretaker Government between 1958 and 1960, the **State Law and Order Restoration Council (SLORC)** carried out a more ambitious program of expanding the boundaries of **Rangoon (Yangon)** by establishing 10 new towns, of which the three largest are Hlaing Thayar, Shwepyithar, and Dagon Myothit (further divided into North, East, and South Dagon). These new settlements incorporated territories lying west of the Hlaing River and east of Ngamoeyeik Creek, the city's traditional boundaries. As many as 450,000–500,000 people moved, or were moved, to these new towns (other estimates are lower). They included a large number of persons subject to **forced relocation**, not only squatters but also people who had supported the demonstrations of **Democracy Summer** and had to rebuild their homes in remote areas lacking basic amenities. Although some people relocated voluntarily, for example, civil servants who were granted parcels of land and wealthy people who bought houses in luxury developments, the SLORC's establishment of the new towns reflects the weakness of individual property rights in Burma, where the state is recognized as having ultimate authority over land. *See also* HUMAN RIGHTS IN BURMA; YANGON CITY DEVELOPMENT COMMITTEE.

NIBBANA. *Neikban* in Burmese, known as *nirvana* in English; the ultimate goal of **Buddhism**, meaning liberation from *samsara* or the cycle of rebirth and suffering. The original meaning of the term is the "extinguishing" of the flame of life, like a candle snuffed out. The concept is extremely difficult for even learned Buddhists to understand, and most ordinary believers in Burma are more attracted by the prospect of a pleasant rebirth (perhaps as a rich man or a celestial being) or by the idea of *nibbana* as simply a serene paradise. Gotama **Buddha** was able to pass into *nibbana* at death, after achieving Enlightenment. *Nibbana* stands above the 31 levels of existence, including hell, animal life, the human world, and the realms of gods and incorporeal celestial beings, which comprise Buddhist cosmology. *See also* KAMMA; KUTHO.

NONGOVERNMENTAL ORGANIZATIONS (NGOs) IN BURMA. Nongovernmental organizations (NGOs) and international nongovernmental organizations (INGOs) have been deeply involved in

Burma since the **State Law and Order Restoration Council** seized power in 1988. Amnesty International, Human Rights Watch, and other well-known INGOs began drawing world attention to the new regime's **human rights** abuses, and new NGOs were established by Burmese exiles and their overseas supporters, including the Free Burma Coalition, the Burma Project of the Soros Foundation, ALTSEAN-Burma, the Karen Human Rights Group, and the Shan Human Rights Foundation. Based in neighboring countries, such as **Thailand**, Western countries, or **Japan**, these groups have been successful in using **information technology**, such as the Internet, to increase awareness of a country that previously was largely ignored by the international community. Some of them have also played a role in getting Western governments to enact **sanctions** against the military regime. Such NGOs as the Burmese Relief Centre and the Burma Border Consortium assist Burmese **refugees** in Thailand.

Other NGOs or INGOs have operated inside the country since the early 1990s, providing assistance in public **health**, family planning, and community development. Narcotics and the **AIDS** epidemic have been special areas of concern. Such groups include Médecins sans Frontières-Holland, Médecins du Monde, CARE Myanmar, World Vision Myanmar, Save the Children Fund (United Kingdom and United States), Population Services International, and the Adventist Development and Relief Agency. NGOs are required to sign a formal Memorandum of Understanding (MOU) with a government agency, usually the Ministry of Health, and are expected to work closely with local Peace and Development Councils, the **Union Solidarity and Development Association**, and GONGOS (government-organized nongovernmental organizations), such as the **Myanmar Maternal and Child Welfare Association**, Myanmar Medical Association, and Myanmar Anti-Narcotic Association. They also must avoid involvement of any kind that the State Peace and Development Council regards as "political," including contacts with the **National League for Democracy (NLD)**.

After her release from house arrest in 1995, **Aung San Suu Kyi** asked that NGOs working in Burma consult with the NLD, a condition that, given the restrictions imposed by the regime, is impossible for them to satisfy; in a 1998 interview, she said that NGOs should not work inside Burma at all, but rather focus their resources on helping refugees in neighboring countries. The controversy over the legitimacy of NGO/INGO work inside Burma focuses on two issues: whether the aid given by these groups benefits the SPDC regime more than the people, and whether people in local communities can be meaningfully helped as long as the military-dominated power structure remains unchanged. *See also* UNITED NATIONS IN BURMA.

NORDIC COUNTRIES AND BURMA. Although they do not have significant historical ties with Burma, the nordic countries (Sweden, Denmark, Norway, and Finland) have been particularly active in providing the Burmese prodemocracy movement with moral and material support, aiding Burmese **refugees**, and calling upon the post-1988 military regime to recognize the results of the **General Election of May 27, 1990**. In 1991, the Norwegian Nobel Committee awarded the Peace Prize to **Aung San Suu Kyi**; the Norwegian government established ties with the **National Coalition Government of the Union of Burma** after it was set up in late 1990 and has provided funding for the Democratic Voice of Burma radio station, which broadcasts Burmese programs from Norway. Although Sweden and Denmark coordinate their Burma policies with those of the **European Union**, the Swedish foreign minister, the late Anna Lindh, was strongly committed to focusing international attention on the Burma crisis. In the 1990s, Sweden cosponsored resolutions in the General Assembly of the **United Nations** condemning the post-1988 military regime's violations of **human rights**. **Nongovernmental organizations** in all four countries have been active in addressing Burma-related issues.

NU, U (THAKIN NU) (1907–1995). Independent Burma's first prime minister, who began his political career as a **student** activist during the 1930s. Born on May 25, 1907, in Wakema, **Myaungmya (Myoungmya)** District south of **Bassein (Pathein)**, he was a graduate of **Rangoon (Yangon) University**. His election to the presidency of the **Rangoon University Students Union (RUSU)** in 1935 ensured control of the organization by radicals. The following year, his expulsion from the school, along with **Aung San**, led to the student strike of February–May. This made both Nu and Aung San figures of importance on the national political scene. In 1937, he joined the **Dobama Asiayone**

or **Thakin Party** (thus, he was widely known as "Thakin Nu") and was also a founder of the **Nagani Book Club**. Interned by the British between 1940 and 1942, he served as foreign minister in the pro-Japanese wartime government of Dr. **Ba Maw** from 1943 to 1945. At war's end, he was vice president of the **Anti-Fascist People's Freedom League (AFPFL)** and succeeded to the presidency following the **assassination of Aung San** on July 19, 1947, negotiating the **Nu–Attlee Agreement** with the British government in October of that year.

U Nu was prime minister during the periods 1948–1956, 1957–1958, and 1960–1962. His political vision encompassed non-Marxist socialism, construction of a modern welfare state, and **Buddhism**. Though he ceded power to General Ne Win's **Caretaker Government** in October 1958, his **Pyidaungsu (Union) Party** won the February 1960 election, and Burma had two more years of civilian government under his prime ministership.

Between 1954 and 1956, U Nu sponsored the **Sixth Great Buddhist Council**, on the 2,500th anniversary of the Buddha's attainment of *nibbana* (*nirvana*), in which Buddhist monks and lay scholars produced an authoritative version of the **Tipitaka** (Buddhist scriptures). Though a strong backer of religious tolerance, U Nu proposed that Buddhism be made the state religion, a measure popular with the **Burman (Bamar)** voters that probably assured his 1960 election victory. A constitutional amendment to this effect was passed in August 1961, but it alienated religious minorities, including Christians among the **Kachins** and other border area nationalities. U Nu's hosting of the Federal Seminar in February 1962, however, reflected his willingness to talk with ethnic minority leaders about granting the border area **states** more autonomy. U Nu's government was overthrown in the coup d'état of March 2, 1962, and he and other political leaders were imprisoned.

U Nu was able to leave Burma in 1969 after his participation in the **Internal Unity Advisory Board (IUAB)**, and headed an anti-Ne Win insurgency, the National United Liberation Front, based in Thailand. This proved ineffectual, and he quit as chairman in 1972, returning to Burma in 1980 following Ne Win's announcement of a general amnesty. Though retired from political life and devoting himself to religion, he announced a "parallel government" on September 9, 1988, establishing his own cabinet with himself as prime minister, on the grounds that following the 1962 coup d'état the **Constitution of 1947** had never been formally abrogated. Because of his refusal to dissolve the parallel government, the **State Law and Order Restoration Council** kept him under house arrest from December 1989 to April 1992. His party, the League for Democracy and Peace, failed to win a seat in the **General Election of May 27, 1990**. He died on February 14, 1995.

U Nu was internationally respected as one of the founders of the Non-Aligned Movement. At home, he always preferred discussion to the use of brute force, and his government, though not without its flaws, was the most democratic Burma ever experienced.

NU–ATTLEE AGREEMENT. Officially, the "Treaty between the Government of the United Kingdom and the Provisional Government of Burma Regarding the Recognition of Burmese Independence and Related Matters," signed by U **Nu** and Prime Minister Clement Attlee on October 17, 1947, in London. Defense and financial agreements were also signed. The British Parliament passed the Burma Independence Bill on December 10, 1947, and U Nu's government chose January 4, 1948, as an auspicious date for the ending of British rule. *See also* AUNG SAN–ATTLEE AGREEMENT.

NUMEROLOGY. The belief that certain numbers are auspicious or inauspicious, widespread in Burma. For example, if the number of passengers in a bus is considered unlucky, the driver may place a rock in the vehicle, representing an additional passenger. **Ne Win** was well known for his belief that the number 9 was lucky. This was reflected in his **demonetization** order of September 1987, replacing old **kyat** notes with denominations of 45 and 90; the power seizure by the **State Law and Order Restoration Council**, occurring on September 18 (1 + 8 = 9), 1988; and the date of the **General Election of March 27, 1990** (2 + 7 = 9). The rather unrealistic figure that the military government gives for the number of national ethnic groups, 135 (1 + 3 + 5 = 9), may also reflect this obsession. The **Four Eights (8.8.88) Movement** began on August 8, 1988, because oppositionists believed that eight is an inauspicious number for rulers, representing anarchy and destruction of the old order. *See also* ASTROLOGY; *YEDAYA*.

NUNS, BUDDHIST. Although Gotama **Buddha** established an order of nuns (*bhikkuni*) during his lifetime, the **Sangha** of Burma and other Theravada **Buddhist** countries does not include **women**, since the ordination rites for them were lost to the Theravada tradition. Inscriptions indicate that there may have been ordained nuns during the **Pagan (Bagan) Dynasty.**

Despite the lack of equal status with monks in modern Burma, many women become ascetics (often referred to as *sila-shin*, "owners of good moral conduct," or *dasa-sila*, "observers of the 10 precepts"), shaving their heads and wearing pink robes. They are estimated to number around 30,000 (compared to 300,000 monks), and large communities of nuns live in **Sagaing** and **Mingun.** Their activities are essentially the same as male monks: **meditation** and study of the **Pali** Canon. Women are still ordained as nuns in Mahayana Buddhist countries, such as China and Korea, and some Buddhists have suggested that the Mahayana rites could be used to start a new order of *bhikkuni* in Burma and other Theravada countries.

– O –

OFFICE OF STRATEGIC STUDIES (OSS). Widely described as a "think tank" collecting information on matters of domestic and international importance to the **State Peace and Development Council** regime, the OSS, a **Military Intelligence** organ, was established in the mid-1990s and had five areas of responsibility: international issues, narcotics, security, ethnic minority affairs, and science and the environment. It organized and participated in international conferences involving academic and official participants from countries of the **Association of Southeast Asian Nations (ASEAN)** and beyond. Although formally superior to the **Directorate of Defense Services Intelligence** within the Ministry of Defense hierarchy, its importance had declined even before the purge of Military Intelligence head **Khin Nyunt** in October 2004. Many observers believe the OSS was set up to give Khin Nyunt a strategic command, justifying his promotion to lieutenant general in 1994. *See also* MILITARY INTELLIGENCE, ORGANIZATION OF.

OFFICERS' TRAINING SCHOOL (OTS). One of Burma's two main institutions for training commissioned officers, the other being the **Defence Services Academy.** Established in 1948, it is located in Bahtoo. Since 1988, most OTS cadets have been university graduates, with a smaller number of noncommissioned officers without college degrees. The course lasts for nine months, and almost all graduates receive commissions from the **Army.** Prominent OTS graduates have included Senior General **Than Shwe** and former SPDC Secretary-1 and prime minister **Khin Nyunt.** *See also* TATMADAW.

OIL AND NATURAL GAS. Burma possesses abundant oil and natural gas resources, located both onshore and offshore. During the **Konbaung Dynasty,** "earth oil" was extracted from wells around **Yenangyaung (Yaynangyoung),** in present-day **Magwe (Magway) Division.** The wells were operated by *twinza,* "well-eaters," whose usufruct right was hereditary. During the British colonial period, the Burmah Oil Company, a Scottish-owned corporation, extracted oil from wells at Yenangyaung, Myingyan, and Chauk, and Burma exported oil products to India. The company continued its operations until it was nationalized by the **Burma Socialist Programme Party** regime in the 1960s. During the socialist period, the energy sector languished. Although attempts were made to increase oil production and discover new offshore fields with the cooperation of foreign oil companies, sustained increases in production could not be achieved. After the **State Law and Order Restoration Council (SLORC)** seized power in September 1988, socialist economic policies were dropped and the way cleared to exploit hydrocarbon resources with the full participation of foreign oil companies. Beginning in 1989, 18 European, American, and Japanese companies paid large "signature bonuses" to the SLORC to do onshore exploration from **Mon State** in the south to **Sagaing Division** in the north, but they failed to find major new deposits. Most had quit the country by 1993, after spending hundreds of millions of dollars. Burma became increasingly dependent on oil imports, and much locally produced oil was sold on the **black market.**

Offshore, deposits of natural gas proved more promising. The US$1.2 billion **Yadana Pipeline Project** in the Andaman Sea became the largest **foreign investment** in Burma; this joint venture comprising the Myanmar Oil and Natural Gas Enterprise (MOGE),

Total of France, Unocal of the **United States**, and the Petroleum Authority of **Thailand** to export natural gas to Thailand has gained the Burmese government as much as US$400 million in annual revenues. A second field, Yetagun, is also being developed. In early 2004, it was announced that a third natural gas field, called the "Shwe [Golden] Prospect," located off the coast of **Arakan (Rakhine) State** in the Bay of Bengal, was exploited by a consortium of MOGE, South Korean, and Indian energy firms. It will provide India with natural gas and bring the **State Peace and Development Council** between US$800 million and US$3 billion in yearly revenue.

Energy exports are ideal sources of hard currency for the SPDC because the extraction of hydrocarbons takes place in remote areas offshore, has—unlike the establishment of new manufacturing industry—almost no impact on society in central Burma, and is completely under the control of MOGE and its foreign partners. Cases of **forced labor** and **forced relocation** associated with the Yadana and Yetagun projects have raised international concern, and many activists fear that construction of a pipeline to India in connection with the Shwe Prospect will result in similar hardship for people in western Burma. *See also* OIL FIELD WORKERS' STRIKE.

OIL FIELD WORKERS' STRIKE (1938). Sparked by a dispute over holidays between Burmese oil field workers at wells at Chauk and **Yenaungyaung (Yaynangyoung)** and the British-owned Burmah Oil Company, the strike, which began in January 1938, was organized by local branches of the **Dobama Asiayone** and soon developed into a movement with strong political and anticolonial overtones. But most of the 12,000 laborers involved were back at work by October 1938, and strike leaders sought to revive the movement by organizing a 400-mile march from the oil fields to **Rangoon (Yangon)** by way of **Magwe (Magway)** in the following month. On January 8, 1939, the marchers arrived at the **Shwe Dagon Pagoda**, and their supporters, including workers at the **Syriam (Thanlyin)** oil refinery, farmers, firemen, bus drivers, as well as members of the **Sangha**, women's groups, *tats,* and **Rangoon University Students Union**, held massive demonstrations, although the authorities thwarted a Dobama-organized general strike. The oil field strike was the beginning of the modern labor movement in Burma, witnessing the establishment of the All Burma Trade Union Congress. Known as the "1300 Revolution" (1938–1939 was the year

1300 in the **Burmese Era**), it also anticipated the massive prodemocracy demonstrations of 1988, the "1350 Revolution," in which huge crowds of townspeople joined with activists to protest the **Ne Win** government. *See also* AUNG GYAW, BO.

OKKALAPA, NORTH AND SOUTH. New **townships** in **Rangoon** **(Yangon)**, established during the **Caretaker Government** period of General **Ne Win** (1958–1960). They are located to the north and northeast of downtown Rangoon. To deal with the problems of squatters and overcrowding in the city center, Rangoon's new mayor, a military officer, relocated as many as 170,000 squatters by mid-1959, of whom 75,647 and 64,441 were placed in North and South Okkalapa, respectively. During **Democracy Summer** in 1988, the largely poor and working-class population of these townships bitterly resisted the **Tatmadaw**, suffering many casualties; residents of North Okkalapa built a memorial to the martyrs of the **Four Eights Movement**, which was torn down after the **State Law and Order Restoration Council** seized power on September 18, 1988. *See also* NEW TOWNS (RANGOON); THAKETA.

OPIUM. Burma's most profitable cash crop. Opium and its derivatives, especially **heroin**, generate hundreds of millions of dollars in revenue annually. Raw opium latex is extracted from the pods of the opium poppy (*Papaver somniferum*), which is cultivated in remote, hilly parts of **Shan** and **Kachin States**. Because of soil and climatic conditions, the most productive areas are the **Wa District** and **Kokang**, both located along the border with China east of the **Salween (Thanlwin) River**, though areas close to the border with **Thailand** also account for significant production. For generations, local farmers have found that growing opium is more profitable than other crops, although their income is small compared to the profits made by middlemen and the leaders of drug-financed armed groups, such as the former "kings of the Golden Triangle," **Lo Hsing-han** and **Khun Sa**. After the **People's Republic of China** forcefully ended opium production and consumption inside its borders, the Golden Triangle—consisting of eastern Burma, northern Thailand, and Laos—supplied international demand for illicit opiates. The demand for heroin increased during the Vietnam War, when it was used widely by **U.S.** troops stationed in

Southeast Asia. Drug trafficking routes connected growing and refining areas in Shan and Kachin States with international markets by way of Thailand, but in the 1990s traffickers opened new routes through China's Yunnan Province—creating a Chinese drug-abuse problem comparable to that of the period before 1949. Injection of heroin has contributed to a massive **AIDS** epidemic, both in Burma and neighboring countries.

At the beginning of the 21st century, Burma vies with Afghanistan for the dubious distinction of being the world's largest producer and exporter of opiates (in other parts of the Golden Triangle, poppy cultivation has been largely suppressed in northern Thailand, and most Laotian opium is grown for local use). Production increased during the early and mid-1990s, in part because **cease-fires** gave armed groups, such as the **United Wa State Army (UWSA)**, greater freedom to expand poppy cultivation; according to the U.S. Department of State, production reached a high of 2,560 metric tons of opium in 1996, compared to 1,100 metric tons in 1986. However, a steady decrease in production has occurred since 1996, falling to 865 metric tons in 2001. Acreage under poppy cultivation has also decreased substantially. The **State Peace and Development Council (SPDC)** claims that the decline shows the effectiveness of its drug eradication policies. In Kokang, the SPDC authorities have been able to carry out drug-eradication programs, especially following a mid-1990s power struggle among leaders of the **Myanmar National Democratic Alliance Army/Party** that gravely weakened this armed group. The UWSA, however, is much stronger, and has succeeded in keeping central government officials out of its territories. Nevertheless, the UWSA leadership promised to end poppy cultivation by 2005. The SPDC pledges to eradicate opium production nationwide by 2014.

Although there is no hard evidence that top leaders of the SPDC are directly involved in the drug economy, drug exports generate huge profits that have been "laundered" through the regular economy. Many "new capitalists" in **Rangoon (Yangon)** have close ties to drug-producing areas, including the retired Lo Hsing-han and his son, Stephen Law. Among foreign countries, especially the United States, there is sharp disagreement over whether the military regime is sincerely committed to drug eradication. Another problem is that neither the government nor the ethnic armed groups have seriously addressed the problem of the massive outflow of Burma-produced **amphetamines** into Thailand. *See also* DRUG ECONOMY.

ORWELL, GEORGE (PSEUDONYM OF ERIC BLAIR, 1903–1950). The author of *Animal Farm* and *Nineteen Eighty-four*, whose first novel, *Burmese Days*, and essays, such as "A Hanging" and "Shooting an Elephant," reflected his experiences in Burma from 1922 to 1927 as a young officer of the Indian Imperial Police. Posted to **Myaungmya (Myoungmya)**, Twante, Insein (now **Insein Township**), **Syriam (Thanlyin)**, **Moulmein (Mawlamyine)**, and Katha (in **Upper Burma**), he described his service as "five boring years within the sound of bugles." His view of colonialism—that it enslaved colonized and colonizer alike and involved unconscionable brutality—evolved during this time. As a police officer dealing with criminal cases, he became familiar with the darker side of empire and decided, after returning to England in 1927, to quit the service and pursue a literary career. One of his earliest published essays, "A Hanging," is an eloquent critique of capital punishment based on his experience at a colonial jail, probably at Moulmein. *Burmese Days*, first published in the United States in October 1934, has such vividly drawn characters that his British publisher, Gollancz, hesitated to publish it until changes were made that reduced the possibility of libel (since then, the American edition has been seen as authoritative). Apart from descriptions of natural beauty, *Burmese Days* is unrelentingly dark, but it is also probably the best novel in the English language about the country. *See also* COLLIS, MAURICE.

OTTAMA, U (1897–1939). A pivotal figure in modern Burmese political history, the first of the "political *pongyis*" members of the **Sangha** who agitated against British colonial rule. A native of **Sittwe (Sittway)** in **Arakan (Rakhine)**, he went to Calcutta to study and was deeply influenced by the ideas of the Indian National Congress. He also resided in **Japan**, teaching **Pali** in Tokyo. Returning from Japan in 1919, he became involved in the emerging political movements of the time, writing articles for the nationalist newspaper, *Thuriya* (*The Sun*), preaching in villages, establishing branches of the *wunthanu athin*, and becoming famous for writing an open letter to the governor of the province, Reginald Craddock, demanding that he "go home." While conservative monks avoided any involvement in politics, U Ottama, an excellent public speaker, preached that monks should not concentrate on achieving *nibbana* before the people were freed from (colonial) oppression, an idea linking **Buddhism** and politics that in different forms remained important until the **Ne Win** era (1962–1988). In 1921, he was imprisoned for sedition after making a political speech, receiving a harsh sentence that inspired mass protests. Between that year and his death in 1939, he spent much time in jail, and in his latter years endured illness, poverty, and neglect at the hands of a younger generation of Burmese nationalists. He was one of the founders of the **General Council of Sangha Sammeggi** and, inspired by the *khadi* movement led by Mahatma Gandhi in India, advocated a boycott of British goods in favor of Burmese-made ones, such as *pinni* or homespun cloth. *See also* DYARCHY; WISARA, U.

OVERTURNING THE OFFERING BOWL. A boycott of **Tatmadaw** personnel and their families by **Buddhist** monks in the summer of 1990. The shooting of two monks by the army in **Mandalay** during a popular demonstration on August 8 and other heavy-handed treatment of members of the **Sangha** by the authorities led senior abbots at monasteries in Mandalay to declare in late August that monks should not accept offerings given by soldiers or their families or participate in army-sponsored ceremonies, a severe form of "excommunication." The protest spread from Mandalay to other cities, including monasteries in **Rangoon (Yangon)**, the "offering bowl" being "overturned" so as not to accept offerings from soldiers. The **State Law and Order Restoration Council** responded by raiding monasteries, arresting monk activists, and pressuring senior monks to cancel the boycott. *See also* YEDAYA.

– P –

PA-AN (HPA-AN). The capital of **Karen (Kayin) State**, with a population estimated at 59,078 in 1996. Located on the eastern bank of the **Salween (Thanlwin) River**, its inhabitants are **Burmans (Bamars)**,

Mons, and **Muslims**, as well as **Karens (Kayins)**. Nearby is the monastery where the **Thamanya Sayadaw** resided until his death in November 2003.

PACIFICATION OF BURMA (1885–1890). The Third Anglo-Burmese War lasted only two weeks, from its outbreak on November 14, 1885, until the occupation of **Mandalay** on November 28. But the countrywide uprisings that followed, involving thousands of rural-based guerrillas, surprised the British, who expected that the Burmese people would be grateful for having been liberated from the tyranny of King **Thibaw**'s court. After being appointed chief commissioner of Burma in March 1886, Sir Charles Crosthwaithe launched a "pacification" campaign, involving more than 40,000 British and Indian troops and military police, which succeeded in imposing order in most parts of **Upper** and **Lower Burma** by 1887 (British authority over border areas where **Shans**, **Kachins**, and **Chins** resided was not effectively imposed until the end of the decade). This was accomplished through the use of mobile cavalry operations, summary executions, and the **forced relocation** of communities that supported rebels, a method that was especially effective in tearing up the social roots of guerrilla resistance. Some of the harsher measures were criticized in the British newspapers and Parliament. Crosthwaithe claimed that when villagers were unwilling to give information on rebel movements, "the only open course was to make them fear us rather than the bandits."

The intensity of the popular resistance and its appearance even in areas that had been under British rule for decades, such as the delta of the **Irrawaddy (Ayeyarwady River)**, was caused in Upper Burma by the breakdown of governmental institutions during the last years of Thibaw's reign and the desire of bandit gangs to take advantage of an anarchic situation. In Lower Burma, rebels were inspired by their Upper Burma counterparts. But the uprising also had a patriotic theme, especially when members of the royal family, such as the Myinzaing Prince, a surviving son of King **Mindon**, were involved. In the Shan States, the **Limbin Confederacy**, led by another royal prince, first opposed King Thibaw, then the British. Patriotic movements attempted to restore the traditional political and social order, though not necessarily by a scion of the **Konbaung Dynasty**, and it was often difficult to tell the difference between a bandit (*dacoit*) and a patriotic leader. In some areas, members of the **Sangha** actively aided the resistance, anticipating the anti-British "political *pongyis*" of the 1920s. British use of **Karen (Kayin)** levies to suppress the rebellion, encouraged by some Christian **missionaries**, fueled ethnic antagonism.

Although the uprisings were largely suppressed by 1890, the British resorted to similar pacification measures in dealing with the **Saya San (Hsaya San) Rebellion** of 1930–1932, the last major Burmese rural uprising. *See also* ANGLO-CHIN WAR.

PADAUNGS. Also known as *Kayans*, an ethnic minority nationality related to the **Karens (Kayins)**, speaking a Tibeto-Burman language, who live for the most part in **Kayah (Karenni) State**. They are most famous for their "giraffe women," who place heavy copper or brass rings around their necks (according to **James G. Scott**, weighing as much as as much as 50–60 pounds), depressing the rib cage and elongating the neck. It is unclear why some (not all) Padaung women traditionally submitted to such disfigurement; some observers speculate that it was to make them unappealing to the **Burmans (Bamars)**, who captured "hill tribe" women in slave raids. Since the British colonial period, the "giraffe women" have been a popular trademark of "exotic" Burma, and in recent years the **tourist** industry along the Thai–Burma border has been accused of exploiting them for profit. A Padaung armed group, the Kayan New Land Party, was founded in 1964 but signed a **cease-fire** with the **State Law and Order Restoration Council** in July 1994.

PAGAN (BAGAN). One of the most famous archeological sites in Southeast Asia, comparable to Angkor in Cambodia. It is located on the east bank of a bend in the **Irrawaddy (Ayeyarwady) River** in **Mandalay Division**. The Pagan region is bounded on the northeast by the village of Nyaung-U and on the south by Pagan New Town (Bagan Myothit). Over 2,000 **pagodas**, temples (*pahto*), *umin* (temples built to resemble caves), and other religious buildings, erected mostly during the **Pagan (Bagan) Dynasty** between the 11th and 13th centuries, are found within a 41-square-kilometer (16-square-mile) area, along with a roughly equal number of unexcavated and unidentified mounds. Most of the pagodas and temples are built of brick. Wooden buildings of the old palace of the Pagan kings, on the banks of the Irrawaddy, no longer exist. The most notable monuments include the **Shwezigon** and Shwesandaw **Pagodas** and the **Manuha**, **Ananda**, Dhammyangyi, and Thatbyinnyu Temples. Over the centuries, the Burmese kept many of these monuments in good repair. Modern archeological investigation began in the British colonial era. Gordon H. Luce did extensive research and writing on Pagan, as did the Burmese scholar Dr. Than Tun.

An earthquake in 1975 damaged many of the monuments, but they were largely restored with the assistance of UNESCO, which has designated Pagan a World Heritage Site. The post-1988 military government has carried out ambitious alterations of many of the temples since the mid-1990s, which have been criticized for being unfaithful to their original design. Also criticized is a 60-meter (200-foot) concrete viewing tower, completed in 2005, which is seen as an eyesore by locals and foreigners alike. The **State Peace and Development Council (SPDC)** regards Pagan as a major center for international **tourism**, an important source of foreign exchange. According to journalistic reports, the SPDC has allowed the construction of a large hotel in the area.

Pagan has long been a center for the production of high-quality **lacquerware**. In 1990, the government forced residents of the old village of Pagan, located among the monuments, to relocate to open fields, now known as Pagan New Town, causing them considerable hardship.

PAGAN (BAGAN) DYNASTY (1044–ca. 1325). Pagan (Bagan) was a small **Burman** city-state established on the banks of the **Irrawaddy (Ayeyarwady) River** in what is now **Mandalay Division** in the ninth century CE. After King **Anawrahta** (r. 1044–1077) became its ruler, he unified **Upper** and **Lower Burma**, establishing what is sometimes called the "First Burmese (Myanmar) Empire." Pagan was one of the post powerful states in Mainland Southeast Asia until its invasion by the armies of the Mongol emperor, Khubilai Khan, in the late 13th century. Best known for its thousands of **pagodas** and temples (*pahto*), it set the pattern for subsequent Burman and Burmese states, especially its official sponsorship of Theravada **Buddhism** and the **Sangha**. Its end is obscure: The last Pagan monarchs, Sawnit (r. 1298–1325) and Uzana (1325), were apparently powerless puppets, and with their passing the Burman capital was established principally at **Sagaing** (1315–1364) and **Ava (Inwa)** (1364–1555).

Monarchs of the Pagan Dynasty	Year of Accession
Anawrahta	1044
Sawlu	1077
Kyanzittha	1084
Alaungsithu	1112
Narathu	1167
Naratheinhka	1170
Narapatisithu	1173
Nantaungmya	1210
Kyaswa	1234
Uzana	1250
Narathihapate	1254
Kyawswa	1287
Sawhnit	1298
Uzana	1325

Source: D. G. E. Hall, *A History of South-East Asia*. London: Macmillan, 1964.

Because the near-desert region in which Pagan is located had little **agricultural** potential, the dynasty was economically dependent on a complex of irrigated **rice** fields, especially at **Kyaukse**. *See also* ANANDA PAHTO; DRY ZONE; KONBAUNG DYNASTY; KYANZITTHA, KING; MANUHA TEMPLE; MONS; NARATHIHAPATE, KING; SHIN ARAHAN; SHWEZIGON PAGODA; TOUNGOO DYNASTY.

PAGODA. A structure, usually built of bricks or stone, that houses holy relics or other items associated with **Buddhism**. "Pagoda" is derived from Sanskrit, meaning a relic shrine. In Burmese, the word *zedi* (*chedi*), derived from **Pali**, or *paya* is used. Pagodas of all sizes are found throughout the country and are one of the most distinct features of the landscape. **Stupa**, also derived from Sanskrit, is a generally synonymous term for pagoda used in English.

With some exceptions, such as the Botataung and the **Maha Vizaya Pagoda** in **Rangoon (Yangon)**, pagodas in Burma are solid structures. Temples containing an inner chamber or chambers where devotees enter are commonly known in Burmese as *pahto* and are often likened to holy caves. Both pagodas and *pahto* are found in large numbers at **Pagan (Bagan)**.

Pagodas contain a sealed relic chamber, where items associated with Gotama **Buddha**'s person, such as his hair, teeth, or bones, or his personal possessions, are stored. The **Shwe Dagon Pagoda** in Rangoon and the **Shwemawdaw** in **Pegu (Bago)** both are said to contain hairs of the Buddha, and the Shwe Dagon also is said to contain the possessions of three earlier Buddhas; thus, it is known as the "four relic pagoda." Buddhist scriptures, Buddha images, or replicas of holy relics may be substituted for authenticated relics, usually the case when ordinary villagers or merit-seeking individuals build their own *paya*. The patron or builder of a pagoda, known as a *paya-taga*, earns a great deal of merit (Burmese, *kutho*) from the enterprise, while those who restore an old pagoda or donate jewels or other treasure earn lesser amounts of merit.

The prototype for the pagoda is the stupa built at Sanchi in India in the third century BCE, which is said to resemble an inverted alms bowl. The bell-shaped pagoda form, most recognizable in stupas, such as the Shwe Dagon, Shwemawdaw, and **Shwesandaw** in **Prome (Pyay)**, is traced to early Sri Lanka and some of the stupas found at Pagan, such as the **Shwezigon**, built in the 11th and 12th centuries CE.

Buddhist pagodas are not the dwelling places of gods, and thus the devotee does not worship there or address prayers to deities. But an elaborate "pagoda religion" has emerged within **Buddhism** that stresses the importance of venerating or paying respect to religious sites and Buddha relics. Many pagodas, however, have *nat* shrines on their premises, where people pray to supernatural beings for good fortune or protection. *See also* ARCHITECTURE, RELIGIOUS.

PAHTO. A building, usually constructed of brick or stone, used for **Buddhist** devotions or **meditation**. In English, *pahto* are often referred to as "temples." In contrast to **pagodas**, which are usually solid and contain holy relics, *pahto* have an interior chamber or chambers that devotees can enter from the outside. They are often built to resemble caves. The most important *pahto* are found at the old royal capital of **Pagan (Bagan)**. *See also* ARCHITECTURE, RELIGIOUS.

PALAUNGS. An ethnic minority nationality who live in **Shan State**, especially **Tawngpeng** state, where they had their own *sawbwa* during the dynastic and colonial periods. They speak a Mon-Khmer language, and their culture has been heavily influenced by neighboring **Shans (Tai)**. Living in upland areas, they have practiced slash-and-burn (swidden) **agriculture**. They also cultivate tea leaves as a cash crop, used to make pickled tea or *let-hpet*, which is popular with the **Burmans (Bamars)**. Although their indigenous **religion** is animist, many Palaungs have become Buddhists. A Palaung armed group, the Palaung State Liberation Organization/Army, operated in northern Shan State, but in April 1991 it signed a **cease-fire** with the **State Law and Order Restoration Council**; a small breakaway group, the Palaung State Liberation Front, has rejected the truce.

PALI. The sacred language of Theravada **Buddhism**, in which the **Tipitaka**, also known as the Pali Canon, is written. It originally was a Prakrit (vernacular or spoken) language of ancient India (Sanskrit was India's original literary language). Pali developed its own literary forms, which had a profound impact on the development of the **languages** and **literatures** of Burma and its Southeast Asian neighbors. Members of the **Sangha** study the Pali scriptures as part of their religious devotions, and Burmese governments for many centuries have sponsored examinations in which monks recite the Pali texts from memory. Just as Western European languages are dependent on Latin- and Greek-derived words for much of their vocabulary, Pali-derived words are indispensable for modern users of the **Burmese (Myanmar) language**.

The Pali Text Society, established in Britain in 1881, has translated much of the Canon into English. The most widely known Pali text, the *Dhammapada*, serves as an introduction to the teachings of Gotama **Buddha**.

PANGLONG CONFERENCE (1947). Although a first Panglong Conference was held in March 1946, the term is generally used to refer to the second conference, held February 7–12, 1947, at the town of the same name in what is now **Shan State**. At the conference, **Aung San** and leaders of the **Kachin, Chin**, and **Shan** communities agreed to a basic framework for the Union of Burma, incorporating both **Burma Proper** and the **Frontier Areas**. It was held against the background of the January 1947 **Aung San–Attlee Agreement**, which recognized the inclusion of the two regions in the new independent state. The conference resulted in the agreement to establish **Kachin State**, recognition of the autonomy of the *sawbwas* within Shan State, and the inclusion of the **Chins** in Burma. Further commitments were made to ensure fair and equal treatment of the Frontier Area peoples through representation in the highest levels of government and economic development. The **Frontier Areas Committee of Enquiry** was charged with further investigating minority sentiment—especially among the smaller groups.

Aung San's accommodating attitude at Panglong won the trust of minority leaders, but the **Karennis (Kayahs)**, who regarded their states as essentially independent, did not commit themselves to joining the Union, and the **Karens (Kayins)**, who demanded a separate state under British protection, refused to participate. The decisions made at the conference were embodied in the **Constitution of 1947**, which combined the features of both a federal and a unitary state. The anniversary of the conclusion of the conference, February 12, is celebrated as Union Day. *See also* ADMINISTRATION OF BURMA, BRITISH COLONIAL PERIOD; NATIONAL UNITY.

PANTHAYS. Chinese Muslims from Yunnan Province, who migrated in large numbers to the Burma–China border region following the suppression by the Chinese government of a Muslim rebellion between 1856 and 1873. Many settled in the **Wa** district and **Keng Tung** in **Shan State**, but lacking land of their own, they made their living as mule drivers, leading caravans back and forth across the Burma–China border and as far south as **Rangoon (Yangon)**. In **Mandalay** and other towns, the Panthays have built mosques to serve their own community. Some observers believe the Panthays are descended from Arab or Central Asian Muslims who were brought to Yunnan by Khubilai Khan in the 13th century and intermarried with local women but kept their Islamic faith. *See also* KOKANG.

PA-OS. An ethnic nationality found in **Shan, Karen (Kayin), Mon,** and **Kayah (Karenni) States** with an estimated population of between one and two million. Known as *Taungthu* ("Mountain People") in the **Burmese (Myanmar) language**, they are considered to be the second largest ethnic group in Shan State, after the **Shans (Tai)**, and are found mostly in the southern and western parts of the state. They speak a Tibeto-Burman **language** closely related to the **Karen (Kayin)** language but consider themselves a separate ethnic group rather than a Karen subgroup. According to Pa-O legend, they are descended from a king of **Thaton** who reigned in the sixth century BCE, but they suffered oppression and dispersal after King **Anawrahta** conquered Thaton in 1057. Their traditional black or indigo outfits are said to be a symbol of that subjugation.

The majority of Pa-Os are adherents of **Buddhism**, which has been strongly influenced by the religion of their Shan neighbors. The famed "hot-air balloon festival" observed at the end of the Buddhist lent in **Taunggyi**, featuring large balloons made in fanciful shapes out of traditional paper and lit with candles, is celebrated by both Pa-Os and Shans. Most Pa-Os are farmers, growing such crops as tobacco, *thanapet* leaves (used for wrapping cheroots), and mustard leaves.

There has been a history of Pa-O resistance to the central government since Burma achieved independence in 1948. The first armed group was the *Pa-O Lam Bhu*, or Pa-O Union. The Pa-O National Organization/Army was a member of the National Democratic Front (1976) and the **Democratic Alliance of Burma** (1988) but signed a **cease-fire** with the **State Law and Order Restoration Council** in March 1991; a non-cease-fire group, the Pa-O People's Liberation Organization, is based on the border opposite the Thai town of Mae Hong Son.

PARLIAMENTARY DEMOCRACY PARTY (PDP). Established in August 1969 by former prime minister U **Nu** after he went into exile and including other prominent political figures, such as Bo **Let Ya**, Bohmu **Aung**, and Bo Yan Naing. The PDP's armed wing, the Patriotic Liberation Army, operated an insurgency along the Thai–Burma border, commanded by Bo Let Ya. In 1970, it formed a united front with three noncommunist, ethnic minority movements (the **Karen**

National Union, the Chin Democracy Party, and the **New Mon State Army**), known as the National United Front. However, the movement fell apart after U Nu quit as PDP president in 1973 and left for India.

PATRIOTIC BURMESE FORCES (PBF). The name given to the **Burma National Army (BNA)** by **Lord Louis Mountbatten**, Supreme Allied Commander for South East Asia, in the closing months of **World War II.** It seems to have been suggested by **Aung San**, and was first used in connection with a victory parade held in **Rangoon (Yangon)** on June 23, 1945. Having risen against the Japanese on March 27, the BNA posed a problem for the victorious Allies because its support was needed in operations against retreating enemy forces, but British colonial officials considered its commander, Aung San, a collaborator. Mountbatten took a liberal view and negotiated with Aung San over disarmament of the BNA/PBF and its integration into a new **Burma Army**, a policy that was fully worked out at the **Kandy Conference** in September 1945. *See also* ANTI-FASCIST ORGANIZATION; SLIM, GENERAL WILLIAM; TATMADAW, HISTORY OF.

PATRON–CLIENT RELATIONSHIPS. In Burma as well as other Asian countries, patron–client relationships are important in business, politics, and daily life; they are especially vital in societies where the rule of **law** is weak and protection must be sought from powerful and influential persons. Patron–clientism suffused Burmese society during the monarchical period, when elites were composed neither of hereditary aristocrats (as in Europe) nor meritocratic officials (as in China), but rather of men who enjoyed the king's trust and favor who were subject to his whims. In such a context, power was personal, not institutional.

During the **Burma Socialist Programme Party** era (1962–1988), **black market** entrepreneurs sought military and BSPP party patrons, who could give them protection in exchange for economic rewards, on which the officials in turn became dependent in an **economy** of great scarcity. This pattern has continued under the **State Law and Order Restoration Council/State Peace and Development Council**, arguably becoming more pervasive because the "state capitalist" system established after 1988 made available more money (including **foreign investment**) and more opportunities for profitable ties between business and officials. Burmese often comment that if a person has good connections to top **Tatmadaw** personnel, especially members of the SPDC, he or she can make huge profits quickly on enterprises that otherwise would not be economically viable; this includes the government's granting of exclusive import–export licenses to favored businesspeople who would have been unable to obtain them had economically rational criteria, for example, cost-competitiveness, been applied.

Throughout Burmese society, people seek the aid of influential persons who are relatives, went to the same school or university, served in the same Tatmadaw unit, or came from the same township. But such ties can produce unpredictable results. If a patron, such as a high-ranking military officer, is disgraced or purged, his clients will suddenly be cut off from lucrative opportunities and may even be arrested for corruption. Although loyalty and trust are much-esteemed Burmese social values, Burmese society is very volatile, and it is difficult for a someone to be loyal to a patron who might suddenly lose power.

PAYA (HPAYA). The word in the **Burmese (Myanmar) language** that is commonly employed to refer to **pagodas**, but it may be used in connection with other **Buddhist** holy places or objects, such as Buddha images, or even persons, including Gotama **Buddha** himself. During the British colonial period, ordinary Burmese often referred respectfully to Burmese civil servants as *paya gyi* (great lord). Thus the word can refer to any object, place, or person deemed worthy of veneration.

PEACE TALKS (1963–1964). Discussions held by the **Revolutionary Council (RC)** of General **Ne Win** and the **Communist Party of Burma** and ethnic minority armed groups. Ne Win claimed the civil war was ruining the country and that any insurgent group willing to recognize the **"Burmese Road to Socialism"** could participate in the new political system. On April 1, 1963, the RC declared a general amnesty, and on June 11 invited insurgent leaders to come to **Rangoon (Yangon)** to participate in the talks, guaranteeing safe passage.

However, once it became clear that the RC expected total surrender, the talks stalled. Only one small **Karen (Kayin)** faction laid down its arms. In support of the peace process, the "People's Peace Committee," whose prestige was bolstered by the patronage of the revered Thakin **Kodaw Hmaing,** held a march from Minhla to Rangoon in November and a rally in front of Rangoon City Hall that was attended by as many as 200,000 people. The Peace Committee was seen as a threat by the RC, especially after another rally was scheduled for **Mandalay,** and a wave of arrests and detentions followed. The general amnesty expired on January 31, 1964, without having achieved tangible results.

PEACOCK. The royal bird of Burma, whose splendid plumage symbolizes the sun (in Burmese legend, the kings are descended from the *naymyo* or the "solar race"). A peacock displaying its tail appeared on a white field in royal flags during the late **Konbaung Dynasty.** During **World War II**, the motif was adopted by both the British colonial government and the nominally independent state headed by Dr. **Ba Maw** in 1943–1945. A different motif from the peacock displaying its tail is the "fighting peacock," its posture symbolizing resistance to colonial rule, used by student activists of the **Rangoon University Students Union** and the **All Burma Students Union** during the 1930s; it is also associated with the **Democracy Summer** movement of 1988. A flag adopted by several prodemocracy groups since 1988 displays a red field, a yellow fighting peacock, and a white star. *See also* GALON; HONGSA.

PEGU (BAGO). The capital of **Pegu (Bago) Division,** with a population estimated at 188,831 in 1996, making it one of Burma's largest cities. The city is best known as the site of the **Shwemawdaw Pagoda** and the Shwethalyaung Reclining Buddha image. Known historically as **Hanthawaddy,** Pegu was one of Burma's most important royal capitals, under both the **Mon** dynasty established by King **Wareru** and the **Burman (Bamar) Toungoo Dynasty.** The **State Law and Order Restoration Council/State Peace and Development Council** has carried out excavations at the site of King **Bayinnaung**'s 16th-century Kanbawzathadi Palace and has partially reconstructed it.

Pegu was captured and destroyed by King **Alaungpaya** in 1757, following a Mon uprising and invasion of **Upper Burma**. Located 80 kilometers northeast of **Rangoon (Yangon)** along major north–south road and rail routes linking it with **Mandalay**, it was once a major Southeast Asian port city, but its prominence was eclipsed by removal of the Burmese capital to **Ava (Inwa)** in 1635, Alaungpaya's 1757 conquest, and the silting of the Pegu River, which cut off the town from the sea.

PEGU (BAGO) DIVISION. One of Burma's 14 **states** and **divisions**, with an area of 39,404 square kilometers (15,214 square miles) and an estimated population in 2000 of over five million (1983 census figure: 3,799,791). The divisional capital is **Pegu (Bago)**, one of Burma's historically most important cities, and the division is divided into four **districts** (Pegu, **Prome [Pyay]**, Tharrawaddy [Thayarwady], and **Toungoo [Taungoo]**) and 28 **townships**. Topographically it includes the **Pegu (Bago) Yoma**, a range of low-lying hills that in the past was heavily forested, as well as fertile lowlands that are formed by alluvium from the **Irrawaddy (Ayeyarwady) River** and its tributaries. The Irrawaddy is a major artery of transportation and forms most of the division's western border with adjacent **Irrawaddy (Ayeyarwady) Division**. Centrally located, Pegu Division is also bounded by **Arakan (Rakhine) State**, **Magwe (Magway) Division**, **Mandalay Division**, **Mon State**, **Karen (Kayin) State**, and **Rangoon (Yangon) Division**.

Pegu Division is Burma's second-largest producer of **rice**. **Forestry** is also economically important, along with the production of oil seeds, tobacco, and sugarcane. The delta of the **Sittang (Sittaung) River** is located in the southern part of the division and empties into the Gulf of **Martaban (Mottama)**, while the Pegu (Bago) River rises in the Pegu Yoma and connects the cities of Pegu and **Rangoon (Yangon)**. Ethnically, the population is made up of **Burmans (Bamars)**, the majority, **Mons**, **Karens (Kayins)**, **Shans**, and others. After Burma became independent in 1948, the Pegu Yoma, being difficult to penetrate, became a "liberated area" for the **Communist Party of Burma**, although the central government had cleared the hills of most communist insurgents by the mid-1970s.

PEGU (BAGO) YOMA. A narrow range of hills or low-lying mountains (*yoma* means "mountain range" in the **Burmese [Myanmar] language**) that runs north to south from Mount **Popa** near Myingyan in **Mandalay Division** to Singuttara (Theingottara) Hill, where the **Shwe Dagon Pagoda** is located in **Rangoon (Yangon).** The average elevation is between 475 meters (1,500 feet) and 610 meters (2,000 feet), and its highest elevated point, Sinhna-maung Taung, is 821 meters (2,694 feet). Though not one of Burma's highest mountain ranges, the Pegu Yoma's terrain is difficult to traverse and (in the past, at least) densely forested, making it an ideal base for insurgencies. In December 1931, the **Saya San (Hsaya San) Rebellion** against the British began on Alantaung ("Flag Hill") in the Pegu Yoma near Tharrawaddy, and after independence the mainstream **Communist Party of Burma** established "liberated areas" in the mountain range, which the **Tatmadaw** could not entirely suppress until the mid-1970s. *See also* ARAKAN (RAKHINE) YOMA.

PEOPLE'S COUNCILS (PCs). In the political system established by the **Constitution of 1974**, popularly elected bodies on the **state/ division, township,** and ward/village tract levels that were responsible for public administration, **law** and order, and other functions. Encouraged to exercise "local autonomy under central leadership" (perhaps a contradiction), they were in fact tightly controlled by state and **Burma Socialist Programme Party** organs on the central or national level according to the Leninist principle of "democratic centralism."

PEOPLE'S VOLUNTEER ORGANIZATION (PVO). An association of veterans of the **Patriotic Burmese Forces** who had not been mustered into the post–World War II **Burma Army,** established on December 1, 1945. It functioned as a paramilitary group loyal to **Anti-Fascist People's Freedom League** president **Aung San.** After his **assassination** in July 1947, it split into two factions, the "Yellow Band" PVO led by Bohmu **Aung,** which remained loyal to the government during the insurrections that erupted in 1948–1949; and the "White Band" PVO, which went underground on July 28, 1948, and allied itself with the **Communist Party of Burma.** The "White Band" contained a majority, about 60 percent, of PVO personnel, but many surrendered their arms during a 1958 amnesty. Old PVO leaders played a peripheral role in the prodemocracy uprising of 1988.

PERFORMING ARTS, TRADITIONAL. *Pwe* is the **Burmese (Myanmar) language** term used to denote various types of performing arts, including dance, plays, the Burmese equivalent of vaudeville (*anyeint pwe*), and marionettes. Especially in rural areas, such performances take place in conjunction with **pagoda** festivals, *shinbyu* ceremonies, and other special events. Burmese dance genres are derived from Indian and Thai models but also have been inspired by *nat* worship. One of the most striking dance forms imitates the movements of marionettes. As in Japan and some other Asian countries, puppet plays (*yokthe pwe*) became popular because of customary disapproval of men and **women** performing together on the stage, considered an invitation to public immorality. Dance dramas are inspired by the Buddhist **Jataka Tales** (*zat pwe*) or the Indian *Ramayana* (*Yamazat*); Thai (*Yodaya*) models inspired much play writing during the late **Konbaung Dynasty** period. A more modern form of play, the *pya zat*, is a kind of musical comedy that is said to have been inspired by silent movies. Some genres, such as *pya zat* and puppet plays, have suffered a decline in popularity because of competition from **motion pictures** and the proliferation of "video huts," especially in urban areas. *See also* MUSIC, TRADITIONAL AND MODERN.

PHAUNG DAW U IMAGES. Three images of the **Buddha** and two of his disciples, reportedly made in the 12th century, located in the Phaung Daw U Monastery on the shores of **Inle Lake** in **Shan State.** They have been covered with so much gold leaf that it is impossible to see the original figures. During the Phaung Daw U Festival in September–October, four of the five figures are carried around the villages on the shore of the lake in an elaborate boat, while the smallest image remains behind to guard the monastery. One of the most important Shan **Buddhist** celebrations, the festival draws thousands of visitors.

PHEUNG KYA-SHIN (PENG JIASHENG, 1931–). A **Kokang** Chinese who fought in Jimmy Yang's Kokang Revolutionary Force against the **Ne Win** regime in the 1960s but went with his younger brother Pheung Kya-fu (Peng Jiafu) to the **People's Republic of China** and, in 1968, returned as commander of the Kokang People's Liberation Army, which merged with the armed forces of the **Communist Party of Burma**. Serving as Kokang's civil administrator, he was active in the **opium** trade since at least the early 1970s. In early 1989, Pheung initiated a mutiny against the CPB leadership that resulted in the dissolution of the party. He signed a cease-fire with the **State Law and Order Restoration Council**, and his armed force, now legalized in the eyes of the military regime, became known as the **Myanmar National Democratic Alliance Army/Party**. Pheung has been a major figure in Burma's post-1988 **drug economy**, responsible for a rapid expansion of opium and **heroin** exports, although he was driven out of Kokang in 1992 by a rival, Yang Molian, a scion of Kokang's ruling Yang clan. By the late 1990s, however, he had reasserted his position as the territory's most powerful warlord and cooperated closely with the **State Peace and Development Council**. *See also* LO HSING-HAN.

PLURAL SOCIETY. Term that describes social and economic institutions under colonial rule, first used by **J. S. Furnivall**, a retired member of the Indian Civil Service who served for a long time in Burma and was critical of the government's laissez faire economic policies. In a plural society, ethnic groups preserve their own cultural, linguistic, and religious identity—resisting assimilation—while interacting with each other primarily in the marketplace, through commercial transactions. Furnivall described this as "different sections of the community living side by side, but separately, within the same political unit" (*Colonial Policy and Practice, 1948*). An ethnic division of labor emerges that marginalizes some groups; most Burmese were poor farmers, but the capitalist, professional, and working classes comprised almost exclusively foreigners: European, **Chinese**, and **Indian** expatriates and migrants. Because the colonial government defined its role exclusively as imposing law and order and ensuring favorable conditions for profitable operations by foreign-owned firms, it did nothing to change the plural society structure. When economic conditions deteriorated during the 1930s, there were violent clashes between different groups, especially Burmese and Indians.

The plural society paradigm has been used to describe other former colonial countries, such as **Malaysia**, where post-independence governments sought to break the pattern by cultivating a Malay middle class (the New Economic Policy); in Burma, the plural society problem was dealt with by nationalizing ("Burmanizing") economic enterprises after 1962 and expropriating the property of Chinese and Indian businesspeople, causing many of them to leave the country. The result was economic stagnation. *See also* ANTI-INDIAN RIOTS; ECONOMIC POLICY, BURMA SOCIALIST PROGRAMME PARTY ERA.

POLITICAL PARTY REGISTRATION LAW (SEPTEMBER 27, 1988). To prepare for a "multiparty democratic general election," the **State Law and Order Restoration Council** repealed the 1964 Law Safeguarding National Unity, which made the **Burma Socialist Programme Party** the only legal political party, on September 19, 1988, and a week later decreed the Political Party Registration Law, which enabled groups to acquire recognition as parties from the Election Commission. By the end of October 1988, 66 parties had been registered, growing to 171 by the end of the year. By mid-1989, 233 parties had been registered, although the Election Commission subsequently "deregistered" all but 93 parties, which were allowed to contest the **General Election of May 27, 1990.** Among the 93 eligible parties were the **National League for Democracy** and the **National Unity Party.** *See also* PYITHU HLUTTAW ELECTION LAW.

PONGYI (HPOUNGYI). In the **Burmese (Myanmar) language**, literally "great glory," used to refer to members of the **Sangha** who have been ordained (thus excluding *koyin*, or novices) and have pursued the monk's life for an extended period of time. When speaking Burmese, a layperson will use the term to address a monk, as a title, and the monk will use it to refer to himself. *Pongyis* are considered to be, in terms of their spiritual status, "sons of the Buddha" and fundamentally different from ordinary human beings (*lu* in Burmese). *See also PAYA (HPAYA);* SAYADAW (*HSAYADO*).

POPA, MOUNT. Located about midway between **Pagan (Bagan)** and **Meiktila** in **Mandalay Division**, what is popularly known as "Mount Popa" is actually the core of an extinct volcano, rising 737 meters (2,200 feet) above the Myingyan Plain. It is the site of shrines devoted to the *nats*. Often called "Burma's Mount Olympus," the *nat* cult flourished there long before King **Anawrahta** established the official pantheon of the **Thirty-seven Nats**. A popular destination for pilgrims, it hosts two important *nat-pwe*, in spring and winter, and is widely known as the "temple mount" (*daung kalat*). It should not be confused with the actual Mount Popa, which is located nearby and has an altitude of over 1,500 meters (4,500 feet).

POPULATION. There are no accurate figures on the population of **Lower** and **Upper Burma** before the British colonial period. According to one estimate, the population in 1785, early in the reign of King **Bodawpaya**, was 4.7 million (rounded), of whom 3.5 million lived in Upper Burma. That a much smaller number (1.2 million) seem to have lived in fertile Lower Burma probably reflects the devastation resulting from the suppression of the **Mons** in the late 18th century by King **Alaungpaya** and his successors. Following the British colonial occupation, the populations of both areas were roughly equal, due largely to the migration of farmers from Upper to Lower Burma after the **Second Anglo-Burmese War** (1852). The colonial government's decennial censuses reported a country-wide population of 8.1 million in 1891, 10.5 million in 1901, 12.1 million in 1911, 13.2 million in 1921, 14.7 million in 1931, and 16.8 million in 1941. **World War II**, the **Japanese occupation**, and civil war after 1948 did not halt population growth: in 1951, a population of 19.1 million was recorded, and by 1961 it had reached 22.2 million. Between 1901 and 1983, annual population growth varied between 0.87 and 2.32 percent.

After independence in 1948, the collection of accurate demographic figures was hampered by unrest and insurgency, especially in border areas where ethnic minorities lived and carved out "liberated areas." The **Burma Socialist Programme Party (BSPP)** government carried out the last national census in 1983: a total population of 35.3 million people was counted at that time. It was estimated to be 43.1 million in 1993, 46.4 million in 1997, and between 48 and 50 million at the start of the 21st century. The U.S. government published an estimate of 42,510,537 for July 2003 (*CIA World Factbook*, 2004). Estimates of annual population growth rates also vary widely, from 0.52 percent to 1.7 percent.

There is general agreement that ethnic majority **Burmans (Ba-mars)** comprise roughly two-thirds of the total population, although an accurate ethnic breakdown has not been available since colonial times, if even then. The largest minority groups are believed to be the **Shans** and **Karens**. During the colonial period, many **Indians** and **Chinese** migrated to Burma, but their numbers declined dramatically during **World War II** and, after the establishment of the BSPP regime, by **Ne Win** in 1962.

By Asian standards, Burma is not a densely populated country, with an average of 74 persons per square kilometer. Only 27 percent of the population lives in urban areas, reflecting the undeveloped state of the industrial economy even after liberalization policies were adopted by the **State Law and Order Restoration Council** (the urbanization average for Southeast Asia is 37 percent). Because of deepening rural poverty, however, the urban population seems to be growing in recent years relative to the population as a whole because large numbers of poor villagers now work in urban factories or construction sites. There are no accurate figures on the populations of the major cities; **Rangoon (Yangon)** has between 4.5 and 5 million residents and **Mandalay**, 600,000 to 800,000. Also, there are no credible statistics on new immigrants from the **People's Republic of China (PRC)**, who are believed to number as many as several hundred thousand, especially in Upper Burma and **Shan State**. Along with large **refugee** populations in neighboring countries, such as **Thailand** and **Bangladesh**, Chinese in-migration represents an important demographic change in post-1988 Burma. Another factor is the impact of **AIDS**: In 2005, the country had an estimated 600,000 people afflicted with HIV/AIDS, and the epidemic has had a significant impact on mortality rates and population growth, especially because most of the victims are young people. Life expectancy at birth for both sexes is 55.8 years, which is low compared to Burma's neighbors, including Thailand (71.2 years). *See also* HEALTH.

PRESS SCRUTINY BOARD (PSB). The chief censorship organ of the Burmese government, which has exercised strict control over publication of books, periodicals, and magazines during both the **Burma Socialist Programme Party** and the **State Law and Order Restoration Council/State Peace and Development Council** eras.

According to guidelines promulgated in July 1975, the PSB can halt publication of, among other things, items considered "harmful to national solidarity and unity." Because of the ambiguity of the guidelines, almost any publication, even if nonpolitical, is liable to censorship. After 1988, for example, references to things associated with **Aung San Suu Kyi** were not permitted (e.g., the Nobel Prize). Because the PSB requires that publishers submit books and magazines after they are printed, rather than as manuscripts, there is a strong financial incentive for self-censorship, especially because paper is expensive and in short supply. Objectionable material is torn out of publications or inked-over, with popular monthly magazines being special targets of censorship. *See also* HUMAN RIGHTS IN BURMA; MASS MEDIA IN BURMA.

PROME (PYAY). One of Burma's major cities, on the eastern bank of the **Irrawaddy (Ayeyarwady) River** in the western part of **Pegu (Bago) Division**. Its population was estimated at 104,537 in 1996. Located on principal north–south transportation routes—by water, road, and rail—it is best known among Burmese for the **Shwesandaw Pagoda**. On the outskirts of town are the ruins of the **Pyu** city of **Sri Ksetra (Thayekhittaya)**, which contains the cylindrical Bawbawgyi Pagoda, a ninth-century structure quite different in design from typical Burmese **pagodas**.

PWE. Traditional performances, including song, instrumental music, dance, plays (set to music), and comedy routines, which are sponsored on numerous occasions, including festivals related to **pagodas**, *shinbyu,* and **ear-boring** ceremonies; life-cycle occasions, such as birth, marriage, and death; and sometimes simply when a sponsor desires to host one. Traditionally, *pwe* are held out of doors, often in the street, and have an informal atmosphere, spectators drifting in and out. Vivid descriptions of *pwe* are found in **James G. Scott's** *The Burman: His Life and Notions* and **George Orwell's** *Burmese Days. See also* ANYEINT; MUSIC, TRADITIONAL AND MODERN; *NAT-PWE*; PERFORMING ARTS, TRADITIONAL.

PYIDAUNGSU (UNION) PARTY. The new name for the "Clean" faction of the **Anti-Fascist People's Freedom League** led by U **Nu,**

adopted in March 1960. It won a landslide victory in the general election of February 1960 but subsequently split into two factions. Its internal problems paved the way for the military coup d'état of General **Ne Win** in March 1962.

PYINMANA. A town located 320 kilometers (200 miles) north of **Rangoon (Yangon)** in the southern part of **Mandalay Division.** Pyinmana was the site of the headquarters of the **Burma Defence Army** during **World War II** and an insurgency by the **Communist Party of Burma** after independence in 1948. Its population in 2005 was estimated at around 98,000. Although situated near a major north-south road between Rangoon and **Mandalay**, its relative remoteness, on the **Sittang (Sittoung) River**, with mountains and the ethnic minority areas of **Shan, Kayah**, and **Karen States** lying to the east and southeast, may have been a factor in the decision of the **State Peace and Development Council (SPDC)** to make Pyinmana, or rather, a heavily fortified compound located a few kilometers outside the town, Burma's new national capital. On November 6, 2005, civil servants in a truck convoy left Rangoon to take up their posts at the new site. The official name of the new capital will be *Nay Pyi Daw* ("Place of the King").

The military junta's motivations for the capital's relocation, which was veiled in secrecy and poorly organized (there was insufficient food and housing at the new site), remain obscure. Some observers believe the SPDC was fearful of an Iraq-style invasion of Burma by the **United States**, which might include an amphibious landing on the coast near Rangoon. The need to exercise greater pressure on the ethnic minorities, especially the **Shans** and **Karens (Kayins)**, is probably also a factor, especially since the October 2004 purge of Lieutenant General **Khin Nyunt**, head of **Border Area Development** Programs since 1989, injected a new element of uncertainty into relations between the junta and the border area armed groups. Moreover, Burma's military elite, especially Senior General **Than Shwe**, are very superstitious, and **astrology** and *yedaya* probably played a major role in their decision to quit Rangoon. But most fundamentally, against a background of continued economic crisis, it seems that the SPDC was afraid of a recurrence of **Democracy Summer** in Burma's cities and wanted to construct a tightly controlled, combined military camp and capital in a remote area to insulate themselves from urban social tensions. The move also seems to reflect a return to an isolationist **foreign policy**, a desire to minimize foreign ties (except possibly with **China**) in a manner similar to that of the 1962–1988 regime of General **Ne Win**. Relocation of the capital is not without precedent in Burmese history: King **Thalun** (r. 1629–1648) moved the capital from **Pegu (Bago)** to **Ava (Inwa)** in central Burma, and it was relocated several times between Ava, **Amarapura**, and Mandalay during the **Konbaung Dynasty**. *See also* TATMADAW AND BURMESE (MYANMAR) SOCIETY.

PYITHU HLUTTAW (PEOPLE'S ASSEMBLY). The unicameral national legislature, defined as the "highest organ of state power" in the political system established by the **Constitution of 1974**. Its members were popularly elected for terms of four years, though this could be shortened or extended. In the **General Election of May 27, 1990**, candidates ran for seats in the People's Assembly (485 seats were contested out of a total of 492), but the legislature was never allowed to form a government. *See also* GANDHI HALL DECLARATION; PYITHU HLUTTAW ELECTION LAW.

PYITHU HLUTTAW ELECTION LAW (MAY 31, 1989). The **State Law and Order Restoration Council (SLORC)** decreed the law to prepare for the **General Election of May 27, 1990**. It specified that the election would be held for "representatives" from the constituencies of the **Pyithu Hluttaw** and laid out in detail qualifications of voters and candidates, the criteria necessary to recognize votes as valid, and other matters. Its wording was a source of considerable confusion, since the Pyithu Hluttaw, described in Article 41 of the **Constitution of 1974** as the "highest organ of State power," was regarded by the democratic opposition and many foreign governments as a governing body rather than, as the SLORC later implied, a constitution-drafting body. When the **National League for Democracy** won a landslide victory in the election, it was expected that a transfer of power would occur. *See also* POLITICAL PARTY REGISTRATION LAW.

PYUS. A people speaking a Tibeto-Burman language, who established states in the valley of the **Irrawaddy (Ayeyarwady) River** during the early centuries CE and are often described as the "advance guard" of the **Burmans (Bamars)**. Most of what we know about them comes from the Buddhist pilgrims I Tsing and Hsuan-tsang, the official history of the T'ang Dynasty (618–906), and other Chinese sources, as well as extensive excavations that have been carried out since British colonial times at **Sri Ksetra (Thayekkhittaya)**, one of the Pyus' major cities. Deeply influenced by **India** and possibly ruled for a time by an Indian dynasty, the Pyus practiced a **religion** that combined Hindu and Buddhist elements. According to the Chinese, they exercised suzerainty over 18 states and nine walled cities. Apart from Sri Ksetra, they had sizeable urban centers at Beiktano (in present-day **Magwe [Magway] Division**) and Halingyi (in **Sagaing Division**). The Pyus paid tribute to **Nan Chao** and may have been conquered by that state in the ninth century CE.

According to Chinese descriptions, they had a high level of culture. At the beginning of the ninth century, a band of Pyu musicians accompanying a Nan Chao mission to the T'ang capital of Ch'ang-an gave a performance before the emperor. A didactic verse by the great Chinese poet Po Chü-I recommended that the emperor pay more attention to the sufferings of the peasants than to the exotic music of *P'iao* (Pyu): "Music of P'iao, in vain you raise your din/Better were it that my Lord should listen to that peasant's humble words." No trace remains of the Pyus as a people today; they were probably assimilated by the Burmans.

– R –

RAIL TRANSPORT. The first railroad was opened for service in 1877 under British rule, connecting **Rangoon (Yangon)** with **Prome (Pyay)**. By 1941, Burma had an extensive rail system, totalling 4,600 kilometers (2,852 miles) of track, including the spectacular Gokteik Viaduct in what is now **Shan State**, constructed by American engineers between 1899 and 1903. Most rail links were inoperable by the end of **World War II**, and the system further suffered from the insurgencies and instability of the late 1940s and early 1950s. According to government statistics, Burma's track mileage totalled 5,837 kilometers (3,619 miles) in 1997–1998. There has been construction of new rail links since the **State Law and Order Restoration Council** seized power in 1988. Like the wartime **Thai–Burma Railway**, these projects have often involved the use of **forced labor**.

RAM-UK. "Lord (*uk*) of the soil/land (*ram*)," referring to the chiefs of the **Chins**, whose authority encompassed as many as several hundred villages, in which case he was the leader of a tribe. He had the authority to distribute land to cultivators and was high priest officiating over sacrifices to the *Khua-hrum* (local guardian deities), head of the community, and commander in war. The authority of the *ram-uk* was tightly bound to the Chins' animistic religion because, as lord of the land, he had a special relationship with the deities who protected it and the people who lived on it. When the British issued the Chin Hills Regulations in 1896, they refused to recognize the authority of the *ram-uk*, who had strenuously opposed the pacification of **Chinram**, but this was reversed after the **Anglo-Chin War** of 1917–1919, partly to gain the goodwill of the tribal elites.

RANCE, HUBERT. British army general who served as the head of the Civil Affairs Service (Burma) from July to October 1945 and was appointed Reginald Dorman-Smith's successor as governor of Burma in August 1946. He established a friendly working relationship with **Aung San**, which facilitated a peaceful resolution of the independence issue, as reflected in the January 1947 **Aung San–Attlee Agreement**.

RANGOON INCIDENT. On October 9, 1983, operatives from **North Korea** placed a bomb in the Martyrs' Mausoleum north of the **Shwe Dagon Pagoda** in **Rangoon (Yangon)** that killed 21 people, including four ministers in the cabinet of the president of **South Korea**, Chon Doo Hwan, who was beginning a state visit to five Asian countries. Chon himself narrowly escaped assassination because of a delay in his arrival at the monument for a wreath-laying ceremony. Security forces tracked down three North Koreans, one of whom was killed and the others put on trial and sentenced to death. Burma immediately broke off relations with Pyongyang, which before the bombing had been close and cordial. The incident was deeply embarrassing to the government of **Ne Win**, and many observers attribute it to security lapses and disarray in **Military Intelligence** following the purge of **"MI" Tin Oo** earlier that year. *See also* KHIN NYUNT.

RANGOON (YANGON). Burma's capital and largest city from the British colonial era until 2005. Its population was 2,513,123 when the last official census was taken in 1983, but at the beginning of the 21st century it was estimated at between 4.5 and 5 million. The city is located in a lowland alluvial area, at the confluence of the Rangoon (Yangon) River (which is called the Hlaing River farther upstream) and Pazundaung Creek (known upstream as Ngamoeyeik Creek), although expansion of its territory during the **Caretaker Government** and **State Law and Order Restoration Council** periods placed its eastern limits along the Pegu (Bago) River and its western limits in new townships across the Rangoon/Hlaing River. Rangoon is not on the **Irrawaddy (Ayeyarwady) River** but is connected to it by the Twante Canal. Apart from the rivers, the city center's most prominent geographic features are Singuttara (Theingottara) Hill, where the **Shwe Dagon Pagoda** is located, and **Kandawgyi** and **Inya Lakes.**

Rangoon was never a royal city like **Pagan** or **Mandalay**, but its early history is intimately linked to legends concerning the Shwe Dagon Pagoda, where relics of Gotama **Buddha** and three of his predecessors are enshrined. The site was originally a **Mon** fishing village, **Dagon.** After **Alaungpaya** subjugated the Mons, he established *Yangoun* ("End of Strife") in 1755 as his kingdom's primary port. It became the center of British colonial power after the **Second Anglo-Burmese War** (1852) and the capital of the independent Union of Burma after 1948. Since the early 20th century, Rangoon has been the country's principal arena of political conflict, especially during the struggle for independence in the 1930s and 1940s and again during the **Democracy Summer** in 1988.

Rangoon is the country's major center of finance, industry, and communications with the outside world. Its port is the largest in the country, and the international airport at **Mingaladon** north of the city center has the greatest traffic among Burmese airports. Highways, inland waterways, and railways link it with most other major cities and towns, including Mandalay, **Moulmein (Mawlamyine)**, and **Pegu (Bago)**.

Since economic liberalization policies were adopted in 1988, industrial parks financed with foreign private investment have been established in outlying townships, and new foreign-financed luxury hotels downtown make Rangoon the center of Burma's **tourism** sector. The city boasts the country's major universities, including **Rangoon (Yangon) University** and the **Rangoon Institute of Technology** (Yangon Technological University). After 1988, many university facilities were moved to outlying districts, apparently to discourage **student** political activism. This includes a new institution, **Dagon University**, established in the mid-1990s.

The modern city owes its layout to the British, who after 1852 constructed a modern downtown area with a rectangular grid of streets centered on the **Sule Pagoda**. The central business district still contains **Chinese** and **Indian** communities that trace their roots to the colonial period and traditionally dominated commerce. Major government ministries are also located here, and just north of the district the fortified **Defence Services Compound** served as the command headquarters of the **Tatmadaw** until this was moved to a location north of Inya Lake, Eight Mile Junction. Because of the threat of civil unrest, the military presence in Rangoon is large though low profile, including extensive installations in Mingaladon Township.

The State Law and Order Restoration Council transformed Rangoon's landscape by establishing 10 new satellite townships; resettling as many as 500,000 of the central city's residents there; and embarking on the construction of new roads, bridges, and other infrastructure. Rangoon's planning and infrastructure development is the responsibility of the **Yangon City Development Committee**, established in 1990. Its chairman serves concurrently as city mayor. Austere and run down during the **Burma Socialist Programme Party (BSPP)** period (1962–1988), Rangoon today looks increasingly like other Asian metropolises, including widening gaps between a small affluent class characterized by conspicuous consumption (including patronage of newly opened **golf** courses) and a growing number of desperately poor people who survive by working in the informal sector.

During the colonial era, Rangoon was a multiethnic city; more than two-thirds of its residents were non-Burmese, especially sojourners from British-ruled India. However, the **Japanese occupa-**

tion of 1942–1945 and nationalization policies under the BSPP regime forced Westerners and many foreign Asians to leave, and persons of nonindigenous ancestry comprised less than 8 percent of the population in 1983. Apart from **Burmans (Bamars)**, there are a substantial number of **Karen (Kayin)** residents, especially in **Insein** Township.

In mid-2005, it was disclosed that the **State Peace and Development Council** planned to move the headquarters of the Tatmadaw and Ministry of Defence from Rangoon to a heavily fortified compound outside the town of **Pyinmana**, located in Mandalay Division. At that time, it was unclear whether Pyinmana would replace Rangoon as capital or serve as a second capital. But in early November 2005, when civil servants in large numbers were moved in truck convoys from Rangoon to Pyinmana, it became apparent that the military regime was determined to relocate not only the military but civil components of government to the new site, which has the official name of *Nay Pyi Daw* ("Place of the King"). The action is reminiscent of the decision of King **Thalun** (r. 1629–1648) to move the country's capital from **Pegu (Bago)** to **Ava (Inwa)**.

RANGOON (YANGON) DIVISION. One of Burma's 14 **states** and **divisions**, it has an area of 10,171 square kilometers (3,927 square miles), making it the smallest of Burma's regional jurisdictions, and an estimated population in 2000 of 5.56 million (1983 census figure: 3,965,916). The divisional capital is **Rangoon (Yangon)**, which is Burma's largest city and until 2005 was the national capital. Rangoon Division comprises four **districts** (East, West, South, and North Rangoon [Yangon]) and 45 **townships**, of which 34 are currently located within the capital's city limits. The topography is level, formed by alluvial deposits from the region's many rivers and creeks, although Singuttara (Theingottara) Hill, where the **Shwe Dagon Pagoda** is located, is the southernmost extension of the **Pegu (Bago) Yoma**. Rangoon Division is Burma's most densely populated, with an average of 525 persons per square kilometer (1,360 persons per square mile); the population is most concentrated in Rangoon's Pabedan Township, located in the old Central Business District, with 77,220 persons per square kilometer (200,000 persons per square mile). However, the division also includes the remote and thinly populated Cocos Islands, in the Andaman Sea, which have functioned as a naval base and a place of exile for (political) prisoners. Apart from Rangoon, major towns in the division are Htaukkyant (site of a large British Commonwealth war cemetery), Hlegu, Hmawbi, **Syriam (Thanlyin)**, Kyauktan, and Twante.

Although **agriculture** is not unimportant to Rangoon Division's economy (despite the post-1988 creation of **new towns**, which have incorporated crop lands), it is Burma's most urbanized region and contains the country's major industrial, mercantile, and financial enterprises, including industrial estates established with **foreign investment** in Rangoon city's outlying areas, such as **Mingaladon Township**. Most of Burma's major universities, including the **University of Rangoon (Yangon)**, **Dagon University**, and **Rangoon (Yangon) Institute of Technology**, are located there, as well as central government ministries and the headquarters of the **Tatmadaw**. It has one of only two international airports in the country (the other is at Mandalay) and is the main sea and air gateway to the outside world.

Rangoon Division has an ethnically diverse population. Aside from a **Burman (Bamar)** majority, there are significant communities of **Karens (Kayins)**, especially in **Insein Township**, **Mons**, **Arakanese (Rakhines)**, **Shans**, and Burmese citizens of **Chinese** and **Indian** ancestry, as well as the country's largest concentration of expatriates, including Chinese, Indians, Westerners, Japanese, and persons from countries belonging to the **Association of Southeast Asian Nations**. Rangoon Division's urban environments are diverse. Newly modernized downtown areas resemble Bangkok or Kuala Lumpur, with their high-rise hotels and condominiums, and middle-class areas, such as Bahan Township, have many large houses. But many of the new towns resemble impoverished rural villages, while adjacent suburbs contain affluent "gated communities" that resemble those of Southern California. Although ethnic segregation seems to be breaking down, Karen and Indian **Muslim** communities still maintain a large measure of coherence and identity. Since 1988, large areas in Rangoon Division have been allocated by the government for new **Buddhist** monasteries, schools, and **pagodas**.

RANGOON (YANGON) GENERAL HOSPITAL INCIDENT (AUGUST 10, 1988). After the hospital staff hung signs in front of the colonial-era building calling for an end to **Tatmadaw** shooting of demonstrators, army units fired into the hospital compound with automatic weapons, killing and wounding nurses and some bystanders. The incident was one of the most important in turning the general population of **Rangoon (Yangon)** against the military. *See also* DEMOCRACY SUMMER.

RANGOON (YANGON) INSTITUTE OF TECHNOLOGY (RIT). Originally the Department of Engineering at **Rangoon (Yangon) University**. A new campus at Gyogone, **Insein** Township, was constructed in 1958–1961 with assistance from the Soviet Union. RIT became completely independent of Rangoon University in 1964, as part of a general university reorganization carried out by the **Ne Win** regime. The institute is best known to the outside world for the **Tea Shop Incident** of March 12, 1988, a fight between RIT **students** and town youths, which took place at the Sandar Win Teashop adjacent to the campus and escalated into a large-scale student demonstration. In 1998, RIT's name was changed to Yangon Technological University; the following year, a new campus was opened in Hlaing Thayar Township west of the Hlaing River. *See also* EDUCATION, HIGHER; MAUNG PHONE MAW; WHITE BRIDGE INCIDENT.

RANGOON (YANGON) UNIVERSITY. Burma's oldest degree-conferring institution of **higher education**, formally established in 1920 by the British colonial government. The Rangoon University Act was controversial because the new institution had little autonomy and offered a curriculum along British lines that was designed to train a small number of élite civil servants. Instruction was in English rather than Burmese. In protest, a **student** strike was organized in November 1920. After 1935, when Ko **Nu** became president of the **Rangoon University Students Union (RUSU)**, the scenic campus along the shores of **Inya Lake** and the area around the **Shwe Dagon Pagoda**, where students established strike centers, became sites of student activism that played a vital role in the struggle for independence.

The pre–World War II university had four basic components: University College, Judson College (a Baptist missionary institution), the Teachers Training College, and the Medical College. There were also postgraduate courses in Law and Engineering.

Ethnic minorities, especially **Karens (Kayins)**, were well represented at Judson College (often nicknamed "Karen College"); most **Burman (Bamar)** students attended University College, which in the late 1930s had 800 male and 200 female students. According to Mi Mi Khaing, the women were happily idolized and fussed over by the exuberant male students. Apart from RUSU and political activism, the campus was kept lively by activities such as the Rangoon University Boat Club, which held regattas on Inya Lake, and frequent *anyeint* performances.

Student freedoms were sharply curtailed after the **July 7, 1962 Incident**, when the military demolished the RUSU building. The **Ne Win** regime reorganized Burma's university system in 1964, and RU became the Rangoon Arts and Sciences University (RASU), offering courses in natural sciences, social sciences, and humanities, while the medical, education, and economics faculties were split off to become separate institutions. RASU had affiliated colleges at Botataung, Hlaing, Kyimyindine, and Prome (Pyay), as well as a Workers College and the Yangon Cooperative Degree College, though these were reorganized and consolidated during the 1990s. In 1997–1998 its faculty numbered 945 and the student body 13,539.

Following the massive demonstrations of **Democracy Summer** in 1988, the **State Law and Order Restoration Council/State Peace and Development Council** kept the campuses of RASU and other universities closed for much of the time until 2001, although student demonstration broke out at RASU in 1991 and 1996. The military regime has also built new universities, located far outside Rangoon's city center, to make it difficult for students and ordinary citizens to mingle. The future of Rangoon University is unclear. *See also* DAGON UNIVERSITY; RANGOON (YANGON) INSTITUTE OF TECHNOLOGY.

RANGOON UNIVERSITY STUDENTS UNION (RUSU). Established as a **student** body organization in the 1920s to promote campus life, RUSU played a central role in the political struggles of the 1930s and after Burma became independent in 1948. The election of Ko **Nu** as its president in 1935 marked the beginning of its radical phase. When he and Ko **Aung San**, editor of the RUSU magazine and member of its executive committee, were expelled from **Ran-**

goon (Yangon) University in 1936 for opposing the university's British authorities, a RUSU-organized student strike led to their reinstatement. Both RUSU and a new student organization, the **All Burma Students Union**, supported the **Oil Field Workers' Strike** of 1938. After World War II, RUSU was strongly influenced by the **Communist Party of Burma**; in the 1950s, leadership of the union was bitterly contested by procommunist students and the "Democratic Students Organization," which was sponsored by the **Socialist Party**. During the **Caretaker Government** period (1958–1960), many procommunist students were arrested, some being exiled to the Cocos Islands.

After the establishment of the **Revolutionary Council** in March 1962, **Ne Win** took a hard line against student activism. In the early morning following the **July 7, 1962 incident**, in which many students were killed by **Tatmadaw** troops, the RUSU building on the edge of the university campus was demolished, allegedly on orders from Ne Win, although he blamed Brigadier **Aung Gyi**. During the demonstrations of 1988 there were demands that RUSU be reestablished and its historic brick building rebuilt. At the beginning of the 21st century, however, the place where the building stood remains vacant and fenced off. *See also* EDUCATION, HIGHER.

RAZADARIT, KING (r. 1385–1423). One of Burma's most prominent **Mon** kings, he was an able ruler who fought protracted wars with the state of **Ava (Inwa)** in **Upper Burma** and with the **Tai** states of Ayuthaya and Lan Na (Chiang Mai). During his reign the royal capital of **Hanthawaddy** (modern-day **Pegu [Bago]**) was one of Southeast Asia's most prosperous port cities. Like his successors **Shinsawbu** and **Dhammazedi**, he made generous donations to the **Shwe Dagon Pagoda** and to the **Shwemawdaw** in Pegu. *See also* LOWER BURMA; WARERU.

REFUGEES. Because of **human rights** abuses and deteriorating economic conditions, the number of Burmese refugees has increased dramatically since the **State Law and Order Restoration Council (SLORC)** seized power in September 1988. Among the first refugees were an estimated 8,000–10,000 activists who left following the new military regime's suppression of the **Democracy Summer** movement.

This group, mostly **students** but also including teachers, civil servants, and members of the **Sangha**, was largely urban and **Burman (Bamar)**. Based along the lengthy Thai–Burma border, many joined the **All Burma Students' Democratic Front (ABSDF)** and fought together with other members of the **Democratic Alliance of Burma (DAB)** against the SLORC. By the mid-1990s, however, a majority of these activists had left the border area and settled in Bangkok, Chiang Mai, and other parts of **Thailand**, or went farther afield to **Japan**, North America, or Western Europe. Smaller groups of student refugees settled in **China** and **India**. Since 1988, a steady stream of Burman and ethnic minority intellectuals, artists, and members of the **Pyithu Hluttaw** who won seats in the **General Election of May 27, 1990**, have also gone abroad, fleeing persecution.

By far the largest number of refugees are members of ethnic minorities who have, either directly or indirectly, been targets of the **"Four Cuts"** strategy of the **Tatmadaw**, aimed at removing popular support for such insurgent movements as the **Karen National Union**. These include **Shans, Karennis, Karens (Kayins)**, and **Mons**, most of whom have fled across the border into Thailand. They can be divided into two groups: a relatively stable population of Karens, Mons, and Karennis, numbering 120,000–130,000, who live in refugee camps along the Thai–Burma border; and a much larger group of people from **Shan State**, as many as one million, who work as illegal or semilegal laborers inside Thailand. India has an estimated 52,000 refugees, mostly **Chin, Bangladesh** about 120,000 Muslim **Rohingyas**, and China an undetermined number of **Kachins**. Although most Burmese refugees live in neighboring countries, there is a large number of Rohingyas in **Malaysia** and the Middle East. The total number of Burmese refugees is unknown, but is probably between one and two million.

The conventional distinction between *political refugees*, who are fleeing persecution at home, and *economic refugees,* who are seeking a better livelihood abroad, is not especially useful in Burma's case because many in the latter category, especially ethnic minorities, are fleeing truly desperate conditions caused by the policies of the **State Peace and Development Council**. They include minority **women** and girls who have been drawn into the **sex industry** in northern Thailand because of extreme economic deprivation (an estimated

20,000–30,000 in the early 1990s). Internally displaced persons, victims of **forced relocation** numbering between 600,000 and one million, often become refugees. Although educated refugees have been able to create an intellectually active exile community in neighboring countries or the West, the great majority endure great insecurity and deprivation outside their homeland. *See also* FORCED LABOR.

REGIONAL MILITARY COMMANDS (RMC). Before 1988, the **Army (Tatmadaw Kyi)** conducted its operations on the regional level through nine Regional Level Commands, which after the establishment of the **State Law and Order Restoration Council** were expanded to 12. At the beginning of the 21st century, the RMC are the Northern Command (**Kachin State**, headquartered in **Myitkyina**); Northwestern Command (**Sagaing Division**, headquartered in Monywa); Northeastern Command (northern **Shan State**, headquartered in **Lashio**); Central Command (**Mandalay Division**, headquartered in **Mandalay**); Eastern Command (southern Shan State, headquartered in **Taunggyi**); Triangle Command (eastern Shan State, headquartered in **Keng Tung**); Western Command (**Arakan [Rakhine]** and **Chin States**, headquartered in **Sittwe [Sittway]**); Southwestern Command (**Irrawaddy [Ayeyarwady] Division**, headquartered in **Bassein [Pathein]**); Southern Command (**Pegu [Bago]** and **Magwe [Magway] Divisions**, headquartered in **Toungoo [Taungoo]**); Rangoon (Yangon) Command (**Rangoon [Yangon] Division**, headquartered in **Mingaladon** Township); Southeastern Command (**Mon** and **Karen [Kayin] States**, headquartered in **Moulmein [Mawlamyine]**); and the Coastal Region Command (**Tenasserim [Tanintharyi] Division**, headquartered in **Mergui [Myeik]**). RMC commanders are of major general (two-star) rank, but at the beginning of the 21st century, they were not included in the **State Peace and Development Council** junta.

RELIGIONS IN BURMA. According to the *CIA World Factbook* (2005), 89 percent of Burma's population are adherents to **Buddhism**, 4 percent are Christians (3 percent Baptist and 1 percent Roman Catholic), 4 percent are **Muslims**, 1 percent are animists, and 2 percent are adherents of other religions. Burmese government figures are similar: 89.2 percent Buddhist, 5 percent Christian, 3.8 percent

Muslim, 1.2 percent animist, 0.5 percent Hindu, and 0.2 percent other. Burma's national identity has been intimately connected with Theravada Buddhism since the 11th century, when King **Anawrahta** of the **Pagan Dynasty** made it the official religion (thus the popular saying, "to be Burmese is to be Buddhist"). During the dynastic period, **Burman (Bamar)**, **Mon**, **Arakanese (Rakhine)**, and **Shan** rulers gave generous donations to the Buddhist **Sangha** and sponsored **pagoda**-building projects. The old kings were also charged with upholding doctrinal orthodoxy by appointing a respected senior monk as head of the *Sangha* (known as the *Thathanabaing* in the **Burmese [Myanmar] language**). From at least the Pagan period, there were minority communities of Hindus and Muslims, and in later centuries Christians, whose presence was generally tolerated.

The British colonial regime was religiously neutral, refusing to appoint a *Thathanabaing*, but allowed Christian **missionaries** to proselytize, especially among ethnic minority peoples, such as the **Karens (Kayins)**, **Chins**, and **Kachins**. Thus, defense of the Buddhist religion became a major theme in early 20th-century nationalism. The British also encouraged the immigration of people from the Indian subcontinent, most of whom were Hindus or Muslims, greatly increasing the size of these religious minorities, especially in **Lower Burma**. This contributed to violent communal clashes during the 1930s between Burmese Buddhists and Hindu or Muslim Indians. Burma's status as a secular state continued after it became independent in 1948, but in August 1961, with the backing of Prime Minister U **Nu**, parliament passed a constitutional amendment making Buddhism the official religion. The **Revolutionary Council** established in March 1962 by General **Ne Win** nullified this measure, and since then Burma officially has remained secular (this is reflected in the **Constitution of 1974**, which was abrogated in 1988). However, the post-1988 **State Law and Order Restoration Council/State Peace and Development Council** military junta has patronized senior monks and devoted scarce resources to ambitious pagoda projects, including replacement of the *hti* or finial on the **Shwe Dagon Pagoda** in 1999. By acting as Buddhism's patrons, imitating the old Burmese kings, the military regime seeks to acquire legitimacy in the eyes of the religious majority. Minorities, especially Muslims, have had their religious activities restricted by the state and, at times, have been targets of mob violence. In contemporary Burma, all citizens are required to carry an identity card that shows their religion, which exposes minorities to discrimination by officials. The issue of religious adherence is complicated by the fact that, among the Buddhist majority, many, if not most, people also practice forms of animism, that is, veneration of gods or spirits known as *nats*. In traditional Burmese homes, a small *nat* shrine often supplements a Buddhist altar. Other forms of supernaturalism are widespread among Buddhists, for example, the old belief that certain amulets and **tattoos** can make a person invulnerable to bullets and the practice of *yedaya*, a form of magic designed to prevent misfortune. "New religions" have also emerged, especially among ethnic minorities living in the mountainous border areas, such as **God's Army** among some Karens. Such religions typically blend animist, Christian, and Buddhist elements.

Religious values remain strong in Burmese society, in contrast to some neighboring Asian countries. This is due in part to isolation during the socialist period (1962–1988), which limited the impact of secular and modern trends. Moreover, most Burmese (about three-quarters of the population) live in rural areas, where old religious values and superstitious beliefs remain largely unchallenged. Among those Burmese who can afford it, generous donations (*dana*) to Buddhist monks or pagodas are an important means of enhancing social prestige, and even gaining influence with the military elite. Perhaps most fundamentally, the consolations of religion are essential to people living in a nation that lacks the rule of law and where insecurity is the lot of rich and poor alike. *See also* ASTROLOGY; BUDDHA, GOTAMA; BUTTERFLY SPIRIT; CONGREGATION OF THE SANGHA (1980); DHAMMA; INDIANS IN BURMA; JATAKA TALES; JEWS IN BURMA; JUDSON, ADONIRAM; *KUTHO* (MERIT); MEDITATION; *NAT-PWE*; *NIBBANA*; NUNS, BUDDHIST; PALI; *PAYA*; *PONGYI*; SHIN ARAHAN; SHINBYU; STUPA; THAGYA MIN; *VINAYA*; WEIKZA; YOUNG MEN'S BUDDHIST ASSOCIATION.

RESISTANCE DAY. *See* ARMED FORCES DAY (MARCH 27).

REVOLUTIONARY COUNCIL (RC). Following the coup d'état of March 2, 1962, General **Ne Win** set up the Revolutionary Council as a martial law body, exercising supreme executive and legislative authority in place of institutions established by the **Constitution of 1947**, which had been abrogated. Originally composed of 17 officers of brigadier or colonel rank (apart from the chairman, Ne Win, who was a general), it was reorganized in 1971 (following the first congress of the **Burma Socialist Programme Party**) as a 15-member body, including four civilians. Several of the original RC members, including Brigadier **Aung Gyi**, were Ne Win's comrades in the **Fourth Burma Rifles**. The Revolutionary Council exercised executive power through a regional-local hierarchy of **Security and Administration Committees (SACs)**. Following implementation of the **Constitution of 1974**, it was abolished. *See also* ADMINISTRATION OF BURMA, BURMA SOCIALIST PROGRAMME PARTY ERA.

RICE. Burma's staple food, the most important part of the meal for most people. Burmese people are among the world's largest rice consumers: A per capita average of 186 kilograms of cleaned rice is eaten annually, which provides around 75 percent of their caloric intake. Rice is also a major element in the development of the country's history and cultures. Paddy rice cultivation became synonymous with civilization in lowland or plateau areas inhabited by **Mons, Burmans (Bamars), Arakanese (Rakhines)**, and **Shans (Tai)** because it made possible a high standard of living (compared to hill-dwelling peoples, who engaged in shifting **agriculture**) in which Indo-Buddhist civilization, including the building of **pagodas** and royal support for the **Sangha**, flourished. Irrigated rice fields, principally at **Kyaukse** and Minbu, were the economic foundation of the **Pagan Dynasty**, providing it with surpluses of food that supported a powerful and militarily expansive state from the 11th to 13th centuries. After **Lower Burma** was annexed following the **Second Anglo-Burmese War** in 1852, the British encouraged the migration of farmers from **Upper Burma**, who cleared land in the delta of the **Irrawaddy (Ayeyarwady) River** and grew rice for export. This experiment in "industrial agriculture," assisted by British investment in transportation and rice mills and the opening of the Suez Canal, was so successful that, before **World War II**, Burma was the world's largest supplier of the grain to world markets (over three million tons annually).

After Burma became independent in 1948, it lost this distinction, largely because of insurgency and the ill-conceived agricultural policies of the **Burma Socialist Programme Party** regime (1962–1988). During the socialist era, an inefficient and corrupt distribution system, coupled with periodic droughts and floods, caused serious rice shortages and periodic urban unrest. During the late 1970s, success in increasing rice harvests was achieved through the promotion of high-yield varieties under the **Whole Township Extension Program**. To ensure a dependable supply of rice to politically restive urban areas, the **State Peace and Development Council (SPDC)** has expanded irrigation facilities, promoted double cropping, and opened up new land for rice cultivation. But because there has been limited investment in fertilizers, pesticides, farm mechanization, and storage facilities, and most rice lands, being rain-fed, are hostage to the seasonal monsoon, ensuring adequate rice supplies for a growing population continues to be a major preoccupation of the military government. In April 2003, the SPDC announced a radical liberalization measure for the rice trade, which would allow farmers to sell rice to private citizens at market prices, although it is unclear whether the policy is being consistently implemented because coercive state procurement seems to continue in various localities, such as **Arakan (Rakhine) State**. In the mid-1990s, about 72 percent of Burma's cropland was devoted to rice, or 6.5 million hectares. As mentioned, most rice lands are rain-fed, lying in the lowland, alluvial region of the Irrawaddy Delta or in coastal areas of Arakan, while irrigated rice fields, about 18 percent of the total, are found principally in Mandalay, **Sagaing**, and **Pegu (Bago) Divisions**.

As in other parts of Southeast and East Asia, paddy rice cultivation in Burma requires the sowing of seed grain in nursery beds; after the seeds have sprouted and started to grow, they are transplanted to amply watered and plowed paddy fields, a task requiring intensive labor. After about four months, the crop is ready for harvesting, which requires more intensive labor. Because there is very little farm mechanization in Burma, both transplanting and harvesting involve backbreaking work, and farmers cannot harvest their crops without hiring extra laborers. *See also* ECONOMY AND ECONOMIC POLICY, STATE LAW AND ORDER RESTORATION COUNCIL/STATE PEACE AND DEVELOPMENT ERA.

RIOT POLICE (*LON HTEIN*). Detachments of special police, essentially a paramilitary unit, used for crowd control, separate from the regular People's Police Force of the **Ne Win** era. Commanded by **Sein Lwin**, they killed hundreds of protesting **students** in March and June 1988, especially during the **White Bridge Incident** of March 16. After martial law was declared in **Rangoon (Yangon)** in early August 1988, the **Tatmadaw** took over public order functions in the capital. Citizens' hopes that the army would act better than the Riot Police were severely disappointed. *See also* DEMOCRACY SUMMER; MYANMAR POLICE FORCE; MYEINIGONE MARKET INCIDENT; TEA SHOP INCIDENT.

ROAD TRANSPORT. In 1996–1997, according to government statistics, Burma had a total of 30,153 kilometers (18,695 miles) of roads, of which 16,439 kilometers (10,192 miles) were unpaved. Most major roads run south to north, along the valleys of the **Irrawaddy (Ayeyarwady)** and **Sittang (Sittoung) Rivers**. Road networks serving the **states** are much less developed than those in central Burma, though an extensive road network, financed by **China**, has been built in recent years in **Shan State** near the China–Burma border (apparently not included in the above statistics). The condition of most roads, including the paved ones, is poor, because of the severe rainy season, wear-and-tear by overloaded trucks, and poor maintenance. Rural communities are obliged by the authorities to keep roads in a minimal state of repair, a major reason for **forced labor**.

ROHINGYAS. **Muslims** who live in **Arakan (Rakhine) State**, mostly in the northern area bordering on **Bangladesh**. Unlike other ethnic minorities, they are not recognized as citizens by the Burmese government, but are considered illegal aliens. Numbering around 1.4 million, they have been objects of systematic persecution by the **Ne Win** regime and the **State Law and Order Restoration Council/State Peace and Development Council**. In a classic "divide-and-rule" strategy, both military regimes have enlisted Arakanese **Buddhists** in attacks on Rohingya communities, and, after evicting the Muslims, allowed the Arakaneses Buddhists to occupy their lands. In a 1978 operation called *Naga Min* ("Dragon King"), the **Tatmadaw** swept through Rohingya areas in search of illegal aliens, forcing over

200,000 (some sources say 300,000) to flee to Bangladesh, where they were housed in **refugee** camps until largely repatriated under **UN** auspices. In 1991–1992, a similar operation resulted in the flight of around 280,000. In 2003, some 21,000 Rohingyas remained in Bangladesh **refugee** camps, and an estimated 100,000 were illegal aliens, not recognized by the Dhaka government, living outside the camps. A large number of Rohingyas live in other countries, especially **Malaysia** and the Middle East.

The history of the Rohingyas is controversial because the Burmese government claims they are descended from Bengali residents of Chittagong District (now in eastern Bangladesh) who migrated into Arakan after the British annexed it in 1824–1826, and thus cannot be recognized as a legitimate Burmese ethnic nationality. A portion of northern Arakan was a part of British Bengal until 1937. Rohingya spokesmen claim their community is descended from Arabs and other migrants who settled on the Arakan coast as early as the ninth century CE. This contention is supported by historical scholarship showing that Muslim communities flourished in the Kingdom of **Arakan (Rakhine)** for many centuries before the coming of the British. Moreover, Arakan occupied areas of what is now Bangladesh during the 16th and 17th centuries.

During the opening months of **World War II**, there was severe communal violence between Rohingyas and Arakanese Buddhists, the former supporting the British and the latter the Japanese-backed **Burma Independence Army**. After independence, *mujahadin* operating in northern Arakan tried to establish an autonomous state run under Islamic law. Yet antigovernment insurgency among Rohingyas has been on a comparatively small scale; in 1998, two factions of the Rohingya Solidarity Organization (RSO) and the Arakan Rohingya Islamic Front (ARIF), which operated from bases in Bangladesh, joined together to form the **Arakan Rohingya National Organization (ARNO)**. *See also* CITIZENSHIP LAW; HUMAN RIGHTS IN BURMA; MIN BIN; MRAUK-U.

RUSSIA (SOVIET UNION), RELATIONS WITH. Under Prime Minister U **Nu**, the Burmese government sought to remain neutral and nonaligned in the late 1940s and early 1950s, when the Cold War was beginning to intensify. Diplomatic relations with the Soviet

Union were established in 1949; the prime minister visited Moscow in 1955, but did not refrain from telling Soviet leader Nikita Khrushchev not to give moral and other support to the **Communist Party of Burma**. Bilateral relations were troubled following the discovery in the 1950s that the KGB was using the Soviet embassy in **Rangoon (Yangon)** as a center for espionage. But the Soviets funded a number of important aid projects, including a hospital in **Taunggyi**, the new campus of **Rangoon (Yangon) Institute of Technology** in Gyogon, **Insein Township**, and the **Inya Lake** Hotel, which for many years was Burma's most modern accommodation. During the **Burma Socialist Programme Party (BSPP)** era (1962–1988), Moscow recognized the **Ne Win** regime as a "socialist-oriented state," although Ne Win did not espouse orthodox Marxist–Leninist ideology. The Russians constructed a large dam in central Burma, the Kyaikmauk Taung Dam, but it was poorly designed and never provided adequate water for irrigation.

The year 1988 saw the collapse of the BSPP socialist regime and 1991 the Soviet Union itself. Though suffering economic and political ills, the new Russian Federation has sought to obtain influence with the **State Peace and Development Council**—and also earn some hard currency—by selling the regime Mig-29 fighter jets in 2001 and a 10-megawatt nuclear reactor the following year. The latter sale fueled fears, probably unfounded, that the military junta was planning to develop nuclear weapons. Russia is also training several hundred **Tatmadaw** personnel. Post-1988 Burma also has arms trade ties with parts of the former Soviet Union, such as Ukraine.

– S –

SAGAING. The capital of Sagaing Division, located on the west bank of the Irrawaddy (Ayeyarwady) River, across from Mandalay. With an estimated population of 60,798 in 1996, it is one of Burma's historically most important cities, having served as a royal capital in the 14th century and for a few years in the 18th century (1760–1764), under the **Konbaung Dynasty**. The Sagaing Hills contain a large number of Buddhist monasteries, and the city is well known as a center of study and meditation; many **Buddhist nuns** (silashin) reside there.

Nearby is the 17th-century **Kaunghmudaw Pagoda**. See also AMA-RAPURA; AVA (INWA).

SAGAING DIVISION. One of Burma's 14 **states** and **divisions**, with an area of 93,701 square kilometers (36,178 square miles), making it Burma's second largest regional jurisdiction, and an estimated population in 2000 of 5.3 million (1983 census figure: 3.8 million). The divisional capital is **Sagaing**, which was briefly a royal capital and is located across the **Irrawaddy (Ayeyarwady) River** from **Mandalay**. Presently, Sagaing is a major center for **Buddhist** study and **meditation**, with many monasteries located on Sagaing Hill. Sagaing Division comprises eight **districts** (Sagaing, **Shwebo**, Monywa, Katha, Kalay, Tamu, Mawlaik, and Hkamti) and 37 **townships**. To the north and west, it shares a long border with India, and the **Chindwin (Chindwinn) River** runs through the division from north to south. The Chindwin joins the Irrawaddy River at the place where Sagaing, **Magwe (Magway)**, and **Mandalay Divisions** meet.

Sagaing Division's topography is complex: In the south, it is mostly lowlands, but hills and mountains are found to the north and the west, especially along the border with India (the Patkai Range and the Naga Hills). Nwemauk Peak is one of Burma's highest mountains, at 3,827 meters (12,553 feet). Although **Burmans (Bamars)** form the majority of the population, there are also significant numbers of **Shans**, **Chins**, and **Nagas**. **Forest** resources are abundant, although they are being depleted. Important crops include **rice**, maize, wheat, millet, groundnuts, sugarcane, sesame, pulses and beans, and sunflowers. Livestock raising and freshwater fisheries are also economically important. Many of Sagaing Division's abundant resources reach India by way of border trade.

Shwebo (Yadanatheinkha), located to the northwest of Sagaing city, was the hometown and royal capital of King **Alaungpaya**, who established the **Konbaung Dynasty** in 1752.

SAGAING MASSACRE (AUGUST 8, 1988). At the beginning of the **Four Eights Movement**, several thousand demonstrators converged on a police station in **Sagaing** and were shot at by police and troops. Reportedly, 537 persons were killed (the official figure was 31), and witnesses report that police dumped many of the bodies into the **Irrawaddy (Ayeyarwady) River**. Outside of **Rangoon (Yangon)**, the incident in Sagaing was probably the worst, in terms of casualties, to occur during **Democracy Summer**.

SALE (SALAY). Located on the banks of the **Irrawaddy (Ayeyarwady) River** in **Magwe (Magway) Division** southwest of Chauk, Sale contains more than one hundred religious monuments from the **Pagan Dynasty** era. They are smaller in scale than the **pagodas** and *pahto* at **Pagan (Bagan)**, so some scholars believe they may have been built by commoners or minor aristocrats. Little archeological research has been done at Sale, and **tourists** visit the area infrequently.

SALWEEN (THANLWIN) RIVER. One of Burma's major river systems, which flows in a north–south direction and bisects **Shan State**. Its headwaters are located in Tibet, and its length inside of Burma is 1,600 kilometers. The Salween empties into the Gulf of **Martaban (Mottama)** at **Moulmein (Mawlamyine)**. Territories located east of the river in **Shan State**, especially **Kokang** and the **Wa** districts, have traditionally enjoyed great independence from the central government in **Rangoon (Yangon)** and have been major producers of **opium** and other narcotics. Unlike the **Irrawaddy**, the turbulent Salween is navigable for only very short stretches and until recently has played a negligible role in the country's economy. However, in recent years, there have been proposals to dam the river to generate hydroelectric power and facilitate navigation. This is highly controversial because the Salween is one of the last major unexploited rivers in Southeast Asia, and damming its upper reaches would have a negative environmental impact on areas where **Shans** and other ethnic minorities live. *See also* MEKONG RIVER.

SAMSARA. The cycle of rebirth and suffering that all living things must endure until they attain *nibbana* (nirvana). In **Buddhist** cosmology, there are 31 levels of existence, ranging from the deepest hell to heavenly realms inhabited by incorporeal beings. Simply put, the sum total, or nature, of an individual's meritorious or evil deeds (*kamma*) over a lifetime determines the place of rebirth. Because Buddhists do not believe in the existence of an immortal soul (the doctrine of *anatta*), the manner in which a being passes from one life to another has been a matter of considerable speculation. Ordinary Burmese people often simply assume the existence of a soul separate from the body, sometimes described as a **butterfly spirit**. Although humans inhabit only the fifth level of existence, which is inferior to that of gods or celestial beings, humans alone can achieve Enlightenment and pass into *nibbana*. See also BUDDHA, GOTAMA; *KUTHO*.

SAN YU, U (1918–ca. 2001). Close associate of **Ne Win** who served as president of the Socialist Republic of the Union of Burma when the former retired from that post in 1981. He retired from all his posts following the **Burma Socialist Programme Party's Extraordinary Congress** in July 1988.

SANCTIONS. Following the seizure of power by the **State Law and Order Restoration Council (SLORC)** on September 18, 1988, **Japan**, European countries, and the **United States** halted the flow of official development assistance (ODA). This was the beginning of international sanctions against the new military government, which accelerated during the next decade, especially after the SLORC refused to recognize the results of the **General Election of May 27, 1990**. Daw **Aung San Suu Kyi** backed comprehensive sanctions as a means of forcing the regime to democratize and halt **human rights** abuses. The moral authority of the 1991 Nobel Peace Prize winner galvanized activists worldwide, who called for Burma to become the "South Africa of the 1990s" (because the *apartheid* regime in that country had supposedly been forced out of power by a coordinated international boycott).

The member countries of the **European Union** have implemented an array of sanctions, including suspension of all ODA, except for humanitarian purposes, an arms embargo and halt to defense cooperation, bans on the issuance of visas to high-ranking regime officials, and withdrawal of GSP privileges from Burma (because of **forced labor**). In 1996, the EU adopted a "Common Position" on Burma that was reaffirmed and strengthened in 2000 and 2003. The U.S. government approved a nonretroactive ban on American investment in the country on May 20, 1997. Following the **"Black Friday" Incident** of May 30, 2003, the Bush Administration signed into law the "Burmese

Freedom and Democracy Act," a set of more severe measures that include a ban on imports from Burma and financial transactions between Americans and entities connected in any way to the **State Peace and Development Council (SPDC)**. A number of American states and cities passed "selective purchasing laws" in the 1990s designed to penalize companies that did business in Burma, but the Massachusetts law was overturned by the U.S. Supreme Court. Although by 2003 some new Japanese ODA projects had been initiated, the Tokyo government did not approve **aid** on the scale given during the **Ne Win** era before 1988 because of financial considerations and pressure from the United States. Because of American, Japanese, and European influence over multilateral institutions, such as the World Bank and the Asian Development Bank, Burma was effectively barred from receiving their support, at least on a major scale.

Supporters of tough sanctions and "constructive engagement" (capital investment in the country to promote social change and eventual democratization) are bitterly at odds. In a 1997 essay in the Hong Kong–based magazine *Far Eastern Economic Review*, Ma Thanegi, a former associate of Daw Suu Kyi, claimed that sanctions hurt the people without effectively changing the behavior of the regime. Some observers argued that although business-oriented investment or aid should be (partially) banned, Burma desperately needed humanitarian aid. Critics of sanctions noted that the 2003 trade embargo by Washington threw tens of thousands of women factory workers out of work because Burma exported US$300–400 million in textiles to the United States, and that sanctions by Western countries have had little real impact because the SPDC has close economic ties with **China, India**, and members of the **Association of Southeast Asian Nations**. In fact, it seems that neither sanctions nor constructive engagement have had much influence on the behavior of the SPDC, which is willing to risk economic overdependence on China and to sacrifice the welfare of the people to keep itself in power. *See also* ECONOMY AND ECONOMIC POLICY, STATE LAW AND ORDER RESTORATION COUNCIL/STATE PEACE AND DEVELOPMENT COUNCIL ERA; "VISIT MYANMAR YEAR".

SANDA WIN (1953–). Favorite daughter of **Ne Win**, whose failure to pass an English-language examination in order to study at a medical school in Britain was said to have led to a reinstatement of English in Burmese school curricula. After the power seizure by the **State Law and Order Restoration Council**, she was rumored to have formed close ties with SLORC Secretary-1 **Khin Nyunt**. However, even if it existed, a "Sanda Win–Khin Nyunt axis" exercised little influence over post-1988 politics. Widely criticized for building her own personal business empire, she was placed under house arrest following discovery of a **coup d'état attempt (March 2002)** involving her husband and sons. *See also* EDUCATION, HIGHER.

SANGHA. The **Buddhist** monastic order, whose members live according to strict rules (*vinaya*) and have the solemn responsibility of conserving and promulgating the teachings of Gotama **Buddha**. They are not "priests" in the sense of ministering to a congregation or serving as intermediaries between the human and divine worlds, although laypeople may acquire merit (Burmese, *kutho*) through donations (*dana*) to monks. Monks are also the primary teachers of the religion (*dhamma*) to laypeople. As highly respected exemplars of Buddhist wisdom and discipline, studying religious texts, the **Tipitaka**, and practicing **meditation**, their primary task is to prepare for entry into *nibbana*. Since at least the time of the **Pagan (Bagan) Dynasty**, they have been the most highly respected group in Burmese society. In contemporary Burma, they function as the most important social institution, with the possible exception of the **Tatmadaw**.

Although "forest monks" often live a hermetic existence, most members of the Sangha live in monasteries (*kyaung*) in towns and villages throughout Burma. In 1988, they numbered around 300,000, including both *rahan* (ordained monks) and *samanera* (novices). The Sangha in Burma is divided into nine orders (*gaing*), of which the largest by far, containing almost 90 percent of all monks, is the Thudhamma. Of near equal importance is the Shwegyin sect, which was patronized by King **Mindon**. Differences between the orders are not so much doctrinal as interpretational, focusing on how the *vinaya* rules should be followed (e.g., the proper wearing of saffron robes).

Members of the Sangha are often referred to as *pongyi* ("great glory"), while the head monk of a monastery, or a highly respected senior monk, is given the title *sayadaw*. Women cannot enter the Sangha, although those who aspire to a religious life often become the equivalent of **nuns** (*silashin*), without benefit of ordination. Like monks, they shave their heads and live according to strict monastic rules. Ordination of women was once practiced in Theravada countries but has died out.

Historically, the relationship between the Sangha and the Burmese state has been complex, complementary, and sometimes antagonistic. In precolonial times, Burmese kings assumed responsibility for reforming or purifying the monastic orders and appointing a senior monk, the *Thathanabaing*, to oversee them. During the colonial period, the British policy of religious neutrality is said to have contributed to the monkhood's poor discipline and low quality at the time. Many monks, most notably **U Ottama** and **U Wisara**, became politically active. In May 1980, **Ne Win** convened the **Congregation of the Sangha of All Orders** to reassert state control over the monks. Although young monks participated in the demonstrations of **Democracy Summer**, the post-1988 military government has been largely successful in gaining the compliance of conservative senior members of the Sangha. *See also* ALL BURMA YOUNG MONKS UNION; OVERTURNING THE OFFERING BOWL; *SHINBYU*.

SAW, U (1900–1948). A major colonial-era political leader, who took the name *Galon U Saw* after serving as a defense attorney for **Saya San (Hsaya San)** in 1931. He established the *Myochit* or Patriot Party in 1938, and served as Burma's prime minister in 1940–1941 under the system established by the **Government of Burma Act**. However, he was arrested by the British on his way home from a 1941 trip to Britain and the United States after attempting to make contact with the Japanese legation in Lisbon, Portugal, and spent **World War II** imprisoned in Uganda, East Africa. Brought back to Burma in 1946 by the sympathetic governor, Reginald Dorman-Smith, he expected, with the governor's backing, to assume a leadership position, but he was eclipsed in popularity by **Aung San**, for whom he developed a strong antagonism (in part stimulated by his belief that Aung San attempted to have him assassinated). A member of the delegation that went to London to confer with Prime Minister Clement Attlee in January 1947, he refused to sign the **Aung San–Attlee Agreement**. Gunmen loyal to U Saw assassinated Aung San and six other leaders on July 19, 1947. U Saw apparently believed that with Aung San and the rest of his Executive Council out of the way, it would be possible for him to become the first prime minister of independent Burma. But U Saw was promptly arrested, put on trial, and sentenced to death in December 1947, the sentence being carried out in May of the following year. *See also* AUNG SAN, ASSASSINATION OF; SAYA SAN (HSAYA SAN) REBELLION; *TAT*.

SAW MAUNG, GENERAL (1928–1997). First Chairman of the **State Law and Order Restoration Committee (SLORC)**, concurrently serving as prime minister, defense minister, and commander of the **Tatmadaw** (senior general) following the SLORC seizure of power on September 18, 1988. His military career began in 1949; after rising through the ranks, he became Tatmadaw chief of staff in 1985. A hard-liner loyal to **Ne Win** and close to **Sein Lwin**, he was forced to retire as SLORC chairman on April 23, 1992, for reasons of health and was succeeded by the vice chairman, General **Than Shwe**.

SAWBWA (SAO PHA). The **Burmese (Myanmar) language** rendition of the **Shan language** word *sao pha* (*chao fa* in the Thai language), literally meaning "lord of the heavens" and referring to the hereditary rulers of the **Shan States** of eastern Burma or, more broadly, also to the rulers of **Shan (Tai)**-dominated polities found in other parts of Burma and neighboring countries, including China's Yunnan Province. The term is most frequently used to refer to the 14–16 rulers of the major Shan States during the British colonial period who, together with other rulers of lower rank, *myosa* and *ngwekhunhmu*, were sometimes collectively called *Saophalong* (Burmese, *Sawbwagyi*), "great lords." The rulers enjoyed a measure of autonomy under the British, although their powers were significantly reduced by the establishment of the Federated Shan States in 1922. Before they relinquished their "feudal" authority to the Union of Burma in April 1959, the *sawbwa* maintained their own courts, *haw* (royal palaces), and local administrations, although they were carefully supervised by officials of the colonial government. The Burmese, strongly influenced by socialist ideology, tended to view the traditionally minded *sawbwa* as feudal relics who exploited their downtrodden subjects, but in fact many of them were well educated, quite popular, and played important roles in national politics during the U **Nu** period and the

Shan resistance against the **Ne Win** regime. These included **Sao Shwe Taik**, *sawbwa* of **Yawnghwe**, who was the first president of the Union of Burma, and his wife, the **Yawnghwe** *Mahadevi* (a title for the *sawbwa's* wife) Sao Nang **Hearn Kham**, who served as leader of the first Shan State Army, established in 1964. *See also* PANGLONG CONFERENCE; SHAN STATE.

SAYA SAN (HSAYA SAN) REBELLION (1930–1932). The largest rural uprising during the British colonial period, caused by economic distress, harsh taxation measures, and land foreclosures. Its leader, Saya San (Hsaya San), was a practitioner of traditional medicine, **alchemy**, and **astrology** who was also an active member of the radical faction of the **General Council of Burmese Associations (GCBA)**. Before the revolt, he served as the chairman of a special GCBA committee surveying abuses of power by government officials and traveled to different parts of **Lower Burma** to compile a record of such abuses. This experience, and the general ineffectiveness of the GCBA's nonviolent tactics, convinced him that only an armed uprising could improve the lot of Burmese villagers. Quietly, he established a "**Galon** Army," and initiated a revolt on December 23, 1930, in Tharrawaddy District, north of **Rangoon (Yangon)** in what is now **Pegu (Bago) Division**. Among the rebels' first actions was the killing of local village headmen, who were widely perceived as instruments of British rule.

Although Saya San's headquarters at Alantaung ("Flag Hill") in the **Pegu Yoma** was captured by colonial troops on December 31, the revolt spread to other parts of Lower Burma, including **Insein**, Henzada (Hinthada), **Pegu (Bago)**, **Toungoo (Taungoo)**, **Prome (Pyay)**, Pyapon, and Thayetmyo, and also to the **Shan States**. Resorting to guerrilla tactics, the insurgents offered stubborn resistance to colonial police and military forces until mid-1932. According to British reports, rebel activity was so widespread that authority had collapsed in some districts.

After the capture of his headquarters, Saya San fled to Upper Burma and then to the Shan States, hiding out at Nawngkio in **Hsipaw**. When his forces were defeated in an engagement with colonial troops, he attempted to get to his hometown of **Shwebo** but was betrayed and captured in August 1931. Brought before a Special Tribunal, he was sentenced to death by hanging on August 28. The sentence was carried out on November 28 at Tharrawaddy jail. Both Dr. **Ba Maw** and "Galon" U **Saw** gained national prominence by defending him.

The revolt caught the British by surprise. They brought reinforcements from the Indian Army to Burma, where they were combined with military police, newly recruited civilian police, and **Karen (Kayin)** and **Chin** levies to create a force of more than 23,000 men. Martial law was imposed. More than 1,300 insurgents were killed, 9,000 arrested, and 126 rebels, including Saya San, executed. In some districts, the colonial police used methods similar to the **"Four Cuts"** policy of the **Tatmadaw** to deprive the guerrilla resistance of local support networks, including **forced relocation.**

The revolt was poorly organized and equipped; peasant rebels had few rifles, and, to protect themselves from British bullets, resorted to magical **tattoos,** spells, and amulets. The official British report on the uprising attributed it to the gullibility and superstition of Burmese villagers and described Saya San as an opportunistic charlatan. Little attention was paid to peasant grievances, including **rice** prices so low that farmers fell deeper and deeper into debt and did not have enough income to feed their families, a situation that the colonial government did next to nothing to alleviate. Many of the districts where rebels received the most popular support were those in which farmers had lost their land to **Indian** moneylenders. Peasant resentment was also stimulated by the government's strict prohibitions against their using timber from forest reserves.

The colonial authorities made much of the fact that Saya San designated himself *Thupannaka Galuna Yaza* (the Galon King) and constructed a "palace" at Alantaung, reflecting his desire to expel the Westerners and restore the old order. Although his thinking may have been reactionary, it reflected the widespread perception among ordinary Burmese that the colonial government was illegitimate.

Many urban Burmese, including students at **Rangoon (Yangon) University,** admired Saya San and his followers. But a new generation of nationalists, including those who joined the **Dobama Asiayone,** recognized that a restoration of the precolonial order was impossible. When **Aung San** and the **Thirty Comrades** received military training from the Japanese on the eve of **World War II,** their goal was to establish a modern state, defended by a modern army. In U Maung Maung's words, "[T]he Saya San Rebellion, fundamentally the people's revolution, ended an epoch of modern Burmese history, a period of uneasy alliance of traditionalism with modern politics" (*From Sangha to Laity*, 1980, 105).

SAYADAW (*HSAYADO*). In the **Burmese (Myanmar) language**, the term literally means "royal teacher," but it is used today to refer to senior or highly respected members of the **Sangha**, including the heads of monasteries (*kyaung*). When speaking Burmese, a layperson will use the term to address a senior monk, that is, as a title. The *sayadaw* is renowned for his superior knowledge of the **Pali** Canon or **meditation** techniques and sometimes has a national or even international reputation, for example the **Mahasi Sayadaw**. *See also* **PONGYI**.

SCOTT, JAMES GEORGE (1851–1935). A prominent writer and British colonial civil servant. Born in Scotland, the son of a minister, he began his career as a journalist in Malaya, was a schoolteacher at Saint John's College in **Rangoon (Yangon)**, and also worked as a correspondent for the *Rangoon Gazette*, writing under the name *Shway Yoe* ("Golden Honest"). His most famous book, *The Burman: His Life and Notions*, was published in 1882 and introduced British audiences to a hitherto unknown land. After **Upper Burma** was occupied during the **Third Anglo-Burmese War**, Scott, having passed the bar examinations, returned to Burma and served on the Burma Commission, retiring in 1910. He was almost entirely involved in the **Shan States**, becoming Superintendent for the Northern Shan States in 1891 and Superintendent for the Southern Shan States from 1902 to 1910. Scott established **Taunggyi** as the administrative center for the Shan States (it is now the state capital). He served briefly as chargé d'affaires in Bangkok in the mid-1890s.

Every inch an imperialist and a product of his times, Scott had remarkable courage and the ability to communicate effectively with local leaders, including the **Shan (Tai)** princes, or *sawbwas*. He is said to have introduced **soccer (football)** to Burma; it is now the country's favorite game. His encyclopedic knowledge of Burma and especially the Shan States is reflected in his five-volume *Gazetteer of Upper*

Burma and the Shan States (1901) and *Burma: A Handbook of Practical Information* (1906, 1921). Although a century old, these classics are still consulted and quoted by Burma watchers and travelers today, including his comments on the remote and little-known **Was**.

SEAGRIM, HUGH P. (1909–1944). British officer who worked with **Force 136** during **World War II** to establish an anti-Japanese base in the hills of what is now **Karen (Kayin) State**, near the Thai–Burma border. Operating on his own with a small force of **Karens (Kayins)** after the Japanese occupied Burma in early 1942, he established radio communication with India in October of the following year and sent a Karen agent to **Rangoon (Yangon)** to contact Karens and anti-Japanese **Thakins** in the city. Sent on a punitive expedition to locate Seagrim's base in the Karen hills, the Japanese *Kempeitai* (military police) caused such a reign of terror that Seagrim decided to give himself up in order to spare the Karens further retaliation. He was executed at Rangoon on September 22, 1944, but he and his Karen comrades had succeeded in opening up a line of communication between the British in India and disaffected **Burman** and Karen elements. His story is told by Ian Morrison in *Grandfather Longlegs*, and to this day he remains a hero among the Karens. *See also* JAPANESE OCCUPATION.

SECURITY AND ADMINISTRATION COMMITTEES (SACs). During the **Revolutionary Council** period (1962–1973), administrative bodies whose chairmen were military officers, found on the **state/ division, township**, and ward/village tract levels of local and regional administration. SACs were placed in a hierarchy below the Security and Administration Central Committee, which was directly responsible to the Revolutionary Council chaired by General **Ne Win**. This "transitional," military-dominated governmental structure anticipated the hierarchy of Law and Order Councils (after 1997, Peace and Development Councils) established after the **State Law and Order Restoration Council** seized power in September 1988. *See also* ADMINISTRATION, BURMA SOCIALIST PROGRAMME PARTY ERA.

SEIN LWIN (1924–). A close associate of **Ne Win** who briefly served as chairman of the **Burma Socialist Programme Party (BSPP)** and as Burma's president in 1988. He joined the **Burma Defence Army** in 1943, and after the war served in the **Fourth Burma Rifles** under Ne Win's command. He killed Saw **Ba U Gyi** during operations against the **Karen National Union** insurgents in 1950, and commanded the troops who fired on **Rangoon (Yangon) University student** demonstrators during the **July 7 Incident** in 1962, causing many fatalities. As commander of the **Riot Police** (*Lon Htein*), he was responsible for the shooting of hundreds of student demonstrators in March 1988, earning himself the name "the Butcher of Rangoon." Following the **BSPP Extraordinary Congress** on July 23–25, 1988, he was unexpectedly promoted to the two highest state and party posts. The **Four Eights Movement**, organized by **Min Ko Naing** and other student activists, led to his resignation on August 12, but at the cost of hundreds more casualties in **Rangoon (Yangon)** and elsewhere. Since 1988, he has lived in obscurity. Though valued by Ne Win for his loyalty and willingness to do the regime's dirty work, he was universally hated. *See also* DEMOCRACY SUMMER; TEA SHOP INCIDENT; WHITE BRIDGE INCIDENT.

SEX INDUSTRY IN BURMA. The commercialization of sex and the victimization of "sex industry workers" have become major problems in many Southeast Asian countries, including Burma. During the **Burma Socialist Programme Party** period (1962–1988), the country's isolation from its neighbors inhibited the growth of a sex industry, but this changed after the **State Law and Order Restoration Council** ended socialist policies of self-sufficiency in 1988 and promoted international economic ties. A report in late 1993 by Human Rights Watch, an international **nongovernmental organization (NGO)**, disclosed that, by that time, an estimated 20,000 Burmese **women**, mostly members of ethnic minorities, were working in Thai brothels, and that the number was increasing by 10,000 annually. Most of the women suffered harsh working conditions and abuse, and many were exposed to **AIDS**. By the beginning of the 21st century, prostitution inside Burma was also recognized as a growing problem; because of deteriorating economic conditions, women entered the sex industry not only in **Rangoon (Yangon)** and other large cities, but also in rural areas. Along with the use of **heroin**, the domestic sex industry was a major cause of the country's AIDS epidemic, one of Asia's worst. Critics of American **sanctions** against the **State Peace and Development Council** argued that the July 2003 embargo on exports to the United States closed down textile factories and forced many unemployed women workers to turn to prostitution. *See also* HUMAN RIGHTS IN BURMA.

SHAN LANGUAGE. A member of the Tai-Kadai group of **languages.** It is monosyllabic and tonal, the number of tones more complex than the **Burmese (Myanmar) language** of the Sino-Tibetan group. The same combination of consonants and vowels, pronounced with different tones, has different meanings. Most speakers live in **Shan State**, with other speakers in **Kachin State, Kayah (Karenni) State,** and **Burma Proper.** The Shan language and those of **Thailand** and Laos are closely related; important dialects include those of the *Tai Khun* of **Keng Tung** and the Hkamti Shan in Kachin State. The Shan script has been influenced by the Burmese writing system.

SHAN NATIONALITIES LEAGUE FOR DEMOCRACY (SNLD). In the **General Election of May 27, 1990**, the SNLD was the political party that won the second largest number of seats, 23 out of 56 contested in **Shan State**, surpassed nationwide only by the **National League for Democracy** (392 seats).

SHAN PLATEAU. A large elevated region, with an average altitude of 900 meters (3,000 feet), located in **Shan State** between the valley of the **Irrawaddy (Ayeyarwady) River** to the west and the **Salween (Thanlwin) River** to the east. It is criss-crossed by several mountain ranges, running generally in a north–south direction.

SHAN STATE. In land area, the largest of Burma's **states** and **divisions**, covering 155,801 square kilometers or (155 square miles). It contains 11 **districts** (**Taunggyi**, Loilem, **Lashio**, Muse, Kyaukme, Kunlong, Laukkai, **Keng Tung**, Monghsat, Monghpyak, and Tachilek), which are subdivided into 54 **townships**. Shan State is bisected by the **Salween (Thanlwin)** River. West of the Salween, the **Shan Plateau**, an upland region with an average elevation of 900 meters, comprises most of its land area. There are rugged mountain ranges east of the river and in the northern and western parts of the state. Shan State borders **Mandalay** and **Sagaing Divisions** to the west, **Kachin State** to the north, and **Karen (Kayin)** and **Kayah (Karenni) States** to the south. The state forms part or all of Burma's international borders with **China** to the northeast, Laos to the east (the two are separated by the **Mekong River**), and **Thailand** to the southeast. The largest lake is **Inle Lake**, located near the state capital, **Taunggyi**.

The 1983 census, the last one taken, recorded 3,716,841 inhabitants; exact figures on the present population are not available, but it was estimated at 4.8 million in 2000. The flow of **refugees** into neighboring Thailand since the mid-1990s has probably had a significant demographic impact. Aside from Taunggyi, which in 1983 had 108,231 inhabitants (134,023 estimated in 1996), major cities and towns include Keng Tung, **Hsipaw**, Lashio, and **Kalaw**.

Shan State is one of Burma's most ethnically diverse regions. The **Shans (Tai)**, who comprise around half of the population, are valley dwellers who cultivate **rice** and have adopted Indo-Buddhist civilization. Their states, traditionally governed by *sawbwas* and other local dynastic rulers and ideologically and institutionally similar to those of the **Burmans** and **Mons**, trace their roots to at least to the 13th century, and probably earlier. Other important ethnic groups (there are around 35 in all) include the **Pa-O, Palaung, Kachin, Wa, Lahu, Akha**, and **Kokang** Chinese. In contrast to the valley-dwelling Shans, these groups commonly live in upland areas and traditionally practice shifting **agriculture** (*taungya*), growing dry rice, buckwheat, and maize. Shan State cash crops include tea, coffee, oranges, pineapples, and sugarcane. Its **forests**, once covering three-quarters of the land area, have been heavily depleted. Many of the upland peoples, especially the Wa and Kokang Chinese in northeastern Shan State, grow **opium** poppies. Although quantities of exports and acreage under poppy cultivation have declined in recent years, Shan State is still one of the world's major sources of opium, **heroin**, and **amphetamines**.

After the British pacified the region in the late 1880s, they governed what is now Shan State indirectly, allowing the rulers of 43 constituent states (in 1905, 15 *sawbwas* and 28 chiefs of lower rank, known as *myosas* and *ngwekhunhmu*) considerable autonomy; in 1922, the Federated Shan States was established, with its administrative center at Taunggyi. However, in contrast to **Burma Proper**, the **Shan States** were not economically developed, with the exception of the lead and silver mines at Bawdwin (Namtu). Although the **Burma Road** ran from Lashio to the Burma–China border, the Shan States were one of the few areas in Burma to escape devastation during **World War II**, its rulers recognizing the **Japanese occupation**. The Japanese gave the eastern Shan States of Keng Tung and Mong Pan to their ally, Thailand, but the remaining states were included in the nominally "independent" Burma proclaimed by them in August 1943. At the February 1947 **Panglong Conference**, the Shan rulers agreed to join the Union of Burma, although they gained important concessions embodied in the **Constitution of 1947**, including the right to secede 10 years after independence. The first president of the Union of Burma was a Shan, Sao **Shwe Taik**, *sawbwa* of **Yawnghwe**. In April 1959, the Shan rulers agreed to relinquish their "feudal" authority, though they remained popular with their former subjects, and some of them became involved in antigovernment insurgency.

Following the **Kuomintang (KMT, Guomindang)** intrusions of 1950, Shan State became a war zone. **Tatmadaw** units sent to fight the KMT often wreaked havoc on local populations, leading to the first Shan antigovernment insurgency, the *Noom Suk Harn* ("Young Brave Warriors"), started in 1958. By the 1960s, especially after the abolition of the 1947 Constitution's parliamentary and semifederal institutions by the **Revolutionary Council**, Shan State had become host to a growing number of local militias and warlord armies, including the nationalist Shan State Army and **Ka Kwe Ye** units, such as those led by **Lo Hsing-han** and **Khun Sa**, two drug-dealing warlords later notorious as "kings of the Golden Triangle." In January 1968, the **Communist Party of Burma (CPB)** established a base along the Shan State–China border, which was generously supported by the **People's Republic of China** and became the best-equipped and most powerful insurgency fighting the central government during the 1970s and 1980s. Following the CPB's breakup in early 1989, its constituent ethnic units signed **cease-fires** with the **State Law and Order Restoration Council**. The cease-fires, especially one agreed to by Khun Sa, commander of the **Mong Tai Army**, in January 1996, fundamentally changed the balance of power in Shan State. The post-1988 military regime was able to exert unprecedented power in central and southern parts of the state, ordering massive **forced relocations** and causing the movement of hundreds of thousands of refugees to Thailand; moreover, the drug-dealing **United Wa State Army**, formally an ally of the **State Peace and Development Council (SPDC)**, became the most powerful ethnic armed group, with territory along the Thai–Burma border as well as the border with China. Many areas of Shan State are now sites of SPDC-sponsored **Border Area Development** programs, including an opium poppy crop substitution project in Kokang. Following the loss of their traditional rulers and protectors, the Shans have become targets for regime-instigated **human rights** abuses, as well as attempts by the central government to "Burmanize" their traditional culture and religion. *See also* CHINESE IN BURMA; FEDERAL MOVEMENT; FRONTIER AREAS; INTHA; MINERAL RESOURCES; PANTHAYS; SHAN NATIONALITIES LEAGUE FOR DEMOCRACY (SNLD); SHAN STATE ARMY (SOUTH); TAUNGGYI.

SHAN STATE ARMY (SSA) (SOUTH). An ethnic armed group that continues to resist the **State Peace and Development Council (SPDC)**. After **Khun Sa** signed a **cease-fire** with the SPDC's predecessor, the **State Law and Order Restoration Council**, in January 1996, the Shan State Army (South) was constituted from contingents of the drug warlord's **Mong Tai Army**. Its commander is Colonel Yord Serk, who has fought as an insurgent since the age of 17. Its armed strength is estimated at between 1,000 and 2,000 guerrillas. In contrast to Khun Sa's armed group, the SSA (South) claims to be suppressing the traffic in **opium** and **heroin** in the territories it controls. It operates in central Shan State, and the post-1988 military regime has subjected as many as 300,000 **Shans** in the region to **forced relocation** in an effort to undercut the SSA (South)'s popular bases of support. It has also encouraged the **United Wa State Army** to enclose and contain the Shan guerrillas, which has caused border tensions and fighting with **Thailand**. The

SSA (South), formerly known as the Shan United Revolutionary Army (SURA), has made alliances with other non-cease-fire groups, the **Karen National Union**, the **Karenni National Progressive Party**, and the **Chin National Front**. *See also* HUMAN RIGHTS IN BURMA.

SHAN STATES. The term refers to both to a unique kind of polity established by **Shans (Tai)** in various parts of Burma since at least the 13th century and a group of such polities, known as the Federated Shan States after 1922, which enjoyed a measure of autonomy under their own rulers—commonly known as *sawbwa* (*sao pha*), *myoza,* and *ngwekhunhmu*—during the British colonial period.

Known as *möng* in the **Shan language**, the traditional Shan polity was established in valleys and lowland areas where wetland **rice** could be cultivated. Ideologically and institutionally, it resembled the states of lowland Burma, especially its promotion of close ties between the state and **Sangha**. Principally in what is now **Shan State** but also in parts of **Kachin State** and other areas, Shans lived clustered in or around a fortified city and exercised influence over adjacent hill peoples, such as the **Palaung**, **Wa**, and **Akha**, a hierarchical distribution of power and authority that, on a higher level, included the *möng's* ceremonial and sometimes actual subordination to a larger state, such as the **Konbaung Dynasty** or the British colonial regime. Located near **Burman (Bamar)** power centers, the western states of **Hsipaw, Hsenwi**, and **Tawngpeng** were open to Burmese influences, while **Keng Tung**, east of the **Salween (Thanlwin) River**, was subject to more influence from **Thailand** and even **China**. Within Shan society was a marked distinction between the noble and commoner classes, as well as a separate group of "outcastes," slaves and persons in "unclean" professions, such as butchery. Shan chronicles record the establishment of an important state at Mogaung in present-day Kachin State in 1215. Keng Tung was established in the late 13th century.

Following the **Third Anglo-Burmese War**, the British succeeded in "pacifying" the Shan States by 1888; the Shan States Act, passed the following year, established a system of British residents responsible to the Superintendents of the Northern and Southern Shan States. The rulers were given "writs of authority" (*sanads*) that confirmed their claims to the throne and were promised minimal interference in their internal affairs as long as they enforced law and order. According to the *Imperial Gazeteer of India*, published in 1905, the Northern Shan States consisted of 5 entities as well as the remote and unsettled **Wa states**, and the Southern Shan States consisted of 38 entities, for a total in the two areas of 43 states. After **World War II, Kokang** was also recognized by the British as a full-fledged Shan State. Only around 14 to 16 states (including Kokang after 1945) were ruled by full-fledged *sawbwa*, the others being ruled by the lower-ranking chiefs known as *myosa* and *ngwekhunhmus*. In the early 20th century, the colonial authorities also recognized the existence of four Shan States lying within the districts of **Burma Proper**: Mong Mit, Hsawnghsup, Singaling Hkamti, and Hkamti-long.

Some Shan states were extensive: Keng Tung encompassed over 31,000 square kilometers (12,000 square miles) and had more than 190,000 residents in the early 20th century. But others were tiny principalities, such as Namtok, which comprised only 32 square kilometers (20 square miles) and had a population of 778 (1905 figures). But they were structurally similar and shared these similarities with Shan polities outside of Burma, such as those in northern Thailand, Laos, and China's Yunnan Province.

The establishment of the Federated Shan States and the Federal Council of Shan Chiefs in 1922 marked a trend toward centralization and rationalization. Each ruler was obliged to remit part of his tax revenues into a common Federal Fund, which paid for public works, the police, and social services. Shan rulers, including the first president of the Union of Burma, Sao **Shwe Taik**, signed the agreement that resulted from the 1947 **Panglong Conference**, which recognized their traditional status and the autonomy of their polities. During the 1950s, the imposition of martial law by the central government following the incursions of the **Kuomintang** and **Tatmadaw** abuses of local populations eroded the rulers' authority. In March 1959, the Shan State Council, composed of the rulers, agreed to relinquish their "feudal" privileges. In April, each of them signed an agreement with the **Caretaker Government** of General **Ne Win** terminating his status, in exchange for compensation. The long and colorful history of the Shan States was at an end, but the consequence was not modernization and development but rather an anarchic situation in which the

Shans and other ethnic minorities have endured war and oppression. *See also* CONSTITUTION OF 1947; FEDERAL MOVEMENT; *HAW*; KARENNI STATES.

SHANS (TAI). Burma's most numerous ethnic minority, comprising an estimated 9 percent of the total population (more than 4 million people). They call themselves *Tai*. The Burmese name for them, *Shan*, apparently shares a common origin with *Siam*, the old country name for **Thailand**. The **Shan language** belongs to the Tai-Kadai group. As members of the larger Tai ethnic-linguistic group, they share close affinities with the people of Thailand and Laos, as well as Tai minorities in Vietnam, China, and India. Although most Shans live in **Shan State**, where other minority groups have been assimilated to their language and culture over the centuries, they are also found in significant numbers in **Kachin State, Kayah (Karenni) State**, and parts of **Burma Proper**. There are important dialectical and cultural differences among them, particularly between those who live in western Shan State, where they have been subject to strong Burmese influences, and the *Tai Khun* of **Keng Tung**, whose location remote from the center of Burman power has resulted in closer ties to the northern Thais and Chinese. A community of *Hkamti Shans* lives in Kachin State's **Hukwang Valley** and the upper reaches of the **Chindwin (Chindwinn) River**.

The history of Shan/Tai migration into Burma is unclear: It may have occurred as early as the first millennium CE, and involved the fortunes of the non-Han Chinese state of **Nan Chao**. By 1215, a Shan state had been established at Mogaung, in what is now Kachin State. The Mongol emperor Khubilai Khan's conquest of what is now China's Yunnan Province in the mid-13th century caused further waves of Tai migration.

Apart from language, a number of features constitute the distinctness of the Shans: Their religion is a distinct variety of Theravada **Buddhism**, with its own **Sangha**, holy sites, and artistic/architectural expression; unlike the "hill tribes" with whom they often live in proximity, they are cultivators of wetland **rice**; their political organization, a hereditary "feudal" system under a prince or *sawbwa* (*saohpa*) who was based in a fortified city-state (*möng*), is unique, although it has been adopted by other ethnic groups, such as the **Karenni**; and their material culture includes distinct characteristics, such as the wearing of trousers rather than a *longyi*. From the 14th to the 16th centuries, the Shans were the most powerful group in **Upper Burma**, although after the rise of the **Toungoo Dynasty** they were driven out, and many Shan principalities fell under Burmese suzerainty.

Since Burma became independent in 1948, the Shans have endured unbroken war and insurgency; the **State Law and Order Restoration Council/State Peace and Development Council** has used a "divide and rule" strategy (**cease-fires**) in Shan State since 1988 that has weakened their armed groups and exposed them to major **human rights** violations and compulsory cultural "Burmanization." Many Shans have left Burma to become "invisible" **refugees** in Thailand, hoping to find employment and refuge from persecution.

SHIN ARAHAN (ca. 11th CENTURY CE). A **Mon** monk, whom King **Anawrahta** (r. 1044–1077), founder of the **Pagan (Bagan) Dynasty**, charged with converting his subjects to the orthodox doctrines of Theravada **Buddhism**. He was also patronized by Anawrahta's successor, **Kyanzittha** (r. 1044–1112), and his image can be found inside the **Ananda Pahto**, which Kyanzittha ordered built.

SHINBYU. The major life-cycle ritual for nearly all male believers in Burmese **Buddhism**, the initiation of boys into the **Sangha**, although their sojourn as *koyin* or novice monks in a monastery is usually brief. The ceremony begins with a festive procession, the initiates being dressed in princely garb, like Gotama **Buddha** before his renunciation of the world. The ritual usually entails considerable expense, and sponsors gain much *kutho* (merit), because *shinbyu* is seen as a means of propagating the religion. Parents play an important role in the initiation, but when the boy's head is shaved and he dons the robes of a monk, they must do him obeisance. Through *shinbyu* the boy becomes a "dignified person." A life-cycle ritual for small girls, **ear boring**, often occurs at the same time as the initiation. Although it is a common practice for boys in Theravada Buddhist countries to spend some time in a monastery, it is especially important in Burma.

SHINSAWBU, QUEEN (r. 1453–1472). Burmese name for a **Mon** Queen of the **Wareru** Dynasty, called *Bannya Thaw* in the **Mon Language**. A daughter of **Razadarit**, she is renowned as a wise ruler and a devout Buddhist. Shinsawbu was married to the **Burman** king of **Ava (Inwa)** but fled to **Hanthawaddy** (modern-day **Pegu [Bago]**) in 1430, accompanied by two members of the **Sangha** who were her teachers, one of whom was **Dhammazedi**. Religiously inclined, she donated her weight in gold to gilding the **stupa** of the **Shwe Dagon Pagoda**, raised its height, and carried out extensive renovations of the pagoda grounds. After retiring from public life, she resided at **Dagon**, within sight of the pagoda. Her son-in-law, the former monk Dhammazedi (r. 1472–1492), succeeded her in 1472. Together, they are two of the most illustrious Mon monarchs, and she was the only woman to have ruled a major Burmese state.

SHITTHAUNG (SITTAUNG) TEMPLE. One of the most important **Buddhist** temples located in **Mrauk-U (Myohaung)** in **Arakan (Rakhine)**. Its name means "eighty thousand images." Built by King **Min Bin** in 1536, it is of rectangular shape, built of stone (unlike the monuments of **Pagan [Bagan]**, which are largely of brick), and is surmounted by numerous bell-shaped **stupas**. The temple's design, and the images and carvings found within, are representative of a distinct Arakanese style of Buddhist art and **architecture**.

"SHOE QUESTION." As in other Asian countries, it is the custom in Burma for people to doff their shoes before entering a house; on **pagoda** platforms and other sites associated with **Buddhism**, neither footwear nor stockings may be worn. These customs became issues in relations between the Burmese and British on two occasions in the 19th and 20th centuries. During the last years of King **Mindon's** reign in the 1870s, the British Indian government ordered its resident in **Mandalay** to refuse to take off his footwear when attending royal audiences, on the grounds that this was humiliating. As a result, the king refused to see any British envoys in person, as did his son and successor **Thibaw**, greatly hampering diplomatic communications.

The shoe question emerged in a different form in the second decade of the 20th century when the **Young Men's Buddhist Association** and other groups called for strict observance of the ban on footwear in pagodas; a respected member of the **Sangha**, the **Ledi Sayadaw**, wrote a treatise on the issue, "On the Impropriety of Wearing Shoes on Pagoda Platforms," which generated nationwide support for the ban. After a violent incident in which monks attacked shoe-wearing European visitors in Mandalay in 1919, the colonial government recognized the authority of pagoda trustees to exclude such persons. An exception was made for policemen and soldiers on duty, which was much resented by the Burmese.

Many British held the opinion that because they had previously been allowed to visit pagodas with their shoes on, the ban was simply a way of humiliating them; the matter stirred up considerable bitterness between British and Burmese, and before independence in 1948, most Westerners avoided such sites as the **Shwe Dagon Pagoda** that had previously been major **tourist** attractions. For the Burmese, success in getting the government to recognize the ban was a moral victory against the seemingly all-powerful British Empire.

SHWE DAGON PAGODA. Although it is not the tallest Buddhist **pagoda** in Burma, a distinction enjoyed by the **Shwemawdaw Pagoda** in **Pegu (Bago)**, the Shwe Dagon is regarded as the country's holiest Buddhist site, a place of pilgrimage and devotion for millions of people who congregate at its base each year. It is located on Singuttara (Theingottara) Hill, the southernmost elevation of the **Pegu (Bago) Yoma** mountain range, north of the central business district of modern **Rangoon (Yangon)** and west of **Kandawgyi Lake**. According to legend, Gotama **Buddha** gave eight of his hairs to two traveling merchants from a country known as *Ukkala* or *Okkala*, identified as the region around Rangoon. When they returned home from India, they located the hill and built a chamber to enshrine the holy relics with the assistance of *nats*, and discovered relics of the three earlier Buddhas of the present era: the staff of the Kakussanda Buddha, the robe of the Kassapa Buddha, and a water filter belonging to the Konagamana Buddha. Devotees believe the relics of all four Buddhas are still housed within the pagoda, giving it unmatched religious and devotional significance. Another legend relates that the Indian Emperor Asoka visited the Shwe Dagon in the third century BCE and sponsored its repair. A small **Mon** fishing settlement, **Dagon**, grew up around the site of the pagoda as early as the 11th century CE, giving the pagoda its name ("Golden Dagon").

Over the centuries, the Shwe Dagon Pagoda received generous donations from both **Mon** and **Burman (Bamar)** monarchs. The 15th-century Mon queen **Shinsawbu** was the first to gild the pagoda, offering her weight in gold and also donating a *hti* or umbrella to the pagoda's summit; her successor, **Dhammazedi**, carried out further renovation and donated a series of stone inscriptions that relate the pagoda's history. Both kings **Tabinshwehti** and **Bayinnaung**, Burman rulers who established their capital at **Pegu (Bago)** in the 16th century, carried out extensive renovations. After the pagoda was damaged in an earthquake in 1768, King **Hsinbyushin** repaired it, donated a *hti*, and raised it to its present height of 99 meters (326 feet). King **Mindon** donated a new *hti* for the pagoda in 1871, but the British authorities refused to allow him to come down to Rangoon to present it in person because this might indicate recognition of his sovereignty over **Lower** as well as **Upper Burma**. The **State Peace and Development Council** carried out extensive renovation of the pagoda in 1999, including replacement of Mindon's *hti*. *See also* SHWE DAGON PAGODA, ARCHITECTURE AND LAYOUT; SHWE DAGON PAGODA, POLITICAL SIGNIFICANCE OF.

SHWE DAGON PAGODA, ARCHITECTURE AND LAYOUT. The **Shwe Dagon Pagoda** is dense with religious and symbolic meaning. In physical terms, it can be understood in terms of three components: the 99-meter (326-foot)-high **stupa**, said to contain the relics of the four Buddhas of the present era, including eight hairs of Gotama **Buddha**; the **pagoda** platform upon which it is built, which is roughly rectangular in shape and five hectares in area; and clusters of devotion halls (*tazaung*), shrines, smaller stupas, and other sites that crowd the platform and reflect both the complexity of the Burmese **Buddhist** tradition and its syncretic association with subordinate non-Buddhist beliefs in gods and spirits (*nats*) and occult figures (*weikza*).

The stupa is believed to be solid, though a newspaper article published in 1968 tells of a person who claimed to have entered a tunnel many years before and discovered the "Relic Chamber" deep within. During their occupation of the pagoda platform, the British dug tunnels inside it. It is covered on the outside by gold leaf, which is replaced at regular intervals by devotees, although the "banana bud" is covered with gold plates. The total amount of gold adorning the stupa is estimated to be over three tons.

The bell-shaped stupa, raised above the platform on a plinth, is built up on successive, tapering levels, each with a distinct name relating to its physical appearance: the "square" and "octagonal terraces," the "bands," the "bell," the "twisted turban" molding, the "lotus," the "banana bud," the "umbrella" (*hti*), and the "diamond bud." Both the seven-tiered umbrella and the diamond bud are elaborate metal structures, studded with **gemstones**, bells, and small Buddha images. A flag-like device called the "vane" extends from the diamond bud near the apex of the stupa, whose structure in totality represents the different levels of worldly existence reaching up to the attainment of *nibbana* (*nirvana*).

The pagoda platform is approached by way of four stairways on the north, east, south, and west sides. The southern stairway is considered the main entrance, flanked at its base by two enormous *chinthe* (lions). All stairways except the western one (which was fitted recently with an escalator) contain small shops selling a wide variety of devotional items, such as flowers, beads, and sandalwood Buddha images. Pilgrims make their way around the platform in a clockwise direction.

The variety of buildings clustered around the stupa is overwhelming: shrines (planetary posts) for each of the eight days of the **Burmese week**; small stupas ringing the main stupa; devotional halls for each of the four Buddhas of the present era, located at the four cardinal directions; the Naung Daw Gyi (Elder Brother) pagoda, which is, according to legend, where the eight hairs of Gotama **Buddha** were kept before being encased in the main stupa; a sacred banyan tree; *nat* and *weikza* images and shrines; a reproduction of the Maha Bodhi stupa in India; and the stone inscriptions of King **Dhammazedi** that relate the pagoda's history. A distinctive feature of many of the buildings located on or approaching the platform is the classical Burmese *pyat-that* or tiered roof structure, originally built of wood, which makes a striking contrast with the immense solidity of the main stupa. Despite chronic shortages of electricity in **Rangoon**

(Yangon), the Shwe Dagon Pagoda is usually illuminated at night, an impressive site. *See also* ARCHITECTURE, RELIGIOUS; SHWE DAGON PAGODA; SHWE DAGON PAGODA, POLITICAL SIGNIFICANCE OF.

SHWE DAGON PAGODA, POLITICAL SIGNIFICANCE OF. Although primarily a religious site, the **Shwe Dagon Pagoda** has functioned as a contested public space of great importance during the colonial and postcolonial periods. It was occupied by British troops during the **First Anglo-Burmese War** of 1824–1826, and again in 1852 following the annexation of **Rangoon (Yangon)** and **Lower Burma** during the **Second Anglo-Burmese War**. Because of its strategic location, part of the **pagoda** platform, including the western staircase, was occupied by British troops between 1852 and 1929. Although maintenance of the pagoda remained in Burmese **Buddhist** hands and a Board of Trustees for this purpose was established in 1885, the remains of British soldiers were buried at the site (later removed), and part of the grounds was at one time used as an ammunition dump. The British also attempted to tunnel into the base of the pagoda. By the second decade of the 20th century, this continuing desecration, together with the unwillingness of Western visitors to the pagoda (and other Buddhist sites) to doff their shoes, had become political issues, taken up by the **Young Men's Buddhist Association** and the General Council of Buddhist Associations (later the **General Council of Burmese Associations**), which saw defense of the Buddhist religion as part of their nationalist program.

Participants in the **students'** strike against the act that established **Rangoon (Yangon) University** gathered at the Shwe Dagon on December 3, 1920, and a monument at the southwest corner of the pagoda platform commemorates this event. Subsequent student strikes, in 1936 and 1938–1939, used the pagoda and its environs as bases of operation, and it was an objective of a massive march undertaken in support of the 1938 **Oil Field Workers' Strike**. After World War II, Bogyoke **Aung San** made political speeches from the pagoda hill. On August 26, 1988, his daughter **Aung San Suu Kyi** made a speech in the public grounds adjoining the pagoda, attended by huge crowds, which marked the beginning of her leadership of the prodemocracy movement.

The military regime established on September 18, 1988, has sought to "occupy" the pagoda both physically and ideologically. In 1999, the **State Peace and Development Council** sponsored large-scale renovation, including replacement of the bejewelled *hti* (umbrella) at its apex, which had been donated by King **Mindon** in 1871. Official photographs show Lieutenant General **Khin Nyunt** and other high SPDC officers at the apex of the pagoda, presiding over installation of the new *hti*, images that advertise their spiritual worthiness and high status.

SHWE KYIN, NAI (1913–2003). Also known as Nai Ba Lwin (*nai* is a title for an adult male in the **Mon language**); **Mon** leader, founder, and president of the **New Mon State Party**. Born near **Moulmein (Mawlamyine)**, he studied at **Rangoon (Yangon) University** and served in the British navy. He was jailed by the Burmese government for participating in the uprising of 1948, became a leader of the Mon People's Front after his release from jail, and established the New Mon State Party in July 1958. Participating in various insurgent **united fronts**, he cooperated closely with the **Karen National Union** and became vice chairman of the **Democratic Alliance of Burma** in 1988. However, Nai Shwe Kyin signed a **cease-fire** with the **State Law and Order Restoration Council** in June 1995. After signing the cease-fire, he resided at Moulmein until his death in March 2003.

SHWE TAIK, SAO (1894–1962). Prominent **Shan (Tai)** leader and the Union of Burma's first president. Educated at the Shan Chiefs' School in **Taunggyi**, he served in the British army for 20 years and in 1927 was chosen as successor to his uncle as *sawbwa* of **Yawnghwe** by the state's council of ministers. After **World War II**, he initially opposed the policy of Prime Minister Clement Attlee's government to merge **Burma Proper** with the **Frontier Areas** in an independent Burma, but compromises reached with **Anti-Fascist People's Freedom League** President **Aung San** at the **Panglong Conference** of February 1947 persuaded him to sign the agreement that concluded the historic conference. He served as president of the Union of Burma from 1948 to

1952. From 1952 to 1960, he was speaker of the upper house of parliament, the Chamber of Nationalities. An advocate of reform and modernization in the **Shan States**, he endorsed the formal relinquishment of authority by the *sawbwas* to the Shan State government in 1959, but also played an important role in the **Federal Movement**. When General Ne Win seized power and shut down parliamentary government in March 1962, Sao Shwe Taik's house in **Rangoon (Yangon)** was surrounded by troops, and his youngest was son killed. He died at **Insein Jail** under ambiguous circumstances in November 1962. *See also* HEARN KHAM, SAO NANG.

SHWEBO. Located in **Sagaing Division** west of the **Irrawaddy (Ayeyarwady) River**, a town with an estimated population of 68,654 in 1996. It is renowned as the hometown of King **Alaungpaya**, founder of the **Konbaung Dynasty**, who briefly made it his royal capital (*Yadanatheinkha*) and base for the conquest of **Upper** and **Lower Burma**. Nearby are villages, Monhla and Chantha, where Portuguese followers of **Felipe de Brito** were exiled after the conquest of **Syriam (Thanlyin)** by King **Anaukpetlun** in 1613. Descendants of these people, who retained their Catholic religion, are known as **Bayingyi**. Shwebo was known as *Moksobomyo*, "town of the hunter Po," referring to Alaungpaya's early career.

SHWEMAWDAW PAGODA. A major **pagoda**, located in **Pegu (Bago)**, which is said to contain hair and tooth relics of Gotama **Buddha**. The **stupa** is 114 meters high and similar in bell-shaped design to the **Shwe Dagon Pagoda**, but taller. Legends trace its origins to the lifetime of the Buddha. Its history goes back more than a thousand years to early **Mon** kingdoms in the area, and it has always been considered of special significance to the Mon people. In 1912 and 1917, it was damaged by **earthquakes**, and was completely destroyed, with some loss of life, in an earthquake that occurred in May 1930. The Shwemawdaw was rebuilt in the early 1950s and is again one of the principal **Buddhist** sites in **Lower Burma**. *See also* ARCHITECTURE, RELIGIOUS; *HTI*.

SHWESANDAW PAGODA. A major **pagoda**, located on a hillside in **Prome (Pyay)**, said to contain hair relics of Gotama **Buddha**. It is

100 meters high, and, like the **Shwe Dagon**, **Shwemawdaw**, and **Kyaiktiyo** pagodas, is a major site of Buddhist pilgrimage in **Lower Burma**. *See also* ARCHITECTURE, RELIGIOUS.

SHWEZIGON PAGODA. One of the principal **Buddhist** monuments of **Pagan (Bagan)**, said to contain relics from the body of Gotama **Buddha**. It was built during the reigns of Kings **Anawrahta** (r. 1044–1077) and **Kyanzittha** (r. 1084–1113). Its design anticipates later Burmese pagodas, including the **Shwe Dagon**. Apart from Buddhism, the Shwezigon is associated historically with veneration of the **Thirty-seven Nats**, statues of whom are found near the pagoda platform. *See also* ARCHITECTURE, RELIGIOUS; PAGAN DYNASTY.

"SIDECARS" (*SAIQ-KA*). Three-wheeled, human-powered vehicles (trishaws) that are still popular in Burma's cities and towns, despite the increasing use of secondhand cars, buses, and other motor vehicles. Sidecars are made from sturdy bicycles, to which a third wheel has been attached parallel to the rear wheel. Two seats, facing front and back, are fitted between the rear wheels, and can accommodate two or more persons, including children sitting in a passenger's lap, as well as baggage. The design is different from the well-known Vietnamese *cyclo*, in which the two wheels and seats are fitted in front of the driver. Cheap and convenient for people on short errands, the owners rent them out to operators, who must pay them a fixed amount of money before they have take-home pay.

SINGAPORE, RELATIONS WITH. After the **State Law and Order Restoration Council (SLORC)** seized power in September 1988, Singapore forged close economic and security ties with the new military government. In late 1988, it became the first country to supply the SLORC with arms, brought by ship to **Rangoon (Yangon)** in October of that year, and it remains one of the most important sources of sophisticated weapon systems for the **State Peace and Development Council (SPDC)**. Singapore has served as a middleman in arms purchasing deals between Burma and third countries, such as Israel, and has provided "cyber-warfare" technology to **Military Intelligence**. In the economic field, statistics show that Singapore is the largest provider of **foreign investment** (US$1.49 billion by the late 1990s, though Chinese investment, for which the figures are undisclosed, may be larger) and Burma's second-largest trading partner. The Singapore government has rebuffed international criticisms of its support of the SPDC by claiming that engagement with Burma, in both the economic and national security spheres, is a vital national interest. *See also* MALAYSIA, RELATIONS WITH.

SINO-BURMESE. Persons of mixed **Chinese** and **Burman (Bamar)** or Burmese parentage. Although the number of **Chinese in Burma** was small compared to **Indians** during the British colonial period, Sino-Burmese generally had an easier time assimilating into Burmese society than **Anglo-Burmese** or Indo-Burmese, especially if they adopted Burmese customs, **language**, and the **Buddhist** religion as practiced in the country. Chinese ancestry does not seem to have been a barrier for many Sino-Burmese to become prominent, the most famous example being **Ne Win (Shu Maung)**. However, such persons would generally hide, or downplay, their Chinese roots. *See also* ANTI-CHINESE RIOTS.

SINYETHA PARTY. Known in English as the "Poor Man's Party," a political group formed in 1936 by Dr. **Ba Maw.** Its capture of 16 seats in the 1936 legislative election enabled Ba Maw to form a minority government. After his government's fall in February 1939, it became an opposition party and in October joined with the **Dobama Asiayone** and the **All Burma Students Union** in the **Freedom Bloc.**

SITTANG (SITTOUNG) RIVER. A major river system flowing from the **Pegu (Bago) Yoma** to the Gulf of **Martaban (Mottama)** for a length of about 500 kilometers. The Sittang Valley is home to a densely populated agricultural region. A bridge across the Sittang was the site of a major engagement between British and Japanese forces in February 1942. *See also* IRRAWADDY (AYEYARWADY) RIVER; SALWEEN (THANLWIN) RVER; WORLD WAR II IN BURMA (MILITARY OPERATIONS).

SITTWE (SITTWAY). The capital of **Arakan (Rakhine) State,** known as *Akyab* during the British colonial era, a Bengali name. Its population was estimated at 135,033 in 1996. Located at the mouth of the Kaladan River, where it empties into the Bay of Bengal, it became an important seaport and center for **rice** milling during the British colonial period. Before **World War II**, commercial aircraft flying into **Rangoon (Yangon)** from India and points west often stopped off at Sittwe.

SITWUNDAN. Local militias or territorial armies, numbering about a hundred, established with the encouragement of the government of Prime Minister U **Nu** in 1948 to counterbalance the **Burma Army**'s dependence on ethnic minorities, especially **Karens (Kayins)** and **Kachins**. When the **Karen National Union** uprising began in January 1949, the *sitwundan* played a decisive role in defending **Rangoon (Yangon)** from the rebels and quelling the "multicolored" communist and ethnic nationalist insurgencies. Major General **Ne Win**, who became head of the armed forces after the resignation of General **Smith Dun**, commanded the *sitwundan. See also* KA KWE YE; TATMADAW, HISTORY OF.

SLIM, GENERAL WILLIAM (1891–1970). One of the ablest generals of **World War II**. He commanded Allied troops in Burma during the Japanese invasion of December 1941–June 1942 and presided over their retreat, largely intact, to northeastern India. He recognized the importance of air support for ground operations and backed Brigadier Orde Wingate's **Chindit** operations in 1943–1944. Slim repulsed the Japanese **Imphal Campaign** in March–June 1944 and, as commander of the million-man-strong XIVth Army, retook Burma from the Japanese in 1945. His use of deceptive tactics in the capture of **Meiktila** and **Mandalay** in February–March was highly successful, and the Allied offensive against the Japanese in central Burma turned into a rout. During a meeting with **Aung San** in May 1945, he gained the latter's cooperation for joint operations against the retreating Japanese forces, although he also warned him that he and his officers might be punished for collaborating with the Japanese. *See also* MOUNTBATTEN, LORD LOUIS; PATRIOTIC BURMESE FORCES; WORLD WAR II IN BURMA (MILITARY OPERATIONS).

SLORC ANNOUNCEMENT NO. 1/90. Opposition parties, especially the **National League for Democracy**, won a landslide victory in the **General Election of May 27, 1990**, but the **State Law and Order Restoration Council (SLORC)** refused to allow formation of a government of elected **Pyithu Hluttaw** representatives. On July 27, 1990, it promulgated "Announcement No. 1/90," which declared that a transfer of power to civilian authorities could not take place until a new constitution was drafted, and that the elected representatives were responsible for doing so. It also declared that the junta, a martial law regime "not bound by any constitution," had exclusive legislative and judicial power and exercised administrative authority with the assistance of lower-level governmental bodies. The junta gave the **National Convention**, first convened in 1993, the responsibility of drafting a new basic law. Signed by SLORC Secretary-1 **Khin Nyunt**, Announcement 1/90 expressed the SLORC's determination to maintain complete control over the political transition process. *See also* GANDHI HALL DECLARATION.

SMIM HTAW BUDDHAKETI (r. 1740–1747). Following an uprising in **Lower Burma** against the **Burman** state at **Ava (Inwa)** in 1740, Smim Htaw, a member of the **Sangha**, became ruler of a restored **Mon** state at **Hanthawaddy** (modern-day **Pegu [Bago]**). His multiethnic supporters included Burmans and **Karens (Kayins)**, as well as Mons. Attempting to capture Ava, he occupied **Prome (Pyay)** and **Toungoo (Taungoo)**, although an offensive north along the **Irrawaddy (Ayeyardwady) River** was repulsed. He gained a reputation for just and gentle rule, but was indecisive, and was overthrown in a palace coup in 1747. The successor was his chief minister, **Binnya Dala (Bannya Dala)**. Mon nationalists regard Smim Htaw Buddhaketi as one of their major historical figures.

SMITH DUN, GENERAL (1906–1979). A **Karen (Kayin)** officer who fought on the British side in **World War II** and was appointed commander of the **Burma Army** when independence was proclaimed in January 1948. In January 1949, he was obliged to resign because of the insurrection instigated by the **Karen National Union**; he was succeeded by **Ne Win**. Ne Win's appointment marked the beginning of the systematic "Burmanization" of the **Tatmadaw**. Smith Dun's experiences are recounted in his biography, *Memoirs of the Four-Foot Colonel*.

SOCCER (FOOTBALL) IN BURMA. Burma's most popular sport, soccer was introduced to the country during the British colonial period, allegedly by **James G. Scott**, who claimed the Burmese had a talent for it "because they like to fight." In his famous essay "Shooting an Elephant," **George Orwell** describes the tensions that emerged during games played by European and Burmese teams. During the early **Ne Win** period, Burma had the strongest team in the Southeast Asia region, winning the Asian Games soccer championship twice. Though the quality of the team later declined, its successes against fellow members of the **Association of Southeast Asian Nations** in recent years have stirred national pride.

Like **Thingyan** and popular music, soccer offers occasions for ordinary Burmese to blow off steam. A number of observers have reported that in domestic matches, when a civilian team plays one fielded by the **Tatmadaw**, there are often lusty cheers for the former and boos for the latter. At present, it is estimated that Burma has 20,000 soccer players, organized into 600 clubs. *See also* SPORTS, TRADITIONAL.

SOCIALIST PARTY OF BURMA (SPB). Established at the end of **World War II** and led by Thakin Mya, its president, U **Ba Swe**, and U Kyaw Nyein. It was the principal rival of the **Communist Party of Burma** during the postwar independence struggle, and after independence was the most powerful group inside the **Anti-Fascist People's Freedom League (AFPFL)** united front. U Ba Swe and U Kyaw Nyein served in the cabinets of Prime Minister U **Nu**, Ba Swe also serving as prime minister in 1956–1957. The party also exercised its influence through its affiliates, the All Burma Peasants' Organization and the Trade Union Congress (Burma), the latter being the largest trade union federation in the country during the 1950s. Within the SPB, there was intense debate about what form socialism should take, Marxism or a more moderate "Burmese" version. Left-wing socialists (known as "Red Socialists"), favoring the former, broke away from the party and the AFPFL and formed the Burma

Workers and Peasants Party in 1950. When the AFPFL split in 1958, the mainstream Socialists inside the League constituted the "Stable" faction, a rival to Prime Minister U Nu's "Clean" faction.

SOE, THAKIN (1905–1989). A prominent communist leader, member of the **Dobama Asiayone**, and a founding member of the **Communist Party of Burma (CPB)** when it was established in August 1939. During **World War II**, he served as secretary general of the CPB, but he broke with the mainstream communists and established his own party, the Communist Party–Red Flag, in February 1946. Until captured by government troops in 1970, he operated underground, mostly in the **Arakan (Rakhine) Yoma** region. Granted amnesty by the **Ne Win** regime in 1980, he played a peripheral role in the prodemocracy movement of 1988, as a patron of the Unity and Development Party.

SOE WIN. Lieutenant general, commander of the **Air Force**, and First Secretary (Secretary-1) of the **State Peace and Development Council (SPDC)**. Following the purge of **Khin Nyunt** in October 2004, he was also appointed Burma's prime minister. A graduate of the 12th class of the **Defence Services Academy**, he rose to the position of SPDC Secretary-2 in February 2003 as successor to Lieutenant-General **Tin Oo**, who died in a helicopter crash in **Karen (Kayin) State** on February 19, 2001. On August 25, 2003, he replaced Khin Nyunt as Secretary-1. He is close to Senior General **Than Shwe** and is a hard-liner, refusing to compromise with the democratic opposition. He reportedly ordered troops to fire on protesters during the **Rangoon General Hospital Incident** in August 1988 and was also partly responsible for the **"Black Friday" Incident** in May 2003. *See also* STATE PEACE AND DEVELOPMENT COUNCIL, INTERNAL DYNAMICS.

SPORTS, TRADITIONAL. Although **soccer (football)** is Burma's most popular sport, traditional sports have a wide following. The aim of *chinlon*, a game played with a cane or rattan ball (similar to *takraw* in Thailand or *sepak raga* in Malaysia), is for players to keep the ball in the air using only the feet or legs; a variant is played with a net, like volleyball. *Le-thwei* is a form of kick-boxing similar to Thailand's *muay thai*, though rougher and with more informal rules; the loser in a match is the one who wipes blood from his face a certain number of times. *Le-thwei* matches frequently occur at *pwe*, and national championships are held at Aung San Stadium in **Rangoon (Yangon)**. For poor but tough young men, the sport promises a kind of upward mobility, or at least winnings from matches to supplement meagre earnings. A form of wrestling similar to Japanese *sumo* is found in **Arakan (Rakhine) State**, and traditional regattas involving long boats with many rowers are often held on Rangoon's **Kandawgyi Lake**.

SRI KSETRA (THAYEKKHITTAYA). Capital of the **Pyus** from the fifth to the ninth centuries CE, located at Hmawza near **Prome (Pyay)** in what is now **Pegu (Bago) Division**. Chinese chroniclers described it as a large city with a circular wall (8.5 miles in circumference), 12 gates, and more than a hundred monasteries, where gold and silver currency was used (coins were not minted by the Burmese until the mid-19th century). It was a major seaport, being located at that time near the sea. The Archeological Survey of India began excavations on the site in 1907. Today, the most prominent features of the Sri Ksetra ruins are remains of the wall and several **pagodas**, including the cylindrical-shaped Bawbawgyi and the conical Payagyi and Payama, which have a design distinct from later pagodas, being strongly influenced by India. G. E. Harvey describes Sri Ksetra as "the most extensive site in Burma, larger than any city the Burmese ever built, possibly because the whole population dwelt inside the wall" (*History of Burma*, 1967, 12).

STATE. *Pyi-ne* (plural: *pyi-ne-myar*) in the **Burmese (Myanmar)** language; refers to the major unit of territorial administration below the national level (along with **divisions**) and above the **district** and **township** levels. There are seven states: **Arakan (Rakhine), Chin, Kachin, Karen (Kayin), Kayah, Mon,** and **Shan**. Under the **Constitution of 1947**, the states, which generally corresponded to the territory of the colonial-era **Frontier Areas**, had quasi-federal powers and were recognized as the homelands of the major ethnic minorities. However, the distinction between states and divisions (which also number seven) became administratively and politically irrelevant after the **Constitution of 1974** was adopted, and the new constitution being drafted by the reconvened **National Convention** may weaken their identity further by granting smaller ethnic groups, such as the **Was**, "autonomous regions." At present, each state is under the authority of a "Peace and Development Council" composed of **Tatmadaw** officers, under the command of the **State Peace and Development Council**.

STATE COUNCIL. In the political system established by the **Constitution of 1974**, one of the two major executive organs of the national government, the second being the Council of Ministers. Composed of the prime minister and 14 members chosen by the **Pyithu Hluttaw** from among its members and another 14 chosen from **state**- and **division**-level People's Assemblies, its role was to "direct, supervise and coordinate" the operations of central and regional/local government organs. Chairman of the State Council was ex officio president of the Socialist Republic of the Union of Burma and head of state: **Ne Win** from 1974 to 1981, **San Yu** from 1981 to 1988, **Sein Lwin** July–August 1988, and Dr. **Maung Maung** August–September 1988.

STATE LAW AND ORDER RESTORATION COUNCIL (SLORC). The martial law regime that seized power on September 18, 1988. Reorganized as the **State Peace and Development Council (SPDC)** in November 1997, it is a junta consisting of the highest-ranking military officers. According to **SLORC Announcement No. 1/90**, issued in July 1990, it was not bound by any constitution and exercised sole legislative, executive, and judicial authority (as does its successor the SPDC). The name in Burmese is *Naing-ngandaw Nyein Wut Pyi Pya Yae* (shortened to *Na-Wa-Ta*), which literally means "Committee for the Construction of Tranquility and Obedience in the Country."

The SLORC was proclaimed over the state radio on the afternoon of September 18. It ordered the armed forces to suppress popular opposition in **Rangoon (Yangon)** and other localities, resulting in as many as 1,000 civilian deaths in the capital alone. Its seizure of power is sometimes erroneously referred to as a "coup d'état" similar to the one on March 2, 1962, which brought General **Ne Win** to power. But it was neither an action by the military against a government of which it disapproved (SLORC commanders were loyal to retired leader Ne Win) nor a *putsch* carried out by a single military faction against rivals (because the top levels of the **Tatmadaw** remained united behind the new junta). Its legal, or extralegal, status appears to have been inspired by the concept of "an aid to civil power," found in the British colonial-era code of laws, in which the military may be empowered to intervene "in a state of extreme emergency" to protect lives and property. According to some sources, Dr. **Maung Maung**, serving as president at the time, advised SLORC chairman General **Saw Maung** about the use of this legal justification on the eve of the takeover.

The mission of the SLORC was defined in four objectives: restoration of law and order; facilitation of transportation and communications through adequate security; provision of the people with food and other basic necessities; and successful staging of democratic, multiparty elections after the three prior objectives have been met. Although SLORC leaders repeatedly emphasized the transitional nature of military rule and the need to establish a democratically elected civilian government, reformulation of the junta's objectives in the more vague **Three Main National Causes** ("Non-Disintegration of the Union," "Non-Disintegration of National Solidarity," and "Consolidation of Sovereignty") in the early 1990s indicated that the transition process would be a lengthy one. Regime spokesmen defined the SLORC's role as historically analogous to that of the 1962 **Revolutionary Council**, which over a dozen years prepared the way for establishment of a new constitutional order, the Socialist Republic of the Union of Burma.

On the **state/division, township**, and ward/village tract levels, Law and Order Restoration Councils composed of lower-ranking military officers were established to control the civil administration, in a pattern similar to the post-1962 **Security and Administration Committees**.

At the time of its formation, the SLORC junta consisted of 19 members: Chairman General **Saw Maung** (later Senior General), who served concurrently as commander in chief of the Tatmadaw, prime minister, defense minister, and foreign minister; vice chairman lieutenant general **Than Shwe**, concurrently commander of the **army**; Secretary-1 Brigadier (later Lieutenant General) **Khin Nyunt**, who was also head of **Military Intelligence**; Secretary-2 Colonel **Tin Oo**; the commanders of the **navy** and **air force**; the adjutant-general;

the quartermaster general; the commanders of the Bureaus of Special Operations 1 and 2; and the heads of the country's nine **regional military commands** (later expanded to 12). The most important change in SLORC personnel was the retirement of Saw Maung as SLORC chairman on April 23, 1992 and his replacement by Than Shwe.

STATE PEACE AND DEVELOPMENT COUNCIL (SPDC). Established on November 15, 1997, the State Peace and Development Council is the successor of the original post-1988 martial law regime, the **State Law and Order Restoration Council (SLORC)**. In Burmese, its name is *Naing-ngandaw Aye Chan Tar Yar Yae Hint Phont Phyo Yae*. The name change, emphasizing "peace" rather than "order," was probably motivated by the junta's desire to improve its image, but substantial changes in personnel also occurred.

The four top SLORC leaders, Chairman and Senior General **Than Shwe**, Vice Chairman General **Maung Aye**, Secretary-1 Lieutenant General **Khin Nyunt**, and Secretary-2 Lieutenant General **Tin Oo**, retained their positions, but a Secretary-3, Lieutenant General Win Myint, was added, along with newly appointed commanders for the **navy** and **air force** and for six of Burma's 12 **regional military commands**. Altogether, the SPDC at its inception had 19 members.

The personnel changes infused new blood into the junta and purged SLORC and cabinet members (the cabinet was also reshuffled) who were considered excessively corrupt. Fourteen retired generals were appointed to a powerless "Advisory Board," but this was dissolved in June 1998.

In February 2001, Secretary-2 Tin Oo was killed in a helicopter crash; in November, Secretary-3 Win Myint was dismissed on corruption charges. By early 2003, the junta had been reshaped into a 13-member body that included a new Secretary-2, Air Force Lieutenant General **Soe Win**, who on orders of Than Shwe replaced Khin Nyunt as Secretary-1 in August of that year. Khin Nyunt was appointed prime minister (one of Than Shwe's posts), widely considered a demotion. In October 2004, Khin Nyunt was charged with corruption, arrested, and dismissed from his posts as prime minister and director of **Military Intelligence**. *See also* STATE PEACE AND DEVELOPMENT COUNCIL, INTERNAL DYNAMICS.

Members of the State Peace and Development Council (as of January 1, 2005)

NAME AND RANK	POSITION
1. Senior General THAN SHWE SHWE	Chairman of SPDC; Commander-in-Chief of Defence Services (*Tatmadaw*)
2. Deputy Senior General MAUNG AYE	Vice-Chairman of SPDC; Deputy Commander-in-Chief of Defence Services (*Tatmadaw*); Commander-in-Chief (Army)
3. General THURA SHWE Mann	Member of SPDC; Joint Chief of Staff of the Army, Navy and Air Force
4. Lieutenant General SOE WIN	SPDC Secretary 1; Air Defence General
5. Lieutenant-General THEIN SEIN	SPDC Secretary 2; Adjutant General
6. Lieutenant-General THIHA THURA TIN AUNG MYINT OO	SPDC Member; Quartermaster General
7. Lieutenant-General KYAW WIN	SPDC Member; Chief of Armed Forces Training
8. Lieutenant-General TIN AYE	SPDC Member; Chief of Military Ordnance
9. Lieutenant-General YE MYINT	SPDC Member; Chief of Bureau of Special Operations-1 (covering Kachin, Chin States, Mandalay, Magwe, and Sagaing Divisions)
10. Lietenant-General AUNG HTWE	SPDC Member; Chief of Bureau of Special Operations-2 (Kayah, Shan States)
11. Lieutenant-General KHIN MAUNG THAN	SPDC Member; Chief of Bureau of Special

	Operations-3 (Pegu, Rangoon, Irrawaddy Divisions, Arakan State)
12. Lieutenant-General MAUNG BO	SPDC Member; Chief of Bureau of Special Operations-4 (Karen, Mon States, Tenasserim Division)

STATE PEACE AND DEVELOPMENT COUNCIL (SPDC), IN-TERNAL DYNAMICS. Because of the secrecy of its operations and tight state control of sensitive information, knowledge of the internal political dynamics of the military SPDC junta is limited, though rumors abound. Before the purge of Lieutenant General **Khin Nyunt** in October 2004, he and SPDC Vice Chairman **Maung Aye** differed on a number of important policy issues and had their own supporters within the **Tatmadaw**; Khin Nyunt's power base was within **Military Intelligence**, while Maung Aye's was within the ranks of the regular army. The former supported limited economic opening to the outside world, close relations with the **People's Republic of China**, and development of the border areas where minority nationality armed groups have signed **cease-fires** with the central government. Maung Aye was more conservative in economic policy, suspicious of outside influences, and advocated a hard line toward the minorities. Both opposed political liberalization, but while Maung Aye and his supporters have advocated harsh treatment of **Aung San Suu Kyi** and the **National League for Democracy**, Secretary-1 was believed to have favored a more subtle and manipulative approach, to divide the opposition. Few observers believed that differences between the two leaders would result in a split in the Tatmadaw.

Traditional Burmese political culture tends to favor strong, personal leaders, such as **Ne Win**. The post–Ne Win era, under both the SPDC and the previous **State Law and Order Restoration Council**, has been a transition period in which "collegial dictatorship" has resulted in policy paralysis and indecisiveness on such issues as economic reform. At the beginning of the 21st century, SPDC Chairman Senior General **Than Shwe** has emerged as Ne Win's successor as a "one man" leader, while Khin Nyunt has been purged and Maung Aye has apparently lost power. Than Shwe's worldview is deeply conservative and isolationist, and it is unlikely that he would undertake needed reforms of the political economy. Moreover, he is personally antagonistic to Daw Suu Kyi and may have had a hand in the "**Black Friday**" Incident of May 30, 2003, which was instigated by members of the **Union Solidarity and Development Association (USDA)**, of which he is the patron. In August 2003, Than Shwe relieved the "moderate" Khin Nyunt of his post as SPDC Secretary-1, appointing him prime minister. This was seen by most Burma watchers as a demotion. Khin Nyunt's arrest and dismissal as prime minister 14 months later confimed his waning power, rather than representing a sudden, fundamental change in SPDC factional dynamics. With most of Khin Nyunt's Military Intelligence subordinates forcibly retired or arrested, it seemed that Than Shwe had further consolidated his power, and that his most loyal subordinates, Prime Minister **Soe Win** and General **Thura Shwe Mann**, are also in the ascendant. With a single line of authority running from Than Shwe through his subordinates to the rank and file below, the period of SPDC transition and "collegial dictatorship" may be over.

STEVENSON, HENRY NOEL COCHRANE. British colonial official who advocated establishment of a political/administrative unit consisting of the peoples of the **Frontier Areas** separate from an independent Burma. At the beginning of **World War II**, Stevenson was superintendent of the **Chin** Hills, and he organized and commanded the Chin Levies to fight the Japanese. In 1943, he published *The Economics of the Central Chin Tribes*. At war's end, he was appointed director of the Frontier Areas Administration by the governor, Reginald Dorman-Smith, and made his **United Frontier Union** proposal, which, if adopted, would have created a jurisdiction within the British Commonwealth for the "hill tribes." Excoriated by the **Anti-Fascist People's Freedom League (AFPFL)** for promoting "divide and rule," his proposal was rejected by the Labour government of Clement Attlee.

Although responsive to the demands of the AFPFL and **Aung San**, the Attlee government was ignorant of or indifferent to the sentiments of the ethnic minority peoples, though they had loyally supported Britain during the war. Against a background of five-and-a-half decades of ethnic insurgency and civil war, Stevenson's repeated warnings on the need for London to promote the economic and social development of the Frontier Areas and to recognize their aspirations was highly prescient. *See also* AUNG SAN–ATTLEE AGREEMENT; FRONTIER AREAS COMMITTEE OF ENQUIRY; PANGLONG CONFERENCE.

STUDENT DEMONSTRATIONS (1996). The year 1996 witnessed the largest student demonstrations in **Rangoon (Yangon)** since the **Democracy Summer** of 1988. In October 1996, a fight between students of **Rangoon (Yangon) Institute of Technology** and the auxiliary police resulted in arrests of the former. Although they were released, other students were detained for protesting against police brutality; this inspired demonstrations in early December. In the evening of December 6, some 1,000 students (with thousands of people looking on) held a protest at Hledan Junction near **Rangoon (Yangon) University**, demanding, among other things, reestablishment of the students' union. In the early morning of December 7, the couple of hundred students remaining at the junction were attacked by troops and **Riot Police** wielding fire hoses. The leaders were arrested, but "hit-and-run" protests continued. The 1996 demonstrations convinced the **State Law and Order Restoration Council** to keep universities closed during most of the remainder of the 1990s and to reorganize colleges and universities to prevent student activism. *See also* EDUCATION, HIGHER; FOUR EIGHTS MOVEMENT; STUDENTS, HISTORICAL ROLE OF; TEA SHOP INCIDENT; U THANT INCIDENT.

STUDENTS, HISTORICAL ROLE OF. Beginning in the early 20th century, university and high school students played an active and sometimes leading role in struggles against British colonial rule. Following independence in 1948, they organized opposition movements against the government in power, especially after **Ne Win** established the **Revolutionary Council** in 1962. The first important student movement, the boycott against the act that established **Rangoon (Yangon) University**, began on December 3, 1920 (celebrated as Burma's National Day). By the mid-1930s, the **Rangoon University Students Union** had become radicalized, and a second major student strike took place in February 1936 when two of its leaders, Thakins

Aung San and **Nu**, were expelled from the university by the British authorities. Students also protested in December 1938 after some students were arrested for assisting the **Oil Field Workers' Strike**. Most students respected Prime Minister U Nu, a highly educated man. Despite the influence of the **Communist Party of Burma** on campuses, his government generally treated student demonstrators leniently. Under Ne Win, the government's attitude changed completely, as reflected in the **July 7, 1962 Incident**, in which a large number of students were shot dead by the **Tatmadaw**. Despite high casualties inflicted by the authorities and the imprisonment of thousands of students, their opposition persisted stubbornly throughout the 1962–1988 period, when Ne Win was in power, including the People's Peace Committee demonstrations (1963), the Southeast Asian Games demonstrations (1969), the **U Thant Incident (1974)**, protests demanding the release of imprisoned students (1975), the movement commemorating the birth centenary of Thakin **Kodaw Hmaing** (1976), and student protest over the **demonetization** order of September 1987. The year 1988 saw the most massive expression of student militancy in the history of independent Burma, beginning with the demonstrations of March at the **Rangoon (Yangon) Institute of Technology** and Rangoon University and culminating in **Democracy Summer**.

After the **State Law and Order Restoration Council** seized power in September 1988, many student oppositionists went to the border areas to fight the new military regime, their most important organization being the **All Burma Students' Democratic Front**. Some activists, such as **Min Ko Naing**, chose to work inside the country. By keeping the campuses closed during much of the period between 1988 and 2001, offering an increasing number of courses through distance education, intensifying **Military Intelligence** surveillance of students, and moving universities outside Rangoon's city center to remote locations, the authorities largely succeeded in curtailing student activism, although demonstrations broke out briefly in December 1996. *See also* ALL BURMA FEDERATION OF STUDENTS UNIONS; ALL BURMA STUDENTS UNION; AUNG GYAW, BO; DAGON UNIVERSITY; DEMOCRATIC PARTY FOR A NEW SOCIETY; EDUCATION, HIGHER; MAUNG PHONE MAW; PEACE TALKS; TEA SHOP INCIDENT; WHITE BRIDGE INCIDENT.

STUPA. A term generally synonymous with **pagoda** (*zedi* in the **Burmese [Myanmar] language**), but referring especially to the mound or spire surmounting a relic chamber containing objects associated with the person of Gotama **Buddha**. The oldest is the Great Stupa at Sanchi, India, built by the Emperor Ashoka in the third century BCE. The Burmese form of stupa appears to be derived from bell-shaped Sri Lankan designs. The exteriors of many of the most important Burmese stupas, such as the 99-meter (326-foot)-high **Shwe Dagon Pagoda**, are gilded. *See also* ARCHITECTURE, RELIGIOUS; SHWEMAWDAW PAGODA; SHWESANDAW PAGODA; SHWEZIGON PAGODA.

SULE PAGODA. When the colonial city of **Rangoon (Yangon)** was constructed in a rectangular grid pattern by British engineers after the **Second Anglo-Burmese War**, the Sule Pagoda was chosen as the town center. Reputed to be over 2,000 years old, it is 46 meters high and is believed to contain a hair relic of Gotama **Buddha**. Aside from its location in the city center, surrounded by lively streets and shops, the pagoda's most striking feature is a large image of the Sule *Nat*, an ogre (*bilu*) who converted to Buddhism, who points with his hand toward the place where the **Shwe Dagon Pagoda** stands. The pagoda is also known by its **Mon** name, *Kyaik Athok*. Since the colonial era, the area around the Sule Pagoda and Rangoon City Hall has frequently been the site of popular rallies and demonstrations. *See also* DEMOCRACY SUMMER.

SUPAYALAT, QUEEN (1859?–1925). A secondary queen of King **Thibaw** (r. 1878–1885) who quickly gained control over the last monarch of the **Konbaung Dynasty** with the backing of a court faction and played a major role in the fatal decision of Thibaw's government to take a hard line against the British. Ferociously jealous of her weak husband, greedy, and cruel (though contemporary sources may exaggerate), she was exiled with him to Ratnagiri, in **India**, following the **Third Anglo-Burmese War**. In the closing years of her life, she was allowed to return to **Rangoon (Yangon)**, where she lived in near penury, largely ignored by a new generation of Burmese patriots. F. Tennyson Jesse provides a vivid picture of her in *The Lacquer Lady*.

SUZUKI KEIJI, COLONEL (1894–1967). Japanese military officer who, in the guise of a correspondent for the *Yomiuri Shimbun* newspaper, "Minami Masuyo," traveled to Burma in 1940 to collect intelligence and make contacts with nationalists. His talks with Thakin **Kodaw Hmaing**, Dr. Thein Maung, and Thakin Mya convinced him that **Japanese** support of a well-organized Burmese uprising against the British could serve Tokyo's war aims, including shutting down the **Burma Road**. When Thakins **Aung San** and Hla Myaing left Burma for **China** in search of foreign support for the independence movement, Suzuki arranged in November 1940 to have them brought to Tokyo. Imperial General Headquarters made Suzuki head of the **Minami Kikan** (Minami Organ), established on February 1, 1941. He undertook the training of the **Thirty Comrades** at Hainan, China, and made them the nucleus of the **Burma Independence Army (BIA)**, which was established soon after war broke out in December 1941. Assuming the Burmese name **Bo Mogyo** (Commander Thunderbolt), which had prophetic associations, he served as commander of the BIA until June 1942, when he was transferred back to Japan. Dr. **Ba Maw** compared him to Lawrence of Arabia, "an adventurer with something like a sense of mission" (*Breakthrough in Burma*, 1968, 111). Most Burmese nationalists who worked with him believed his support for immediate Burmese independence was sincere. U **Nu** quotes him as saying that if the Burmese really wanted independence, they should take up arms, even against the Japanese. This opinion was obviously not shared by the regular Japanese military, who wanted to fully exploit Burma's human and natural resources for the war effort. *See also* JAPANESE OCCUPATION.

SYRIAM (THANLYIN). Now part of the **Rangoon (Yangon)** municipal area, located across the Pegu (Bago) River from downtown Rangoon. It is a town of historical importance. In the early 17th century, the Portuguese **Felipe de Brito** made it his personal appanage, until it fell to King **Anaukpetlun** in 1613. During the eighteenth century, there were competing British and French "factories" (trading depots) at Syriam, but after its fall to King **Alaungpaya** in July 1756, Rangoon became Burma's principal port. Little remains of this colorful past, save for some Portuguese ruins and an old **Armenian** church. During the British colonial period, a large oil refinery was built at Syriam. It was destroyed as part of the British "policy of denial" to the invading Japanese in 1942, but was reconstructed after **World War II**. A Chinese-built bridge spans the Pegu River between Rangoon and Syriam, making it unnecessary to take a ferry between the two places.

– T –

TABINSHWEHTI, KING (r. 1531–1550). Second monarch of the **Toungoo (Taungoo) Dynasty**, he restored the fortunes of the **Burmans (Bamars)** by conquering the **Mon** state of **Hanthawaddy** (modern day **Pegu [Bago]**) in **Lower Burma** in 1539, extinguishing the line of monarchs established by **Wareru**, and extended his realm to the south by occupying **Martaban (Mottama)**, **Moulmein (Mawlamyine)**, and **Tavoy (Dawei)**. To the north, he captured **Prome (Pyay)** and campaigned in **Upper Burma**, where the **Shans** had occupied **Ava (Inwa)**. Recognizing the equality of Mons and Burmans, he established Hanthawaddy as his royal capital in 1546. He sought unsuccessfully to subjugate **Arakan** and Siam **(Thailand)**, and was assassinated by Mon rebels in 1550. *See also* BAYINNAUNG.

TARONS (TARONGS). One of Burma's smallest and most isolated ethnic groups, who live near **Hkakabo Razi** in northern **Kachin State**. Their existence was confirmed only in 1954, when they were encountered by a **Tatmadaw** detachment carrying out a "flag march" to the Burma–China border. They have been called the only Mongoloid "pygmy tribe" in existence, though their short stature may be due to poor nutrition and inbreeding within the small population. In 1997, a group of Kachin Christians from **Myitkyina** visited the Tarons and discovered that they had intermarried with neighboring (Rawang) **Kachins**, and only a handful were "pure-blooded."

TAT. "Army" in the **Burmese (Myanmar) language**. During the early 20th century, the **Young Men's Buddhist Association** advocated the establishment of military training corps for young Burmese men, but it was only in 1930 that the *Ye Tat* (People's Army) was established, under the auspices of the **General Council of Burmese Associations**. It became extremely popular, especially in the countryside, although the British colonial government prohibited its training with real weapons. The *Ye Tat* played an important role in National Day and other celebrations and was much imitated, especially by political parties and **student** activist groups. The **Dobama Asiayone** established its own *tat*, as did the **Rangoon University Students' Union.** Dr. **Ba Maw's Sinyetha Party** had a paramilitary unit called the *Dahma Tat* (*dahma* being a hewing knife used by farmers), and U **Saw** organized the **Galon** *Tat*, which often attacked the meetings of rival political groups and behaved like the Blackshirts of Mussolini (whom U Saw admired). By 1939, the *Galon Tat* had reached a strength of around 100,000.

TATMADAW. The armed forces of the Union of Myanmar. Because this Burmese term contains the honorific suffix *"daw,"* many persons critical of the **State Peace and Development Council (SPDC)** regime prefer the generic term *sit tat* ("army"). But Tatmadaw remains the most common term to describe the armed forces in the **Burmese (Myanmar) language**, having been first used by its founder, General **Aung San.**

The Tatmadaw comprises three services: the **Army (Tatmadaw Kyi), Navy (Tatmadaw Yay),** and **Air Force (Tatmadaw Lei).** Of the three, the Army is the most important in terms of political influence, number of personnel, and historical role in fighting both domestic and foreign opponents of the central government. Since 1988, all three services have undergone significant expansion in personnel and equipment. In the late 1980s, the total number of Tatmadaw personnel was 186,000. By the end of the 20th century, this number exceeded 400,000, with the largest increase in the Army. Economic difficulties in the early 21st century seem to have precluded further expansion to a stated goal of 500,000.

The Tatmadaw is under the authority of the Ministry of Defence, which in 2005 was headed by Senior General **Than Shwe**, who served concurrently as chairman of the SPDC and commander in chief of the armed forces. The Ministry of Defence functions both as a government department and as an integrated command headquarters for the three services, and was located in the walled and heavily guarded **Defence Services Compound** in downtown **Rangoon (Yangon)** before being relocated to a new headquarters at Eight Mile Junction, north of **Inya Lake.** In 2005, Tatmadaw and defense ministry headquarters were transferred to the new national capital outside of **Pyinmana**, in **Mandalay Division**. Since 1989, the commander in chief of the Tatmadaw has been a senior (five-star) general, the commander of the Army has been a full (four-star) general, and the commanders of the Navy and Air Force have been lieutenant (three-star) generals. Burma is divided into 12 **Regional Military Commands (RMC)**, increased from nine during the 1990s. Each RMC commander is an Army officer of major general (two-star) rank.

Unlike the armed forces in most Western countries, the Tatmadaw plays primarily an internal security role. For example, **Light Infantry Division** 11, a rapid response force, was established to keep order in Rangoon after the 1988 unrest. However, enhanced numbers and new equipment also give it greater ability to project its power beyond its borders, especially in historically tense and complex relations with **Thailand**. *See also* ADMINISTRATION OF BURMA, STATE LAW AND ORDER RESTORATION COUNCIL/STATE PEACE AND DEVELOPMENT COUNCIL ERA; MYANMAR POLICE FORCE; TATMADAW AND BURMESE (MYANMAR) SOCIETY; TATMADAW, ECONOMIC ROLE; TATMADAW, HISTORY OF.

TATMADAW AND BURMESE (MYANMAR) SOCIETY. When Bogyoke **Aung San** and his comrades established the **Tatmadaw** during **World War II**, he described it as an armed force serving the people and working in close collaboration with them. Two developments after independence in 1948, however, made its status as a "people's army" problematic. First, communist and ethnic minority rebellions in 1948–1949 led to a "Burmanization" of the rank and file, especially the officer corps, including the retirement of the **Karen (Kayin)** commander in chief, General **Smith Dun**, and his replacement by **Ne Win**. The Tatmadaw's **Burman (Bamar)** perspective was reflected in the harsh treatment meted out to populations in **Shan State** during the 1950s, when the army launched attacks against the **Kuomintang (Guomindang)** invaders. By the late 1960s, most major ethnic minorities and many small ones had their own insurgent groups, and members of these communities regarded the Tatmadaw as a foreign army of occupation.

Second, the monopolization of economic and political power by the armed forces after Ne Win established the first martial law regime, the **Revolutionary Council**, in March 1962 led to the emergence of the Tatmadaw as a privileged caste who were increasingly separate in lifestyle and living standards from the civilian majority, both in ethnic minority and Burman areas. Military officers, using their privileged access to goods at subsidized prices, were able to enrich themselves in the **black market**, even though the Ne Win regime (1962–1988) was, in principle, socialist and committed to ending the "exploitation of man by man."

After the **State Law and Order Restoration Council (SLORC)** was established in September 1988, the alienation of the army from Burmese society accelerated. During 1988's **Democracy Summer**, Tatmadaw-perpetrated massacres in **Rangoon (Yangon), Sagaing**, and elsewhere made the army an object of hatred and fear among Burmans, who, unlike the minorities, had previously held soldiers in high esteem. Throughout the country, civilian populations were forced by the army to engage in unpaid labor (**forced labor**), a practice that was not new in 1988 but was enforced with unprecedented severity. After the abandonment of socialism in 1988, moreover, economic liberalization policies have given high-ranking military officers new opportunities to make money and indulge in conspicuous consumption, such as luxury homes, cars, and **golf** memberships, while many ordinary Burmese, including lower-ranking soldiers, do not have enough to eat.

The military has its own systems of schools, universities, hospitals, and other social services, which are usually of better quality than those available to civilians. Officers and men live in special areas on the outskirts of major towns and cities, such as **Mingaladon** in northern Rangoon, which resemble the "cantonments" of the British colonial era, an ironic development for an army that prides itself on its anticolonial past. *See also* HUMAN RIGHTS IN BURMA.

TATMADAW, ECONOMIC ROLE OF. Both in terms of control of economic enterprises and defense expenditures by the central government the **Tatmadaw** has played a dominant role in the economy of Burma. After **Ne Win** established the **Revolutionary Council** in March 1962, he ordered the nationalization of private firms, both foreign and domestic, in the name of the **"Burmese Road to Socialism."** Some 15,000 enterprises, large and small, were brought under government ownership in 23 state corporations. Management of the corporations became the responsibility of inexperienced and often corrupt military officers. After the establishment of the **State Law and Order Restoration Council** in 1988, the socialist economic system was, in principle, abandoned, and the private sector, both domestic and foreign, was given a greater economic role. But the Tatmadaw has remained the largest economic player through ownership and control of combines such as the **Union of Myanmar Economic Holdings, Ltd. (UMEH)**, established in 1990, and the Myanmar Economic Corporation. These entities are involved in the majority of joint ventures established with foreign companies. Other state-owned enterprises fall under Tatmadaw control, and few civilian businesspeople in Burma are able to survive without a close informal, if not formal, relationship with high-ranking military officers.

Although statistics are unreliable, defense expenditure in the late 1990s was estimated to be between 30 and 40 percent of total government budgets, not counting "hidden" subsidies, such as free electric power for military units. This amounted to around 4 percent of Burma's Gross National Product. Generous budgets for the Tatmadaw have resulted in serious neglect in other areas, especially spending for **education** and **health** care, which are regarded by many observers as being lower than during the 1962–1988 socialist period. *See also* DEFENCE SERVICES INSTITUTE (DSI); ECONOMY AND ECONOMIC POLICY, BURMA SOCIALIST PROGRAMME PARTY ERA; ECONOMY AND ECONOMIC POLICY, STATE LAW AND ORDER RESTORATION COUNCIL/STATE PEACE AND DEVELOPMENT COUNCIL ERA.

TATMADAW, HISTORY OF. Although the dynastic states of precolonial Burma and British colonial Burma had their own armed forces, the present Burmese armed forces, the **Tatmadaw**, date their history to the establishment of the **Burma Independence Army (BIA)** in December 1941. Its leadership consisted of Japanese officers, members of the **Minami Kikan**, and the **Thirty Comrades**, including **Aung San** and **Ne Win**. After the Japanese drove the British out of Burma and set up their own military administration, the BIA was reorganized as the **Burma Defence Army (BDA)**. Burma became nominally independent in August 1943 within the Japanese

"Greater East Asia Co-Prosperity Sphere," and the BDA was replaced by the **Burma National Army (BNA)**. Aung San, considered by Burmese people to be the founder of the Tatmadaw, served as war minister in the cabinet of **Dr. Ba Maw**, while **Ne Win** became the BNA's commander in chief.

After Aung San ordered the BNA to rise up against the Japanese on March 27, 1945 (Resistance Day, known today as **Armed Forces Day**), the British recognized it as the **Patriotic Burmese Forces (PBF)**. Following the **Kandy Conference** of September 1945, the British established a new **Burma Army**, composed of BNA/PBF veterans and the old **colonial armed forces**, which were composed of ethnic minority troops who had remained loyal to them during the war. This was a highly unstable arrangement. The largely **Burman (Bamar)** PBF men regarded themselves as genuinely "patriotic soldiers" (*myochit sittha* in the **Burmese [Myanmar] language**) and the ethnic minority rank and file as "rightists" and "mercenary soldiers" (*kyesar sittha*) because they had fought on the side of the British. However, the latter outnumbered the former (11 of 15 infantry battalions were minority troops), and the commander in chief of the postwar Burma Army was a **Karen (Kayin)**, General **Smith Dun**.

During the communist and ethnic minority uprisings of 1948–1949, most ethnic minority officers and men mutinied or were purged, leaving only a rump of the Burma Army loyal to the central government: the ex-PBF forces, commanded by Ne Win. With the support of local levies known as *sitwundan*, Ne Win succeeded in rolling back the "multi-colored insurgents." During the 1950s, the Tatmadaw, now primarily a Burman armed force (especially on the officer level), underwent substantial internal reorganization and rationalization, designed to make it a more efficient fighting force and insulate it from both civilian oversight and political factionalism. When the army-run **Caretaker Government** assumed power from 1958 to 1960, the Tatmadaw, described almost as a "state within the state," played an increasingly dominant economic and social, as well as political, role in national life.

The two martial law regimes established in March 1962 and September 1988, the **Revolutionary Council** and the **State Law and Order Restoration Council**, asserted a monopoly of military control over almost all aspects of society in central Burma. But although the Tatmadaw was a tough, effective fighting force during the 1962–1988 period, battling communist and ethnic rebels in the border areas; after 1988, it expanded into a *rentier* class, more concerned with holding onto power and making money than with giving the nation and its diverse peoples a vision for the future. *See also* TATMADAW; TATMADAW AND BURMESE (MYANMAR) SOCIETY.

TATTOOS AND TATTOOING. Until recently, tattoos were widely used in Southeast Asia for decoration of the body, and Burma was no exception. Most rural **Burman (Bamar)** men had tattoos of a dark bluish hue, usually extending from the waist to the knees, which reminded colonial-era British observers of a tightly fitting pair of shorts. The designs were commonly of animals, *nats*, *bilus* (demons), and stylized letters of the Burmese alphabet. Young men underwent the ordeal of tattooing by a *se saya* (tattoo master), using natural pigments (lampblack gave the bluish hue) and primitive but elaborately decorated needles, to make themselves attractive to **women** and exhibit their manly stoicism (men boasted of having large areas of skin tattooed at one time in spite of the terrible pain). Additional tattoos were often placed on the arms, chest, or back. Some designs had magical as well as aesthetic appeal; along with other charms, they were believed to make the bearer invulnerable to swords or bullets, help in winning the affections of a young woman, or defend against snake bite or black magic. Many of the peasant soldiers who joined **Saya San's Rebellion** in 1930 had special charms tattooed on their bodies to protect them from British bullets. Burman women rarely had tattoos, and never in visible places.

Some of Burma's ethnic minorities, such as the **Shans** and the **Chins**, have their own tattoo traditions. Shan men often had elaborate decorations over their entire bodies, exceeding in complexity those of the Burmans. Chin women had geometric decorations tattooed on their faces. During the 20th century, the use of tattoos declined widely throughout the country, a consequence of modernization. By the 1990s, only a few old men could be seen with tattooed thighs. But tattooing has not died out entirely among younger men, and health experts warn that the use of infected needles is a significant cause of the spread of **AIDS**.

TAUNGGYI. The capital of **Shan State**, with a population of 108,231 persons when the last census was taken in 1983 and an estimated 134,023 people in 1996. It stands at an elevation of 1,430 meters (4,690 feet) above sea level. Its multiethnic population includes not only **Burmans (Bamars)** and **Shans (Tai)**, but also **Chinese** and people from **India** and Nepal, reflecting both historical connections with China and the town's British colonial past. Because of its healthful climate and strategic location at the entrance to the **Shan States**, **James G. Scott** established it as the Shan States' administrative center in the early 20th century. It was the site of the Shan Chiefs' School, which offered the rigors of a British public school education to Shan royalty. Located near **Inle Lake** in the old Shan State of **Yawnghwe (Nyaungshwe)**, it has been an enterprising center of the **black market** trade since the "**Burmese Road to Socialism**" was imposed in 1962.

TAVOY (DAWEI). The capital of **Tenasserim (Tanintharyi) Division**, Tavoy had a population estimated at 95,903 in 1996. A port city on the Andaman Sea, it alternated between Burmese and Thai control during the 18th and early 19th centuries before being occupied by the British in 1826. The **Yadana Pipeline** runs nearby, and a new railroad between Tavoy and Ye attracted much attention internationally during the 1990s because of the use of **forced labor**. The city and surrounding areas are home to the **Tavoyans**, a people closely related to the **Burmans (Bamars)**.

TAVOYANS. An ethnic minority living in and around **Tavoy (Dawei)** in **Tenasserim (Tanintharyi) Division**. Linguistically and culturally, they are closely related to the **Burmans (Bamars)**.

TAWNGPENG (TAUNGPENG). Located west of the old **Shan State** of **Hsenwi**, Tawngpeng was described as a "Shan State," though most of its inhabitants were **Palaung** and it was ruled by a Palaung *sawbwa*. Its capital, Namhsan, contained the ruler's *haw*, which was destroyed in **World War II**. With an area of 2,430 square kilometers (938 square miles), Tawngpeng was rich because of the cultivation of tea, enjoyed throughout Burma, and the Bawdwin silver mine in the hills around Namhsan. *See also* MINERAL RESOURCES.

TEA SHOP INCIDENT (MARCH 12, 1988). Against a backdrop of economic distress, the **tea shop** incident, which occurred in northern **Rangoon (Yangon)** on the evening of Saturday, March 12, 1988, was the small spark that led to the massive demonstrations of **Democracy Summer** and the end of the **Burma Socialist Programme Party** regime. The most commonly accepted account is that a fight broke out at the Sanda Win Teashop between students of nearby **Rangoon Institute of Technology** (RIT, now Yangon Technological Institute) and local youths over the choice of music to be played on the shop's cassette player. One of the students was injured by a local youth, who was arrested but later released on bail because his father was chairman of the local **People's Council.** On March 13, units of the *Lon Htein* (**Riot Police**) attacked RIT students who were protesting this abuse of power, and at least two students, including **Maung Phone Maw**, were killed. *See also* WHITE BRIDGE INCIDENT.

TEA SHOPS. Tea shops are an essential part of social life in Burma, places for refreshment, conversation, and just passing the time. Business is often conducted in these shops, and in a society where the state-run **mass media** have little credibility, they are good places to swap rumors or political opinions. For this reason, **Military Intelligence** informers are frequent customers.

The tea is usually served with milk and sugar, though thin Chinese tea is also provided free of charge. Tea shops also sell a wide variety of tea snacks, usually Chinese- or Indian-style, along with other items, such as cigarettes. Some tea shops are quite elaborate, but others, especially in the villages, are little more than open-air stalls equipped with small wooden tables and chairs. *See also* TEA SHOP INCIDENT.

TEAK. *Kyun* in Burmese, historically Burma's most important **forest** resource. Teak (*Tectonia grandis*) is a deciduous tropical hardwood that grows best in upland areas, often reaching tremendous height (50 meters) and girth (5 meters). Easily identified by their large leaves, teak trees grow in mixed forests, where they comprise no more than 10 to 15 percent of all arboreal species. Durable and insect-resistant, a tree can take as long as 150 years to reach maturity. Traditionally a royal monopoly, teak was used for the construction of Buddhist monasteries, royal palaces, and substantial housing, as well as furniture and elaborate wooden ornamentation, the latter being a well-developed art in Burma. In the 18th and 19th centuries, the British used it extensively for shipbuilding. After the **Second Anglo-Burmese War**, they established a strict system of forest conservation that delivered high yields without depleting forest reserves, making teak an important colonial-era export. The system continued, with some modifications, until the untrammeled commercialization of forestry under the **State Law and Order Restoration Council** after 1988. Although *Tectona grandis* is found in Thailand, China, Indonesia, and India, the world's most extensive stands of teak, 70 percent of the total, are found in Burma. Because of foreign exploitation and the popularity of teak for use in furniture and flooring, however, they are being rapidly depleted, especially along the Thai and Chinese borders. *See also* ARCHITECTURE, RELIGIOUS; ARCHITECTURE, TRADITIONAL; THIRD ANGLO-BURMESE WAR.

TENASSERIM (TANINTHARYI) DIVISION. One of Burma's 14 **states** and **divisions**, it has an area of 43,346 square kilometers (16,736 square miles) and an estimated population in 2000 of 1.35 million (1983 census figure: 917,247). The divisional capital is **Tavoy (Dawei)**. Tenasserim Division comprises three **districts** (Tavoy, **Mergui [Myeik]**, and Kawthaung) and 10 **townships**. It is elongated in shape, extending from **Mon State** in the north to Burma's southernmost point at Kawthaung (formerly Victoria Point). It forms a long border with Thailand on the east, defined geographically by the Tenasserim Yoma (mountain range). To the west, it fronts the Andaman Sea and includes the **Mergui (Myeik) Archipelago**, an abundant marine environment with tropical reefs and diverse sea life. Ethnically, **Burmans (Bamars)** form the majority, while minorities include **Tayoyans, Karens (Kayins), Mons**, and the **Moken**, or "Sea Gypsies," who live a nomadic existence in the Mergui Archipelago.

Tenasserim Division's climate and environment are more closely akin to those of Island Southeast Asia (Indonesia and Malaysia) than to continental Burma. It has abundant tropical fruits (coconuts, durians, mangosteens, and rambutans, among others) and is Burma's most important producer of **betel nut**. Fishing and fisheries are economically important, including the breeding of prawns, which are exported to foreign countries. While **Mogok (Mogoke)** in **Mandalay Division** has its rubies, the Mergui Archipelago produces high-quality pearls. Mining, especially for tin and tungsten, is economically important, and the cultivation of rubber and palm oil is being expanded.

THAGYA MIN. Also known as Sakka or Sakra, in Burmese popular religion he is the King of the Gods, sometimes identified as the king of the *nats*, who corresponds to the Hindu god Indra. During **Thingyan**, Thagya Min is said to descend to earth to judge human beings. He inscribes the names of good people in a book bound with gold and those of sinners in a volume with covers of dog skin. He is also protector of the **Buddhist** religion, who received the hair of Gotama **Buddha** in a golden bowl when the latter cut it off to become a hermit. Like the Greek god Zeus, he is often depicted as punishing wrongdoers with thunderbolts.

THAI–BURMA RAILWAY. Railway built by the Japanese during **World War II**, which connected the Bangkok–Singapore line at Bangpong, **Thailand**, with the Ye–**Moulmein** (Yay, **Mawlamyine**) line at Thanbyuzayat, in what is now **Mon State**. It was 415 kilometers (257 miles) long, ran through **Three Pagodas Pass**, and made it possible for the Japanese to have direct rail links between Singapore, Malaya, Thailand, and Burma. At a time when shipping was increasingly threatened by Allied submarines, the railway was a top strategic priority and was completed in record time, between October 1942 and August 1943. Service began on October 25, 1943.

It is often called the "Railway of Death" because so many Allied prisoners of war (POWs) and Asian slave laborers perished during its construction. Of 61,806 POWs, 12,399 (over 20 percent) died of starvation, disease, and maltreatment. The number of Asian laborers, known as *romusha* in Japanese, probably exceeded 300,000, of whom as many as 100,000 may have died. POW and Japanese sources agree that the *romusha*, who came from Burma, Thailand, Indonesia (mostly Java), Malaya, and Vietnam, were treated even more harshly than the POWs, and lacked any sort of medical care. On the Burmese side of the border, laborers were forcibly recruited into the *Chwe Tat* or "Sweat Army" of Dr. **Ba Maw**'s government.

The rail line was repeatedly attacked by Allied aircraft and fell into disuse after the war. A popular novel about the railway, Pierre Boulle's *Bridge on the River Kwai*, contains a number of inaccuracies. During the 1990s, a new rail line constructed between **Tavoy (Dawei)** and Ye by the **State Law and Order Restoration Council**, which also used forced laborers, is often compared to the original "Railway of Death." *See also* FORCED LABOR; YE–TAVOY RAILWAY.

THAILAND (SIAM) AND BURMA. By the 16th century, two powerful states flourished in the valleys of the the Chao Phraya and **Irrawaddy (Ayeyarwady) Rivers**, the Siamese Tai state of Ayuthaya and the **Toungoo Dynasty** of the **Burmans (Bamars)**, whose king, **Tabinshwehti** (r. 1531–1550), established his capital at **Hanthawaddy** (modern **Pegu [Bago]**) and unsuccessfully attempted to conquer Siam in 1548. His successor, **Bayinnaung** (r. 1551–1581), subjugated Chiang Mai (now in northern Thailand) and accepted the surrender of Ayuthaya in 1564; he began his campaign in 1563 after the king of Siam refused to give him two sacred **white elephants**. Because of an uprising by the former Siamese king, Bayinnaung was obliged to recapture it in 1569, sacking the Siamese capital and placing the country under the rule of a puppet king, Thammaraja. Thammaraja's son, Phra Naret (Naresuan, who became king of Siam in 1590), successfully threw off the Burmese yoke in 1584 and fought a series of defensive and offensive wars against Bayinnaung's successor, Nanda Bayin (r. 1581–1599). In 1592, Phra Naret killed the Burmese crown prince, Nanda Bayin's son, in single combat on the backs of elephants, an episode that made him one of Thailand's most revered national heroes. The Siamese asserted control over **Tavoy (Dawei)** in what is now **Tenasserim (Tanintharyi) Division** in 1593.

Hostilities between the two states continued intermittently throughout the 17th and early 18th centuries. In 1759–1760, **Alaungpaya** (r. 1752–1760), founder of the **Konbaung Dynasty**, laid siege to Ayuthaya, but he died during the campaign, and his son **Hsinbyushin** (1763–1776) launched a new invasion in 1765. Three Burmese columns entered Siam by way of Chiang Mai, **Three Pagodas Pass**, and Tenasserim, capturing and pillaging the Siamese capital in April 1767. The Siamese king was killed, and Hsinbyushin's victorious armies brought thousands of prisoners of war back to **Up-per Burma**.

The fall of Ayuthaya (it was never rebuilt) is considered one of Thailand's greatest national calamities. But a half-Chinese Siamese general, Pya Taksin, led a successful resistance and established a new dynasty at Thonburi, near modern Bangkok. He was overthrown in 1782 by another general, Maha Chakri, who moved the capital to Bangkok and established the dynasty that reigns in Thailand today. Maha Chakri (known as King Ramathibodi, or Rama I) defeated several attempts by King **Bodawpaya** (r. 1781–1819) to conquer Siam, though he was not able to recover Tenasserim, which remains part of Burma today. Burma ceased to be a threat after the **First Anglo-Burmese War**, and relations between Siam and British Burma were peaceful. However, Japanese armies based in Thailand, formally Japan's ally, invaded Burma at the beginning of **World War II**.

A key element in Burma–Siam conflicts were the **Mons**, who previously ruled states in **Lower Burma** and sought Siamese help to prevent their domination by Burman kings. When Alaungpaya extinguished Mon independence in the mid-18th century, many Mons fled to Siam, where they attained high civil and military office under Rama I and his successors.

In 1917, Siamese prince Damrong Rajanubhab published a history of the centuries-long hostility between the two countries, *Our Wars with the Burmese* (*Thai Rop Phama*), which had a major influence on the development of Thailand's view of its national history, as found in school textbooks and popular culture. In his view, not only were the Burmese a savage and aggressive people, but Siam was defeated in war only when it was unprepared and divided against itself. Kings who rallied the people, such as Phra Naret and Rama I, waged successful wars of national liberation against an imperialist enemy.

More recent scholarship has cautioned against casting the history of the 16th to 18th centuries in a 20th-century conceptual framework. The 24 Thai–Burmese wars described by Damrong between 1539 and 1767 were wars between monarchs rather than nations, and many prominent Siamese (including Phra Naret's father) were willing to accept Burmese overlordship. Premodern Burma and Siam shared similar ideological preconceptions, derived from their common Indo-Buddhist civilization. One of these was that the ruler was not the leader of a national community, but a man endowed with abundant *hpoun* (power/authority) that legitimized his wartime victories over peoples near and far.

Images of Burma as the "enemy nation" are still strong in Thailand. Popular Thai motion pictures such as *Suryothai* and *Ban Rajaan* have revived them. But relations between the Thai government and the **State Peace and Development Council (SPDC)** are generally cordial, strengthened by complementary economic interests.

In Burma, images of the Thais have not, until recently, been especially negative. After King Hsinbyushin's armies brought back Siamese musicians and dancers from the sack of Ayuthaya, the Burmese gained an appreciation for their refined *Yodaya* (Ayuthaya) styles, which deeply influenced their own theater, music, and the arts. *Yodaya* became synonymous with elite or courtly art forms. However, the post-1988 military regime has encouraged anti-Thai sentiment from time to time, symbolized by its construction of a statue of Bayinnaung at Tachilek in **Shan State**, a town overlooking the Thai border, and its periodic campaigns against the "perfidious Siamese" in the state-run **mass media**. *See also* THAILAND, RELATIONS WITH.

THAILAND, RELATIONS WITH. Sharing both a common Indo-Buddhist civilization and many centuries of antagonism, the governments of Burma and Thailand followed fundamentally different courses after **World War II**. Under both U **Nu** and **Ne Win**, Burmese policies emphasized socialism and nonalignment (as well as isolationism after Ne Win's **Revolutionary Council** was established in 1962), while Thailand's leaders promoted friendly relations with the **United States**, close economic connections with Western countries and **Japan**, and an anticommunist agenda, as reflected in Bangkok's charter membership in the Southeast Asia Treaty Organization in 1954 and the **Association of Southeast Asian Nations (ASEAN)** in 1967 and its active support for the American war in Indochina, including sending troops to South Vietnam. Thai leaders, most of whom had conservative military backgrounds, were suspicious of socialism in any form and also feared the power of the **Communist Party of Burma**. They used border-area insurgent movements, especially the

Karen National Union (KNU) and the **New Mon State Party (NMSP)**, as "buffers" against the Burmese. These insurgent groups carried out trade across the border, especially at **Three Pagodas Pass**, exporting Burmese raw materials, including **teak**, in exchange for consumer goods from Thailand that supplied Burma's **black market**. Ethnic minority armies in **Shan State**, such as the **Mong Tai Army** exported **opium** and **heroin** to international markets through Thailand, but although the trade earned corrupt Thai officials large payoffs, it had relatively little impact on Thailand's own society.

Guided by Washington's Cold War strategies, Thailand's behavior earned the distrust of the Burmese in other ways, especially when it became apparent that Bangkok and Washington backed the **Kuomintang (Guomindang)** incursions into Shan State in the early 1950s. Relations reached an all-time low when Thailand offered sanctuary to former Prime Minister U Nu's **Parliamentary Democracy Party (PDP)** in 1969; in 1970, the PDP became part of a **united front**, the National United Liberation Front, which sought unsuccessfully to overthrow the Ne Win regime.

In the late 1980s, Thailand's prime minister, Chatichai Choonhavan, talked about "replacing battlefields with marketplaces" in post–Cold War Mainland Southeast Asia. Burma–Thailand relations underwent a fundamental transformation in 1988, following the establishment of the **State Law and Order Restoration Council (SLORC)** and the end of Burmese-style socialism. In December of that year, the Thai Army commander, Chaovalit Yongchaiyuth, led a delegation to **Rangoon (Yangon)** to talk with SLORC chairman General **Saw Maung**. The new Burmese military regime was desperate for cash, and the Chaovalit–Saw Maung summit led to the SLORC's awarding concessions to Thai companies to exploit **forest** resources along the border; these earned the regime over US\$110 million annually between 1989 and 1993. The SLORC also granted Thai companies offshore fishing contracts. The **Yadana Pipeline Project**, the largest single **foreign investment** project in Burma, was built in the 1990s to supply Thailand with natural gas extracted from the Gulf of **Martaban (Mottama)**.

Closer cooperation between the Thai military and the **Tatmadaw** after 1988 put an end to the ethnic minority insurgents' buffer status.

They lost the freedom to operate on Thai soil, while Tatmadaw units were sometimes allowed to attack KNU units from the Thai side of the border. In 1990, Burmese troops occupied Three Pagodas Pass, formerly controlled by the KNU and the NMSP; in 1995, they captured the major KNU base at **Manerplaw.**

Although economic engagement and closer relations brought monetary rewards to Thai elites, the country has suffered from the consequences of Burmese social and political instability. Hundreds of thousands of **Karen (Kayin), Mon, Karenni,** and **Shan (Tai) refugees,** as well as **Burman (Bamar)** student exiles, fled to Thailand in the wake of the SLORC power seizure and Tatmadaw **"Four Cuts"** campaigns. Most of these refugees lacked documentation, and many became illegal workers inside Thailand. Powerful new drug-dealing armies in Shan State, especially the **United Wa State Army (UWSA),** flooded the country with cheap **amphetamines,** creating a major drug epidemic nationwide that especially targeted young people. Growth of Chinese influence has also worried Thai leaders, and the flow of cheap Chinese consumer goods into Burma has disappointed businesspeople who had hoped the country would become part of a Thailand-centered economic zone.

Along the long, poorly demarcated Thai–Burma border, an unpredictable mix of the Thai Army and Border Police, Tatmadaw troops, **cease-fire** armed groups (such as the UWSA), and non-cease-fire groups (such as the KNU and the **Shan State Army-South**) has led to periodic outbursts of armed conflict. One of the worst incidents occurred in February 2001, when Thai and Tatmadaw artillery units exchanged fire across the border at Mae Sai-Tachilek, an event that stimulated a paroxysm of anti-Thai propaganda in Burma's state-run **mass media,** including glorification of the 16th-century conqueror-king **Bayinnaung,** who subjugated Siam in the 1560s.

On the Thai side, old images of the Burmese as the "enemy nation" have revived in popular films such as *Ban Rajaan* (about a band of villagers who, Alamo-like, fought to the death against an 18th-century Burmese onslaught) and *Suryothai* (about a legendary queen who died fighting the Burmese invader from the back of an elephant).

But Thai attitudes toward Burma since 1988 have been complex. As Thailand moved from military domination of politics to government by elected civilian politicians, many "civil society" activists expressed strong sympathy for their prodemocracy counterparts in Burma and also helped Burmese refugees. The Thai media, including the English-language *Nation* and *Bangkok Post*, have provided detailed reports on violations of **human rights** inside Burma and along the border. The Democrat Party government of Prime Minister Chuan Leekpai was one of the few within the Association of Southeast Asian Nations to express reservations about admitting Burma as an ASEAN member in 1997. Under Chuan's successor, Prime Minister Thaksin Shinawatra, business interests have had a dominant voice in the making of Burma policy, meaning that other factors have not been allowed to interfere with smooth bilateral relations. *See also* THAILAND (SIAM) AND BURMA.

THAKETA. A **new town** in **Rangoon (Yangon)**, established during the **Caretaker Government** period of General **Ne Win** (1958–1960). It is located to the northeast of downtown Rangoon, across the Pazundaung/Ngamoeyeik Creek. To deal with the problems of squatters and overcrowding in the city center, Rangoon's new mayor, a military officer, relocated as many as 170,000 squatters by mid-1959, of whom 55,050 were brought to Thaketa. During **Democracy Summer** in 1988, the township was the site of intense antigovernment resistance. *See also* OKKALAPA, NORTH AND SOUTH.

THAKIN. Meaning "master" in the **Burmese (Myanmar) language**, the term was used by Burmese during the colonial era to address British people, roughly equivalent to *sahib* in India (*thakinma* was used to address a woman). The **Dobama Asiayone** appropriated the term to refer to members of their own party, asserting that the Burmese rather than the British were the true masters of the country (thus, the Dobama Asiayone was widely known as the "Thakin Party," and its members as "Thakins"). As a title, it is presently used to refer to individuals who were members of the party or who actively participated in the struggle for independence, for example, Thakin **Aung San** or Thakin **Nu**. *See also* BO.

THALUN, KING (r. 1629–1648). Monarch of the **Toungoo Dynasty**, who came to the throne after the assassination of his brother,

Anaukpetlun. He is best remembered for moving the capital of his kingdom from **Pegu (Bago)** to **Ava (Inwa)** in **Upper Burma**. This was a momentous decision, because it isolated the royal capital from foreign contact and deprived the state of that cultural and economic stimulation that made Ayuthaya, capital of Siam, one of Southeast Asia's major cities. Although Pegu's port was of doubtful use because of silting, there was some thought of establishing a new capital at **Syriam (Thanlyin)**, across the Pegu (Bago) River from present-day **Rangoon (Yangon)**. In contrast to his predecessors, Thalun's reign was largely peaceful. He promoted administrative reform, the composing of the first law code (*Dhammathat*) in the **Burmese (Myanmar)** language, expansion of the irrigation facilities at **Kyaukse**, and a detailed land survey, carried out in 1638.

THAMANYA SAYADAW (1910–2003). The Baddantha Vinaya Sayadaw, a highly respected member of the **Sangha**, known as the "Thamanya Sayadaw" because he established a monastery on Thamanya Hill, 40 kilometers southeast of **Pa-an (Hpa-an)**, the capital of **Karen (Kayin) State**. A community of around 7,000 families grew up around the monastery, where the *sayadaw* promoted welfare projects and a "zone of peace," free of the strife afflicting adjacent areas. Of **Pa-O** ethnicity, he was widely believed to have possessed a spiritual status approaching Buddhahood. Unlike most other senior monks, he refused to accept the patronage of the **State Peace and Development Council**, but received **Aung San Suu Kyi** at his monastery twice, in October 1995 and June 2002, following her release from house arrest. He passed away at the age of 93 on November 29, 2003, while being brought back to Thamanya from a hospital in **Rangoon (Yangon)**.

THAN SHWE (1933–). Senior general, chairman of the **State Peace and Development Council (SPDC)**, and concurrently commander in chief of the Defence Services, minister of defence, and minister of agriculture. He also served as prime minister until this post was given to SPDC Secretary-1 **Khin Nyunt** in August 2003. Born in 1933 in **Kyaukse**, near **Mandalay**, he entered the military in 1953, completing the course at the **Officers' Training School** (ninth), serving in the Psychological Warfare Department before assuming commands in

Shan and **Karen (Kayin) States** that assured him rapid promotion. Appointed commander of the Southwest Military Region in 1983, he attained the rank of lieutenant general four years later. He was appointed vice chairman of the **State Law and Order Restoration Council (SLORC)** when it was established on September 18, 1988, and also served as commander in chief of the Army. He succeeded Senior General **Saw Maung** as SLORC chairman on April 23, 1992, and remained in the same post when the SLORC was reorganized as the **State Peace and Development Council** in November 1997.

Regarded by outsiders in the 1990s as an aging, neutral figure, who delayed retirement in order to stem rivalries between Khin Nyunt and **Maung Aye**, Than Shwe has often been underestimated. Observers now see him as the successor to **Ne Win** as the country's unitary "strong man," though he lacks the deceased leader's prestige and historical role in the independence movement. Than Shwe is a highly conservative figure, apparently willing to sacrifice Burma's post-1988 open-door policies to preserve the military-dominated status quo. Lacking personal charisma, he is a reclusive leader, preferring to exercise his power ambiguously and from behind the scenes. *See also* STATE PEACE AND DEVELOPMENT COUNCIL, INTERNAL DYNAMICS.

THAN TUN, THAKIN (1911–1968). A prominent nationalist and communist leader. He was a member of the **Dobama Asiayone** and a founding member of the **Communist Party of Burma (CPB)** when it was established in August 1939. Although he served as agriculture and transport minister in the wartime government of Dr. **Ba Maw**, he played a central role in organizing anti-Japanese resistance, along with his brother-in-law, war minister **Aung San**. Than Tun served as general secretary of the **Anti-Fascist People's Freedom League** from May to August 1946, when the CPB was expelled from the League. In March 1948, he led the mainstream CPB underground and two years later was chosen to be the party's chairman, a post he held until he was assassinated by his bodyguard in the **Pegu (Bago) Yoma** on September 24, 1968.

THANAKHA. A tree (*Linoria acidissima*) whose bark is ground and mixed with water to make a traditional cosmetic for **women**. Applied to the face and arms as a yellowish paste, it serves as a skin moisturizer and sunscreen. Mothers use it to protect their children's skin. Though Burmese women who can afford them increasingly use Western-style cosmetics, *thanakha* remains very popular because it is cheap and effective. Readily available in markets, there are several grades, and it can be purchased in solid, powder, or liquid form.

THANT, U (1909–1974). Serving as secretary general of the **United Nations**, U Thant was arguably the best-known Burmese on the international stage until **Aung San Suu Kyi** won the Nobel Peace Prize in 1991. A close associate of U **Nu**, he served as minister of information in his cabinet from 1948 to 1953 and became the prime minister's secretary from 1954 to 1957. In the latter year, he was appointed Burma's ambassador to the United Nations, where he was secretary general from 1961 to 1971. Following his death in November 1974, his remains were taken back to **Rangoon (Yangon)**. President **Ne Win**'s refusal to give U Thant the honor of a state funeral (because of his closeness to U Nu, who had led the **Parliamentary Democracy Party** insurgency on the Thai–Burma border until 1973) aroused major antigovernment demonstrations, the **U Thant Incident** of December 1974.

THATON. A town in **Mon State** north of **Moulmein (Mawlamyine)**, the site of a thriving trade center and **Mon** kingdom in **Lower Burma** that was captured by King **Anawrahta** in 1057. The king, Manuha, was brought by Anawrahta back to **Pagan (Bagan)**. Little remains of its former glory, except for the ruins of city walls. *See also* MANUHA TEMPLE.

THEIN PE MYINT, THAKIN (1914–1978). A leading left-wing politician. During **World War II**, he resided in India, where he coordinated anti-Japanese resistance inside Burma with the backing of the British. Although elected secretary general of the **Communist Party of Burma** in 1945, he did not follow the CPB mainstream when it went underground in March 1948. Active in legal left-wing parties, in 1956 he became a member of parliament representing the **National Unity Front**. After 1962, he advised the **Revolutionary Council** of General **Ne Win** and became a member of the **Burma Socialist Pro-**

gramme Party. He is also well known for his short stories, novels, and political memoirs.

THIBAW, KING (r. 1878–1885). Last monarch of the Konbaung Dynasty, he was chosen by court factions to succeed his father, Mindon (r. 1853–1878), because the 19-year-old youth was considered pliable. He soon fell under the influence of his secondary queen, Supayalat, who, with the aid of a powerful minister, the Taingda Mingyi, arranged a massacre of royal relatives in early 1879 that made the king, probably undeservedly, notorious. This was done to eliminate rivals for the throne, a time-honored practice. A weak ruler who never took advantage of his royal prerogative (multiple wives), he feared plots by surviving royal princes and never left Mandalay Palace. Although some historical details are unclear, his ministers apparently sought an alliance with France, including provision of arms, to counteract British influence, thinking that Britain's involvement in Afghanistan (where the British resident had been assassinated in 1879) would prevent them from taking a strong hand in Upper Burma. But British economic and imperial interests in India and Lower Burma converged to create a climate for war, which began on November 14, 1885, following Thibaw's refusal of an ultimatum that demanded British control over Burmese foreign policy. When Mandalay was captured on November 28, Thibaw and Supayalat were exiled to Ratnagiri, India, where the king died in 1916. The sad spectacle of the royal couple being brought in a lowly bullock cart to a steamer on the banks of the Irrawaddy (Ayeyarwady) River, while thousands of their subjects mourned their banishment, marked a decisive end to Burma's old order. See also ANGLO-BURMESE WAR, THIRD.

THINGYAN. The Burmese New Year, a three- to four-day period that falls during the first half of April, the hottest time of year. It is believed that during this time, Thagya Min, King of the Gods, visits earth to check up on humans' behavior. Practitioners of astrology determine the exact time of his arrival and departure. Thingyan is also known as the Water Festival because people douse each other with water, including strangers walking along the street. Water pistols (traditionally made of bamboo), pails, and even fire hoses are used to get people thoroughly wet. Apart from members of the **Sangha**, high-status people are not spared, though their subordinates pour water on them respectfully. The streets of towns and villages all over Burma are packed with lively crowds, and the celebrations are often raucous. Neighborhoods, companies, and government departments sponsor special curbside stages, called *pandals*, where performances are given, including Western-style rock concerts.

In recent years, economic hardship and political restrictions have made Thingyan a rare opportunity to publicly let off stream. Because the behavior of the crowds is sometimes unpredictable, the **State Peace and Development Council** authorities warn them to conduct the festivities in a "dignified" manner. *See also* CALENDAR, BURMESE.

THIRTY COMRADES. The group of Burmese nationalists recruited by **Aung San** after he returned to Burma from Japan in February 1941, who formed the core of the **Burma Independence Army (BIA)**. Secretly brought out of Burma in batches between March and July 1941, the men were trained by Japanese officers of the **Minami Kikan** during April–October on the island of Hainan, China. After the outbreak of war, they were moved to Bangkok and became officers of the BIA, formally established on December 28, 1941. During their training on Hainan, they were divided into three groups: the first, including Aung San (whom the Japanese recognized as the most talented of the Thirty Comrades), were to assume top command and administrative positions in the new army; a second group, including **Ne Win**, were to carry out guerrilla and sabotage actions behind British lines; and the third group, composed of younger men, were to assume field command positions. They assumed Burmese *noms de guerre* emphasizing their courage and prowess (e.g., Thakin Shu Maung was Bo Ne Win, "Commander Bright as the Sun").

Ranging in age from 19 to 35 (the average age was 24), more than half of the Thirty Comrades were members of the left-leaning **Thakin Kodaw Hmaing** faction of the **Dobama Asiayone**; a minority, including Ne Win and Tun Oke, came from the Dobama's **Ba Sein** faction, which was rightist. Ne Win alone achieved a dominant position in postwar Burma, as commander of the armed forces in 1949 and head of the **Revolutionary Council** in March 1962. Some of the Thirty Comrades, such as **Bo Let Ya** and **Bohmu Aung**, took high office in **Anti-Fascist People's Freedom League** governments; others, such as Bo Yan Aung and Bo Zeya, became prominent leaders of the **Communist Party of Burma**. In the 1990s, a handful of surviving Thirty Comrades called for reconciliation between the **State Law and Order Restoration Council/State Peace and Development Council** and Aung San's daughter, **Aung San Suu Kyi**.

THIRTY-SEVEN NATS. Also known as the "Thirty-Seven Lords," the pantheon of *nats* first established by King **Anawrahta** in the 11th century. To 36 deities, whose number has cosmological meaning, the monarch decreed that **Thagya Min**, the divine protector of **Buddhism**, be added, making 37. Although membership in the pantheon has changed over time, the number has remained constant. They include **Min Mahagiri** and his sister, Lady Golden Face; the Little Lady, a cheerful *nat* who plays with children; the Old Man of the Banyan Tree, who died of leprosy; and a king of Chiang Mai (now in **Thailand**) who was taken prisoner by **Bayinnaung**. All but three (including Thagya Min) were executed, died under other tragic or violent circumstances, or perished from disease. Their elevation to special status reflected the need to placate them, to prevent their angry spirits from doing harm to the living. *See also* MOUNT POPA; *NAT PWE*.

THREE MAIN NATIONAL CAUSES. The self-defined mission of the **State Law and Order Restoration Council** martial law regime and its successor, the **State Peace and Development Council**. The three causes are "Non-Disintegration of the Union," "Non-Disintegration of National Sovereignty," and "Consolidation of National Sovereignty." The underlying assumption is that military rule in some form is essential for preserving **national unity** and defending the country's independence from foreign interference. The Three Main National Causes appear on the front pages of practically all government-approved publications, often accompanied by sets of four "political," "economic," and "social objectives," and the "People's Desire," for example, to "crush all internal and external destructive elements as the common enemy."

THREE PAGODAS PASS. Known as *Payathonzu* in the **Burmese (Myanmar) language**, Three Pagodas Pass is a historically important trade and invasion route that links Burma's **Karen (Kayin) State** and **Thailand**'s border town of Sangklaburi. Before 1988 the settlement at Three Pagodas Pass, controlled by the **Karen National Union (KNU)** and the **New Mon State Party (MNSP)**, was a profitable "toll gate," where taxes were levied by the insurgents on cross-border and **black market** trade, including the export of **teak** from Burma. However, on July 23, 1988, disputes between the KNU and the NMSP over revenues erupted into full-scale fighting, with casualties on both sides. Although a truce between the two groups was negotiated, the **Tatmadaw** seized control of Three Pagodas Pass in early 1990 and now operates a trading post and sawmills there. *See also* MAE SOT-MYAWADDY; THAILAND (SIAM) AND BURMA.

THURA SHWE MANN (ca. 1947–). General, close to Senior General **Than Shwe**, who is joint chief of staff of the **Army, Navy,** and **Air Force** and the third-ranking member of the **State Peace and Development Council.** A member of the 11th class of the **Defence Services Academy,** he is considered a likely successor to **Than Shwe** and General **Maung Aye** in the highest positions in the junta.

THURIYA (THE SUN). One of the most important **Burmese (Myanmar) language** newspapers during the British colonial period, established by U **Ba Pe** in 1911. In 1935, it was purchased by U **Saw,** who used it to promote his own political agenda. *Thuriya's* inflammatory articles in 1938 played a major role in sparking rioting against **Indians** and **Muslims** in **Rangoon (Yangon),** during which almost 200 people were killed. *See also* ANTI-INDIAN RIOTS.

TIN OO, "MI" (1928–1997). Powerful head of **Military Intelligence** (thus "MI"), **State Council** member, and joint secretary of the **Burma Socialist Programme Party,** he was considered **Ne Win**'s heir apparent until arrested and given a life sentence in 1983 for corrupt practices. His sudden fall was attributable in part to his unpopularity with regular **Tatmadaw** commanders, who feared the information he obtained as MI head might be used to blackmail them, but more fundamentally to Ne Win's concern that he was becoming too powerful. His power base of loyal supporters within the intelligence apparatus was largely independent of Ne Win's control. Tin Oo remained in prison, most of the time at **Insein Jail**, until the 1990s, when he was released, apparently viewed by the **State Law and Restoration Council** as harmless. His successor as head of Military Intelligence was **Khin Nyunt**. *See also* RANGOON INCIDENT.

TIN OO, SECRETARY-2 (1940–2001). Lieutenant general and second secretary of the **State Law and Order Restoration Council** and, after 1997, the **State Peace and Development Council**. A hardliner who repeatedly called for the "annihilation" of **Aung San Suu Kyi** and the **National League for Democracy**, he was the target of an assassination attempt in March 1997, a parcel bomb that killed his eldest daughter. The government claimed that it had been sent by Burmese exiles based in **Japan**. On February 19, 2001, he died in an apparently accidental helicopter crash in **Karen (Kayin) State**.

TIN PE, BRIGADIER. A close confidant of General **Ne Win** and veteran of the **Fourth Burma Rifles**, he served in the cabinet during the **Caretaker Government** period (1958–1960) and was member of the **Revolutionary Council** when it was established in March 1962. A leading theorist of the "**Burmese Road to Socialism**," his influence over economic policy following the resignation of the pragmatic Brigadier **Aung Gyi** from the Council in 1963 was paramount. But Tin Pe's doctrinaire, Eastern European–type socialist ideas caused economic disaster, and he was obliged to resign from the Revolutionary Council in 1968. Thereafter, economic policy was largely formulated by the civilian economist U **Ba Nyein**. *See also* ECONOMY AND ECONOMIC POLICY, BURMA SOCIALIST PROGRAMME PARTY ERA.

TIN U, "NLD" (1927–). Chairman of the **National League for Democracy (NLD)** and a prominent opposition leader, Tin U served as **Tatmadaw** chief of staff and defense minister from 1974 to 1976. He was dismissed in March 1976 on charges of dealing in the black market and given a seven-year jail sentence in January 1977 for failing to report the **coup d'état attempt (July 1976)** against **Ne Win**, of which he allegedly had prior knowledge. Observers believe that Ne Win purged him on trumped up charges because he was becoming too popular in the army and among civilians. Tin U had urged restraint in handling the demonstrations arising from the December 1974 **U Thant Incident**, and many younger officers, including the coup plotters, were loyal to him (they were later purged or passed over for promotion in favor of Ne Win loyalists).

Released during a general amnesty in 1980, Tin U devoted himself to studying **Buddhism** and law and was prominent during the protests of 1988. In September 1988, he joined with Daw **Aung San Suu Kyi** and **Aung Gyi** in a coalition that became the National League for Democracy after the September 18 seizure of power by the **State Law and Order Restoration Council**. Following Aung Gyi's departure from the NLD in December 1988, he became the party's chairman. In July 1989, he was placed under one-year house arrest, then given a prison sentence with hard labor. After his release, Tin U worked closely with Aung San Suu Kyi to revive the NLD, which was an object of sustained repression, and he was again placed in detention following the **Black Friday Incident** of May 30, 2003. As of late 2003, the state of his health and conditions of imprisonment remained uncertain. *See also* DEMOCRACY SUMMER; IN-SEIN JAIL; TRADE MINISTRY INCIDENT.

TIPITAKA (TRIPITAKA). The scriptures of **Buddhism**, known as the "Three Baskets": the *Sutta Pitaka* or Discourses of Gotama **Buddha**; the **Vinaya** *Pitaka*, rules for the **Sangha**; and the *Abhidhamma Pitaka*, a lengthy and difficult treatment of Buddhist philosophy and psychology. The *Tipitaka* is in **Pali**, the sacred language of Theravada Buddhism. Both King **Mindon** and Prime Minister U **Nu** convened special assemblies of Buddhist monks and other scholars to correct errors in the translation and transmission of the scriptures. *See also* GREAT BUDDHIST COUNCIL, FIFTH; GREAT BUDDHIST COUNCIL, SIXTH.

TOUNGOO (TAUNGOO). A town near the **Sittang (Sittoung) River** in northern **Pegu (Bago) Division**, the site of a powerful **Burman (Bamar)** kingdom in the 14th to 15th centuries whose rulers established the **Toungoo Dynasty**. It is located on major north-south high-way and rail arteries linking **Mandalay** with **Rangoon (Yangon)**.

TOUNGOO (TAUNGOO) DYNASTY (1486–1752). Sometimes called the "Second Burmese (Myanmar) Empire" because, like the **Pagan (Bagan)** and **Konbaung Dynasties**, it unified the country. Historians generally divide it into two periods. The first, spanning the reigns of **Minkyinyo** (r. 1486–1531), **Tabinshwehti** (r. 1531–1550), **Bayinnaung** (r. 1551–1581), and Nanda Bayin (r. 1581–1599), witnessed the **Burman (Bamar)** conquest of the **Mons** in **Lower Burma** and the **Shans**, who had occupied **Ava (Inwa)** in 1527, and the kingdom emerged as a major power in Mainland Southeast Asia, conquering Siam in the 1560s.

Monarchs of the Toungoo Dynasty	Year of Accession
Minkyinyo	1486
Tabinshwehti	1531
Bayinnaung	1551
Nandabayin	1581
interregnum	1599–1605
Anaukpetlun	1605
Minredeippa	1628
Thalun	1629
Pindale	1648
Pye	1661
Narawara	1672
Minrekyawdin	1673
Sane	1698
Taninganwe	1714
Mahadammayaza Dipati	1733 (to 1752)

Source: D. G. E. Hall, *A History of South-East Asia*

The second period, coming on the heels of an invasion of Lower Burma by Siam and **Arakan** and a chaotic interregnum (1599–1605), is commonly called the *Restored Toungoo Dynasty* or the *Nyaungyan Dynasty*. King **Anaukpetlun** (r. 1605–1628) reestablished order, with his capital at **Pegu (Bago)**, but his brother **Thalun** (r. 1629–1648) moved the capital back to **Ava (Inwa)**. This was a significant development because Pegu had been one of Southeast Asia's major seaports (though it suffered from silting), while Ava was located inland, in **Upper Burma**, isolated from the outside world. The capital remained in Upper Burma until 1885, and narrow ethnocentrism characterized Burmese rulers' views of the world, with the exception of King **Mindon**. Thalun's successors were ineffective, and the country suffered greatly from Chinese invasions in the mid-seventeenth century. The dynasty fell when **Binnya Dala** captured Ava in 1752. *See also* ALAUNGPAYA; BRITO, FELIPE DE; SYRIAM.

TOURISM IN BURMA. The beginnings of modern tourism in Burma can perhaps be traced to the opening of the Suez Canal in 1869, which dramatically cut seaborne travel time between Europe and Asia, or to the opening of the Strand Hotel on the waterfront of **Rangoon (Yangon)** in 1901, providing the colonial capital with its first international class hotel. After World War I, steamships remained the most important means of getting to Burma from Europe, but Rangoon was also linked with Europe and South Asia by air, principally by British carrier Imperial Airways, and the Strand had several competitors. The unwillingness of Western tourists to take off their shoes and stockings upon entering the compounds of **pagodas**, the "**Shoe Question**," became a major political controversy following World War I. Travelers wanted to see the famous **Shwe Dagon Pagoda** up close, but their qualms about going shoeless were interpreted by Burmese activists as disrespect to the **Buddhist** religion. **World War II** and insurgency following Burma's achievement of independence from British colonial rule in 1948 hampered development of the tourism sector, but before **Ne Win** established the **Revolutionary Council** in March 1962, Rangoon was well-equipped with tourism facilities compared with many other Asian capitals, including one of the region's more modern airports in **Mingaladon Township**.

The Ne Win regime (1962–1988) adopted a policy of isolationism, which included the banning of foreign tourists (travelers could only lay over in Rangoon for 24 hours), although seven-day visas were introduced in 1970 to generate foreign exchange. Facilities, including the now-decrepit Strand Hotel, were minimal, and travelers found the dual currency system (use of U.S. dollars in some places and *kyats* in others) confusing and inconvenient. But Union of Burma Airways, the national carrier, took the more intrepid foreign tourists to **Inle Lake** in **Shan State**, **Mandalay**, and **Pagan (Bagan)**, places that remain the top three tourist destinations outside of Rangoon in the early 21st century. From Mandalay, tourists customarily have visited nearby sites, such as the old royal capitals **Ava (Inwa)**, **Amarapura**, and **Sagaing**, and the colonial-era hill station **Maymyo (Pyin Oo Lwin)**.

After 1988, the **State Law and Order Restoration Council** made development of the tourism sector a top priority, hoping to emulate neighboring **Thailand**, where tourism generates billions of U.S. dollars in revenue annually. Tourist visas were extended from 7 to 28 days. But the SLORC faced opposition from **Aung San Suu Kyi** and her international supporters, who urged foreigners not to visit because tourism dollars allegedly helped keep the military regime in power. In preparation for **"Visit Myanmar Year"** in 1996–1997, new luxury hotels were constructed in Rangoon, Mandalay, and elsewhere; private airlines were set up as joint ventures with foreign companies; and tourist sites were upgraded (including the moat around **Mandalay Palace**, which allegedly renovated using **forced labor**). The impact of tourism on the environment has been controversial; a 60-meter concrete tower was opened at Pagan in 2005 for the benefit of tourists who wanted a view of the plain, dotted with pagodas and temples, but the structure has been criticized for being too large and poorly designed. Formerly inaccessible parts of the country, such as the **Mergui (Myeik) Archipelago**, have been opened for tourism exploitation, but this has often had negative impacts on local people, such as the **Mokens** ("Sea Gypsies"), who live among the islands. Because of poor infrastructure and the continuing international boycott movement, it is unlikely that Burma will rival Thailand as a tourism destination in the near future, but its hospitable people and historic, often beautiful landscapes promise travelers a taste of an "unspoiled" Asia. *See also* AIR TRANSPORT, CIVIL; INVESTMENT, FOREIGN; "JUMPING CAT MONASTERY"; LACQUERWARE; SEX INDUSTRY IN BURMA.

TOWNSHIP. A unit of local administration established by the British during the colonial period. It was also part of the four-level administrative structure defined by the **Constitution of 1974**: the national level, the **state/division** level, the township level, and the ward/village tract level. Under the **State Peace and Development Council**, the **district**, composed of four or five townships, has been reintroduced as an administrative unit. Although district Peace and Development Councils are frequently headed by a **Tatmadaw** officer of lieutenant-colonel rank, township Peace and Development Councils are often headed by military veterans, while the township government head is a local resident appointed by the Ministry of Home Affairs. Burma presently is divided into 324 townships, which are further subdivided into wards or village tracts. *See also* ADMINISTRATION OF BURMA, BRITISH COLONIAL PERIOD; ADMINISTRATION OF BURMA, STATE LAW AND ORDER RESTORATION COUNCIL/STATE PEACE AND DEVELOPMENT COUNCIL ERA.

TRADE MINISTRY INCIDENT (SEPTEMBER 17, 1988). After troops fired on demonstrators from the roof of the Trade Ministry on Strand Road in downtown **Rangoon (Yangon)**, an angry crowd surged into the building, intent on killing them. They were dissuaded from doing so by opposition leaders **Aung Gyi** and U **Tin U**, but the crowd took away the soldiers' weapons. **Military Intelligence** director **Khin Nyunt** later cited the incident as an example of how Burma was slipping into anarchy, attempting to justify the power seizure by the **State Law and Order Restoration Council** on September 18, 1988. *See also* DEMOCRACY SUMMER.

TRANSPORT. *See* AIR TRANSPORT, CIVIL; RAIL TRANSPORT; ROAD TRANSPORT; WATER TRANSPORT.

– U –

U THANT INCIDENT (1974). After former UN Secretary-General U **Thant** died in November 1974, President **Ne Win** denied him a formal state funeral, ordering that his body be buried at the **Rangoon (Yangon)** city cemetery at Kyandaw. U Thant was a close associate of U **Nu**, the former prime minister who led an antiregime movement based in Thailand between 1969 and 1973. Ne Win also apparently begrudged U Thant the international stature he enjoyed. Thousands of people came to the Kyaikkasan grounds in Rangoon to pay respects to his remains, and on December 5, 1974, university **students** took possession of his coffin, bringing it to the Main Campus of **Rangoon (Yangon) University**. It was housed in the Convocation Hall, where tens of thousands came to pay respects and Buddhist monks offered chants.

Negotiations between the government and students might have prevented a confrontation. Ne Win conceded that U Thant's remains could be buried in a cemetery park near the **Shwe Dagon Pagoda**. But militant students took control of the situation, constructing a mausoleum for the late secretary-general on the site of the demolished **Rangoon University Students' Union** building. It became the focus for intense antiregime protest, including speeches critical of Ne Win. Threatened by what seemed to be a popular as well as student uprising, Ne Win ordered the **Tatmadaw** to storm the campus in the early morning of December 11. They seized the coffin, which was buried at the site near the Shwe Dagon, and killed an undetermined number of students. Many other students were arrested. Demonstrations and riots broke out around the city, and the authorities reportedly killed hundreds of protesters. The U Thant incident was the largest example of student militancy since the **July 7, 1962 incident**. In many ways, it was a precursor of **Democracy Summer** and the protests in early 1988 that led up to it. *See also* LABOR STRIKES.

UNION OF MYANMAR ECONOMIC HOLDINGS, LTD (UMEH). Established in 1990, a military-owned business conglomerate with enterprises in numerous sectors, including trade, financial services, **tourism**, and real estate. Believed to be the largest single company in Burma, it has formed joint ventures with foreign companies. Its assets are owned by both the Ministry of Defence and **Tatmadaw** units, personnel, and army veterans. *See also* DEFENCE SERVICES INSTITUTE.

UNION SOLIDARITY AND DEVELOPMENT ASSOCIATION (USDA). Burma's largest and most important mass movement organization, established in September 1993 by the **State Law and Order Restoration Council** with Senior General **Than Shwe** as its patron.

It is not a political party but a "social organization," registered with the Ministry of Home and Religious Affairs. At the beginning of the 21st century, its membership numbers between 10 and 15 million. The USDA is administered through a hierarchy of offices on the central, **state/division**, **district**, **township**, and ward/village tract levels.

The USDA's purpose is to organize support for the military regime's policies on the grassroots level. For a nominal fee (five *kyats*), individuals can join and have access to free courses on practical and ideologically oriented subjects, including computer training, English, and "**Buddhist** culture." Membership may also make it easier for persons to enjoy favorable treatment at the hands of government or military officials, including employment, while those who refuse to join may be harassed.

However, members are expected to make considerable contributions in terms of time and labor, including attendance at rallies. USDA mass rallies have frequently been organized to criticize **Aung San Suu Kyi** and the **National League for Democracy**. The USDA is considered responsible for a mob attack on her and other NLD leaders in **Rangoon (Yangon)** in late 1996 and the **"Black Friday" Incident** of May 30, 2003. It has considerable economic resources at its disposal through ownership of land and enterprises and can establish joint ventures with foreign partners.

UNITED FRONTIER UNION (UFU). A post–**World War II** proposal made by **H. N. C. Stevenson**, director of the Frontier Areas Administration, to establish a province under British rule, including the **Frontier Areas** but excluding most of **Burma Proper**. Based on the belief that the ethnic minority peoples, who had been loyal to Britain during the war, did not want to live in a **Burman (Bamar)**-dominated state, the UFU would have joined together what are now **Chin State**, **Kachin State**, the **Shan** and **Karenni States**, **Karen (Kayin)**-inhabited parts of Toungoo (Taungoo) District and the Salween District, and what are now **Mon State** and **Tenasserim (Tanintharyi) Division**. Stevenson organized the March 1946 Panglong Conference (known as the First Panglong Conference) to introduce the idea to Frontier Area leaders, but it aroused the implacable opposition of Burmese nationalists, who accused him of following a colonial "divide and rule" policy. Although

Stevenson lobbied for the United Frontier Union in London, the proposal was rejected by the Labour government of Clement Attlee, which promised **Aung San** that Britain would adhere to the principle that Burma Proper and the Frontier Areas would form a single independent state. *See also* AUNG SAN–ATTLEE AGREEMENT; PANGLONG CONFERENCE.

UNITED FRONTS (ANTIGOVERNMENT INSURGENTS). Ethnic nationalist, leftist, and **Burman (Bamar)** insurgent groups have established united fronts to topple the central government since independence, but their effectiveness has been undermined by geographic remoteness, ideological and factional differences, and the often-effective tactics of the **Ne Win** and **State Law and Order Restoration Council/State Peace and Development Council** regimes to divide them against themselves. The most important were the National United Liberation Front (NULF), which brought together the **Parliamentary Democracy Party (PDP)** of former Prime Minister U **Nu**, the **Karen National Union (KNU)**, the **New Mon State Party (NMSP)**, and the Chin Democracy Party in 1970. After its collapse, ethnic minority leaders established a new grouping in 1976, the National Democratic Front (NDF), which in addition to the KNU and MNSP also included the **Kachin Independence Army/Organization**, the **Karenni National Progress Party**, the **Chin National Front**, and seven other armed groups. In principle, it remained operative in 2005, although overshadowed by the **Democratic Alliance of Burma**, established in November 1988, which includes a broad array of minority, Burman, and political exile groups. *See also* CEASE-FIRES.

UNITED NATIONALITIES LEAGUE FOR DEMOCRACY (UNLD). An umbrella organization of minority nationality political parties established in 1989. Its 19 constituent parties, including the **Shan Nationalities League for Democracy**, the **Arakan League for Democracy**, and the Mon National Democratic Front, won about 50 seats in the **May 27, 1990 General Election**. Between June 29 and July 2, 1990, the UNLD held a conference in **Rangoon (Yangon)** and adopted a program based on federalism. On August 19, 1990, the

UNLD and the **National League for Democracy** formed an alliance, but in 1992 the **State Law and Order Restoration Council** banned the UNLD, although it has operated in exile as the United Nationalities League for Democracy-Liberated Areas.

UNITED NATIONS IN BURMA. Burma joined the United Nations in 1948, after becoming an independent nation. U **Thant**, a prominent political figure close to Prime Minister U **Nu**, served as UN secretary-general from 1961 to 1971, the first Asian to hold this post. A number of other Burmese nationals have served in the United Nations in various capacities, including **Aung San Suu Kyi**. After the **State Law and Order Restoration Council** was established in September 1988, the United Nations became involved in issues concerning **human rights**, **refugees**, human development, and **drugs**. UN agencies with a presence in the country include the United Nations Development Program (UNDP), the International Drug Control Program (UNIDCP), the UN Population Fund (UNFPA), the Food and Agriculture Organization (FAO), the UN High Commissioner for Refugees (UNHCR), the UN Children's Fund (UNICEF), the International Labour Organization (ILO), and the World Health Organization (WHO).

In 1992, the UN Commission on Human Rights nominated a "special rapporteur" to investigate the human rights situation in Burma, encourage the government to make improvements, and make a report to the UN General Assembly and the Human Rights Commission. In 2003, this post was filled by Dr. Paulo Sergio Pinheiro, a Brazilian academic and legal scholar. In addition, UN Secretary-General Kofi Annan designated a "special envoy," Razali Ismail, a Malaysian diplomat, who traveled many times to Burma to promote reconciliation between the **State Peace and Development Council (SPDC)** and Daw Suu Kyi. The SPDC has also entered into intensive interactions with the ILO over the issue of **forced labor**.

UNITED STATES, RELATIONS WITH. American ties with Burma go back to before the **First Anglo-Burmese War**. **Adoniram Judson**, a Baptist preacher, arrived in the country in 1815 and was followed by other American Baptist **missionaries**, who made many converts among the **Karens (Kayins)**, **Chins**, and **Kachins**. During **World War II**, American troops fought alongside Chin, Kachin,

Naga, British, and Chinese troops in northern Burma; **Merrill's Marauders** fought bloody battles in 1944 to capture **Myitkyina** and its airfield from the Japanese.

Before Burma became formally independent, the government signed an educational exchange agreement with Washington under the Fulbright Program in late 1947, and the United States began providing the country with **foreign aid** in 1950. But relations were troubled by Washington's support for **Kuomintang (Guomindang)** forces operating in **Shan State**, and Prime Minister **U Nu** ended the aid agreement over this issue in 1953. Aid was resumed in 1956, but following the loss of two Burmese air force planes in 1961 after they had intercepted a cargo plane from Taiwan bringing American supplies to the Kuomintang, there was a new crisis in relations, and anti-U.S. demonstrations flared up in **Rangoon (Yangon)**. U Nu's government regarded backing for the Kuomintang intruders by the U.S. Central Intelligence Agency (CIA) as a deliberate attack on Burma's sovereignty and independence.

After **Ne Win** established the **Revolutionary Council** in March 1962, relations with the United States and other Western countries were reduced. Although ongoing American aid agreements continued until their expiry, the Fulbright Program was shut down, and the activities of private organizations, such as the Ford and Asia Foundations, ended. However, the United States continued to give low-profile military assistance, a total of US$80 million between 1958 and 1970, which included the training of **Tatmadaw** officers at U.S. facilities. Modest educational and cultural exchanges were also reestablished after 1970. By the mid-1970s, Washington was providing assistance for **drug**-eradication programs, including helicopters and other equipment, to interdict the export of **opium** and **heroin** across Burma's borders. According to some American critics, the U.S. government also made available defoliants, similar to "Agent Orange," to destroy poppy fields inside Burma, but the Ne Win regime used them indiscriminately against civilian ethnic minority populations. By the 1980s, the United States had become an important provider of economic aid, though the amounts were small compared to those given by **Japan** and West **Germany**.

Democracy Summer and the seizure of power by the **State Law and Order Restoration Council** in 1988 led to a fundamental change in relations. Much of the Tatmadaw's violence against civilian demonstrators took place near the U.S. embassy on Merchant Street in downtown Rangoon, and Ambassador Burton Levin was outspoken in criticizing the new regime's hard line. **Aung San Suu Kyi** soon gained admirers among influential Americans, including Ambassador Levin and Stephen Solarz, a U.S. congressman with a special interest in Asian affairs. American aid, a total of US$16 million, was suspended. Aside from humanitarian aid, it has not been resumed.

The administrations of Presidents George Bush and Bill Clinton both urged the post-1988 military regime to respect the results of the **General Election of May 27, 1990.** President Clinton's secretary of state, Madeleine Albright, visited Daw Suu Kyi in Rangoon after her release from house arrest in July 1995 and took a strong personal interest in her situation. The U.S. State Department, in its annual *Country Reports on Human Rights Practices,* criticized the junta's **human rights** violations, though the U.S. Drug Enforcement Agency (DEA) had a different perspective, advocating better ties with the SLORC to carry out drug eradication more effectively. A community of prodemocracy Burmese exiles and activists emerged in Washington, D.C., after 1988 and received substantial moral and material support from the U.S. government, including the strong backing of an influential Republican Senator, Mitch McConnell of Missouri. Government-funded Radio Free Asia broadcasts news in the **Burmese (Myanmar) language** to provide Burmese listeners with an alternative to the official **mass media.**

After 1988, the United States blocked financial assistance to the SLORC/SPDC by the World Bank, in which it has a major voice, and other multilateral lenders. Major **sanctions** were imposed by President Clinton in 1997 (a nonretroactive ban on American investments) and by President George W. Bush (bans on financial transactions and imports of Burmese products to the United States) following the **"Black Friday" Incident** of May 30, 2003 (renewed in 2004 and 2005). However, these measures did not affect the **Yadana Pipeline Project**, in which a U.S. oil company, Unocal, had a share. Business interests inside the United States opposed sanctions for economic reasons, and some critics argued that the 2003 import ban was counterproductive, harming ordinary Burmese workers rather than the military junta.

The **State Peace and Development Council** has assailed the United States in the official media as a neoimperialist power and has warned its people that Washington might attempt an invasion of their country similar to that of Iraq. Civil servants have been given special military training to prepare for this eventuality. But official anti-Americanism seems to find limited resonance among ordinary people, whose main concerns are daily economic woes rather than a neoimperialist replay of Iraq and Afghanistan. *See also* EUROPEAN UNION, RELATIONS WITH.

UNITED WA STATE ARMY (UWSA). At the beginning of the 21st century, the most powerful ethnic minority armed group in Burma, with a strength of 20,000 men and a notorious reputation as Southeast Asia's best organized "narco-army." Although statistics are unreliable, it is believed to make as much as US$550 million a year from the sale of **opium, heroin**, and **amphetamines** to international markets. The UWSA was established in November 1989, after a mutiny by ethnic commanders led to the breakup of the **Communist Party of Burma**, and was one of the first armed groups to sign a **cease-fire** with the **State Law and Order Restoration Council (SLORC)**. Its leader since 1989 has been **Bao Youxiang**, who also became chairman of its political wing, the United Wa State Party, after its first chairman, Chao Ngi Lai, died of a stroke in 1995. Its headquarters are at Panghsang, a Burma–China border town that has grown prosperous through the **drug** trade.

The UWSA not only controls the traditional **Wa States** region east of the **Salween (Thanlwin) River** in **Shan State** but also occupies extensive territories along the Thai–Burma border, especially around Tachilek and Mong Yawn (Mong Yun). Both locations enable it to export large amounts of drugs by way of Yunnan Province in **China** and northern **Thailand**. To consolidate its control over the southern region, in 1999 the UWSA began to relocate some 100,000 **Wa** villagers to the Burma–Thai border; there were many instances of **forced relocation**, and the new settlers suffered because of inadequate supplies and because their new homes were in a hotter climate than their native highlands. Moreover, many of the original inhabitants of the resettlement areas, mostly **Shan** and **Lahu**, were driven from their villages.

After the cease-fire with the SLORC was signed, the cultivation and export of opium and heroin in areas under UWSA control increased tremendously. Bao Youxiang has promised that his territories will be "opium free" by 2005, but nothing has been done about the trade in cheap amphetamines (known in the Thai language as *yaabaa*, "crazy medicine"), 80 percent of which is controlled by the UWSA.

The UWSA has proven to be both a blessing and a curse for the **State Peace and Development Council**. It has played an effective role in the junta's "divide and rule" strategies in Shan State: UWSA pressure contributed to **Khun Sa**'s decision to sign a cease-fire in January 1996, causing the breakup of his **Mong Tai Army**, which had been strong enough to frustrate the military regime's objective of controlling central and southern Shan State. But the UWSA is powerful enough to deny the **Tatmadaw** access to its own territories, in contrast to the situation in **Kokang**, where the **Myanmar National Democratic Alliance Army**, another cease-fire group, is much weaker and internally divided. The UWSA's aggressive behavior has led to occasional border clashes with the Thai Army, though border problems have not prevented political and business leaders in Bangkok from pursuing profitable relations with the SPDC.

Flush with cash from drug dealing, the UWSA has expanded into a variety of businesses. It controls the Myanmar May Flower Group, a **Rangoon (Yangon)**-based enterprise that includes one of Burma's largest private banks, and has a stake in Yangon Airways, a private airline that caters to Burma's tourist trade. Reports by the few outsider observers to enter Wa territory indicate that while UWSA leaders like Bao are fabulously wealthy, ordinary Wa people endure some of the worst poverty in Burma.

UPPER BURMA. A term used by the British in the 19th and early 20th centuries to refer to those territories ruled by the **Konbaung Dynasty** until the **Third Anglo-Burmese War** (1885). Upper Burma was sometimes referred to as "**Ava**," the name of a royal capital. It includes present-day **Mandalay**, **Magwe (Magway)**, and **Sagaing Divisions**, and its chief urban center is **Mandalay**, Burma's last royal capital. It is bisected by the **Irrawaddy (Ayeyarwady) River**, traditionally the main artery of transportation. Like **Lower Burma**, Upper

Burma has a strong geographic and historical identity. Largely isolated from the outside world by mountain ranges that separate it from China, India, and Thailand, it is the home of the **Burmans (Bamars)** and is relatively homogeneous ethnically. Except for irrigated areas, such as **Kyaukse**, its agricultural potential has been limited by lack of water. During the colonial era, both regions constituted **Burma Proper**, in contrast to the **Frontier Areas**. *See also* ADMINISTRATION OF BURMA, BRITISH COLONIAL PERIOD; DRY ZONE.

– V –

VINAYA. *Wini* in the **Burmese (Myanmar) language**, the 227 rules that all members of the **Sangha** are expected to observe. They are found in the *Vinaya Pitaka*, one of the three "baskets" of the **Buddhist** scriptures (**Tipitaka**), and are divided into eight categories, depending on their importance, and the sanctions used in punishing transgressions of them, ranging from prohibitions against killing and sexual intercourse to detailed prescriptions concerning how the saffron robe is to be worn, the time for taking meals, and proper relations within the monastic community and with laypeople. Practically every aspect of human behavior is affected, and differences between the various sects (*gaing*) of Burmese Buddhism generally concern divergent interpretations of *vinaya* rules, rather than doctrine.

"VIP GRIDS." Because of the poor state of the electric power–generating infrastructure, including the dilapidated Baluchaung Hydroelectric plant in Kayah State, which had been built with Japanese war reparations in the 1950s, electric power in **Rangoon (Yangon)** and other areas is intermittent, especially during the dry season. To obtain electricity during blackouts and brownouts, residents use Chinese- and Japanese-made generators, which are noisy, polluting, and sometimes undependable, or purchase electricity from those who have a reliable source. Intermittent power cuts do great damage to machinery, especially computers. However, high-ranking **Tatmadaw** officers and other VIPs ("very important persons") live in areas where electricity is available 24 hours a day, seven days a week, the "VIP Grids," which include **Bogyoke Ywa** ("generals' villages").

"VISIT MYANMAR YEAR" (1996–1997). A campaign carried out by the **State Law and Order Restoration Council (SLORC)** to bring 500,000 foreign visitors to Burma in 1996–1997. In anticipation of the huge money-making potential of **tourism**, the SLORC entered into joint ventures with foreign companies to build luxury hotels and establish two new airlines, Air Mandalay and Yangon Airways, to carry tourists between favored destinations, especially **Rangoon (Yangon), Mandalay, Pagan (Bagan)**, and **Inle Lake** in **Shan State**. Some old hotels, like the Strand in Rangoon, were completely renovated, and tourist visas were lengthened from 7 to 28 days. However, after her release from house arrest in July 1995, **Aung San Suu Kyi** urged an international boycott of "Visit Myanmar Year," claiming that tourist revenues would support an illegitimate regime and that the development of many tourist sites, like the moat of **Mandalay Palace**, involved **forced labor** and **forced relocation**. The campaign never reached its goal of half a million visitors (it was closer to 200,000), and Daw Suu Kyi's opposition to international tourism embittered already-delicate relations between her and members of the SLORC. *See also* SANCTIONS.

– W –

WA STATES. A region of northeastern **Shan State**, between the **Salween (Thanlwin) River** and the Chinese border, south of **Kokang** and northwest of **Keng Tung**, which is the homeland of the **Was**. With an area of about 6,000 square miles, one-tenth the area of Shan State, it is extremely remote and mountainous. Neither the British nor the governments of independent Burma succeeded in imposing effective control. According to **James George Scott**, writing in 1906: "the Wa States are . . . not administered, and not very thoroughly explored, but the boundary has been mapped and notified to the Chinese Government" (*Burma: A Handbook of Practical Information*, [1921] 1999, 2). Once the **Communist Party of Burma** established its headquarters at Panghsang on the Chinese border in 1968, the Wa

States felt the impact of war and heavy Chinese influence. Until recently, the core of the Wa States, an area of about 2,600 square kilometers (1,000 square miles), was inhabited by the "Wild Wa," a fierce group of headhunters who lived in well-fortified hilltop villages and were ruled by *ramang* (chiefs), the heads of a confederation of three or four villages. Beyond this, there appears to have been no stable political organization, making the term "states" rather misleading. Headhunting seems to have stopped only in the 1970s. In 1989, the **United Wa State Army** established its headquarters at Panghsang and divided the original Wa States into 11 districts. The area remains one of Burma's poorest and most undeveloped, dependent on the cultivation of **opium** poppies.

WARERU, KING (r. 1287–1296). Though probably Tai, Wareru founded a powerful **Mon** dynasty in **Lower Burma**. He was an officer at the court of the king of Sukhothai, in what is now **Thailand**, who allegedly eloped with the king's daughter to **Martaban (Mottama)** in 1280–1281, where he helped Mon rebels expel the **Burmans (Bamars)** from the region. Killing his principal Mon ally and establishing himself as an independent ruler with Martaban as his capital (it was later moved to **Hanthawaddy**), he is renowned for having sponsored the compiling of Burma's first *Dhammathat*, or law code. His descendants, **Razadarit** (r. 1385–1423), **Shinsawbu** (r. 1453–72), and **Dhammazedi** (r. 1472–92), presided over a Mon golden age, but the last ruler of Wareru's line, Takayutpi, was overthrown by **Tabinshwehti** in 1539. *See also* TOUNGOO DYNASTY.

WAS. An ethnic minority group who live in northeastern **Shan State** and adjacent areas of China's Yunnan Province, though before the coming of the **Shans (Tai)** they were more widespread and were probably the original inhabitants of **Keng Tung**. Of importance to the Wa people is Lake Nawngkhio (Nawng Kheo), near the present Chinese border, which is said to be their mythic place of origin. They speak a language belonging to the Wa-Palaung subgroup of the Mon-Khmer language group; in recent years, heavy Chinese influence has resulted in the widespread use of Mandarin.

Their homeland, the **Wa States**, bounded by the **Salween (Thanlwin) River** on the west and the Chinese border on the east, south of

Kokang, is composed of mountains and steep-sloped hills and has little agricultural potential, leaving the Wa poor and undeveloped. Slash-and-burn **agriculture** has left many of the slopes denuded of vegetation. To generate income, they have become heavily dependent on the cultivation of **opium** poppies, the drug being exported to neighboring countries by the **United Wa State Army (UWSA)**.

During the British colonial period, the Wa States were so remote that only in 1937 were officials of the colonial regime, two in number, posted there. Both the Shans and the British divided the Wa into two groups: the "Tame Wa," who were exposed to **Buddhism**, influenced by Shan customs and were usually part of the jurisdiction of a Shan *sawbwa,* and the "Wild Wa," who lived in the remotest areas, were animists, and practiced head-hunting (a "skull grove" outside of Wa villages was believed to ensure good harvests and protection from disease and calamity). The Wild Wa had a fearsome reputation, which kept intruders out, and their hilltop villages were strongly fortified. In **James G. Scott**'s words, "(t)he race is brave, independent, energetic, ingenious, and industrious. . . . The taking of a head is a sacrificial act, not an example of brutal ferocity" (*Burma: A Handbook of Practical Information*, [1921] 1999, 141).

The remoteness of the Wa States left them out of the mainstream of Burmese and even **Frontier Area** history; they were not included in the 1922 Shan States Federation and were largely untouched by **World War II**. Although some Wa fighters joined Shan State insurgencies, it was only with the establishment of a strong **Communist Party of Burma (CPB)** base on the China–Burma border in January 1968 that their region was fully opened to outside influences, primarily from **China**. They formed a majority of the CPB's People's Army, often serving as "cannon fodder" in pitched battles with the **Tatmadaw**. Now they serve as soldiers in the 20,000-man strong UWSA. According to Shan sources, Wa women outnumber men three to one because of the decades of bitter warfare.

No one can say with confidence how many Wa there are. The UWSA claimed in 1994 that they numbered half a million. In the late 1990s, the armed group began relocating 100,000 of them from their mountain homeland to the Thai–Burma border area, around Mong Yawn, part of a UWSA strategy to acquire a strategic position in southern Shan State from which to export **drugs**, especially **amphet-**

amines, to Thailand. The significant Wa presence in the south was made possible by the surrender of **Khun Sa's Mong Tai Army** in January 1996, but it has caused great hardship, both to the relocated Wa and to Shan and **Lahu** people who were forced to leave their villages. The Wa have always been good fighters and now constitute the strongest ethnic minority armed group in Burma, but while the leadership, including UWSA commander **Bao Youxiang**, grows rich on the drug trade, ordinary Wa remain among the poorest people in Burma and lack even the most elementary social services.

WAT ZOM KHAM (WAT JONG KHAM). A major **Buddhist** site in **Keng Tung**, eastern **Shan State**, which according to legend stands at a place visited by Gotama **Buddha** during his lifetime, but probably dates from the late 13th century, when Keng Tung was established. The **stupa**, 38 meters high, is said to contain six strands of the Buddha's hair. The use of the term *wat* to refer to the site (and others in Keng Tung) reflects affinities with **Thailand**, where the word is used to refer to Buddhist temples and **pagodas**.

WATER TRANSPORT. Burma is blessed with navigable rivers, especially the **Irrawaddy (Ayeyarwady)** and **Chindwin (Chindwinn)**, and river transport was long the principal mode of transport between **Upper** and **Lower Burma**. Navigable rivers are estimated to total 6,452 kilometers (4,000 miles), of which about half are in the Irrawaddy Delta. **Rangoon (Yangon)** has been connected to the Irrawaddy River by the 35-kilometer-long (22-mile-long) Twante Canal since the late 19th century, when it was constructed by the British. During the colonial period, river boats carried more passengers and freight than **rail transport**; in central Burma, the Scottish-owned **Irrawaddy Flotilla Company** operated a virtual monopoly, squeezing out local competitors. When Burma attained independence in 1948, the Irrawaddy Flotilla and the Arakan Flotilla Companies were nationalized and merged under the Inland Water Transport Board (known as the Inland Water Transport Corporation after 1972). Since 1988, **China** has invested heavily in Burma's water transport facilities, including both powered vessels and barges.

Coastal shipping is extensive. Oceangoing vessels are owned by Myanmar Five Star Line, a state corporation established in 1959, and the major port is Rangoon, whose facilities are being modernized. Since the **Ne Win** era, many young Burmese men have served in the world's merchant marine as a way of earning hard currency, though not necessarily on Burmese-registered ships.

WEEK, BURMESE. The traditional Burmese week has eight rather than seven days; to accommodate this, Wednesday morning and afternoon in the Western system each count as a separate day. As in many other societies, individual character is said to be determined by the day on which people are born, for example, those born on Tuesday are honest, those on Saturday bad tempered, etc. A person born on a "compatible" day of the week with one's own is considered a desirable marriage partner. In early childhood, a very detailed horoscope (Burmese, *sada*) is often drawn up by a practitioner of **astrology** to guide the child through his or her life. Each day of the week has its own planet, animal, and cardinal direction. The platforms of **pagodas** (most famously the **Shwe Dagon Pagoda**) frequently contain shrines set at appropriate points of the compass for each day of the week.

WEIKZA. Also *wei'za*, a practitioner of occult or supernatural arts who acquires special powers through **alchemy**, magic amulets, mantras, magic letters (Burmese "runes"), and other devices, and can aid people in distress. Belief in *weikzas* and the growth of cults (*gaing*) associated with them seem to be relatively modern developments, perhaps a response to the shock of British colonial occupation. They are neither members of the **Sangha** nor *nats*, but are an important element in the folklore of popular **Buddhism**. Although occult figures going back at least to the **Pagan Dynasty** are identified by Burmese sources as *weikzas*, along with the devout **Mon** king, **Dhammazedi** (r. 1472–1492), the most prominent example is **Bo Bo Aung**, a contemporary and adversary of King **Bodawpaya** (r. 1782–1819). Belief in these figures seems to flourish in times of stress and uncertainty. Although the governments of U **Nu** and **Ne Win** attempted to suppress the more extreme *weiksa* cults in favor of orthodox Buddhist practices, the cults retained their popularity, even among military officers who supposedly espoused modernist, socialist ideology. Apparently, they remain important in the religious life of Burmese people under the **State Peace and Development Council.**

WHITE BRIDGE INCIDENT (MARCH 16, 1988). Also known as the "White Bridge Massacre," an incident that took place on an embankment along the western shore of **Inya Lake** in **Rangoon (Yangon)**, where student demonstrators marching from **Rangoon University** to the **Rangoon Institute of Technology** were attacked by the **Riot Police (Lon Htein)**. According to a letter written to **Ne Win** by **Aung Gyi** on June 8, 1988, almost 300 students were killed, many drowned in the lake by Riot Police personnel. *See also* DEMOCRACY SUMMER; TEA SHOP INCIDENT.

WHOLE TOWNSHIP EXTENSION PROGRAM. In the late 1970s, the **Burma Socialist Programme Party** regime sought to increase agricultural yields by promoting the cultivation of high-yield varieties of **rice**, which had been initially developed at the International Rice Research Institute (IRRI) in the Philippines. In the 1977–1978 planting year, the varieties were introduced to two townships, and by 1982–1983 had spread to more than 50 percent of the country's rice lands. The program was initially a great success: Paddy yields also increased by 50 percent. But these increases could not be sustained because of variable weather conditions and inadequate investment in fertilizers, pesticides, and farm mechanization. Also, the state threatened many farmers with expropriation of their land if they did not plant the new varieties. However, many Burmese consumers found them less tasty than traditional varieties of rice. *See also* AGRICULTURE; ECONOMY AND ECONOMIC POLICY, BURMA SOCIALIST PROGRAMME PARTY ERA.

WIN TIN, U (1930–). A distinguished journalist and writer, at present one of Burma's most prominent political prisoners. He served as editor of the *Hanthawaddy* newspaper until 1978, when the presentation of a paper critical of the **Burma Socialist Programme Party** at a writers' circle he sponsored resulted in his losing his post and the *Hanthawaddy* being closed down by the government. Between 1978 and 1988, he was a freelance writer, then became active in the Burma Writers' Union during 1988 and secretary to the executive committee of the **National League for Democracy**, advising Daw **Aung San Suu Kyi** and other NLD leaders. Imprisoned in June 1989 for allegedly having a telephone conversation with an antistate element, his prison sentence was extended without trial three times, and he remained confined as of mid-2005. Suffering from ill health, he has been kept since 1997 in guarded hospital wards at **Insein Jail** and Rangoon General Hospital.

WISARA, U (1888–1929). One of the most prominent "political *pongyis*," U Wisara was born near Monywa in what is now **Sagaing Division** and decided to devote his life to the **Buddhist** religion around the age of 20. When monastic superiors chastised him for becoming involved in politics, he and like-minded young monks established their own monastic community in Pakkoku, now in **Magwe (Magway) Division**. In 1923, he went to **Rangoon (Yangon)**, associated with **U Ottama**, and under his sponsorship spent two years in India. Upon returning home, U Wisara made political speeches and was repeatedly imprisoned by the colonial authorities. His hunger strikes while in jail to be allowed to observe the *vinaya* rules (especially wearing saffron robes rather than a convict's outfit), as well as abuses inflicted by his jailors, ruined his health. He was arrested and jailed one last time in April 1929. He died on September 19, 1929, after a 166-day hunger strike, undertaken to persuade the authorities to respect the rights of jailed monks. He became a martyr of the independence movement, and in 1940 a statue of him was erected near the **Shwe Dagon Pagoda**, where it stands today.

WOMEN IN BURMESE SOCIETY. During the British colonial period, European observers were impressed by the apparent equality of the sexes in Burmese society, claiming, as **James George Scott** did, that "a married Burmese woman is much more independent than any European woman even in the most advanced states" (*The Burman*, [1883] 1963, 52). Women not only managed household finances but also played a major role in retail trade, their business acumen widely considered superior to that of the average Burmese man. This is still true today; for example, the wives of high-ranking military officers have made large amounts of money from private and **black market**

businesses, while their menfolk, in **Ne Win**'s words, "only know how to fight."

Traditionally, Burmese women have been free of the stifling restrictions of the patriarchal family system, such as those found in China, India, and Japan. In patriarchal systems, the primary role of the woman is to provide a male heir for her husband's family, with whom she lives, largely severing her ties with her own parents and siblings. In the Burmese case, the **family system** is bilateral (descent through both the father's and mother's line, rather than the father's alone), and married women remain close to their own parents. Inheritances are shared between sons and daughters, rather than by sons only, and a divorced woman is entitled to take away from the failed marriage her own property, which even in traditional law was recognized as different from that of her husband. Burmese parents with several daughters but no sons would not be considered especially unfortunate; if the daughters marry well (e.g., a military officer), they can generously support their parents in their old age.

Most fundamentally, there is none of the strong discrimination against the birth and upbringing of daughters in Burma that one finds in India or some East Asian countries, and female infanticide appears to be rare. According to recent UN statistics, there are 101 women and girls per 100 males in Burma's rural areas and 100 females per 100 males in urban areas, a natural ratio. In India, the ratios are 96 females per 100 males in rural and 88 females per 100 males in urban areas, reflecting the widespread practice of abortion of female fetuses and the overall lower survival rates of girls due to harsh treatment or neglect, compared to boys.

In precolonial Burma, educational opportunities for girls were available at village monastery schools, although females could not (and cannot) become members of the **Sangha** (the practice of ordaining **nuns** having been lost to the Theravada branch of **Buddhism**). In the colonial and postcolonial eras, a large percentage of the student bodies at the **University of Rangoon (Yangon)** and other institutions have been women. They have freely entered the professions. For example, Daw **Khin Kyi**, wife of **Aung San** and mother of **Aung San Suu Kyi**, served as Burma's ambassador to India, and such women as Ludu Daw Amar have been prominent on the literary scene. However, the freedoms that Burmese women enjoy are not equivalent to 100-percent equality with men in terms of social roles.

In the religious sphere, women are not only prohibited from joining the Sangha, but it is also believed that only men can achieve *nibbana*; women cannot enter certain holy places, such as the upper platform of the **Shwe Dagon Pagoda** or the space directly in front of the **Maha Muni Buddha Image** in **Mandalay**. The *shinbyu* ceremony for young boys entering the monkhood far overshadows girls' coming-of-age rite, the **ear-boring** (*natwin*) ceremony.

Men are commonly believed to possess a certain authority or power (*hpoun*) that would be diminished if they find themselves placed in any situation where their inferior position to women is apparent, for example, sitting below a woman on a crowded bus or ferry boat or allowing their heads to pass beneath a woman's garments on a clothesline. Burmese women are expected to show deference to men, especially their husbands, even if this is only for show. A major reason for the strong antipathy that Senior General **Than Shwe** and other members of the **State Peace and Development Council (SPDC)** feel toward Aung San Suu Kyi is her insistence upon expressing her opinions frankly and interacting with them as equals. Her behavior is seen as very "Western" and antipathetic to traditional values, though she is also greatly admired for her courage. It is probably significant that during its long history, Burma has had only one major female ruler, the **Mon** Queen **Shinsawbu**.

Military values and military control of the political system since 1962 have resulted in a decline in Burmese women's social status, compared to the parliamentary and even British colonial eras. Burma is one of the few countries (another being Saudi Arabia) where women at present hold no important government posts. Ethnic minority women have suffered worst of all from **human rights** abuses, including the apparently systematic rape of **Karen (Kayin)** and **Shan** women by **Tatmadaw** officers and men.

Even in central Burma, economic stagnation and the deterioration of **health** and **educational** services since 1988 have had an especially harsh impact on women's lives. The recent growth in the **sex industry**, which previously had not been a major social problem, reflects the fact that for both ethnic minority and **Burman** women with families to support, few other types of employment are widely available.

More than 40,000 Burmese women work in brothels in neighboring Thailand. **Nongovernmental organizations** have been established to deal with women's issues, some of which enjoy the patronage of the wives of SPDC generals, but for the great majority of women, facing a grim day-to-day struggle to survive, the freedoms enjoyed by their mothers and grandmothers are a distant dream.

WORLD WAR II, ETHNIC MINORITIES IN. World War II and the **Japanese Occupation** transformed relations between the indigenous and nonindigenous ethnic minorities and the **Burman (Bamar)** ethnic majority. In **Lower Burma**, the Japanese invasion and anti-**Indian** incidents led to the departure of more than half a million persons of South Asian descent in early 1942. They returned to the British-ruled subcontinent, often overland under conditions of great hardship. Only a few went back to Burma after the war, meaning that South Asians (including people from what are now India, Pakistan, and Bangladesh) exercised significantly reduced economic and social influence compared to before 1941. The Overseas **Chinese** and **Sino-Burmese** sometimes suffered harsh treatment at the hands of the Japanese, but apparently not the systematic atrocities endured by the Chinese in Singapore and Malaya. The **Anglo-Burmese** (Eurasians) seem not to have been systematically persecuted, but they lost the favorable connections provided by British rule. Violent race riots broke out between Buddhist and Muslim residents of **Arakan** after British authority there collapsed in early 1942.

Generally loyal to the British, the **Karens (Kayins)** of the **Irrawaddy (Ayeyarwady) River** Delta region and the hills east of the **Sittang (Sittoung) River** endured atrocities at the hands of the **Burma Independence Army** and the Japanese, and organized guerrilla resistance with the help of **Force 136**. The British supplied the hill Karens with weapons, which they used with great effect against retreating Japanese troops in 1945. Although Dr. **Ba Maw** and General **Aung San** tried to win their trust, Karen wartime experiences engendered strong opposition to their inclusion in any Burman-dominated state, leading to the 1949 uprising by the **Karen National Union.**

With a few exceptions, the **Kachins**, **Chins**, and **Nagas**, who lived along Burma's mountainous borders with India and China, supported the British. This was because of traditionally close ties between their leaders and the colonizers (including in many cases a common Christian faith), the inclusion of these groups in the **colonial armed forces**, and the fact that many hill areas were not firmly under Japanese control. These groups, along with the hill Karens, played a significant role in the Allied recapture of Burma in 1944–1945. The **Shans**, whose *sawbwa* (*saohpa*) or rulers were confirmed in their semifeudal status under Japanese rule, remained largely aloof from the war, though many Shans were alienated by the Japanese decision to give the states of **Keng Tung** and Mongpan to Thailand in 1943.

In conclusion, the war, which enshrined the politics of armed violence, broke down Burma's multiethnic **plural society** and shattered the ethnic peace that had been imposed by the British since the late 19th century. The Japanese-supported government of Dr. Ba Maw, moreover, espoused a specifically Burman cultural and national identity, creating Burma's first "postcolonial state." Though Ba Maw and Aung San sought ethnic inclusiveness, many of their subordinates (especially in the armed forces) were afflicted by Burman chauvinism. Among minorities, such as the Kachins and Karens, fighting alongside the British and Americans gave them the experience they needed when they began insurgencies against the Rangoon government after the war. *See also* MYAUNGMYA MASSACRES; PANGLONG CONFERENCE; WORLD WAR II AND BURMA (MILITARY OPERATIONS).

WORLD WAR II IN BURMA (MILITARY OPERATIONS). Burma was the site of some of the largest battles of World War II. Following the outbreak of war between Japan and Britain on December 8, 1941, the Japanese air force carried out bombing raids against **Rangoon (Yangon)** and other targets, causing considerable demoralization. Elements of the Japanese Fifteenth Army, based in Thailand, had captured Kawthaung (Victoria Point, Burma's southernmost point), **Tavoy (Dawei)**, **Mergui (Myeik)**, and the key town of **Moulmein (Mawlamyine)** by the end of January 1942, and crossed the **Sittang (Sittoung) River** in late February (British orders to demolish the Sittang Bridge on February 23, while some of their forces were still east of the river, remain highly controversial). Rangoon was evacuated by the British and occupied by the Japanese on March 9. Between March and May 1942, the Fifteenth Army succeeded in driving north along the **Irrawaddy (Ayeyarwady) River** and the **Pegu (Bago)-Mandalay** road, thwarting British plans to maintain control of **Upper Burma** with the assistance of Chinese Nationalist **(Kuomintang)** troops concentrated at **Toungoo (Taungoo)**. **Mandalay** fell on May 1. **Lashio** was captured on May 8, and the **Burma Road** was cut. Allied forces staged a retreat overland to northeastern India, their troops ravaged by disease and starvation. But they remained largely intact, to fight another day.

Japanese victory in the first Battle of Burma can be attributed to superior numbers, superior mobility and maneuverability (British forces were repeatedly outflanked and encircled), control of the air (reflecting the technical superiority and greater numbers of the Japanese Zero fighter compared to its Allied counterparts), and the support provided by the **Burma Independence Army (BIA)**. The BIA's contribution was as much psychological as military because its fighting alongside Japanese troops gave rise to Burmese hopes, ultimately disappointed, that a victorious Japan would grant their country immediate independence.

The year 1943 witnessed an unsuccessful British attempt to dislodge the Japanese from their positions in what is now **Arakan (Rakhine) State**, and the more successful incursion of the **Chindits** deep into Japanese-held territory in northern Burma, an operation that did much to raise Allied morale. The South-East Asia Command under Vice-Admiral Lord **Louis Mountbatten** was established in August, with responsibility for joint Allied operations in the Indian Ocean and adjacent areas.

The ill-advised **Imphal Campaign** of March–June 1944 cost the Japanese as many as 80,000 casualties, undermining the Fifteenth Army's ability to defend Upper Burma. An American force, nicknamed **Merrill's Marauders**, moved along the **Ledo Road** and captured the airfield near **Myitkyina** (now the capital of **Kachin State**) in May 1944. British XIVth Army commander General **William Slim**, one of the Allies' ablest field commanders, began an offensive from India into northern Burma in late 1944. By February 1945, British forces had crossed the Irrawaddy; in early March, they captured the strategically important town of **Meiktila**, south of **Mandalay**. Mandalay itself was secured on March 19, although **Mandalay Palace** was incinerated in Allied air attacks. The push into southern Burma was slowed only by the start of the monsoon, and Japanese forces began a desperate retreat from central Burma toward the Sittang River and the Thai–Burma border, where **Karen (Kayin)** guerrillas killed many of them. Rangoon, evacuated by the Japanese, was recaptured without a fight on May 2–3.

Allied military successes in 1944–1945 were attributable to their growing material superiority over the Japanese, both in weapons and troop support. The stubborn insistence of Japanese commanders that their men could achieve victory through will power alone, with little or no logistical support, needlessly wasted many lives. Japanese infantrymen often lacked both food and bullets. Moreover, Allied commanders had learned from the bitter experiences of 1942 to exercise greater flexibility and mobility in operations. The effective use of armor on the plains of central Burma and airdrops to supply troops on the ground (e.g., the Chindit incursions and the battle of the "Admin Box" in Arakan in 1944) were also decisive factors. The uprising of the **Burma National Army** against the Japanese on March 27, 1945, provided the Allies with important sources of intelligence, though a greater contribution was probably made by Karen and other guerrillas organized by **Force 136**.

Burma was devastated twice by large-scale fighting, in 1942 and 1944–1945. Japanese forces in the country totaled 303,501, but only 118,352 were repatriated to Japan after the war. British and Commonwealth casualties amounted to 73,909, of whom more than half were from the British Indian Army. Nationalist Chinese casualties during 1942 appear to have been tremendous, though uncounted. There are no reliable statistics on the number of Burmese soldiers and civilians who died during the war, but after December 1941 it was men with guns, rather than politicians or civil servants, who determined the country's future. *See also* JAPANESE OCCUPATION; PATRIOTIC BURMESE FORCES; WORLD WAR II, ETHNIC MINORITIES IN.

WUNTHANU ATHIN. "Patriotic" or "nationalist associations" (**Ba Maw** translates *wunthanu* as "racially faithful ones") established in rural villages that were closely associated with the **General Council** of **Burmese Associations (GCBA)** and the **General Council of Sangha Sammeggi (GCSS)**. They played a major role in political mobilization against British colonial rule before the **Saya San (Hsaya San) Rebellion** of 1930–1932. Thousands of these associations operated on the local level, charged with promoting pride in Burmese tradition, national identity, and the **Buddhist** religion and with agitating against oppressive measures such as the 1907 Village Act, which imposed heavy **forced labor** burdens on the populace. "Political *pongyis*" played a key role in their activities. Because local *wunthanu athin* leaders constituted, in a sense, an alternative source of authority to the village headmen appointed by the British, they were subject to harsh government measures.

– Y –

YA NAING, BO (1919–1989). *Nom de guerre* of Ko Tun Shein, one of the **Thirty Comrades** and son-in-law of Dr. **Ba Maw**. He played a leading role in the **Rangoon University Students Union** and the **All Burma Students Union** from 1938 to 1941, and after the **Burma Independence Army** was established in December 1941, won distinction as a commander fighting the British at Shwedaung, near **Prome (Pyay)**. In 1944–1945, he was commandant of the military academy established by the Japanese at **Mingaladon**. After **World War II**, he was active in opposition politics. In 1969 he joined the **Parliamentary Democracy Party** of U Nu and became one of the commanders of the former prime minister's antigovernment insurgency based in the Thai–Burma border area. He returned to Burma following an amnesty proclaimed by **Ne Win** in 1980, but after the power seizure by the **State Law and Order Restoration Council** in September 1988, he helped U Nu organize his own party, the League for Democracy and Peace.

YADANA PIPELINE PROJECT. One of the largest joint ventures funded by **foreign investment** in Burma since 1988 (US$1.2 billion), constructed by a consortium consisting of the Myanmar Oil and Gas Enterprise, the French oil company Total, Unocal of the United States, and the Petroleum Authority of Thailand. With a length of 666 kilometers, the pipeline extends from the Yadana natural gas field in the Andaman Sea, just south of **Rangoon (Yangon)** over water and land, a land corridor in northern **Tenasserim (Tanintharyi) Division** reaching to **Thailand**, where the gas is used to generate electricity. The project is controversial for two reasons: It generates as much as US$400 million in revenues annually for the **State Peace and Development Council**, and construction of the pipeline and associated facilities involved extensive **forced labor** and **forced relocation** in Tenasserim Division, especially of **Karen (Kayin)** and **Mon** villagers. Security was provided by the **Tatmadaw**, which applied the "**Four Cuts**" policy to local insurgents and their civilian supporters. A similar project was initiated at the Yetagun natural gas field, involving Japanese, British, and Malaysian partners. Both projects were targets of campaigning by international **nongovernmental organizations**, and Unocal was brought to court in the **United States** for complicity in **human rights** abuses.

YANGON CITY DEVELOPMENT COMMITTEE (YCDC). In May 1990, the **State Law and Order Restoration Council (SLORC)** established the YCDC as an agency on the same level as the Cabinet, exercising considerable autonomy. Its membership, numbering between 7 and 15, is appointed by the SLORC (known after 1997 as the **State Peace and Development Council**), and its chairman serves concurrently as Mayor of **Rangoon (Yangon)**. Its responsibilities are wide-ranging: establishment and management of **new towns**; infrastructure projects, such as highways, reservoirs, and parks; land-use administration; control of illegal residents; and the collection of taxes to be used on city projects. It has the authority to enter into joint ventures with foreign companies and borrow funds from abroad, and has evolved into one of the country's largest business conglomerates, operating hotels and **golf** courses. A similar agency has been established for **Mandalay**, although the Mandalay City Development Committee seems to exercise less autonomy.

YAWNGHWE (NYAUNGSHWE). One of the **Shan States**, whose last *sawbwa*, Sao **Shwe Taik**, was the first president of the Union of Burma (1948–1952) and a prominent leader of the **Federal Move-**

ment. Located in southwestern **Shan State**, it had a land area of around 3,600 square kilometers (1,400 square miles), and its most prominent feature was **Inle Lake**. The town of Yawnghwe near the lakeshore is the site of the *haw* of the Yawnghwe *sawbwas*. Located nearby is **Taunggyi**, the Shan State capital. *See also* INTHA.

YEDAYA (YADAYA). Magical rituals used by many Burmese to prevent misfortune. Building a **pagoda** is considered an effective method. In late 1961, the government of U **Nu** ordered the construction of 60,000 sand pagodas throughout the country to prevent the occurrence of a terrible calamity, possibly a world war, predicted for the following year. **Ne Win**, a devoted practitioner of *yedaya*, is said to have decreed that cars in Burma must drive on the *right* rather than *left* side of the road (the previous practice, inherited from British colonial days) to neutralize the threat of an insurgency; the former cancels out, or counteracts, the latter. When the **State Peace and Development Council** (**SPDC**) sponsored construction of a complex to house a gigantic Buddha image made of white stone at Min Dhamma Hill in northern **Rangoon (Yangon)**, it included a large marble replica of a **Buddhist** monk's offering bowl on the platform surrounding the image. The stone bowl is right side up, meant to counteract the threat of a monks' boycott of the **Tatmadaw**, known as **Overturning the Offering Bowl** and symbolized by the bowl turned upside down.

Yedaya is closely associated with the practice of **astrology** because practitioners of the art claim to foretell inauspicious days, on which special ritual measures need to be taken. Some monks are skilled in devising *yedaya* rituals, which are also sometimes used to obtain a desirable thing, such as a promotion or a lover's affections. Many Burmese believe that the success of both Ne Win and the SPDC junta in holding onto power is almost entirely due to their skill in using *yedaya* rituals, which allegedly have rescued them from repeated misfortunes. *See also* NUMEROLOGY.

YENANGYAUNG (YAYNANGYOUNG). A city in **Magwe (Magway) Division**, with a population estimated at 81,745 in 1996. Though it has little to offer tourists, it is historically and economically important as a center for the production of **oil** since before

British colonial times. Clusters of oil wells can be seen just outside the town. *See also* OIL FIELD WORKERS' STRIKE.

YE–TAVOY (YAY–DAWEI) RAILWAY. A project initiated by the **State Law and Order Restoration Council** in 1993 to link the railhead at Ye (Yay) in **Mon State** with **Tavoy (Dawei)**, the capital of **Tenasserim (Tanintharyi) Division**. Its purpose was to facilitate transportation links with Burma's resource rich but undeveloped southern region. Construction involved the **forced relocation** and **forced labor** of mostly **Mon** and **Karen (Kayin)** residents; by the mid-1990s, as many as 300,000 local people were drafted annually to do uncompensated labor on the project, which critics called the "Second Railway of Death." Many fled and became **refugees** on the Thai–Burma border. *See also* HUMAN RIGHTS IN BURMA; THAI–BURMA RAILWAY.

YOUNG MEN'S BUDDHIST ASSOCIATION (YMBA). A national movement that emerged during the first decade of the 20th century to defend **Buddhism** from the corrosive effects of British colonial rule. In the context of the "separation of religion and state" under the British, it was not a political organization, although many of the issues it raised had political ramifications. As early as 1897, a Buddha Sasana Noggaha Association had been established in **Mandalay** to revitalize the religion; in 1902, laypeople established the Ashoka Society in **Bassein (Pathein)** to promote a modernistic Buddhism. Inspired both by the Young Men's Christian Association (YMCA) movement and developments among Buddhists in Sri Lanka, educated laymen established the first YMBA branch in **Arakan (Rakhine)** in 1902; by 1906, there was a branch in **Rangoon (Yangon)**, followed by the establishment of some 50 more branches in cities and towns nationwide. YMBA members were mostly urban and well educated. The association maintained student hostels, encouraged laypeople to observe Buddhist precepts, and sponsored seminars and discussions on religious topics. In 1916, it called on the government to legally prohibit footwear in **pagoda** precincts, which had become an intensely controversial issue because many Europeans refused to doff their shoes and stockings during visits to the **Shwe Dagon Pagoda** and other holy sites. The General Council of Buddhist Associations served as the YMBA's national association and held annual conventions; this became the **General Council of Burmese Associations** in 1920, the most important political organization in the country before the **Saya San (Hsaya San) Rebellion** of 1930–1932. *See also* "SHOE QUESTION."

– Z –

ZARGANA. Popular Burmese comedian whose stage name means "tweezers" and who is a dentist. He frequently satirized government corruption and incompetence during the **Ne Win** era (1962–1988) and was jailed for refusing to stop lampooning the **State Law and Order Restoration Council** after it assumed power in September 1988. On one occasion, he was detained after doing a street routine implying that the 1996–1997 **"Visit Myanmar Year"** campaign would encourage prostitution. *See also* HUMAN RIGHTS IN BURMA; MOUSTACHE BROTHERS.

Bibliography

CONTENTS

INTRODUCTION

Following the tumultuous events of 1988, Burma's political, social, and humanitarian crises gained international attention. Before that year, the country was largely isolated from the rest of the world and was of interest to only a small number of scholars and specialists. But as this bibliography shows, a growing quantity of recent publications deal with human rights and ethnic minority issues, the dynamics of military rule, the democratic opposition, and the country's postsocialist "open" economy (including the controversy over whether foreign countries should implement sanctions against the State Peace and Development Council or engage with it economically).

In addition, the diffusion of online information services since the mid-1990s has given both the democratic opposition and the military regime a new medium through which to present their views. Probably the single greatest change in Burma-related information over the past decade has been the crucial role of the Internet in reporting developments inside the country to a worldwide audience. For example, the unrest in Rangoon connected with labor strikes and the U Thant incident in 1974, arguably a precursor for the more massive demonstrations of 1988, was little known outside the country. It merited brief discussion in an essay by Raja Segaram Arumgam in the 1975 edition of *Southeast Asian Affairs*, and it was only in 1989 that Andrew Selth published a detailed English-language account ("Death of a Hero: The U Thant Disturbances in Burma, December 1974"). However, the Alternative ASEAN Network on Burma (Altsean), a Bangkok-based NGO, provided via e-mail attachment a detailed and thoroughly cited report on the May 30, 2003, attack on Aung San Suu Kyi and her supporters in northern Burma ("Briefing: Black Friday and the Crackdown on the NLD") only 12 days after the event. Doubtless the full story of "Black Friday" will not be known for many years, but the speed, volume, and ubiquity of online information delivery means that Burma is no longer a "closed" country despite the efforts of the SPDC to control domestic information technology and present an alluring face to the outside world.

One of the oldest online information sources is the *BurmaNet News* (www .burmanet.org), which was established in 1994 and provides an electronic "clipping file" of newspaper and periodical articles; it is posted to subscribers about five times weekly. But the most comprehensive source is the Online Burma/Myanmar Library (www.burmalibrary.org), which encompasses a vast and growing amount of information on contemporary developments and some older sources, such as the *Burma Press Summary*, a digest of articles from the *Working People's Daily* compiled during the late 1980s and early 1990s. Through the Online Burma Library, one can also access scores of other Burma-related sites. *The Irrawaddy* online (www.irrawaddy.org) is another excellent and timely source, which provides daily updates on developments inside the country. The British Broadcasting Corporation also releases informative articles on Burma through its online news site (news.bbc.co.uk) as well as its special Burma page (www.bbc.co.uk/burmese). For readers seeking SPDC perspectives, the online *Myanmar Times and Weekly Review* (www.myanmar.com/myanmartimes) is upbeat, colorful, and sometimes informative; however, following the purge of Prime Minister Khin Nyunt and his Military Intelligence subordinates in fall 2004, the future of both the online and hardcopy *Myanmar Times* remains in doubt.

For many years, the most detailed English language sources on developments in Burma have been the Thailand-based dailies *Bangkok Post* and *Nation* and the Hong Kong–based weeklies *Asiaweek* and *Far Eastern Economic Review*. Throughout the 1990s, Bertil Lintner, a *Review* correspondent with a special interest in Burma's ethnic minority areas, was considered by many observers to be one of the most informative journalistic sources on the country. But *Asiaweek* has ceased publication, and in 2004 the *Far Eastern Economic Review* ended its newsmagazine format. Articles on Burma turn up occasionally in the pages of such publications as *The New York Times* and the *International Herald Tribune*. But outside of Thailand, the tendency for the country to slip between the cracks of the mainstream media makes the online sources even more essential.

Annual summaries of events in Burma are published in the January–February issue of the University of California's *Asian Survey* and *Southeast Asian Affairs*, the latter published yearly by the Institute of Southeast Asian Studies in Singapore. The *Asia Yearbook,* published by the *Far Eastern Economic Review,* has been discontinued, but annual issues going back to the Ne Win era provide detailed descriptions of politics, economics, and foreign relations. Hardcopy periodicals specializing in Burma include *The Irrawaddy* magazine, published monthly by the same people who operate *The Irrawaddy* online, and the quarterly *Burma Debate,* supported by the Burma Project of the Open Society Institute in New York.

On the events of 1988—the prodemocracy demonstrations, the emergence of Aung San Suu Kyi as opposition leader, and the bloody seizure of power by the State Law and Order Restoration Council (predecessor of the SPDC)—the principal source remains Lintner's *Outrage: The Struggle for Democracy in Burma*; unfortunately, Japanese journalist Tanabe Hisao's *Biruma Minshuka Undō* (Burma's Democracy Movement) has not been translated into English. Dr. Maung Maung's last published work, *The 1988 Uprising in Burma*, reveals more about the mind of Ne Win's principal "intellectual" spokesman than it does about what took place in the streets of Rangoon, Mandalay, or Sagaing. Daw Aung San Suu Kyi's *Freedom from Fear and Other Writings* includes her epochal "Speech to a Mass Rally at the Shwedagon Pagoda" on August 26, 1988. Further descriptions and analyses of 1988—on what happened and why—are much needed.

Useful reference works on politics include *To Stand and Be Counted: The Suppression of Burma's Members of Parliament*, published by the All Burma Students' Democratic Front, and *Democracy and Politics in Burma: A Collection of Documents*, edited by Marc Weller. Gustaaf Houtman's *Mental Culture in Burmese Crisis Politics: Aung San Suu Kyi and the National League for Democracy* includes both a criticism of the "state-building" paradigms of Burmese politics—chiefly Robert H. Taylor's 1987 work, *The State in Burma*—and an interesting attempt to link the confrontation between the SLORC/SPDC and Daw Suu Kyi to Buddhist values and contrasting concepts of power. Like E. Sarkisyanz's *Buddhist Backgrounds of the Burmese Revolution*, published in 1965, it is one of the few Western-language discussions of Burma's modern intellectual history and its connection with politics. On this topic, see also Aung San Suu Kyi's lengthy essays in *Freedom from Fear*: "Intellectual Life in Burma and India under Colonialism" and "Literature and Nationalism in Burma."

The Tatmadaw, Burma's armed forces, are central to any understanding of Burmese political dynamics. Two recent books—Mary Callahan's *Making Enemies: War and the State in Burma* and Andrew Selth's *Burma's Armed Forces: Power without Glory*—provide detailed discussions of its history and development. Concerning the impact of military rule on daily life, see Christina Fink's *Living Silence: Burma under Military Rule*.

Veteran Burma specialist David Steinberg's *Burma: The State of Myanmar* is a comprehensive introduction to present-day political, economic, and social conditions. In the early 1990s, many economists described postsocialist, natural resource–rich Burma as "the next Asian tiger"; more recently, they have debated why, despite promising fundamentals, the country's economy remains in a state of perpetual crisis. Good analyses are being written by a group of economists at Australia's Macquarie University in the form of *Burma Economic Watch*, accessible at www.econ.mq.edu.au/BurmaEconomicWatch. Official economic statistics are notoriously unreliable, but the Economist Intelligence Unit's *Burma/Myanmar: Country Profile* and *Burma/Myanmar: Country Reports* are among the most credible sources for economic trends, including GDP and inflation figures. For historical economic data, see Teruko Saito and Lee Kin Kiong's *Statistics on the Burmese Economy: The 19th and 20th Centuries*.

Burma's crises in human rights, health, and education are described in detail in Chris Beyrer's *War in the Blood: Sex, Politics and AIDS in Southeast Asia*; Human Rights Watch's *A Modern Form of Slavery: Trafficking of Burmese Women and Girls into Brothels in Thailand*; and the Asian Human

Rights Commission's *Voice of the Hungry Nation*. Human rights conditions in the country have been closely monitored since 1988 by international non-governmental organizations (INGOs), such as Amnesty International and Human Rights Watch, as well as the United Nations Commission for Human Rights, the U.S. Department of State, and the International Labour Organization, all of which have published detailed reports. The Shan Human Rights Foundation and the Karen Human Rights Group publish information on conditions in ethnic minority areas.

The two most comprehensive accounts of ethnic politics remain Bertil Lintner's *Burma in Revolt: Opium and Insurgency since 1948* and Martin Smith's *Burma: Insurgency and the Politics of Ethnicity*, both of which came out in revised editions in the late 1990s. Lintner's work is especially valuable for its appendixes, including a detailed chronology and brief descriptions of the bewilderingly diverse individuals and organizations involved in ethnic and communist insurgency. Chao-Tzang Yawnghwe's *The Shan of Burma: Memoirs of a Shan Exile* was published in 1987 but remains an invaluable source on this group's recent history; on the Chins, see works by Lian Sakhong, especially *In Search of Chin Identity: A Study in Religion, Politics and Ethnic Identity;* on the Mons, Ashley South's *Mon Nationalism and Civil War in Burma: The Golden Sheldrake*; and on the Karens, Jonathan Falla's *True Love and Bartholomew: Rebels on the Burmese Border* and Ananda Rajah's "Ethnicity, Nationalism and the Nation-State: The Karen in Burma and Thailand."

New contributions to the academic study of Burmese history include Thant Myint-U's *The Making of Modern Burma* and articles by Michael W. Charney, Jacques Leider, Victor Lieberman, Guy Lubeigt, Sunait Chutintaranond, and Dr. Than Tun. Michael Aung-Thwin's views on Burmese history, as reflected in his 1998 book *Myth and History in the Early History of Burma: Paradigms, Primary Sources and Prejudices*, are controversial in their attempt to turn British colonial historiography on its head. Amply and attractively illustrated, Pamela Gutman's *Burma's Lost Kingdoms: The Splendour of Arakan* describes a little known but culturally and historically distinct region that until 1784 was independent of the Burman state.

Although academic studies of dynastic history reach limited audiences, the bibliography shows the continued popularity of publications about World War II by British and American writers, especially war veterans. Historian Louis Allen's massive and authoritative *Burma: The Longest War, 1941–1945* not only provides details on the various military campaigns (with maps), but also includes both the Allied and Japanese perspectives and an interesting account, taken from Japanese sources, of General Mutaguchi Renya's disastrous decision to initiate the 1944 Imphal Campaign, an invasion of northeastern India. Another valuable source is Christopher Bayly and Tim Harper's *Forgotten*

Armies: The Fall of British Asia, 1941–1945, published in 2004, which recounts wartime events in Burma, India, and the Malay Peninsula.

One of the best histories of the "Thirty Comrades" is Izumiya Tatsuro's *The Minami Organ*, translated into English by U Tun Aung Chain and published in Rangoon in 1985. For those interested in Japanese soldiers' experiences in the Burma war, see Kazuo Tamayama and John Nunneley, *Tales by Japanese Soldiers*. Eric Lomax's *The Railroad Man* is a story of wartime memories and reconciliation from a former POW who worked on the infamous Thai–Burma Railway.

The standard sources on Burmese Buddhism remain Melford E. Spiro's *Buddhism and Society: A Great Tradition and Its Burmese Vicissitudes*, E. Michael Mendelsohn's *Sangha and State in Burma: A Study of Monastic Sectarianism and Leadership*, and Winston L. King's *A Thousand Lives Away: Buddhism in Contemporary Burma*. But more recent studies on Buddhism include those by Guy Lubeigt, Hiroko Kawanami, Bruce Matthews, and Juliane Schober. Articles on *nat*-worship have been published by Bénédicte Brac de la Perrière and Sarah Bekker. The history of Christian missionary activity in Burma is also well documented, for example, Janet Benge and Geoff Benge in *Adoniram Judson: Bound for Burma*.

Relatively little in dynastic era or modern Burmese literature that has yet to be translated into English or other Western languages. Maureen Aung-Thwin's translation of Ma Ma Lay's *Not out of Hate* was published in 1991, but to this writer's knowledge there exist no—or at least no readily available—English translations of Burma's premier nationalist writer, Thakin Kodaw Hmaing (see Aung San Suu Kyi's discussion of him in "Literature and Nationalism in Burma"). Lack of attention to the country's contemporary literature may reflect the poor conditions under which writers and publishers must operate, the lack of translators outside Burma who could make the best writing available to a global audience, and perhaps also the intense focus on the part of Burmese intellectuals on immediate, political issues. Anna J. Allott's *Inked Over, Ripped Out: Burmese Storytellers and the Censors* provides a sample of recent short stories and a discussion of the heavy state control that writers must endure.

The country's sophisticated artistic and architectural heritage is reflected in such attractively illustrated studies as Sylvia Fraser-Lu's *Burmese Crafts Past and Present*, Alexandra Green and T. Richard Blurton's *Burma: Art and Archeology*, Ralph Isaac and T. Richard Blurton's *Visions from the Golden Land: Burma and the Art of Lacquer*, and Pierre Pichard's monumental, multivolume *Inventory of Monuments at Pagan*. Noel Singer's *Old Rangoon: City of the Shwedagon* recalls the city's precolonial and colonial past, with excellent photographs. *Myanmar Design: Art, Architecture and Design of Burma* by John

Falconer et al. is an attractively packaged introduction to the country's architecture, visual arts, and handicrafts. Irene Moilanen and Sergey S. Ozhegov's *Mirrored in Wood: Burmese Art and Architecture* is also recommended. Finally, a large number of outstanding works on Burma fall in the "Travel and Description" category: not only the classic *The Burman: His Life and Notions* by J. G. Scott ("Shway Yoe"), first published in the 1880s, but also post-1988 works, such as Sue Arnold's *A Burmese Legacy: Rediscovering My Family*, Rory MacLean's *Under the Dragon: Travels in a Betrayed Land*, and Andrew Marshall's *The Trouser People: A Story of Burma in the Shadow of the Empire*, all of which provide vivid and sometimes disturbing images of life in military-ruled Burma.

I. GENERAL

1. Bibliographies and Research Guides

Bečka, Jan. *Historical Dictionary of Myanmar*. Metuchen, N.J.: Scarecrow Press, 1995.

Burma: A Study Guide. Edited by Ronald A. Morse, Helen L. Loerke, et al. Washington, D.C.: Woodrow Wilson International Center for Scholars, Asia Program, 1987.

Burmese Studies in Japan, 1868–1985: Literary Guide and Bibliography. Edited by the Burma Studies Group. Tokyo: Burma Research Group, Tokyo University of Foreign Studies, 1985.

Guide to Universities' Central Library. Rangoon: Union of Myanmar, Ministry of Education, Dept. of Higher Education, Universities Central Library, 1999.

Herbert, Patricia, M. *Burma*. World Bibliographical Series 132. Santa Barbara, Calif.: ABC Clio, 1991.

———. "List of Burmese Pro-Democracy [August–September 1988] Publications in the British Library." *South-East Asia Library Group Newsletter* 34–35 (December 1990): 25–38.

Shulman, Frank Joseph. *Burma: An Annotated Bibliographical Guide to International Doctoral Dissertation Research on Burma, 1898–1985*. Lanham, Md.: University Press of America, in association with the Woodrow Wilson International Center for Scholars, 1986.

Sun Laichen. "Chinese Historical Sources on Burma." *The Journal of Burma Studies* 2 (special issue) (1997).

Tuchrello, William P. "A Survey of Selected Resources for the Study of Burma." *Crossroads* 4, no. 1 (Fall 1988): 128–51.

2. Directories, Handbooks, Statistical Abstracts, and Yearbooks

Bunge, Frederica M., ed. *Burma: A Country Study*. 3rd ed. Area Handbook Series. Washington, D.C.: The American University, Foreign Area Studies, 1983.

The Far East and Australasia. London: Europa Publications, 1969–.

Hla Tun Aung. *Myanmar: The Study of Processes and Patterns*. Rangoon: Ministry of Education, National Centre for Human Resources Development, 2003.

Human Rights Year Book 1998, Burma. Washington, D.C.: Human Rights Documentation Unit, National Coalition Government of the Union of Burma; NCGUB Information Office, 1998.

Scott, James George. *Burma: A Handbook of Practical Information*. Bibliotheca Orientalis. London: Daniel O'Connor, 1921; Bangkok: Orchid Press, 1999.

Socialist Republic of the Union of Burma. *Burma: 1983 Population Census*. Rangoon: Ministry of Home Affairs, 1986.

Statistical Yearbook for Asia and the Pacific/Annuaire Statistique pour l'Asie et le Pacifique. Bangkok: United Nations Economic and Social Commission for Asia and the Pacific (ESCAP), 1966–.

Statistical Yearbook 2002. Rangoon: Central Statistical Organization, 2002.

3. Guides

Burma Action Group. *Burma: The Alternative Guide*. 2nd ed. London: BAG, 1995.

Eliot, Joshua, and Jane Bickersteth. *Myanmar (Burma) Handbook*. Bath, England: Footprint Handbooks, 1997.

Globetrotter Travel Map: Myanmar. London: Old Saybrook, 1999. Scale 1:1,700,000.

Martin, Steven, et al. *Myanmar (Burma)*. 8th ed. Footscray, Victoria: Lonely Planet, 2002.

Saw Myat Yin. *Culture Shock! Burma*. Singapore: Times Books International, 1994.

———. *Cultures of the World: Burma*. Singapore: Times Books International, 1990.

Tun Shwe Khine. *A Guide to Mahamuni*. Rakhine Book Series. Rangoon: U Hla Sein, 1996

4. Travel and Description

Abbott, Gerry. *Inroads into Burma: A Travellers' Anthology*. Oxford in Asia Paperbacks. Kuala Lumpur, Malaysia: Oxford University Press, 1997.

––––––. *Back to Mandalay: An Inside View of Burma.* Bromley, England: Impact Books, 1990.

Ainsworth, Leopold. *A Merchant Venturer Among the Sea Gypsies: Being a Pioneer's Account of Life on an Island in the Mergui Archipelago.* Bangkok: White Lotus, 2000.

Allott, Anna J. "Burma." In *The Traveller's Literary Companion to Southeast Asia,* Edited by Alastair Dingwall. Brighton, England: In Print Publishing, 1994.

Arnold, Sue. *A Burmese Legacy: Rediscovering My Family.* London: Sceptre, 1995.

Aung Aung Taik. *Visions of Shwedagon.* Bangkok: White Lotus, 1989.

Boucaud, André. *Birmanie: sur la piste des seigneurs de la guerre.* Paris: L'Harmattan, 1985.

Boudignon, Françoise. *A Letter from Burma.* Rangoon: UNICEF, 1984.

Cangi, Ellen Corwin. *Faded Splendour, Golden Past: Urban Images of Burma.* Oxford in Asia Paperback. Kuala Lumpur, New York: Oxford University Press, 1997.

Collis, Maurice. *Land of the Great Image: Being the Experiences of Friar Manrique in Arakan.* London: Faber & Faber, 1953.

––––––. *Lords of the Sunset: A Tour in the Shan States.* London: Faber & Faber, 1938.

Dhida Saraya. *Mandalay: The Capital City, Center of the Universe.* Bangkok: Muang Boran Publishing, 1995.

Everada, Ellis. *Burma: Encountering the Land of the Buddhas.* Gartmore, Scotland: Kiscadale Publications, 1994.

Falconer, John, David Odo, and Mandy Sadan. *Burma: Frontier Photographs 1918–1935.* Edited by Elizabeth Dell. London: Merrell, 2000.

Grant, Colesworthey. *Rough Pencillings of a Rough Trip to Rangoon in 1846.* Bangkok: White Orchid, 1995.

Hall, Fielding H. *The Soul of a People.* London: Macmillan, 1898.

Ivanoff, Jacques, and Thierry Lejard, in collaboration with Luca Gansser and Gabriella Gansser. *A Journey Through the Mergui Archipelago.* Bangkok: White Lotus, 2002.

Khin Myo Chit, and Paw Oo Thet. *Festivals and Flowers of the Twelve Burmese Seasons.* Bangkok: Orchard Press, 2002.

Khoo Thwe, Pascal. *From the Land of Green Ghosts: A Burmese Odyssey.* New York: HarperCollins, 2002.

MacLean, Rory. *Under the Dragon: Travels in a Betrayed Land.* London: Flamingo, 1999.

Marshall, Andrew. *The Trouser People: A Story of Burma in the Shadow of the Empire.* Washington, D.C.: Counterpoint, 2002.

Mi Mi Khaing. *Burmese Family*. Bombay, [India]: Longmans Green, 1946.

Mirante, Edith T. *Burmese Looking Glass: A Human Rights Adventure and a Jungle Revolution*. New York: Grove Press, 1993.

O'Connor, Vincent Clarence Scott. *The Silken East: A Record of Life and Travel in Burma*. 2 vols. London: Hutchinson, 1904; Bangkok: White Lotus, 1993.

Rajanubhab, Damrong. *Journey Through Burma in 1936: A View of Culture, History and Institutions*. Bangkok: River Books, 1991.

Sangermano, Father Vincentius. *A Description of the Burmese Empire, Compiled Chiefly from Burmese Documents*. Translated from the Italian and Latin by William Tandy, with a preface and note by John Jardine. London: Susil Gupta, 1966.

Schramm-Evans, Zoe. *Dark Ruby: Travels in a Troubled Land*. London: Pandora, 2000.

Scott, James G. (Shway Yoe). *The Burman, His Life and Notions*. London: Macmillan, 1883; New York: Norton, 1963.

Sell, Julie. *Whispers at the Pagoda: Portraits of Modern Burma*. Bangkok: Orchid Press, 1999.

Shades of Gold and Green: Anecdotes of Colonial Burmah, 1886–1948. New Delhi: Asian Educational Services, 1998.

Strachan, Paul. *Mandalay: Travels from the Golden City*. Gartmore, Scotland: Kiscadale Publications, 1994.

Takano, Hideyuki. *The Shore Beyond Good and Evil: A Report from Inside Burma's Opium Kingdom*. Reno, Nev.: Kotan, 2002.

Win Pe et al. *Rangoon: Green City of Grace*. Rangoon: Yangon City Development Committee, 1999.

II. HISTORY

1. General

Cady, John F. *The United States and Burma*. The American Foreign Policy Library. Cambridge, Mass.: Harvard University Press, 1976.

Hall, D. G. E. *Burma*. London: Hutchinson University Library, 1960.

Renard, Ronald D. "For the Fair Name of Myanmar: They Are Being Blotted out of Burma's History." In *Burma: Myanmar in the Twenty-First Century—Dynamics of Continuity and Change*. Edited by John J. Brandon. Bangkok: Thai Studies Section, Chulalongkorn University, 1997.

———. "Minorities in Burmese History." In *Ethnic Conflict in Buddhist Societies*. Edited by K. M. de Silva et al. London: Pinter Publishers, 1988.

Seekins, Donald M. *The Disorder in Order: The Army-State in Burma Since 1962*. Bangkok: White Lotus, 2002.

Taylor, Robert H. *The State in Burma*. Honolulu: University of Hawaii Press, 1987.

Tinker, Hugh. *The Union of Burma*. London: Oxford University Press, 1959.

Trager, Frank N. *Burma: From Kingdom to Republic*. New York: Frederick A. Praeger, 1966.

2. Prehistory

Ba Maw. "The First Discovery in the Evolution of Anyathian Cultures from a Single Site in Myanmar." *Myanmar Historical Research Journal* 2 (June 1998): 97–105.

———. "Research on the Early Man in Myanmar." *Myanmar Historical Research Journal* 1 (1995): 213–20.

Hla Myo Nwe. "Sophisticated Stone Age Imagery at Padahlin." *Myanmar Perspectives* 5 (December 1996): 55–57.

Houtman, Gustaaf. *Human Origins, Myanmafication and "Disciplined" Burmese Democracy*. London: Pekhon University Press, 2000.

Nyunt Han, Win Maung, and Elizabeth Moore. "Prehistoric Grave Goods from the Chindwin and Samon River Regions." In *Burma: Art and Archeology*. Edited by Alexandra Green and T. Richard Blurton. Chicago: Art Media Resources, 2002.

Than Tun. "Prehistoric Researches in Myanmar." In *Traditions in Current Perspective: Proceedings of the Conference on Myanmar and Southeast Asian Studies 15–17 November 1995, Yangon*. Rangoon: The Universities Press, 1996.

3. Dynastic History (1st Millennium to 19th Century CE)

Aung-Thwin, Michael. *Myth and History in the Historiography of Early Burma: Paradigms, Primary Sources, and Prejudices*. Singapore: Institute of Southeast Asian Studies, 1998.

———. *Pagan: The Origins of Modern Burma*. Honolulu: University of Hawaii Press, 1985.

Aye Kyaw. "Crimes Against Religion in the Penal Codes of Burma, Thailand and the Philippines." *Journal of the Siam Society* 76 (1988): 217–26.

———. "Religion and Family Law in Burma." *Journal of the Siam Society* 80, no. 2 (1992): 59–65.

——. "The Sangha Organization in Nineteenth Century Burma and Thailand." *Journal of the Siam Society* 72 (1984): 166–96.

——. "Status of Women in Family Law in Burma and Indonesia." *Crossroads* 4, no. 1 (Fall 1988): 100–20.

Bennett, Paul J. *Conference under the Tamarind Tree: Three Essays in Burmese History.* Monograph Series No. 15. New Haven, Conn.: Yale University Southeast Asian Studies, 1971.

Charney, Michael W. "The 1598–99 Siege of Pegu and the Expansion of Arakanese Imperial Power into Lower Burma." *Journal of Asian History* 28, no. 1 (1994): 39–57.

——. "A Reinvestigation of Konbaung-era Burman Historiography on the Relationship Between Arakan and Ava (Upper Burma)." *Journal of Asian History* 34, no. 1 (2000): 53–68.

——. "Shallow-draft Boats, Guns, and the Aye-ra-wa-ti: Continuity and Change in Ship Structure and River Warfare in Precolonial Myanma." *Oriens Extremus* 40, no. 1 (1997): 16–63.

Department of History, University of Rangoon. *Glimpses of Glorious Pagan.* Rangoon: The Universities Press, 1986.

Eleven Mon Dhammasat Texts. Translated by Nai Pan Hla and Ryuji Okudaira. Tokyo: The Center for East Asian Cultural Studies for U[NESCO] (The Toyo Bunko), 1992.

Fransch, Tilman. "Some Reflections on the Burmese Dhammathat with Special Reference to the Pagan Period." In *Tradition and Modernity in Myanmar 1.* Edited by U. Gärtner and J. Lorenz. Münster/Hamburg: 1994.

Gutman, Pamela. "The Pyu Maitreyas." In *Traditions in Current Perspective: Proceedings of the Conference on Myanmar and Southeast Asian Studies 15–17 November 1995, Yangon.* Rangoon: The Universities Press, 1996.

Harvey, G. E. *History of Burma: From the Earliest Times to 10 March 1824, the Beginning of the English Conquest.* London: Frank Cass, 1967.

Huxley, Andrew. "Buddhism and Law: The View from Mandalay." *Journal of the International Association of Buddhist Studies* 18, no. 1 (1995): 47–95.

——. "The Importance of the Dhammathats in Burmese Law and Culture." *The Journal of Burma Studies* 1 (1997): 1–17.

——. "The Village Knows Best: Social Organization in an Eighteenth-Century Burmese Law Code." *Southeast Asia Research* 5, no. 1 (March 1997): 21–39.

Koenig, William J. *The Burmese Polity, 1752–1819: Politics, Administration, and Social Organization in the Early Kon-Baung Period.* Ann Arbor: Center for South and Southeast Asian Studies, University of Michigan, 1990.

Lehman, F. K. "Symposium on Societal Organization in Mainland Southeast Asia Prior to the Eighteenth Century; Freedom and Bondage in Traditional

Burma and Thailand (with Discussion)." *Journal of Southeast Asian Studies* 15 (September 1984): 233–44, 266–70.

Leider, Jacques P. "Arakan's Ascent during the Mrauk U Period." In *Recalling Local Pasts: Autonomous History in Southeast Asia.* Edited by Sunait Chutintaranond and Chris Baker. Chiang Mai, Thailand: Silkworm Books, 2002.

Lieberman, V. "Political Consolidation in Burma Under the Early Konbaung Dynasty 1752–c. 1820." *Journal of Asian History* 30, no. 2 (1996): 152–68.

——. "Provincial Reforms in Taung-ngu Burma." *Bulletin of the School of Oriental and African Studies* 43, no. 3 (1980): 548–69.

——. "Reinterpreting Burmese History." *Comparative Studies in Society and History* 29 (January 1987): 162–94.

——. "The Transfer of the Burmese Capital from Pegu to Ava." *Journal of the Royal Asiatic Society* 1 (1980): 64–83.

Lubeigt, Guy. "Ancient Peninsular Trade Roads and Rivalries over the Tenasserim Coasts." In *Commerce et Navigation en Asie du Sud-Est, XIVe-XIXe siècle (Trade and Navigation in Southeast Asia, 14th–19th Centuries).* Edited by Nguyên Thê Anh and Yoshiaki Ishizawa. Paris: Harmattan, 1999.

——. *Pagan (Xe-XILLe Siècles): Capitale d'un Empire Médiéval Indochinois.* Paris: Ed. Kailash, 1997.

——. *Pagan, du Passé au Présent: Contribution à la Géographie Historique d'une Capitale Médiévale Indochinoise.* Paris: Ed. Kailash, 1998.

Myint Myint Than, Daw. "Mindon's Measure Against Bribery and Corruption." *Historical Research Journal* 1, no. 1 (1993–1994): 31–36.

Myo Thant Tyn. "Oo Shwe O: Myanmar Scientist of Konbaung Period." In *Traditions in Current Perspective: Proceedings of the Conference on Myanmar and Southeast Asian Studies 15–17 November 1995, Yangon.* Rangoon: The Universities Press, 1996.

Nai Pan Hla. "Old Terracota Votive Tablets and New Theories." In *Traditions in Current Perspective: Proceedings of the Conference on Myanmar and Southeast Asian Studies 15–17 November 1995, Yangon.* Rangoon: The Universities Press, 1996.

Okudaira Ryuji. "A Hypothetical Analysis on 'Theravâda Buddhist State at its Height' Under King Badon with Special Reference to *Manugye Dhammathat* (1782 Manuscript)." In *Traditions in Current Perspective: Proceedings of the Conference on Myanmar and Southeast Asian Studies 15–17 November 1995, Yangon.* Rangoon: The Universities Press, 1996.

Rajanubhab, Damrong. *Our Wars with the Burmese: Thai-Burmese Conflict, 1539–1767.* Bangkok: White Lotus, 2001.

Sunait Chutintaranond. "The Image of the Burmese Enemy in Thai Perceptions and Historical Writings." *Journal of the Siam Society* 80, no. 1 (1992): 89–99.

———. "King Bayinnaung in Thai Perception, Historical Writings and Literary Works." In *Traditions in Current Perspective: Proceedings of the Conference on Myanmar and Southeast Asian Studies 15–17 November 1995, Yangon.* Rangoon: The Universities Press, 1996.

———. "Leading Port Cities in the Eastern Martaban Bay in the Context of Autonomous History." In *Recalling Local Pasts: Autonomous History in Southeast Asia.* Edited by Sunait Chutintaranond and Chris Baker. Chiang Mai, Thailand: Silkworm Books, 2002.

Sunait Chutintaranond and Than Tun. *On Both Sides of the Tenasserim Range: History of Siamese-Burmese Relations.* Bangkok: Institute of Asian Studies, Chulalongkorn University, 1995.

Tamura Katsumi. "Tradition of Urban Cosmology in Burma." *East Asian Cultural Studies* 27 (March 1988): 49–58.

Than Tun, Dr. "A Bagan Temple's Main Gate: Is There Any Significance When It Opens in Any Other Direction Except East?" *Myanmar Historical Journal Research* 2 (June 1998): 106–8.

———. *Essays on the History and Buddhism of Burma.* Edited by Paul Strachan. Whiting Bay, Scotland: Kiscadale Publications, 1988.

Tun Aung Chain. "The Banya Sein Uprising 1774." *Myanmar Historical Research Journal* 2 (June 1998): 127–36.

———. "The Deposition of Kyazwa: A Reconsideration of the Inscriptional Evidence." *Historical Research Journal* 1, no. 1 (1993–1994): 1–6.

———. "Pegu in Politics and Trade, Ninth to Seventeenth Centuries." In *Recalling Local Pasts: Autonomous History in Southeast Asia.* Edited by Sunait Chutintaranond and Chris Baker. Chiang Mai, Thailand: Silkworm Books, 2002.

Walker, Andrew. *The Legend of the Golden Boat: Regulation, Trade and Traders in the Borderlands of Laos, Thailand, China, and Burma.* Honolulu: University of Hawaii Press, 1999.

4. Colonial and Pacific War Era (19th–20th Centuries CE)

Allen, Lewis. *Burma: The Longest War 1941–1945.* London: Cassell, 2000.

Allott, Anna J. *The End of the First Anglo-Burmese War: The Burmese Chronicle Account of How the 1826 Treaty of Yandabo was Negotiated.* Bangkok: Chulalongkorn University, 1994.

Aung San Suu Kyi. *Aung San of Burma.* 2nd ed. Edinburgh: Kiscadale Publications, 1991.

Aung-Thwin, Michael. "'The British Pacification' of Burma: Order without Meaning." *Journal of Southeast Asian Studies* 16 (September 1985): 245–61.

Aye Kyaw. *Voice of Young Burma.* Ithaca, N.Y.: Cornell University Southeast Asia Program, 1993.

Ba Maw. *Breakthrough in Burma: Memoirs of a Revolution, 1939–1946.* New Haven, Conn.: Yale University Press, 1968.

Bakshi, Akhil. *The Road to Freedom: Travels through Singapore, Malaysia, Burma, and India in the Footsteps of the Indian National Army.* New Delhi: Odyssey Books, 1998.

Bayly, Christopher, and Tim Harper. *Forgotten Armies: The Fall of British Asia, 1941–1945.* London: Allen Lane, 2004.

Bečka, Jan. "The Role of Buddhism as a Factor of Burmese National Identity in the Period of British Rule in Burma (1886–1948)." *Archiv Orientalni* 59 (1991): 389–405.

Bierman, John. *Fire in the Night: Wingate of Burma, Ethiopia, and Zion.* New York: Random House, 1999.

Bjorge, Gary J. *Merrill's Marauders: Combined Operations in Northern Burma in 1944.* Fort Leavenworth, Kan.: Combat Studies Institute, U.S. Army Command and General Staff College, 1996.

Brookes, Stephen. *Through the Jungle of Death: A Boy's Escape from Wartime Burma.* London: John Murray, 2000.

Brown, Ian. "The Economic Crisis and Rebellion in Rural Burma in the Early 1930's." In *Growth and Distribution and Political Change: Asia and the Wider World.* Edited by Ryoshin Minami, Kwan S. Kim, and Malcolm Falkus. Basingstoke, England: Macmillan, 1999.

———. "Tax Remission and Tax Burden in Rural Lower Burma During the Economic Crisis of the Early 1930's." *Modern Asian Studies* 33, no. 2 (1999): 383–403.

Bryant, Raymond L. "Fighting over the Forests: Political Reform, Peasant Resistance and the Late Colonial Burma." *Journal of Commonwealth and Comparative Politics* 32 (1994): 248–65.

———. "From Laissez-faire to Scientific Forestry: Forest Management in Early Colonial Burma, 1826–85." *Forest and Conservation History* 38 (1994): 160–70.

———. *The Political Ecology of Forestry in Burma, 1824–1994.* London: C. Hurst, 1997.

Building the Death Railway: The Ordeal of American POWs in Burma, 1942–1945. Edited by Robert S. La Forte. Wilmington, Del.: S.R. Books, 1993.

Cady, John F. "Our Burma Experience of 1935–1938." In *Essays on Burma.* Edited by John P. Ferguson. Contributions to Asian Studies 16. 1981.

Chaikin, Rosalind B. *To My Memory Sing: A Memoir Based on Letters & Poems from Sol Chick Chaikin, an American Soldier in China, India, Burma During World War II.* Monroe, N.Y.: Lib Res., 1997.

Chalker, Jack, and Edward Dunlop. *Burma Railway Artist: An Artist at War in Singapore, Thailand & Burma, 1942–45.* Philadelphia: Trans-Atlantic Publications, 1994.

Collis, Maurice. *Into Hidden Burma: An Autobiography*. London: Faber & Faber, 1953.

——. *Trials in Burma*. 1938; reprint Bangkok: Ava Publishing House, 1996.

Falconer, John, David Odo, and Mandy Sadan. *Burma: Frontier Photographs 1918–1935*. Edited by Elizabeth Dell. London: Merrell, 2000.

Fergusson, Bernard Baron Ballantrae. *Beyond the Chindwin: An Account of Number Five Column of the Wingate Expedition into Burma, 1943*. Large print ed. Oxford, England: ISIS, 1999.

Fischer, Edward. *The Chancy War: Winning in China, Burma, and India in World War Two*. New York: Orion Books, 1991.

Fraser, George MacDonald. *Quartered Safe Out Here: A Recollection of the War in Burma with a New Epilogue: Fifty Years On*. London: HarperCollins, 2000.

Furnivall, John S. *Colonial Policy and Practice: A Comparative Study of Burma and Netherlands India*. Cambridge, England: Cambridge University Press, 1948.

——. *The Fashioning of Leviathan*. Canberra: The Department of Anthropology, Research School of Pacific Studies, The Australian National University, 1991.

——. *An Introduction to the Political Economy of Burma*. Rangoon: Burma Book Club, 1931.

Ghosh, Parimal. *Brave Men of the Hills: Resistance and Rebellion in Burma, 1825–1932*. Honolulu: University of Hawaii Press, 1999.

Gordon, John W. *Wings from Burma to the Himalayas*. Prescott, Ariz.: Wolfe, 1992.

Grant, Ian. *Burma 1942: The Japanese Invasion; Both Sides Tell the Story of a Savage Jungle War*. Chichester, England: Zampi, 1999.

——. *Burma, the Turning Point: The Seven Battles on the Tiddim Road Which Turned the Tide of the Burma War*. 2nd ed. Chichester, England: Zampi, 1995.

Gumbrell, Royston. *A Man of Twenty Summers: A Personal Account of a Young Infantryman's Experiences in India and Burma during World War Two (1939–1945)*. n.p.: R. Gumbrell, 1999.

Hall, Leslie G. *The Blue Haze: Incorporating the History of "A" Force, Groups 3 & 5, Burma-Thai Railway, 1942–1943*. Kenthurst, Australia: Kangaroo, 1996.

Hayward, David K., ed.-in-chief. *Eagles, Bulldogs & Tigers: History of the 22nd Bomb Squadron in China, Burma, India*. Huntington Beach, Calif.: The Association, 1997.

Hellings, David. *A Civil Servant in Burma: A Memoir of Harold Arrowsmith Brown*. Bristol, England: J.W. Arrowsmith, 1997.

Hickey, Michael. *The Unforgettable Army: Slim's 14th Army in Burma*. Tunbridge Wells, England: Spellmount, 1992.

Hooker, M. B. "The 'Chinese Confucian' and the 'Chinese Buddhist' in British Burma, 1881–1947." *Journal of Southeast Asian Studies* 21, no. 2 (September 1990): 384–401.

Htin Aung, Maung. *Lord Randolph Churchill and the Dancing Peacock: British Conquest of Burma*. New Delhi, 1990.

Humphreys, Roy. *To Stop a Rising Sun: Reminiscences of Wartime in India and Burma*. Phoenix Hill: Alan Sutton, 1996.

Izumiya Tatsuro. *The Minami Organ*. 2nd ed. Translated by U Tun Aung Chain. Rangoon: Higher Education Department, 1985.

Jowers, John Edward. *Getting My Knees Brown: The War Diary of 14239274 Signalman John Edward Jowers, 1st January 1943–28th April 1946, While Serving in India, Burma and Thailand with 228 Indian Wing Signal Section, 6 Indian Air Formation Signals*. Harrow, England: J. E. Jowers, 1997.

Khin Yi. *The Dobama Movement in Burma 1930–1938*. Ithaca, N.Y.: Cornell University Southeast Asia Program, 1988.

Kin Oung. *Who Killed Aung San?* Bangkok: White Lotus, 1993.

Kinvig, Clifford. *River Kwai Railway: The Story of the Burma-Siam Railroad*. London: Brasseys, 1992.

Law-Yone, E. M. "Dr. Ba Maw of Burma." In *Essays on Burma*. Edited by John P. Ferguson. Contributions to Asian Studies 16. 1981.

Lewin, Ronald. *Slim: The Standardbearer*. Ware, England: Wordsworth Editions, 1999.

Lomax, Eric. *The Railway Man*. New York: W.W. Norton, 1995.

M & R: A Regimental History of the Sikh Light Infantry 1941–1947. Bath, England: J. D. Hookway, 1999.

MacGarrigle, George L. *Central Burma*. Washington, D.C.: U.S. Army Center of Military History, 1996.

McBride, Glen (Glenorchie). *D-Day on Queen's Beach Red: An Australian's War from the Burma Road Retreat to the Normandy Beaches*. Brisbane, Australia: Professor G. McBride, 1994.

McCormack, Gavan, and Hank Nelson, eds. *The Burma-Thailand Railway: Memory and History*. St. Leonards, Australia: Allen & Unwin, 1993.

McCrae, Alister. *Scots in Burma*. Edinburgh: Kiscadale Publications, 1990.

McCrae, Alister, and Alan Prentice. *Irrawaddy Flotilla*. Classic Works on Myanmar Studies Series. Paisley, England: James Paton, 1978.

McEnery, John H. *Epilogue in Burma, 1945–48: The Military Dimension of British Withdrawal*. Tunbridge Wells, England: Spellmount, 1990.

McGeoch, Ian. *The Princely Sailor: Mountbatten of Burma*. London: Brassey's, 1996.

Marshall, Harry I. *The Karens of Burma*. Burma Pamphlets 8. London: Longmans, Green, 1945.

Maung Maung, U. *Burmese Nationalist Movements, 1940–1948*. Edinburgh: Kiscadale Publications, 1989.

———. *From Sangha to Laity: Nationalist Movements of Burma 1920–1940*. Australian National University Monographs on South Asia 4. New Delhi: Manohar, 1980.

Means, Gordon. "Human Sacrifice and Slavery in the 'Unadministered' Areas of Upper Burma During the Colonial Era." *Sojourn: Journal of Social Issues in Southeast Asia* 15, no. 2 (October 1 1999): 184–221.

Monteiro, Irene-Anne. *Camp Four–Kanburi: The True Story of a POW and Survivor of the Infamous Death Railway on the Siam-Burma Border*. Edinburgh: Pentland Press, 1997.

Morgan-Jones, D., et al. "The Burma Campaigns 1942–1945." *Commentary Journal of the Royal Army Medical Corps* 146, no. 3 (2000): 256–70.

Morris, Jones, W.H. "Thirty-Six Years Later: The Mixed Legacies of Mountbatten's Transfer of Power." *International Affairs* 59 (Autumn 1983): 621–28.

Mountbatten of Burma, Louis Mountbatten, Earl. *Personal Diary of Admiral the Lord Louis Mountbatten, Supreme Allied Commander, South-East Asia, 1943–1946*. London: Collins, 1988.

Mukherjee, A. *British Colonial Policy in Burma; An Aspect of Colonialism in South East Asia 1840–1945*. New Delhi: Abhinav Pub., 1988.

Mya Han, Archbishop. "Japanese Studies in Myanmar (1910–1945)." *Myanmar Historical Research Journal* 2 (June 1998): 150–62.

Nagarajan, S. "Tamils of Burma and the Second World War." *Bulletin of Asian Studies: Osaka University of Foreign Studies (Ajia Gaku Ronso)* IV (1994): 71–84.

Naw, Angelene. *Aung San and the Struggle for Burmese Independence*. Chiang Mai, Thailand: Silkworm Books, 2001.

Nelson, Hank, and Gavan McCormack. *The Burma-Thailand Railway*. Concord, Mass.: Paul & Company Publishers Consortium, 1994.

Ni Ni Myint. *Burma's Struggle against British Imperialism, 1885–1895*. Rangoon: The Universities Press, 1983.

Painter, Robin. *A Signal Honour: With the Chindits and the 14th Army in Burma*. London: Leo Cooper, 1999.

Palace, Wendy. "Sir John Jordan and the Burma Border 1906–12." *Asian Affairs* 30, no. 3 (October 1999): 317–24.

Pearn, B. R. *A History of Rangoon*. Rangoon: American Baptist Mission Press, 1939.

Philipps, Bob. *KCS Burma: CBI Air Warning Team, 1941–1942*. Manhattan, Kan.: Sunflower University Press, 1992.

Prefer, Nathan N. *Vinegar Joe's War: Stilwell's Campaign for Burma*. Novato, Calif.: Presido, 2000.

Richards, C. J. *The Burman: an Appreciation*. Burma Pamphlets 7. London: Longmans, Green, 1945.

Rooney, David. *Burma Victory: Imphal, Kohima and the Chindit Issue*. London: Arms and Armour Press, 1992.

Schendel, Willem Van. "Origins of the Burma Rice Boom, 1850–1880." *Journal of Contemporary Asia* 17, no. 4 (1987): 456–72.

———. *Three Deltas: Accumulation and Poverty in Rural Burma, Bengal and South India*. Newburry Park, Calif.: Sage Publications, 1991.

Selth, Andrew. *Australia's Relations with Colonial Burma, 1886–1947*. Clayton, Australia: Monash Asia Institute, Monash University, 1994.

———. "Race and Resistance in Burma, 1942–1945." *Modern Asian Studies* 20 (July 1986): 483–507.

Shipster, J. N. *Mist Over the Rice Fields: A Soldier's Story of the Burma Campaign 1943–45 and Korean War 1950–51*. London: Leo Cooper, 2000.

Silverstein, Josef, ed. *The Political Legacy of Aung San*. Rev. ed. Ithaca, N.Y.: Cornell University Southeast Asia Program, 1993.

Singer, Noel F. *Old Rangoon: City of the Shwedagon*. Gartmore, Scotland: KiscadalePublications, 1995.

Singh, Surendra Prasad. *Growth of Nationalism in Burma, 1900–1942*. Calcutta: Firma KLM Pvt., 1980.

Slim, William Joseph, Viscount. *Defeat into Victory: Battling Japan in Burma and India, 1942–1945*. With a new introduction by David W. Hogan Jr. New York: Cooper Square Press; distributed by National Network, 2000.

Smith, Dun. *Memoirs of the Four-Foot Colonel*. Southeast Asia Program Data Paper 113. Ithaca, N.Y.: Cornell University Press, 1980.

Snodgrass, Judith. "Colonial Constructs of Theravâda Buddhism: Current Perspectives on Western Writing on Asian Tradition." In *Traditions in Current Perspective: Proceedings of the Conference on Myanmar and Southeast Asian Studies 15–17 November 1995, Yangon*. Rangoon: The Universities Press, 1996.

Stevenson, H. N. C. *The Hill Peoples of Burma*. Burma Pamphlets 6. London: Longmans, Green, 1945.

Tamayama, Kazuo, and John Nunneley. *Tales by Japanese Soldiers*. Cassell Military Paperbacks. London: Cassell, 2000

Tanabe, Hisao. "Japanese Ex-Soldiers' View on Burma Appeared in Their War Memoirs [sic]." In *Burma and Japan: Basic Studies on their Cultural and Social Structures*. Edited by The Burma Research Group. Tokyo: Tokyo University of Foreign Studies, 1987.

Tarling, Nicholas. *The Fall of Imperial Britain in South-East Asia*. Singapore: Oxford University Press, 1993.

Tate, D. J. M. *The Making of South-East Asia.* Vol. 2, *The Western Impact: Economic and Social Change.* Kuala Lumpur, Malaysia: Oxford University Press, 1979.

Taylor, Robert H. "Disaster or Release? J. S. Furnivall and the Bankruptcy of Burma." *Modern Asian Studies* 29, no. 1 (February 1995): 45–64.

———. *Marxism and Resistance in Burma: Thein Pe Myint's Wartime Traveler.* Athens: Ohio University Press, 1984.

Tinzar Lwyn. "The Mission: Colonial Discourse on Gender and the Politics of Burma." *New Literatures Review* 24 (Winter 1992): 5–22.

Turrell, Robert Vicat. "Conquest and Concession: The Case of the Burma Ruby Mines." *Modern Asian Studies* 22 (February 1988): 141–63.

The U.S. Army and World War II: Selected Papers from the Army's Commemorative Conferences. Washington, D.C.: Center of Military History, United States Army, 1998.

Webb, G. H. "Kipling's Burma; a Literary and Historical Review." *Asian Affairs* 15 (June 1984): 163–78.

Wilkinson, Wynyard R. T. *Indian Silver, 1858–1947: Silver from the Indian Sub-continent and Burma Made by Local Craftsmen in Western Forms.* London: W. R. T. Wilkinson, 1999.

Willis, G. R. T. *No Hero, Just a Survivor: A Personal Story with Beaufighters and Mosquitoes of 47 Squadron RAF over the Mediterranean and Burma 1943–1945.* Huddersfield, England: Robert Willis, 1999.

Woodward, Mark R. "When One Wheel Stops: Theravada Buddhism and the British Raj in Upper Burma." *Crossroads* 4, no. 1 (Fall 1988): 57–90.

Yang Li. *The House of Yang: Guardians of an Unknown Frontier.* Sydney, Australia: Bookpress, 1997.

Yoon, Won Z. *Japan's Scheme for the Liberation of Burma: The Role of the Minami Kikan and the "Thirty Comrades."* Athens: Ohio University Center for International Studies, 1973.

5. Post-Independence Era (1948–1987)

Aung-Thwin, Michael. "1948 and Burma's Myth of Independence." In *Independent Burma at Forty Years: Six Assessments.* Edited by Josef Silverstein. Ithaca, N.Y.: Cornell University Southeast Asia Program, 1989.

Aye Saung. *Burman in the Back Row: Autobiography of a Burmese Rebel.* Hong Kong: Asia, 1989, 2000.

Badgley, John. "Burma's Military Government: A Political Analysis." *Asian Survey* 2, no. 6 (August 1962): 24–31.

Burma Socialist Programme Party. *The System of Correlation of Man and His Environment.* Rangoon: BSPP, 1973.

Callahan, Mary P. *Making Enemies: War and State Building in Burma*. Ithaca, N.Y.: Cornell University Press, 2003.
Chao-Tzang Yawnghwe. *The Shan of Burma: Memoirs of a Shan Exile*. Singapore: Institute of Southeast Asian Studies, 1987.
Davies, Philip H. J. "Legacies of Secret Service: Renegade SOE and the Karen Struggle in Burma, 1948–50." In *The Clandestine Cold War in Asia, 1945–65: Western Intelligence, Propaganda and Special Operations*. Portland, Ore.: Frank Cass, 2000.
Elliott, Patricia. *The White Umbrella*. Bangkok: Post Books, 1999.
Maung Maung, Dr. *Burma and General Ne Win*. Rangoon: Religious Affairs Department Press, 1969.
Maung Maung Gyi. "Foreign Policy of Burma since 1962: Negative Neutralism for Group Survival." In *Military Rule in Burma since 1962: A Kaleidoscope of Views*. Edited by F. K. Lehman. Singapore: Maruzen Asia, 1981.
Mya Maung. "The Burma Road to Poverty: A Socio-Political Analysis." *The Fletcher Forum* 13, no. 2 (Summer 1989): 271–94.
———. "Cultural Value and Economic Change in Burma." *Asian Survey* 4, no. 3 (March 1964): 757–64.
Nu, U. *Saturday's Son*. Translated by Edward Law-Yone. New Haven, Conn.: Yale University Press, 1975.
Ono Toru. "The Development of Education in Burma." *East Asian Cultural Studies* 20, nos. 1–4 (March 1981): 107–34.
Raja Segaram Arumgam. "Burma: A Political and Economic Background." In *Southeast Asian Affairs, 1975*. Singapore: Institute of Southeast Asian Studies/Heinemann Asia, 1975.
———. "Burma: Political Unrest and Economic Stagnation." In *Southeast Asian Affairs, 1976*. Singapore: Institute of Southeast Asian Studies/Heinemann Asia, 1976.
Remond Htoo, Saw. "The Massacre of the University Students in Rangoon 1962, July 7." Unpublished paper presented at the Opening Ceremonies of the Center for Burma Studies, Northern Illinois University, July 28, 1987.
Sargent, Inge. *Twilight Over Burma*. Honolulu: University of Hawaii Press, 1994.
Selth, Andrew. *Death of a Hero: The U Thant Disturbances in Burma, December 1974*. Research Paper 49. Brisbane, Australia: Griffith University Centre for the Study of Australian-Asian Relations, 1989.
Silverstein, Josef. *Burma: Military Rule and the Politics of Stagnation*. Ithaca, N.Y.: Cornell University Press, 1977.
———. *Burmese Politics: The Dilemma of National Unity*. New Brunswick, N.J.: Rutgers University Press, 1980.
———. "The Other Side of Burma's Struggle for Independence." *Pacific Affairs* 58, no. 1 (spring 1985): 98–108.

Sola, Richard. *Chine-Birmanie: Histoire d'une Guerre Secrète, 1949–1954.* Paris: Sudestasie, 1990.

Steinberg, David I. *Burma's Road toward Development: Growth and Ideology under Military Rule.* Boulder, Colo.: Westview Press, 1981.

——. "Burma under the Military: Toward a Chronology." *Contemporary Southeast Asia* 3, no. 3 (December 1981): 244–85.

——. "Burmese Economics: The Conflict of Ideology and Pragmatism." In *Military Rule in Burma since 1962: A Kaleidoscope of Views.* Edited by F. K. Lehman. Singapore: Maruzen Asia, 1981.

——. "Neither Silver nor Gold: The 40th Anniversary of the Burmese Economy." In *Independent Burma at Forty Years: Six Assessments.* Edited by Josef Silverstein. Ithaca, N.Y.: Cornell University Southeast Asia Program, 1989.

Thaung, U. *A Journalist, A General and An Army in Burma.* Bangkok: White Lotus, 1995.

Tinker, Hugh. "Burma's Struggle for Independence: The Transfer of Power Thesis Re-examined." *Modern Asian Studies* 20 (July 1986): 461–81.

Tun, M. C. "Secretariat No More." In *Asia Yearbook 1973.* Hong Kong: Far Eastern Economic Review, 1973.

Wiant, Jon. "Tradition in the Service of Revolution: The Political Symbolism of *Taw-hlan-ye-khit.*" In *Military Rule in Burma since 1962: A Kaleidoscope of Views.* Edited by F. K. Lehman. Singapore: Maruzen Asia, 1981.

6. The Political Crisis of 1988

Aikman, David. "Armies Rampant." *Time* 132 (October 3, 1988): 30–32.

Aung Chin Win Aung. *Burma and the Last Days of General Ne Win.* Indianapolis, Ind.: Yoma, 1996.

Aung Gyi, U. "Letter to General Ne Win." *Burma Debate* IV, mo. 3 (July/Aug. 1997): 25–30.

Aung San Suu Kyi. *Freedom from Fear and Other Writings.* 2nd ed. London: Penguin, 1995.

Birth: Voices from the 1988 Uprising in Burma. Ithaca, N.Y.: Nonviolence Empowerment Organizations (NEO).

"Burma (Special Section)." *World Press Review* 35 (November 1988): 26–28.

Burma Watcher. "Burma in 1988: There Came a Whirlwind." *Asian Survey* 29, no. 2 (February 1989): 174–80.

Levin, Burton. "Reminiscences & Reflections." *Burma Debate* 3 (1998): 4–12.

Lintner, Bertil. *Outrage: Burma's Struggle for Democracy.* Hong Kong: Review Publishing, 1989.

Maung Maung, Dr. *The 1988 Uprising in Burma.* Monograph 49. New Haven, Conn.: Yale Southeast Asia Studies, 2000.

Moksha Yitri. "The Crisis in Burma: Back from the Heart of Darkness?" *Asian Survey* 29, no. 6 (June 1989): 543–58.

Tanabe Hisao. *Biruma Minshuka Undō, 1988: Dokyūmento* [*Document: Burma's Democracy Movement, 1988*]. Tokyo: Nashi no Ki Sha, 1989.

III. CONTEMPORARY BURMA (MYANMAR)

1. Population, Ethnicity, and Languages

Allott, A. J., and John Okell. *Burmese (Myanmar) Dictionary of Grammatical Forms.* Richmond, England: Curzon, 2000.

Armstrong, Ruth M. *The Kachins of Burma.* Bloomington, Ind.: Eastern Press, 1997.

Ba Han, Dr. *The University English-Myanmar Dictionary.* Rangoon: Win Literature, 1996.

Bauer, Christian. "Language and Ethnicity: The Mon in Burma and Thailand." In *Ethnic Groups Across National Boundaries in Mainland Southeast Asia.* Edited by Gehan Wijeyewardene. Singapore: Institute of Southeast Asian Studies, 1990.

Chappell, Hilary. "The Benefactive Construction in Moulmein Sgaw Karen." *Linguistics of the Tibeto-Burman Area* 15, no. 1 (Spring 1992): 11–30.

Dessaint, William, and Alain Dessaint. "Opium and Labor: Social Structure and Economic Change in the Lisu Highlands." *Peasant Studies* 19, nos. 3–4 (Spring–Summer 1992): 147–77.

Dessaint, William, and Avounado Ngwâma. *Au Sud des Nuages: Mythes et Contes Recueillis Oralement Chez les Montagnards Lissou (Tibéto-Birmans),* Paris: "L'Aube des Peuples," Editions Gallimard, 1994.

Evans, Grant, Christopher Hutton, and Khun Eng Kuah. *Where China Meets Southeast Asia: Social and Cultural Change in the Border Region.* New York: St. Martin's Press, 2000.

Falla, Jonathan. *True Love and Bartholomew; Rebels on the Burmese Border.* Cambridge, England: Cambridge University Press, 1991.

Fiskesjö, Nils Magnus Geir. "The Fate of Sacrifice and the Making of Wa History." Ph.D. Thesis, Department of Anthropology and Department of East Asian Languages and Civilizations, University of Chicago, 2000.

Forbes, Andrew D. W. "History of Panglong, 1875–1900: A 'Panthay' (Chinese-Muslim)." *Muslim World* (Hartford, Conn.) 78 (January 1988): 38–50.

Hayami, Yoko. "Karen Tradition According to Christ or Buddha—The Implications of Multiple Reinterpretations for a Minority Ethnic Group in Thailand." *Journal of Southeast Asian Studies* 27, no. 2 (September 1996): 334ff.

Hayami, Yoko, and Susan M. Darlington. "The Karen of Burma and Thailand." In *Endangered Peoples of Southeast and East Asia: Struggles to Survive and Thrive.* Edited by Leslie E. Sponsel et al. Westport, Conn.: Greenwood, Press, 2000.

Heppner, Kevin. "Manerplaw's Federal University: An Experiment in Ethnic Harmony in the Midst of Revolution." *Thai-Yunnan Project Newsletter* 16 (March 1992): 22–26.

Howard, Michael C. *Textiles of the Hill Tribes of Burma.* Bangkok: White Lotus, 1999.

Kammerer, Cornelia Ann. "Customs and Christian Conversion Among Akha Highlanders of Burma and Thailand." *American Ethnologist* 17 (May 1990): 277–91.

Khai, Chin Khua. "Dynamics of Renewal: A Historical Movement Among the Zomi in Myanmar." Ph.D. Thesis, Intercultural Studies, Fuller Theological Seminary, 1999.

Khin Maung Kyi. "Indians in Burma: Problems of an Alien Subculture in a Highly Integrated Society." In *Indian Communities in Southeast Asia.* Singapore: Times Academic Press, 1993.

Khin Maung, M. Ismael. *Estimates of Burma's Mortality, Age Structure, and Fertility, 1973–83.* Honolulu, Hawaii: East-West Population Institute, East-West Center, 1990.

Lintner, Bertil. *The Kachin: Lords of Burma's Northern Frontier.* Peoples and Cultures of Southeast Asia. Thailand: Teak House, 1997.

———. *Land of Jade.* Edinburgh: Kiscadale Publications, 1990.

Moe K. Tun. *Education for the Development of the Marginalized Karen in Burma.* Bangkok: Burma Issues, 1998.

Mya Than. "Jairampur: A Profile of an Indian Community in Rural Burma." In *Indian Communities in Southeast Asia.* Singapore: Times Academic Press, 1993.

Nai Pan Hla. *The Significant Role of the Mon Language and Culture in Southeast Asia.* Part I. Tokyo: Tokyo University of Foreign Studies, Institute for the Study of the Languages and Cultures of Asia and Africa, 1992.

Peltier, Anatole-Roger. "Régards sur la Litterature Classique Khun de Birmanie." *Bulletin De L'Ecole Française D'Extrême-Orient* 87 (2000): 193–214.

Rajah, Ananda. "Ethnicity, Nationalism, and the Nation-State: The Karen in Burma and Thailand." In *Ethnic Groups Across National Boundaries in Mainland Southeast Asia.* Edited by Gehan Wijeyewardene. Singapore: Institute of Southeast Asian Studies, 1990.

Rastorfer, Jean-Marc. *On the Development of Kayah and Kayan National Identity: A Study and A Bibliography*. Bangkok: Southeast Asian Publishing House, 1994.

Sakhong, Lian H. *In Search of Chin Identity: A Study in Religion, Politics and Ethnic Identity in Burma*. Nordic Institute of Asian Studies, Monograph Series No. 91. Copenhagen: NIAS Press, 2003.

———. *Religion and Politics Among the Chin People in Burma (1896–1949)*. Uppsala, Sweden: Uppsala University, 2000.

South, Ashley. *Mon Nationalism and Civil War in Burma: The Golden Sheldrake*. London: Routledge-Curzon, 2003.

Tooker, Deborah E. "Identity Systems of Highland Burma: Belief, Akha zan, and a Critique of Interiorized Notions of Ethno-Religious Identity." *Man* 27 (December 1992): 799–819.

Van Bik, Rolling. "The Chin National Front and Chin Nationhood." *Burma Debate* III (November/December 1996): 30–33.

Wijeyewardene, Gehan. "Ethnicity Policy in Burma." *Thai-Yunnan Project Newsletter* 14 (September 1991): 17.

2. Economics and Economic Engagement

Aditjondro, George. "Dictators United: The Suharto-SLORC Business Connection." *Multinational Monitor* 18 (1997): 11–14.

Badgley, John. "The Burmese Way to Capitalism." In *Southeast Asian Affairs 1990*. Singapore: Institute of Southeast Asian Studies, 1990.

Brunner, Jake. *Logging Burma's Frontier Forests: Resources and the Regime*. Washington, D.C.: World Resources Institute, 1999.

"Burma: Gas Exports—and Endless Problems Asia's Latest Gas Contender is Stifled by Its Military, Corruption and the Limited Opportunities Offered by Thailand Energy Economist." *Thailand Energy Economist* 226 (2000): 16–19.

Buszynski L. "Thailand and Myanmar—The Perils of Constructive Engagement." *Pacific Review* 11, no. 2 (1998): 290–305.

Capital Flows Along the Mekong: The Complete Guide to Investing in Cambodia, Laos, Myanmar & Vietnam. 2 vols. Hong Kong: Asia Law & Practice, 1996.

Carter, George Francis. "Rice Shortage to Hit Home." *Far Eastern Economic Review* 136 (April 16 1987): 76.

Cook, Paul. "Myanmar: Experience with Aid and Management Development during Transition." *Public Administration and Development* 13, no. 4 (October 1993): 423–34.

———. "Policy Reform, Privatization, and Private Sector Development in Myanmar." *South East Asia Research* (SOAS, London University) 2, no. 2 (September 1994): 117–40.

Cook, Paul and Martin Minogue. "Economic Reform and Political Change in Myanmar." *World Development* 21 (July 1993): 1151–61.

Country Profile. London: The Economist Intelligence Unit (annual publication).

Country Report. London: The Economist Intelligence Unit (quarterly publication).

Economy of Burma. Parts 1 and 2. New Delhi: Washington, D.C.: Library of Congress Office; Library of Congress Photoduplication Service, 1998–1999.

Fujisaka, Sam, Keith Moody, and Keith Ingram. "A Descriptive Study of Farming Practices for Dry Seeded Rainfed Lowland Rice in India, Indonesia, and Myanmar." *Agriculture, Ecosystems & Environment* 45 (May 1993): 115–28.

Hirouchi, Kaori. "Japan's Official Foreign Aid to Burma: Contradiction and Motivation." Master's Thesis, Clark University, 1998.

Hobson, J. S. Perry, and Roberta Leung. "Hotel Development in Myanmar: Politics and the Human-Resources Challenge." *The Cornell Hotel and Restaurant Administration Quarterly* 38 (February 1997): 60–71.

Innes-Brown, Marc, and Mark J. Valencia. "Thailand's Resource Diplomacy in Indochina and Myanmar." *Contemporary Southeast Asia* 14, no. 4 (March 1993): 332–51.

Kanayama, Hisahiro. *Expectations and Reality: The Economic & Political Transition of Vietnam & Myanmar*. Tokyo: Institute for International Policy Studies, 1995.

Kane, Robert E., and Robert C. Kammerling. "Status of Ruby and Sapphire Mining in the Mogok Stone Tract." *Gems & Gemology* 27 (Fall 1992): 152–74.

Khin Maung Nyunt. *Foreign Loans and Aid in the Economic Development of Burma 1974/75 to 1985/86*. Bangkok: Chulalongkorn University Printing House, 1990.

Kiryu Minoru, ed. *ASEAN and Japanese Perspectives on Industrial Development and Reforms in Myanmar: A Survey of Selected Firms*. Bangkok: Chulalongkorn University Printing House, 1998.

——. *Industrial Development and Reforms in Myanmar: ASEAN and Japanese Perspectives*. Bangkok: White Lotus, 1999.

——. "Performance and Prospects of the Myanmar Economy." In *Southeast Asian Affairs 1992*. Singapore: Institute of Southeast Asian Studies, 1992.

McCarthy, Stephen. "Ten Years of Chaos in Burma: Foreign Investment and Economic Liberalization Under the SLORC-SPDC, 1988 to 1998." *Pacific Affairs* 73, no. 2 (Summer 2000): 233–62.

Mya Maung. "The Burma Road from the Union of Burma to Myanmar." *Asian Survey* 30, no. 6 (June 1990): 602–24.

——. *The Burma Road to Capitalism: Economic Growth Versus Democracy*. Westport, Conn.: Praeger, 1998.

———. *The Burma Road to Poverty*. New York: Praeger, 1991.

Mya Than. "Agriculture in Myanmar: What Has Happened to Asia's Rice Bowl?" In *Southeast Asian Affairs 1990*. Singapore: Institute of Southeast Asian Studies, 1990.

———. "Economic Co-operation in the Greater Mekong Subregion." *Asian-Pacific Economic Literature* 11, no. 2 (November 1997): 40–57.

———. "Little Change in Rural Burma: A Case Study of a Burmese Village (1960–80)." *Sojourn* 2, no. 1 (February 1987): 55–88.

———. *Myanmar's External Trade: An Overview in the Southeast Asian Context*. ISEAS Current Economic Affairs Series. Singapore: Institute of Southeast Asian Studies. 1992.

Mya Than and Joseph L. H. Tan, eds. *Myanmar Dilemmas and Options*. Singapore: Institute of Southeast Asian Studies, 1990.

Mya Than, Myat Thein, and Maw Than. *Financial Resources for Development in Myanmar: Lessons from Asia*. Singapore: Institute of Southeast Asian Studies, 2000.

Myat Mon. "The Economic Position of Women in Burma." *Asian Studies Review* 24, no. 2 (June 2000): 243–55.

Myat Thein. "The Economics of Farm Size and Land Policy in the Transition to a Market Economy." *Sojourn* 12 (April 1997): 124–34.

———. *Improving Domestic Resource Mobilization in Myanmar*. Singapore: Institute of Southeast Asian Studies, 1999.

Myat Thein and Maung Maung Soe. "Economic Reforms and Their Impact on Agricultural Development in Myanmar." *ASEAN Economic Bulletin* 15, no. 1 (April 1998): 13–29.

Nishizawa, Nobuyoshi. "Recent Economic Changes in Myanmar." *Kobe University Economic Review* 0, no. 40 (1994): 1–16.

Philip, Janette, and David Mercer. "Commodification of Buddhism in Contemporary Burma." *Annals of Tourism Research* 26, no. 1 (January 1999): 21–54.

Rana, Pradumna B., and Naved Hamid, eds. *From Centrally Planned to Market Economies: The Asian Approach*. Vol. 3, *Lao PDR, Myanmar and Viet Nam*. Hong Kong: Oxford University Press for the Asian Development Bank, 1996.

Schermerhorn, John R., Jr. "Terms of Global Business Engagement in Ethically Challenging Environments: Applications to Burma." *Business Ethics Quarterly* 9, no. 3 (July 1999): 485–505.

Schmidt, Michael J. "Working Elephants (Used for Logging in Burma)." *Scientific American* 274 (January 1996): 82–87.

Steinberg, David I. "International Rivalries in Burma: The Rise of Economic Competition." *Asian Survey* 30, no. 6 (June 1990): 587–601.

———. "Japanese Economic Assistance to Burma: Aid in the 'Tarenagashi' Manner?" *Crossroads* 5, no. 2 (1990): 51–107.

———. "Liberalization in Myanmar: How Real Are the Changes?" *Contemporary Southeast Asia* 15, no. 2 (September 1993): 161–78.

Talib, Azizah. "Monetary Policy in Myanmar: An Update (1979–1990)." In *Monetary Policy in the SEACEN Countries: An Update*. Kuala Lumpur, Malaysia: The South East Asian Central Banks (SEACEN), 1993.

Walker, Andrew. "The Myanmar Trade Fair: Tachilek 21–31 December 1993." *Thai-Yunnan Project Newsletter* 24 (March 1994): 8–9.

Wijeyewardene, Gehan. "Traders of Jade, Traders of Rice: The Anguish of the DAB." *Thai-Yunnan Project Newsletter* 24 (March 1994): 1–4.

Wong, John. "Why Has Myanmar Not Developed Like East Asia?" *ASEAN Economic Bulletin* 13, no. 3 (March 1997): 344–58.

Yao Jianguo. "Sino-Myanmar Trade Develops Apace." *Beijing Review* 34 (August 19, 1991): 38–39.

Young, Kenneth B. *An Economic Assessment of the Myanmar Rice Sector: Current Developments and Prospects*. Fayetteville: Arkansas Agricultural Experiment Station, 1998.

3. Politics

Burma Students Democratic Front. Orchestra Burma, 2000. Available at www .orchestraburma.org/politics/absdf/Absdf%20Index.htm.

Allott, Anna J. "The Media in Burma and the Pro-Democracy Movement of July–September 1988." *South-East Asia Library Group Newsletter* 34–35 (December 1990): 17–24.

Aung Hla. "Using the Internet in the Cyberwar Between Burma Activists and the Military Government of Burma 1998." Master's Thesis, University of Maryland, College Park, 1998.

Aung San Suu Kyi. *Freedom from Fear and Other Writings*. Rev. ed. Edited by Michael Aris. London: Penguin Books, 1995.

———. "In Her Own Words: Interview with Daw Aung San Suu Kyi." *Burma Debate* IV, no. 5 (November/December 1997): 21–27.

———. *Letters from Burma*. New York: Penguin, 1997.

———. "An Opening Keynote Address: The NGO Forum on Women Beijing 1995, 31 August 1995." *Burma Debate* 11, no. 4 (August/September 1995): 16–19.

———. *The Voice of Hope*. New York: Seven Stories Press, 1998.

Bečka, Jan. "The Military and the Struggle for Democracy in Burma: The Presentation of the Political Upheaval of 1988 in the Official Burmese Press." *Archiv Orientalni* 61 (1993): 63–80.

Brown, David. "The Ethnocratic State and Ethnic Separatism in Burma." In *The State and Ethnic Politics in Southeast Asia*. London: Routledge, 1994.

Burma, Country in Crisis. New York: Burma Project, Open Society Institute, 1998.

Callahan, Mary P. "Burma in 1995: Looking beyond the Release of Aung San Suu Kyi." *Asian Survey* 36, no. 2 (February 1996): 158.

Carey, Peter, ed. *Burma: The Challenge of Change in a Divided Society*. Basingstoke, England: Macmillan, 1997.

Danitz, Tiffany, et al. *Networking Dissent: Cyber Activists Use the Internet to Promote Democracy in Burma*. Washington, D.C.: United States Institute of Peace, 2000.

Democratic Alliance of Burma. Publications. Part 1. New Delhi; Washington, D.C.: Library of Congress Office; Library of Congress Photoduplication Service, 1998.

Diller, Janelle M. "Constitutional Reform in a Repressive State: The Case of Burma." *Asian Survey* 33 (April 1993): 393–407.

"Extracts from a Personal Statement by Khon Mar Ko Pan Regarding the SLORC's National Convention." *Thai-Yunnan Project Newsletter* 21 (June 1993): 10–12.

Fink, Christina. *Living Silence: Burma under the Military Rule*. New York: Zed, 2001.

Ghosh, Amitav. "Burma (Aung San and Daw Aung San Suu Kyi)." *The New Yorker* 72 (August 12, 1996): 38–54.

Gravers, Mikael. *Nationalism as Political Paranoia in Burma. An Essay on the Historical Practice of Power*. 2nd rev. ed. London: NIAS-Curzon, 1998.

Guyot, James. "Burma." In *Rethinking Political Development in Southeast Asia*. Edited by Norma Mahmood. Kuala Lumpur, Malaysia: University of Malaya Press, 1994.

———. "Myanmar in 1989: Tatmadaw V." *Asian Survey* 30, no. 2 (February 1990): 187–95.

———. "Myanmar in 1990: The Unconsummated Election." *Asian Survey* 31, no. 2 (February 1991): 205–11.

Guyot, James F., and John Badgley. "Burma in 1988: Perestroika with a Military Face." In *Southeast Asian Affairs 1989*. Singapore: Institute of Southeast Asian Studies, 1989.

Haseman, John B. "Burma in 1987: Change in the Air?" *Asian Survey* (February 1988).

———. *Destruction of Democracy: The Tragic Case of Burma*. New York: Asian Affairs, 1993.

———. "Turmoil in Burma: There Came a Whirlwind." *Asian Defence Journal* (August 1989).

Heppner, Kevin. "Manerplaw's Federal University: An Experiment in Ethnic Harmony in the Midst of Revolution." *Thai-Yunnan Project Newsletter* 16 (March 1992): 22–26.

Herbert, Patricia. "List of Burmese Pro-Democracy [August–September 1988] Publications in the British Library." *South-East Asia Library Group Newsletter* 34–35 (December 1990): 25–38.

Hoffmann, Ralf. "Traditional Political Culture and the Prospects for Democracy in Burma." In *Tradition and Modernity in Myanmar 3–2.* Edited by U. Gärtner and J. Lorenz. Münster/Hamburg, 1994.

Houtman, Gustaaf. *Mental Culture in Burmese Crisis Politics: Aung San Suu Kyi and the National League for Democracy.* Monograph Series 33. Tokyo: Tokyo University of Foreign Studies, Institute for the Study of Languages and Cultures of Asia and Africa, 1999.

International IDEA. *Challenges to Democratization in Burma: Perspectives on Multi-lateral and Bilateral Perspectives.* Stockholm: Institute for Democracy and Electoral Assistance (IDEA), 2001.

Leehey, Jennifer. "Message in a Bottle: A Gallery of Social/Political Cartoons from Burma." *Southeast Asian Journal of Social Science* 25, no. 1 (1997): 151–55.

Lin Xixing. "Burma's Political Situation before the General Election." *Thai-Yunnan Project Newsletter* 10 (September 1990): 14–17.

Lintner, Bertil. *Aung San Suu Kyi and Burma's Unfinished Renaissance.* Clayton, Australia: Center of Southeast Asian Studies, Monash University, 1990.

——. *Burma in Revolt: Opium and Insurgency Since 1948.* Boulder, Colo.: Westview Press, 1994.

Matthews, Bruce. "Buddhism Under a Military Regime: The Iron Heel in Burma." *Asian Survey* 33 (April 1993): 408–23.

——. "The Present Fortune of Tradition-Bound Authoritarianism in Myanmar." *Pacific Affairs* 71, no. 1 (Spring 1998): 7–23.

May, Ronald James, Emily Rudland, and Morten B. Pedersen. *Burma-Myanmar: Strong Regime, Weak State?* Adelaide, Australia: Crawford House Publishing, 2000.

Mya Maung. *Totalitarianism in Burma: Prospects for Economic Development.* New York: Paragon House, 1992.

Politics and Government in Burma. Parts 1 & 2. New Delhi; Washington, D.C.: Library of Congress Office; Library of Congress Photoduplication Service, 1999.

Rotberg, Robert I., ed. *Burma: Prospects for a Democratic Future.* Cambridge, Mass.: The World Peace Foundation and Harvard Institute for International Development/Brookings Institute Press, 1998.

Seekins, Donald M. "Burma in 1998: Little to Celebrate." *Asian Survey* 39, no. 1 (January/February 1999): 12.

———. "Burma in 1999: A Slim Hope." *Asian Survey* 40, no. 1 (Jan./February 2000): 16–24.

———. Myanmar: Secret Talks and Political Paralysis." In *Southeast Asian Affairs 2002*. Singapore: Institute of Southeast Asian Studies, 2002.

Sein Win. "Sustaining Burma's Hopes for Freedom." *Journal of Democracy* 5 (April 1994): 144–49.

Siemers, Gunter. "Myanmar 1992: Heading for A Guided Democracy." In *Southeast Asian Affairs 1993*. Singapore: Institute of Southeast Asian Studies, 1993.

Silverstein, Josef. "Aung San Suu Kyi: Is She Burma's Woman of Destiny?" *Asian Survey* 30, no. 10 (October 1990): 1007–19.

———. "Burma's Uneven Struggle." *Journal of Democracy* 7 (October 1996): 88–102.

———. "Change in Burma?" *Current History* 94 (December 1995): 440–43.

———. "Civil War and Rebellion in Burma." *Asian Survey* 21, no. 1 (March 1990): 114–34.

———. "The Idea of Freedom in Burma and the Political Thought of Daw Aung San Suu Kyi." *Pacific Affairs* 69 (Summer 1996): 211–28.

———. *Two Papers on Burma*. Department of Social Change Research School of Pacific and Asian Studies. Canberra: Australian National University, 1996.

Skyful of Lies, B.B.C., V.O.A.: Their Broadcasts and Rebuttals to Disinformation. Rangoon: The News and Periodicals Enterprise, 1988.

Smith, Martin. *Burma: Insurgency and the Politics of Ethnicity*. Rev. and updated ed. London: Zed Books, 1999.

Sola, Richard. *Birmanie: La Révolution Kidnappée (1981–1995)*. Paris: L'Harmattan, 1996.

Steinberg, David I. *Burma: Prospects for Political and Economic Reconstruction*. Cambridge, Mass.: World Peace Foundation, 1997.

———. "Burma/Myanmar: Under the Military" In *Driven by Growth: Political Change in the Asia-Pacific Region*. Rev. ed. Singapore: Institute of Southeast Asian Studies, 1999.

———. *Burma, the State of Myanmar*. Washington, D.C.: Georgetown University Press, 2000.

———. "Crisis in Burma." *Current History* 88 (April 1989): 185–88.

———. "Myanmar in 1991: The Miasma in Burma (Part of a Symposium on Asia in 1991)." *Asian Survey* 32 (February 1992): 146–53.

———. "Myanmar 1991: Military Intransigence." In *Southeast Asian Affairs 1992*. Singapore: Institute of Southeast Asian Studies, 1992.

Sundhaussen, Ulf. "Indonesia's New Order: A Model for Myanmar?" *Asian Survey* 35, no. 8 (August 1995): 768–80.

Taylor, Robert H, ed. *Burma: Political Economy under Military Rule*. New York: St. Martin's Press, 2000.

———. "Change in Burma: Political Demands and Military Power." *Asian Affairs* 22 (June 1991): 131–41.

———. "The Evolving Military Role in Burma." *Current History* 89 (March 1990): 105–8.

Ten Years on: A Parliament Denied: Burma's Struggle to Convene the People's Parliament. Bangkok: Alternative A[SEAN] Network on Burma, 2000.

Thawnghmung, Ardeth Maung. *Behind the Teak Curtain: Authoritarianism, Agricultural Policies and Political Legitimacy in Rural Burma/Myanmar*. London: Kegan Paul, 2004.

Thomson, Curtis N. "Political Stability and Minority Groups in Burma." *Geographical Review* 85 (July 1995): 269–85.

Tin Maung Maung Than. "Myanmar Democratization: Punctuated Equilibrium or Retrograde Motion?" In *Democratization in Southeast and East Asia*. Edited by Anek Laothamatas. Chiang Mai, Thailand: Silkworm Books, 1997.

———. "Neither Inheritance nor Legacy: Leading the Myanmar State since Independence." *Contemporary Southeast Asia* 15, no. 1 (June 1993): 24–63.

To Stand and Be Counted: The Suppression of Burma's Members of Parliament. Bangkok: All Burma Students' Democratic Front, Documentation and Research Centre, 1998.

Tortured Voices: Personal Accounts of Burma's Interrogation Centres. Bangkok: All Burma Students' Democratic Front, 1998.

Web of Conspiracy Complicated Stories of Treacherous Machinations and Intrigues of BCP UG, DAB, and Some NLD Leaders to Seize State Power. Rangoon: The News and Periodicals Enterprise, 1991.

Weller, Marc., ed. *Democracy and Politics in Burma: A Collection of Documents*. Manerplaw, Burma: G.P.O. of the National Coalition Government of the Union of Burma, 1993.

Wijeyewardene, Gehan. "The Defeat of Khun Sa." *Thai-Yunnan Project Newsletter* 32 (June 1996): 3–5.

Yawnghwe, Chao-Tzang. "The Orientalization of Burmese Politics? A Research Agenda." *Burma Debate* VII, nos. 1 & 2 (Fall 2000): 10–13.

———. "The Political Economy of the Opium Trade: Implications for Shan State." *Journal of Contemporary Asia* 23, no. 3 (1993): 306–26.

———. "The Politics of Authoritarianism: The State and Political Soldiers in Burma, Indonesia, and Thailand." Ph.D. Thesis, University of British Columbia, 1997.

4. Foreign Relations and Security-Military Affairs

Ball, Desmond. *Burma and Drugs: The Regime's Complicity in the Global Drug Trade*. Canberra: Strategic and Defence Studies Centre, Australian National University, 1999.

——. *Burma's Military Secrets: Signals Intelligence (SIGINT) from the Second World War to Civil War and Cyber Warfare*. Bangkok: White Lotus, 1998.

Bert, Wayne. "Chinese Policy toward Democratization Movements: Burma and the Philippines." *Asian Survey* 30, no. 11 (November 1990): 1066–83.

Buszynski L. "Thailand and Myanmar—The Perils of Constructive Engagement." *Pacific Review* 11, no. 2 (1998): 290–305.

Groves, Tim. "'Burma' Joins Japan's Newspeak Blacklist." *Kyoto Journal* 29 (1995): 136–39.

Guay, Terence. "Local Government and Global Politics: The Implications of Massachusetts' 'Burma Law'." *Political Science Quarterly* 115, no. 3 (Fall 2000): 353–76.

Liang, Chi Shad. *Burma's Foreign Relations: Neutralism in Theory and Practice*. New York: Praeger, 1990.

Lu, Yun. "Ruili: China's Southwestern Gate to Burma." *Beijing Review* 30 (May 25, 1987): 22–24.

Malik, J. Mohan. "Sino-Indian Rivalry in Myanmar: Implications for Regional Security." *Contemporary Southeast Asia* 16, no. 2 (September 1994): 137–56.

Maung Aung Myoe. *Building the Tatmadaw: The Organisational Development of the Armed Forces in Myanmar, 1948–98*. Canberra: Strategic and Defence Studies Centre, Australian National University, 1998.

——. *Officer Education and Leadership Training in the Tatmadaw: A Survey*. Canberra: Strategic and Defence Studies Centre, Australian National University, 2000.

——. *Neither Friend nor Foe: Myanmar's Relations with Thailand since 1988: A View from Yangon*. IDSS Monograph 1. Singapore: Institute of Defence and Strategic Studies, 2002.

Ott, Marvin C. *Burma: A Strategic Perspective*. Washington, D.C.: National Defense University, Institute for National Strategic Studies, 1996.

Overholt, William H. "Dateline Drug Wars: Burma: The Wrong Enemy." *Foreign Policy* 77 (winter 1989/1990): 172–91.

Pradhan, Swatanter, K. *New Dimensions in Indo-Burmese Relations*. New Delhi: Rajat, 2000.

Saito, Teruko. "Japan's Inconsistent Approach to Burma." *Japan Quarterly* 39 (January/March 1992): 17–27.

Seekins, Donald M. "Burma-China Relations: Playing with Fire." *Asian Survey* 37, no. 6 (June 1997): 525–39.

———. "Japan's Aid Relations with Military Regimes in Burma, 1962–1991: The *Kokunaika* Process." *Asian Survey* 32, no. 3 (March 1992): 246–62.

———. "The North Wind and the Sun: Japan's Response to the Political Crisis in Burma, 1988–1996." *Journal of Burma Studies* 4 (1999): 1–33.

Selth, Andrew. *Burma's Armed Forces: Power without Glory.* Norwalk: Eastbridge, 2002.

Singh, S. "The Sinicization of Myanmar and Its Implications for India." *Issues and Studies* 33, no. 1 (January 1997): 116–33.

Steinberg, David I. "Burma/Myanmar and the Dilemmas of U.S. Foreign Policy." *Contemporary Southeast Asia* 21, no. 2 (August 1999): 283–311.

———. "Japanese Economic Assistance to Burma: Aid in the 'Tarenagashi' Manner?" *Crossroads* 5, no. 2 (1990): 51–107.

Tin Maung Maung Than. "Burma's National Security and Defence Posture." *Contemporary Southeast Asia* 11, no. 1 (June 1989): 40–60.

5. Human Rights

Allott, Anna J. *Inked Over, Ripped Out: Burmese Storytellers and the Censors.* New York: Pen American Center, 1993.

Amnesty International. *Myanmar—Exodus from the Shan State.* London: International Secretariat, 2000.

Apple, Betsy. *School for Rape.* Bangkok: EarthRights International, 1998.

Bamforth, Vicky, Steven Lanuouwand Graham Mortimer. *Conflict and Displacement in Karenni: The Need for Considered Approaches.* Chiang Mai, Thailand: Burma Ethnic Research Group, 2000.

Bangladesh/Burma: Rohingya Refugees in Bangladesh, The Search for a Lasting Solution. New York: Human Rights Watch/Asia, 1997.

Burma: Children's Rights and the Rule of Law. New York: Human Rights Watch, 1998.

Burma, Entrenchment or Reform: Human Rights Developments and the Need for Continued Pressure. New York: Human Rights Watch/Asia, 1995.

Burma: Extrajudicial Execution, Torture and Political Imprisonment of Members of the Shan and Other Ethnic Minorities. London: Amnesty International, 1988.

Burma: Human Lives for Natural Resources, Oil & Natural Gas. Chiang Mai, Thailand: The Southeast Asian Information Network and the All Burma Students' Democratic Front, Chiang Mai University, 1994.

Burma: Human Rights, Foreign Trade, Aid and Investments. Brussels, Belgium: International Confederation of Free Trade Unions (ICFTU), Department of Free Trade Union Rights, 1994.

Burma/Bangladesh: Burmese Refugees in Bangladesh: Still No Durable Solution. New York: Human Rights Watch, 2000.

Burma/Thailand: Unwanted and Unprotected: Burmese Refugees in Thailand. London: Human Rights Watch, 1998.

Dispossessed: Forced Relocation and Extrajudicial Killings in Shan State. Chiang Mai, Thailand: The Shan Human Rights Foundation, 1998.

Forgotten Victims of a Hidden War: Internally Displaced Karen in Burma. Bangkok: Burma Ethnic Research Group and the Friedrich Naumann Foundation (BERG), 1998.

Human Rights Violations Relevant to the 1998 United Nations Commission on Human Rights, Geneva, Switzerland. Bangkok: Altsean Burma, 1998.

IMAGES/ASIA in collaboration with ALTSEAN-BURMA. *Report on the Situation for Muslims in Burma.* Bangkok: Forma Asia, 1997.

International Labour Organisation. *Forced Labour in Myanmar (Burma): Report of the Commission of Inquiry Appointed under Article 26 of the Constitution of the International Labour Organisation to Examine the Observance by Myanmar of the Forced Labour Convention, 1930.* Geneva: ILO, 1998.

Iyer, Venkat. *Acts of Oppression: Censorship and the Law in Burma.* London: Article 19, 1999.

Lang, Hazel. *Fear and Sanctuary: Burmese Refugees in Thailand.* Ithaca, N.Y.: Cornell University Southeast Asia Program, 2002.

Lewa, Chris. *All Quiet on the Western Front?: The Situation in Chin State and Sagaing Division, Burma.* Chiang Mai, Thailand: Images Asia, 1998.

Life in the Country: Continued Human Rights Violations in Burma (Special Emphasis on Far Southern and South-Eastern Regions: Tenasserim Division and Mon State). Bangkok: Mon Information Service, 1997.

A Modern Form of Slavery: Trafficking of Burmese Women and Girls into Brothels in Thailand. New York: Asia Watch and The Women's Rights Project, Human Rights Watch, 1993.

Myanmar: The Climate of Fear Continues, Members of Ethnic Minorities and Political Prisoners Still Targeted. New York: Amnesty International U.S., 1993.

Myanmar: Conditions in Prisons and Labour Camps. London: Amnesty International, 1995.

Myanmar: Ethnic Minority Rights under Attack. London: Amnesty International, 1997.

Myanmar: "In the National Interest": Prisoners of Conscience, Torture, Summary Trials Under Martial Law. London: Amnesty International, 1990.

Myanmar: The Kayin (Karen) State Militarization and Human Rights. London: Amnesty International, 1999.

Myanmar—"No Law at All": Human Rights Violations under Military Rule. New York: Amnesty International, 1992.

Myanmar: Update on the Shan State. London: International Secretariat, 1999.

Myanmar (Burma): Continuing Killings and Ill-Treatment of Minority Peoples. London: Amnesty International, 1991.

People's Tribunal on Food Scarcity and Militarization in Burma. *Voice of the Hungry Nation.* Hong Kong: Asian Human Rights Commission, 1999.

Shan Human Rights Foundation. *Uprooting the Shan.* Chiang Mai, Thailand: SHRF, 1996.

To Stand and Be Counted: The Suppression of Burma's Members of Parliament. Bangkok: All Burma Students' Democratic Front, Documentation and Research Centre, 1998.

Tortured Voices: Personal Accounts of Burma's Interrogation Centres. Bangkok: All Burma Students' Democratic Front, 1998.

Venkateswaran, K. S. *Burma, Beyond the Law.* London: Article 19, 1996.

6. Social and Public Health Issues

Ba-Thike, Katherine. "Abortion: A Public Health Problem in Myanmar." *Reproductive Health Matters* (May 9, 1997): 94–100.

Beyrer, Chris. "The Health and Humanitarian Situation of Burmese Populations along the Thai-Burma Border." *Burma Debate* 6, no. 3 (Fall 1999): 4–13.

———. *War in the Blood: Sex, Politics and AIDS in Southeast Asia.* Bangkok: White Lotus; London: Zed Books, 1998.

Dessaint, William, and Alain Dessaint. "Opium and Labor: Social Structure and Economic Change in the Lisu Highlands." *Peasant Studies* 19, nos. 3–4 (Spring–Summer 1992): 147–77.

Drug Control: U.S. Supported Efforts in Burma, Pakistan, and Thailand. Washington, D.C.: Report to Congress 1988.

Evans, Kiri. *Cost Effectiveness of Primary Education in Myanmar.* Rangoon: UNICEF, 1994.

Khin Maung Naing, Cho Nwe Oo, and Tin Tin Oo. "A Study on the Aetiology of Endemic Goitre in Lowland Burma." *European Journal of Clinical Nutrition* 43 (October 1989): 693–98.

Muller, H. J. "Women in Urban Burma-Social Issues and Political Dilemmas." *Women's-Studies-International-Forum* 17, no. 7 (November/December 1994): 609–20.

Naing Oo. "Urbanization and Economic Development in Burma." *Sojourn* 4, no. 2 (August 1989): 233–60.

Out of Control 2: The HIV/AIDS Epidemic in Burma: A Report on the Current Status of the HIV/AIDS and Heroin Epidemics, Policy Options and Policy Implications. Thailand: Southeast Asian Information Network, 1998.

Renard, Ronald D. *The Burmese Connection: Illegal Drugs and the Making of the Golden Triangle*. Boulder, Colo.: Lynne Rienner, 1996.

Report of the Preliminary Joint Survey Team on Opium Production and Consumption in the Union of Burma." *Thai-Yunnan Project Newsletter* 22 (September 1993): 20–23.

The Role of NGOs in Burma. Milton Keynes, England: World Vision, 1995.

A Situation Analysis of Children and Women in Myanmar. Rangoon: United Nations Children's Fund, 1990.

Swan, June Angela "Utilization of Mental Health Services Among Myanmar Americans." Ph.D. Dissertation, California School of Professional Psychology, Los Angeles, 1993.

Tin May Than and Ba Aye. "Energy Intake and Energy Output of Burmese Farmers at Different Seasons." *Human Nutrition* 39c (January 1985): 7–15.

Women's Report Card on Burma. Bangkok: Alternative A[SEAN] Network on Burma, 2000.

7. Religion, Religion in Society

Barden, Stanley. *The Golden Rock of Kyaik-Tiyo*. Cornwall, England: United Writers, 1997.

Bates, Alice Buhl. *For All Time: The Story of Ann Judson*. Birmingham, Ala.: New Hope, 1998.

Bekker, Sarah M. "Transformation of the Nats: The Humanization Process in the Depiction of the Thirty-Seven Lords of Burma." *Crossroads* 4, no. 1 (Fall 1988): 40–45.

Benge, Janet, and Geoff Benge. *Adoniram Judson: Bound for Burma*. Seattle: YWAM, 2000.

Brac de la Perrière, Bénédicte. "The Burmese Nats: Between Sovereignty and Autochthony." *Diogenes (International Council for Philosophy and Humanistic Studies)* 174 (1996): 45–60.

———. "'Etre épousée par un Naq': Les Implications du Mariage avec l'Esprit dans le Culte de Possession Birman (Myanmar)." *Anthropologie et Sociétes* 22, no. 2.

———. "Musique et Possession Dans le Culte des Trente Sept Naq Birmans." *Cahiers de Litérature Orale* 35 (1994): 177–88.

Dowling, Nancy H. "Burmese Lokapalas: A Problem of Identification." *Journal of the Siam Society* 70 (1982): 86–99.

Fransch, Tilman. "A Buddhist Network in the Bay of Bengal: Relations Between Bodhgaya, Burma and Sri Lanka, ca. 300–1399." In *From the Mediterranean to the China Sea: Miscellaneous Notes*. Edited by Glaude Guillot et al. Wiesbaden, Germany: Harrassowitz, 1998.

————. "An Eminent Buddhist Tradition: The Myanmar Vinayadharas." In *Traditions in Current Perspective: Proceedings of the Conference on Myanmar and Southeast Asian Studies 15–17 November 1995, Yangon.* Rangoon: The Universities Press, 1996.

————. "Some Reflections on the Burmese Dhammathat with Special Reference to the Pagan Period." In *Tradition and Modernity in Myanmar 1.* Edited by U. Gärtner and J. Lorenz. Münster/Hamburg, 1994.

Gatellier, Marie. "Les images du Temple Phaung Daw U sur le lac Inlé en Union de Myanmar (Birmanie)." In *Péninsule Indochinoise (collectif): Notes sur la Religion et la Culture dans la Péninsule Indochinoise.* Paris: L'Harmattan, 1994.

Hayami, Yoko. "Karen Tradition According to Christ or Buddha—The Implications of Multiple Reinterpretations for a Minority Ethnic Group in Thailand." *Journal of Southeast Asian Studies* 27, no. 2 (September 1996): 334ff.

Houtman, Gustaaf. "The Biography of Modern Burmese Buddhist Meditation Master U Ba Khin: Life before the Cradle and Past the Grave." In *Sacred Biography in the Buddhist Traditions of South and Southeast Asia.* Edited by Juliane Schober. Honolulu: University of Hawaii Press, 1997.

Jordt, Ingrid. "Bhikkhuni, Thilashin, Mae-chii: Women Who Renounce the World in Burma, Thailand, and the Classical Pali Buddhist Texts." *Crossroads* 4, 1 (1988): 31–39.

Kammerer, Cornelia Ann. "Customs and Christian Conversion Among Akha Highlanders of Burma and Thailand." *American Ethnologist* 17 (May 1990): 277–91.

Kawanami, Hiroko. "Buddhist Nuns in Transition: The Case of Burmese Thila-Shin." In *Indian Insights: Buddhism, Brahmanism and Bhakti.* Edited by P. Connolly and S. Hamilton. London: Luzac Oriental, 1997.

————. "Jyosei to Bukkyo Shugyo [Women and Buddhist Practice]." In *Myanma: Shinko, Matsuri, Seikatsu [Myanmar, Belief System, Festivals and Life].* Edited by R. Okudaira. Tokyo: Bijitsu, 1977.

————."Women in Buddhism Revisited." In *Women, Power and Resistance.* Edited by T. Cosslett et al. Buckingham, England: Open University Press, 1997.

King, Winston L. *A Thousand Lives Away: Buddhism in Contemporary Burma.* Berkeley, Calif.: Asian Humanities Press, 1989.

Ling, Samuel Ngun. *The Meeting of Christianity and Buddhism in Burma: Its Past, Present, and Future Perspectives.* Tokyo: International Christian University, 1998.

Lubeigt, Guy. "Dana: From the Religious Concept to its Practical Manifestations in the Burmese Buddhist Environment = Dana: du Concept Religieux à ses Manifestation Pratiques en Milieu Bouddhique Birman." *Social Compass* 40, no. 2 (June 1993): 233–59.

Nu, U. "Nats." *Crossroads* 4, no. 1 (Fall 1988): 1–12.

Ray, Niharranjan. *Brahmanical Gods in Burma: A Chapter of Indian Art and Iconography.* Singapore: Myanmar Rare Book Publications, 1998.

Sarkisyanz, E. *Buddhist Backgrounds of the Burmese Revolution.* The Hague: Martinus Nijhoff, 1965.

Schendel, Jörg. "Christian Missionaries in Upper Burma, 1853–85." *South East Asia Research* 7, no. 1 (March 1999): 61–91.

Schober, Juliane. "Buddhist Just Rule and Burmese National Culture: State Patronage of the Chinese Tooth Relic in Myanmar." *History of Religions* 36 (February 1996): 218–43.

———. "In the Presence of the Buddha: Ritual Veneration of the Burmese Mahamuni Image." In *Sacred Biography in the Buddhist Traditions of South and Southeast Asia.* Edited by Juliane Schober. Honolulu: University of Hawaii Press, 1997.

———. "The Path to Buddhahood: The Spiritual Mission and Social Organization of Mysticism in Contemporary Burma." *Crossroads* 4, no. 1 (fall 1988): 13–30.

Shwedagon Zedi All-Round Perpetual Renovation Committee. *Historic Record of the Hoisting of the Gold Umbrella on the Shwedagon Pagoda.* Rangoon: Shwedagon Board of Trustees Office, 1999.

Spiro, Melford E. *Burmese Supernaturalism.* Expanded ed. New Brunswick, N.J.: Transaction, 1996.

Strong, John S. *The Legend and Cult of Upagupta.* Lawrenceville, N.J.: Princeton University Press, 1991.

———. *Relics of the Buddha.* Buddhisms: A Princeton University Press Series. Princeton, N.J.: Princeton University Press, 2004.

Temple, Richard Carnac. *The Thirty-Seven Nats: a Phase of Spirit-Worship Prevailing in Burma.* Arran-Edinburgh, Scotland: Kiscadale Publications, 1992.

Tin Maung Maung Than. "The Sangha and Sasana in Socialist Burma." *Sojourn* 3, no. 1 (February 1988): 26–61.

Tooker, Deborah E. "Identity Systems of Highland Burma: 'Belief', Akha zan, and a Critique of Interiorized Notions of Ethno-Religious Identity." *Man* 27 (December 1992): 799–819.

IV. CULTURAL EXPRESSION

1. Literature

Allott, Anna J. "Burma." In *The Traveller's Literary Companion to Southeast Asia.* Edited by Alastair Dingwall. Brighton, England: In Print Publishing, 1994.

——. "Half a Century of Publishing in Mandalay." *The Journal of Burma Studies* 1 (1997): 83–106.

——. "The Study of Burmese Literature." In *Southeast Asian Languages and Literatures: A Bibliographical Guide to Burmese, Cambodia, Indonesian, Javanese, Malay, Minangkabau, Thai and Vietnamese.* Edited by E. Ulrich Kratz. New York: Tauris Academic Studies, 1996.

Bechert, Heinz. *Burmese Manuscripts.* 3 vols. Wiesbaden, Germany: Steiner, 1978–1996.

Comparative Studies on Literature and History of Thailand and Myanmar. Bangkok: Institute of Asian Studies, Chulalongkorn University, 1997.

Esche, Annemarie. "Myanmar Prose Writing: Traditions and Innovation in the 20th Century." In *Traditions in Current Perspective: Proceedings of the Conference on Myanmar and Southeast Asian Studies 15–17 November 1995, Yangon.* Rangoon: The Universities Press, 1996.

Hla Pe. *Burmese Proverbs.* London: John Murray, 1962.

Khin Ma Kyu. *Les Femmes de Lettres Birmanes.* Paris: Harmattan, 1994.

Khin Myo Chit. *A Wonderland of Pagoda Legends.* Illustrated by Paw Oo Thet. Rangoon: U Hla Htay, 1996.

Khin Than, U. *Twelve Tales.* Rangoon: Nu Yin Press & Publishing House, 1995.

Kyaw Maung Maung Nyunt. *Careless Talk and Other Memories of a Myanmar Village.* Rangoon: Thwe Thwe Than Publishing House, 2000.

Ma Ma Lay. *Not Out of Hate.* Translated by Maureen Aung-Thwin. Athens: Ohio University Press, 1991.

Minamida, Midori. "Between Fact and Fiction: Thein Pe Myint's Two Long Novels in the 1960s." *Bulletin of Asian Studies: Osaka University of Foreign Studies (Ajia Gaku Ronso)* III (1993): 71–118.

Saw Tun, U. "The Development of Political Themes in Min-Thuwun's Poetry." *The Journal of Burma Studies* 1 (1997): 107–24.

Silverstein, Josef. "Burma Through the Prism of Western Novels (Review Article)." *Journal of Southeast Asian Studies* 16 (March 1985): 129–40.

Webb, G. H. "Kipling's Burma: A Literary and Historical Review." *Asian Affairs* 15 (June 1984): 163–78.

Zaw Gyi and Alan Nichols, eds. *The Words Cry Out: New Writing by Burmese in Exile.* Potts Point: Australia-Burma Support Group, 1995.

2. Architecture, Plastic, and Visual Arts

"Ancient Arakan." *Arts of Asia* 17 (March/April 1987): 96–109.

Ancient Buddhist Art from Burma. Singapore: Taisei Gallery, 1993.

Archaeological Department, Socialist Republic of the Union of Burma. *Pictorial Guide to Pagan.* Rangoon: Ministry of Culture, 1979.

Broman, Barry. "Relics of the Raj: Colonial Architecture in Myanmar." *Arts of Asia* 27 (November–December 1997): 88–97.

Ciochon, Russell L., and Jamie James. "The Power of Pagan." *Archaeology* 45 (September/October 1992): 34–41.

Di Crocco, Virginia M. "Early Burmese Ceramics from Sriksheta and Pagan and the Problem of the Identification of the Piao Kingdom of the Chinese Chronicles." In *Southeast Asian Archaeology 1990*. Edited by Tam Glover. Hull, England: Centre of Southeast Asian Studies, University of Hull, 1992.

———. "Silver Coins: Evidence for Mining at Bawzaing in the Shan State Circa 6th–8th Century A.D." *Journal of the Siam Society* 80, no. 2 (1992): 125–28.

Dove, Victor. "Two Capitals of Burma: Pagan and Mandalay." *Arts of Asia* 17 (May/June 1987): 135–40; 17 (July/August 1987): 136–39.

Dumarçay, Jacques. "The Palaces of Burma." In *The Palaces of South-East Asia: Architecture and Customs*. Translated by Michael Smithies. Singapore: OUP, 1991.

Falconer, John, et al. *Myanmar Style: Art, Architecture and Design of Burma*. Hong Kong: Periplus Editions, 1998.

Fraser-Lu, Sylvia. "Ancient Arakan." *Arts of Asia* 17 (March/April 1987): 96–109.

———. *Burmese Crafts Past and Present*. Gartmore, Stirling: Kiscadale, 1992.

———. "Frog Drums and Their Importance in Karen Culture." *Arts of Asia* 13 (September–October 1983): 50–63.

———. "Kalagas: Burmese Wall Hangings and Related Embroideries." *Arts of Asia* 12 (July–August 1982): 73–82.

———. "Sadaik–Burmese Manuscript Chests." *Arts of Asia* 14 (May–June 1984): 68–74.

Gatellier, Marie. "Le Temple Shitthaung 'a Myohaung Depositaire Des Traditions de L'Arakan." *Arts Asiatiques* xlvii (1993): 110–26.

———. "Les images du Temple Phaung Daw U sur le lac Inlé en Union de Myanmar (Birmanie)." In *Péninsule Indochinoise (collectif). Notes sur la Religion et la Culture dans la Péninsule Indochinoise*. Paris: L'Harmattan, 1994.

Green, Alexandra, and T. Richard Blurton. *Burma: Art and Archaeology*. London: The British Museum, 2002.

Hasson, Haskia. *Ancient Buddhist Art from Burma*. Bangkok: White Lotus, 1993.

Hein, Don. "Ceramic Production in Myanmar—Further Evidence on Old Traditions." In *Traditions in Current Perspective: Proceedings of the Conference on Myanmar and Southeast Asian Studies 15–17 November 1995, Yangon*. Rangoon: The Universities Press, 1996.

Herbert, Patricia. *The Art of the Painted Books in Burma*. Edinburgh: Kiscadale Publications, 1991.

Howard, Michael C. *Textiles of the Hill Tribes of Burma*. Bangkok: White Lotus, 1999.

Isaacs, Ralph, and Richard T. Blurton. *Visions from the Golden Land: Burma and the Art of Lacquer*. London: British Museum, 2000.

Karow, Otto. *Burmese Buddhist Sculpture: The Johan Moger Collection*. Bangkok: White Lotus, 1991.

Le Bonheur, Albert. "Bronze Burmese Buddha Acquired by the Musée Guimet, Paris." *Arts Asiatiques* 45 (1990): 126–27.

Lefferts, H. Leedom Jr. "Contemporary Burmese Earthenware." *Crossroads* 4, no. 1 (Fall 1988): 121–27.

Lubeigt, Guy. *Shwe-Gyi-Htô, l'art de la Tapisserie Brodée en Birmanie*. Paris: Ed. Kailash, in press.

———. "Vernacular Architecture of Some Ethnic Minorities in Burma (Shan, Môn, Kachin, Yakaing, Chin)." In *Encyclopaedia of Vernacular World Architecture*. Cambridge, England: Cambridge University Press, 1997.

Mitchiner, Michael. "The Date of the Early Funanese, Mon, Pyu, and Arakanese Coinages ('Symbolic Coins')." *Journal of the Siam Society* 70 (1982): 5–12.

Moilanen, Irene. "Last of the Great Masters? Woodcarving Traditions in Myanmar, Past and Present (Buddhism)." Ph.D. Dissertation, Jyvaskylan Yliopisto, Finland, 1995.

Moilanen, Irene, and Sergey S. Ozhegov. *Mirrored in Wood: Burmese Art and Architecture*. Bangkok: White Lotus, 1999.

Moore, Elizabeth H. "Contemporary Paintings in Burma." *Arts of Asia* 22 (September/October 1992): 150–53.

———. "Monasteries of Mandalay: Variation in Architecture and Patronage." In *Traditions in Current Perspective: Proceedings of the Conference on Myanmar and Southeast Asian Studies 15–17 November 1995, Yangon*. Rangoon: The Universities Press, 1996.

Moore, Elizabeth, and San San Maw. "Flights of Fancy, Hintha and Kinnaya, the Avian Inspiration in Myanmar Art." *Oriental Art* 41, no. 2 (1995): 25–31.

Moore, Elizabeth H., Hansjorg Meyer, and U Win Pe. *Shwedagon: Golden Pagoda of Myanmar*. London: Thames and Hudson, 1999.

Pichard, Pierre. *Inventory of Monuments at Pagan*. Gartmore, Scotland: Kiscadale Publications, 1992.

———. *The Pentagonal Monuments of Pagan*. Bangkok: White Lotus, 1991.

———. "Sous Les Voûtes De Pagan." *Arts Asiatiques* xlvii (1993): 86–109.

Reith, Charlotte. "Comparison of Three Pottery Villages in Shan State, Burma." *The Journal of Burma Studies* 1 (1997): 45–82.

Shwe Mann Maung. "The Largest Alloy Buddha Image." *Myanmar Perspectives* 2 (April 1997): 82–83.

Singer, Noel F. *Old Rangoon, City of the Shwedagon*. Gartmore, Scotland: Kiscadale Publications, 1995.

———. "Palm Leaf Manuscripts of Myanmar, Burma." *Arts of Asia* 21 (January/February 1991): 133–40.

Stadtner, Donald M. "An 'Extraordinary Folly'?" *Archaeology* 53, no. 3 (May/June 2000): 54–59.

———. "A Fifteenth-Century Royal Monument in Burma and the Seven Stations in Buddhist Art." *Art Bulletin* 73 (March 1991): 39–52.

Than Tun, Dr. "A Bagan Temple's Main Gate: Is There any Significance When It Opens in Any Other Direction Except East?" *Myanmar Historical Journal Research* 2 (June 1998): 106–8.

Thanegi, M. "Traditional Myanmar Pottery." *Arts of Asia* 27, no. 1 (January–February 1997): 66–70.

3. Performing Arts

Diamond, Catherine. "Burmese Nights: The Pagoda Festival Pwe in the Age of Hollywood's 'Titanic'." *New Theatre Quarterly* 16, no. 3 (August 2000): 227–48.

Khin Mya Kyu. "The Music of Myanmar." *Unesco Courier* 45 (March 1992): 48–49.

Maung Sein Tun. *Best of the Best Jokes of Zar Ga Na*. Long Beach, Calif.: Maung Sein Tun, n.d.

Thanegi, Ma. *The Illusion of Life: Burmese Marionettes*. Bangkok: White Orchid, 1994.

White Elephants and Golden Ducks: Enchanting Musical Treasures from Burma. San Francisco: Ko Ko Lay, n.d.

Win Pe. "The Myanmar Female Solo Dance." *Myanmar Perspectives* II (April 1997): 41–42.

———. "Myanmar Pure Dance." *Myanmar Perspectives* II (June 1997): 30–32.

About the Author

Donald M. Seekins was born in New York. He obtained his B.A. in Asian studies at Cornell University and his M.A. and Ph.D. in political science from the University of Chicago. He is currently professor of Southeast Asian Studies in the College of International Studies at Meio University in Okinawa, Japan. Prior to joining Meio University, he was professor of political science in the Department of Law and Political Science at the University of the Ryukyus in Okinawa, Japan, and research professor in the Foreign Area Studies Department of The American University in Washington, D.C. In 1988–1989, he was a Fulbright Visiting Lecturer at the University of the Ryukyus and in 1995 was a guest professor in the College of Letters and Social Sciences of the University of Malaya, Kuala Lumpur, Malaysia. Long interested in Burma, he first visited the country in 1970, during the height of Ne Win socialism, and has frequently returned to do fieldwork after 1988. He is presently working on a monograph about social, economic, and cultural changes in the city of Rangoon during the post-1988 period.

Breinigsville, PA USA
19 April 2010
236251BV00002BA/1/P